The Story of the Royal Horticultural Society
1804–1968

Plate I

JOHN WEDGWOOD, FOUNDER OF THE SOCIETY

HAROLD R. FLETCHER

The Story of
the
Royal Horticultural Society
1804–1968

OXFORD UNIVERSITY PRESS
for
THE ROYAL HORTICULTURAL SOCIETY
1969

Oxford University Press, Ely House, London W. 1

GLASGOW NEW YORK TORONTO MELBOURNE WELLINGTON
CAPE TOWN SALISBURY IBADAN NAIROBI LUSAKA ADDIS ABABA
BOMBAY CALCUTTA MADRAS KARACHI LAHORE DACCA
KUALA LUMPUR HONG KONG TOKYO

© Oxford University Press 1969

PRINTED IN GREAT BRITAIN
BY W & J MACKAY & CO LTD, CHATHAM

Dedicated to all those
who in many capacities
have given great service to
The Royal Horticultural Society
and yet are not mentioned
in the following pages

Acknowledgement

It is a matter of the most profound regret to me that Mr. A. Simmonds did not live to see published *The Story of the Royal Horticultural Society*.

Mr. Simmonds not only had given a lifetime of service to the Society—he had held executive positions for forty years—but for so long had been the Society's unofficial historian, as his many contributions to the Society's *Journal* on various people and events in the Society's history and as his *Horticultural Who was Who* abundantly show. On his retirement in 1962, he accepted the Council's invitation to write the story of the Society and towards this end he had for several years, in spite of failing health, accumulated a great mass of material. From this he produced a first draft.

At this stage, on behalf of the Council, I undertook to prepare the work for the press, regarding it as the greatest possible privilege to take up the task which this most devoted servant of the Society had laid down.

I have acknowledged the Society's immense debt to Mr. Simmonds in the following pages. Here I record my own great sense of gratitude to him for the 350 or so pages of typed manuscript which he handed to me, as well as for the assistance and encouragement he gave me during the time I was writing the story in its present format.

Mr. Simmonds sincerely believed that I had figured him far too prominently in the *Story*, for in his draft, not unnaturally, he had mentioned himself in the most impersonal of terms. This, of course, is not my view. Neither is it the view of the President and my friends on the Society's Council and staff who have been kind enough to read and criticize the manuscript. Nor, I believe, will it be the view of countless others who know of Mr. Simmonds' association with the Society. Many of these have provided me with much interesting information about the Society not to be found in the literature. To all I extend my thanks and to none more than to the associate, for some fifteen years, of the Rev. W. Wilks—Mr. A. Ogilvie-Gaskell of Praa Sands. Cornwall.

Contents

Part Four

THE KENSINGTON ADVENTURE—AND DISASTER (1858–1885)

Part Five

RECOVERY: SIR TREVOR LAWRENCE & THE REV. WILLIAM WILKS (1885–1919)

Part Six

FROM ONE WAR TO THE OTHER (1919–1945)

Part Seven

ON THE CREST OF THE WAVE (1945–1968)

List of Illustrations

Colour Plates

Black and White Plates

LIST OF ILLUSTRATIONS

(Except where otherwise specified all the photographs, including those
from original portraits, are by J. E. Downward.)

INTRODUCTION

IN THE EIGHTEENTH CENTURY GARDENING AND HORTICULTURE IN Britain, in England especially, had been largely dominated by Philip Miller, gardener to the Worshipful Company of Apothecaries at their Botanic Garden at Chelsea, and a Fellow of the Royal Society, and by some of Miller's Scots assistants. Though Miller had been born at either Deptford or Greenwich, in 1691, his father was a Scotsman and he himself would employ only Scotsmen. The Chelsea Garden had been founded as the Garden of the Society of Apothecaries in London in 1673; in 1712 Dr. (afterwards Sir Hans) Sloane had purchased the freehold of the Manor of Chelsea, including the Garden, and in 1722 had conveyed the Garden by deed to the Society of Apothecaries 'to the end that the said garden might at all times thereafter be continued as a Physick Garden, and for the better encouraging and enabling the said Society to support the charge thereof, for the manifestation of the power, wisdom and glory of God in the works of the creation, and that their apprentices and others might better distinguish good and useful plants from those that bore resemblance to them, and yet were hurtful and other the like good purposes'.

Shortly after Sloane's deed of conveyance Miller was appointed head gardener at Chelsea and in 1724 published his first work, the two-volume *The Gardeners and Florists Dictionary, or A Complete System of Horticulture*, which he dedicated to the Apothecaries' Company. Four years later he demonstrated his skill as a cultivator by communicating to the *Philosophical Transactions of the Royal Society* a paper on 'A Method of Raising some Exotic Seeds which have been judged almost impossible to be raised in England'. His horticultural skill at this time was very much needed, for plants from overseas were coming into the country in large numbers, hot-houses for their cultivation were multiplying, and many such plants were grown and flowered at Chelsea for the first time in cultivation; plants from the Cape, Siberia, North America, and the West Indies, to the extent that the Garden at Chelsea was said to exhibit the treasures of both the Indies. Miller determined to impart the knowledge he had acquired of these new plants to others, and in 1731 published his monumental work *The Gardeners Dictionary*, of which Linnaeus

1

said that it was not simply a dictionary of gardening but of botany as well, and which earned for him, overseas, the title of 'Prince of Gardeners'. From the time of its publication until his death in 1771 eight editions of the work were to be published, with a further eight editions during the first thirty years of the nineteenth century. He also issued the *Gardeners Dictionary* in an abridged form.

In 1889 a writer in the *Publishers' Circular* gave some interesting particulars regarding Miller's *Dictionary*, particulars which had remained buried in a petition dated 1759.

The demand for such a work would, at that time, naturally be circumscribed, and it is rather surprising that the folio edition at three guineas should have been only nine years in selling, and that an abridgement in quarto should have been sold in seven years. . . . Philip Miller was evidently a man with a due regard for posterity, because he stipulated in the original agreement that either he himself or his heirs for ever were to be paid a sum of £40 for each and every impression. This apparently did not 'cover' any new matter, as he was paid £94 for the fifty sheets added in the 1752 edition. And seven years afterwards, when the dictionary came out in sixpenny weekly numbers, he received thirty copies, and cash to make up £300. In 1768 he received £200 for additions, whilst the abridgements of 1764 and 1771 each represented £120 to him. These figures are extremely interesting, as indicating that, even in an age of shams and shoddy, of barren philosophy and stereotyped theology, the tastes for the higher occupations of outdoor life were becoming extremely popular. The charming essays of Addison and Steele had given a great impetus to gardening, and Miller's somewhat stupendous tome appeared just when it was most likely to sell.

Miller lived to see the number of plant species cultivated in Chelsea increased fivefold. In 1731 about a thousand were in cultivation; when he died in 1771 there were rather more than five thousand. And many people, 'Curious Delighters in Flowers' as Miller called them, were interested in growing these plants. When Miller retired from Chelsea in 1770 he was succeeded by one of his Scots pupils, William Forsyth, who remained at Chelsea until 1784, when he was appointed Royal Gardener at Kensington, and during his régime Chelsea lost much of the glory Miller had won for it. But as the King's Gardener at Kensington he was to make a great name for himself as the originator of 'Forsyth's Plaister' and as the writer of the *Treatise on the Culture and Management of Fruit Trees* of 1802.

By 1789 some 5,500 species were in cultivation at Kew when Aiton published his *Hortus Kewensis* or a catalogue of the plants cultivated in the Royal Botanic Gardens at Kew. Aiton had been Miller's assistant at Chelsea from 1754 to 1759—another of his Scots gardeners—and had been appointed the first Curator at Kew in 1759, when Princess Augusta initiated a botanical garden of some nine acres in the region of Kew House, a garden which occupied a position about fifty yards south-west of the present Orangery. The first unofficial Director was the Earl of Bute, a botanist of some distinction; the second Joseph Banks, also un-official, was far more distinguished. Aiton served as Curator for thirty-four years. His three-volume *Hortus Kewensis* of 1789 not only listed the 5,500 species which were in cultivation at Kew but classified them according to the Linnaean system, gave their country of origin, the date of their introduction and by whom they were introduced. When Aiton died in 1793 his son William Townsend Aiton succeeded him, having the entire management of both the Royal Gardens of Kew and Richmond, and in 1810–13 publishing a second enlarged edition of his father's work, in five volumes. King George III, Banks, and the two Aitons raised the Kew Gardens to great eminence, and Banks, by his championing of plant exploration, was the means of enriching the gardens of Britain with many new plants of great horticultural and botanical merit.

Banks, William Townsend Aiton, and Forsyth were to play an im-portant role in the formation of the Royal Horticultural Society.

Over a hundred years before the publication of *Hortus Kewensis*, in 1683 in fact, another botanical garden catalogue of plants had been published, James Sutherland's *Hortus Medicus Edinburgensis*, 'a catalogue of the plants in the Physical Garden at Edinburgh, containing their most proper Latin and English names'. Sutherland had been appointed the first 'Intendent' of the Physic Garden which Dr. Andrew Balfour and Dr. Robert Sibbald had established on a piece of land, 40 feet by 40 feet—a portion of the Royal Gardens at Holyroodhouse—and which they had stocked with many hundreds of plants from the garden of their mutual friend, Patrick Murray, Laird of Livingston, as well as with plants of their own. Not surprisingly, the Garden soon became too small, apparently was abandoned, and in 1676 the lease was obtained from the town council of the garden attached to Trinity Church and Hospital —and Sutherland was appointed intendent of this garden. He was, moreover, but not until twenty years later, given the title of Professor of Botany in the town's College. Around 1695 there was another garden on the ground surrounding the College buildings—and Sutherland was placed in charge of this garden also. Not content with this additional garden, Sutherland took over part of the Royal Garden at Holyrood known as the King's Garden, quite distinct from the original plot at St. Anne's Yards, and there began to grow vegetables and medicinal herbs. This garden was Sutherland's first step towards royal patronage, for in 1699 he became King's Botanist under a Warrant of William III. Thus in the eighteenth century three Physic Gardens existed in Edinburgh— the Royal Garden (at Holyrood), the town's (at Trinity House), and the

3

College (at the University), and James Sutherland was in charge of them all. In the course of time the College Garden was to be discontinued, the Royal Garden and the town's garden combined, and in 1763 the combined Physic Garden was transferred to a site in Leith Walk where John Hope, keeper of the garden and Professor of Botany, greatly enlarged the collection of plants in the garden, and conducted experiments on such plant physiological matters as growth in length and in width, the effects of light and of gravity, movement of sap and healing of wounds.

The publications of Miller, Aiton, and Forsyth were by no means the only important publications of the eighteenth century. There were those of another Scotsman, John Abercrombie, born at Prestonpans in East Lothian in 1726, and for a time a gardener at Kew. In 1767 *Every Man His Own Gardener* was published, under the authorship of Mawe and Abercrombie. The work is by the latter, who, fearing that the book might not succeed, offered Thomas Mawe, head gardener to the Duke of Leeds, twenty pounds for the use of his name as author on the title-page. Mawe accepted and *Every Man* was published 'By Mr. Mawe, Gardener to His Grace the Duke of Leeds, and Other Gardeners' and sold at '4*s.* bound'. The work was a tremendous success, but only in the seventh edition of 1776 did Abercrombie add his own name to the title-page as joint author with Mawe. By this time confidence in himself was established (he was in the process of becoming the father of two sons and sixteen daughters), and in his later works he was to describe himself on his title-pages as 'Author of *Every Man His Own Gardener*', even embellishing later editions of *Every Man* with a full-length profile portrait of himself. About 1770 Abercrombie established himself as a nurseryman near Hackney and thereafter published many works on practical gardening: *The Garden Mushroom* (1779), *The Complete Forcing Gardener* (1781), *The Complete Wall Tree Pruner* (1783), *The Propagation and Botanical Arrangements of Plants and Trees* (1784), *The Gardener's Pocket Dictionary* and *The Gardener's Daily Assistant* (1786), *The Universal Gardener's Kalendar*, *The Gardener's Vade Mecum*, and *The Hothouse Gardener* (all 1789) —and, about 1789 or 1791, *The Gardener's Pocket Journal* which by 1857 was to reach its thirty-fifth edition.

The years of Abercrombie's authorship were also noteworthy in that they witnessed the birth of the first periodical devoted to scientific horticulture. William Curtis, who in 1772 had been a demonstrator at the Chelsea Physic Garden, and who, in 1777 had produced the first part of the beautiful *Flora Londinensis*—a description, with illustrations, of the wild flowers growing in the vicinity of London—launched in 1787 *The Botanical Magazine, or 'Flower Garden Displayed*, in which the most ornamental foreign plants, cultivated in the open ground, the greenhouse

4

and the stove, are accurately represented in their natural colours'. The price was one shilling per part of three hand-coloured plates, and the publication was issued from Curtis's Botanic Garden at Lambeth Marsh. As editor, Curtis prefaced the first volume of *The Botanical Magazine* thus:

The present periodical publication owes its commencement to the repeated solicitations of several Ladies and Gentlemen, Subscribers to the Author's Botanic Garden, who were frequently lamenting the want of a work, which might enable them, not only to acquire a systematic knowledge of the Foreign Plants growing in their gardens, but which might at the same time afford them the best information respecting their culture—in fact, a work, in which Botany and Gardening (so far as relates to the culture of ornamental Plants) or the labour of Linnaeus and Miller, might happily be combined.

In compliance with their wishes, he has endeavoured to present them with the limited information of both authors, and to illustrate each by a set of new figures drawn always from the living plant, and coloured as near to nature, as the imperfection of colouring will admit.

He does not mean, however, to confine himself solely to the Plants contained in the highly esteemed works of those luminaries of Botany and Gardening, but shall occasionally introduce new ones, as they may flower in his own Garden, or those of the curious in any part of Great Britain.

At the commencement of this publication, he had no design of entering the province of the Florist, by giving figures of double or improved Flowers, which sometimes owe their origin to culture, more frequently to the sportings of nature; but the earnest entreaties of many of his Subscribers have induced him so far to deviate from his original intention, as to promise them one, at least, of the flowers most esteemed by Florists.

The encouragement given to this work, great beyond the Author's warmest expectations, demands his most grateful acknowledgements, and will excite him to persevere in his humble endeavours to render Botany a lasting source of rational amusement, and public utility.

The *Magazine* was launched with three beautiful plates of *Iris persica*, *Rudbeckia purpurea* (now *Echinacea purpurea*), and *Eranthis hyemalis*, now naturalized in Britain, but then much less common, and 3,000 copies of this first part were sold. The plates were the work of Sydenham Teast Edwards, son of a Welsh schoolmaster, who probably was responsible for all but about seventy-five of the first 1,720 plates. When Curtis died in 1799 his friend John Sims took over the general management and editorship of the *Magazine* and for a time many South African plants, new to cultivation, were figured. For ten years *The Botanical Magazine* was alone in the field of superbly illustrated scientific horticultural writings. Then, in 1797, entered its first rival, *The Botanist's Repository*, with plates by Henry C. Andrews. The *Repository* was more restricted than the *Magazine*, described mostly newly introduced or rare plants,

5

and only ten volumes were issued. Andrews was later to produce works on heathers, geraniums, and roses—and to marry the daughter of John Kennedy, of the renowned nursery firm of Lee & Kennedy.

The Gardens at Edinburgh, founded in 1670, at Chelsea, founded in 1673, and at Kew, founded in 1759, were by no means the only physic or botanic gardens growing plants from Britain and from overseas. Trinity College, Dublin, possessed a Physic Garden as early as 1711 and Dr. Henry Nicholson, the first lecturer in botany, published a pamphlet on it in 1712—*Methodus plantarum in horto medico collegii Dublinensis, jamjam dispondendarum*. Many years later, under the direction of Edward Hill who was first Lecturer in, and later Professor of, Botany, from 1773 to 1800, the Garden was transferred to the neighbourhood of Harold's Cross. Hill apparently was paid a salary of £130 per annum, out of which he agreed to meet the wages of two permanent gardeners and to hire the services of two others for the months of March to September. In 1806 the College Board took possession of slightly over three acres of land at Ballsbridge for the foundation of a botanical garden and the following year James Townsend Mackay, the first Curator, began to lay out the grounds. J. T. Mackay was born in Kirkcaldy, Fife, and was the brother of John Mackay who was Superintendent of the Edinburgh Botanic Garden in 1800. In 1832, and again in 1848, the College extended the gardens and the entire design was the creation of J. T. Mackay. The College was to be extremely fortunate in its Curators; two especially were to figure in the history of the Royal Horticultural Society, Frederick Moore and Frederick William Burbidge.

At Oxford there was the oldest Botanic Garden in Britain, founded and endowed as a physic garden by the Earl of Danby in 1621 for the study of drug plants or 'simples'. It was laid out on the site of the old Jews' burying-ground opposite Magdalen College, from whom the Garden is still leased by the University. It occupies the same site today. The magnificent gateway, the Danby Gate, designed by Inigo Jones, was erected in 1632. Not until 1642 was the garden ready for occupation, and then Danby appointed Jacob Bobart, an old Brunswick soldier, as keeper, having failed to secure the services of John Tradescant, gardener to Charles I. Bobart began to build up his collection of plants, mainly for their interest in medicine, and by 1648 was able to publish a catalogue which listed the names of some 600 native plants and some 1,200 plants from abroad, all of which were established in the Garden. Such teaching as was done at the Garden was done by Bobart and later by Bobart's son, who died in 1719.[1] Some years later Dr. William Sherard, a distinguished patron of botanical science who had given

---

[1] The first Chair of Botany in Britain was established at Oxford in 1669 and Robert Morison was appointed the first Professor.

plants to the Garden, books to the library, and £500 towards the enlargement of the conservatory, endowed a Chair of Botany, and Dr. Dillenius was appointed the first Sherardian Professor of Botany in 1734 and greatly added to the interest of the collection in the Garden during the thirteen years of his office. His successor, however, Humphrey Sibthorp, who held the Chair from 1747 to 1783, appears to have had little interest in the Garden and, although his son John, who was in the Chair from 1783 to 1795, attempted to introduce many of the plants he had seen on his travels in Greece, his efforts met with little success. Not for another forty years was real progress to be made at the Oxford Botanic Garden.

Of botany in Cambridge during much of this period, Sir J. E. Smith, the first president of the Linnean Society, said: 'Botany slept from 1734 till 1761, when Walker raised it from a deep slumber. The Professor had neither salary nor students.'[1] The Professor was John Martyn, who practised medicine in Chelsea and journeyed to Cambridge, until 1734, to deliver his lectures. After 1734 the lectures were discontinued, for there was neither a Botanic Garden nor students, and no one cared. However, as he was on the point of retiring, in 1761, Richard Walker, the Vice-Master of Trinity, bought and presented to the University five acres of land in the centre of Cambridge, land on which now stands the Cavendish Laboratory and other University buildings, for the purposes of a botanic garden. Thomas Martyn, who had succeeded his father as Professor of Botany, sought the help of his friend Philip Miller of Chelsea in the layout of the garden, and Philip Miller's son, Charles, was appointed the first Curator in 1762. Miller, however, stayed only until 1770, when he went to the East Indies and when Martyn took upon himself the duties of Curator. He himself left Cambridge in 1776, and, because he was still University Professor of Botany and Walker Reader in Botany, returned to Cambridge almost annually for the next twenty-four years to give courses of lectures. During most of this time he was writing a new edition of Miller's *Gardeners Dictionary*, which, arranged in the main according to the Linnaean system, appeared in four folio volumes in 1803–7, under Miller's name, and for which Martyn was paid £1,000. Not unnaturally, by the turn of the century the Cambridge Garden was not in very good shape and it was not until the nineteenth century was well advanced that progress was to be made.

In the botanic gardens of the eighteenth century, all of which were destined to play important roles in the affairs of the Royal Horticultural Society, were to be found many of the native plants enumerated in Hudson's *Flora Anglica* (1762), Lightfoot's *Flora Scotica* (1777), and in Threlkeld's *Synopsis Stirpium Hiburnicum* (1727); plants from Europe and

[1] *Journal of the Royal Horticultural Society*, LXV (1940), p. 173.

a few from North America introduced by John Gerard in the sixteenth century; the early seventeenth-century introductions from Europe and North America of John Parkinson, whose *Theatricum Botanicum* (1640) describes nearly 3,800 plants; the seventeenth-century introductions of the two Tradescants, including many plants for the herbaceous border of the future—phlox, lupin, michaelmas daisy,—and of Dr. Compton, Bishop of London from 1675 to 1713, described by Loudon as 'the great introducer of foreign trees in this century'.[1] and who in his garden at Fulham grew oaks, hollies, cedars, junipers, maples, magnolias, hickories, liquidambars, hawthorns, dogwoods, robinias, and much else. In the seventeenth century nearly 500 hardy trees and shrubs were introduced into Britain, including 108 from Europe, 300 from North America, three from Chile, thirteen from China, six from Japan, and two from the Cape of Good Hope.

And there were the eighteenth-century introductions, notably those from America, of the Quaker botanist Peter Collinson, who in the middle of the century was living at Ridgeway House, Mill Hill, where he made a rich collection of plants. In America, Collinson had two great friends, John Bartram, another Quaker, and Mark Catesby, and they were the means by which Collinson was able to introduce so many American plants to Britain; sugar maples, tulip trees, magnolias, michaelmas daisies, dog's-tooth violets, gentians—and *Lilium superbum*, which flowered for the first time in Europe in Collinson's garden in 1738. Many of the plants still flourished in 1800, when Collinson's house and garden came into the possession of R. A. Salisbury, one of the founders of the Royal Horticultural Society. Indeed, several were still flourishing in 1835 when Loudon visited the garden; a *Platanus* was 40 feet high and $1\frac{1}{2}$ feet in diameter a foot from the base; a deciduous cypress was 48 feet high and the stem $1\frac{1}{2}$ feet in diameter; a stem of *Pinus pinaster* was 3 feet in diameter and *Pinus cembra* with a stem nearly 2 feet in diameter was between 50 and 60 feet high; a tulip tree was nearly 30 feet high with a 9-inch stem; cedars with 4-foot stems 30–40 feet high had a branch spread of 60 feet in diameter; a sweet chestnut had a 5-foot stem with branches extending 30 feet on either side; there was a *Quercus ilex* with a branch spread of 35 feet; a weeping willow 50 feet high; an *Arbutus* with stem $1\frac{1}{2}$ feet in diameter and branches extending 20 feet; a handsome variegated holly covering a space 18 feet in diameter; a box 15 feet high; two Portugal laurels each covering a space 40 feet in diameter; and much else.

Another remarkable collection of trees was to be found in the garden of Dr. John Fothergill at Upton House, West Ham. When Loudon visited the garden early in 1835 the hybrid poplar, *Populus* x *canadensis*

[1] *Arboretum et Fruticetum Britannicum*, I (1838), p. 41.

was 100 feet high, and the Lombardy poplar, *P. nigra* 'Italica', 120 feet high; Turner's hybrid oak, *Quercus* x *turneri*, was a fine specimen of 50 feet, whilst the Turkish hazel, *Corylus colurna*, formed a most handsome tree with a trunk 5 feet in circumference; two very large cedars had trunks 9½ feet in diameter[1] 6 feet from the base; there was a large cork oak, *Quercus suber*, a great *Robinia*, whilst *Koelreuteria paniculata* and *Cupressus sempervirens* 'Horizontalis' were both 40 feet high.

In the second half of the eighteenth century there were the introductions resulting from the voyages of exploration; from Cook's three voyages, the first (1768–71) with Joseph Banks and Dr. Solander the naturalists on board, the second (1772–5) with J. R. and G. Forster, and the third (1776–9) with Dr. William Anderson and David Nelson; from the expedition of Vancouver during which Archibald Menzies introduced the monkey puzzle. Banks, on Cook's first great voyage of exploration through the Pacific, had seen many plants which he believed should be grown in Britain, and when he became Director of Kew he began to send plant collectors to various parts of the world and so inaugurated a new era of plant introduction. The first to journey from Kew was Francis Masson, who collected at the Cape from 1772–3, in the Canaries and the Azores from 1778–82, in Spain and Portugal from 1783–5, and at the Cape again, as well as in the interior, from 1786–95; and from these expeditions there reached Britain the first South African heaths which were to become immensely popular during part of the nineteenth century, the *Senecio* species from which the florist's cineraria has been evolved, Cape pelargoniums which were to give rise to the garden geraniums so popular for bedding-out purposes, echiums, proteas, the Canary Island broom, and *Ixia viridiflora*, which created a great sensation when its soft pea-green flowers first opened at Kew.

Of the nurseries of the time which stocked the introductions of the last three centuries, the most renowned, and for a time the most extensive, was the Brompton Park Nursery, which had been established in 1681. In 1700 it was over 100 acres in extent, was owned by London & Wise, who employed twenty men and two women, and in an account of the parish of Kensington in 1705 it was said 'that if the stock of these nurseries were valued at one penny per plant, the amount would exceed £40,000'. Evelyn, in his preface to the translation of Quintinye's *Compleate Gard'ner*, published in 1693, had this to say:

The proprietors, Mr. George London, Chief Gardener to Their Majesties, and his associate, Mr. Henry Wise, are recommended for their assiduity and industry; they have not made gain the only mark of their pains, but with extraordinary and rare industry endeavoured to improve themselves in the

---

[1] London must surely have meant 'in circumference'.

mysteries of their profession; from the great advantages and now long experience they have had, in being employed in most of the celebrated gardens and plantations which this nation abounds in, besides what they have learned abroad, where horticulture is in high reputation . . . the grounds and gardens of noblemen and persons of quality, which they have planted *ab origine*, and which are still under their care and attention, justify what I have said in their behalf.

From time to time during the course of the century the nursery changed hands and gradually decreased in size, so that by 1800 it was owned by Gray, Wear & Co., and was little over thirty acres in extent.

The Fulham Nursery of Christopher Gray was founded early in the eighteenth century. It was noted especially for its American plants, many of which Gray had received from collectors in America and many of which he had bought at the sale of Dr. Compton's trees. In 1740 he issued a catalogue of his plants—which Philip Miller may have written —and in 1767 published Catesby's *Hortus Europae Americanus*, in the preface of which it is said that

Mr. Gray of Fulham has, for many years, made it his business to raise and cultivate the plants of America, from whence he has annually fresh supplies, in order to furnish the curious with what they want; . . . through his industry and skill, a greater variety of American forest trees and shrubs may be seen in his garden than in any other place in England.

At the beginning of the nineteenth century Gray had fine specimens of *Quercus suber*, *Celtis occidentalis*, *Ailanthus altissima*, *Koelreuteria paniculata*, *Diospyros virginiana* and *Magnolia grandiflora*. The latter probably was the first of its kind to be introduced to England, and, after thousands of plants had been propagated from it, died about 1810, when the trunk was nearly 5 feet in circumference and the branch spread over 20 feet in diameter.

The largest maidenhair tree, *Ginkgo biloba*, or *Salisburia adiantifolia* as it was then called, which had been introduced into England around 1754, was to be found in the nursery of James Gordon of Mile End, London. In 1835 it was 55 feet high and had a stem girth of 5 feet 5 inches at one foot from the ground. At that time the nursery was in the hands of James Thompson and was much reduced in size. From the 1750s it had been in the Gordon family and James Thompson's father, Archibald, had secured possession at the turn of the century. Of James Gordon, John Ellis, who imported many American seeds and was a correspondent of Linnaeus, writing to the latter on 25 April, 1758, said:

If you want a correspondent here that is a curious gardener, I shall recommend you to Mr. James Gordon. . . . This man was bred under Lord Petre and Dr. Sherard, and knows systematically all the plants he cultivates. He has more knowledge in vegetation than all the other gardeners and writers on gardening in England put together; but he is too modest to publish anything. If you send him anything rare, he will make you a proper return. We have got a rare double Jessamine (Gardenia) from the Cape, that is not described; this man has raised it from cuttings, when all other gardeners have failed in the attempt. I have lately got him a curious collection of seeds from the East Indies, many of which are growing, but are quite new to us.

Another correspondent of Linnaeus was James Lee, a native of Selkirk, who about 1745 became joint partner, with Lewis Kennedy, of the nursery at Hammersmith known as the Vineyard; at the beginning of the century the land was, in fact, a vineyard, producing considerable quantities of Burgundy annually. Through foreign botanists and other correspondents and through the efforts of their own collectors—in North America, South America, and at the Cape—they gradually developed a large nursery stock and in 1774 the nursery published its catalogue of seventy-six pages, listing hardy trees and shrubs, herbaceous plants, greenhouse plants, plants for a dry stove or glass-house, stove plants, fruits, kitchen garden seeds, seeds of evergreen trees and shrubs, of deciduous trees and shrubs, of perennial flowers, of annual flowers, of biennial flowers, and seeds to improve land such as clover, trefoil, flax, hemp, and lentils. Loudon, in his *Encyclopaedia* in 1822, was to describe the nursery as 'unquestionably the first nursery in Britain, or rather the world'.

About the middle of the eighteenth century the Hackney nursery of Loddiges had been founded by a German, John Busch, and taken over by a Dutchman, Conrad Loddiges, early in the 1770s, and through William Bartram, son of John Bartram, Loddiges had introduced many American plants. Gradually the nursery came to specialize more or less in greenhouse plants, so that early in the nineteenth century it contained, according to Loudon, the best general collection of greenhouse and hothouse exotics of any commercial garden, excelling especially in tree ferns, members of the ginger family, and in palms, of which over eighty species were stocked. For the better display and cultivation of all these plants, before 1820 a large hothouse 80 feet long, 60 feet wide, and 40 feet high, heated by steam, had been erected, so that at this time the nursery could boast of 1,000 feet of glass, two houses being devoted to camellias. Stocks were also quickly acquired of the newly introduced Cape Heaths which were another of the Hackney specialities, as they were of William Rollison of Tooting.

As for Scotland, in 1717 John McAslan founded a nursery in Glasgow and many years later took his son-in-law, Robert Austin, into partnership with him. Either under the name of McAslan & Austin, or, later, as Austin & McAslan, the firm remained in being until after the Second

World War, the first and longest-established nursery in Scotland; in the latter part of the eighteenth and early part of the nineteenth century it was to become famous for the development of the Scots rose—many varieties of which were to be sent to Kew and the Gardens of the Royal Horticultural Society. The dominant name in the nursery trade in Scotland in the eighteenth century, however, was that of Dickson. In 1729 Robert Dickson had founded a nursery at Hassendeanburn in Teviotdale and twenty years later was supplying trees to many of the big estates in Scotland. Another son started the famous Edinburgh firm of Dickson & Co., which by the end of the eighteenth century was in the forefront of the seed and nursery trade, issuing in 1794 a *Catalogue of Hot-house, Green-house, Hardy and Herbaceous plants; flowering and evergreen plants, fruit and forest trees, alphabetically arranged.* The preface stated:

We by no means pretend to be in possession of all the plants mentioned in this catalogue; perhaps no botanic garden in Europe can boast of such a treasure; notwithstanding, we are determined to increase our collection, and make it as complete as possible, to *supply* the demands of the public.

Some thirty years later the firm was able to offer 46 asters, 28 chrysanthemums, 24 dahlias, 18 delphiniums, 24 gentians, 34 irises, 21 lilies, 58 daffodils, 24 phlox, 32 primulas, 35 saxifrages, 31 violas, 28 maples, 8 arbutus, 41 azaleas, 25 heaths, 10 kalmias, 47 willows, 20 viburnums, all the American magnolias as well as the Chinese *Magnolia denudata*, the Himalayan *Rhododendron arboreum*, 487 hybrid roses, 146 named varieties of apple and the same of pear, and 194 varieties of gooseberry.

In Dickson's Leith Walk Nursery, in Edinburgh, John Claudius Loudon was to receive his training towards the close of the century.

Like Dickson & Co., the Lawson Seed and Nursery Company of Edinburgh, established in 1770, catered for every branch of the horticultural trade. Other nurseries, on the other hand, were much more specialized and one such was the Aberdeen Nursery of Messrs. Reid, which was devoted chiefly to the cultivation of forest trees, especially of Scots pine and larch. That there was scope for the production of such plants on a vast scale is obvious from the fact that between 1774 and 1826 the fourth Duke of Atholl was to plant 14,083,378 larches and 13,348,222 trees of other kinds. The Duke of Atholl was by no means the only planter of trees on a large scale; neither was he the first. The Earls of Tweeddale at Yester from shortly after 1660 had planted 6,000 acres, to the extent that John Macky in *A Journey through Scotland* (1723) commented:

The palace of Yester . . . stands in the middle of the best planted park I ever saw; the park walls are about eight miles in circumference; and I dare venture to say, there is a million of full grown trees in it. In short, it's larger, as well walled, and more regularly planted than Richmond in Surrey.[1]

In the early years of the eighteenth century the Earl of Haddington began massed planting at Tyninghame; 'many millions of trees . . . in a sandy down or links . . . and they thrive mightily. He hath also laid out several avenues through his park, which when full grown, will be as noble as any in Britain', wrote Macky. About 1705 the Earl of Haddington began to plant holly hedges; and 130 years later there were to be nearly 3,000 yards of them. One walk, 743 yards long, had holly hedges on either side 11 feet in breadth and 15 feet high.

Even in the eighteenth century the transplanting of large trees had been mastered. On 30 October 1762 Collinson wrote of Lord Petre:

. . . he was my intimate friend, the ornament and delight of the age he lived in. He went from his house at Ingatestone in Essex, to his seat at Thorndon Hall in the same county, to extend a large row of elms of the park behind the house. He removed, in the spring of the year 1734, being the 22d. of his age, twenty-four full grown elms about sixty feet high and two feet diameter: all grew finely, and now are not known from the old trees they were planted to match. In the year 1738 he planted the great avenue of elms up the park from the house to the esplanade: the trees were large, perhaps fifteen or twenty years old.[2]

How Petre accomplished this Collinson does not relate. But it *is* known how, almost a century later, in 1821–3, William McNab, principal gardener at the Royal Botanic Garden, Edinburgh, moved the entire contents of the Garden in Leith Walk to the new site in Inverleith, including a yew, some 200 years old, which still stands today[3] where McNab planted it. McNab invented a transplanting machine specially for the purpose, a somewhat cumbersome and crude version of the tree-transplanting machines of today, but obviously efficient for all that. The transplanting operation was described in *The Planter's Guide* (1825) by Sir Henry Steuart of Allanton in Lanarkshire:

The method adopted was to raise as great a mass or ball of earth as possible with the plants, and that was carefully matted up in order to preserve it entire. The plants were then put upon a platform with four very low wheels, in an upright position . . . and transplanted about a mile and a half to the new garden. In removing the trees, owing to the immense friction occasioned by the lowness of the wheels, ten and twelve horses were occasionally employed; so that the procession through the suburbs for many days, consisting

[1] p. 30, op. cit., p. 26.
[2] Quoted by Lambert in *Transactions of the Linnean Society*, X (1811), p. 273.
[3] Unfortunately blown down on 25 January 1968.

of men and horses, and waving boughs, presented a spectacle that was at once novel and imposing. The citizens of Edinburgh were surprised and delighted with the master of an art which seemed more powerful and persuasive than the strains of Orpheus, in drawing after it, along their streets, both grove and underwood of such majestic size—

Threicio blandius Orpheo
Auditam moderari arboribus fidem.[1]

Throughout the eighteenth century, though there were many fine gardeners in Scotland—many of them seeking their fortune in England—there were remarkably few fine garden designers. Of course, most of the gardens in Scotland were of the formal type, hardly to be distinguished from the majority of such in England, and required very little designing. Such great gardens as were designed were in large measure the work of the English garden designers such as London & Wise, who planned the garden at Hatton, the seat of the Earl of Lauderdale. One or two other gardens were designed by distinguished architects as a by-product of their architecture; Sir William Bruce, architect of Holyrood and his own garden at Kinross House, is an example. However, there was in Edinburgh a portrait painter, Alexander Nasmyth, who before he died in 1840 was to achieve a reputation as a garden designer, being employed by Sir James Hall at Dunglass, Haddingtonshire, and by John, the fourth Duke of Atholl, at Dunkeld. Still, in spite of the lack of designers, gardens in Scotland were being laid out in the eighteenth century, gardens which one day were to become famous in their various ways: Culzean, Brodick, Tyninghame, Balcaskie, Biel, Crathes, Drummond, Hopetoun, Lochinch. And throughout the century there was, of course, the fine seventeenth-century formal 'great garden' of Pitmedden.

Even so there was little in Scotland in the eighteenth century to compare with the gardens in England; little to compare with the seventeenth-century gardens at Woburn Abbey in Bedfordshire, Chatsworth in Derbyshire, Hatfield in Hertfordshire, Penshurst Place in Kent, or Cliveden in Buckinghamshire; little to compare with the eighteenth-century landscapes of Stourhead in Wiltshire, Castle Howard, Broughton Hall, and Duncombe Park in Yorkshire, Killerton and Bicton in Devon, Hagley Hall in Worcestershire, St. Paul's Walden Bury in Hertfordshire, Clevedon Court in Somerset, Frogmore in Berkshire, and Dropmore in Buckinghamshire; nothing to compare with the early eighteenth-century landscapes of Wise at Blenheim and Kensington Palace and at Melbourne Hall in Derbyshire; with the Charles Bridgeman landscape at Stowe, north of Buckingham; with the landscapes of

[1] *The Planter's Guide* (1825), p. 64.

William Kent, at Claremont and Esher in Surrey, Stowe, and at Rousham north of Oxford—Kent, who with his ha-ha 'leaped the fence and saw that all nature was a garden'; nothing to compare with the 'Capability' Brown landscapes of Blenheim and Chatsworth, Castle Ashby in Northamptonshire, Longleat in Wiltshire, Syon House near Brentford, Audley End House in Essex, Harewood in Yorkshire, Chilham Castle in Kent, Ickworth and Heveningham Hall in Suffolk, Westen Hall in Staffordshire, Sheffield Park in Sussex, Corsham Court in Wiltshire; nothing to compare with Humphry Repton's landscapes —and his Red Books—at Bulstrode and Cobham in Kent, Welbeck in Nottinghamshire, Luscombe in Devon, Anthony in Cornwall, Tatton Park and Rode in Cheshire, and Sheringham Park in Norfolk.

Throughout the land every establishment of any stature had its walled kitchen garden, which, in Scotland at any rate, was the most typical component of the estate, a mixture of flowers, fruits, and vegetables, often situated at a distance from the house and in which the head gardener practised his cultural skills. In the walled garden walls, of course, played a most important role. They were used not only as architectural features and for shelter but for forcing fruit; the back of a wall was heated by a series of ovens sometimes placed below ground level and, on the wall, grapes, peaches and nectarines were forced. Lean-to lights were kept in position on the wall until danger from spring frosts was past. Such walls with their movable lean-to lights were in use even after hot-houses and vineries had become the vogue. Pineapple pits were in use in the first half of the century and the fruits could be sold for half-a-guinea a time. In Scotland they were first ripened by James Justice round about 1750. Though Scotland was not regarded as a fruit-growing country, by the end of the century close on a hundred named varieties of apple were grown, some sixty pears, some twelve cherries, over twenty plums, about six apricots, about twelve peaches, about six nectarines, over a dozen grapes, about twenty-four gooseberries, six raspberries, and four currants.

In England there were many more, and towards the end of the eighteenth century there was already much confusion in their nomenclature. This was evident from the collection of hardy fruits, which its owner, Leonard Phillips Jnr., claimed to be the largest collection ever assembled, occupying 'about six acres of ground in the Portsmouth road, about a quarter mile beyond Vauxhall Turnpike'.[1] And the stated object of the collection was to clear up the muddled nomenclature. This was precisely what the Royal Horticultural Society was to do some twenty to twenty-five years later.

Scotland, in the eighteenth century, may not have had the great

[1] *Jl R. hort. Soc.*, LXXIX (1954), p. 363.

landscape gardeners and landscaped gardens which wrought such a change in the English scene, but the country certainly had its share of flower gardens (flowers played a very minor role in the landscaped gardens of the seventeenth and eighteenth centuries), of florists' flowers, and of florists' societies. Even Repton himself designed one flower garden—at Valleyfield on the Firth of Forth; '. . . flower gardens on a small scale may, with propriety, be formal and artificial', Repton had said. For the most part, however, the flower gardens, both in Scotland and in England, were the small cottage gardens, and the flowers cultivated were in the main tulips, auriculas, carnations, pinks, anemones, ranunculus, hyacinths, and polyanthus. These were the eight flowers defined as florists' flowers in the rules of the florists' societies. The original florists were mostly Flemish or French weavers who had fled to England in the sixteenth century and, by the eighteenth century, were well established, and held their shows in East Anglia and in the industrial area of the Midlands, as well as parts of Scotland.

In Scotland the cheapest flowers were the most popular; tulips, for instance, because of their high price, were never so popular with the working-class florists as carnations or pinks, and no one, anywhere in Britain, was so successful with the cultivation of the florists' pink as were the 'operative manufacturers' of Paisley. Pinks were already very popular plants by 1780. By 1790 seeds of pinks from London had been obtained and, although most of the seedlings were quite ordinary, a few showed a pattern of lacing. The laced seedlings were carefully segregated, propagated from seeds, and then selected, to the extent that by the early years of the nineteenth century a wide range of laced pinks of superior form were to be distributed all over the country.

The English equivalent of the Paisley Pink was undoubtedly the auricula, and Lancashire, Cheshire, Yorkshire, and the neighbourhood of London—districts in which the Continental refugees had settled—were in large measure the centres of auricula cultivation in the seventeenth, eighteenth, and nineteenth centuries. By the middle of the seventeenth century the auricula exhibited all manner of flower colours —white, yellow, yellow-brown, orange, cherry, red, violet, purple, tawny, olive, purple and white striped, purple and yellow striped. Gradually flowers with paste and flowers with meal were bred. By the middle of the eighteenth century green-edged and white-eyed flowers had been raised and further new 'breaks' were still to come—and the florists' auricula, the 'Show' auricula of today, was to reach the peak of perfection in the middle of the nineteenth century.

Thus the eighteenth century was an age of garden-making and tree-planting on a vast scale; an age during which new plant material was accumulating from overseas and was being tested and tried in nurseries and in gardens great and small, and being illustrated in the few horticultural publications available; an age during which fruits and flowers—and vegetables—were being improved; an age during which small societies were springing up throughout the country. Surely the time was ripe for the establishment of a Society for the study and advancement of horticulture in all its branches and for the co-ordination of the horticultural activities of the country.

At any rate there was one man who thought so and, on 29 June 1801, he expressed his thoughts in a letter written from Etruria, his home in Staffordshire.

Part One
The Early Years
(1804 - 1810)

CHAPTER ONE

THE FOUNDERS AND THE FOUNDATION

Etruria.
June 29, 1801.

Dear Sir,

I have been turning my attention to the formation of a Horticultural Society, and have drawn up such heads as have appeared to me necessary for the first formation of the Society. It would be proper to add a preamble, just stating the ideas of the first founders of the Society, and intimating that we wish to clash with no society at present instituted whose plans are different from ours. By this means we shall give no offence to any party. By not binding ourselves to publish annually we shall not be obliged to expose ourselves to the world in an imperfect state by publishing papers not worth making public. When you have read the enclosed, I shall be happy to have your opinion on it.

I expect to be in London about the middle of July, and I hope that you will have so settled your plans that you will be able to give me your company at Coote when I leave town the middle of August. I mention it to you now, that you may have time to arrange your affairs, that I may not be disappointed again. When you come again, I hope you will make some stay with me.

There is now a fine opportunity to try any experiments on trees, but nobody to do it. My stay is so uncertain that I have not begun to do anything, for I could do nothing effectually, as I must do every individual thing with my own hands. My direction now is Etruria, Staffordshire.

Believe me ever Yours Truly,

JOHN WEDGWOOD

P.S. If you should see Sir Joseph Banks, will you be so good as to ask him his opinion of the plan, and learn how far we might have a chance of having his patronage of the scheme.

W. Forsyth, Esq.,
Royal Gardens, Kensington.

John Wedgwood was a son of Josiah Wedgwood, the great potter, William Forsyth gardener to King George III, and Sir Joseph Banks President of the Royal Society and Royal Adviser to the Gardens at Kew.

Quite clearly Wedgwood had been turning his attention to the project to some profit, as the text of the enclosure to which he refers shows.

That a Society be formed to be called 'The Horticultural Society'.

That the object of this Society shall be to collect every information respecting the culture and treatment of all plants and trees, as well culinary as ornamental.

That every new member shall be balloted after a Society of original members has been formed, and that every such member at his admission shall pay one guinea besides his annual subscription.

That a certain number of honorary members may be elected, who shall be admitted to the sittings of the Society without paying any subscriptions; that two black balls be sufficient to reject such honorary candidate.

That the Society shall from time to time publish a volume of papers of the same size and form as the Transactions of the Adelphi Society,[1] and that each Member shall be entitled to a copy, but no honorary member unless he has furnished a paper judged worthy of publication.

That the Society shall annually choose a President, four Vice-Presidents, a Committee of Inspection, and a Secretary.

That the Committee shall have the power of selecting the papers for publication, and that no paper shall be published before it has been read at a sitting of the Society.

That no paper shall be published which does not treat of horticultural subjects.

That it shall be considered within the intention of this Society to give premiums for improvements in horticulture, whenever it shall be judged expedient so to do.

Some time during the following month the letter and enclosure were given, or sent, by Forsyth to Banks, who returned them on 31 July 1801, with a note saying 'I approve very much the idea,' and adding that he would be honoured to be an original member. This note is in the possession of the Royal Horticultural Society, but the whereabouts of Wedgwood's historic letter and enclosure is not known. Certainly they were available to Andrew Murray in 1863 when he published *The Book of the Royal Horticultural Society*; the text of them forms part of the Appendix.

During the following months the matter was discussed by Wedgwood and Forsyth in correspondence and no doubt, also, whenever they met, for at this time the former was spending several weeks of the year in

[1] The Society for the Encouragement of Arts, now the Royal Society of Arts, founded 1754.

Sir Joseph Banks, Bt.

Charles Francis Greville

Plate 1. FOUNDERS OF THE SOCIETY

W. T. Aiton

R. A. Salisbury

William Forsyth

James Dickson

Plate 2. FOUNDERS OF THE SOCIETY

London. Thus, in September 1801 Wedgwood wrote that he had met W. T. Aiton, gardener to H.M. the King at Kew, and had 'mentioned our horticultural society to him, which he much approved'; and on 22 January 1802, 'I have shown the proposal for our new Society to the Marquess of Lansdowne who desired me to add his name to the list of subscribers, as did also Mr. Jervis of Darlaston, in Staffordshire, who is one of the best gentleman gardeners I am acquainted with.'

Wedgwood was corresponding again with Forsyth, on 8 March 1802, when he wrote:

On the other side you have a kind of preface to the Rules of our intended Society, which I have drawn up at my leisure. I must trouble you to fix some hour that I can spend with you to talk this matter over, and put things in a train that we may put our intentions in execution. Since I saw you I have written to Dr. (J. E.) Smith [President of the Linnean Society], explaining our intention, and hoping to have his concurrence in the scheme. He has given me a very obliging answer, and desired me to use his name as I thought proper. I hope that we shall thus steer clear of all jealousies and animosities with other societies.

HORTICULTURAL SOCIETY

In almost all the counties of Great Britain are now established Societies for the improvement of Agriculture, which have been attended with more or less success, by the introduction of new breeds of cattle, or new instruments of husbandry, &c. Some of these societies have considered orchards as a branch of agriculture which deserved peculiar attention, and have given premiums accordingly:— For example, the Society for the Encouragement of Arts, &c. in the Adelphi, and the Bath Agricultural Society. This last society has given a premium for raising new sorts of apples from the pippin. These appear to be the only instances where any branch of gardening has been encouraged by the agricultural societies, and they only so far as they are considered in an agricultural point of view. It is now proposed to form a society for the sole purpose of encouraging Horticulture in its different branches, to form a repository for all the knowledge which can be collected on this subject and give a stimulus to the exertions of individuals for its farther [sic] improvement. It is well known to all persons who have made enquiries on this subject, that there are various facts relevant to gardening confined to small districts, which would be of general service if communicated. These facts will be collected by the society, and the knowledge of them generally dispersed over the country. The following rules and regulations have been drawn up as the basis of the society, by which it will be clearly seen that there is no intention of interfering with any other society whatsoever, but, on the contrary, a wish to concur in the general improvement of the country.

Whether or not a meeting of Forsyth and Wedgwood took place is not known, but in an undated letter of 1802 Wedgwood is anxious 'to hear if you have made any progress towards getting a meeting for establishing our Horticultural Society. If you are at leisure any morning this week I will call on you.'

Clearly Wedgwood had no desire to take the lead in the formation of the society he had conceived; he gave the initiative to Forsyth. Possibly he himself was too busy; certainly he was greatly preoccupied. The London bank in which he was a partner was not flourishing and the products of the family pottery in Staffordshire were deteriorating both in quality and in quantity. Moreover war was anticipated, volunteers were everywhere being recruited and John and his brother Josiah were each commanding a company. Even his gardener was troublesome and in the autumn of 1802 had to be discharged for inefficiency.

Given the initiative Forsyth hardly reacted with alacrity, possibly because he, too, was occupied in 1801 with the compilation of his *Treatise on the Culture and Management of Fruit Trees* which was published the following year and which some critics considered was in large measure a copy of an earlier work by Thomas Hitt. Be this as it may, the book was a success, three editions being issued in less than two years.

Not until Wednesday, 7 March 1804, was the Society's inaugural meeting held, in the house of the bookseller Mr. Hatchard,[1] in Piccadilly, London, for, as the minutes of the meeting record, 'the purpose of instituting a Society for the Improvement of Horticulture'. Apart from Wedgwood and Forsyth the meeting was attended by five others; the Rt. Hon. Sir Joseph Banks, the Rt. Hon. Charles Greville, Richard Anthony Salisbury, William Townsend Aiton, and James Dickson. 'Mr. Wedgwood was requested to take the Chair' and 'A paper which had been circulated among a few Friends by Mr. Wedgwood was read'. The contents of this paper, save that no mention is made of honorary members, are essentially those of Wedgwood's enclosure which accompanied his letter to Forsyth of 29 June 1801. Before the meeting closed it was

resolved that this paper be approved as the Foundation of the New Society but that the Rules proposed in it be not considered as confirmed until the Society has actually met; that the Original Society shall consist of Twenty Eight Members, to be recommended by the Gentlemen present, and confirmed by the Approbation of the next Meeting; that each Person present shall have the Privilege of recommending three Persons for the Approbation of the next Meeting; that each Person do pay the Sum of one Guinea towards defraying the Expenses of the Meeting, and other necessary expenses; that Mr. Wedgwood be requested to act as Treasurer at present; that he be re-

---

[1] Mr. Hatchard's business still bears his name and is conducted on the same site, 187 Piccadilly. The building now bears a commemorative tablet which was unveiled on 7 March 1932 by the Hon. H. D. McLaren, the then President of the Society (*Jl R. hort. Soc.*, LVII (1932), p. 157).

quested to order the Paper he has been so good as to produce with the Minutes of this Meeting to be printed and to send Ten Copies to each Member present; that this Meeting be adjourned to Wednesday next, the 14th Instant, then to meet at the same Place.

What manner of men were these who thus founded the Royal Horticultural Society? Four were amateur gardeners and one of the four an eminent botanist; two were professional gardeners; the other a nurseryman and seedsman; and with one possible exception they were all quite remarkable apart from their connection with the Society and their horticultural interests.

Wedgwood[1] (1766–1844) (Plate I), thirty-eight at the time, was the most junior of the party. He was the eldest of three sons of Josiah Wedgwood, founder of the world-famed pottery at Etruria, near Newcastle under Lyme, Staffordshire, and an associate of those extraordinary men—Erasmus Darwin, Joseph Priestley, James Watt, and Matthew Boulton among them—who called themselves the Lunar Society, 'the most remarkable group of thinkers and inventors in the eighteenth century, which had a more potent effect upon civilization than that of any society in history'.[2] Susannah, John Wedgwood's sister, was to marry one of Erasmus Darwin's sons, Robert, and become the mother of Charles Darwin, author of *The Origin of Species* (1859), still the most important biological work ever written.

After some schooling at Hindley and at Bolton-le-Moors in Lancashire, John studied chemistry in Newcastle under Lyme. This pleased his father, who, realizing the importance of a knowledge of this subject to the family business, happily wrote to his partner 'the boys drink in knowledge like water. . . . Jack is very deep in chemical affinities.' Subsequently John and his next brother Josiah entered Edinburgh University, where they gave special attention to mineralogy as well as to chemistry. After a short apprenticeship at the pottery they spent two years on the Continent, visiting Paris, Rome, and Naples, before settling down to work. In 1790 their father retired from an active part in the business and the firm was reconstituted under the name of Wedgwood, Sons & Byerley. However, two years later John became a junior partner in the London and Middlesex Bank (absorbed by Coutts & Co. in 1816) and shortly afterwards ceased to be a partner in the pottery.

In 1794 he married Miss Louisa Jane Allen, whose elder sister had previously become the wife of his brother Josiah. For a time he lived at Tallaton in Devon, subsequently moving to London, to Devonshire Place, where doubtless he made the acquaintance of William Forsyth—

[1] *Jl R. hort. Soc.*, LVI (1931), p. 65.
[2] Hesketh Pearson in *Doctor Darwin* (1930), p. vii.

for his hobby was gardening. And no doubt it was his hobby which, in 1797, caused him to make his home at Cote House, Westbury, near Bristol, where he was happy growing grapes, pineapples, peaches, and ornamental plants under glass, planting an orchard, building a wall for plums, and cultivating out of doors azaleas, dahlias, tulips, and carnations, and many another flower. On at least one occasion Forsyth visited him to advise him on his garden.

Although the garden at Cote House was prospering, the old family business was not. In fact, since the death of Josiah Wedgwood the elder, in 1795, the pottery had deteriorated rapidly, for Josiah the second lacked his father's administrative and business ability. Consequently in an endeavour to revive the family firm, John rejoined it in 1800, frequently staying in Staffordshire and, when not there, always being consulted on most matters. It was on one of his visits to Staffordshire that he wrote the letter to Forsyth suggesting the foundation of a horticultural society. At this time a volunteer army was being formed and in 1803 both John and Josiah were captains commanding companies. As most of the men in the ranks were the firm's employees, 'great were the complaints of the foremen at the time lost by these men in learning to drum and fife'.

John continued to reside at Cote House until the beginning of 1805, when, owing to the ill success of the bank into which he had placed the greater part of the fortune inherited from his father, he was obliged to sell the property. He moved temporarily to Maer Hall, Staffordshire, and later to Etruria, where he remained until 1810. Thereafter he moved restlessly from place to place before settling finally at Seabridge, near Newcastle under Lyme. Wherever he lived, however, he took the greatest possible pleasure and interest in his gardens, and in spite of his greatly reduced circumstances never failed to make them the admiration of all who saw them. His Garden Book,[1] now one of the treasures of the Society's Lindley Library, tells us that in 1827, in his garden at Kingscote, he grew eight kinds of broccoli, celery, borecole, brussels sprouts, nine kinds of cabbage, early frame peas, malta beans, carrots. During the next fifteen years he was to cultivate over a hundred different varieties of apple, including many of Thomas Andrew Knight's seedlings, over twenty kinds of pear, over twelve kinds of cherry, peaches and nectarines, twelve different raspberries, and over thirty different strawberries. In 1831 disaster hit him:

April 22nd. On coming home this day and looking over my garden found it in great confusion, having been entirely neglected. No Onions, no Carrots, no Parsnips, no red Beets. All my early Peas gone, the seed beds evidently in

[1] E. A. Bunyard, *Jl R. hort. Soc.*, LVI (1931), p. 196.

many cases not dug, only raked over. The Broccoli in holes all gone; luckily we had provided against this by sowing beds of Broccoli of different sorts.

After having finished the flower garden and after carefully looking over the garden, I immediately discharged Hooper for his entire neglect during my absence. The only crops that are at all promising are some of the crops of Peas and Beans. The seed beds of Savoys and Kales are evidently sown without an atom of dung put to them. The Runner and Kidney Beans are tolerable.

Kingscote wasn't the first garden to suffer from lack of personal supervision—and it certainly wasn't the last.

Fruit and vegetables apart, he cultivated about thirty different paeonies, phloxes and trilliums from America, many bulbs and corms, including over fifty kinds of crocus and eight species of ixia, over a hundred and fifty pelargoniums, over two hundred kinds of dahlia, many chrysanthemums, camellias, roses and carnations, and, perhaps most remarkable of all, many alpines, including androsace and gentian.

Very sadly, owing to partial loss of sight, he had to renounce gardening in 1843 and went to live with one of his sons at Tenby, where he died on 24 January the following year, and where he was interred in the burial ground of the parish church.

William Forsyth[1] (1737–1804) (Plate 2), gardener to King George III at Kensington and St. James's and sixty-six or sixty-seven years of age, was probably the oldest of those present at the inaugural meeting. Born at Old Meldrum in Aberdeenshire, he emulated many other enterprising Scotsmen by moving to England in 1763, at the age of twenty-six. For some time he worked under the illustrious Philip Miller, the greatest gardener-botanist of his time, who had been in charge of the Apothecaries' Garden at Chelsea since 1722 and had published the monumental *Gardeners Dictionary* in 1731. Subsequently Forsyth became gardener to the Duke of Northumberland at Syon House, but in 1770 returned to Chelsea to succeed Miller (who had retired in his eightieth year) at a salary of sixty pounds per annum 'with lodging rooms in the green-house, and coals'.

With great energy he entered upon his duties in 1771 and soon removed a number of large trees which were considered injurious to the growth of those plants for which the Garden had more particularly been designed. Arrangements were made for 'a great interchange of exotic plants . . . between the [Apothecaries] Society and various Noblemen, Gentlemen and others'. And in 1774 he began to construct probably the first rock garden in Britain, using forty tons of old stone from the Tower of London, flints and chalk, and lava brought from Iceland by Sir Joseph Banks two years before. This was Forsyth's greatest contribution

[1] *Jl R. hort. Soc.*, LXVI (1941), pp. 319, 374.

to the Garden, which never again was to attain the supremacy it had had under Miller; certainly it lost some of its pre-eminence under Forsyth's régime. Even so, when, in 1784, he was appointed to the charge of His Majesty's Garden at Kensington, and resigned from Chelsea, he received the thanks of the Chelsea committee for his great care of the Garden.

Two years before leaving Chelsea he helped to found the Society for Promoting Natural History. The first meeting was held at a Mr. Dean's, The Corner House, The Turnpike, Pimlico, which appears to have stood on the site of Hobart House, Grosvenor Place. Eaton Square did not exist, and the King's Road, along which Forsyth would walk from the Physic Garden at Chelsea, ran entirely through fields between Sloane Square and Grosvenor Place. After the first year meetings were held in various places, usually in taverns and coffee houses, 'once every month on the Monday next following the Full Moon, at seven o'clock in the evening'. The normally dark roads were naturally safer under the light of the moon. The meetings were largely occupied with official business and the exhibition of specimens among which minerals and fossils bulked disproportionately. Several very prominent naturalists, including J. E. (later Sir James) Smith, anonymous writer of the text of Sowerby's thirty-six-volume *English Botany*, and Samuel Goodenough (later Bishop of Carlisle), an authority on British seaweeds, became members. However, they, and no doubt others, quickly became dissatisfied with the way the Society's affairs were conducted, Goodenough writing to Smith in 1787:

The present Society goes on in the usual way of having a fossil or plant go round the table; nothing is or can be said about it. It is referred to a committee to consider; the committee call it by some name and send it back to the society. The society desires the committee to reconsider it. In the meantime nothing is done; indeed it does not appear to me that any of them can do anything.

But Smith and Goodenough could; the Linnean Society was formed in 1788 with Smith the first president and Goodenough the treasurer. Forsyth's old Society struggled on for another thirty-four years, until in 1822 its assets were handed over to the Linnean. The ivory gavel now used by the president of the latter Society is the one which belonged to the Society for Promoting Natural History.

Now that he was the King's gardener at Kensington and St. James's, Forsyth perforce had to turn his attention to the cultivation of fruit and vegetables, for the royal household drew its supplies of these largely from Kensington Gardens. His task was not easy, because many of the fruit trees were in poor health, canker being rife in the apples and gumming in the stone fruits. Consequently it was necessary to head-back many of the trees and to remove numerous large branches. Naturally great wounds were formed and, to encourage the formation of callus over these, as well as to help to hide them, Forsyth coated them with a mixture of cow dung, lime, wood ashes, sand, soap suds, and urine, beaten into the consistency of the plaster which is used by builders. In like manner he used this same 'plaster' or 'composition' on elms, oaks, and other trees where branches had to be removed, extravagantly claiming that, by so doing, he could restore trees which were so diseased and hollow that nothing remained but the outer bark, and render them as sound as they had been before being injured. By disclosing his method, at a time when England was at war with Napoleon and the provision of sound oak for shipbuilding was essential, in 1789 he gulled a Parliamentary Commission, which inspected his experiments, into reporting to the Treasury 'that Mr. Forsyth's Composition is a discovery which may be highly beneficial to individuals and the public'. As a result, Treasury recommended the King to grant to Forsyth a reward which is generally understood to have been £1,500, although the amount does not appear to have been published officially. Much elated, Forsyth advertised his plaster far and wide and wrote of it in his small book entitled *Observations on the Diseases, Defects and Injuries in all kinds of Fruit and Forest Trees*, published in 1791 and reprinted at the end of his *Treatise on the Culture and Management of Fruit Trees* (1802). Forsyth and his experiments were famous all over the country and Wedgwood clearly believed him to be the obvious person to whom to put his ideas regarding the proposed horticultural society. No doubt he was thinking of Forsyth's experiments when he wrote to Forsyth on 29 June 1801 'there is now a fine opportunity to try any experiments on trees'. One man was not impressed by Forsyth's experiments—Thomas Andrew Knight, who was to prove to be one of the most significant figures in British horticulture and the Horticultural Society and who severely criticized Forsyth's 'Plaister', his experiments, and his writings, from 1802 until Forsyth died in 1804.

The memory of this shrewd Scotsman is kept green in the genus of spring-flowering shrubs named by Vahl in his honour—the genus *Forsythia*.

By far the most outstanding of the seven founders was Sir Joseph Banks[1] (1743–1820) (Plate 1). The only son of William Banks, M.P., of Revesby Abbey in Lincolnshire, he was schooled both at Harrow and Eton, at which latter establishment he developed a great interest in natural history and especially in plants and insects. In 1760, at the age of seventeen, he entered Christ Church, Oxford, and there remained for three years. His father having died in 1761, Banks, on coming of age,

[1] Edward Smith, *Life of Sir Joseph Banks* (1911).

inherited the family fortune, which gave him an income of about £6,000 a year. Unlike most wealthy young men of his day, he did not make the 'grand tour' of Europe. Instead he frequented the company of those most interested in botany and other natural sciences, made full use of the Chelsea Physic Garden and of Philip Miller's vast knowledge of plants, and thus gradually and unconsciously equipped himself with the knowledge that was to enable him soon to lay the foundations of Kew as a botanical institution of international importance. In 1766–7 he botanized in Newfoundland and Labrador (and, whilst abroad, was elected a Fellow of the Royal Society), and introduced into cultivation in Britain *Rhododendron canadense*, the 'Rhodora' whose rosy-purple flowers open before the leaves appear, and the close ally of the rhododendrons, the evergreen rose-flowered *Kalmia polifolia*.

As a result of representations made by the Royal Society, it was arranged in 1768 that the ship *Endeavour*, under the command of Captain James Cook, should voyage to the South Pacific, primarily to observe, in 1769, the passage of the planet Venus over the disc of the sun. Banks was quick to realize the wonderful opportunities for botanical study this expedition would give, and at his request the Royal Society obtained permission for him and his party of seven others to accompany the expedition, at his own expense. The party included his friend the Swedish botanist and favourite pupil of Linnaeus, Daniel Carl Solander, who later became Banks's librarian, and two artists. Thus in 1768 Banks set out on Cook's first great voyage of exploration through the Pacific, visiting Madeira, Rio de Janeiro, Tierra del Fuego, Tahiti, New Zealand, Australia (where he saw the plants, locally known as honeysuckle, which later were to commemorate his name—*Banksia*), the Dutch East Indies, South Africa, and St. Helena, before returning in July 1771. From all points of view the expedition was a great success. Banks was lionized and was taken by the President of the Royal Society to meet the King, George III. The two became close friends.

Banks was due to accompany Cook on the latter's second voyage, in 1772, and had arranged to take with him a suite of fifteen, which was to include two horn players. To accommodate them all, as well as the £5,000-worth of equipment which Banks had bought, Cook had to be turned out of the *Resolution*'s main cabin and a separate round-house had to be built on the deck for his own use. However, this additional accommodation rendered *Resolution* top-heavy and in danger of capsizing, and it had to be removed. If Banks insisted on taking his suite, all members of it would have to pack into the original deck space as best they could. This Banks refused to do and, after unavailingly protesting to the Admiralty, he withdrew from the expedition. Instead of travelling with Cook, he journeyed to Iceland, where he collected a great number of specimens of plants and other objects of natural science, including lava for the construction of Forsyth's new rock garden at Chelsea. In 1778, at the age of thirty-five, he was unanimously elected President of the Royal Society and held this office until his death forty-two years later. A fine naturalist and polite autocrat, with unique experience in his own field, he was well suited to preserve and enhance the Royal Society's authority on matters of science. From 1778 his large house in Soho became his chief residence and the resort of innumerable persons of standing not only in science but in the arts as well, for he was much interested in the latter, being Secretary of the Society of Dilettanti from 1778 to 1797. He was created a baronet in 1781, a K.C.B. in 1795 and a Privy Councillor in 1797, and few non-political projects of public importance seem to have been undertaken without his being consulted. It was very natural indeed that Wedgwood should be anxious to secure his patronage for the Horticultural Society.

Through his influence with George III, the Royal Pleasure Gardens at Kew began to assume the role of a botanic garden, and vast numbers of plants from overseas were sought and obtained from correspondents or from collectors dispatched specially for the purpose. And, of course, he maintained his own garden, at his country house, Spring Grove, Isleworth. Although he cultivated interesting, newly-introduced ornamental plants, to judge from the papers he submitted to the Horticultural Society for publication in *The Transactions*, he appears to have been interested mostly in fruits. Thus he contributed papers on the management of strawberries, the cultivation of American cranberries, the ripening of a second crop of figs, and on an apple called 'Spring Grove Codlin'. It is possible, of course, that his apparent special interest in fruit may have been thrust upon him by his gardener to whom he once referred as 'my gardener who, of course, is my master'. It cannot have been difficult for the gardener to prove himself master, for during the last fifteen years of his life Banks was greatly crippled by gout, often losing the use of his limbs and having to be carried around in a chair.

No doubt Banks was responsible for William Townsend Aiton (Plate 2) attending the inaugural meeting, for, like Forsyth, Aiton was in the service of George III, having been gardener to His Majesty at Kew since 1793, when he had succeeded his father in this post on a strong recommendation from Banks. The father, William Aiton (1731–93), was a Lanarkshire man who had come to England in 1754, had worked with Philip Miller in the Chelsea Physic Garden (as Forsyth later did) before moving to Kew in 1759. Thirty years later he published the *Hortus Kewensis*, or a *Catalogue of the plants cultivated in the Royal Botanic Gardens at Kew*, a three-volume work in which 5,500 species are named, diagnosed, and classified according to the Linnaean system. Aiton described himself as 'Gardener to His Majesty' and at his death he was sometimes called 'His Majesty's Principal Gardener at Kew'.

William Townsend Aiton (1766–1849) was the eldest son, born at Kew and reared there during the early years of Banks's association with the establishment. At the age of sixteen he was assisting his father in the Garden and appears to have received training not only as a cultivator and as a botanist but also as a landscape gardener, for it is on record that before he had attained the age of twenty-seven he had been employed in the latter capacity by the Duke of Kent and other noblemen and gentlemen. With the assistance of Banks and Dr. Dryander, Banks's librarian, he published, in 1810–13, a second enlarged edition of his father's *Hortus Kewensis*, in five volumes, and in the following year, for the use of practical gardeners, a catalogue, or epitome, of the earlier work, with additions that brought the total number of species to 11,013.

The two Aitons, with Banks and George III, raised Kew to a prominent position in the botanical and horticultural worlds, and between them carried over the superintendence of the Gardens from the very end of the reign of George II into the reign of Victoria. However, in 1820 both the King and Banks died, and thereafter W. T. Aiton, who lived to be eighty-three, witnessed the gradual decadence of the Gardens in his charge. Both father and son are buried in the churchyard of St. Anne's Church, Kew Green.

It is possible that Banks was also responsible for the attendance at the inaugural meeting of his bachelor friend, the Hon. Charles Francis Greville[1] (1749–1809) (Plate 1), attending the inaugural meeting, for they were both office-holders in the Society of Dilettanti, Banks as secretary and his friend as Very High Steward. Greville was the second son of the first Earl of Warwick of the Greville family.[2] Whilst in his early twenties he was of sufficient standing in the scientific world to be elected a Fellow of the Royal Society. His particular interest lay in precious stones in their natural state, of which, throughout his life, he amassed a fine collection—diamond, ruby, sapphire, emerald, topaz, and rubillite. He also gave much attention to meteorites, and indeed the only paper he appears to have delivered before the Royal Society was 'An account of some Stones said to have fallen on the Earth in France; and of a Lump of Native Iron said to have fallen in India'. In 1774, at the age of twenty-five, he entered Parliament as one of the Members for Warwick, and in 1783 he was appointed Treasurer of the Household and sworn of the Privy Council. Eleven years later he became Vice-

[1] *Jl R. hort. Soc.*, LXVII (1942), p. 219.
[2] He is not to be confused with Charles Greville (1762–1832) or with his son Charles Cavendish Fulke Greville (1794–1865) of the *Greville Memoirs*. They belong to the Fulke Greville family of Wilbury.

Chamberlain of the Household, a post he continued to hold for ten and a half years. His parliamentary career was somewhat chequered, for in 1790 he lost his seat at Warwick, returned to the House of Commons five years later as Member for Petersfield, only to be defeated at a general election the following year. Although he was never again in Parliament, he continued to act as Vice-Chamberlain of the Household and was the holder of his appointment at the time of the inaugural meeting.

In some ways Greville was the most interesting member present at the inaugural meeting. In 1782 he had given up his house in Portman Square and had moved to Edgware Row, where for the next four years he lived happily with a household consisting of the remarkably lovely teenage girl at that time known as Emma Hart, and her mother, who managed the housekeeping well and economically. The small house was furnished in beautiful taste and with works of art which he had collected with the connoisseur's discretion and financial prudence, and it was more with the eye of an art connoisseur than that of a lover that Greville appears to have regarded Emma. He treated her with the greatest kindness, provided her with teachers in music and singing and encouraged her to read and to take an intelligent interest in ancient coins, fine engravings, and mezzotints. She was introduced to Romney, at whose studio in Cavendish Square she became a frequent visitor when Greville was engaged in his parliamentary duties, and Romney, so captivated by her beauty, painted no fewer than twenty-four portraits of her.

In the meantime, on his visits to London, Greville's uncle, Sir William Hamilton (1730–1803), H.M. Ambassador at Naples, and a widower in his fifties, had become greatly attracted to the pretty 'tea-maker of Edgware Row', and in 1786 Emma and her mother left London for Naples—temporarily, as they thought, but, as it turned out, permanently—to live with Sir William. Greville was not greatly averse to the change, for he was finding it more and more difficult to make both ends meet and had realized that he must either marry an heiress or become a pauper. He did neither. The story of how Emma stayed in Naples, eventually becoming Lady Hamilton and subsequently Nelson's mistress, has many times been told and many hard words have been written about Greville's actions and motives as revealed by the Hamilton-Nelson papers and embroidered by the imaginations of authors. Perhaps the best judge of Greville's conduct throughout the whole of this period is the one-time illiterate girl who, as Lady Hamilton, wrote in 1794:

I congratulate you, my dear Mr. Greville, with all my heart on your appointment to the Vice-Chamberlainship. You have well merited it and all your friends must be happy at a change so favourable, not only for your pecuniary circumstances, as for the honner [sic] of the situation. May you long enjoy it

31

with every happiness that you deserve. I speak from my heart, I don't know a better, honester or more amiable and worthy man than yourself; and it is a great deal for me to say this, for whatever I think I am not apt to pay compliments.

In 1784 William Hamilton had entrusted to Greville the care of his Welsh estate. Milford Haven seemed to have possibilities of becoming an important centre similar to the Tyne and other large rivers and Greville enthusiastically began to develop the estate. The town was laid out in American fashion and Greville secured the passage of an Act 'to enable Sir William Hamilton . . . to make and provide Quays, Docks, Piers and other Erections, and to establish a Market' at Hubberston and Pile. At frequent intervals he reported progress to his uncle, though Sir William, far away in Naples, was quite unable to appreciate all that was happening and wrote: 'I have sign'd, sealed and returned the paper but . . . I know no more of my affairs in Wales than the man in the moon.' However, once he had seen for himself he wrote further to Greville: 'My visit to Milford last year convinced me of the propriety of all your operations there.' At his death in 1803 he left to Greville, his sole executor, rather more than £7,000 and his Welsh estate, so that at the time of the formation of the Horticultural Society Greville was freed from financial worries.

It is not clear when he began to take a keen interest in gardening. It is known, however, from Emma Hart's housekeeping accounts that he employed a jobbing gardener in 1784 when he was living at Edgware Row. In 1790 he moved to a rather larger house at Paddington Green, where there was not only more room for his cabinets of minerals, and for his pictures and other works of art, but also a large garden in which, according to Sir James Smith, 'the rarest and most curious plants, from various climates, were cultivated with peculiar success, and always devoted to the real advancement of science'. At least fourteen of the plates in the *Botanical Magazine* and similar works were painted from specimens in his garden and he is credited by contemporary writers with the introduction of *Lilium concolor*, the bright scarlet erect-flowered lily from China; a more or less double rose-coloured form of the tree paeony, *Paeonia suffruticosa* 'Rosea'; a semi-double red-flowered cultivar of *Camellia japonica*; *Adina globiflora*, a tender pretty evergreen shrub with globose heads of small yellow flowers; *Marantochloa dichotoma*, a close ally of the gingers; the magnolia everyone now knows as *M. liliflora*; *Michelia figo*, related to the magnolias; and a good semi-double rose-pink flowered form of *Prunus japonica*.

He died on 23 April 1809 a few months after the genus *Grevillea* had been named, by Robert Brown, in honour of 'the right honourable Charles Francis Greville . . . a gentleman eminently distinguished for his acquirements in natural history, and to whom the botanists of this country are indebted for the introduction and successful cultivation of many rare and interesting plants'.

James Dickson[1] (1738 or 1739–1822) (Plate 2), a nurseryman and seedsman living over his business premises in Covent Garden, was a friend both of Banks and of Forsyth, and one of them may have asked him to attend the meeting on 7 March 1804. As he had taken part, sixteen years before, in the foundation of the Linnean Society in 1788, (and thus holds the distinction of having been the founder of two world-famed societies), it was possibly thought that he would have ideas as to how a horticultural society should be formed and constituted. Dickson was a Scotsman, born at Kirke House, Traquhair, Peeblesshire, who came to England as a young man and worked as an improver in the famous nurseries of Jeffrey & Co., whose grounds extended from Brompton Road to Kensington Gore on the site now occupied by the Natural History Museum, the Imperial College of Science, and the Albert Hall. Subsequently he held several posts as a gardener before opening a shop in Covent Garden in 1772 and establishing a business, as a nurseryman and seedsman, which continued until his death fifty years later.

Shortly after arriving in London he was fortunate enough to become known to Banks, who was able to assist him in many ways. Thus, when in 1781 the Trustees of the British Museum became dissatisfied with their gardener, Banks persuaded Dickson to tender for the post. The tender was accepted and Dickson retained the contract for the rest of his life. Among his other customers were William Forsyth and Sir Francis Drake, Master of the Household.

It is rather remarkable that this nurseryman and horticulturist who was interested in vegetables and alpine plants should have become an eminent botanist chiefly noted for his studies on mosses, fungi, and grasses. In 1785 he commenced the publication of his *Fasciculi Plantarum Cryptogamicarum Britanniae*, a quarto work in four parts containing 400 descriptions. This work brought great scientific prestige to Dickson and upon it his reputation as a botanist was largely built. Although he made no mention of having received assistance from anyone, it would appear that a great deal of credit should have been given to a botanist named John Zier, a Pole by birth, who lived in London and seems to have assisted more than one author. Dickson also published *A Collection of Dried Plants, named on the authority of the Linnaean Herbarium* in seventeen folio fascicles each containing twenty-five species, and a *Hortus Siccus Britannicus*, in nineteen folio fascicles. Much of the material for his publications was collected during tours into Scotland. On one such tour, in 1789, when he was the first to discover the rare little rock-cress, *Draba*

[1] *Jl R. hort. Soc.*, LXVIII (1943), p. 66.

rupestris, on Ben Lawers, he was accompanied by a young medical student who later became famous for his explorations in Africa, and whose sister Dickson married after his first wife had died—Mungo Park.

He himself died in 1822 and the inscription on his tombstone in the churchyard of All Saints, Sanderstead, about two miles south of Croydon, has it that he was

A MAN OF POWERFUL MIND,
AND OF SPOTLESS INTEGRITY,
WHOSE SINGULAR ACUTENESS AND ACCURACY
IN THE MOST DIFFICULT DEPARTMENTS OF BOTANY,
HAVE RENDERED HIS NAME CELEBRATED
WHEREVER THAT SCIENCE IS KNOWN.

Those were the words of the first president of the Linnean Society, Sir James Edward Smith.

Apart from the portrait of him at the age of eighty-two (Plate 2), his memory is most effectively preserved in the genus of plants *Dicksonia*, consisting chiefly of handsome tree-ferns, which was named in his honour by L'Heritier in 1788.

Richard Anthony Salisbury[1] [*né* Markham] (1761–1829) (Plate 2), also in the Banksian circle and forty-two at the time of the inaugural meeting, was the one of the seven founders who was to take the most active part in the Society's early life. The only son of Richard Markham, a cloth merchant in Leeds, he was a botanist of distinction as well as a keen amateur gardener, believing, not altogether logically, that he had inherited a taste for botany from Henry Lyte, the botanist and antiquary whose sister was an ancestor of Salisbury's mother. At about the age of twenty he had commenced his studies at the University of Edinburgh, and there, apparently, had become acquainted with Mrs. Anna Salisbury, a connection of his maternal grandmother, who, in 1785, had given him £10,000 in three per cents to enable him to pursue his studies in botany and gardening, on the condition that he took the sole surname of Salisbury. Not unnaturally, this he did.

On coming down from the University he lived on one of his father's properties at Chapel Allerton near Leeds, was elected to the Royal Society in 1787 and became one of the first Fellows of the Linnean Society the following year. At Chapel Allerton he cultivated an unusually wide range of plants, both in the open and under glass, and was constantly adding to his collection through correspondence with such people as Banks, John Sims the editor of the *Botanical Magazine*, and

[1] *Jl R. hort. Soc.*, LXIX (1944), pp. 59, 95.

many Continental botanists. Thus on one occasion he received from Banks a collection of seeds of no fewer than 154 different species of East Indian plants and in writing to Banks about them said: 'Between 40 and 50 are already up, that were *not* in my collection before!!' That he was not only willing to acquire plants, but, like every true gardener, equally willing to share his plants with others, is evident from a letter to Sims: 'By the mail coach which leaves Leeds tonight I have sent you some large Bulbs which I have just received in the state you see. I hope you may get something new; we have spread all the earth they came in upon a Hotbed and several plants are appearing we do not know or even guess at.'

In 1796 he published in an octavo volume of 422 pages the *Prodromus Stirpium in Horte ad Chapel Allerton vigentium*, a catalogue of the plants in his garden, listing with his usual thoroughness not only cultivated species but weeds, fungi, and algae as well. Having a somewhat fastidious taste in the matter of plant names, whenever the usual name of a plant was not exactly as he would have chosen it he gave the usual one, but at the same time proposed a new one which he thought more appropriate. This one book, in fact, contains many dozens of new names which have never been adopted by other botanists and few books have littered the pages of *Index Kewensis* with so many useless synonyms. No doubt it was this coining of new names for well-known plants that induced the Rev. Dr. Goodenough to write to James Edward Smith in 1797:

Salisbury's nomenclature is, I think, extremely improper, not to say ridiculous. I am sorry that he has persisted in his errors even to printing them. I was present at a very warm dispute between him and Dryander, who in his blunt rough manner finished his argument with 'If this is to be the case with everybody, what the devil is to become of botany?'

In December 1796 Salisbury married Caroline Staniforth (not Stainforth, as stated in the *Dictionary of National Biography*), and their only child, a daughter, was born the following year. Apparently Mrs. Salisbury was not happy and, in 1798, left her husband and returned to her father with the infant. There followed protracted proceedings in which Mr. Staniforth and his other son-in-law, Joseph Beckett, endeavoured not only to obtain satisfactory provision for Mrs. Salisbury and her child but also to show that no such woman as Mrs. Anna Salisbury (the benefactress) had existed: 'all was fraud, fiction and deceit. . . . He is over ears and head in debt. . . .' It would appear that in order to defeat his relations Salisbury fraudulently represented himself to be insolvent and succeeded in deceiving not only them but the Lord Chancellor's Bankruptcy Commission as well. Moreover, he took pride in his astuteness, writing in 1806:

Having fallen into the hands of sharpers, it was necessary to invent *ruse contre ruse*, and no easy matter to affix the great seal to deeds which revoked the settlements I had in my generosity made upon my wife; indeed nothing but the supposition of my being a total bankrupt and the most positive evidence that I did not retain a single penny of hers, could have induced the Chancellor to do this.

His marriage broken up, early in 1800 he moved from Yorkshire to Mill Hill, Middlesex, where he purchased Ridgeway House, formerly the famous home and garden of Peter Collinson, the naturalist and antiquary, and now part of Mill Hill School, though the house and garden no longer exist. There, among 'venerable Chestnuts, Magnolias, Cembra Pines, Cedars and Cypresses, relics of Peter Collinson's labours,' and with other treasures like *Orchis militaris* and *O. purpurea*, 'where they had no doubt been planted by Mr. Peter Collinson' (who had been dead for over thirty years), and many different kinds of narcissi and other old favourites he had brought from Yorkshire, he continued his gardening activities. And there he was living at the time of the inaugural meeting. However, two years later he moved to 18 Queen Street, Edgware Road. The street is now Harrowby Street and is a turning off Edgware Road some 600 yards from the Marble Arch. This was his home for the rest of his life, and here he cultivated a tiny garden, thirty feet square, in which he contrived to grow several hundreds of rare plants in pots, including *Lilium concolor*, received, no doubt, from Greville, which he was the first to describe and name, and of which he wrote: 'it produced six flowers upon a stem in my smoaky court.'

How Salisbury served the Society for ten years after its foundation will be related in later pages. He died on 23 March 1829 and was buried in the churchyard of St. Mary's, Paddington Green, a few yards from the house in which his old colleague, Charles Greville, had lived. In 1797, the year of his daughter's birth, James Edward Smith had paid him a charming tribute when naming in his honour one of the most ancient of existing flowering plants we know as the Maidenhair tree. In describing *Salisburia adiantifolia* Smith wrote: 'The genus is named in honour of Richard Anthony Salisbury Esq., F.R.S. and F.L.S., of whose acuteness and indefatigable zeal in the service of botany no testimony is necessary in this Society [the Linnean], nor in any place in which his writings have reached.' It was unfortunate that in 1771 Linnaeus had named the same plant *Ginkgo biloba*, by which name it must be, and is, known. And more unfortunate still that, from about 1802, until which time Salisbury and Smith had been good friends, the two quarrelled almost continuously on matters botanical for several years.

Such were the men who attended the inaugural meeting on 7 March 1804.

CHAPTER TWO

THE EARLY MEETINGS

THE SECOND MEETING WAS HELD, AS ARRANGED, ON 14 MARCH 1804, except that Wedgwood could not attend and Sir Joseph Banks was in the Chair. The minutes record that in addition 'Mr. Hawkins attended, and informed the Meeting, that he would certainly have been present, on the 7th of March, if he had been in Town', and it was 'Resolved that Mr. Hawkins be considered as one of the Founders of the Society, and have the Privilege of recommending three Persons to be Members of this Society.'

John Hawkins (1758?–1841) was a friend of Wedgwood's, a Fellow of the Royal Society, a man of wealth who collected minerals and works of art, and a keen botanist and gardener. He had married the sister of John Sibthorp, Professor of Botany at Oxford from 1783 to 1795, and had accompanied Sibthorp to Greece in 1787 when the latter was collecting material for his monumental *Flora Graeca*. When Sibthorp died in 1796 Hawkins became one of his executors and for the rest of his life had much to do with the posthumous publication of Sibthorp's great work which appeared in ten volumes from 1806 to 1840. Hawkins, a member of the well-known Cornish family, died in Cornwall, at Trewithen, and his garden there was to be developed into one of the greatest of twentieth-century gardens by a future member of the family, an authority on Asiatic magnolias, the late Mr. George Johnstone (1882–1960).

Each of the members present at the second meeting proceeded to nominate three persons all of whom were unanimously approved, and it was 'Resolved that a printed Letter be sent to each Gentleman so nominated, acquainting him with his Nomination, and requesting him, if he chooses to belong to the Society, to signify such his Intention, in a letter directed to Mr. Salisbury, at Mr. Hatchard's, Piccadilly.' It was decided that the next meeting should be held a fortnight later at the same time and place, and it was agreed 'That each Member who chooses shall have the Option of proposing Candidates at the next Meeting, each of whom shall be immediately ballotted for, and in case of Two Thirds of the Members present vote for him he shall be considered duly

37

elected.' Thereafter election would be rather more difficult, for it was also 'Resolved that all Candidates who shall in future be proposed, be recommended in Writing, on the personal Knowledge of Three Members at least, and their Certificate hung up in the Meeting Room of the Society for Two Meetings before they are ballotted for.'

At the third meeting, held on 28 March, with Wedgwood in the Chair, it was reported that as favourable replies, either written or oral, had been received from those persons who had been approached, the following twenty-eight had become the 'Original Society':

William Townsend Aiton	John Hawkins
John Townsend Aiton	A. H. Haworth
The Rt. Hon. Sir Joseph Banks, Bt.	George Hibbert
The Marquis of Blandford	Dr. John Coakley Lettsom
George Caswall	John Maitland
Lord Cawdor	Charles Miller
William Corbett	John Leigh Philips
James Dickson	William Price
The Marquis of Exeter	William Rashleigh
Thomas Forsyth	R. A. Salisbury
William Forsyth	Capt. George Sedley
William Forsyth Junr.	Dr. James Edward Smith
The Rt. Hon. Charles Greville	James Vere
John Hall	John Wedgwood

A further thirty-two names 'were then proposed by the Members present, which were put to the Vote, and all admitted Members' and the Chairman was desired to write to them. 'It was resolved to take into Consideration at the next Meeting the Rules and Regulations of the Society, when the Chairman was desired to wait on Sir Joseph Banks, to beg his Assistance in framing a Set of Rules' and the meeting then adjourned for a fortnight.

Wedgwood also presided at the fourth meeting, held on 11 April, and 'laid before the Meeting a Paper containing the Outlines of the Rules for the Society, which being read, It was resolved that a Committee of Seven Persons be appointed to draw up the Rules of the Society, and that Three be a Quorum. The following Gentlemen were appointed of the Committee:—

The Earl of Dartmouth	John Hawkins Esq.
The Rt. Hon. Sir Joseph Banks	Dr. Sims
A. B. Lambert Esqr.	Mr. Dickson
R. A. Salisbury Esqr.	Mr. Wedgwood as Chairman.'

The Committee met next morning and, after drawing up part of the Rules, adjourned until the following day (13 April), when 'The Committee finished drawing up the Rules for the Horticultural Society, which they desire to lay before the General Meeting of the Society for their Consideration on the 25th Instant.' At the meeting on 25 April, when Salisbury presided, the 'Regulations . . . for the future Guidance of the Society were then read and with some Alterations and Additions (which the Chairman was desired to enter in the Book the Committee had prepared) were unanimously approved and confirmed.' Incidentally, another minute of that day reveals the circumstances in which the Society came to hold its earliest meetings 'at Mr. Hatchard's House': 'A letter from Mr. Gillam, to the Earl of Dartmouth, was read, in which he communicates a Minute of the Society for Bettering the Condition of the Poor, granting Leave for the Horticultural Society to meet in their Apartment at Mr. Hatchard's, at the request of the Earl of Dartmouth.' Finally it was decided that the next meeting of the Society should be held on 'Wednesday, the 2nd of May, at One o'Clock, and the Anniversary Meeting of the Society, when they are to choose a President, Treasurer, & Secretary, will be on May 30th, being the first Wednesday after Whitsun Week'.

Salisbury was again in the Chair on 2 May, when 'Balloting Lists were unanimously ordered to be printed, for the Election of Officers and Council of the Society, and sent to every Member of the Society, before the 30th Day of May, the Day fixed for the Anniversary.' Mr. Bartholomew Peacock, No. 7 High Street, Lambeth, was recommended as a clerk to the Society, by Mr. Hatchard, and so became the Society's first employee.

The Earl of Dartmouth presided at the first 'Anniversary Meeting' held as arranged on 30 May 1804.

The Society proceeded to ballot, and after the Urns had remained on the Table the time prescribed by the regulations the Ballot for the Council was drawn: And the following Gentlemen were declared duly elected for the ensuing Year,

W. Townsend Aiton Esqr.	Lord Middleton
Rt. Hon. Sir Josh. Banks	Mr. Chas. Miller
Sir Wm. Blizard	Mr. Chas. Minier
Rt. Hon. Isaac Corry	Wm. Meyer Esqr.
The Earl of Dartmouth	Mr. Wm. Price
Mr. Jas. Dickson	R. A. Salisbury Esqr.
Mr. Wm. Forsyth	Jas. Sims M.D.
Rt. Hon. Chas. Greville	John Trevelyan Esqr.
Sir C. Hawkins Bt.	Jas. Vere Esqr.
John Hawkins Esqr.	John Wedgwood Esqr.
Mr. Thos. Hoy	

The Ballot for the Officers was then drawn, and the following Persons were also declared duly elected for the ensuing Year.

> The Earl of Dartmouth[1]........President
> John Wedgwood Esqr. ....Treasurer
> The Revd. Mr. Cleeve ....Secretary.

While the minutes of the period merely record the election of the officers, no doubt their selection was the subject of a good deal of discussion between the ambitious William Forsyth and some of the other founders. In a letter written subsequently to Sir Joseph Banks, Thomas Andrew Knight (who was himself to become President in due course) said: 'Mr. Forsyth was, I have reason to believe, to have been at the Head of the Horticultural Society; and Dr. Anderson, I suppose, looked to the office of Secretary.' Whether Forsyth did or did not visualize himself as President, he certainly had the idea that the best person to be Secretary would be his brother Scot, James Anderson, LL.D., an agricultural journalist and the editor-proprietor of a short-lived periodical called *Recreations in Agriculture*. Anderson had published a long article on 'Mr. Forsyth's Discoveries', had advertised his book, and had advised him how to answer those who doubted the extravagant claims which he made for his 'composition'. However, there were those who did not hold Anderson in such high esteem, for in a letter to Forsyth, John Wedgwood wrote: 'Since we last met I have been employed in the business of the Society and have been talking about the election of a Secretary, and am sorry to say that I find so strong a prejudice against Dr. Anderson that I should advise his friends not to propose him.' As a result Anderson was not proposed and the Rev. Alexander Cleeve (1748–1805) became the first Secretary.[2]

Nothing seems to be known as to how or when Cleeve became interested in horticulture. After education at Eton, matriculation at Queen's College, Oxford, at the age of sixteen, and ordination in Cambridge, he was appointed vicar of Wooler, a parish in Northumberland, in 1780, which office he held until his death in 1805, although he officiated there only from May 1780 to June 1781. In the latter year

---

[1] The Rt. Hon. George Legge, third Earl of Dartmouth, K.G. (1753–1810). Born 3 October 1753. He entered Parliament in 1778 as Member for Plymouth, and subsequently represented other constituencies. In 1801 he was sworn of the Privy Council and became President of the Board of Control. He succeeded his father on 15 July 1801. In 1802 he became Lord Steward of the Household, and in 1804 Lord Chamberlain. He was a Fellow of the Linnean Society and had been President of the earlier Society for Promoting Natural History. He was made a Knight of the Garter in 1805, and died on 1 November 1810. At Sandwell Hall, Staffordshire, he maintained a fine garden. (See Plate 4.)

[2] *Jl R. hort. Soc.*, LVIII (1933), p. 320.

this absentee vicar let the tithes of Wooler and the glebe lands to a far-mer, at a rent of £200, under the burden of paying fifty pounds to a curate—and moved to Edinburgh, where he soon established his position and where he stayed for nineteen years before moving to London in 1800 to become chaplain to the Duke of Portland (later Prime Minister of England) and lecturer at Trinity Chapel, Knightsbridge.

At this date (30 May 1804) about ninety-three Members had been enrolled and they included many well-to-do and influential people, of whom ten were peers or the sons of peers.

At the next ordinary meeting on 6 June Lord Dartmouth was in the Chair; only five others were present and the only business was the receipt of eight letters intimating that the writers consented to their election. A month later, on 4 July, with seven members present, 'The President announced to the Meeting the following Gentlemen as Vice Presidents, & directed the Secretary to acquaint them thereof.

Sir Josh. Banks, Bt.	R. A. Salisbury
Mr. Dickson	Jas. Sims, M.D.[1]
Rt. Honble. Chas. Greville	John Wedgwood Esqr.'

When next the Society met, on 7 November, 'A Letter was read from Dr. James Anderson, of Isleworth, requesting to withdraw himself from the Society, which was agreed to'. His friend, William Forsyth, had died on 25 July, and it may be concluded that Dr. Anderson realized that he was not popular with the rest of the Council.

The record number of thirty-one new Members was elected at the last meeting of the year, held on 5 December, and the minutes of that day were also noteworthy in that they recorded the first gift to the Society. 'A Letter was read from Dr. Lettsom[2], with a Letter from Mr. John

---

[1] James Sims (1741–1820), M.D., physician, with a lucrative practice in London. President of the Medical Society of London for twenty-two years. Not to be confused with Dr. John Sims, who edited the *Botanical Magazine* from 1801 to 1826.

[2] John Coakley Lettsom, M.D., F.L.S., F.R.S. (1744–1815). Born 22 November 1744, he was a well-known Quaker physician, with a very large and lucrative practice based on Basinghall Street, and with a country house and well-labelled garden at Camberwell. He was one of the twenty-eight 'original Members' and was energetic, indefatigable and philanthropic, and engaged in a great variety of controversies. His habit of signing his Latin prescriptions 'I. Lettsom' gave rise to the following rhyme of which there were many versions:

> When any sick to me apply
> I physics, bleeds and sweats 'em;
> If after that they choose to die,
> Why, Verily! I. Lettsom.

He was a friend of Forsyth's and the father-in-law of Colonel John Elliot, who was Treasurer, 1809–28. He died 1 November 1815.

Wagstaffe of Norwich, who desired the Society's acceptance of a donation of five Pounds, & the Meeting ordered the thanks of the Society to
be presented to Mr. Wagstaffe, Thro' Dr. Lettsom.'

At the first meeting in January 1805 it was decided that in future the
meetings should be changed from the first Wednesday to the first Tuesday in each month. Forsyth's place on the Council was filled by Aylmer
Bourke Lambert, F.R.S. (1761–1842), who was an ardent botanist and
for forty-six years a Vice-President of the Linnean Society. He formed at
Boyton, Wiltshire an extensive herbarium especially rich in Siberian
and American plants, and with the help of his paid assistant published
in 1832 'one of the most sumptuous botanical works ever issued', *A
Description of The Genus Pinus*. Also at this meeting 'The Regulations of
the Society were revised and 250 Copies thereof ordered to be neatly
printed, together with a List of the Members, and one Copy directed
to be delivered to such of the Members as should apply to the Clerk
for it.'

As the Society was nearing the end of its first year, Mr. Hatchard
applied for rent for the use of his room in Piccadilly, a subject which
apparently had not previously been discussed. He was subsequently paid
various sums, but how much was rent and how much was in respect of
some service, such as printing, is not clear. However, one result of his
request for rent was a resolution 'that the Secretary do write to the
Secretary of the Linnaean Society, and desire to know whether the
Linnaean Society will consent to allow this Society to hold their Meetings in their Apartment, & if so what rent they will wish and desire, on
condition of the Meetings of this Society being held at such hours as do
not interfere with those of the Linnaean Society.' The Linnean Society
being willing to provide the desired accommodation in return for an
annual rent of twenty-five guineas, from 5 March 1805, the meetings
were held at 10 Panton Square, and that arrangement continued until
the autumn of 1805, when both Societies moved to 9 Gerrard Street,
Soho.

At the time Mr. Hatchard raised the question of rent Bartholomew
Peacock, whom he had recommended for the post of clerk, asked 'what
salary the Society would be pleased to allow him'. It was accordingly
decided 'that the sum of Thirty pounds be paid to Mr. Peacock for his
Salary, and in consideration of the extraordinary trouble attending the
execution of his office during the first year of the institution of the
Society'; furthermore 'that the Council be requested to engage Mr.
Price, the Clerk of the Linnaean Society, to act as Clerk also to the
Horticultural Society for a salary of Twenty pounds p. annum.' Within
a few days there was a further decision 'that the sum of Twelve guineas
and a half be paid to the Revd. A. Cleeve, in addition to what he has

already received, for his services as Secretary hitherto.' In 1806 Price's salary was raised to twenty-five guineas, and in 1810 to thirty pounds on the understanding that he corrected the proofs of the *Transactions*. The following year it was 'Resolved that Mr. Price be appointed under Secretary to the Society at £50 a year Salary, He providing a clerk to attend.'

CHAPTER THREE

THE OBJECTS OF THE SOCIETY

ON 5 MARCH 1805 A COMMITTEE OF SEVEN, UNDER THE CHAIRMANSHIP of Sir Joseph Banks, was appointed 'for the purpose of preparing a Prospectus declaratory of the intentions of this Society, to be submitted to the Public' and to 'report to the next General Meeting, on any subjects which they may think likely to promote the success of the Society'. The Committee met at Banks's house two days later and on several other occasions. Apparently, however, the seven decided that the prospectus was not one which any of them individually, or all of them collectively, could satisfactorily frame, and that it would be better to hand the task to Mr. Thomas Andrew Knight, who, although not one of the twenty-eight 'Original Members', but to whom Banks had written on 29 March 1804, 'I have taken the liberty of naming you an original member', seemed best equipped to outline the course which the Society should pursue. Knight, the friend of Banks, was a newly elected Fellow of the Royal Society and a farmer and horticulturist, particularly interested in the breeding of new fruit trees. Since 1795 he had conducted with Banks a voluminous correspondence describing his horticultural experiments and his observations on plant physiology. And since 1795 he had been publishing his experiments and observations in the *Philosophical Transactions of the Royal Society of London*. His 'Observations on the Grafting of Trees' of 1795 had discussed inheritance of decay among fruit trees and the propagation of debility by grafting. His 'Experiments on the Fecundation of Vegetables' of 1799 had discussed experiments with peas, begun in 1787, which quite clearly showed that he was observing dominance, recessive behaviour and heterosis almost eighty years before Mendel's day, although, of course, he failed to recognize the true Mendelian significance of his experiments. And in 1805 he was working on his great paper 'On the Direction of the Radicle and Germen during the Vegetation of Seeds', which was read before the Royal Society the following year and which describes the influence of gravitation and centrifugal force on the responses of seedlings.

Knight accepted the task of writing the prospectus and at the next General Meeting, on 2 April, his paper was read by Sir Joseph Banks and the Council was requested to have printed 250 copies for distribution among the Members of the Society and to give leave to the periodical journalists to reprint the text.

The paper, *Introductory Remarks relative to the Objects which the Horticultural Society have in view*, an immensely important document in the history of the Society, reads as follows:

Were it possible to ascertain the primeval state of those vegetables which now occupy the attention of the gardener and agriculturist, and immediately, or more remotely, conduce to the support and happiness of mankind; and could we trace out the various changes which art or accident has, in successive generations, produced in each, few inquiries would be more extensively interesting. But we possess no sources from which sufficient information to direct us in our inquiries can be derived; and are still ignorant of the native country, and existence in a wild state, of some of the most important of our plants. We, however, know that improved flowers and fruits are the necessary produce of improved culture; and that the offspring, in a greater or less degree, inherits the character of its parent. The austere Crab of our woods has thus been converted into the Golden Pippin; and the numerous varieties of the Plumb, can boast no other parent than our native Sloe. Yet few experiments have been made, the object of which has been new productions of this sort; and almost every ameliorated variety of fruit appears to have been the offspring of accident, or of culture applied to other purposes. We may therefore infer, with little danger of error, that an ample and unexplored field for future discovery and improvement lies before us, in which nature does not appear to have formed any limits to the success of our labours, if properly applied.

The physiology of vegetation has deservedly engaged the attention of the Royal and Linnaean Societies; and much information has been derived from the exertions of those learned bodies. Societies for the improvement of domestic animals, and of agriculture in all its branches, have also been established, with success, in almost every district of the British Empire. Horticulture alone appears to have been neglected, and left to the common gardener, who generally pursues the dull routine of his predecessor and, if he deviates from it, rarely possesses a sufficient share of science and information to enable him to deviate with success.

The establishment of a national society for the improvement of Horticulture has therefore long been wanted; and if such an institution met with a degree of support proportionate to the importance of its object: if it proceed with cautious circumspection to publish well ascertained facts only, to detect the errors of ignorance, and to expose the misrepresentations of fraud; the advantages which the public may ultimately derive from the establishment, will probably exceed the most sanguine hopes of its founders.

Horticulture, in its present state, may with propriety be divided into two distinct branches, the useful, and the ornamental: the first must occupy the principal attention of the members of the Society, but the second will not be neglected; and it will be their object, wherever it is practicable, to combine both.

Experience and observation appear to have sufficiently proved, that all plants have a natural tendency to adapt their habits to every climate in which art or accident places them: and thus the Pear-tree, which appears to be a native of the southern parts of Europe, or the adjoining parts of Asia, has completely naturalized itself in Britain, and has acquired, in a great number of instances, the power to ripen its fruit in the early part even of an unfavourable summer; the crab tree has in the same manner adapted its habits to the frozen regions of Siberia. But when we import either of these fruits, in their cultivated state, from happier climates, they are often found incapable of acquiring a perfect state of maturity even when trained to a south wall.

As the Pear and Crab tree, in the preceding cases, have acquired powers of ripening their fruits in climates much colder than those in which they were placed by nature, we have some grounds of hope that the Vine and Peach tree may be made to adapt their habits to our climate, and to ripen their fruits without the aid of artificial heat, or the reflection of a wall; and though we are at present little acquainted with the mode of culture best calculated to produce the necessary changes in the constitution and habit of plants, attentive observation and experience will soon discover it; and experiments have already been made, which prove the facility of raising as fine varieties of fruit in this country, as any which have been imported from others.

Almost every plant, the existence of which is not confined to a single summer, admits of two modes of propagation; by division of its parts, and by seed. By the first of these methods we are enabled to multiply an individual into many; each of which, in its leaves, its flowers, and fruit, permanently retains, in every respect, the character of the present stock. No new life is here generated; and the graft, the layer, and cutting, appear to possess the youth and vigour, or the age and debility, of the plant, of which they once formed a part. [The diseased state of young grafted trees of the Golden Pippin, and the debasement of the flavour of that fruit, afford one, amongst a thousand instances, which may be adduced, of the decay of those varieties of fruit which have been long propagated by grafting, &c.] No permanent improvement has therefore ever been derived, or can be expected, from the art of the grafter, or the choice of stocks of different species, or varieties: for, to use the phrase of Lord BACON, the graft in all cases overruleth the stock, from which it receives aliment, but no motion. Seedling plants, on the contrary, of every cultivated species, sport in endless variety. By selection from these therefore we can only hope for success in our pursuit of new and improved varieties of each species of plant or fruit; and to promote experiments of this kind the Horticultural Society propose to give some honorary premiums to those who shall produce before them, or such persons as they shall appoint, valuable new varieties of fruit, which, having been raised from seeds, have come into existence since the establishment of the institution.

In the culture of many fruits, without reference to the introduction of new varieties, the Society hope to be able to point out some important improvements. Several sorts, the Walnut and Mulberry for instance, are not produced till the trees have acquired a very considerable age; and therefore, though the latter fruit is highly valued, it is at present very little cultivated. But experiments have lately been made, which prove that both Walnut and Mulberry trees may be readily made to produce fruit at three years old; and there appears every reason to believe, that the same mode of culture would be equally successful in all similar cases.

In training Wall trees there is much in the modern practice which appears defective and irrational: no attention whatever is paid to the form which the species or variety naturally assumes, and be its growth upright, or pendent it is constrained to take precisely the same form on the wall.

The construction of Forcing houses appears also to be generally very defective, and two are rarely constructed alike, though intended for the same purposes; probably not a single building of this kind has yet been erected, in which the greatest possible quantity of space has been obtained, and of light and heat admitted, proportionate to the capital expended. It may even be questioned, whether a single Hot bed has ever been made in the most advantageous form; and the proper application of glass, where artificial heat is not employed, is certainly very ill understood.

Every gardener is well acquainted with methods of applying manure, with success, to annual plants; for these, as EVELYN has justly observed, having but little time to fulfil the intentions of nature, readily accept nutriment in almost any form in which it can be offered them; but trees, being formed for periods of longer duration, are frequently much injured by the injudicious and excessive use of manure. The gardener is often ignorant of this circumstance; and not infrequently forms a compost for his Wall trees, which for a few years stimulating them to preternatural exertion, becomes the source of disease, and early decay.

It is also generally supposed, that the same ingredients, and in the same proportion to each other, which are best calculated to bring one variety of any species of fruit to perfection, are equally well adapted to every other variety of that species, but experience does not justify this conclusion, and the Peach in many soils acquires a high degree of perfection, where its variety, the Nectarine, is comparatively of little value; and the Nectarine frequently possesses its full flavour in a soil, which does not well suit the Peach. The same remark is also applicable to the Pear and Apple; and as defects of opposite kinds occur in the varieties of every species of fruit, those qualities in the soil, which are beneficial in some cases, will be found injurious in others. In those districts where the Apple and Pear are cultivated for cyder and perry, much of the success of the planter is found to depend on his skill, or good fortune, in adapting his fruits to the soil.

The preceding remarks are applicable to a part only of the objects, which the Horticultural Society have in view; but they apply to that part in which the practice of the modern gardener is conceived to be most defective, and embrace no inconsiderable field of improvement.

In the execution of their plan, the committee feel that the Society have many difficulties to encounter, and, they fear, some prejudices to contend with; but they have long been convinced, as individuals, and their aggregate observations have tended only to increase their conviction, that there scarce exists a single species of esculent plant or fruit, which (relative to the use of man) has yet attained its utmost state of perfection; nor any branch of practical horticulture which is not still susceptible of essential improvement: and, under these impressions, they hope to receive the support and assistance of those who are interested in, and capable of promoting, the success of their endeavours.

Clearly Knight conceived horticulture as a practical science and the newly formed Society as a scientific one. There would be no place for the spurious experimentation of a Forsyth.

When reporting on any matters which they thought likely to promote the success of the Society the seven committee members appointed for this purpose no doubt had in mind the rent and salaries for which the Society was responsible, and on 2 April 1805 Sir Joseph reported that the Committee

had particularly adverted to the necessity of Economy in the infancy of an Institution, which must look forward to great expenses to form a permanent establishment, viz. the purchase of a House, a Charter etc. That in consequence of this R. A. Salisbury Esq. had offered his services to act as Secretary to the Horticultural Society, without any emolument and in case of his absence the revd. George Glasse[1] had offered his assistance to the Secretary gratis. That the Council of the Linnaean Society had agreed to permit the Horticultural Society to meet in their Apartments for the Annual Sum of Twenty five guineas.

It was then resolved unanimously, that the offer of R. A. Salisbury to act as Secretary be accepted; that the Thanks of the Society should be transmitted by R. A. Salisbury Esq. to the Council of the Linnaean Society, for having admitted them into a temporary participation of their rooms at so moderate a price; that the thanks of the Society be given to the Revd. A. Cleeve for his useful labours as Secretary; that the Council be desired to allow him such remuneration as they shall think sufficient; and that he be entitled to attend all the Meetings of the Society in future.

Unfortunately he died before the end of the year.

In 1805 the Anniversary Meeting was held on 11 June. Wedgwood was not present. He appears to have had difficulty in attending to the Society's affairs at this time, and at the Anniversary Meeting in 1806 retired from the treasurership. Three years later, on 7 February 1809, presumably because he found it impossible to attend the meetings, he resigned from the Society. On his retiring from the treasurership he was succeeded by the Rt. Hon. Charles Greville, who continued in that office until his death in 1809.

[1] Presumably the Rev. George Henry Glasse (1761–1809), the classical scholar who ran through a large fortune in sixteen years and, having become financially embarrassed, hanged himself while mentally deranged.

From the beginning of 1805 the Society's calendar assumed a rather definite pattern. Until 1809 there were normally eight General Meetings each year, one on the first Tuesday in each of the first six months, one in November, and one in December. The Chair was occupied by the President or one of the Vice-Presidents, and the average attendance was eleven, the highest being thirty-four at the Anniversary Meeting in June 1809.

The essential business at these meetings was the election of new members, of whom there were eighty-two in this period, bringing the total to one hundred and seventy-seven. Every person for election was required to sign the Obligation Book undertaking to pay his subscription and comply with the Bye-Laws and, having paid his admission fee and first year's subscription, was formally admitted to the Society by the President (or, in his absence by the presiding Vice-President) taking the newcomer's hand and saying, 'I do, by the Authority, and in the Name of the Horticultural Society of London, admit you a Member thereof.'

At most General Meetings one or more papers were read. Not unnaturally, Banks was a frequent contributor during the first five years of the Society's history, discussing the introduction of the potato into the United Kingdom, the hill wheat of India, the inuring of tender plants in the British climate, the revival of an obsolete method of managing strawberries, the cultivation of American cranberries in his garden at Spring Grove, Isleworth, the horticultural management of the Spanish or sweet chestnut, and the forcing-houses of the Romans.

Knight, however, was even more prolific, contributing nineteen papers during the same period on such subjects as alpine strawberries, peaches and peach-houses, apples, new and early fruits, training and grafting of fruit trees, the construction of forcing-houses and hot beds, onions, and potatoes. Clearly, at this time discussion centred mostly on fruits and vegetables. Indeed, to the end of 1809 only six papers were concerned with ornamental plants; R. A. Salisbury discussed the cultivation of *Polianthes tuberosa*, the tuberose, and species of dahlia; John Wedgwood likewise spoke on the dahlia as it grew in northern Britain; A. H. Haworth, the entomologist, on the cultivation of crocuses; Joseph Knight, of the Chelsea nursery which was later purchased by James Veitch, on *Pistia* and its relatives, and John Dunbar, gardener to Thomas Fairfax, on *Linum usitatissimum*, the flax.

When the Council considered a paper to be of sufficient importance it was printed in the Society's *Transactions*, which first appeared in 1807, and which roughly corresponded to the present-day Society's *Journal*. It was a quarto publication, containing handsome hand-coloured plates which to this day are among the finest to be found in horticultural literature. Five parts, and a few extra papers, comprised Volume I, which was completed in four years. The *Transactions* had a considerable sale to the public, as well as being distributed to Members, and the number of copies printed gradually rose from about five hundred to as many as 2,500 in 1822.

Later, shows were to become an important feature of the Society's meetings, but rather remarkably during these early formative years an exhibit of any kind was most unusual. The first recorded one was at the meeting of the Council on 8 April 1805, when 'A Potatoe was exhibited by Mr. [Charles] Minier likely to prove a valuable variety, the peculiar property of which is, that its tubers form so late in the season and have so thin a skin that they may be used through the winter, like young Potatoes.' To the meeting of 2 December two specimens of kohlrabi, a green and a red variety, were sent, but by whom was not recorded. In February 1806 (not 1805, as stated in the *Transactions*) James Dickson, one of the founders and a Vice-President, brought from Covent Garden Market specimens of a variety of *Brassica napus*, or rape, which had long been cultivated on the Continent, and the paper which he read on the subject was duly printed.[1] Apparently nothing more was exhibited until the December meeting of 1806, when seventy different varieties of apple were shown by Arthur Biggs, gardener to Mr. Isaac Swainson at Twickenham, an exhibit for which Mr. Biggs received the Society's Silver Medal. Again in May 1808 'Several new varieties of Apples which were tasted and proved excellent were exhibited by Mr. Minier.' At the following December meeting 'Specimens of both purple and white Broccoli exceedingly fine, the whites seven inches in diameter, the purple nine inches in diameter, were exhibited by Mr. Grange', fruiterer of Piccadilly. The only noteworthy ornamental plants shown during the years 1805–9 seem to have been '*Ranunculus pedatus* from Hungary, *Rosa caucasica* of Denon's Catalogue with flower buds then upon it in the open Air, & *Anemone palmata* in flower' exhibited by Mr. Biggs on 7 March 1809.

It is from such humble beginnings that the magnificent shows of today have grown. Today the Society considers, as indeed it has done so for over a hundred years, that one of its most important functions is to guide its Fellows and the public in the choice of the best kinds and varieties of plants for various purposes. As is well known, this is done by the bestowal of awards (e.g. the First Class Certificate, the Award of Merit, etc.) on plants which one or other of a series of committees, appointed largely for this purpose, consider meritorious. However, in its early years, anxious to avoid 'the possibility of misapprehension, of jealousy, or jar, among a numerous and diversified Association', the Society took care to avoid any appearance of expressing what might be regarded as an official

---

[1] *Transactions of the Horticultural Society of London*, 1 (1807), p. 26.

opinion about any paper or exhibit submitted to it, as may be gathered from the following announcement which was repeatedly made in the *Transactions*:

It is likewise necessary . . . to remark that it is an established rule of this Society, to which they will always adhere, never to give their opinion, as a body, upon any subject, either of Nature or Art, that comes before them. And therefore the thanks which are proposed from the Chair, to be given to the Authors of such Papers as are read at the General Meetings, or to the Persons who send fruits or other vegetable productions, or exhibit Inventions of various kinds to the Society, are to be considered in no other light than as a matter of civility, in return for the respect shewn to the Society by these communications.

The policy here outlined continued until 1858.

The Society's account books for these early years have not been preserved, and while the minute books record some of the payments made they reveal practically nothing about receipts. The first indication that the Society's financial position was fairly sound is a Council minute of 24 July 1806, resolving 'that the Treasurer purchase Three Hundred pounds Stock in 3 p.c. Consols in the Name of the Rt. Hon. Sir Jos. Banks, Bart., K.B., the Rt. Hon. Chs. Greville and Mr. James Dickson'. Exceptionally, in the following year the result of the annual audit was recorded in the following minute:

The Treasurer's Accounts were examined and found just as follows—

Ballance audited 20th May, 1806	£246 18.	5.
Revd. to 19th May, 1807.	251 3.	0.

Paid		
Purchase of £300 in 3 p.c. Anny.	185 15.	0.
Printer's Bill &c.	93 9.	1.
Annual Expenses.	86 18.	2.
	366 2.	3.
Ballance in the Treasurer's Hands	131 19.	2.

Besides the above Ballance and the £300 3 p.c. there is due about £260 arrears to the Society.

During the next ten years the holding in Consols appears to have been increased to £1,000, and in 1816 a further £400 was invested.

The Society's year began at what was called the Anniversary Meeting, at which the President, Treasurer, and Secretary for the ensuing year were elected, and a fourth of the Council seats were vacated and refilled. For the first few years the meeting was held at the beginning of June, and then for some years in the first week in May. Each year, in the late afternoon following the Anniversary Meeting, or on a date soon afterwards, as many members as found it possible dined together. At first the Anniversary Dinner was held at the Crown and Anchor Tavern in the Strand. Members' tickets were 10s. 6d. each, and 'extra expenses', which in 1807 amounted to £6. 4s. 0d., were borne by the Society. From 1810 to 1816 the Dinner was transferred to the Freemasons' Tavern, Great Queen's Street, Lincoln's Inn Fields, but in 1816 the charge for a ticket had increased to 15s. and the extra expenses to £16. 18s. 0d. This was considered to be too extravagant and the following year all dined at the Thatched House Tavern, the site of which was later partly occupied by the Conservative Club, St. James's Street. As this Dinner was more satisfactory and as the extra expense fell to £9. 17s. 0d., the function was held in the same place in 1818. For the next three years Willis's Rooms in King Street, St. James's Square, was the venue, and from 1822 to 1826 the Freemasons' Tavern all over again. Meanwhile the cost of a ticket had risen from 15s. to £1, and finally in 1826 to one guinea, while the bill for extras in that year was £90. 12s. 6d.

At first the Anniversary Dinner was confined to Members, but in 1811 a Fellow was permitted to bring a friend. By 1822 official guests were being invited to dine, and in this year Sir Humphry Davy (President of the Royal Society) and Sir James Smith (President of the Linnean Society), both Honorary Members of the Society, accepted the invitation. The dinners were especially noted for the dessert, which was provided by Members (called Fellows from 1809 onwards), some of whom were chiefly interested in fruit and vied with each other in produce of the highest quality. For example, to the 1822 Dinner Mr. Thomas Baldwin, gardener to the Marquis of Hertford and himself a Fellow, sent four remarkably large pineapples, one of which weighed 8 lb. 14 oz. Tables loaded with fruits of this nature no doubt were a ravishing sight and apparently others besides Society Members were anxious to see the spectacle. This, at first, the Council would not countenance and ordered that no person be admitted to see the dessert before the Anniversary Dinner unless introduced by a member of the Society possessing a dinner ticket. Now, at this period, and indeed until 1830, only men were eligible for membership and thus ladies could not attend the Society's meetings or dinners. However, some ladies knew of these displays of fruit, wished to see them, and agitated accordingly, to the extent that in 1824 it was 'ordered that each Steward do have two tickets to admit ladies into the Gallery during the dinner'. So important did this annual competition in the production of choice fruits become that in the following year 'It was resolved that the Anniversary Dinner

Plate 3. Thomas Andrew Knight (President of the Society 1811–1838)

The Earl of Dartmouth (1804–1810)   The Duke of Devonshire (1838–1858)

Prince Albert (1858–1861)   The Duke of Buccleuch (1862–1873)

Plate 4. PRESIDENTS OF THE SOCIETY

for the present year should be deferred till such time as the Strawberries in the Gardens near London shall be in perfection,' and the Dinner was held on 23 June.

Early in 1808 the matter of a Charter, which had first been discussed by Banks's 'Prospectus' Committee, was again raised and at a meeting of the Council on 5 January, with Sir Joseph in the Chair, the Secretary was asked to inquire of the proper steps to be taken to procure such a Charter and of the expenses attending it. When Council met in April the President, Banks, Greville, and Salisbury were unanimously appointed to form a committee to conduct the whole of the business with the President's solicitor, Mr. Hanrott. In March 1809 Mr. Hanrott was paid £300 towards the expenses of the Charter, and the following month informed the Society that he hoped to deliver the Charter with the Great Seal in the course of the next few days and requested an additional £130 which he hoped would cover the whole expense. No doubt this was the hope of the Council also, for £130 was more than was available. So they 'Ordered by an unanimous ballot that the Treasurer do pay to Mr. Hanrott the sum of £130, and there not being a sufficient ballance in his hands, & the Secretary [R. A. Salisbury] having offered to lend that sum to the Society', it was 'Resolved unanimously, that his offer be accepted & that he be allowed 5 p.c. Interest for the same.' The Charter, dated 17 April 1809, was delivered a few days later, and at a meeting of the Council on 25 April 'A letter from Messrs. Hanrott and Metcalf, Solicitors, offering their gratuitous services to the Society in procuring the Charter, was read & the unanimous thanks of the Society ordered to be sent to them.' At the same time 'It was proposed by Mr. Dickson, seconded by Col. Elliot & unanimously resolved, that the Gold Medal of the Society [which was at this time being negotiated], as soon as executed, be sent to Sir Joseph Banks and the Gilt Medal to Messrs. Hanrott & Metcalf.' In actual fact the medal was not available until 1811, when a silver-gilt medal was presented to each of the partners, Philip August Hanrott and Thomas Metcalf.

The Charter, which is reproduced as Appendix II, established the Society's first name as 'The Horticultural Society of London', and those constituting it, who had hitherto been referred to as 'Members', were now designated 'Fellows', with two additional categories, viz. 'Honorary Members' and 'Foreign Members'. From the time of the Society's inauguration there had been a Council consisting of the President and twenty other members, five of whom retired each year. The Charter provided for a Council of fifteen (including the President), three of whom should retire each year on the first day of May.

The Charter required the Council to make 'Bye-Laws', and with that object in view a committee of six was appointed in 1811. It appears not to have acted very quickly and, moreover, the product of their labours not to have met with general approval, for in 1815 a committee of the whole Council was appointed to consider and frame the Society's Laws, taking those of the Royal and Linnean Societies as their guide. The result of their deliberations was submitted to the Fellows in January 1816, and three months later it was agreed to publish the new Code of Bye-Laws.

As early as 1808, the Society felt the need for a medal to express its approbation, and the President, Banks, and Greville were asked to have such a medal executed with all possible speed. However, eleven months were to elapse before 'The Drawings of a Medal having been presented by Dr. Batty through the Rt. Hon. Sir Joseph Banks, the thanks of the Society were ordered to be sent to him.' Apparently Dr. Batty's design was not considered entirely satisfactory, for in July 1809 it was 'Resolved, that a Premium of Twenty pounds be offered to Artists for the best Drawing of a basket of Fruit & Flowers intended for the Medal of the Horticultural Society—the Drawings to be sent sealed up to the Secretary . . . on or before Michaelmas Day next with a private mark for each.' It was only when such drawings as were submitted as a result of the Society's advertisement in the public press were considered to be quite unsatisfactory that the first design of Dr. Batty was adopted. The obverse of the medal showed a greenhouse in a garden setting, and the reverse bore the god of gardens being decked with flowers by Flora and being offered fruits by Pomona (Plate 22).

As soon as executed, the first specimen of the Gold Medal was presented to Banks on 5 June 1811, 'for his unremitted and important services to the Society, from its first institution'. At first the medal was produced in gold, silver-gilt, and silver, but later also in bronze. The medal in silver was often used to recognize good exhibits at the Meetings, and the first of this nature was presented 'To Mr. Arthur Biggs, gardener to Isaac Swainson, Esq., for his exhibition of Apples, produced in his master's garden at Twickenham, under his superintendance.' During the five years commencing in 1811 the total number of medals presented was twenty, three being gold, three silver-gilt, and fourteen silver.

In 1812 the god of the gardens side of the medal was made into the Society's seal, which was used for the next ninety-one years. Then in 1903 some doubted whether the seal was still in order, for by this time the Society had changed its name from 'The Horticultural Society of London' to 'The Royal Horticultural Society'. The solicitor, however, was able to report that the original seal was still perfectly valid. Even so, in 1907 it was decided that a new seal should be made, similar to the original but incorporating the Society's current name; this is the seal now used.

In the early part of the nineteenth century letters were not enclosed in envelopes, but were folded with the writing inside and closed by means of warm wax flattened by a seal bearing some indication of the sender. In 1817 the Council decided that the Society should have such a seal for its correspondence consisting of a figure of Flora surrounded by the words 'Horticultural Society of London'. However, when it was realized that this would be too costly it was agreed that a wreath of vine leaves should be substituted for Flora. Even this was not to be, for the seal engraver maintained that such a design could not be satisfactorily executed. 'An apple tree in fruit was therefore ordered.' It was with this decision in mind that over a century later an apple tree in fruit was chosen for the Society's present device.

The formation of a library was one of the Society's earliest activities. The first recorded gift of books was one of five French horticultural works presented in November 1806 by Dr. Sims, and the first recorded purchase was of the *Annales du Museum d'Histoire Naturelle* and of the first edition of Miller's *Gardeners Dictionary*, in the following month. By 1813 the Society's books were sufficiently numerous to warrant the purchase of a book-case, costing £22. 10s 0d., which was accommodated in the Council Room of the Linnean Society. Four years later, when the Horticultural Society's offices were moved from the Linnean Society's premises to the first floor of 21 Church Street,[1] where there was more ample accommodation, a Library Committee consisting of five Members of Council was appointed to meet from time to time and to advise the Council on books suitable for the Society's Library and to arrange for the binding of such books as required it. At its first meeting, in June 1817, the Committee recommended the purchase of eleven books, including Redouté's *Les Roses* and Aiton's *Hortus Kewensis*. Fairly frequent purchases followed, one of which, made during 1818, consisted of the forty-third volume (published in 1816) of Curtis's *Botanical Magazine*, and the volumes of Edwards's *Botanical Register* from its commencement in 1815. As the library increased in size, so did the number of users and borrowers of books. Among the latter was J. C. Loudon, the famous horticultural journalist and landscape architect, who joined the Society in 1817 and, apparently, retained books for far too long, for when he wished to borrow Columella's *De Cultu Hortorum* 'It was ordered that this request be complied with when the books now in Mr. Loudon's possession are returned.'

The Society has always been encouraged in its work by the patronage of the Royal Family. When, in 1816, Queen Charlotte became its first royal patron, William Hooker, the botanical artist, was commissioned

[1] Meetings still continued to be held in the Linnean Society's Rooms in Gerrard Street, Soho.

to prepare an illuminated page for Her Majesty's signature in the Obligation Book. Thus began a practice which has been continued to the present day and the Library contains a unique collection of the autographs of British and foreign patrons and Honorary Fellows beautifully embellished on vellum. The latest addition is the autograph of Her Majesty Queen Elizabeth II.

By 1810 the Society was firmly established. It had its Charter and Bye-Laws, its publications, and had begun to build its library; regularly it held its meetings. And in this year the Earl of Dartmouth, who, as first President, had guided the fortunes of the Society through these first formative years, died on 1 November.

Interlude
to Parts One and Two

DURING THESE EARLY YEARS OF THE SOCIETY ONE MAN WAS LAYING the foundations of a career which is without parallel in the history of horticulture—John Claudius Loudon (1783–1843).[1] Born at Cambuslang, in Lanarkshire, at the home of his mother's only sister (his father was a farmer living at Kerse Hall, near Gogar, about five miles from Edinburgh), he was sent to school, and to live with an uncle, in Edinburgh. His favourite pursuits were writing and drawing and his teacher prophesied that he would become one of the best writers of the day; this he did, though possibly not in the sense his master forecast. In drawing he became so proficient that when he was allowed to start a career as a landscape gardener he was at once made draughtsman and assistant to Mr. John Mawer, a nurseryman and landscape gardener at Easter Dalry, near Edinburgh. As Mawer died before his assistant was sixteen, Loudon continued his training in the same profession with Mr. Robert Dickson in Leith Walk. He boarded with Dickson, and attended classes in botany, chemistry, and agriculture, under Dr. Coventry, Professor of Agriculture in the University of Edinburgh. No doubt he was also a frequent visitor to the Botanic Garden, then also in Leith Walk, when Daniel Rutherford, uncle of Sir Walter Scott, was keeper. Certain it is that he worked prodigiously and developed the habit, which he continued for many years, of sitting up, two nights in every week, to work and to write.

At the age of twenty, in 1803, the year before the inaugural meeting of the Society, he came to London and immediately called on Mr. James Sowerby, the botanical artist, at Lambeth. As he had brought with him, mostly from Dr. Coventry, many letters of recommendation to gentlemen of landed property, he was quickly accepted into the Banksian circle and extensively employed as a landscape gardener in various parts of England. In London he was immensely impressed by the great gloominess of the gardens of its public squares, planted, as they were, almost entirely with evergreens, particularly with Scotch pine, yew, and

[1] Jane Loudon, *A short account of the Life and Writings of John Claudius Loudon* (1847).

57

spruce. Before the end of 1803 he had published in *The Literary Journal* an article entitled 'Observations on laying out the Public Squares of London', in which he condemned the prevailing taste and advocated mingling deciduous trees with evergreens, recommending sycamore, the oriental and occidental plane, and the almond as trees best able to tolerate the smoke of the city. His suggestions were not unheeded.

Loudon was not in London at the time of the inaugural meeting. He was back again in Scotland, altering the Palace Gardens at Scone, in Perthshire, for the Earl of Mansfield, and laying out the grounds of other noblemen and gentlemen, directing the planting and managing of woods, and all the time accumulating new ideas which he incorporated into his book, published in 1804, with the somewhat forbidding title *Observations on the Formation and Management of Useful and Ornamental Plantations; on the Theory and Practice of Landscape-gardening, and on gaining and embanking Land from Rivers or the Sea.* In addition to stating his youthful ideas on the functions of a landscape architect, the work clearly shows that its author, even at this stage in his career, had a considerable knowledge of trees and shrubs, in the same fashion as *A short Treatise on some Improvements made in Hothouses* of 1805 illustrates his knowledge of the management of hot-houses, in which subject he had been interested since the time he had worked with John Mawer.

In 1805 he was in England again, actively engaged in the practice of landscape gardening. He was also writing on this matter and, in so doing, criticizing the work of Repton towards whose latter work he had some bias. His writings were illustrated by beautiful copperplate engravings of landscapes drawn by himself. Towards the end of 1806, when returning from a landscaping project in Caernarvonshire and having to travel on the outside of a coach all through the night in the rain, he caught a violent chill. The chill brought on rheumatic fever which resulted in a permanently stiff left knee which was to trouble him for the rest of his life. While recuperating from the fever in a farmhouse at Pinner called Wood Hall, he had time to paint (some of his landscapes were exhibited at the Royal Academy), to learn German, to think, and to write up his journal—a task he had begun at the age of fifteen, and which he was to continue for thirty years. An entry in 1806 reads thus: 'Alas! how have I neglected the important task of improving myself! How much I have seen, what new ideas have developed themselves, and what different views of life I have acquired since I came to London three years ago! I am now twenty three years of age and perhaps one third of my life has passed away, and yet what have I done to benefit my fellow-men?'

At this time more than a third of his life had passed; by the standards of most men he had benefited his fellows considerably—though as nothing compared to the extent he *was* to help them. Moreover, he was to benefit himself; he took up farming.

Wood Hall, the farm at Pinner where he had been staying, was to be let. Impressed by the imperfect state of the husbandry here and elsewhere in England, and realizing the potential of the soil, he persuaded his father to move to Wood Hall in 1807. The following year, from Wood Hall, he wrote the pamphlet *An immediate and effectual Mode of raising the Rental of the Landed Property of England; and rendering Great Britain independent of other Nations for a Supply of Bread Corn. By a Scotch Farmer, now farming in Middlesex.* The pamphlet caused a great deal of interest, to the extent that General Stratton of Tew Park in Oxfordshire offered Loudon a portion of his property, if he would undertake the management of the remainder and introduce Scottish farming to Oxfordshire. Loudon took up the offer, began work on the farm called Great Tew at Michaelmas 1808, and there remained until February 1811, Stratton being pleased with the improvement effected and paying him well for his lease and stock. By the end of 1812, as a result of his farming and landscape-gardening endeavours, he had amassed upwards of £15,000—and determined to seek for further horticultural and other knowledge, by travelling abroad. For the next eighteen months he was on the Continent.

On 25 November 1809 the Edinburgh nurseryman Thomas Dickson called a few friends to his house to discuss the possibilities of forming a horticultural society in Scotland. The friends called a general meeting of professional and amateur gardeners in the Physicians' Hall, George Street, on 5 December; the Hall has long since disappeared and the National Commercial Bank of Scotland now stands on the site. At this meeting the Caledonian Horticultural Society was instituted. Dr. Andrew Duncan took the Chair, a Council was formed, Walter Nicol and Patrick Neill agreed to act as Joint Secretaries, and the Earl of Dalkeith was elected President; and the object of the Society was 'the encouragement and improvement of the best fruit, the most choice flowers and the most useful culinary vegetables'.

By 1824 the Society received its first Royal Charter. As early as 1811 the Council had appointed a committee 'to look out for a proper place for a garden', but not until shortly after 1820 did the Society come into possession of ten acres of ground known as Herd's Hill on the lands of Inverleith. The Garden gradually became so great a strain on the resources of the Royal Caledonian Horticultural Society that in 1864 it was added to the Botanic Garden.

In Ireland there are records of a flower show being held at Donnybrook, County Cork, in 1817, and in all probability this show was organized by the Horticultural Society of Ireland. However, the Society apparently went into abeyance. Then, in 1830, a meeting was called at 90 Abbey Street, Dublin, to reconstitute the old Society, with the Earl of Leitrim as President, for 'the improvement of horticulture in all its branches, ornamental as well as useful'. The new Society prospered; in 1838 Queen Victoria granted her patronage, the Society was designated the Royal Horticultural Society of Ireland, membership increased, and the shows became some of the most important social events in Dublin.

In the meantime, in Ireland, John Underwood, a Scotsman, had been appointed the first Curator of the Botanic Garden at Glasnevin. The Garden had been founded in 1790, when the Irish Parliament had voted £300 to the Dublin Society (now the Royal Dublin Society) towards the foundation of a national garden for Ireland. Underwood had been recommended by William Curtis, the founder of *The Botanical Magazine*, and acted as Curator from 1798 until he died in 1834, during most of this period having the scientific advice of Dr. Walter Wade, the Dublin Society's Professor of Botany. And between 1800 and 1804 Underwood published the *Catalogue of Plants in the Dublin Society's Botanic Garden*.

In 1803, the year Loudon left Scotland for London, William Kerr,[1] a gardener at Kew, left London for Canton in China, sent there by Sir Joseph Banks, at a salary of £100 a year, to collect plants for the Kew Royal Gardens. He stayed in Canton, apart from the time he spent on expeditions to Java and the Philippines, until 1812, when he was appointed superintendent of the Colonial Botanic Gardens at Colombo, Ceylon, a post he held until his death two years later. Thus he was the first botanical collector to reside in China for more than a few weeks. Kerr's first consignment of living plants from Canton, purchased from Canton nursery gardens, was transmitted to Kew by Captain Kirkpatrick in the *Henry Addington* in 1804, the year of the Society's inaugural meeting, and included *Nandina domestica*, that relation of the barberries somewhat resembling a bamboo, two conifers—the handsome pyramidal *Juniperus chinensis* and the not so handsome *Cunninghamia lanceolata* (the dead shoots remain on the plant far too long and give it an untidy appearance), the commonest trumpet lily of South China, now called *Lilium brownii* var. *viridulum* (but received at Kew under the name of *Lilium japonicum*), and the so-called 'Ogre Lily' of Japan, *Lilium tigrinum*, which, apart from *L. candidum*, probably has a longer history in cultivation than any other lily, having been raised for over a thousand years by the Chinese, Japanese and Koreans as an article of food. Even though it was sterile, William Townsend Aiton quickly recognized the horticultural possibilities of this vigorous orange-red flowered lily and straight away began to propagate it by means of the purplish bulbils in the axils

[1] Bretschneider, *History of European Botanical Discoveries in China* (1898), p. 189.

of the leaves of the hairy purple stems. By 1812 over 10,000 bulbs had been propagated at, and distributed from, Kew. It is still widely grown, though many commercial stocks have become infected by virus and, albeit not decreased in vigour, they are nevertheless dangerous neighbours for more susceptible species. Today many fertile strains and hybrids of this lily are grown, in colours of lemon-yellow, salmon, and pink; in the future there will be many more. Other plants which Kerr sent to Kew during the next two or three years included the double-flowered form of the plant which commemorates his name, *Kerria japonica*, and the climbing rose which honours the name of his sponsor, *Rosa banksiae*.

At this time not only Kew but also enlightened amateurs were importing plants from China and elsewhere, and none was more successful than Sir Abraham and Lady Amelia Hume.[1] And no one was more successful in cultivating these introductions than their distinguished gardener at Wormley Bury, in Hertfordshire, James Mean. An uncle of Sir Abraham had been a director of the Honourable East India Company; two of his cousins were employed in its service—one as captain of one of the Company's ships, the other, Alexander Hume, in charge of the English factory at Canton. Probably it was through the good offices of the latter that the Humes procured their Chinese plants, among the more outstanding being *Magnolia denudata* (at that time called *M. conspicua*), planted at Wormley Bury in 1801; *Paeonia suffruticosa* var. *papaveracea*, planted in 1802 and first blooming in 1806 with glorious single white flowers, 10 inches across, the papery petals purple-blotched at the base—the plant by 1826 growing 7 feet high, 40 feet in circumference, and carrying 660 buds; *Camellia japonica* 'Lady Hume's Blush', planted in 1806, the beautiful, double, perfectly imbricated flowers being figured for the first time in 1811 in the *Botanist's Repository*; seven different chrysanthemums, the 'Rose' and the 'Buff' in 1798, the 'Golden Yellow' and the 'Quilled Yellow' in 1802, the 'Spanish Brown' in 1806, and the 'Quilled White' and the 'Large Lilac' in 1808. Only one other chrysanthemum was introduced to Britain during this period, the 'Sulphur Yellow', by Thomas Evans of Stepney in 1802. Could this enlightened pair of gardeners have foreseen the tremendous interest the gardening and horticultural worlds were to take in chrysanthemums, camellias, magnolias, and paeonies? In 1809 Sir Abraham introduced from China 'Hume's Blush Tea-scented China Rose'. Unfortunately Lady Amelia was not to see the plant in flower, for in the year it arrived at Wormley Bury she died. Her name is commemorated by the genus *Humea*, for it was in her greenhouse that Amaranth Feathers or the Incense Plant, *Humea elegans*, flowered for the first time in Britain, in

[1] *Jl R. hort. Soc.*, LXVI (1941), p. 308; ibid., LXXXIX (1964), p. 497.

1804. Remarkably enough, some 130 years later, another owner of Wormley Bury was to be similarly honoured. Major Albert Pam, for some years an active member of the Council of the Society, was the first to flower *Pamianthe peruviana*.

The flowering of 'Hume's Blush Tea Rose' in Colvill's Nursery in 1810 was regarded as of some importance. At any rate in that year special arrangements were made by both the British and French Admiralties for the safe transit of plants of the new rose to the Empress Josephine at Malmaison, in spite of the fact that England and France were still at war. The history of the rose since that time has shown that the importance of Hume's introduction was not exaggerated. Although it is not now regarded as a true Tea Rose it has proved to be an important ancestor of these roses and, crossed with the Bourbon, Noisette and Yellow China Roses towards 1830, gave rise to typical Tea Roses. Another significant event in the history of the rose during this period also took place in Colvill's Nursery. In 1805 Parson's 'Pink China Rose' gave rise to the 'Dwarf Pink China', a miniature then known in England as *Rosa lawrenceana* and now as *R. chinensis* var. *minima*, or the Fairy Rose. In France, where Louis Noisette introduced it, it was called 'Bengale Pompon' and in 1868 became a grandparent of the first Poly-Poms, and ancestor of the Poulsen Roses. Moreover, Parson's 'Pink China', introduced to the French Island of Bourbon (Réunion) in 1810 and planted as a hedge along with the 'Autumn Damask Rose', hybridized with the latter and by so doing became a grandparent of the French Bourbon Rose and thus an ancestor of the Teas, Hybrid Perpetuals, and Hybrid Teas.

Only two years after the Society was formed John Sutton established the House of Sutton to deal chiefly in flour and in agricultural seeds.[1] From these rather simple beginnings the firm has progressed and prospered and none has done more for the seed industry and for the millions who love a garden and love to plant a garden. Certainly no horticultural establishment, through the activities of its various officers, has contributed more to the welfare of the Society, whose history it almost (apart from two years) encompasses, than has Sutton's at Reading.

[1] *Jl. R. hort. Soc.*, LXXXI (1956), p. 234.

Part Two

Thomas Andrew Knight and Joseph Sabine
(1810 - 1838)

CHAPTER FOUR

HEADQUARTERS

THE EARL OF DARTMOUTH, THE SOCIETY'S FIRST PRESIDENT, HAVING died on 1 November 1810, the Council, at its meeting on 6 December, unanimously resolved that Thomas Andrew Knight[1] (1759–1838) (Plate 3), of Downton Castle, be recommended to the Society for President, and the Council's choice was endorsed at the General Meeting on 1 January 1811, when Knight was also re-elected to the Council.

The new President was destined to preside with great distinction over the Society for the next twenty-seven years. He was the younger brother of Richard Payne Knight, the scholar, poet, and patron of the arts who collected Greek bronzes and Claude drawings, and who also had certain ideas on landscape design. The brothers had inherited much wealth and property from their father, wealth originally derived from the mines and ironworks around Madeley in Shropshire. Whereas Richard Payne had collected rare coins, gems, and bronzes on which he had spent a fortune and which he bequeathed on his death to the British Museum, Thomas Andrew's interests were almost entirely in agriculture and horticulture.

Schooled first at Ludlow and then at Chiswick, he went up to Balliol in 1778 or 1779, but came down from Oxford in 1780 and lived for the next ten years with his mother at Maryknowle, near Ludlow, devoting most of his time to the study of natural science. As early as 1786 he had begun the series of experiments in the grafting of fruit trees which was later to form the subject of his first written contribution to pomology. In 1791 he married Frances Felton, lived first at Elton Hall, a small Queen Anne house between Maryknowle and Downton, acquired a farm and a hot-house and entered on a programme of horticultural and agricultural experiments which continued without interruption until his death. He was especially interested in the breeding of improved varieties of fruits and vegetables and in plant physiology. His meeting with Sir Joseph Banks in 1795 was clearly the turning-point in his life, for until then he had been somewhat shy and retiring, and at the age of thirty-six had written and published nothing. The stimulation he received from Banks changed all this, for in 1799 he wrote to Banks: 'If I have become a

[1] *Jl. R. hort. Soc.*, LXIII (1938), p. 319.

troublesome scribbler to you, I must claim your pardon on the ground that you have made me such; for without the attention I have been honoured with from you, I am certain I should never (in print) have scribbled at all.'

Apart from his contributions to the *Transactions* of the Horticultural Society and the *Philosophical Transactions* of the Royal Society of London, his 'scribblings' are to be found in his many letters to Banks,[1] all of which give a fair picture of his activities. The letter written on 8 August 1805 is one such. He speaks of the water-wheel which he had constructed in his garden and which was to play an important role in the establishment of the law of geotropism; he gives his views on the connection between berberis and rust on wheat; discusses mildew on peas in relation to moisture conditions; describes a pruning experiment on young apple trees, his breeding work on early grapes, and the cultivation of the potato. At this time he was also breeding new cider-apple types by crossing the Siberian Crab with local cider varieties in order to induce hardiness; attempting to combine earliness with hardiness in new varieties of grape; designing a new forcing-house for grapes, as well as for strawberries; and experimenting on the growing of melons.

Such a man was obviously a potential leader of the Horticultural Society, especially since, in 1805, he had drawn up the memorandum on the objects of the Society with such distinction. In 1806 he had been elected to the Council and under the Bye-Laws had retired at the Anniversary Meeting in 1810, by which time he had contributed fifteen papers on horticultural matters to the Society's *Transactions*.

In the meantime his elder brother Payne had found the responsibilities of maintaining 'the stone mansion in castellated style' called Downton Castle, which he had built for himself near Ludlow, too much; he left the Castle and moved into a cottage in the grounds. Thereupon Andrew and his family occupied Downton and there he lived and worked for the next thirty years, managing the estate of 10,000 acres. He was

a landowner who was his own agent, a farmer and stock-breeder actively engaged in the experimental breeding of cattle, sheep, horses, dogs and poultry; but above all a horticulturist with a detailed research programme in plant breeding, pomology and plant physiology. He seems to have experimented with everything, from the potato to the Persian melon and the pineapple, and in all his experiments he recorded facts and figures either in his memory, which was proverbial for its retentive powers, or in note-books and memoranda which he must have written in his own hand.[2]

[1] Dawson, Warren R. (ed.), *The Banks Letters* (1958).
[2] *Jl R. hort. Soc.*, LXIII (1938), p. 319.

From the start the President made it clear that he could not accept responsibility for the day-to-day conduct of the Society's business; this must be left to the other officers. Benjamin Price, who in 1811 had been promoted to Assistant Secretary, was probably a very busy man, but not a very businesslike one. In addition to his usual secretarial duties, he corrected the proofs of the *Transactions*, was responsible for the distribution and sale of these, as well as for keeping the accounts of subscriptions paid and in arrears. R. A. Salisbury, the Hon. Secretary, was not conditioned to fixed office hours; in any case, being engrossed in botanical studies and in his own gardening activities, he left all the routine to Price, who, with no pretence to being a horticulturist, was doubtless usually at a loss to give a satisfactory answer to any member who called at the Society's headquarters hoping to receive enlightenment on some gardening problem. Moreover, the Treasurer, John Elliot, who succeeded Greville in 1809 and held the office of Treasurer continuously for the next twenty years, appears to have regarded his duties as beginning and ending with the custody of such money as was from time to time passed to him for banking or investment; the question of whether the correct amounts were being handed to him appears to have caused him little concern. This is all rather surprising, for Elliot, unlike Salisbury, was a businessman; he was the managing director of what was then Elliot's Brewery (subsequently owned by Messrs. Watney, Combe & Reid) situated in Palace Street, Westminster, just off Victoria Street. He lived in Pimlico Lodge, adjoining the brewery, where his garden, of about twenty acres, extended from Vauxhall Bridge Road to the present site of the Army & Navy Stores. Part of Victoria Street runs through, and the Roman Catholic Cathedral has been built on, the garden in which John Elliot so successfully cultivated grapes and other fruits. On one occasion he communicated to the Society a 'Description of a moveable Frame for training Vines in a House, to protect them from frost and to facilitate the Operation of Pruning'. The frame, which was hinged at the eave and suspended from the ridge by wires running over pulleys, allowed of the vines being lowered away from the glass, or raised close to it, at will. An exhibit of his grapes was to receive a Banksian Medal in 1821. In 1804 he married the only daughter of John Coakley Lettsom, much to the latter's pleasure, as a letter of his to William Forsyth well shows.

> Sambrook Court.
> Feb. 20, 1804.

Dear Mr. Forsyth,

. . . By the change my only Daughter is soon likely to undergo, I shall claim Colonel Elliot of Pimlico, my Son, whom I desire to visit you, and I am sure you will take a pleasure in showing him your hospital of Invalids [i.e. the trees whose wounds had been treated with Forsyth's much vaunted 'plaister'].

I am as well persuaded that he will be happy to see you at Pimlico, where he possesses a magic habitation, with 20 acres of useful and ornamental land. Altho' in the City of Westminster, he is about erecting hot and greenhouses, which will altogether render his residence a paradise, and I know you like to see a terrestrial one; which indeed is an excellent preparation for enjoying a celestial one, but altho' you have a fair title to the latter, I hope you will long be kept out of possession, and that you may long continue to enjoy the former is the wish of

Yr. frd.

J. C. LETTSOM

By his marriage Elliot had fifteen children, one of whom provided the lymph for the vaccination of Queen Victoria as a child. In those days calf lymph was not used and one child was vaccinated from the arm of another. When Pettigrew, the Duke of Kent's surgeon, was entrusted with the selection of a child from whom the future Queen of England should be vaccinated, he was especially anxious to choose a healthy infant with a known good personal and family medical history, for it was then thought possible to convey certain diseases in the operation. His choice fell on little Edmund Elliot, the grandson of his 'dear friend, Dr. Lettsom'. The operation having been performed, the Duchess of Kent expressed her indebtedness in a letter saying that Princess Victoria

was going on as well as possible, thanks to Mrs. Elliot's great kindness which will never be forgotten by the Duke and herself [i.e. the Duchess of Kent]. If Mrs. Elliot will do her the favour of calling any day between two and three o'clock, and send up her name to Baroness de Spaeth, she will immediately take her into the nursery that she may judge *herself* how the little infant thrives. The Duke joins with her in anxious enquiry after the dear little boy from whom the lymph was taken, and the Duchess, in conveying to Mrs. Elliot the Duke's best remembrance, is particularly desired also to bring him to the recollection of Colonel Elliot.

With Price overworked and receiving little or no direction from Salisbury, and with Elliot not treating his treasuring responsibilities as seriously as he might have done, it is hardly surprising that by 1814 the Society's records and accounts had become somewhat muddled. How far Price was personally to blame is not known. But he *was* blamed for his lack of horticultural knowledge, the Council insisting that he, occupying the post of Assistant Secretary, must be conversant in horticultural matters and capable of performing the duties of the Secretary in the latter's absence. Accordingly, in 1815, Price was summarily relieved of his office and Thomas Hare was appointed in his stead. Price, supported by the opinion of two lawyers whom he consulted, disputed the Council's right to treat him thus, but in the end thought it wise to resign. His successor found it impossible to reconcile the accounts, and a small committee which endeavoured to do so, and which produced a very long and detailed report, concluded that 'It is scarce possible to conceive that such irregularity and confusion could have existed in any Books purporting to record the proceedings of any Society.'

The report, which was presented in March 1816 by two members of Council, John Cresswell and Joseph Sabine, was really the work of the latter. It not only gave particulars of all Price's sins of commission and omission, but set forth a year's programme of things which should in future be done.

Joseph Sabine, F.R.S. (1770–1837), was born at Tewin, Hertfordshire, and was the elder brother of Captain Edward Sabine, the astronomer, who later became General Sir Edward Sabine and successively Secretary, Treasurer, and President of the Royal Society. Joseph was educated at the Bar and practised until 1808, when he was appointed one of ten Inspectors-General of Assessed Taxes. In 1816 the Government of the day apparently considered that the department was overstaffed and dispensed with the services of seven of Sabine's colleagues. He, however, continued in office until his post was abolished in 1835, receiving in salary and travelling expenses an income which averaged £1,200 per annum.

Sabine had joined the Society in 1810, had been elected to the Council in 1812, and had become a Vice-President three years later. Once on the Council, and with his training, it is not unreasonable to suppose that he sensed the possibility of the Society's accounts being not all that they should have been; and not unreasonable to suppose that he conceived the idea of turning the matter to his own advantage when the opportunity occurred. In the autumn of 1814, for some unrecorded reason, Salisbury was unable to attend to the Society's affairs and during his absence, at a Council Meeting, Sabine moved that the Society's Gold Medal be given to Salisbury 'for his various communications and for his unceasing attention to the Duties of his Office and the Interests of the Society'. The motion was carried unanimously and Salisbury no doubt was very delighted and quite unsuspecting of what was soon to come—Sabine's report on the affairs and management of the Society.

The report was ostensibly an indictment of Price, the Assistant Secretary, and contained no adverse reference to Salisbury, the Secretary. The latter, however, could hardly miss its implications and resigned from his post with effect from the forthcoming Annual General Meeting. And at the same Council Meeting at which Salisbury's impending resignation was announced it was resolved that Sabine, who was presiding, be recommended to fill the vacancy. On this same day, doubtless with due regard to the feelings of Salisbury, who was present, Sabine gave notice of his intention to propose Sir James Edward Smith, Salisbury's old enemy, as an Honorary Fellow of the Society.

Sabine was ambitious, energetic, and enthusiastic, and to him belongs much of the credit and most of the blame for the rise and fall of the fortunes of the Society during the next fourteen years. In 1830, as a result of the findings of another committee of inquiry, he, too, was compelled to resign, and the *Gardener's Magazine* to say of him, 'he it is, and he alone, who by a system of concealment and monopoly of power has brought the Society to the brink of ruin'.[1] Did he, one wonders, recall the treatment he had given Salisbury?

Before long Sabine found that the roster of duties outlined in his report was more than he and Hare, the Assistant Secretary, could manage. Accordingly, in February 1817, it was decided to employ a clerk, at fifty pounds per annum, to work from 11 a.m to 4 p.m. on six days of each week. Hare, who at that time was receiving exactly the same salary as the clerk was to be paid, was also expected to work similar hours. Not unnaturally, it was soon found necessary to double Hare's salary, but at the beginning of 1818 he intimated that he wished to resign; his duties, which had progressively increased since he entered upon his office, had greatly exceeded his expectations and appeared to be taking up almost all his time; his professional occupations were being most seriously encroached upon; he was unable to foresee the extent of extra duties. He was succeeded, at a salary of £100 by, John Turner, a protégé of Sabine, who had previously arranged for him to read the papers at a General Meeting, 'his style of reading being much approved'. Early in 1818 the clerk also resigned, and his successor bore the burden of work for less than a month, to be replaced by one Thomas Whisfield Tindal. From these and subsequent happenings it appears that Sabine was inclined to expect too much of his subordinates and probably he was not a very good judge of men.

Undoubtedly he himself devoted much more time and energy to the Society's affairs than Salisbury had ever done, and the Society soon became a much more active body. He was a great correspondent and made contact with the leading horticulturists not only in all parts of the British Isles but in many foreign countries also. The Society's Meetings became more lively affairs, and the exhibits both more numerous and larger. By about 1818 every kind of fruit and vegetable appeared in its season, and while most exhibits consisted of a single dish or vase, others were quite imposing, as when Mr. Joseph Kirke showed from his Brompton nursery seventy-two varieties of apple, or when Messrs. Whitley, Brame & Milne sent from their garden at Fulham a collection of dahlia flowers consisting of more than two hundred varieties—'splen-

[1] *Gardener's Magazine*, vi (1830), p. 252.

did beyond description'. The exhibitors, moreover, were not confined to the British Isles; Dr. J. B. van Mons sent from Brussels a large collection of pears, and Monsieur L. C. Noisette, the eminent French nurseryman, several packages of various fruits which arrived too late for one of the usual Meetings, with the result that a special Meeting was held to examine them.

While exhibits of fruit and vegetables were still the more numerous, flowers and ornamental plants were becoming a regular feature, and among those shown at this period were aralias, aucubas, azaleas, carnations, chrysanthemums, dahlias, *Datura arborea*, geraniums, gourds, hydrangeas, irises, *Lathyrus grandiflorus*, lilies, *Lobelia* species, *Lycium chinense*, magnolias, paeonies, *Pittosporum* species, primulas, roses, *Sarracenia purpurea*, snowflakes, stocks, tropaeolums, and yuccas. Horticultural 'sundries' also began to appear at the Meetings. Thus in May 1818 Mr. James Kewley, of the New Kent Road, showed 'A Thermometrical Alarum for the purpose of ringing a bell when the temperature of Hothouses, Conservatories &c. shall exceed or fall below the desired degree', and 'The Automatic Regulator for the purpose of regulating the temperature without any personal attention'. On the same day Mr. William Bright, of The Borough, exhibited 'A portable Engine for watering or fumigating'.

At many Meetings seeds, seedlings, cuttings, buds, and scions of new or improved plants were available for distribution to interested Fellows. In most cases the material was brought and presented to the Society by Fellows or others for distribution purposes, but not infrequently it was purchased from foreign nurserymen and seedsmen, and often consisted of such of their specialities as had been tried in England in the preceding year and found superior to the kinds commonly grown in the British Isles. For instance, during 1817–18 there were distributed 200 plants of eleven sorts of broccoli presented by Mr. Hugh Ronalds of Brentford; a collection of vegetable and tree seeds presented by Monsieur Vilmorin of Paris; buds of new cherries and a peach raised by Mr. Knight, the President; vine eyes from the Royal Gardens, Windsor; seeds of Chinese plants sent by Mr. John Livingstone from Macao, Livingstone having been elected a Corresponding Member of the Society in 1817; and from various donors seeds of *Passiflora quadrangularis*, the granadilla, bulbs of *Iris xiphioides*, varieties of celery, pea, beet, brussels sprout, melon, strawberry runners, and cuttings of figs. A notable introduction in 1818 was the American pear 'Seckle', of which twenty-two young trees sent to the Society by one of its Foreign Members, Dr. David Hosack of New York, were distributed to nurserymen and others. With a view to extending the cultivation of new and other desirable fruits, arrangements were made with a number of nurserymen in the outskirts of London for rootstocks in their nurseries to be grafted or budded, on the understanding that after two young trees of each variety had been reserved for the Society's own use, the rest could be sold.

It is clear from the Council minutes that by 1817 the publication of the Society's *Transactions*, with its handsome coloured plates, in which Sabine was particularly interested, had become a considerable undertaking. The cost of the parts produced in that year was £3,043. 15s. 0d., while the principal items on the credit side were:

Delivered to Fellows	£348.	6.	0.
Sold to Members	143.	2.	0.
Sold to Booksellers	760.	7.	6.
	£1,251.	15.	6.

The value of the unsold stock at the end of the year was £2,381. Twelve months later, when the second part of Volume III was ready for printing, Sabine estimated that the prime cost would be £677. 5s. 0d. for 1,250 copies printed; that if 350 of these were taken for the use of the Society, as first profit, the remaining 900 copies might be sold to the booksellers and to the Fellows of the Society at £1. 0s. 0d. each, which would give a profit, besides the 350 copies, of £222. 15s. 0d., or nearly 5s. on each of the 900 copies. The price was accordingly fixed at £1 per copy for Fellows and £1. 6s. 6d. to the public. In December 1818 a set of the *Transactions* was presented to the Prince Regent, who had expressed his desire to become the future patron of the Society, and in his covering letter the Secretary stated that the accompanying list of Fellows had been printed in May of that year, and that in the meantime close on 200 new Fellows had been enrolled.

Early in 1817 the Society had rented the first floor of 21 Church Street for its Library and offices; its Meetings, however, continued for the time being to be held in the Linnean Society's apartments in Gerrard Street, Soho. That arrangement obviously left much to be desired and the Council decided that the Society must purchase its own house as soon as one suitable for all its purposes could be found. In December 1818 the Secretary informed the Council that Mr. Burton, the proprietor of some unfinished houses in Waterloo Street, had made an offer to the Society of one of them. Details were laid before the Council and 'an estimate of the Society's pecuniary resources and expenses having been duly considered' the Council inspected the house in January 1819 and found it to be 'peculiarly suited to the purposes of the Society'. A committee of three was accordingly appointed to consult a surveyor recommended by the Secretary, and to treat with Mr. Burton on the basis of a ground rent of £150 and a purchase price of £2,560 or, if need be, £2,650, on the understanding that the price would include as completely as possible the entire finishing of the house and near-by room with the exception of 'papering and bells to the House and the plaistering and stuccoing of the Meeting Room'.

The Committee was also asked to consider the best means of obtaining £4,000 by way of loan for the purchase, finishing, and furnishing of the House and Meeting Room. It reported that it believed that the most simple plan, and the one most likely to be efficacious, was to raise the £4,000 by way of loan amongst such of the Fellows as might be disposed to lend it upon bonds of £100, interest at the rate of 5 per cent, to be paid annually. The scheme was adopted, and within a month twenty-one Fellows had readily offered to take bonds covering the whole £4,000. Much the largest loan, £1,000, was offered by Mr. (later Sir) Claude Scott, and one of several offers of £200 came from Mr. William Cattley, who grew tropical plants with great success in his garden at Barnet and in whose honour the orchids called cattleyas are named. Bonds were issued accordingly and the premises duly purchased, although Mr. Burton insisted that the price be £2,750, to which sum it was subsequently agreed that a further £250 should be added for 'some alterations which it had been found expedient to make'. Arrangements were made to insure the House for £3,000 against all loss from fire, and the Library Committee was instructed to furnish it without further reference to the Council. Notice was given to the Linnean Society that, having purchased a house with a meeting room attached, the Society would take possession of it on 1 May 1819, and would not require the use of the room in Gerrard Street thereafter.

The House which 'was peculiarly suited to the purposes of the Society' was No. 21 on the west side of what is now called Lower Regent Street, three doors down from Jermyn Street, on part of the site now occupied by the Plaza Theatre. The various parts were provisionally allocated as follows:

Rooms in the basement story, for the residence of the Messenger and Housekeeper; Front Parlour, for the Council and Committee Room; Back Parlour, for the Clerks' Office; Front room on first floor, for the Library; Back room on the first floor, for the Secretary; Second floor, for the Secretary's private office and the Assistant Secretary's residence; Attics, for store and fruit rooms.

The unusual, and for the Society's purposes the particularly good, feature of the premises was 'the Great Room' which more or less corresponded to the present 'New Hall'. It stood at the back, over some coach-houses, separated from the house itself by a 12-foot passage to Jermyn Street, and was reached by a covered bridge from the first floor of the house. It was about 56 feet by 32 feet and was lighted by a skylight.

The Anniversary Meeting, held on 1 May 1819, marked the end of the first fifteen years of the Society's existence. The total number of Fellows was 576, of whom 219 had been elected in the preceding twelve months, and the list included 'many of the most distinguished names in the kingdom, whether rank, character or talent be considered'. In addition there were eleven Foreign Members, who were 'persons of the highest consideration for Botanical and Horticultural knowledge in various parts of the world'.[1] There were also 49 Home and 61 Foreign Corresponding Members who 'could not fail to prove of the highest advantage in promoting the objects of the Society'.[2] The Society was enjoying 'the most cordial and able assistance from the Nurserymen, and Market and Practical Gardeners',[3] and 'No petty jealousies or fears have operated to the prejudice of the Society's views.'[4]

The Society's headquarters, with its '. . . favourable situation and general convenience' which left 'nothing more to wish for on this head', was staffed by the Assistant Secretary, John Turner; correspondence clerk, Thomas Whisfield Tindal; library clerk, Thomas Goode; junior clerk, James Thomas Campin; resident messenger and porter, William Tuson; housekeeper, Mrs. Tuson; and an errand boy. Their total cost was £386 per annum. At headquarters a fairly extensive library had already been formed and was being constantly enlarged by gifts and purchases. A collection of excellent drawings of fruits, in the making of which William Hooker, the artist, was regularly employed, was considerable. In addition the Drawings Committee was forming collections of drawings of ornamental plants, one of which consisted of Chinese plants drawn by artists at Canton under the direction of John Reeves. Reeves (1774–1856) was in the employ of the East India Company as an inspector of tea at Canton and Macao and was one of the Society's most valued overseas correspondents. Early in 1817 the Society gladly accepted his offer to obtain and send home plants, and drawings of plants, and agreed to advance such money as he might require to meet the cost. Twenty-five pounds was sent and in return living plants arrived which, because the Society did not have a garden, were put into the care of Mr. Lee of Hammersmith and of Mr. Wm. Anderson of the Chelsea Physic Garden. By August 1819 the Society possessed 130 drawings of Chinese plants, forty-nine of which, executed by different artists, Reeves had purchased for sixteen dollars. Other drawings followed and in 1821 Council approved the purchase of 218 miscellaneous drawings at half a dollar each.

Not only had the Society acquired its own headquarters; in March 1818 it had also acquired its own small garden—an acre and a half in extent—which, it was considered, had already proved the desirability

[1] *Trans. hort. Soc. Lond.*, 3 (1820), ii.   [2] ibid.   [3] ibid.   [4] ibid.

of one on a more extensive scale which would 'at once become a National School for the propagation of Horticultural Knowledge, and a standard reference for the authenticity of every species of Garden produce'. As the garden would obviously be an additional continuing expense to the Society, Council had raised the subscription. After 1 October 1818 a new Fellow was required to pay the usual admission fee of five guineas, but the annual subscription was raised from two to three guineas, which could be commuted in a single sum of thirty guineas. However this increased subscription seems not to have affected the inflow of new Fellows. In the following year, realizing that it was unwise to treat commutation fees as income, the Council directed that sums paid as compositions should be regarded as capital, and invested.

An announcement at the end of 1819 describes the Society's general arrangements.

The General Meetings of the Society are held at the House of the Society in Regent Street on the first and third Tuesdays in every month, the Chair being taken at One o'clock precisely. At these Meetings Communications made to the Society, on new and important subjects in Horticulture, are read; Fruits, Vegetables and Flowers are exhibited; and Seeds, Cuttings, Grafts and Plants procured by, or presented to, the Society are distributed to the Fellows present. Visitors introduced by a Fellow are admitted to these Meetings. In addition to the Business above-mentioned, new Fellows are admitted, Candidates to become Fellows are ballotted for, and Medals and Premiums, awarded by the Council, are presented.

The Society has an Experimental Garden at Kensington, on the south side of the road leading to Hammersmith, nearly opposite Holland House; which is open to Fellows of the Society, from Two to Six o'clock, in each day of the week, except Sundays. Fellows visiting the Garden, have the privilege of introducing one or more friends, in their company.

Every Candidate for Admission into the Society is to be proposed by three or more Fellows, one of whom must be personally acquainted with him, or with his writings. The Certificate of Recommendation must specify the name, rank, and usual place of residence of the Candidate, who will be ballotted for after the Certificate has been read, at two General Meetings of the Society. The fee to be paid on the Election and Admission of a new Fellow is Five Guineas, and the Contribution to the Society in each year succeeding his Election is Two Guineas, provided he shall have been elected *before* the first of October, 1818; but if *after* that period, it is Three Guineas, which charge is payable on the first of May, but may be compounded for, by those Fellows elected before the first of October, 1818, by the payment of Twenty Guineas, and by those elected after that period, by the payment of Thirty Guineas at any one time, before the Contribution of the current Year becomes due.

Any person exercising the trade or profession of a Gardener, who shall have received a Medal from the Society, or shall have communicated a Paper, which shall have been printed in the *Transactions* of the Society, may, if approved by the Council, be elected, and enjoy all the privileges of a Fellow, upon the payment of One Guinea for his Admission Fee, and One Guinea for his Contribution in each year.

The Corresponding Members are not subject to any payments; they are elected at a General Meeting of the Society, on the recommendation of the Council, being persons who from their knowledge and skill in Horticulture, or from the circumstance of their residing in particular places, are likely, by their communications and assistance, to promote the objects of the Society.

Communications intended to be made to the Society, and Articles designed for Presentation, or Exhibition at the Meetings, may be addressed to the President, or to the Secretary, at the House of the Society, where Mr. John Turner, the Assistant Secretary, is in attendance for the transacting of business, from Eleven to Four o'Clock daily.

Some idea of the Society's financial position may be gathered from the following published

STATE OF THE ACCOUNTS

from May 1, 1819 to May 1, 1820

Received by	£	s.	d.			
Balance of last year's Account	170	11	6			
Money borrowed on Account of New House	4200	0	0			
Admission Fees from Fellows	1030	1	0			
Ditto from Practical Gardeners	5	5	0			
Annual Contributions	932	8	0			
Ditto from Practical Gardeners	10	10	0			
Compositions in lieu of Annual Contributions	1144	10	0			
Transactions sold to Fellows	860	13	6			
Dividends on Stock	64	12	6			
Payments for *Transactions* from Booksellers	1238	5	3	9656	16	9

Paid for			
Purchase and Fitting of New House	3722	15	5
Purchase of Stock	819	0	0
Rent, Taxes, and Insurance of House	68	13	3
Salaries and wages	396	7	9
Furniture &c.	31	0	3
Printing and other Expenses of *Transactions*	2238	10	3
Drawings	84	6	6
Books and Binding	49	18	3
Medals and Rewards	43	4	0

	£	s.	d.			
Printing Lists of Members and Miscellaneous Printing	76	11	0			
Stationery, Stamps, and Diplomas	156	16	0			
Postages, Parcels and Porterage	78	16	8			
Expenses of Meetings	47	7	1			
Foreign Importations	108	18	9			
Housekeeping Expenses	86	3	2			
Permanent Expenses of the Garden	272	12	3			
Rent of Garden, and Gardener's and Garden Clerk's wages	151	3	9			
Current Expenses of the Garden	363	9	11			
Miscellaneous Charges	72	15	8—	8868	9	11

Balance to Bankers to next Year £788 6 10

There is due

From Booksellers to January 1820	1111	6	7
From the Executors of deceased Fellows	4	4	0
For Arrears of Annual Contributions	202	13	0
For Admission Fees	350	14	0
For *Transactions* sold to Fellows	383	2	0
For Contributions due May 1, 1820	1833	6	0

£3885 5 7

Besides which, the Society has in 3 per cent Consolidated
Annuities £2712 17 7 stock.

The Society is indebted to Messrs. Lamb, Bulmer, Rundell,
and Tindal, about £860.

Such were the affairs of the Society when Sir Joseph Banks, to whose
wise guidance, especially in its early years, the Society owed a great
deal of its success, died on 19 June 1820 at the age of seventy-seven,
having been President of the Royal Society of London since 1778, having
played an active role in the affairs of the Linnean Society, the Society
of Antiquaries, and the Society of Arts, having been virtually Director
of Kew (on an unpaid basis) since 1772, having enriched botanical and
horticultural science through the trained plant collectors he arranged
to be sent to various parts of the globe, and having formulated the policy
of close collaboration with the Empire which has since been followed at
Kew. As one Director of Kew has vividly and rightly said, 'He was the
greatest botanical and horticultural impresario the world has ever
known.' Shortly after his death the Council circularized the Fellows to
the effect that, as a testimonial of respect due to his memory, and as a

mark of gratitude for the continued attention and kindness he had shown to the Society, and for the interest he had taken in its welfare, a portrait of him should be placed in the Society's Meeting Room. Council therefore proposed that, under its direction, a copy from an original picture should be executed as speedily as possible, and that the expense should be defrayed by a subscription, not exceeding one pound each, amongst the Fellows. The requisite sum, estimated at £200, was quickly raised and Thomas Phillips, R.A., was commissioned to make a copy, 'with some variations in the drapery &c.', of the portrait which he had executed for the Royal Society. The picture (Plate 1) now occupies the place of honour over the mantelshelf in the Council Room in Vincent Square.

The Society also possesses another portrait of the same period, that of the founder member James Dickson (Plate 2), painted by H. P. Briggs, and presented by him to the Society in 1820, two years before Dickson died.

The Society was to honour the name of Banks still further, for in July 1820 it was decided that a die for a medal, the size of a crown piece, should be prepared; that the medals struck from it should be of silver, and presented to those who exhibited articles of merit at the Meetings, as distinct from those who contributed noteworthy papers or otherwise deserved recognition. It was further decided that the device on the silver medal should be the head of Banks, and that the medal should be called the Banksian Medal. William Wyon of the Royal Mint was commissioned to make the dies, and when in August 1821 they became available, they were sent to Thomason of Birmingham, who was instructed to supply 100 medals in silver for the purposes of the Society, and one in gold for presentation to Lady Banks. Meanwhile, having reviewed the records of the exhibits staged in the preceding twelve months, the Council decided that forty-three merited the award of the silver Banksian Medal. Thereafter, at each Meeting, the merits of the day's exhibits were assessed, and not infrequently none was considered worthy of a Banksian Medal. If an exhibit was judged of sufficient merit and was shown by one who had previously received a medal, the exhibitor was given a specially designed certificate in place of a second medal. The Banksian Medal (Plate 23) is still in use, though the terms governing its award have been changed from time to time.

CHAPTER FIVE

THE GARDEN

THAT IN DUE COURSE THE SOCIETY SHOULD HAVE A GARDEN WAS probably in the minds of at least some of the founders in 1804, but the first definite step to acquire one was not taken until 1815, when it was 'Resolved that a Proposal be made to the Company of Apothecaries respecting the use of a part of their Garden'. Presumably the Apothecaries were not disposed to agree to the proposal, for nothing came of the suggestion. The subject seems not to have been pursued again until the first Council Meeting in 1818, when a committee was appointed 'to consider and report on the expediency of establishing, means of obtaining, and plan of conducting a Garden for the Society'.

The committee moved quickly and three weeks later 'The Council authorized Mr. Sabine to contract for the renting of such small piece of Garden ground as he might deem expedient for the Cultivation of the Fruit trees &c. belonging to the Society until the Society shall become possessed of a regular Garden.' Sabine was also authorized to engage a gardener and quickly secured the services of Charles Strachan at one pound a week, and in March reported 'that he had finally agreed with Mr. Sutton for the piece of ground at Kensington as an Experimental Garden and that Mr. Sutton had signed an agreement'.

This, the Society's first Garden, consisted of one and a half acres of a walled market garden, situated on the south side of the Hammersmith Road, nearly opposite Holland House, and rented at sixty pounds per annum. All was reported to the Fellows in April, and Council explained that the land,

though far from sufficient for the cultivation of even a small part of the objects which come under our superintendence, yet it will aid us essentially in case we are able hereafter to obtain sufficient space for all our purposes, by becoming a depot, in which Fruit-trees and Plants may be collected for removal to a larger Garden. Experiments on the cultivation of particular Classes of Vegetables will also be carried on in the Garden under the direction of a Committee of Management.

With the latter purpose in view it was reported that seeds of nine varieties of peas had already been obtained from France; a few days later seeds of a further eight varieties were acquired. The Garden was quickly equipped with frames, hand-glasses, a potting-shed, and a large pit of an improved type which, after consideration, the committee decided would serve all their purposes and be cheaper than a green-house, as 'the cost would not much exceed £200'. However, two years later a glass-house was built 'for the preservation of the less hardy plants, especially of those received from China'. In June 1818 the Council gratefully accepted for the Garden an offer from Sabine of a collection of narcissi, lilies, crocuses, and other bulbous plants which he said he had no doubt was 'the most complete in the species and varieties of the *Liliaceae*, not only in England, but in the world'.

Trials were made of Continental varieties of vegetables and by mid-summer specimens of the resulting crops were sent to the Society's Meetings. The first of such exhibits from the Garden consisted of three varieties of radish, two of them French, the other Russian. Later came three varieties of turnip, a cabbage, and an early silver-skinned onion 'new to this country', both raised from French seeds. They were followed in September by thirty-nine varieties of dahlia. During the year it was announced at the Meetings that broccoli and celery plants and some young vines could be had by Fellows on application at the Garden, and in October notice was given that duplicates of the collection of bulbs, sixty-seven sorts in all, were ready to be distributed. Strachan, the gardener, proved so satisfactory that in the autumn his salary was raised to eighty pounds per annum. However, very surprisingly, in the following sum-mer it was found 'expedient to discharge' him, and in August 1819, the Garden was entrusted to William Christie, the foreman, until a suitable gardener could be found. Not until March 1820, was the Secretary able to report that Donald Munro had been appointed gardener to the Society at a salary of £105 per annum.

Incidentally it is interesting to note that Sabine, a civil servant with a knowledge of some of the ways of government departments, made a successful application to the Lords of the Treasury for the admittance into the country, free of duty, of foreign plants and seeds.

The acquisition of the small garden at Kensington was obviously a very definite step forward, even though it fell far short of the ultimate aim of Sabine and other enthusiasts. But small though it was its equip-ment and maintenance would involve the Society in considerable ex-pense, in addition to the greatly increased expenditure at headquarters. It seemed likely that several years must elapse before the Society would be able to embark on something much more ambitious. However, in July 1820, Sabine reported that from a communication received from the Rt. Hon. Sir Charles Long,[1] who had recently been elected to the Council, 'it appeared that the government was disposed to assist the Society in the annual Expenses of a Garden by an annual grant of money for that purpose'. Fortunately, or unfortunately, nothing came of this suggested government subsidy. Still, at the time it seemed to open up great possibilities, and the Council immediately requested the Committee appointed in 1818 to resume its activities and 'report on the expediency of establishing, means of obtaining, and plan of conducting a Garden'.

The Committee examined a number of sites in the neighbourhood of Wimbledon, but always the soil was unsuitable. This was the trouble with some land at Hornsey for which the Council negotiated, and indeed were prepared to lease, though the rent was more than they wished to pay. The lease was prevented by a committee of five professional gardeners and nurserymen, who reported that the soil was too wet and the site not capable of adequate drainage. Accordingly it was 'ordered that an advertisement be inserted in the newspapers for a piece of garden-ground within a convenient distance of London, on a long lease; suitably circumstanced, and to contain about thirty acres'. Of the nine offers received the most promising was one of thirty-three acres at Chiswick, belonging to the Duke of Devonshire and let to market gardeners. After the site had been inspected by the President and three other members of the Council, on 14 July 1821, it was agreed that the land should be leased on the terms proposed by the Duke's agents. These included the provision of a private door in the wall separating the site from the grounds of Chiswick House, the Duke's residence, to enable the Duke, and any of his family in residence there, to obtain immediate admission to the Garden, during customary hours, on ringing the door-bell.

The lease was for sixty years, renewable every thirty years for ever, upon a fine certain, and a rent of £300 per annum, with power to the Society to relinquish its obligations at any time upon giving twelve months' notice. To meet the cost of establishing the Garden an appeal was issued to Fellows, stating that His Majesty, as the patron of the Society, had been graciously pleased to give the sum of £500, and that Fellows subscribing ten pounds or more would have the privilege of introducing friends by means of tickets at their disposal, without the necessity of personal introduction. To provide additional money for the maintenance of the Garden it was decided to raise the annual subscription from three to four guineas; 'this addition to the yearly Contributions

---

[1] Charles Long, Baron Farnborough (1761–1838). Politician. M.P. from 1789 till raised to peerage in 1826. In 1820 he was Paymaster-General and was made G.C.B. Married daughter of Sir Abraham Hume, and with her assistance laid out an extensive ornamental garden at his residence at Bromley Hill Place.

will necessarily be voluntary on the part of the Members already elected.' The response to the appeal was good, and by 1 April 1823 the list of contributions totalled £4,891. Not unexpectedly, the suggestion that existing Fellows might desire voluntarily to increase their annual subscriptions failed to produce anything like a unanimous acceptance.

In the meantime a scheme for the layout of the new Garden was prepared. A little more than half was allocated to fruit and vegetables, and about thirteen acres to the ornamental department, including an arboretum of about eight acres.

On 25 February 1822 the Council appointed Mr. John Lindley[1] to the post of Assistant Secretary at the Garden at a salary of £120 per annum. His duties were 'to have superintendence over the collection of plants, and all other matters in the Garden, and to keep all Accounts, Minutes of Report &c., under the direction of the President and Secretary'. Unfortunately, Lindley's authority was only nominal. The real authority was in the hands of Sabine, and he exercised it despotically. Life at Chiswick must have been very frustrating to the young Lindley, then only twenty-three and with unlimited energy and ideas. Fortunately, he remained loyal both to Sabine and the Garden and was destined to take a very active part in the Society's affairs for the next forty-one years. For much of that period, as Assistant Secretary, Vice-Secretary, and for the last five years of his working life as Secretary, he was the backbone of the Society and possibly the greatest servant it has ever had. Born at Catton, near Norwich, the son of a rather unsuccessful nurseryman, he came to London in 1819 and became an assistant in Sir Joseph Banks's library. The first reference to him in the Society's minutes is in 1820, when he was commissioned to draw some single roses, and some larches sent to the Society by the Duke of Atholl. Distinctions came quickly to him. In 1828 he was elected a Fellow of the Royal Society and in 1829 became the first Professor of Botany in the University of London, while in 1841 he helped to found the *Gardener's Chronicle* and became its first editor. (Plate 5.)

The little makeshift garden in Kensington was given up in 1823 and the Council proceeded to lay out the new one in accordance with the prepared plan; roads and paths were constructed; walls, glass-houses, frames, sheds, and offices containing a Council Room were built; hedges, fruit trees, etc., were planted; and extensive trials of vegetables were begun. By March 1823 there was a collection of over 1,200 roses. Of the various fruits it was stated that 'at no period, nor under any circumstances, has such a collection been before formed'. Vegetables examined and classified included 435 samples of lettuce, 260 of peas, and 240 of potatoes, among which the synonyms were found to be 'numerous

[1] *Gardener's Chronicle*, vol. 158 (1965), pp. 386, 409, 434, 457, 481, 507.

almost beyond belief'. There were also large plantings of paeonies, phloxes, irises, and various bulbous plants. In 1825 the greenhouse and stove plants consisted almost entirely of the Society's own importations, e.g. from Reeves, from Potts—the Society's recently appointed collector in China—and from correspondents in Sumatra, Mauritius, Calcutta, Trinidad, and St. Vincent, together with the findings of George Don and others in Sierra Leone, South America and the West Indies. There were, for instance, the handsome stove plants *Ixora undulata* and *Wrightia tinctoria*, the Pala indigo plant, both of which John Potts had sent from India in 1822. Potts had also sent from China a grafted camellia; the graft had died, but the stock had lived and grown and had proved to be the small white-flowered *Camellia euryoides*. Also from China, sent by John Damper Parks in 1824, was the orchid *Coelogyne fimbriata*, which plant formed the plate for the *Botanical Register* t.868, as well as the aspidistra, *Aspidistra lurida. Sarcocephalus esculentus*, the Sierra Leone Peach, with globular heads of flowers like pin cushions, had been sent from Sierra Leone by George Don in 1822. Several plants from Rio were flourishing, including the bulbous *Griffinia hyacinthina* which had arrived from John Forbes in 1823; the biennial rosy-flowered *Cleome rosea* from James McRae the following year; and from David Douglas in 1825 the fine orchids *Brassavola nodosa* and *Oncidium pubes* and the close ally of the gloxinia, *Sinningia helleri*. Chrysanthemums introduced by the Society from China were grown both under glass and trained against walls. In 1824 there were twenty-seven different kinds, purple, rose or pink, lilac, white, yellow, buff or orange, quilled or non-quilled, curled, double, and semi-double. An artesian well was sunk to provide water for a canal for aquatics, and a start was made on an arboretum which, when finished, was intended to contain 'a specimen of every kind of hardy tree and shrub, whether species or variety, capable of enduring the climate of this country'.

The year 1826 saw the publication of a *Catalogue of Fruits cultivated in the Garden of the Horticultural Society of London at Chiswick*. The number of varieties enumerated was 3,825 and the preface stated that 'there exist in the Garden nearly 1,000 more, of less certain authority'. It was hoped that this publication would help to stabilize the nomenclature of fruits and extend the cultivation of the more desirable varieties.

From the outset the Society's policy was to maintain a horticultural, as distinct from a botanic, garden. 'Such plants as cannot be considered either Ornamental or Useful, will be left out of the Collection, or if raised from seeds collected for the Society, or given to it, they will be removed and transferred to other Gardens professedly appropriated to Botanical Sciences.'

The assembling of this large and varied collection of plants in the

Garden was by no means a one-way traffic. There was at the same time a constant and extensive distribution of novelties and plants of proven merit to nurserymen and to public and private gardens throughout the country. Care was taken at all times to comply with the Council's standing instruction not to interfere with the interest of nurserymen, and to avoid distributing 'all such things as are to be obtained generally, and correctly [named] from the Seed shops or Nurseries in London or its vicinity'. Both plants and seeds were sent to British colonies, and to foreign countries generally, if it was thought that they were likely to be useful. Understandably, this policy 'produced a reciprocity of kindness in quarters where supplies [had] been received, which would not have been attainable without the exercise of such an influence'. Quite clearly, during the first half of the nineteenth century, no organization or institution anywhere in the world, including those financed by governments, did so much as the Society to disseminate valuable horticultural plants.

As men alone were eligible for fellowship in the Society, the distribution of plants and seeds was only to men. Exceptionally, and as a matter of sentiment, some of the new chrysanthemums from China were presented to the widow of Sir Joseph Banks, but no other lady is mentioned in the Council minutes until 28 May 1824, when it was 'ordered, that a plant of *Primula sinensis* be given to Mrs. Marryat of Wimbledon'. This lady was the wife of Mr. Joseph Marryat, of 1 Mansion House Street and Wimbledon Common, one of the many Fellows who subscribed to the Garden. Why she was singled out for special treatment is not recorded. The plant with which she was presented had recently been raised at the Garden from the first lot of seeds of this species ever to have been sent to Britain; they had come from Canton through the Society's collector there, John Potts. The next mention of a lady occurs in the minutes only three months later, but in rather different circumstances. In June a letter had been received announcing the desire of the Emperor of Russia to become a Fellow of the Society, and when, in August, Dr. Fischer, the botanist, arrived in Britain sent by the Emperor of Russia to obtain plants for the new Garden at St. Petersburg, the Society gave him a large collection as a present to the Emperor, together with a single plant of *Primula sinensis* as a gift to the Empress Mother. The horticultural development of this primula since that time is ample evidence that the high regard attached to it was abundantly justified.

The name of a third lady appears in the minutes in the following year in an altogether different context. A contractor who had accepted bonds in part payment of his bill for work at the Garden wished to receive cash, and the Secretary reported that 'he had arranged with Lady Dampier to advance the sum of £2,000 on a bond of the Council.'

The establishment of the Garden enabled a start to be made on the educational work which was visualized when, in the *Transactions* of 1820, it was stated that the Society 'looked forward with confidence to that period when, either by their own increased efforts, or by an aid superior to their own, they may effect an establishment, which shall at once become a National School for the propagation of Horticultural knowledge, and a standard reference for the authenticity of every species of Garden produce'.[1] The Society's Garden now provided better facilities for the education of professional gardeners than those to be found anywhere else in this country, or indeed abroad, for the most up-to-date glass-houses were being installed, unequalled collections of fruits were being formed, extensive trials of vegetables were being made, and new ornamental plants, both hardy and tender, were streaming in from foreign correspondents and the Society's own collectors. Consequently arrangements were made for up to thirty-six young men to be trained in the Garden for a period of two years, and for those who proved satisfactory to be put in touch with prospective employers.

In this far-sighted fashion, the Society took the lead, and since then has continued to lead the world in the development of organized horticultural training and education. The story of its endeavours in these matters is one of the most glorious chapters in the Society's history.

These young men, who had to be between the ages of eighteen and twenty-six and 'to have been educated as Gardeners, to be unmarried, and capable of reading and writing moderately well', were designated by the unattractive name (especially today) of 'labourers'; they were expected to undertake any work they were asked to do, and were instructed by the under-gardeners in the various departments through which they passed. Although during the first few years of the operation of the scheme they do not appear to have been required to attend courses of lectures, they were encouraged to make use of a small library provided for them. During the two-year course they were paid fourteen shillings a week. Keen young gardeners were not slow to take advantage of the opportunities which the Garden afforded. By March 1826 no fewer than ninety-two had sought and obtained admission, and of those twenty-nine had been found posts, twenty-seven had been dismissed or had not completed the course, and thirty-six were in training. As applicants for admission included a good many from abroad, in 1826 it was 'ordered that henceforward there shall not be more than three foreigners at one time among the Labourers in the Garden, without special permission'.

On admission each entrant was required to write brief particulars of himself in a book of *Handwriting of Under Gardeners and Labourers* which is

[1] *Trans. hort. Soc. Lond.*, 3 (1820), ii.

still preserved in the Lindley Library. Among the earliest entries is one made by Joseph Paxton, who some twenty-seven years later was knighted for the contribution he made to the success of the Great Exhibition of 1851 by designing and supervising the erection of the Crystal Palace. In the *Book of Handwriting* Paxton states that he was born in 1801, whereas in fact he was born in 1803; it seems likely that this go-ahead young man believed that he would be more acceptable if he were thought to be older and more experienced than he actually was. He acquitted himself so well that in due course he was promoted to be under-gardener in the Arboretum at eighteen shillings a week. While thus employed he became known to the Duke of Devonshire, the Society's landlord, who, when in residence at Chiswick House, was a frequent visitor to the Garden, entering by the private door which, under the terms of the Society's lease, had been provided in the wall which separated his grounds from the Garden. The Duke evidently thought highly of the under-gardener, for when, in 1826, he needed a gardener for his seat at Chatsworth, he offered the post, which carried a weekly wage of twenty-five shillings and a cottage, to Paxton, who accepted it. Paxton vividly describes his departure from Chiswick.

I left London by the Comet coach for Chesterfield, and arrived at Chatsworth at half past 4 o'clock in the morning of the 9th of May, 1826. As no person was to be seen at that early hour I got over the greenhouse gates by the old covered way, explored the pleasure ground, and looked round the outside of the house. I then went down to the kitchen garden, scaled the outside wall, and saw the whole of the place, set the men to work there at 6 o'clock, then returned to Chatsworth, and got Thomas Weldon to play me the water works, and afterwards went to breakfast with poor dear Mrs. Gregory and her niece; the latter fell in love with me, and I with her, and thus completed my first morning's work at Chatsworth before 9 o'clock.[1]

'Poor dear Mrs. Gregory' was the housekeeper at Chatsworth, and her niece was Miss Sarah Brown, whom Paxton married the following year.

In 1825 it was thought desirable to maintain a meteorological journal in the Garden and, although some difficulty was at first found in procuring efficient instruments (with the result that the observations made during this year may not have been reliable), all difficulties were eventually overcome and complete records have been kept at the Society's Garden since 1 January 1826, first at Chiswick and since 1904 at Wisley.

In 1827 the Garden became the scene of the Society's main annual social function. On the whole the Anniversary Dinners had been very

[1] Markham, *Paxton and the Bachelor Duke* (1935), p. 30.

Plate 5. Dr John Lindley (Assistant Secretary at the Garden, Assistant Secretary, Vice Secretary and Secretary of the Society 1822–1863)

Plate 6. 'The Horticultural Fate', a cartoon representing the Fête held at the Chiswick Garden in 1829

pleasant occasions, though some part of the cost of them had had to be met from the Society's funds. But in 1827 the Society's financial affairs were in poor shape and no one was in the mood for a celebration of this kind. In these circumstances it was thought undesirable to hold the usual Dinner. Instead, it was suggested that a public meeting of some kind be held in the Garden, provided that the Society was not involved in expenditure of money and that the Garden was not injured in any way. The idea was welcomed by many, especially because ladies would be allowed to participate—and in the event many did. Thus arrangements were made for a 'Public Breakfast' (later called a 'Fête') to be held in the Garden on Saturday 23 June, and for an exhibition of fruit to be associated with it. The details were entrusted to a committee of Fellows, assisted by twenty-four 'lady patronesses', of whom no fewer than twenty were titled. Tickets cost one guinea each, and the sole power of issuing tickets, apart from those issued by the Committee, was vested in the lady patronesses. Refreshments, which proved to be inadequate, were provided by a professional caterer and a military band helped to give the proceedings a festive air. Nearly 3,000 tickets were issued and 2,843 persons attended. 'It was allowed by all parties that such an assemblage of women of beauty, fashion, and rank, had never before been seen in a garden.' While those Fellows who were not inclined to pay for admission to their own Garden and who considered that many non-Fellows who attended were not in the least interested in horticulture regarded the function as a misuse of the Garden, the official view was that the Fête was very satisfactory, especially as there was a credit balance instead of the deficit which had usually followed the Anniversary Dinner.

A similar Fête was held in 1828, when rules for the issue of tickets were amended in favour of the Fellows, and the arrangements for catering, music, etc., were more elaborate. Fine weather, of course, was essential for the success of these popular society functions, and the third one, held in 1829, was unfortunate in this respect, and, of course, provided much coverage for the daily press. The preparations[1] included 'a long range of tents beginning at the . . . principal entrance [and running] along the gravel walk for nearly the whole length of the grounds, . . . intended as a promenade if the day be fine; a shelter if wet'. There were five refreshment tents, 'distinguished by their colours —blue and pink for the principal one; green . . . for tea, coffee, ices, fruits', and they contained 'tables extending a thousand feet in length for the viands'. 'The stores of Messrs. Gunter [the Caterers, which were] enclosed in a spacious area in the rear [were] a perfect sanctum sanctorum.' Music was provided by the bands of the Royal Artillery 'in their

[1] *Jl R. hort. Soc.*, LXXI (1946), p. 43.

beautiful white uniforms', the Blues, and the First Life Guards, while the Tyrolese Minstrels and Les Trois Troubadours were to perform in the evening. In short, the programme 'had all the elements of the grandest fête; and had the weather been equally favourable it would have been a spectacle equal to the proudest days in the annals of George the Fourth'.

'The doors opened at one o'clock, at which time a long line of equipages graced the high Hammersmith-road, nearly fifteen hundred in number, and extending to Hyde Park-corner.' In spite of a slight drizzling rain during the afternoon, the fashionable throng paraded the Garden where they were able to see, among other newly introduced plants, the now well-known annual *Clarkia pulchella*. But soon after 4 p.m. there 'came on a storm of wind, rain and thunder, attended by a gloom which was quite appalling'. Naturally all who could crowded into the tents, and those who couldn't sheltered under the trees. 'From four to five hundreds were in waiting for the opening of the avenues to the refreshment tents, unprotected from the fury of the elements; and loud were the complaints made in consequence of a rigid adherence to the first arrangements.' Even those under cover were not much to be envied, for the tents were in a valley to which all the water from the higher ground found its way, so that the visitors were 'nearly ankle deep in water oozing from the gravel; shrieks were dreadful, and the loss of shoes particularly annoying'. Some of the men reconnoitred the caterer's 'sanctum sanctorum' and, returning to their fair companions in the marquees, 'brought in their umbrellas dishes (we saw seven in one) containing whole chickens, tongues, &c., together with an abundance of fruit; other gentlemen conveyed Champagne, Burgundy, Claret and Madeira.' 'We cannot conclude . . . without alluding to the conduct of certain *persons* who were not *gentlemen*', wrote the *Morning Post*. The event was the subject of one of Paul Pry's (William Heath's) cartoons entitled 'The Horticultural Fate', which is reproduced as Plate 6 by the courtesy of the Trustees of the British Museum.[1]

The reorganization of the Garden did not allow of any Fête being held there in 1830, but one was held in June 1831, and though it made a small profit it was the last of this kind of function.

In the meantime at the Garden horticulture and horticultural education were prospering. In August 1828, probably at the instigation of Lindley, the under-gardeners and men in the Garden formed an association 'for the purpose of improving themselves in the business of their profession', and the Council, thoroughly approving of the movement, authorized an expenditure of fifty pounds to increase the stock of books in the Garden library. Thus began the Mutual Improvement

[1] *Jl R. hort. Soc.*, LXXI (1946), p. 43, fig. 19.

Society which was the forerunner of the present-day Wisley Lindley Society. In December the young men who had hitherto been designated in Sabine's Rules as 'labourers' were for the first time referred to in the Council minutes as 'students', and no doubt they were happy to see the introduction of hot-water pipes in the pineapple pits and in a curvilinear glass-house, for the former they had had to heat by manure hotbeds and the latter by flues.

At this time valuable work was being done by the Garden staff on the classification of fruits and vegetables. Donald Munro, the Society's gardener, who gave loyal service to the Garden until he retired in 1850, when he was presented with a gold watch and chain—the testimonial of 260 of his friends—classified the pineapple collection chiefly on the serration of the leaves, the colour of the flowers, and the shape of the fruits—cylindrical, pyramidal, globular. Some 450 named types he grouped into fifty-two distinct varieties. Robert Thompson, the under-gardener in the fruit department, classified the apricots, gooseberries, and cherries. On the characters of the size of the fruit and the flavour of the kernel, he grouped the seventy to eighty named kinds of apricot, all of which were growing on the walls in the Garden, into seventeen distinct varieties. The fifty-seven kinds of cherry, all of which had fruited, he grouped according to leaf shape and the shape, colour, and flavour of the fruit. The seventy kinds of gooseberry were representative of two races; the Old English—small, globular-fruited, and erect of habit, and the Lancashire gooseberries with more or less pendulous branches cultivated, especially in Lancashire, for the size rather than the flavour, of the fruits. The two races were further classified according to hairiness and colour of fruit—red, yellow, green, white.

In like manner George Gordon, the under-gardener in the kitchen-garden department, classified the peas. He concluded that the forty-three distinct kinds in cultivation in the Society's Garden possessed 130 synonymous names, and he grouped his forty-three kinds into Dwarfs, Talls, Dwarf and Tall Marrows, Sugars, Imperials, Prussians, Grey Sugars, and Greys. His work on varieties of bean, Gordon stated, was 'to reduce the discordant nomenclature of the seed shops to something like order, to enable the Gardener to know the quality of the sorts he is unaccustomed to cultivate, and above all to prevent his buying the same kind under different names'.[1] Gordon was able to distinguish only eleven distinct kinds from among the forty-three reputed varieties he was cultivating at Chiswick.

Another noteworthy development at the Garden stemmed from the decision, taken in 1836, that no student-gardener at Chiswick in future should be recommended for employment unless he had passed an ex-

[1] *Trans. hort. Soc. Lond.*, 2nd Series (1835), p. 369.

amination which showed not only that he could 'write and spell respectably', was sufficiently acquainted with arithmetic to be able to keep accounts, and was able to measure land and make simple ground plans, but also that he had some knowledge of geography and the elements of botany and plant physiology. This first horticultural examination was welcomed by the *Gardener's Magazine* with an article beginning 'A GRAND step has been taken by the London Horticultural Society,' and expressing the hope that the examination would 'contribute towards that most desirable result, the establishment of a national system of [horticultural] education'. And Loudon, the editor, was not far out when he added: 'The idea of examining gardeners . . . we have no doubt originated with Dr. Lindley, who has thus rendered a most important service to the gardening world.' The first recipient of a First Certificate was John Lumsden, of Inchture, Perthshire, who obtained that distinction on 1 August. On 26 September 'an extra certificate of the first class' was awarded to another young Scotsman, named Robert Fortune, of whom more was to be heard later.

The arrival of orchids and other ornamental plants from tropical America, sent by the Society's collector, Theodore Hartweg, made the provision of more glass-houses at Chiswick a matter of urgency, and in June 1838 the Council 'resolved on ballot' that the building of hot-houses at the Garden be commenced immediately; and a committee was appointed forthwith to give effect to the decision. Clearly, as there had to be a ballot on the matter, not everyone favoured the development. The *Gardener's Magazine* gave only qualified approval, expressing the fear that it would involve a reduction in the good work already done with fruit and vegetables. On the other hand, commenting on the subject in the following February, the *Botanical Register* had this to say:

All who are interested in the cultivation of exotic plants will be glad to learn that the Horticultural Society of London are about to erect a most extensive conservatory in the garden at Chiswick. The whole range, when executed will be one of the most extensive in the world. No association of individuals has ever introduced so large a quantity of beautiful and useful plants into this country as have been procured by the Horticultural Society; but those plants have necessarily been confined very much to hardy species, in consequence of the want of extensive glass houses. It is now to be expected that greenhouse and stove plants will become a great object of attention; the effect of which will doubtless be to improve the ornamental character of tender plants in the same degree as that of hardy collections.[1]

At this time the hardy collections included many Californian annual plants collected by David Douglas and probably the most important of

[1] Edwards, *Botanical Register* (1839), p. 17.

these was a form of the Californian Poppy, *Eschscholtzia californica*, with deep orange flowers and thus distinct from the typical plant which has yellow flowers. As a result of hybridization between Douglas's form and the type there has been developed a great range of colour forms, which come true or almost true from seeds. Other of Douglas's Californian annuals included *Platystemon californicus*, a beautiful small poppy-like plant which well displays its many pale yellow or cream flowers against glaucous grey-green foliage; the deliciously fragrant *Limnanthes douglasii* with bright yellow flowers fading to white at the tips of the petals; several lupins, including *Lupinus nanus* with elegant foliage and blue or lilac flowers, *L. densiflorus* with densely packed spikes of yellow flowers, and *L. hirsutissimus* with flowers of reddish-purple; the very decorative lilac or pink-to-white-flowered *Gilia androsacea*; *Phacelia tanacetifolia* with small bright blue flowers carried in large clusters, and a splendid bee plant; and the lilac and white *Collinsia bicolor*. All are still to be found in the catalogues of today.

Douglas had by no means confined his attentions to sending to Chiswick seeds of annuals. Between 1830 and 1840 many conifers had been raised from his seeds, including *Abies procera*, the Noble Fir, which Douglas had discovered on the south side of the Columbia River in 1825 and had introduced in 1830; *Abies grandis*, the Giant Fir, which he also discovered on the Columbia River in 1825 and had introduced in 1832; the Sitka Spruce, *Picea sitchensis*, which Archibald Menzies had first found at Puget Sound in 1792; the Western White Pine, *Pinus monticola*, which Douglas had found and introduced in 1831; the Monterey Pine, *Pinus radiata*, seeds of which he had sent from California in 1833; the Digger Pine, *Pinus sabiniana*, which he had discovered in California in 1826 and had introduced in 1832; and *Pinus coulteri*, the Big-cone Pine (whose cones are often 14 inches long and weigh up to 4 pounds), which Douglas had introduced in 1832 after it had been discovered in the Santa Lucia mountains by Coulter earlier in the same year.

Douglas's conifer introductions have been eminently successful in cultivation. Not so those which Theodore Hartweg endeavoured to introduce. In 1837 he sent home much coniferous seed and by 1840 there were at Chiswick many seedlings. But the majority of the subjects came from the sub-tropical and warm temperate regions of Mexico and Central America and thus have not proved hardy in Britain. Little or no success attended the efforts to establish *Abies religiosa*, the Sacred Fir, *Juniperus flaccida*, the Mexican Juniper, and *J. mexicana*, the Rock Juniper; or the Twisted-leaved Pine, *Pinus teocote*, *P. oocarpa* and the form of the False Weymouth Pine known as *Pinus pseudostrobus* var. *apulcensis*. Those which have succeeded have done so only in the most sheltered of gardens; *Pinus montezumae*, the Rough Barked Mexican Pine; its form *hartwegii*; and *P. patula*, the Spreading-leaved Pine, all wonderfully beautiful plants.

The tender plants which the Council knew would require greenhouse culture and for which, moreover, the Council was determined to provide, included over one hundred species of orchid as well as many members of the Cactaceae.

CHAPTER SIX

PLANT INTRODUCTION

As a result of the arrangements made in 1817 with John Reeves, the Society received a fairly steady trickle of plants from China; in fact, Reeves was the immediate or indirect source of the introduction from Canton and Macao of Chinese azaleas, camellias, moutan paeonies, chrysanthemums, roses, and many others. A correspondent of Sir Joseph Banks and a keen horticulturist who exercised a great influence on both Chinese and British horticulture, he interested himself in Chinese plants from the moment he arrived in China and was indefatigable in his efforts to introduce these plants to Britain, first establishing them in pots in his own garden. As the *Gardener's Chronicle* was to write in 1856,[1] when Reeves died at the age of eighty-two:

Not a Company's [East India Company] ship at that time sailed for Europe without her decks being decorated with the little portable greenhouses which preceded the present Wardian cases; and what was more, Mr. Reeves succeeded in communicating to the Captains the enthusiasm which animated himself. Nor, indeed, could his exertions for sending home new plants have been crowned with much success had not the good will of the officers been secured; for a voyage from Macao to London was not what it has now become. Doubling the Cape was so difficult an operation that the freight of living plants was continually damaged or thrown overboard in order to clear the decks. And in this way hundreds of plant cases were lost, always however to be replaced by a zeal and perseverance which no disaster could diminish.

No doubt it was to encourage the captains to take care of their cases of plants, and no doubt the suggestion came from Reeves, that at the end of 1820 the Council caused a letter of thanks and the Society's Medal to be sent to each of the captains of nine ships which had brought plants from Canton during that year.

Apart from chrysanthemums, paeonies, azaleas and camellias, Reeves was concerned in the introduction of three remarkable plants. In 1822 he sent from Canton a cherry which by 1830 was growing well in the Society's Garden at Chiswick and which Lindley described as *Prunus*

[1] p. 215.

serrulata. Also in 1822, Joseph Poole, a collector in China employed by Messrs. Barr & Brookes, nurserymen at Newington Green, London, introduced this same species. It was the first double-flowered white cherry to be introduced from China and probably the first 'Japanese' cherry to reach Europe. Who could have foreseen at that time the astonishing popularity of these cherries today? And when Reeves caused to have painted for the Society the Chinese primrose, *Primula sinensis*, who could have foretold its future success as a pot plant for the cool greenhouse, the transformation which would be wrought on it by the plant breeders, and the prominent place it would occupy in the science of genetics? The painting was received by the Society in 1819—and caused so much excitement that Reeves was asked to secure both seeds and plants as quickly as possible. With his usual enthusiasm Reeves sent home both plants and seeds, but unhappily the former died and the latter did not germinate. However, Captain Richard Rawes, of the ship *Warren Hastings*, who, in 1820 had introduced *Camellia reticulata* to Britain, brought home a plant of *P. sinensis* in 1821, gave it to his relative, Thomas Carey Palmer of Bromley in Kent, and the plant was figured in the *Botanical Register* of that year. It is not unlikely that Rawes received his plant from Reeves.

Neither is it unlikely that Reeves was responsible for sending to Britain in 1816 two plants of what is possibly the most beautiful of all climbing shrubs, *Wisteria sinensis*. Discovered in the garden of Consequa, one of the greatest of Chinese merchants, a plant was brought to England in May 1816 by Captain Robert Wellbank in the ship the *Cuffnels* and was given to Charles Hampden Turner of Rook's Nest, Surrey. A few days later Captain Rawes brought a second plant which was given to Palmer. The first plant thrived exceedingly well and was quickly propagated at the Hackney nursery of Loddiges. Two years later Reeves sent a third plant to England, this time to the Horticultural Society; it was later planted in the Society's Garden at Chiswick and grew into one of the most remarkable specimens ever seen in Europe, being described in the *Botanical Register* in 1840 as 'a magnificent specimen 180 feet long covering about 1800 square feet of wall'. In the spring of 1839 it produced 675,000 flowers. The latter are lilac-coloured and fragrant.

In 1816 Reeves made one of his infrequent visits to London, travelling on the *Warren Hastings*, and giving the 100 plants he was bringing with him his own personal attention. His success was great, for of the 100 plants only ten died on the long journey; and his success vastly impressed his friend Dr. John Livingstone, the chief surgeon of the East India Company in China and one of the Society's overseas Corresponding Members. In February 1819 Livingstone wrote a long letter to Sabine on the difficulties of transporting plants from China to England and this letter forms a valuable contribution to Volume 3 of the Society's *Transactions*.[1] For successful transportation there are certain essential requirements:

The plants should be collected in proper time, so as to enable them to be firmly rooted in the soil in which they are to be transported to England; a proper soil should be obtained, wherein they might be planted; they should be arranged in their chests or boxes, accordingly as they require abundant, frequent, moderate, or slight waterings; when on board the covers of the chests should be well closed when the spray is flying over the ship, and opened at all times in temperate and fine weather; the plants should be duly watered with good water, and particular attention be paid to them, from the time the ship arrives at her anchorage in the Thames, till they are landed.

Attention to these requirements was no doubt responsible for Reeves's success, but it was asking a lot from a ship's captain to expect him to do likewise. Livingstone continued:

I am of the opinion, that one thousand plants have been lost, for one, which survived the voyage to England. Plants purchased at Canton, including their chests and other necessary charges, cost six shillings and eight pence sterling each, on a fair average; consequently every plant now in England, must have been introduced at the enormous expense of upwards of £300. It surely, then, becomes a matter of importance to attempt some more certain method of gratifying the English horticulturist and botanist, with the plants of China.

The 'more certain methods' Livingstone proposed should consist of the Society's sending a properly qualified gardener to China.

The gardener should reside at Macao, having a suitable establishment, a house, garden, and native assistants. After defraying all his necessary charges, it might be advisable to make his further emoluments to depend chiefly on the success of the undertaking, by paying him a certain handsome sum for every new plant, with which he enriched the horticultural and botanical stores of England.

The arrangements to be made for the transportation of the plants should be liberal, and beneficial to the parties assisting in it. The owners should be paid the proper freight for the requisite quantity of water; and it would probably be found best for all the parties concerned, to have a person, in each vessel on board which the plants are shipped, sufficiently acquainted with the business of a gardener, to take the entire charge of the plants during the passage.

After an ample stock of all the desirable plants had been secured in England, the gardener might be recalled; but the plan, if successful, is capable of much extension; for if a person of sufficient abilities was appointed, he might

[1] (1820), p. 183.

extend his researches to the Philippine Islands, Cochin-China, the Malay Peninsula and Islands etc. etc. The garden at Macao might become the depository of an extensive collection of the botanical riches of these places, from whence they might be transported to Europe.

Livingstone's ideas were eminently sensible. Unfortunately, they were only partially adopted by the Society. However, it was no doubt due to his letter to Sabine and to the latter's consequential inquiries that in November 1820 Sabine informed the Council that he had received an offer from the proprietor of the East India ship *General Kyd*, which was shortly to journey to Bengal and China, to take on board a representative of the Society who could take charge of any plants put on the ship in China and bring them home for the Society. On being asked to inquire about the cost of such an undertaking, Sabine reported some two weeks later that 'the expense of the whole would not exceed £200, being £100 for the services of the man, and £100 for his board and other expenses'. Thus the Society agreed that John Potts, the Gardener, should make this round trip to Bengal and China, and in this way took up the task of plant introduction soon after the death of Banks, when Kew collectors had been withdrawn from foreign parts.

In February 1822 Council learned of the arrival of a consignment of plants, seeds, and dried specimens dispatched by Potts from Calcutta, and that meanwhile he had gone on to meet John Reeves at Canton and John Livingstone at Macao, whence Potts sent home chrysanthemums, camellias, and other plants from Chinese gardens. Unfortunately forty varieties of Chinese chrysanthemums, corresponding to the drawings in the Society's possession, were lost on the way home. More unfortunately still, Potts became very ill and, though it was hoped that the voyage home would conduce to his recovery, when he arrived at the end of August 1822, 'with a large collection of plants in tolerable order and a very satisfactory journal', he himself 'was in a very weak and dangerous state of health'. In spite of the medical attention and other arrangements which the Council made for his well-being, he died a month after his return at Chiswick. His grave in the churchyard there is marked by a headstone erected by the Society.

Unquestionably his greatest introduction was a vast quantity of seeds of *Primula sinensis*, for it is probably from these particular seeds that our present strains of this popular flower have sprung. For the rest there were certain greenhouse plants such as the greyish-white minutely dark-dotted flowered *Ardisia punctata*, the brilliant rose-purple fruited *Callicarpa rubella*, several camellias, including the grafted *Camellia euryoides*, and a *Hoya*. This last consisted of but a single leaf which Potts gave to Sabine shortly before he died and which he had collected on one of his excursions near Macao. The leaf was carefully planted and in 1824 sent forth from its base a fine shoot which in the following year produced several heads of fleshy pale yellow fragrant flowers. The plant is beautifully figured in Volume 7 of the Society's *Transactions* (1830) and in view 'of the esteem in which he was held by his employers was named in the Garden of the Horticultural Society in compliment to him'—*Hoya pottsii*.

In the summer of 1821, when Potts was on his way to China, via Calcutta, the Secretary's brother, Captain Edward Sabine of the Royal Artillery, was arranging to take part in an expedition to the west coast of Africa, the east coast of South America, and the West Indies, to collect data on the calculation of time in different latitudes. The Society gladly accepted his offer to find accommodation on the ship *Iphigenia* for a gardener. George Don, foreman in the Chelsea Garden (and the oldest son of George Don, the famous nurseryman at Forfar in Scotland, and for a time Curator of the Edinburgh Botanic Garden), was engaged by the Secretary for this purpose and sailed in November 1821, arriving in Sierra Leone in the following February. On 11 April 1822 he proceeded southward along the coast and on 17 May landed on the island of St. Thomas, where he stayed for nearly a month. The Society had instructed him to collect plants and seeds and as much information as possible of tropical fruits, in order that these plants might be represented at the Chiswick Garden. Don was lucky to find many fruits in Sierra Leone at their perfection, and both here and on St. Thomas Island he made interesting collections. In August 1822 Lindley, the Assistant Secretary for the Garden, was sent to Liverpool to clear a consignment of West African seeds, plants, bulbs, herbarium specimens, and lepidopterous insects sent by Don, who himself returned in February of the following year, bringing with him other plants from West Africa and the West Indies.

Considerable success attended the germination of many of Don's seeds and the growth of some of the plants he had introduced at the Society's Garden at Chiswick, where the Stove House was certainly enriched by much new material. Many of these introductions were described by Sabine in 1823 and by Lindley in 1826 in Volumes 5 and 6 respectively of the Society's *Transactions*: guavas; several grapes; the Sierra Leone Peach, *Sarcocephalus esculentus*, with its brownish-red warted soft watery fruit; the Sierra Leone Rough or Grey-skinned Plum, *Parinarium excelsum*, the fruit the size of a Victoria Plum, but the stone much larger and the pulp dry and mealy; *Parkia africana*, the African Locust or Nitta Tree, also with mealy sweet pulp; even fruits of one of the largest trees in the world, *Adansonia digitata* (the stem may be over 30 feet thick), oblong and woody with a mealy pulp—the well-known

Monkey Bread. Fruits apart, there were also several orchids and one very beautiful iridaceous plant which Lindley named in compliment to Captain Edward Sabine for the assistance he had given to Don— *Marica sabinii*. This plant is finely figured in Volume 6 of the *Transactions* and well shows the stiff elegant long leaves and the ultramarine flowers with the brown and orange transverse bars at the base of the petals. The plant is now called *Neomarica caerulea* and is a well-known greenhouse plant.

Sabine reported to the Council 'that he had every reason to be satisfied with the diligence and skill of Mr. Don in the execution of his duties' and it was therefore agreed that he should continue in the Society's service for six months (including a month's leave 'to visit his friends in Scotland') and that he should employ the time in arranging and documenting his collection. At the end of the six months he had not finished, but it was deemed necessary to retain his services, as he was preparing a paper on the fruits of Sierra Leone. In April 1824, over thirteen months after his return, his report was still incomplete. Some months later it was discovered that, 'in direct violation of his instructions and engagements', he had published, in the *Edinburgh Philosophical Journal*, an account of the plants seen and collected by him in Sierra Leone; he was dismissed forthwith. When, later on, he sent another manuscript to the Wernerian Society, the Council stopped its publication and obtained an injunction prohibiting him from publishing anything of a similar nature in England. However, the Wernerian Society *did* publish Don's work, for in the Society's *Memoirs* from 1826 to 1831 can be found Don's *Monograph of the Genus Allium*. Moreover, the Linnean Society published his *Review of the Genus Combretum* in 1826—and made him a Fellow of the Society in 1831. His most important work was printed between the years 1831 and 1837, the four-volume *General System of Gardening and Botany founded upon Miller's 'Gardeners Dictionary'*—an eminently useful book at the time and for many years afterwards. Apart from his own publications, he was also to revise the first Supplement to Loudon's *Encyclopaedia of Plants* and to assist Mrs. Loudon in the editing of the second edition which was issued in 1855. He died the following year.

In September 1821, while George Don was preparing to set out for Sierra Leone, it was learned that the Admiralty and Captain William Owen of His Majesty's ship *Leven* were prepared to allow a plant collector to travel in the vessel which had been appointed to survey the east coast of Africa, visiting *en route* Lisbon, Madeira, Brazil, and the Cape of Good Hope. Sabine therefore engaged a young man named John Forbes, who was recommended by Shepherd, the Curator of the Liverpool Botanic Garden. Forbes sailed in January 1822, and sent home during the year orchids and various other plants from Brazil. In the following spring more plants arrived, this time from the east coast of Africa, but in October 1823 a letter from Captain Owen told the Council the sad news that Forbes had died at Senna, while making his way up the Zambezi in August. Owen clearly had an appreciation of the splendid job of work which Forbes had done and its importance to the Horticultural Society, and tried very hard to engage a successor to Forbes for the rest of the journey. In the end he appointed a German botanist, Herr Hilsenberg, whom he found at Mauritius, 'and thus did all in his power to compensate a loss, which botanical science will long endure'.[1]

Of Forbes's collection, Lindley commented:

The collection . . . is a good example of what skill and industry can effect. It is notorious that importations of seeds or plants from Rio have of late had so bad a reputation that collectors here universally consider them of little importance. The excellent, but unfortunate young man, however, from whom this was received, succeeded, during a very short residence, in getting together, and safely transmitting an assemblage of living plants, small, indeed, but consisting entirely of either novel or extremely rare subjects, and, for its size, certainly one of the best collections ever sent to this country.[2]

In the collection were the striking ally of the pineapple, the Brazilian *Pitcairnea staminea*, with its bright red flowers and long protruding red stamens; the South African labiate, *Leonotis intermedia*, with its whorls of orange-brown hairy flowers; a fine *Gloriosa* from Mozambique, the deep orange-and-yellow-flowered *Gloriosa simplex*; and several orchids, including *Aeranthes grandiflora*, live plants of which Forbes sent home from Madagascar, and which, in the stove at Chiswick, soon produced large, almost translucent, pale greenish-yellow flowers, as well as an orchid which commemorates his name and which he collected at Rio, *Cattleya forbesii*, with large handsome yellowish-green flowers.

His name is also commemorated on a tablet which the Society placed in the chancel of Chiswick church, bearing the inscription:

To the Memory of Mr. John Forbes, A.L.S., a botanical collector in the service of the Horticultural Society of London, who died at Senna, on the Zambezee river, in Eastern Africa, in the month of August, 1823, in the 23rd year of his age. This tablet is erected by the Council of the Society, in testimony of their entire approbation of his conduct while in their service, and of their deep regret at the untimely fate of a naturalist of so much enterprise and promise.

By 1820 interest in the cultivation of the chrysanthemum was growing

[1] *Trans. hort. Soc. Lond.*, 5 (1823), p. iii.
[2] *Trans. hort. Soc. Lond.*, 6 (1824), p. 82.

rapidly and twelve named kinds were being grown in the Society's Garden; 'Purple' had been introduced from France in 1790 and 'Changeable White' had sported from it; 'Sulphur Yellow' had been imported from China by Thomas Evans of Stepney in 1802 and between 1798 and 1808 Sir Abraham Hume had also received from China 'Rose', 'Buff', 'Golden Yellow', 'Quilled Yellow', 'Spanish Brown', 'Quilled White', and 'Large Lilac'; Captain Rawes had brought home 'Tasselled White' in 1816 and Captain John Christopher Lockner 'Superb White' in 1817; the latter had been given to Messrs. Barr & Brookes of Newington Green, who had their own collector, Joseph Poole, at Canton. Obviously this nursery recognized the importance of the chrysanthemum. And so did others; Lee & Kennedy of Hammersmith and James Colvill of King's Road, Chelsea, were both growing them.

The Society's Garden, however, was the place to see them, for in addition to the above there were also growing 'Quilled Flamed Yellow' and 'Quilled Pink', both introduced by Captain Henry Andrews Drummond of the *Castle Huntley* in 1819; as well as ten new kinds which Reeves had sent home in 1820 with Captain Charles Otway Mayne of the *Atlas*—'Early Crimson', 'Large Quilled Orange', 'Expanded Light Purple', 'Quilled Light Purple', 'Curled Lilac', 'Superb Clustered Yellow', 'Semi-double Quilled Pink', 'Semi-double Quilled White', 'Semi-double Quilled Orange', 'Large Pale Purple'.

All these Sabine had named and described in the Society's *Transactions* and he was clearly a great enthusiast of the chrysanthemum. 'They contribute so much to the beauty of our gardens in a fine autumn, and our conservatories in the months of November and December, when scarcely any other plants are in blossom, that they are peculiarly deserving the attention of the ornamental gardener,' he wrote in 1821.[1] He had not only studied these named types growing at Chiswick; he had also studied the paintings, made in China, of forty other Chinese types, paintings which, thanks to Reeves, were in the Society's possession. He realized full well that there were many more in China awaiting introduction. It was his hope, and the Society's, that Potts would bring home some of them. Bitter must have been the disappointment when the plants which Potts collected, corresponding to the Society's paintings, were lost on the voyage home; the contents of two boxes, dispatched on the *Bombay*, were all dead on their arrival in England, whilst two other boxes on the *Inglis* were thrown overboard when the ship ran aground on the homeward voyage. Disappointment but not discouragement; Sabine was too persistent, too enthusiastic, to be discouraged by such a set-back. If Potts had failed, someone else must succeed, and in April 1823 Sabine reported that in accordance with a plan of which the

[1] *Trans. hort. Soc. Lond.*, 4 (1821), p. 526.

Council had approved, another young gardener, John Damper Parks, had embarked on the *Lowther Castle* for China, with instructions 'to collect, amongst other rarities, as many good varieties of Chrysanthemum as possible'.

Parks, of course, soon made the acquaintance of Reeves. 'You could not have placed me under a better person than Mr. Reeves, for he has shown me every attention. Indeed, I may say that I have received more favours as a stranger from Mr. Reeves than I ever did from any gentleman in my life,' he wrote in his journal. Certainly Reeves indoctrinated him into the best means of growing on the plants before they were packed, the best methods of packing, and the attention necessary for them on the journey home, with the result that considerable success attended his expedition. Part of his collection arrived in the spring of 1824 aboard the *General Kyd*, and the rest he himself brought home on the *Lowther Castle*, which reached England the same year.

Of chrysanthemums there were twenty varieties of which sixteen were new. As usual, Sabine named and described these in the *Transactions*.[1] By 1826 forty-eight distinct varieties were growing in the Society's Garden and were causing quite a sensation. Sabine wrote:

In the two last seasons, the exhibition of Chrysanthemums in the Garden of the Society has been generally allowed to be the most splendid one of flowering plants in one mass, that has ever been seen, and superior to any other garden exhibition at even the gayest period of the year.

Chrysanthemums in pots, in full flower, to the amount of about seven hundred, were placed together in one of the curvilinear iron houses, without the admixture of any other plants, and were continued, by changing the pots and the introduction of the later varieties in succession, in a state of perfection and splendour from the end of October to the middle of December; thus enlivening the garden at a period when nothing else existed to attract attention.[1]

For the rest, Parks introduced more plants of *Camellia reticulata*, several new varieties of *Camellia japonica*, the yellow form of the Banksian Rose, the first *Aspidistra* to be seen in England, *Aspidistra lurida*, the greenish-yellow or brownish-flowered orchid *Coelogyne fimbriata* and *Reevesia thyrsoidea*, a warm greenhouse tree, with clusters of white or cream five-petalled flowers, which commemorates the name of that great friend of the Society who, on retiring from China in 1831, came to live in England and to become active in the affairs of the Society, especially of its Chinese Committee.

As originally arranged, Parks ceased to be employed by the Society

[1] *Trans. hort. Soc. Lond.*, 6 (1826), p. 322.

soon after his return, becoming gardener to the Earl of Arran at Bognor and subsequently a nurseryman at Dartford.

When Parks went to China it had been the Council's intention to send two collectors there, but the disturbed state of that country persuaded them to send only one. The other should go to New York instead of China, to collect fruits of American origin and other plants to be found in the neighbourhood. The one chosen for this mission was the young Scot, David Douglas, then on the staff of the Glasgow Botanic Garden. Born at Scone, near Perth, in 1799, Douglas had served his apprentice-ship as a gardener in the gardens of the Earl of Mansfield, who, in 1804, had used the services of Loudon in their layout. About the year 1817 Douglas moved to the garden of Sir Robert Preston at Valleyfield, near Dunfermline, and shortly afterwards to the Botanic Garden at Glasgow. There his interest in plants and his immense industry attracted the attention of Professor W. J. Hooker. He was allowed to take part in the Professor's excursions to the Scottish highlands and assisted in collecting materials for the *Flora Scotica*, on the writing of which Hooker was engaged. And it was Hooker who recommended Douglas to Sabine, as a botanical collector for the Society. (Plate 14.)

In June 1823 Douglas left London for New York with the primary object of obtaining, by gift as far as possible, fruit trees and any other interesting plants, and seeds, as well as information on the latest de-velopments in fruit growing. The Society was, of course, greatly inter-ested in fruits of all kinds and, although its new Garden at Chiswick had been in its possession for only a year, it had already 3,000 fruit trees in its orchard. On 3 August Douglas arrived in New York and quickly received the good services of David Hosack, founder of the Elgin Botanic Garden—the first of its kind in New York—and Thomas Hogg, who had recently left England and had set up in business as a nurseryman and florist. He visited orchards across the Hudson and in Philadelphia before journeying to Amherstburg in Upper Canada, where he was warmly welcomed by Henry Briscoe, a friend of Captain Edward Sabine, the Secretary's brother. Here, and in the other settlements along the Canadian side of the Detroit River, Douglas was able to see apples, pears, plums, peaches, and grapes which in the light loam soil exceeded in size and flavour anything he had yet seen. On 19 October he returned to New York, made another journey to Philadelphia, and visited in New Jersey the large orchards of William Coxe, where he was given several varieties of fruit trees as well as two bottles of seventeen-year-old cider—presents to the President and the Secretary of the Society. He then left New York on 10 December on the *Nimrod*, arriving in London on 9 January 1824.

The Council were delighted with the results of the expedition:

This mission was executed by Mr. Douglas with a success beyond expectation: he obtained many plants which were much wanted, and greatly increased our collection of fruit trees by the acquiring of several sorts only known to us by name. It would be unjust here to omit mentioning the uniform kindness and attention with which he was received in every part of the United States that he visited. It is most gratifying to have to add, that the *presents* of cultivated plants to the Society embraced nearly everything which it was desirous to obtain; and that the liberality with which they were given was only equalled by the hospitality with which the Collector was received.[1]

The unassuming Douglas ('the shyest being almost that I ever saw', Thomas Andrew Knight described him) was also delighted. He had not only gathered a wealth of specimens, met many of America's leading horticulturists and visited gardens, orchards, and nurseries, but, even more to his liking, had botanized in a new exciting country, had found nineteen of the thirty-four species of oak enumerated by Pursh as natives of the vast North American continent, and had seen in Philadelphia specimens collected by the Lewis and Clark expedition to the Pacific in 1804–6; he had even brought one of this expedition's introductions home with him, the Oregon Grape, *Mahonia aquifolium*. The Society's Council also had some knowledge of the plants of the Pacific coast, not only from the Lewis and Clark expedition, but also from the Vancouver expedition, and their appetites were whetted; as many as possible must be introduced to Britain. Who better to be entrusted with this task, and who more anxious to accept it, than Douglas?

Thus on 26 July 1824 Douglas set forth on his second mission for the Society, very necessarily under the protection of the Hudson's Bay Company, for its posts were the only ones in any way civilized in that immense country stretching from California to the Arctic. The Company had promised him the facilities of its posts, as well as a free passage on its ship *William & Mary* to the mouth of the River Columbia and the north-west coast of America. No doubt he was aware of the dangers and hardships which were in store for him and no doubt he was thinking of the fate of two of the three collectors who had worked for the Society before him—Potts and Forbes—when he wrote, describing his departure from England, to his friend, William Beattie Booth, also a native of Scone who had worked in the garden of Scone Palace, joined the Chiswick staff as a labourer in the arboretum department, and a few years later was to be the author of the splendid *Illustrations and Descriptions of the Camellieae*: 'I stood on deck looking on the rocky shores of Cornwall burnished with the splendour of a setting sun—a noble scene. By degrees the goddess of night threw her veil over it and my delightful view of happy England closed—probably for ever.'[2]

[1] *Trans. hort. Soc. Lond.*, 5 (1823), p.v.　　[2] *Gardener's Magazine*, XI (1835), p. 271.

However, England was not closed to him for ever—yet. The first halt was Madeira—an island which 'amazingly gratified' him; this was followed by six weeks' voyage across the Atlantic to South America and on 28 September his arrival at Rio de Janeiro and a stay of two weeks, during which time he was completely enraptured by the rich tropical vegetation, especially by the many orchids; then on down the coast, round Cape Horn and a short stay off the coast of Chile at Juan Fernandez Island, where he planted fruit and vegetable seeds and which he described as 'the Madeira of the South'; another brief stay on one of the Galapagos Islands and then, on 12 February 1825, arrival at the latitude of the Columbia River. Because of stormy weather, it was not possible for six weeks to cross the sandbank at the mouth of the Columbia River (where four years later the *William & Mary* was wrecked with the loss of all hands), and not until 7 April 1825 did the *William & Mary* anchor in Baker's Bay—eight and a half months after leaving England.

Almost immediately Douglas got his first sight of the giant fir Menzies had seen, collected, and sent to England in 1795, which came to be a familiar friend to him during his travels along the Columbia and was to become known as the Douglas Fir. Masses of *Gaultheria shallon* and the salmonberry, *Rubus spectabilis*, also delighted him; they were the first fruits of the joys awaiting him as he began his journey through the virgin country of the Columbia. For two years he journeyed, undertaking dangerous and exhausting expeditions, by canoe, rowboat, on foot, horseback or snowshoe, living in tents, deerskin lodges, huts of cedar bark—or often with no cover at all—and undergoing all manner of privations, running for his life from Indians, eating the skins of animals, twice even having to eat his horse. But at all times he was enraptured by the magnificent scenery. He described it as 'sublimely grand, lofty, well wooded hills, mountains covered with perpetual snow, extensive natural meadows, and plains of deep, fertile alluvial deposit, covered with a rich sward of grass, and a profusion of flowering plants'.[1] The worst of his privations and the most magnificent scenery he encountered on his tremendous overland journey from Fort Vancouver to Hudson Bay. There, on 20 August, the *Prince of Wales* was awaiting him to deliver him safely to Portsmouth on 11 October 1827.

The President and Secretary were greatly relieved at his safe return, for they had been desperately anxious about him. Knight had written to his daughter:

Our collector proposes, when he has sent all he can home by a ship, to march across the continent of America to the country of the United States on this side, and to collect what plants and seeds he can in his journey: but it is

---

[1] Douglas, *Oregon Hist. Quart.*, V (1904), p. 243.

but too probable that he will perish in the attempt. Mr. Sabine says, that if he escapes, he will soon perish in some other hardy enterprise or other. It is really lamentable that so fine a fellow should be sacrificed.[1]

Prophetic words!

The expedition had been an overwhelming success. Much living material and vast quantities of seeds had been introduced of plants which would be hardy out of doors in Britain; so much seed indeed that the Garden was unable to cope with it all and much was distributed among nurserymen and the Fellows. 'Mr. Douglas had throughout his mission acted in the most satisfactory manner and . . . nothing could surpass the zeal and spirit with which he had executed the trust he had undertaken,' Sabine reported to the Council. Douglas, with his usual modesty, wrote, '. . . my humble exertions will I trust convey and enthuse, and draw attention to the beautifully varied verdure of N.W. America.'[2]

The species he introduced—over 200 of them—certainly fulfilled his hope. There were such valuable and indispensable annuals as *Clarkia elegans, Limnanthes douglasii, Collinsia bicolor, Mentzelia lindleyi*. There was the lovely alpine *Douglasia*, ally of the primrose, which Lindley dedicated to him in 1826. There was *Lupinus polyphyllus*, with flowers deep blue, purple, reddish or yellow, and which, crossed with the almost equally variable *Lupinus arboreus* in the course of generations of careful selection, has given rise to a race of strikingly handsome perennials showing a great range of flower colour which we know today as the Russell Lupins. There was the sweet-scented musk of the nineteenth century, *Mimulus moschatus*. There was the fine evergreen *Garrya elliptica*, which throughout the winter carries its elegant silvery catkins, named after Nicholas Garry, the deputy governor of the Hudson's Bay Company, who had been of enormous assistance to Douglas. There was the flowering currant, *Ribes sanguineum*, which Archibald Menzies had first discovered during his voyage round the world, in 1787, and of which Lindley wrote, when describing it in the *Botanical Register* for 1830,[3] '. . . of such importance do we consider it to the embellishment of our gardens, that if the expense incurred by the Horticultural Society in Mr. Douglas's voyage had been attended with no other result than the introduction of this species, there would have been no ground for dissatisfaction.' The cost incurred by this remarkable expedition was under £400.

Lindley continued:

It is not the number of objects that a public body or an individual accomplishes, that creates a claim to public gratitude, so much as their utility; and in this view the gentleman who brought the first live plant of the now common

---

[1] Knight, *Papers*, p. 39.   [2] Letter, 9 June 1827.   [3] Plate 1349.

China Rose to England deserves his country's gratitude in a greater degree than all the collectors who sent plants to Kew for the next twenty years. But if we consider that it is not *R. sanguineum* alone that the Horticultural Society has introduced through the same active traveller, but that the gigantic Pines of North-West America, one of which yields timber superior to the finest larch; *Acer macrophyllum*, the wood of which is as much better than our Sycamore as the species is superior in the beauty and amplitude of its foliage; *Gaultheria shallon*, an evergreen shrub of great merit; have all been secured to this country, and distributed in every direction—to say nothing of the beautiful Lupines, Penstemons, Barberries, Oenotheras, and other plants of less moment—when all this, we say, is considered, it is not too much to assert, that this result alone has justified all the expenditure of the Society's Garden from the commencement, and has stamped it with a character of great national utility which nothing but future mismanagement can shake.

What would be the splendid words with which this great servant of the Society would express these same sentiments today? And what would be the thoughts and emotions of David Douglas could he but see today his introductions of the 1820s; his own fir, first called *Pseudotsuga douglasii* but now known as *Pseudotsuga menziesii*, the Noble Fir, *Abies procera*, the Giant Fir, *Abies grandis*, the Sitka Spruce, *Picea sitchensis*, all valuable timber trees which have effected a revolution in British forestry and greatly helped to transform much of the British landscape?

Douglas did not believe that all Lindley's words were quite so splendid. He had attended the dinner commemorating the second centenary of John Ray and Lindley had made an impromptu speech. 'The beginning was bad, the end was bad and the middle worthy of the beginning and the end, not one sentence worth repeating and the manner of delivery shockingly ill,' Douglas wrote to his friend Hooker on 1 December 1828. Douglas was restless and irritable, hated the climate and life of London and was longing to return to the scene of his triumphs. The opportunity came the following year, when the Society decided to send him once again to western North America with the aim of making known to Britain the plant treasures of California. After paying a farewell visit to his mother at Scone, he sailed on 31 October 1829, and this was, indeed, the last time he was to see the shores of England.

There was more rejoicing at the sight of the wonderful country; more appalling hardships; more magnificent collections sent to the Society; and then tragedy. Through a misunderstanding he resigned from the Society's service in 1832. He was in Honolulu when he heard of the ill fortunes of the Society which had caused the resignation of Sabine, the one responsible for getting him appointed as the Society's collector. Feeling that he must remain loyal to Sabine, he, too, resigned from his position with the Society. Two years later he lost his life in the Hawaiian

Islands under most tragic circumstances. Whether he was murdered and then thrown into a pit into which a trapped bullock had fallen, or whether he accidentally fell into such a pit and was then gored to death will never be known. It was indeed 'really lamentable that so fine a fellow should be sacrificed'. He was buried at Kawaiahao Church in Honolulu.

In 1841 in the churchyard at Scone there was erected a monument 23 feet high, the inscription of which admirably describes the character and work of one of the greatest of the many plant-hunters who scoured the vast American continent in search of new plants for the gardens and landscape of Europe:

Erected by the lovers of botany in Europe in memory of David Douglas, a native of this parish, who, from an ardent love of science and a desire to promote the improvement in botany, visited the unexplored regions on the banks of the Columbia and southward to California, whence he transmitted a great variety of the seeds of valuable trees and flowering plants, adapted to the climate of Great Britain, and who, after devoting ten years of the prime of life in adding to the Arboretum and Flora of Europe, suffered an accidental and lamented death in one of the Sandwich Islands, on the 12th July, 1834, in the 35th year of his age. Endowed with an acute and vigorous mind, which he improved by diligent study, this eminent botanist uniformly exemplified in his conduct those Christian virtues which invested his character with a higher and more imperishable distinction than he justly acquired by his well-earned reputation for scientific knowledge. A dutiful son, a kind and affectionate brother, a sincere friend, he secured by the rectitude of his moral and religious principles, not less than by the benevolence of his disposition, the esteemed regard of all who knew his worth.

In the spring of 1824 the Society gave employment, as a plant-collector, to James McRae, an experienced gardener who had been on the staff of the Botanic Garden at St. Vincent in the West Indies. Arrangements were made for him to sail in September of that year, two months after Douglas had sailed, in H.M.S. *Blonde*, bound for Brazil, the Hawaiian Islands, Chile, and Peru. From various ports he sent home plants and seeds, and returned with still more in 1826, his collection being described as 'very large and of the greatest value to science'. The seeds included fresh nuts of the Monkey Puzzle Tree, *Araucaria araucana*, which was then uncommon and much prized, having been first introduced by Archibald Menzies in 1795. Although McRae's nuts were fairly widely distributed by the Society, the Monkey Puzzle did not become common in cultivation until it was reintroduced by William Lobb in 1844. In the Hawaiian Islands McRae successfully transplanted some European, as well as some native Brazilian, fruits and vegetables. Shortly after his return to England, on the recommendation of the Society, he was appointed superintendent of the Ceylon Botanic Garden.

For the next ten years the Society seems to have been content to cultivate, propagate, and distribute the numerous introductions which were filling the available accommodation at the Garden and occupying the energies and skills of the gardening staff. Moreover, the affairs of the Society generally were in very low water. But in February 1836 the Council, being of the opinion that it was 'expedient that a Collector be sent to the mountainous parts of Mexico', appointed a committee to consider the matter. As a result, on 6 October Theodore Hartweg, employed as a clerk in the Garden, sailed for Vera Cruz. The following February two boxes, containing among other plants sixty species of epiphytic orchids, were received from him. He was obviously a most excellent collector; equally obvious is it that he was greatly hindered in his work by the unsettled state of the country; his report of his travels in Volume 3 of the 2nd Series of the *Transactions* is ample testimony to this. Even so, he crossed the Cordillera and visited Guatemala and Oaxaca, before returning to England in the summer of 1843. During his travels he collected and sent home another 140 species of orchids, various cacti, and many species of other genera, including *Pinus, Cestrum, Achimenes*, and *Fuchsia*; one species of *Fuchsia, F. fulgens*, has proved to be an important plant in hybridization and has been one of the main parents in the development of our modern fuchsias. Naturally most of his numerous introductions were suitable for growing only under glass. Already such houses as there were at Chiswick were overflowing with material the Society's collectors had introduced. Very soon the Society was to be faced with the problem of providing new glass-house accommodation.

CHAPTER SEVEN

'EXHIBITION EXTRAORDINARY'

On 1 January 1826 a coloured etching, $10\frac{1}{2}$ inches by $14\frac{1}{2}$ inches, by George Cruikshank, entitled 'Exhibition Extraordinary in the Horticultural Room',[1] was published by G. Humphrey, of 24 St. James's Street, London. It is a typical example of the work of the great caricaturist, gently and genially satirizing the affairs of the Society and some of those most intimately concerned in these affairs, as well as more general matters. Moreover, this is the earliest published picture of the Society's premises and activities. Several copies still exist and the one in the Society's possession is reproduced as Plate II. Cruikshank was not a Fellow, but he may have attended a Meeting, as Fellows were allowed to introduce friends. However, the note in the bottom left-hand corner of the print—'A. Bird, invt., et delt.'—i.e. designed and drawn by A. Bird, supplies the clue to the source of some of the information. 'Bird' was the nickname of a Fellow, William Henry Merle, of 9 Park Street, Westminster, a well-known humorist who could laugh at himself as well as at others, as in the jingle in *Odds and Ends in Verse and Prose* which he published in 1831:

CONSOLATION FOR THE LOSS OF A NEW HAT

> Poor Bird has lost his dandy hat—
> His friends all weep a loss like that,
> And show their love and wit
>
> By saying—'We had felt less shock,
> If he had merely lost the block
> His hat was wont to fit.'

The room represented in the etching was 'the Great Room', about 56 feet by 32 feet, lit by a skylight, situated at the back of 'the House of the Society', which from 1819 to 1859 was 21 Lower Regent Street, three doors down from Jermyn Street. The walls were ornamented with pilasters, as in the etching, for it is on record that the Council took

[1] *Jl R. hort. Soc.*, LXIX (1944), pp. 324–32.

107

exception to the original 'capitals of the pilasters in the large room', and the furnishings were more or less as shown, the seats of the mahogany benches being 'stuffed and covered with black leather'.

The picture labelled 'Hortus Siccus' (to the left of the central pilaster in the caricature) was of Sir Joseph Banks, who, having died five and a half years previously, was commemorated by a portrait which now hangs in the Council Room.

The bust of 'Penny Royal' was that of King George IV, when Prince Regent, which Council had ordered should be placed in the new Meeting Room and for which they had later sanctioned payment to 'Goblet for bust of Regent—£12'.

The portrait of the lady (top right-hand corner) was imaginary, but no doubt was meant to represent Lady Anne Monson (1714–76). As she was long since dead, the picture was apparently introduced partly as a peg on which to hang the Georgian humour which would have been appreciated at the time by those familiar with the scandal connected with this lady in Toynbee's *Letters of Horace Walpole*. The inscription under the picture is a very much embellished version of what R. A. Salisbury wrote about *Arethusa bulbosa* in Volume 1 of the *Transactions*.

'An Irish Potato Plant', the third picture, was again, of course, purely imaginary.

The Chairman is John Elliot, who had become Treasurer in 1809 and had continued to hold the office for twenty years. During this same period he was also a Vice-President, and as the President resided in Herefordshire and seldom came to town, John Elliot, living in Westminster, just across St. James's Park, frequently took the Chair, and did so on most occasions in 1825.

The man on the Chairman's right is the Honorary Secretary, Joseph Sabine. His unbounded enthusiasm for the development of the Garden resulted in financial difficulties for the Society, and his efforts to raise additional funds naturally necessitated his giving eulogistic accounts of the progress already made. That was doubtless the reason for the quotation which appears on his desk in the cartoon. It is taken from one of Horace's letters to Maecenas written from the farm in the Sabine Hills which Maecenas had given him, and runs '*arvum caelumque Sabinum non cessat laudare*'—'he never flags in praising the Sabine soil and air'.

The figure in spectacles on the Chairman's left, referred to on his desk as 'An highly cultivated specimen—requires glass', is John Turner, the Assistant Secretary, who, it will be recalled, had been appointed in 1818, when he was introduced by Sabine, who stated that 'his style of reading was much approved'. Two years later his initial salary of £100 had been doubled on the understanding that 'it is expected that he shall devote his whole time to the service of the Society', the general tone of the Council

EXHIBITION EXTRAORDINARY in the HORTICULTURAL ROOM.

Plate II A CARICATURE OF A MEETING OF THE SOCIETY IN THE GREAT ROOM IN 1825,
BY GEORGE CRUIKSHANK

minute implying that hitherto he had sometimes been attending to his own affairs during the specified office hours. Future events were to show that he certainly had.

It could be assumed that all the characters in the cartoon were at least frequenters of the Society's Meetings if not actually Fellows; but if this had been the case the print would scarcely have given sufficient fun to have had a wide enough appeal. Thus at least one of the persons represented appears to have had little, if anything, to do with the affairs of the Society; it is the second figure from the left, the man with the traditional sign of a cuckold, labelled 'A variety of hornbeam—a double bearer'. He is Alderman Robert Albion Cox, who, during the year preceding the publication of the cartoon, had obtained before the Lord Chief Justice a verdict of £800 damages against Edmund Kean, the actor, for criminal conversation. Owing to the prominence of the defendant, the case attracted widespread attention, not only in England but also in America, and was the subject of pamphlets, press articles and caricatures. The alderman is scrutinizing, through a glass, a basket containing an infant, labelled 'Keen's Seedling'. Obviously this is an allusion to the strawberry of that name which was raised by an Isleworth market-gardener, Michael Keens. It was one of the outstanding new varieties shown at the Society's Meetings at that period.

The identity of the army officer in the scarlet uniform of the Life Guards of the time is doubtful. Possibly he was a member of the Society, Colonel John Camac, of Brittenham Park, Suffolk; possibly he was another Fellow, James Scarlett of Abinger Hall, Dorking, the lawyer-politician who became Attorney-General the following year (1827) and later Lord Abinger; possibly the 'Scarlet Runner' was a pun on the name. One of his sons was later to lead the cavalry charge at Balaclava.

Even more doubtful is the identity of the one-armed naval officer, 'Heart of Oak, with timber lopp'd—little cultivated at present, the old plants vegetate in the background'. It could have been any one of the twenty-one naval officers, including thirteen admirals, who were Members of the Society in 1825. On the other hand, as has been suggested, the figure could have represented not a particular individual but a particular type of naval man.

According to G. W. Reid's *A Descriptive Catalogue of the Works of George Cruikshank* (1871), Mr. West, Mr. Rogers, Mr. Wilbraham, Mr. Richard Salisbury, Mr. Motheaux, Captain Maxwell, Dr. Henderson, Lord Verulam, and Mr. Labouchere are represented among the other figures. Possibly 'Mr. Rogers' was the poet Samuel Rogers (1763–1855), 'A Passion-flower in full bloom', the third figure from the left. And probably the cause of the passionate outburst, the fourth figure from the left, was R. A. Salisbury, Sabine's predecessor as Honorary Secretary;

not only is there a strong facial resemblance, there is also the acknowledged fact that Salisbury was prone to treading on people's toes.

'Mr. Wilbraham' was probably Roger Wilbraham, M.P., F.R.S., of 11 Stratton Street, Piccadilly, and Twickenham; short and stocky of build, he is possibly the 'Monstrous Medler in full bearing'. He was especially interested in fruits and vegetables and in 1822 had received the Society's Silver Medal 'for the unremitting attention which he has paid to Horticulture, and for the many services rendered by him to the Society during the period in which he acted as a Member of the Council, and a Vice President of the Society'.

By 'Mr. Motheaux' Reid probably meant John Motteux (1765?–1843), of 7 Stratford Place, Beachamwell Hall in Norfolk, and Banstead Place in Surrey, a keen grower and exhibitor of apples and pears and at one time a member of Council. He was also a bachelor, and a very wealthy one, and in 1824 purchased Sandringham as an investment. He never lived there, however, and on his death bequeathed it, and other properties, to the Hon. Spencer Cooper, who sold it to King Edward VII, when Prince of Wales, for £220,000. Motteux was short and stout, and, late in life, grey-whiskered; if he was present at the 'Exhibition Extraordinary' it is difficult to find him in the cartoon.

No 'Captain Maxwell' was a Fellow at that time and indeed the only Fellow of that surname was John Maxwell, M.P., of Pollok, Renfrewshire, the grand-uncle of Sir John Stirling Maxwell the well-known Scottish landowner and arboriculturist who died in 1956, aged ninety. Of his grand-uncle, an officer in the Renfrewshire Militia, Sir John said, 'He was tall and lanky, and in looking at his bust I see he had a fairly substantial nose.' Again it is difficult to place him in the cartoon and Reid was possibly in error in suggesting that any 'Captain Maxwell' was caricatured.

On the other hand, his suggestion that 'Dr. Henderson' *is* present is probably correct, though no one has been able to suggest where. Alexander Henderson, M.D. (1780–1863), was a Fellow, a member of Council and a Vice-President. An Aberdonian, he had taken his medical degree in Edinburgh, and commenced to practise in London about 1808, living at 6 Curzon Street. His practice was apparently not too time-consuming and he gave himself to literary works, one of them being an amusing little book *An examination of the Imposture of Anne Moore called The Fasting Woman, of Tutbury, illustrated by Remarks on the Cases of Real and Pretended Abstinence* which he published in 1813.

The 'Lord Verulam' at the time of the meeting was James Walter, first Earl of Verulam (1775–1845). He was a Fellow and a keen gardener who had been advised on the layout of his garden by W. S. Gilpin, the artist and landscape architect. Some idea of the nature of his garden and of Verulam himself may be gained from an advertisement, in his hand-writing, which is preserved at Gorhambury, St. Albans. 'Gardener—Wages 35 guineas per an. No pines raised. Two Houses and one Green House. Expected to understand forcing Fruit and Flowers and produc-ing all descriptions of Vegetables in the most approved stile. 4 Lab-ourers.' If he *is* in the picture he may be 'An English Crab'. On the other hand, Reid may have had in mind the 'Lord Verulam' of 1871, the date of his catalogue, and if this is the case, then he can only be the 'Sprig of Nobility', for in 1825 the second Earl was only a boy of sixteen. Whether he was sufficiently in the limelight at that age to have merited the satire of Cruikshank is doubtful, although his younger brother, Robert, attained notoriety at the age of fifteen when he hired a post-chaise and pursued a burglar from Gorhambury to London, securing his arrest and transportation.

'Mr. Labouchere' was presumably Pierre Cesar Labouchere, of 4 Hamilton Place, and Hylands, Chelmsford, a partner of the great mercantile firm of Hope. He had a splendid garden, devoted chiefly to fruits, which contained a large fruit cage in which he grew ninety-eight horizontally trained cherry trees and a collection of soft fruits. He also forced fruits, including apricots, raspberries, and melons and twice received medals for his exhibits.

As Reid mentioned 'Mr. West' first, it is not unreasonable to suppose that he is 'The Pink of Fashion or Dandy Lion' on the left of the picture, but no link between this figure and either of the two Fellows of that name or any other 'Mr. West' has been found.

What of the exhibits? Those in front of Banks's portrait and opposite Sabine relate to certain financial scandals of the time. '*Vapor vincit omnia et omnium*' refers to unfortunate investments in new railway com-panies and a notorious steam laundry, which led to a crash on the Stock Exchange in December 1825. 'The New Golden Drop or Marvel of Peru—a native of No-mans land. To be bought in the City—only £500 p^r. leaf!! Cheap as dirt and productive beyond belief', and the 'Com-parative Declension, mine—miner—minus—New Lat. Gr^r' are skits on the prevalent speculation in questionable South American mining companies. The 'Matchless specimens' of 'Rye Coffee', exhibited in a blacking jar and described as 'Almighty Roasters', sold by the 'General Polisher of Mankind', have reference to the 'Radical Breakfast Powder' prepared from roasted rye, wheat, peas, and other things, and sold as a substitute for tea and coffee to those pledged to total abstinence from excisable drinks. Henry Hunt (1773–1835), the radical politician and manufacturer of 'Hunt's Matchless Blacking', was one of the chief pro-ducers and sellers of this *ersatz* drink. His blacking and drink apart, he gained special notoriety as the chairman of the 1819 meeting in St.

Peter's Fields, Manchester, which was broken up by the yeomanry in what was called the 'Peterloo Massacre'.

'Perkins's New Grapehouse. Forced by steam. Warranted not to end in smoke' skits Jacob Perkins's steam gun, which caused great excitement in December 1825 when it was demonstrated at his factory near Regent's Park to a party of army officers, including the Duke of Wellington. Presumably the gun discharged grape-shot and that, not the heating of vineries, accounts for 'Grapehouse' and the bunch of grapes emerging from the muzzle. Had Cruikshank been present at Chiswick a few years later no doubt he would have marked the occasion with another delicious cartoon. In 1832 Jacob's son, Angier March Perkins (1779?–1881), was employed, at the Society's Chiswick Garden, to apply to a small glass-house recently constructed his method of heating by means of numerous small pipes, which was regarded as an important invention. After repeated trials, and after the apparatus had once exploded and at all times proved unmanageable, the idea was abandoned.

'The Specimens of American Acasia' from the 'Trees which must not be too much exposed' and 'thrive best in a Register' are pieces of the wood of *Robinia pseudacacia*, the alleged virtues of which were stoutly proclaimed from about 1825 onwards by William Cobbett (1762–1835), the radical politician, agriculturist, and owner-editor of *Cobbett's Weekly Political Register*, in which journal the activities of his opponents were often 'exposed'.

CHAPTER EIGHT
IN THE DOLDRUMS

THERE SEEMS LITTLE REASON TO DOUBT THAT THE GREAT ACTIVITY
of the Society at this period—the establishment of the house in Regent
Street with its Meetings and Exhibitions on the first and third Tuesday
in every month, the publication of the *Transactions*, the dispatching of
plant-collectors, the conducting of correspondence with numerous
horticulturists overseas, and the formation of the Garden, were all very
largely the fruit of Sabine's energy and initiative. Since he was himself
a keen amateur gardener, the Garden naturally absorbed the greater
part of his personal attention. Announcements about the Garden stated
that 'the immediate superintendance of the Garden is vested in the
President and Secretary', but as the President, Thomas Andrew Knight,
lived in Herefordshire and usually spent only about one month each
year in London, whereas the Society leased a house near the Garden
containing 'apartments for the use of the Secretary when resident in the
Garden', it was obvious that Sabine controlled the Garden for eleven
months of the year, subject to his being occasionally overruled by the
Council. He decreed the time of its opening and closing; he drew up six
'Rules' and nine 'Regulations' governing admission into it, and another
set regarding the distribution of plants, etc., from it, and in both cases
those who paid an annual contribution to the Garden were privileged
and their names marked by asterisks in the annual lists of Fellows. To
Sabine, an Inspector of Assessed Taxes, no doubt such administrative
methods were quite natural; understandably they produced some
resentment among the Fellows, especially those who were not prepared
to contribute annually to the Garden in addition to paying their annual
subscription. One such Fellow doubtless spoke for many others when,
writing to the *Gardener's Magazine* under a pen name, he said, 'I wonder,
indeed, that the members of a (professedly) liberal society should quietly
submit to be classed and regulated, and starred and scheduled, like the
items in a paper of assessed taxes.'

In October 1824 the financial position of the Society was apparently
causing some anxiety, for the Secretary submitted to the Council an
unusually extensive statement of accounts. The estimated value of the

Society's property in Regent Street—the house, furniture, books, drawings, wax models of fruits which had been diligently collected by the Library, and stock of the *Transactions*—was about £15,300. The estimated cost of the Garden for the current year was £3,295. 8s. 0d., and the income, including an allocation of £1,400 from the Society's general funds, was £2,071. 6s. 0d., leaving a deficiency of £1,224. 2s. 0d. There had also been a deficiency in 1823, and 'the Secretary observed that these deficiencies in the annual expenditure of the Garden had arisen from failure of consents on the part of the old Members of the Society to contribute annually an additional guinea towards the Garden, about 1,100 of the Members having returned no answers to the application made to them on the subject.'

As to the immediate future, the position was seen to be as follows:

Estimated annual income	£7,000
Estimated receipts from Garden,	
i.e. admissions and sales	1,000
	£8,000
Estimated expenditure at Regent Street,	
including the *Transactions*	£4,000
Towards liquidation of interest and	
principal of Garden loan	1,000
Estimated expenditure on Garden	3,000
	£8,000

The Council was told that

The above outgoings are calculated by keeping down and avoiding several heads of expenditure, the incurring of which would be very desirable and very beneficial to the objects of the Society, but that if by any extra assistance an addition of £2,000 per annum could be made to the income of the Society, enabling it to expend £5,000 per annum in Regent Street and £4,000 per annum at the Garden, all the objects of the Society might be attained exclusive of the further formation of the Garden.

The Secretary then entered on the particulars of the Formation [of the Garden] account, the total of which up to this time paid or promised amounted to £13,890, and it was considered that to finish up the works in hand without entering on any new works would require about £500, making an outlay on Formation of £14,390, beyond which, unless the amount of subscriptions should accumulate or additional aid be given to the Society, it was not proposed to proceed in Formation works.

The provision to meet the above expenditure was:

Donations to Garden Formation, paid or promised	£5,242	
Compositions in lieu of annual contributions	409	
Miscellaneous receipts	46	
Loan raised in 1823	6,000	
		£11,697
Balance still to be found		2,693
		£14,390

A rider stated that of the donations promised £994 still remained unpaid 'and it was possible that some of these might not be received for some time'. It would have been more realistic to have said 'might never be received'.

On the same day (14 October 1824) Sabine informed the Council that it was necessary that they should meet a contractor's bill for £2,515. 5s. 0d. for work done at the Garden, and that it was proposed that it should be settled by bonds for £2,000 bearing interest from the preceding July and a remittance for the balance. No better course being open to them, 'on consideration' the Council agreed to the proposal.

One would have supposed that, considering that they were being obliged to borrow money to meet expenditure already incurred, the Council would not even have contemplated any further avoidable expense until the necessary funds were actually in hand. But no; Sabine seems to have had visions of a State-aided 'National' institution and an infectious optimism in securing financial assistance from Government. At a Meeting of the Council on 23 July 1825 he 'stated that he had authority to announce the intention of His Majesty's Government to place £5,000 at the disposal of the Council for the purpose of forwarding the formation works at the Garden. . . . He also submitted to the consideration of the Council the plan of certain works proposed by the Garden Committee to be executed in contemplation of receiving the above grant.' These works included the construction of sheds for composts, pots, etc., and for the carpenters; the provision of a tank and a water supply to various glass-houses; the erection of houses for tropical plants, pineapples, and vines; the building of a wall on the east side of the Garden; and the provision of arches for climbers in the Arboretum. When plans and estimates were considered a month later the last two items were deferred, but the rest were ordered to be executed 'as soon as the funds proposed to be furnished by Government were supplied'. Minor increases in the salaries of some of the Garden clerks were made and an additional clerk was appointed to go daily between the Garden and Regent Street.

Incorrigible optimism! Some four months later Sabine had to report that it had been

ascertained that the £5,000 which had been promised to be advanced to the Council by the Government had not been received as was expected, and that now there was no certainty that it would at present be paid; that in consequence of this disappointment none of the works ordered by the Council . . . had been proceeded in except the two new Melon Pits, and one Pine Pit which, on consultation with the Treasurer and Vice-Secretary, appearing to be essential, as well for the preservation of the Pine plants as for the profitable growth of Pines in the ensuing year, should be built. . . . This proceeding was approved.

A further seven weeks having passed, on 19 January 1826,

The Secretary stated that he had not yet had an interview with the Chancellor of the Exchequer on the subject of the proposed assistance from Government, but that as it was certain that the advance would not be made at present, and as there was a considerable number of accounts belonging to the Garden which required immediate settlement, he had, in conjunction with the Treasurer and Vice-Secretary, made arrangements for borrowing the sum of £3,000 of Mr. George Law of Lincoln's Inn upon three bonds of £1,000 each. . . . It was ordered that the loan as offered be taken.

Curiously enough, according to Sabine, the necessity for borrowing this money was not improvident spending. 'The Secretary stated that, on examination of the accounts, it appeared that the deficiency in the income of the Garden had entirely arisen from the smallness of the number of Members who had consented to be charged with the additional guinea to their annual subscriptions, as proposed,' and it was 'Ordered that a letter be prepared and sent to each Fellow of the Society who has neither contributed to the fund for the formation of the Garden nor consented to pay the annual guinea, calling his attention to the subject and requesting an answer as to his intentions.'

Obviously Sabine was very much occupied with the Chiswick Garden, which was the source of his greatest interest. Except on the fortnightly Meeting days, he was content to leave the office work in Regent Street in the hands of his protégé, John Turner, the paid Assistant Secretary, who was entrusted with the receipt of annual subscriptions, commuted subscriptions, and contributions to the cost of the formation of the Garden, and with the settlement of the Society's bills to contractors and tradesmen. Left very largely to his own devices, he, of the agreeable reading voice but by no means agreeable morals, had considerable scope for the manipulation of the Society's accounts and the 'borrowing' of the Society's money for his own purposes, such as the acquisition of a house

The Summer Show at Gore House, Kensington, 16 May 1855 (from *Illustrated London News*, 19 May 1855)

The Society's Garden at Chiswick showing the Conservatory. The photograph was taken about the end of the nineteenth century.

Plate 7

The Society's Garden at Kensington (1862) with Kensington Gardens and Hyde Park in the distance

Part of the Society's Garden at Kensington, looking south.

Plate 8

at Turnham Green. In February 1826 Joseph Davis, the accountant-clerk, reported to Sabine his suspicions that a much larger balance was in Mr. Turner's hands than was supposed. Sabine investigated the matter, and believed Turner's not very plausible story that only a comparatively small sum was involved and was due to his having made temporary loans to tradesmen who were unable to meet their liabilities. So, having 'personally expressed his surprise and displeasure at these advances and directed that the sums so advanced should be charged in the account, and receipts filed for them', he said he would report the matter to Elliot, the Treasurer. Turner accordingly produced amended accounts, but Mr. Barnard, the Vice-Secretary, to whose knowledge the matter had been brought, was not so easily deceived, and drew attention to the fact that 'the receipts delivered for the above sums were receipts . . . from former bills, the dates and amounts on the receipts being altered'. Upon being confronted with this evidence, Turner, after a while, confessed to his misdeeds and, having been told that the Treasurer would now be informed, fled to France. At the same time he let it be known through his relatives that the money he had appropriated, apparently about £764, would be repaid provided that 'he should not be deprived of his office'. To this cool impertinent proposal Sabine, the Vice-Secretary, and the Treasurer all incredibly agreed. Turner's brother and his wife's relations refunded the money, Turner returned to duty, and the matter was hushed up. When the President came to town as usual for the Anniversary Meeting in May, 'Mr. Sabine communicated the above circumstances to him with the reasons which had induced Mr. Elliot, Mr. Barnard and himself to withhold the making of them known, to the propriety of which, he, being assured that it was believed that all matters were now regular, assented.'

So 'Mr. Turner continued to execute the duties of the office regularly, and as the accounts were now made up weekly . . . and every precaution possible taken, no apprehensions were entertained of misconduct.' However, about four months later Davis, the clerk, once again reported to Sabine that he suspected Turner's accounts were not correct, and that various sums had not been paid into the bank. Upon investigation Turner admitted that he had received between £500 and £600 for which he had not accounted, and that apart from his undeclared thefts of the previous years he had embezzled about £223 since his reinstatement in April. Full of contrition, on 5 October he readily signed a bill of sale on his house and any property of his at the office and, realizing that he could hardly hope to escape the consequences of his actions a second time, he once more fled to France. Two days later the matter was at last reported to the Council, who, as 'it appeared that all that prudence could have dictated had been followed, . . . approved of what had

been done, and ordered that the Solicitors . . . be instructed to proceed forthwith to execute the powers given to the Society by the bill of
sale from Mr. Turner of his effects'. The Council caused an official
announcement on the matter to be made to a Meeting of the Society
on 21 November 1826, but naturally knowledge of it had already leaked
out. One of the least important consequences was the publication of a
new edition of Cruikshank's cartoon with the note on Turner's desk
improved by the addition of the words 'Now transplanted to a warmer
Climate'.

One fortunate outcome of Turner's dismissal was the decision 'That
Mr. Lindley [the Assistant Secretary for the Garden] be desired to act
as Assistant Secretary [to the Society as well as to the Garden] until a
successor be regularly appointed.' Lindley was formally elected as
Assistant Secretary in accordance with the Bye-Laws at the Anniversary
Meeting in 1827, after having been required to give security for £1,000.

Once it had become common knowledge, the Turner affair led to a
general feeling of uneasiness among the Fellows, and at one Meeting
alone, in 1827, the resignations of no fewer than sixteen Fellows was
reported. The intake of subscriptions at the beginning of the new year
was smaller than usual, and more liabilities arising from Turner's
embezzlements continued to come to light, bringing the net total deficit
from that cause to £960. Consequently the Council had to obtain a
temporary overdraft of £1,000 from the Society's bankers. In order to
bring in unpaid subscriptions more quickly a collector was appointed to
call on Fellows whose payments were in arrears, receiving five per cent
of what he collected.

One Fellow demanded the immediate discharge of a bond given to
him for a loan of £1,300 and the Treasurer was obliged to appeal to the
bankers once again. Being thus hard pressed for money, the Council was
not unnaturally inclined to clutch at straws, and, recalling that in 1825
Sabine had said that it was the intention of the Government to place
£5,000 at the disposal of the Council for work at the Garden, felt that
this verbal promise, even though unsupported in writing, justified an
application to the Exchequer Bill Loan Commissioners. An application
to the Commissioners for a loan of £5,000 was accordingly made, but
'it appeared from the communication of the Commissioners that the
Security of the Society was not of the description on which their loans
were made'.

Although economies were not easy, a small one was made by reducing
the weekly wage of the Garden 'labourers' from fourteen to twelve
shillings, and by omitting to fill any vacancies occurring among them
until their number had been reduced by eight. In August 1827 the
Council was faced with a long list of unpaid bills, but the Society's

account was already overdrawn and the minutes record that it was ordered that the bills should be settled 'as assets may arise'.

The year 1828 opened badly, for at the first Council Meeting it was reported that twenty-four Fellows had resigned. The Society's account was still overdrawn and all that could be done with a very long list of bills was to decide that they should be 'paid by the Treasurer's draft as assets may arise'. It was 'Ordered that the Secretary do take such steps as shall be deemed advisable to obtain the payment of His Majesty's [King George IV's] Subscription of £500 towards the formation of the Garden,' but although application was made first to one official and then to another, the money was never received. During the year still further examples of Turner's misappropriations came to light, and another £160 of the Society's supposed assets proved to be non-existent. And there were others. In a law action, brought by the caterer for the year's Fête, the Society obtained judgement for £131, but the caterer became bankrupt and neither that sum nor the solicitors' costs amounting to £213 could be recovered from him. At the last Meeting of the year the Council decided to treat as void the elections of ten Fellows who had never paid a subscription, and to remove from the list the names of fifteen Fellows whose arrears of subscriptions, amounting to about £227, seemed unlikely to be forthcoming.

Naturally the Society was the subject of a good deal of criticism, especially in regard to the unsatisfactory way in which its funds were being handled and in its management of the Garden. Several attacks appeared in the press, and one in the *Gardener's Magazine* blamed the President for failing to exercise more control, and in particular for the freedom with which Sabine was allowed to do more or less as he liked in the Garden, where his numerous rules annoyed many Fellows. This outspoken criticism was resented by the Council, who directed that the last number of the *Gardener's Magazine* should be returned to Mr. Loudon (the editor), 'conceiving that they would be wanting in all due feeling towards their respected President were they to accept as a present to the Library of the Society a publication in which such reflections on that gentleman have been made'. One journalist went a little too far, and Sabine reported that he had instituted proceedings against the editor of the *Morning Herald* for various libels which had appeared in that paper against the Society and himself, but that the matter had been settled out of court, as the editor had agreed to apologize and pay thirty pounds for the costs.

Throughout 1829 the Society was in the doldrums. No elections of new Fellows were recorded, but six elections were declared void and fifty Fellows resigned. There was no improvement in the Society's finances. Nicol, the printer of the *Transactions*, presented a bill for

£2,335, and the Council was only too pleased to agree with his suggestion that if the Society had not the means to discharge the whole of the debt he should be given interest-bearing bonds for £2,000. The Chiswick parish raised the assessment for rates on the Garden from £190 to £238 and the solicitors thought it would be unwise to dispute the decision. The third Fête, held in June, and about which it was reported that 'the shew of fruit had been very fine' and that 'notwithstanding the badness of the weather . . . no damage whatever occurred to the Garden', coincided with a calamitous thunderstorm. The marquees, however, fared worse than the Garden and suffered considerable damage, with the result that Mr. Edgington, the contractor, sought the Society's assistance in coping with his loss; but the Council, having trouble enough of their own, declined to go to his aid.

Criticisms of the Society's affairs continued to appear in the press and, at its Meetings, much of the Council's time was occupied in dealing with charges contained in a voluminous correspondence between the Secretaries and Charles Henry Bellenden Ker, F.R.S. (1785?–1871), who lived in Park Road, Regent's Park, where he grew orchids about which he wrote in the *Gardener's Chronicle* under the signature of 'Dodman'. He was an ardent advocate of popular education and at this time was much occupied with parliamentary reforms. Although he was sometimes correct in his criticisms of the manner in which the Society's affairs were conducted, he appears to have been a most cantankerous person. Probably it was thanks to him that at the last Meeting of the year 'The Secretary laid before the Council an Anonymous Pamphlet entitled "A Letter to Thomas Andrew Knight, Esq., President of the Horticultural Society, on the Management of the Garden and Funds of the Horticultural Society of London".'

In 1830 the storm broke. On 15 January an anonymous letter regarding the Society's debts (probably also written by Ker) appeared in *The Times*, and at a Meeting of the Society held four days later notice was given by Mr. Robert Gordon, M.P., and seven other Fellows, of their intention to move at the first Meeting in February for the appointment of a committee 'to enquire into Income and Expenditure, the Debts and Assets, and the past and present General Management of the Society'. A committee of thirteen, under the chairmanship of Mr. Gordon, was accordingly appointed, after the following letter from the President had been read:

Gentlemen, I address the following letter to you, respecting the reported embarrassed state of the funds of this Society with exceedingly painful feelings: but I am very anxious to state to its members the circumstances under which I remained unacquainted till within a few days of the present time, with the existence of such embarrassments.

When the honour of being made president of this Society was first proposed to me (I had never previously, for a moment, entertained a thought of aspiring to the office), I stated in answer, that, if I became president, the distance of my residence, and the nature of my pursuits, must preclude the possibility of my being present in London to attend to the local management of the affairs of the Society; and I only assented to be nominated on the condition that no other person was proposed; and, subsequently, when the wealth and number of the members of the Society had greatly increased, I addressed a similar declaration from the chair, and expressed my willingness to resign my office. I had the reasons, which were very flattering to me, to believe that the Society did not wish me to resign my office; and I retained it, requesting, however, that the members of the Society would not, through 'any tenderness of feeling towards me, retain me in office a single hour to the injury of the Society'. I therefore trust that the local management of the official business of the Society was not amongst the duties which the members who did me the honour to elect me expected me to perform.

In thus exculpating myself, I do not mean to shift or cast any blame upon the other officers of the Society. They were misled by apparently well founded expectations of assistance, which subsequently proved fallacious, to take too large a garden, with too great a consequent establishment, and from that source all our subsequent difficulties appear to me to have sprung. I trust, however, that our present embarrassments will be, without much difficulty, overcome; and I beg to say, that, individually, I shall be happy to contribute my assistance in any way which may aid in restoring to prosperity an Institution which has already done much, and is calculated to do much more, public service. I beg to add, that I would have attended this Meeting, if I could have made myself in any degree useful.

I remain, Gentlemen, &c. &c.

(Sgd.) THOS. AND. KNIGHT

Sabine did not object to the formation of Robert Gordon's committee; in fact, he promised his cordial support by every means in his power. But he clearly realized that his prestige was fast ebbing and before the committee met he made his apologia. He had held the post of Honorary Secretary, without remuneration of any kind, and to the neglect of his own private affairs, for fourteen years; always he had striven to promote the objects of the Society, and he believed that in this he had attained a good measure of success; maybe he had committed errors, maybe he had offended some people; he would assure everyone that the errors had been quite unintentional and that to no one had he meant to be unkind; he was extremely sorry.

At its first meeting the Committee called for audited accounts up to the end of 1829, and when in due course they became available they showed that the Society's liabilities were £19,769, of which £14,700 was in interest-bearing bonds. Various estimates of the value of the Society's assets were made, and it appeared that while the total assets were about equal to the liabilities, much depended upon whether the tangible assets were realized at the Society's leisure or by forced sale, and whether the subscriptions in arrear and those about to become due for the year ending 1 May 1830 would be paid. (Up to this time subscriptions for a year began on 1 May and were not due until the following March.) At the committee's suggestion an appeal for prompt payment of subscriptions was sent to all Fellows.

The committee also asked the Council for their opinion as to what savings might be made in current expenses without injury to the material objects of the Society. The first of the Council's suggestions, born of panic, was to dispose of the Regent Street House and rent smaller offices. As, however, the Regent Street premises, with the large Meeting Room, were peculiarly suited to the Society's needs, it was fortunate that the committee had cooler heads than the Council, and that that particular suggestion was not adopted, though most of the others were. Among those called before the committee was J. C. Loudon, who had used his *Gardener's Magazine* as a powerful vehicle of criticism of the Garden, and who now gave it as his opinion that

the Horticultural Society has no more occasion for a garden than the Society of Arts has for a workshop or a manufactory. . . . there is nothing that has been attempted by the Horticultural Society that could not have been better done by individual gardeners and nurserymen. . . . The garden . . . might be given up without the slightest injury to the advancement of horticulture; and all the objects proposed to be effected by the Society might be attained in a better manner than they possibly can be in any wholesale experimental garden, by the separate experiments of individuals.[1]

Fortunately again, this astonishing suggestion was not adopted.

After several meetings, reference to the Council, and talks with Lindley, the Assistant Secretary, the committee put forward a number of proposals which, on the Council's recommendation, were approved by a General Meeting. As a result, part of the Regent Street house was let, the office staff was reduced, a more businesslike system of accounting was adopted, and economies were effected in postage, porterage, printing and stationery. The surplus stock of the *Transactions* was advertised at half price. Duplicate drawings and unwanted books were sold by auction, and John Reeves in China was asked to stop sending plants and drawings. Steps were taken to dispose of the lease of the gardener's house at Turnham Green in which Sabine had apartments. At Chiswick the staff was reduced, student-gardeners were no longer paid, the horses were sold, forcing and the cultivation of pineapples and other plants under glass was reduced, and vacant land was used for the production

[1] *Gardener's Magazine*, VI (1830), p. 248.

of profitable market-garden crops. About £260 was obtained from an auction of surplus plants, and the distribution of plants from the Garden was extended to all Fellows irrespective of whether they had paid any additional contribution towards the cost of the Garden.

The committee gave particular attention to the verification of the statement that by Sabine's orders the plants in the Garden had not been labelled, and that all visitors had to be attended by one of the staff who was afterwards required to report to Sabine any comments which had been made by one visitor to another. As a result, instructions were now given for all plants to be labelled, for the wasteful and objectionable practice of escorting all visitors to cease, and for the Garden to be open from 9 a.m. to 6 p.m., or sunset if earlier.

Acting on a suggestion from the chairman of the committee of inquiry, Sabine resigned from the secretaryship. At the General Meeting to which the committee rendered its final report a vote of censure on the conduct of Mr. Sabine was proposed, but withdrawn on the earnest and magnanimous recommendation of Mr. Gordon 'as unnecessary and likely to injure the interests of the Society with its creditors and the public in general'. But Loudon and the *Gardener's Magazine* could not refrain from welcoming Sabine's departure with the comment—'he it is, and he alone, who, by a system of concealment and monopoly of power, has brought the Society to the brink of ruin.'[1] However, much as Loudon disliked Sabine and the officious treatment he had received from him, he felt obliged to add—'but he has also been the cause of the greater part of the good done by the Society; and that the Society have done good, even we . . . readily allow.'

Loudon could do none other than readily allow all this. Sabine had succeeded Salisbury as Honorary Secretary in 1816 and had found the Society's accounts in great confusion. He had put these to right, had reorganized the Society and for his work had been awarded the Society's Gold Medal in 1816. He had taken a leading part in the establishment of the Society's Garden, first at Kensington and then at Chiswick. The Garden's collection of fruits, unequalled anywhere in the world, was largely his work, as was the distribution of the best kinds of fruits, vegetables, and flowers, and thus the displacement of inferior kinds, throughout the country. In large measure he could take the credit for the many fine plants which Douglas, and others, had introduced, for it had been mostly owing to his enthusiasm and initiative that the Society's collectors had been sent abroad. Moreover, he had contributed some forty papers to the *Transactions* on such subjects as paeonies, magnolias, dahlias, chrysanthemums, crocuses, passion flowers, tomatoes, and others. But he was a despot and a dictator, and like every other such ruined

[1] *Gardener's Magazine*, VI (1830), p. 252.

much of his good work and brought the cause for which he had striven so hard crashing to the ground. On his resignation the Society's fortunes were in a worse state than they had been twenty years before when he came to the rescue.

In 1830 Sabine had his salary of some £1,200 a year from his government post and now, presumably, the time to devote to his job as Inspector-General of Assessed Taxes. And this he did until he retired in 1835. But he also had time to devote to the affairs of the Zoological Society, of which he was Treasurer and Vice-President, adding many animals to the collection and many ornamental plants to its Garden in Regent's Park. He died in 1837.

Lindley, on the other hand, came out of the affair with flying colours, as indeed would one who, albeit unsuccessfully, had opposed Sabine's ideas and actions. That Lindley had acted thus is shown in a letter he wrote to Sabine on February 12, shortly after the committee had begun its investigations. The letter was among the documents on which the committee based its report and recommendations:

Sir,
 It has been impossible for me to misunderstand what occurred in the Council to-day. Upon being called into their presence, I found that an impression had been made upon them, that certain estimates, prepared by the last Council, and sent to the Committee, had been first assented to by me before the Council, and then dissented from by me before the Committee. It is possible that this impression may have ceased with my disavowal of the charge, and that the Council see that no such stigma attaches to me; but this does not satisfy me. I conceive that you, as a gentleman, and professing to be my friend, were bound not to have allowed any such impression to have existed, as you must have known that I was above suspicion upon such a point. You know perfectly well that I have always protested against the statements by which the Council have frequently been deluded into sanctioning measures and expenditure, which, had they known the real state of the Society's affairs, they could not have countenanced and that I was entirely opposed in opinion to the very heads of estimate objected to by the Committee. You know I have always dissented from any higher value than 2000*l.* being placed upon the library, drawings, and models, which are estimated in the return to the Committee at 3580*l.* You are perfectly aware that I remonstrated against the exaggerated amount of assets in the balance-sheet laid before the Council, and I believe given to Lord Essex so recently as Jan. 22 last; that on account of those exaggerations I did not comply with your request to put a copy of that document into the hands of Mr. Gordon; and that one of my objections to it was the valuing of the *Transactions* at 9691*l.*; the information I had obtained at your request was, that they were only worth 1,000*l.*, as I told you over and over again; and, consequently, you must have known that I could not have assented to a statement in which their value is fixed at 2000*l.* You could not be ignorant that I should have objected to 500*l.* being esti-

mated as the value of the fruit-room and sheds; for you yourself, not a month since, told me that, by the lease, no buildings except the glass-houses at the garden, are the property of the Society. All these things being thus, I think I have a right to enquire why you allowed the Council to suppose that I had assented to their estimates. You may perhaps say that you can explain this to my satisfaction; but I have both seen and heard lately too much of explanations to take them against the evidence of my senses. I see clearly that an intrigue is going on for the purpose of making it appear that I am at one time allowing myself to be identified with those miserable proceedings which have brought the Society to its present state, and to which I have been constantly and openly opposed, and at another disavowing those proceedings before the Committee. I have never been a party to the exaggerations of the Society's means, and concealment of the Society's debts, by means of which many honourable and excellent men in the Council have been unfortunately induced to believe a ruined Society to be in a state of prosperity. I have been steadily opposed to the measures by which that ruin has been brought about; and I do not choose, now, at the eleventh hour, either to be cajoled into a suppression of my opinions, or to allow you to make the world believe that I now, for the first time, entertain sentiments adverse to your proceedings. That there may be no farther misconception upon this and other points, I have written you this letter, a copy of which I shall give to all persons whom it is likely to interest.

I am, Sir, &c.

(Sgd.) JOHN LINDLEY

From the storm Lindley emerged as the holder of the dual appointment of Assistant Secretary and Assistant Secretary for the Garden, at a salary of £300, and the *Gardener's Magazine*[1] referred to him as 'unquestionably a man of extraordinary talent, and no less extraordinary industry', and forecast for him a brilliant future. And the future was to show that Loudon's opinion of Lindley was sounder by far than his opinions on the value of the Garden.

On the resignation of Sabine, Edward Bernard was persuaded to act as Secretary *pro tempore*, and he was succeeded at the Anniversary Meeting by George Bentham. At the same time Robert Henry Jenkinson, the Treasurer who had held office for a year, resigned, and Alexander Seton was elected in his place. As the President had always made it clear that he could not accept responsibility for the day-to-day conduct of the Society's business, and under Sabine's 'system of concealment' had obviously been kept in ignorance of the true state of affairs, the Fellows readily exonerated him from blame and had no hesitation in re-electing him.

George Bentham (1800–84), C.M.G., F.R.S., F.L.S., second son of Sir Samuel Bentham, the naval architect and engineer, had spent part

---

[1] Vol. VI (1830), p. 252.

of his early boyhood in Russia and acquired a knowledge of the Russian language. Later he had lived with his family near Montpellier, France, where he had interested himself in botany and horticulture and had become a Foreign Corresponding Member of the Society. He had returned to England in 1826, first turning his attention to law, but soon devoting himself exclusively to botany and by so doing becoming well known to Sabine and Lindley. In 1830, although a shy and retiring man, and in full knowledge of the Society's desperate position, he was persuaded to allow himself to be elected Honorary Secretary of the Society and continued so to act for eleven years, during this time playing an important role in restoring the Society's fortunes. He named and described many of the plants sent home by Hartweg and Douglas and became recognized as one of the foremost botanists of his day. He collaborated with Sir Joseph Hooker in the production of a *Handbook of the British Flora* (1858) and of *Genera Plantarum* (1862–83), and was joint author with Sir Ferdinand von Mueller of the *Flora Australiensis* (1863–78).

The unsatisfactory state of the Society's finances naturally became common knowledge, and some Fellows feared that they might be held liable for the debts. In the circumstances it was not surprising that during the year 218 Fellows resigned and about two dozen allowed their subscriptions to lapse.

By June 1830 the storm had subsided, and although there was no rush to join the Society, most Fellows were disposed to share the view, expressed in the concluding paragraphs of the committee's report, that the errors which had been committed arose from 'mistaken judgment rather than from want of zeal', and that

The Committee indulge the pleasing belief that there still exists the same kind feeling in favour of the Society by which it was first established and for many years so liberally encouraged; relying upon this feeling, the Committee have no reason to doubt but that, under more economical arrangements and a system of management more efficiently controlled and more generally acceptable to the Fellows, the present embarrassments may be surmounted, the debts gradually liquidated, and the approbation of the public deservedly bestowed upon the useful discoveries, the valuable communications, and the beneficial exertions of the Horticultural Society.

CHAPTER NINE

OUT OF THE DEPRESSION

UP TO THIS TIME MEMBERSHIP OF THE SOCIETY HAD CONSISTED solely of men. However, on 2 June 1830, because several women had let it be known that they were anxious to join the men, those parts of the Charter and Bye-Laws which related to the qualifications of candidates were examined and discussed and, as there appeared to be no clause by which women were disqualified, it was agreed that those who were now desirous of becoming Fellows should be proposed at the Society's next Meeting. Thus, on 15 June five ladies were proposed; the Countess of Radnor, Mrs. Holland, Mrs. Marryat, Mrs. Thornton, and Mrs. Louisa Collier. Lady Radnor was accorded the same privilege as a peer of the realm and was elected forthwith without a ballot, thus becoming the first woman to be a Fellow of the Society. At the next Meeting on 6 July the Countess of Guildford and the Countess of Morton were similarly elected, but the other four ladies had to wait until 20 July, when, in accordance with the usual practice for commoners, their certificates had been read at two Meetings.

Very soon the ladies made their mark; not only did they attend the Meetings but they also exhibited. Probably the first woman to take her plants to the Meetings was Mrs. Marryat, of Wimbledon, the lady who, in 1824, had been given by the Society a plant of *Primula sinensis*; on 17 May 1831 she showed *Boronia serrulata* from New South Wales, a yellow azalea, and some strawberries, and subsequently sent many good exhibits. The lady who made the greatest impression on the Meetings, however, was Mrs. Louisa Lawrence, one of the greatest amateur horticulturists of her day. A daughter of James Trevor Senior, a Buckinghamshire landowner, in 1828 she had married William Lawrence, F.R.S., the great surgeon some twenty years older than herself, and lived at Drayton Green, a little village seven miles west of London, on the way to Oxford. At Drayton she herself designed and laid out a two-acre garden which, in Loudon's view, was the most remarkable of its size in the London neighbourhood. The Lawrences were wealthy and labour was easy to come by; six men—and two women for collecting leaves, etc.—were fully employed in the two acres. In 1838 Loudon saw the manuscript catalogue of her collection; 3,266 different species, varieties, and forms of trees and shrubs and herbaceous plants were listed therein. There were 500 roses—this long before the Hybrid Teas and Hybrid Perpetuals had become the fashion. There were 200 different kinds of heartsease, 140 florists' pelargoniums, and 227 orchids. It was these latter and other hot-house plants that she mostly exhibited; and exhibited to such effect that between May 1833, when she gained her first prize, and May 1838, her exhibits had secured a grand total of fifty-three medals including the Knightian Medal. Obviously she was highly competitive, and her keenest rivals were the Duke of Devonshire and his gardener, Joseph Paxton. Unquestionably she would have regarded her greatest horticultural triumph to be the first flowering in cultivation of the magnificent *Amherstia nobilis*, especially as she was able to forestall, only by a year or two, the Duke of Devonshire at Chatsworth.

This notable event occurred in 1849 at Ealing Park, where the Lawrences had lived since 1840 and where she, not only a fine gardener but also a great beauty, enjoyed many social triumphs. There she was visited by Queen Victoria and the Prince Consort, at nine o'clock in the evening, to see the flowers of the night-flowering cactus; there she held her famous afternoon parties at which the Queen and Prince Consort, several European kings and queens, and the leading members of the English aristocracy, were frequent visitors. And there she died in 1855, when her son, James John Trevor, who was later to become a reforming President of the Society, was twenty-four years of age.

In 1828 Lindley had been appointed Professor of Botany in the University of London, had delivered his inaugural lecture on 30 April 1829, and the Council of the Society had agreed to his attending the University between the hours of 8 and 9 a.m. on each day during May, June and July. Already he had begun to concern himself with the horticultural education of the students at the Garden and now was to do likewise with the Fellows, for in 1831, at the Meeting Room in Regent Street, he gave a series of three fortnightly afternoon lectures on botany applied to horticulture. These proved so popular that in subsequent years the number of lectures was increased to six. Thus were inaugurated the lectures which are so conspicuous a feature of the first day of the present fortnightly Shows at Vincent Square.

No doubt Lindley was also responsible for a further innovation. Until 1831 Fellows had brought to the fortnightly Meetings in Regent Street anything they thought would interest other Fellows, and this continued to be the case. But in 1831 a series of competitions was also held, medals being offered for pineapples in February; camellias in April; rhododendrons in May; azaleas, roses and grapes in June; pineapples and melons in July; and dahlias, roses and grapes in September.

These competitions were repeated in the following year and proved very popular, far too popular, in fact, for the size of the room, which became so crowded that the flowers and fruits could not be seen to advantage. Clearly more space would have to be found, and the only additional space available was at the Garden. Consequently Bentham, the Secretary, suggested that the Garden be used for the staging of Shows in the spring. The Council agreed to the extent that, in 1833, they decided to hold three Shows under canvas at Chiswick, on a Saturday in May, June and July. Fellows would be admitted free of charge and the public by ticket at five shillings each. Refreshments would be provided by a caterer at regulated prices and, if the tickets met with a ready sale, the surplus takings over the cost of the tent, seats, etc., would be 'applied to the hire of bands of music'. The first Show was the only one which was not an unqualified success. The season had been unfavourable, and some growers refrained from exhibiting; even so, some 1,700 people attended. As the finances of the June and July Shows were very satisfactory, Council decided to continue on similar lines in 1834, with the addition of a fourth Show in September. The first three were so successful that, after the third, in July, at which there was an attendance of 3,076, the *Gardener's Magazine* suggested that 'the tent, large as it is, will soon have to be supplemented by separate tents for florists' flowers, fruit and vegetables'.[1] The September Show was also well attended, especially as the fashionable world was out of town; even so it was not held in 1835. Thus began a succession of fine Shows which were continued for a quarter of a century, and did much to promote horticulture throughout the country, for many of the plants exhibited were still little known, and their standard of cultivation was very high. All persons, whether Fellows of the Society or not, were invited to exhibit, and gardeners vied with each other in producing fine specimens, so that the winning of a prize at Chiswick became recognized as the hallmark of a skilful grower. By 1836 the popularity of these Shows had grown to such an extent that for the one held in June 12,000 tickets were sold, and the *Gardener's Magazine* expressed the view that that number

would be doubled if it were more generally known in the metropolis what a brilliant scene the Horticultural Society's Garden presents on the days of exhibition . . . besides a splendid Garden and an exhibition of the finest fruit and flowers that wealth and skill can produce, enlivened by several bands of music, . . . the principal part of the English aristocracy are present, and mix indiscriminately with the tradesman, the mechanic and the gardener. This scene may be enjoyed by men, women and children, for five or six hours, at 3s. 6d. each.[2]

[1] Vol. X (1834), p. 411.   [2] Vol. XII (1836), p. 380.

In 1836 the Council decided that the competitions instituted at the Regent Street Meetings in 1831 should be discontinued, and that competitions should be confined to the Exhibitions in the Garden; that, as formerly, the nature of the exhibits staged at the fortnightly Meetings in Regent Street should be at the discretion of the exhibitors, and that no attempt should be made to classify the exhibits as 'first', 'second', or 'third'; that any number of different exhibits should be eligible for the same medals, and that all persons, whether Fellows of the Society or not, should be allowed to exhibit. Council further decided that in addition to the two existing medals, the Large Medal and the Banksian, a third, the Knightian, bearing the profile of the President, should be struck in gold and silver, that it be ordinarily awarded for 'specimens of Eatable Fruits and Ornamental Stove and Greenhouse Plants', and that the first impression, in gold, be 'presented to Thomas Andrew Knight, Esq., for his numerous and valuable contributions to the *Transactions* of the Society and for the signal services he has rendered to Horticulture by his physiological researches'. Upon being informed of this, the President wrote the following characteristic letter to the Secretary, on 6 May 1836:

My dear Sir,

I feel highly honoured and flattered by the wishes of members of the Horticultural Society of London, that the first impression of their new gold medal should be presented to me, and I shall receive it with very great pleasure, provided I be permitted to subscribe a sum equivalent to its cost, to be employed in liquidation of the debt of the Society, but not upon any other conditions.

I remain, &c.

(Sgd.) T. A. KNIGHT

The die for the medal was made by William Wyon and the first impression from it was not available for the Council's inspection until 21 October 1837.

In October 1826 it had been decided that a number of provincial horticultural societies might apply annually for the grant of a large silver medal to be awarded by the council or committee of the local society 'to any one person within their district, who by his exhibitions, cultivation, or communication on horticultural subjects shall appear to the said Council or Committee to be most deserving of such testimony of merit within the year, provided there shall be one sufficiently deserving in their estimation'. In the first instance the offer had to be made to the horticultural societies of Winchester, Newcastle, Aberdeen, Cambridge, Edinburgh, Dumfries, and Glasgow. In 1834 the applications for medals had become so numerous that the Council decided that in future any approved provincial society desiring a medal should contribute ten guineas per annum, in return for which it would receive a silver Banksian Medal, a copy of the *Transactions* or other publications, and once each year a quantity of fruit scions and seeds of hardy plants for distribution. Thus was started a system of affiliation of kindred societies similar to that now in operation.

In June 1837 William IV, the Society's patron, died, and the Exhibition arranged for 8 July was postponed until 11 July. The following month the Duke of Devonshire, who had joined the Council at the Anniversary Meeting in May, reported that, as requested, he had signed and transmitted the Council's loyal address to Her Majesty Queen Victoria on the occasion of her accession to the throne, and that 'Her Majesty had been graciously pleased to become the Patroness of the Society.' Not until 1842 did the Queen honour the Society with her presence. Then on 14 May she visited the Exhibition at the Garden and expressed to the President her 'great satisfaction at the state of the Garden and arrangements for the Exhibition'.

In the spring of 1838 the President was in his seventy-ninth year and in failing health. In spite of this, he came up to London as usual, in April, partly to seek the advice of his London doctor. He was not able to attend the Council Meeting on 25 April, at which he was nominated for re-election at the Anniversary Meeting on 1 May. When that day arrived he did not feel equal to taking the Chair, and in fact did not leave the house of his daughter, Mrs. Walpole, after reaching London. Greatly respected as he was, he was naturally elected President for the twenty-ninth time. Ten days later, however, he died, and his remains were interred at Wormsley. In the *Athenaeum*, John Lindley wrote of him:

The great object which Mr. Knight set before himself, and which he pursued through his long life with undeviating steadiness of purpose, was utility. Mere curious speculation seems to have engaged his attention but little; it was only when facts had a practical bearing that he applied himself seriously to investigate the phenomena connected with them. For this reason, to improve the races of domesticated plants, to establish important points of cultivation upon sound physiological reasoning, to increase the amount of food which may be procured from a given space of land (all of them subjects closely connected with the welfare of his country), are more especially the topics of the numerous papers contributed by him to various societies. Whoever calls to mind what gardens were only twenty years ago, and what they now are, must be sensible of the extraordinary improvement which has taken place in the art of horticulture during that period. This change is unquestionably traceable, in a more evident manner, to the practice and writings of Mr. Knight than to all other causes combined. . . . Of domesticated fruits, or culinary vegetables, there is not a race that has not been ameliorated under his direction, or immediate and personal superintendence; and if henceforward the English yeoman can command the garden luxuries that were once confined to the great and wealthy, it is to Mr. Knight, far more than to any other person, that the gratitude of the country is due.

The *Gardener's Magazine*, which in the past had been so critical of Knight and of his work, published Lindley's notice in full.

His name is commemorated not only in the Knightian Medal, but also in *Knightia*, a small genus appropriately allied to the genus *Banksia*.

Interlude
to Parts Two and Three

FROM HIS JOURNEY TO THE CONTINENT LOUDON RETURNED IN THE autumn of 1814, having seen practically every important garden and met most of the eminent scientists in northern Europe, only to find that in his absence the £15,000 he had amassed by the end of 1812 had been almost completely dissipated by unfortunate speculations, and that he was in pecuniary difficulties. Straight away he decided that henceforward he would live, and make good his losses, by his pen, and that he would write a history of gardening, incorporating the information he had gathered during his travels and supplementing this by much more which he must first collect by journeying to France and Italy. Thus, after a second four months' trip to Europe in 1819, he began work on the *Encyclopaedia of Gardening*, the first edition of which appeared in 1822. It was an epitome of gardening, remarkable for the immense mass of useful matter it contained as well as for the vast number of line engravings printed with the text instead of on separate pages—an unusual feature at that time. The work had an extraordinary sale and was republished again and again, as well as rewritten, in later years. Loudon's fame as an author was established.

Henceforward he was always to suffer indifferent health and often extreme pain. The rheumatism which had gripped him in earlier years was never to leave him; unskilled treatment was to deprive him of the use of his right arm, which ultimately had to be amputated; two fingers and the thumb of his left hand were to become so contracted as to be useless. None of this was to prevent him from working, and in 1826 he established *The Gardener's Magazine*, which first appeared quarterly, then every two months, and finally every month—the first periodical devoted exclusively, or almost so, to horticultural matters. 'We had two grave objects in view:—' Loudon wrote in the preface of the first volume, 'to disseminate new and important information on all topics connected with horticulture, and to raise the intellect and the character of those engaged in this art.' On these matters, and on many others, Loudon communicated with outspoken conviction his own thoughts and feelings, as well as those of his contributors.

Regularly in the *Magazine*, and in considerable detail, all the affairs of the Horticultural Society were recorded, and its management criticized. The second number contained an attack on the Society, especially an attack on Secretary Sabine, by one who signed himself 'A Fellow of the Society', together with a note by Loudon, who maintained that the objects of the Society were too wide in scope, and who, strangely enough, was appalled at the idea of the Society supplying practical gardeners to those gentlemen in need of them. He considered this to be 'so utterly at variance with the dignity of the Society, that we are astonished it should be persisted in. An institution with "His Sacred Majesty" as a patron, and emperors and kings as members, to keep an office for servants! And while all this is being attended to, the gardening comforts of the laboring classes is totally neglected.'[1] Later he was to become a severe critic of Sabine and of the Society's Garden. Of the Arboretum at the Garden and of Sabine, he was to write in Volume V of the *Magazine*:

When we reflect on this arboretum, we are astonished that such an absurdity could be produced in such an age and in such a country. We can only account for it by reflecting on the preponderating influence, in the council and committees of the Horticultural Society and Garden, of a gentleman, who, though he has not attended to this subject [landscape gardening] certainly possesses great merit in point of zeal, activity and perseverance, and is surpassed by none in describing paeonies, crocuses and chrysanthemums. . . .[2]

The 'absurdity' of the Arboretum could have been debated. The absurdity of Loudon's own proposal to lay out Arthur Seat, a hill of volcanic origin in Edinburgh, as a cemetery, with winding roads to and from the summit which was to be crowned with a building and its sides planted with trees and shrubs, was beyond all debate. Obviously his judgement as a landscape gardener was suspect.

The *Gardener's Magazine* reviewed all newly published books bearing however slightly on gardening matters. In 1828, under the heading 'Hints for Improvements', Loudon gave a considerable notice to a novel called *The Mummy*. It was a tale of the twenty-second century in which mechanical milking machines, mowing machines, air machines, and perfect social services were in use. Loudon was much impressed by what he thought were the scientific talents of the author, whom he longed to meet. The meeting was arranged in February 1830, and to his immense surprise Loudon discovered that the author was a lady—Jane Webb. The pair were married on the fourteenth of the following September— and Loudon immediately began to rewrite the *Encyclopaedia of Gardening*.

At this time there was simmering in Loudon's mind the idea of writing a large-scale work on the trees and shrubs, native and introduced, culti-

---

[1] *Gardener's Magazine*, I (1826), p. 150.   [2] ibid., V (1829), p. 348.

vated in the British Isles. In 1833–4 the idea was put into effect and some 3,000 questionnaires relating to this matter were circulated: some 1,600 replied to his quest for information. In this way was born Loudon's greatest work, the *Arboretum et Fruticetum Britannicum*. He employed draughtsmen, sometimes as many as seven, to prepare drawings of trees and shrubs, often overseeing their work from 7 a.m. until 8 p.m., without sustenance, and then working on the text, with his wife as his amanuensis, until two or three o'clock in the morning. The labour was immense, especially since Loudon was a sick man and in more or less constant pain. The magnificent work, in eight volumes, four of text and four of illustrations, was published in monthly numbers between 1835 and 1838—and on completion Loudon realized that he owed £10,000 to the printer, the stationer, and the engraver who had been employed on the production. For the rest of his life he laboured to clear off the debt, writing more horticultural works and even taking up once again his landscape-gardening work, sometimes advising from his bath-chair.

Loudon died in 1843, and the *Gardener's Magazine* died with him. For some years this publication had not been as remunerative to the Loudons as at the time of their marriage, when it gave them an income of £750 a year. In fact, financially, it had been on the decline since 1832, when Joseph Paxton commenced publication of *The Horticultural Register*, the *Magazine*'s first rival, a copy of which Loudon saw at Chester during a tour of the North of England, when he advised on the laying out of a botanic garden at Birmingham and visited Chatsworth, where Paxton had been head gardener for five years. Paxton was 'not at home' and Loudon was not greatly impressed: 'Chatsworth has always appeared to us an unsatisfactory place . . . we protest against the same edging to flower-beds as are adopted in common shrubberies. . . .' Even so 'all the neighbouring gardeners agree in stating that he [Paxton] has improved the garden department at Chatsworth, and we are happy in adding our testimony to this effect.'[1]

Paxton's *Magazine of Botany* of 1834 was the second great rival to the *Gardener's Magazine*—and was condemned in the latter's pages. 'Paxton's *Magazine of Botany*', Loudon wrote, 'may be useful to manufacturers of articles decorated with figures of plants (porcelain, paper-hangers, cotton, printers): to botanists it is of no use, as the plants are neither new nor described with scientific accuracy.'[2] Fortunately Paxton was one of the least quarrelsome of men and seldom took offence for long. Later the two were to become great friends and, when Loudon died, Paxton was one of those who came to the aid of Jane Loudon.

The horticultural publications of Loudon, and of Paxton, were by no means the only ones during this period. There was, for instance, the

[1] *Gardener's Magazine*, VII (1831), p. 395.　　[2] ibid., X (1834), p. 232.

Botanical Register, launched by James Ridgway in 1815 and, until 1847, publishing coloured plates of exotic plants cultivated in British gardens. But almost more important were the books and catalogues published by nurseries, as a form of advertisement. The *Botanical Cabinet* was one such. This periodical, first issued in 1817, and concluded, after twenty volumes had appeared, with a complete index, in 1833, was the publication of the nursery of Conrad Loddiges & Sons. In its pages are to be found figures of many of the early orchids cultivated in Britain, for Loddiges were among the first to grow them on a commercial scale, from about 1821. In 1839 the nursery published its *Orchideae in the Collection of C. Loddiges & Sons*, one of the first orchid lists to be issued in Britain and containing the names of over 1,600 kinds of orchid. Orchids, of course, at this time were much in demand and the Horticultural Society had contributed in no small way to their popularity; John Lindley had been an early writer on the subject, having written the text to Francis Bauer's *Illustrations of Orchidaceous Plants* of 1830. Loddiges' collection of orchids was to be put up for auction in 1856, shortly before the firm went out of business. But Loddiges were noted for more than orchids. By 1830, when the fifteenth edition of their *Catalogue of Plants* was issued, they stocked over 130 palms, close on 1,500 stove plants, close on 2,000 greenhouse plants, including 300 ericas, nearly 30 *Eucalyptus*, and many Australian and New Zealand plants, an unrivalled collection of nearly 4,000 trees and shrubs, including nearly 1,500 roses and 200 willows, as well as many hardy herbaceous perennial flowering plants and ferns.

Loudon ranked the firm of Chandler & Son, at Vauxhall, with that of Loddiges. General nurserymen, specializing in camellias, chrysanthemums and hollies, they were noted most for their work with the first group. The son, Alfred, in addition to making a name for himself as a painter of Veitch's orchids, painted the camellias raised at his father's nursery. *Camellia Britannica* of 1825, with text by E. B. Buckingham, illustrated hybrids which had been raised as a result of crosses made in 1819. More of his paintings were published in 1831 in *Illustrations and Descriptions of the plants which compose the Natural Order Camellieae and of the varieties of* C. japonica *cultivated in the Gardens of Great Britain;* the text of this work is by William Beattie Booth, who in 1830, in the *Transactions of the Horticultural Society*, had listed and described twenty-three cultivars of *Camellia japonica* which had been brought to England between 1792 and 1830, probably all of them from China, and who, in 1858, was to be appointed Assistant Secretary to the Society.

In the *Arboretum et Fruticetum Britannicum* Loudon considered that the *Catalogue of Roses*, issued in 1836 by Rivers & Son of Sawbridgeworth, Hertfordshire, represented the finest collection in the country. There were 24 Moss Roses, with the dark crimson 'Rouge del Luxembourg' the most recently bred; there were 25 Provence or Cabbage Roses—large fragrant flowers on slender stalks; there were 50 Perpetual or Autumnal Roses, 'the most desirable of all sections'; 89 Hybrid China Roses, 'the most beautiful roses known', including 'George IV' raised by T. Rivers, jun.; 25 cultivars of *Rosa* x *alba* with very glaucous foliage and a wide range of flower colour; 19 Damask Roses, fragrant and thorny; 99 French Roses, cultivars of *Rosa gallica*—'the spotted, striped and marbled roses . . . are very novel and beautiful'; 70 China Roses, cultivars of *Rosa chinensis* which 'from six to eight months in the year form brilliant ornaments to our garden'; 51 Tea-scented China Roses, cultivars of *Rosa odorata*; 53 Climbing Roses—of the Ayrshire, Sempervirens, Multiflora and Boursault sections; 66 Noisette Roses—'a happy intermixture of the China rose with the old musk'; 10 Musk Roses; 38 L'Ile de Bourbon Roses; 16 miniature China Roses, cultivars of *Rosa chinensis* var. *minima*; all these and many which were unclassified. In 1837, Rivers published the *Rose Amateur's Guide*, in the same year that Laffray, the rose breeder of Auteuil, introduced the Hybrid Perpetual 'Princesse Hélène', the first of a race of roses soon to be widely popular in British gardens, and of which certain ones, 'Frau Karl Drushki', 'George Dickson', and 'Hugh Dickson', are still in cultivation.

It was during this period that the most famous work on roses of all time was produced, the three-volume *Les Roses* (1817–24) by Pierre Joseph Redouté, the most popular flower-painter in the whole history of botanical art.

A stocky figure with elephantine limbs; a head like a large, flat Dutch cheese; thick lips; a hollow voice; crooked fingers; a repellent appearance; and—beneath the surface—an extremely delicate sense of touch; exquisite taste; a deep feeling for art; great sensibility; nobility of character; and the application essential to the full development of genius; such was Redouté, painter of flowers, who counted all the prettiest women in Paris among his pupils.[1]

And to this same period belong some of the eight wonderful volumes of Redouté's *Les Liliacées* (1802–16). Both works were for the Empress Josephine.

Rivers, of course, was not alone in growing roses. Colvill, of the King's Road Nursery, Chelsea, had raised *Rosa lawrenceana* (*R. chinensis* var. *minima*) in 1805 and had been concerned in the early history of the China Roses. But Colvill was not a rose specialist; his collection was remarkable and wide ranging and many of his plants were figured and described, along with others from the Bristol Nursery of Miller & Sweet, the King's Road Nursery of Davy, and the Sloane Street Nursery of Tate, in such floral periodicals and monographs as *The Geraniaceae*

[1] J. F. Grille, *La Fleur de Pois* (1853); quoted by Ch. Léger (1945).

(1820–30), *The Cistiniae* (1825–30), *Flora Australasica* (1827–8), the two series of *The British Flower Garden* (1823–38). The text of all these important works was by Robert Sweet, the nurseryman with the botanical frame of mind who for several years was employed by Colvill; the plates were drawn by Edwin Dalton Smith, one of the best floral artists of the time but of whom very little is known. One of the most significant plants to be figured in *The British Flower Garden* was the earliest *Gladiolus* hybrid to be well known—*Gladiolus* x *colvillii*, the result of crossing *G. cardinalis* and *G. tristis*. It was the forerunner of such early-flowering cultivars as 'Ackermannii' and 'The Bride'.

Another plant of remarkable significance to be figured in *The British Flower Garden* (Ser. 1, t. 290) in 1829 was *Rhododendron molle*, which had been introduced from China in 1823; it was destined to become famous as one of the parents of the Mollis hybrids. This was the second Chinese rhododendron to be introduced to Britain, for *R. obtusum* had arrived in 1803. Few rhododendrons had been introduced since the turn of the century; *R. caucasicum* had arrived from Asia Minor in 1803; *R. catawbiense* was introduced from North Carolina in 1809 and was to prove to be the main source of hardiness in the garden hybrids which are still popular in cultivation today; *R. arboreum*, with brilliant red flowers, came from India in 1811; *R. zeylanicum* from Ceylon in 1832; *R. campanulatum* from the Himalayas in 1835, and *R. barbatum* from the same region in 1849, the year in which Joseph Hooker was making his historic rhododendron collections in the Sikkim Himalayas.

During the first half of the nineteenth century rhododendron hybrids began greatly to outnumber the species. The first hybrid, strangely enough, was an accidental crossing, in the London nursery of William Thomson, between the evergreen *R. ponticum* and the deciduous *R. (Azalea) nudiflorum*—the sweet-scented *Azaleodendron* 'Odoratum'. Although it has been stated that Thomson introduced his hybrid in 1820, it was in cultivation in the Royal Botanic Garden in Edinburgh in 1814. The deliberate hybridizing of rhododendrons began about 1820, and *R. ponticum, maximum, catawbiense*, and *caucasicum* were the hardy species involved; by intercrossing and recrossing nurserymen vied with each other in publishing long lists of names in their catalogues and in exhibiting their new plants at the Society's Shows. When once the tender Asiatic *R. arboreum* had flowered it, too, was used in hybridization; in 1826 J. R. Gowen made the celebrated cross between (*R. catawbiense* x *ponticum*) and *R. arboreum* which yielded the hybrid 'Altaclarense', and Michael Waterer of the Knaphill Nursery, hybridizing *arboreum* with *caucasicum*, named the resulting seedlings 'Nobleanum', after his friend Charles Noble of the Sunningdale Nursery. Both these nurseries were to play a most important role in the development of the rhododendron.

In the early 1820s Loudon considered Lee & Kennedy's Vineyard Nursery at Hammersmith 'unquestionably the first nursery in Britain, or rather the world'.[1] The business was then run by James Lee, jun., who intended to instal each of his four sons in a particular department; the seed business, the counting-house, greenhouse exotics and fruit trees, and more fruit as well as hardy plants. The plan failed, however, for he died in 1824, and his son John was the only one old enough to be in the business, of which he took charge. The firm spared no expense in procuring new plants from abroad, and indeed sent their own collectors specially for this purpose; one to North America, another to South America, and, in partnership with the Empress Josephine, another to the Cape of Good Hope, collecting bulbs and ericas. Ericas at this time were extremely popular and even private gardeners were growing several hundred different kinds.

The firm had been concerned with the introduction of the fuchsia; it was now to be concerned with the development of the dahlia, which had been introduced to Europe from Mexico, to the Botanic Garden at Madrid in 1789. There were three forms, and from Spain these forms were introduced to France, and from France to England. In 1803 one form called *D. coccinea* flowered in the nursery of John Fraser in Sloane Square, and another known as *D. rosea* flowered at Vauxhall. The Marchioness of Bute, in 1798, had also endeavoured to introduce all three forms, from Madrid, to Kew. But Kew had been unsuccessful in rearing plants and those from France had also died. However, in 1804 Lady Holland sent seeds from Madrid to Holland House, where seedlings were raised and flowered. There appears to be some doubt as to their fate. However, France had had more success than Britain in the cultivation of these first dahlias, and by 1814 a fully double purple-flowered form, very similar to our modern formal decoratives, was flowering in the garden of Comte Lelieur near Paris. In the course of the next year or two tubers of this form found their way into Lee's Hammersmith nursery, and there, by 1818, the first of the ball-type dahlias was to be seen in Britain. Plants were speedily propagated and the English hybridists got to work. In 1832 the first results of hybridization were seen; 'Inwood's Springwood Rival' was a perfect ball dahlia, possessing short tubular florets with incurved margins and was described as a cupped type. 'Lyne's Springwood Rival' was another ball dahlia which appeared in 1834. In a year or two these flowers were all the rage, a guinea being paid for a new variety, and by 1836 there were hundreds and hundreds of ball types, classified for the show benches—and there were some forty shows in various parts of the country—according to

[1] *Encyclopaedia of Gardening* (1822), p. 1224.

colour: selfs, spotted, striped or bicoloured, laced, flaked, painted, striated, edged, clouded, and picotees.

Gradually the popularity of the ball type was to wane. The breeders were particularly interested in the cupped type, and developed great improvements on 'Inwood's Springwood Rival', improvements which for a time were known as Globe dahlias. Later they became known as Show and Fancy dahlias and were the vogue almost until the turn of the century. It was not until the 1870s that *D. juarezii* was to be introduced from Mexico and to lead to the development of the Cactus dahlia.

A prime mover in the development of the dahlia was the firm of James Veitch & Son at Exeter, where dahlia shows were renowned. John Veitch (1752–1839) had travelled south from Jedburgh and had settled in the West Country as a landscape gardener. In 1808 he founded the Killerton Nursery. Successful as this venture was, John's son James found the distance of eight miles from Exeter disadvantageous to his interests, and in 1832 moved to land at Mount Redford and established what later became known as the Exeter Nursery. At the age of eighteen his son James 'the younger' went to London for two years to work at Chandler's Vauxhall Nursery and especially to study orchid growing. He returned to Exeter, full of new ideas and loaded with orchids, and in 1838 joined his father as partner in the firm of James Veitch & Son. Two young Cornish brothers had been employed by them as gardeners —William and Thomas Lobb. In a very short time they were to bring great renown to the firm as plant-collectors.

In later years several descendants of John Veitch were to serve the Horticultural Society—and horticulture—with great distinction and loyalty.

From its inception the Horticultural Society had encouraged the cultivation of fruits of all kinds and, moreover, had always endeavoured to stabilize the nomenclature of fruits and extend the cultivation of the most desirable types. It was chiefly for this reason that, in 1826, the Society had published its *Catalogue of Fruits*. During the next few years two other works of importance to pomologists were published—and for the same reasons. The first was edited by John Lindley, who appears to have been equally expert as a pomologist as an orchidologist; his three-volume *Pomological Magazine* (1828–30) was reissued in 1841 as *Pomologia Britannica*, and figured and described the most important fruits in cultivation at that time in Britain. The second work was by the Brentford nurseryman and seedsman, Hugh Ronalds (1759–1833), who was one of the most expert pomologists of the time; his *Pyrus Malus Brentfordiensis* of 1831, illustrated by forty-two coloured plates by his daughter, Elizabeth, described almost 180 different kinds of apple and summarized a lifetime of cultivation of this fruit.

The activities of the Horticultural Society, especially those centring round the introduction and distribution of new plants, together with the work of a similar nature of the many enterprising plant nurseries, had an enormous influence on the horticultural activities of many of the landed gentry of the country. Robert Stainer Holford of Westonbirt, Gloucester, is a good example. In 1829 he founded the Westonbirt Arboretum, planting oaks and Scots pine, the North-West American conifers introduced during his lifetime such as the Douglas Fir and the Wellingtonia, as well as many other conifers and broad-leaved trees. Robert Holford's son, Sir George, who was to succeed to Westonbirt in 1892, greatly increased the collection by planting more conifers, many rhododendrons, maples and other genera. The Duke of Bedford, at Woburn Abbey in Bedfordshire, was another who did a great deal of planting of the new introductions and, moreover, sponsored such notable publications as James Ford's *Pinetum Woburnense* in 1839. George Spencer-Churchill, the Marquis of Blandford, seems to have been as enthusiastic as anyone, for at White Knights, Reading, he planted all new plants of every description, and built numerous glass-houses and exotic aquaria. Loudon vowed that the collection was at least the equal of any at a private residence in the empire; there were many conifers, all the known species of magnolia and hawthorn, red and snake-barked maples, horse chestnuts and buckeyes, walnuts, strawberry trees, judas trees, koelreuterias, gleditsias, stewartias, azaleas, rhododendrons, and a vast assortment of hardy herbaceous plants. The Marquis was overwhelmed with enthusiasm and never considered the cost. As early as 1800 he had planted on a wall twenty-two plants of *Magnolia grandiflora* at a cost of five guineas each. He would not hesitate to buy several plants of a rare species and pay twenty or thirty guineas each for them, and in 1804 his account with Lee of the Hammersmith Nursery exceeded £15,000. It is hardly surprising that by 1816 the Marquis was in debt and White Knights was mortgaged for £85,000. Fortunately in the following year he succeeded to the dukedom; and fortunately for the nurserymen his tastes did not change. Over twenty years later, in 1838, Loudon was to write of him: 'He has still the same taste for plants, and indulges it, as far as his limited resources will permit, in the pleasure grounds of Blenheim, where His Grace at present resides.'

His Grace the Duke of Devonshire and his establishment at Chatsworth were the most remarkable of all. Loudon had been severely critical of Chatsworth and of Paxton, and, by implication, of the Duke, but by 1839 he had completely changed his opinion. In the *Gardener's Magazine* of 1839 he wrote:

The Duke of Devonshire has stated to us that he owed his taste in botany and

141

gardening entirely to Mr. Paxton. There are but few persons in the present day whose talents and exertions have conferred more service on the science of botany and gardening than the gentleman to whom the above compliment is paid. A few years only have transpired since Chatsworth, as far as gardening was concerned, was below mediocrity. Its noble owner bestowed neither money nor patronage in advancing the art; in fact he had no taste for gardening. Now he is its best and most influential friend.

The Duke's own story of the transformation of Chatsworth under the hand of Paxton is noted in the *Gardener's Chronicle* of July 1865:

He [Paxton] married Miss Sarah Brown in 1827. In a very short time a great change appeared in pleasure-ground and garden: vegetables, of which there had been none, fruit in perfection, and flowers. Twelve men with brooms in their hands on the lawn began to sweep, the labourers to work with activity. The kitchen garden was so low, and exposed to floods from the river, that I supposed the first work of the new gardener would be to remove it to some other place, but he made it answer. In 1829 the management of the woods was entrusted to him, and gradually they were rescued from a prospect of destruction. Not till 1832 did I take to caring for my plants in earnest. The old greenhouse was converted into a stove, the greenhouse at the gardens was built, the arboretum was invented and formed. Then started up Orchidaceae, and three successive houses were built to receive the increasing numbers. In 1835 the intelligent gardener, John Gibson, was despatched to India to obtain the Amherstia nobilis and other treasures of the East. The colossal new conservatory was invented and begun in 1836; the following year Baron Ludwig was so charmed with its conception that he stripped his garden at the Cape of the rarest produce of Africa. Paxton had now been employed in the superintendence and formation of my roads; he made one tour with me to the West of England, and in 1838 contrived to accompany me for an entire year abroad, in which time, having gone through Switzerland and Italy, he trod in Greece, Turkey, Asia Minor, Malta, Spain, and Portugal. In his absence he managed that no progress should be checked at home. A great calamity ruined the expedition he had set on foot to California; the unfortunate Wallace and Banks, young gardeners from Chatsworth, having been drowned in Columbia River. He went with me in 1840 to Lismore, and in that year the conservatory was finished. The village of Edensor was newmodelled and rebuilt between 1839 and 1841, and the crowning works have been the fountains and the rock-garden.

The *Amherstia* to which the Duke referred was the only plant in Europe for several years, though a rumour that another one had found its way into a nursery in Chelsea caused Lindley to write to the Duke, from the Horticultural Society's Regent Street office:

No, No, No, My Lord, there is no Amherstia in King's Road. Your Grace was quite right in your opinion that the impostor is *Brownea grandiceps*. Instead of deriving its origin from the Temple Gardens of Buddha he has had no more dignified birthplace than the bush round a Demerara sugar plantation. I am so very happy to be able to assure you that your *Amherstia* is as yet the only *Amherstia* in Europe.[1]

And it was the only one in Europe until 1847, when Lord Hardinge, then Governor of the East Indies, presented a plant to Mrs. Lawrence, the great gardener at Ealing Park, who succeeded in inducing her plant to flower for the first time in cultivation two years later. The first flowers were cut and sent to Queen Victoria, and Mrs. Lawrence once again had forestalled her great rival at Chatsworth.

'The colossal new conservatory' of 1836 was really the sequel to the Palm Stove at the Royal Botanic Garden, Edinburgh, which had been opened in 1834, when it was the largest house of its kind in Britain, having been built at a cost of 'upwards of £1,500'. The Chatsworth conservatory, which was built at a cost of close on £12,000, was the horticultural wonder of the age, being visited by nearly 50,000 people annually, and the forerunner of others to come. The most important of these were the vast range of glass-houses built for the Queen at Frogmore at a cost of something like £50,000, and the glorious Palm House at Kew designed by Decimus Burton and built by Richard Turner between 1844 and 1848, even today one of the most lovely and imposing glass-houses in the world.

[1] Lindley's letter is the property of Messrs. James Smith & Sons, of the Darley Dale Nurseries, Derbyshire.

Part Three
Difficult Years
(1838 - 1858)

CHAPTER TEN

TWO GARDENS IN JEOPARDY

THE DUKE OF DEVONSHIRE, FROM WHOM THE GARDEN WAS LEASED, and whose residence at Chiswick House adjoined it, joined the Council on 1 May 1837. On the death of Knight he was elected President at a Special General Meeting convened for the purpose on 19 June 1838, and continued to hold office for the next twenty years. (Plate 4.)

William George Spencer Cavendish, sixth Duke of Devonshire (1790–1858), was a very rich bachelor. In 1826, at the request of the Government, he had undertaken a special mission to Russia on the occasion of the coronation of the Emperor Nicholas, when his retinue was of the most superb character. The mission was said to have cost the Duke £50,000 beyond the allowance made to him by the Government. In the same year he had engaged Joseph Paxton, one of the under-gardeners at Chiswick, as his head gardener at Chatsworth. At this time the Duke had no great interest in horticulture, but his new head gardener at Chatsworth had all the energy and enthusiasm necessary to persuade him to lay out an extensive arboretum, and to erect, among other glass structures, a very large conservatory which gave Paxton the experience to enable him, later, to design the famous Crystal Palace for the Great Exhibition of 1851, an achievement for which he was knighted. In a very short time the Duke was as enthusiastic as Paxton and his wealth provided the means for indulging his enthusiasms and for the furtherance of Paxton's ambitious schemes. In ten years he had become, according to the *Gardener's Magazine* for December 1836, 'The greatest encourager of gardening in England at the present time . . . he has already planted an extensive arboretum . . . and is now erecting a house for palms and other tropical plants. . . . The plan and elevation of this house may be compared to those of a cathedral, the central aisles being wider and higher than the two side aisles. The roof is of the ridge and furrow kind . . . which is admirably calculated for uniting strength with lightness.' Work had begun in 1836 and did not finish until 1840, when Paxton's magnificent conservatory, 277 feet long, 123 feet wide with the ridge of the roof 67 feet high and with some 75,000 square feet of glass, covered exactly one acre.

At this time Devonshire and the Society were intimately concerned with the affairs of Kew Gardens, the property of the Royal Family. During the reign of George III, owing principally to the influence of Sir Joseph Banks, a very large collection of plants had been assembled there. But after the death of Banks no one took the same interest in the Gardens, and when William IV died the Government contemplated their abolition. In January 1838 the Treasury appointed a committee, consisting of Dr. Lindley, Joseph Paxton, and John Wilson, gardener to the Earl of Surrey, to inquire into the management of the Royal Gardens. The report of the committee, which was submitted in February, drew attention to the fact that the main use of the Gardens at that time was to furnish plants for the other royal establishments; that the Gardens were serving no scientific purpose; and that while the public were admitted on week-days and were able to enjoy a pleasant walk, the Gardens had very little educational value, chiefly because the plants were inadequately labelled. 'The importance of public Botanical Gardens', said the report, 'has for centuries been recognized by the governments of civilized states, and at this time there is no European nation without such an establishment, except England.' Such Gardens as Kew were very desirable, for instance, from the point of view of meeting the needs of students at the recently established University of London, and the present Gardens should be put on a scientific basis and should co-operate with the public gardens in the various colonies and dependencies with the object of introducing and disseminating new plants. To that end, the report concluded, the Gardens should be transferred from the Lord Steward's department to that of the Commissioners for Woods and Forests.

The appointment of the Lindley committee and the nature of its report naturally came to the knowledge of the Council of the Society, and in May 1838 the Duke of Devonshire, who had recently joined the Council, signed on its behalf a petition from the Society to the House of Commons for the establishment of a public Botanical Garden at Kew.

However, no action was taken by the Government until February 1840, when Mr. Robert Gordon, then Secretary to the Treasury, asked Lindley to ascertain privately what the Council's reaction would be if the Gardens at Kew were to be abolished and all or part of the plants in the conservatories offered to the Society on the condition that the public had free access to them on one or two days of the week, and on the understanding that the Treasury would not make any grant towards the cost of housing or maintaining them. Naturally the Council had no hesitation in replying that it had learned with great regret of the proposal to abolish the Botanical Gardens at Kew; that the collection at Kew contained many plants of great rarity and beauty which it would

be most desirable for the Society to obtain should the Government ultimately determine to alienate them from the Crown; but that it would
not be possible to admit the public to the Society's Garden free of
charge, and that the cost of removing and providing glass-houses for any
considerable part of the collection would be beyond the Society's means,
at any rate unless assisted by a Treasury grant.

On 3 March 1840 Lord Aberdeen, alluding to the Gardens at Kew,
told the House of Lords that he had been informed that the Horticultural Society, 'which was very well known to be anxious to forward
horticultural pursuits', had 'refused to become parties to a transaction
which had for its object the destruction of those Gardens'. He inquired
if this was the Government's intention. The Government spokesman
thought it wise to allay public disquiet by declaring that there was not,
and never had been, any such intention, and a few days later responsibility for the Gardens was transferred to the Commissioners for Woods
and Forests, as recommended by the Lindley Committee. In 1841 the
establishment was reorganized, the Pleasure Grounds were separated
from the Botanic Garden proper, and Sir William Hooker, F.R.S.,
Regius Professor of Botany in the University of Glasgow, became Director. The gift of plants from the Society's Garden was resumed, and during the next three years no fewer than 174 species of plants were sent
by the Society to Kew, many being new tropical American species
sent home by Hartweg, the Society's collector, while others were Chinese
novelties received from John Reeves. Thus no small part of the credit
for saving Kew Gardens for the nation is due to the Society, and
especially to Lindley, who before he was asked to form his committee
appears to have had his eye on the post of Director of Kew. At any rate,
in 1840, he wrote to Sir William Hooker: 'It is rumoured that you are
appointed to Kew. If so I shall have still more reason to rejoice at the
determination I took to oppose the barbarous Treasury scheme of des-
troying the place; for I, of course, was aware that the stand I made and
the opposition I created would destroy all possibility of my receiving any
appointment.'

It is ironic that, almost immediately afterwards, the Society became
engaged in a long fight to save its own Garden at Chiswick.

In 1840 this Garden was a great credit to the Society and much work
of immense value to the Fellows and the general public had been done
there. One of the most important objects of the Society's Garden has
always been the establishment and maintenance of collections of authen-
tically named specimens of useful, as well as ornamental, plants. Much
of this had been done by 1830 and then for a time the pace had quiet-
ened because of the Society's unsatisfactory financial position. Even so,
in 1840, in the fruit department alone, well over 2,000 cultivars of fruit

were considered worthy of cultivation and indeed annually were being distributed by scions, buds, cuttings, or as plants. There were 910 apples; 510 pears; 160 plums; 60 cherries; 30 peaches; 20 nectarines; 14 apricots; 115 grapes; 50 figs; 24 nuts; 230 gooseberries; 10 currants; 8 raspberries; 24 strawberries.[1]

The collection of vegetables consisted of about 120 cultivars procured in this country and about ninety from abroad. For many years the Society had been purchasing from Messrs. Vilmorin, of Paris, seeds of some of their specialities and had been distributing them to Fellows, thus making more widely known those varieties which had been found after trial in the Garden to be superior to those commonly grown.

The collection of ornamental trees and shrubs, like that of fruits, was 'unrivalled in any other part of the Globe', containing nearly 3,000 species and varieties, exclusive of nearly 1,000 garden roses and about 200 garden varieties of azaleas and rhododendrons. The number of herbaceous perennials was about 2,600 and the average number of hardy annuals sown was between 250 and 300.

During the years 1830–40 vast quantities of plants, seeds, and cuttings had been distributed thus:

	Plants	Packets of seeds	Parcels of cuttings
To Members	90,525	349,903	48,500
To Foreign Countries, Correspondents, etc.	3,870	9,185	5,925
To Her Majesty's Colonies	930	4,506	146
	95,325	363,594	54,571

The number of stove and greenhouse plants at the Garden had been governed by the extent of the limited glass-house accommodation available for their culture, but by 1840 they totalled about 3,770, including some 1,750 orchids and other stove plants, and in 1840 new glass was provided for them.

Although the construction of an extensive range of conservatories and hot-houses had been planned at the first laying out of the Garden, by 1830 the glass consisted of only a 405-foot run of hothouses and 457 feet of glazed pits. In 1835 the Council decided that one half of the clear proceeds of the Garden Exhibition should be used for the construction of the long-delayed conservatories and in 1838 a committee considered various designs. The general plan of a central dome 120 feet in diameter, with two wings, each 185 feet long and 30 feet broad, was

[1] *Trans. hort. Soc. Lond.*, 2nd series, 2 (1842), p. 421.

agreed on, and the work was to be carried out by degrees as funds became available. One wing was completed early in 1840, at an estimated cost, including boiler-house, heating apparatus and adjacent terrace, of £4,500.

For financial reasons the Society had not been able to institute comparative trials of the various methods of heating glass-houses by flues, stoves, and hot water, which were the subject of much experimentation at this period. This important matter had not been entirely neglected, however. In 1832 Perkins's method of heating by means of numerous small pipes had been tried—and found wanting. In 1838 one of Rogers's conical boilers had been applied to the heating of a range of pits 77 feet long, with two-inch pipes, and the experiment had completely fulfilled the expectations that were entertained of its efficiency. This had led to the adaptation of two similar boilers in 1839 to other pits 154 feet in length. Partly because the old apparatus was not as good as one could have wished, and partly because of the greater temperature to which the boilers were exposed, this experiment had not been as satisfactory as the last, but it had led to some important improvements in the construction of the apparatus. An attempt had also been made in 1838 to heat a small range of pits with hot-water pipes warmed by an Arnott stove, but the boiler had proved so defective as to be unfit for use. Finally, a hot-water apparatus had been installed for use in the newly completed first wing of the conservatory, the boilers being placed in a detached building sixty feet from it, and the water conveyed by six-inch pipes in a dry tunnel to the conservatory, where four-inch pipes were used. The installation had been quite satisfactory, and it was concluded 'that all the experience obtained at the Garden goes to demonstrate the great inferiority of flues to hot-water pipes as a mode of heating'.[1]

On the whole the 1840s were not momentous years in the history of the Chiswick Garden. They were, however, noteworthy for the fact that much new material was received from China and America as a result of two of the Society's expeditions, as well as for the fact that progress was made in the provision of further educational facilities for the student-gardeners.

On 25 November 1842 the Council 'Resolved that the recent Treaty with China [the Treaty of Nanking] having rendered several of its ports accessible to British enterprise under regular protection, it is advisable that the Horticultural Society immediately avail itself of the opportunity thus offered for the introduction to Great Britain of the useful and ornamental plants of that immense Empire.' Accordingly the Secretary was authorized to seek out a suitable person to proceed to China as the Society's collector. Thus it was that, early in 1843, Robert Fortune,

[1] *Trans. hort. Soc. Lond.*, 2nd series, 2 (1842), p. 435.

(*above left*)
Lord Bury, later
Earl of Albemarle
(1873–1875)

(*above right*)
Lord Aberdare
(1875–1885)

(*left*) Sir Trevor
Lawrence
(1885–1913)

Plate 9.
PRESIDENTS OF
THE SOCIETY

Sir Trevor Lawrence (1885–1913)　　　Lord Grenfell (1913–1919)　　　Lord Lambourne (1919–1925)

Plate 10. CARTOONS OF PRESIDENTS OF THE SOCIETY BY SPY

after distinguishing himself in the Society's first examination in 1836 and after having been in charge of the hot-house department at the Garden, was selected for this great adventure. During the next nineteen years he was to prove to be one of the most successful plant-collectors, although it was on only the first of his four expeditions that he was the Society's employee. (Plate 14.)

Fortune was born at Blackadder Town in Berwickshire on 16 September 1812.[1] He received his schooling at the parish school at Edrom, served his apprenticeship in the gardens of Mr. Buchan at Kelloe, before being employed for some years at Moredun, near Edinburgh and before entering the Royal Botanic Garden, Edinburgh. For two years or so he worked under the famous and exacting taskmaster, William McNab. The latter must have approved of the young gardener, for in 1840 he recommended him for the vacant post in the hot-house department at Chiswick.

Before leaving for China he was given detailed instructions, drawn up by Lindley with the help of John Reeves, who, having given great service to the Society whilst living in China, was now actively engaged in the Society's affairs whilst living in retirement at Clapham. He, more than anyone, realized the immense opportunities that now lay before the Society for the introduction of Chinese plants, and was a member of the Society's so-called Chinese Committee. The instructions stipulated that 'in all cases you will bear in mind that hardy plants are of the first importance to the Society, and that the value of the plants diminishes as the heat required to cultivate them is increased. Aquatics, Orchidaceae, or plants producing very handsome flowers are the only exceptions to this rule.'

The committee thought it desirable to furnish their collector with certain instruments; a spade and trowels, hygrometers and thermometers—even a life-preserver. Fortune thought he should also be equipped with firearms. When these were refused him he wrote to Lindley on 1 January 1843:

I am much disappointed at the resolution of the Committee with regard to fire-arms, but I still hope that you will endeavour to make them alter their minds upon this subject. I think that Mr. Reeves is perfectly right in the majority of cases—that a stick is the best defence—but we must not forget that China has been the seat of war for some time past, and that many of the inhabitants will bear the English no good will. Besides, I may have an opportunity, some time, to get a little into the country, and a stick will scarcely frighten an armed Chinaman. You may rest assured that I should be extremely cautious in their use and if I found that they were not required they should be allowed to remain at home.

[1] *Gdnr's Chron.*, vol. 161 (1967), p. 14.

At the next meeting of the committee it was resolved that 'Fortune be supplied with fowling piece and pistols, and a Chinese Vocabulary'. On at least three occasions he had cause to resort to the fowling-piece and did so with the greatest composure and competence.

The committee also instructed him '. . . to take out three cases of live plants for the purpose, 1st, of making presents to those who may be useful to you, and, 2nd, of watching the effect upon the plants of the various circumstances to which they may be exposed during the voyage —the facts relating to this will form part of your report'. In this way Fortune and the Society were the first to try out, on a considerable scale, the newly invented Wardian case, which Dr. Nathaniel Bagshaw Ward had described in the *Gardener's Magazine* in 1839 and in his small book *On the Growth of Plants in Closely Glazed Cases* (1842).

Fortune sailed on the *Emu* on 26 February 1843 for Hong Kong and Shanghai. He arrived in Hong Kong in July, but, finding that the island had already been ransacked for plants, moved north to Amoy, which he found more barren than the Canton district. By sea he proceeded still further north, twice narrowly escaping shipwreck in the Formosa Channel. Finally he arrived at Chusan and wrote in glowing terms of the hills covered with azaleas and of the botanical riches of this area. He visited Shanghai and explored the rich plains of the Yangtze Kiang, where he procured chrysanthemums and tree paeonies, the beautiful conifer *Cryptomeria japonica* which was forming dense woods, and, amongst the graves of the natives, the wonderful *Anemone hupehensis* var. *japonica* (then called *Anemone japonica*), which he found in full flower in November, when most other flowers had passed, and described as 'a most appropriate ornament to the last resting places of the dead', for 'flowers which the Chinese plant on or among tombs are simple and beautiful in their kind' and 'no expensive Camellias, moutans, or other of the finer ornaments of the garden are chosen for this purpose'. Early in 1844 he returned to Hong Kong, packed his collections and sent them to England. After revisiting Canton and Macao and seeing the arrival from the north of the moutan paeonies—they were introduced each year—he moved north again at the end of March and visited the tea-growing district of Ningpo, little realizing, no doubt, that the tea plant was to be of so much concern to him in later years.

In January of 1845 he sailed for Manila and collected the wonderful Moth orchid with five-inch flowers, *Phalaenopsis amabilis*, including one plant 'with ten or twelve branching flower-stalks upon it and upwards of a hundred flowers in full bloom'. Thence to northern China again— and the black tea districts of the Fokien province—to Chusan, Shanghai (where he collected several importations from Japan), and Hong Kong. Half his collection he dispatched to England; the other half he took with him to Canton, before leaving for England, where he arrived in 1846. And in October of that year he was thrilled to see the anemone he had dispatched in 1844 in full flower in the Chiswick Garden. It had been treated as a greenhouse plant and had produced its mauve-carmine semi-double flowers the following year, flowers which were immediately painted by Miss S. A. Drake and the painting reproduced in Volume 31 of the *Botanical Register*, t. 66, in December.

Already it had caused quite a sensation at Chiswick, and by the time Fortune saw it there, George Gordon, the superintendent of the ornamental department, had realized that it was perfectly hardy and that it had 'proved itself to be one of the most desirable of herbaceous plants for autumn decoration . . . quite a rival for the purple Chinese chrysanthemum'.[1] And Gordon had noted that 'seeds were only produced by plants growing in the greenhouse, and therefore the plan of raising plants in this way is not worth time and trouble, except that there are chances of obtaining new varieties. I have but little doubt such may be obtained by hybridising the Japan anemone with such kinds as the white *A. vitifolia* from the north of India, or the common garden *A. coronaria.*' In point of fact, Gordon had already hybridized Fortune's plant with *A. vitifolia*, for a hybrid of this parentage, raised at Chiswick, was exhibited in September 1848. The hybrid is now known as *A.* x *elegans* and is the pink 'Japanese Anemone' so common in present-day gardens. At Verdun, about ten years later, it produced a white-flowered bud-sport—*A.* x *elegans* 'Honorine Jobert'—the original white Japanese anemone. Thus all the 'Japanese anemones', so popular and so decorative in present-day gardens in the autumn, are of hybrid origin and are now grouped under the hybrid name of *A.* x *elegans*. £1,800—or a little more—the cost of Fortune's expedition, was surely a small price to pay for the great pleasure which these plants have given, and will continue to give, to countless numbers of people.

But then one could truly say the same of other Fortune introductions of this period; of *Jasminum nudiflorum*, for instance, at first regarded as a valuable greenhouse plant, before it, too, was shown to be among the hardiest of winter-flowering shrubs, never failing to open its glorious primrose yellow flowers despite the most inclement weather; of *Lonicera fragrantissimum*, always flowering fragrantly over Christmas and well into the New Year; of *Spiraea prunifolia*, its twigs wreathed with white double flowers; of *Diervilla* or *Weigela florida* with flowers deep rose without, very pale within, one of the most useful of decorative shrubs; of the semi-evergreen sterile or garden form of the Chinese Snowball Tree, *Viburnum macrocephalum*, with its great hydrangea-like heads of pure white flowers; of *Viburnum tomentosum* 'Plicatum' or 'Sterile', the

[1] *Jl R. hort. Soc.*, II (1847), p. 231.

Japanese Snowball, profuse in its production of long-persisting balls of flowers; of the erect stemmed *Forsythia viridissima*; of the Bleeding Heart or Dutchman's Breeches, *Dicentra spectabilis*, of which Fortune wrote 'Its large purse-like blooms of a clear red colour, tipped with white, and hanging down gracefully from a curved spike, and its moutan like leaves, render it a most interesting plant, and one which will become a great favourite in English Gardens'; and of the Chinese Bell-flower, *Platycodon grandiflorus*, which Lindley believed to be the finest herbaceous plant sent by Fortune from China. Certainly Fortune's journey would have been worth while if he had returned with nothing more than the Japanese Cedar, *Cryptomeria japonica*, now represented in cultivation by so many of its splendid garden cultivars and first introduced by Captain Everard Hume who sent seeds to Kew in 1842; with nothing more than the variable *Rhododendron obtusum*, today represented in our gardens by the immense race of the so-called Kurume azaleas; or the variable *Rhododendron indicum*, again cultivated today in many diverse forms; with nothing more than the plants of the 'Chusan Daisy' as Fortune called them and which he found in a cottage garden on the island of Chusan. Fortune saw great possibilities for hybridizing with 'this modest little flower', which in England attracted little attention. French opinion was different, however; the Chusan Daisy became a great favourite there and introduced a new era in the history of the chrysanthemum, for from them the race of the Pompons was developed.

On his return in 1846 Fortune became Curator of the Chelsea Physic Garden, but in 1848 and again in 1852 he made further expeditions to the Far East as an employee of the East India Company with the object of introducing China tea to India. He also made a fourth journey which was privately financed and took him to Japan, whence he arrived back in January 1862. On each of these expeditions he collected a number of excellent plants which are now fine features of many British gardens.

Theodore Hartweg, who had returned from America in 1843, and had ceased to be employed by the Society in September of that year, was anxious to make a second expedition, and in March 1844 suggested that he should collect plants for the Society in California, travelling via Vera Cruz and Tepic, Mexico. The Council favoured the project, but took well over a year to make the necessary arrangements. Thus it was that Hartweg sailed on his second expedition in October 1845. Unfortunately, owing to a blockade of the Mexican ports by the United States, he had to content himself for many months with collecting plants and seeds in Mexico, and it was not until the summer of 1847 that he was able to reach California, whence he returned in 1848. Many plants were received and distributed by the Society from this brief Californian expedition, but three are of special importance; the summer and autumn scarlet flowering *Zauschneria californica*, the Californian Fuchsia; one of the most popular of Californian Lilacs, *Ceanothus dentatus*, unfortunately often not too hardy in the open, but excellent against a wall; and best of all, *Cupressus macrocarpa*, the Monterey Cypress. On the Island of Guadalupe, off the coast of Lower California, Hartweg found this cypress and was greatly impressed with the gnarled twisted trunks and flattened wind-swept crowns of the old plants. In cultivation it is beautiful, with its bright green fragrant foliage, and has proved to be eminently useful as a shelter tree, especially in coastal districts; and especially useful to Mr. Augustus Smith of Ashlyns, Berkhamsted, who in 1834 succeeded the Duke of Leeds as lessee of the Isles of Scilly from the Duchy of Cornwall, and on the Island of Tresco in the 1840s began to build a house and to make a garden. Shortly after the introduction of the Monterey Cypress, Smith began to plant it as a shelter belt and it is in large measure due to this shelter that Tresco and its great collection of subtropical plants are today famous throughout the horticultural and botanical worlds.

In 1846 another step forward was made with the education of the student-gardeners (still at this period often referred to as 'labourers'), of whom 264 had been admitted to Chiswick during the twenty-five years since the formation of the Garden. Inspired by Lindley, the Garden Committee now recommended the construction of a reading-room for the use of the young men. The Council, being 'anxious to contribute to the improvement of the men', but unable to find the money for a new building, had an empty room at the Garden furnished as a temporary measure, and to the already existing small library added further books, including a number given by interested Fellows, Lindley himself presenting fifty-three volumes. The room was opened for study on the evening of 23 November with a lecture by Lindley, who subsequently gave a series of ten more during that winter and early spring. To encourage serious study, prizes were offered on the results of an annual examination held in August. The annual report to the Fellows stated that 'The Council are strongly impressed with the value of the exertions made by the Vice-Secretary to promote this highly important object, as evinced by the very interesting lectures delivered by him at the Garden, and by his valuable donations to the Garden Library.'

By 1855, for a variety of reasons, not all of them associated with the Garden, the Society was in financial straits. As the Garden absorbed the greater part of the Society's income, its activities had to be curtailed. The Exhibitions had ceased to provide the necessary funds for the maintenance of the Garden and it was therefore profitless to hold them further. Moreover—a bitter pill to have to swallow—the Council was of the opinion that 'the proximity of the great government establishment at Kew [which the Society had done so much to save], accessible as it is by railway and water, and with whose attractions it is hopeless to contend, annually renders the Society's Garden of greatly diminished interest'. Anyway, without the necessary funds the Garden must either be reduced to the bare minimum or else relinquished altogether. The Council proposed not to go the whole way, but to maintain only a small Garden, mostly for experimental purposes. But the Council had reckoned without the President, who hardly ever attended a Council Meeting. There was to be no question of maintaining a smaller Garden on its present site, for the Duke of Devonshire, on whose land the Garden had been developed, insisted that the Society should occupy the entire ground or none at all.

The Council, understandably, was reluctant to relinquish the Garden; if, however, the entire area had to be occupied, obviously much reorganization would be necessary and many economies would have to be made. Towards these ends George McEwan, who had been gardener to the Duke of Norfolk at Arundel, and was in the front rank of his profession, was appointed to the charge of all the Garden's departments and given the title of Superintendent. Unfortunately, he was to hold this post only for fourteen months, for he died in 1858 in his thirty-eighth year. During his brief period at Chiswick, 'he evinced so much skill and energy as to make it a subject of the most lively regret that so great a spirit should have dwelt in so frail a body'.[1] He was succeeded by his assistant and general foreman, Archibald Henderson, who had begun his gardening career at Yester in East Lothian, and had later been gardener to the Earl of Zetland, at Aske Park. He reigned at Chiswick only for a few months, resigning before the year was out and moving to Trentham Gardens.

Robert Thompson, who had been on the Chiswick staff since 1824 and had done much to stabilize the nomenclature of fruit by the preparation of the Society's *Catalogue of Fruits*, and who since 1830 had maintained the meteorological records at the Garden, was given the title of fruit inspector, and continued to give great service to Chiswick for another ten years. No one more deserved the tribute paid to him towards the end of his career in the presentation of a testimonial of £400, raised by private subscriptions. Unfortunately the post of another great gardener, George Gordon, who, with Thompson, had done so much to make the name of Chiswick famous, had to be abolished. An Irishman, who had received his horticultural training in County Meath, Dublin, Bethnal Green, and in the nursery of J. Colvill of King's Road, Chelsea, Gordon came to Chiswick in 1828 at the age of twenty-two, and as a departmental foreman under Munro was thus contemporaneous

[1] *Gdnr's Chron.* (1858), p. 400.

with Thompson as well as with Robert Fortune. For close on thirty years he gave the Society splendid service and acquired a good knowledge of hardy trees and shrubs during the time he was in charge of the Arboretum. He came to be regarded as an authority on conifers, in 1858 publishing the *Pinetum*, which was followed by a Supplement, and a new edition in 1875. He became a friend of Loudon, to whom he was of great assistance in the preparation of the *Arboretum et Fruticetum Britannicum* and the *Encyclopedia of Trees and Shrubs*. After leaving the Society in 1857 he ceased to take a very active part in its activities, and died in 1879.

Lindley endeavoured to make one further economy by offering to renounce his salary as Vice-Secretary, but the Council took the view that it would not be in the interests of the Society to accept the offer.

In its efforts to make the Garden much less of a show-place and much more of an experimental one—the Council was determined that this should be done, and done on fifteen pounds a week—many stove and greenhouse plants and the major part of the tree paeony collection were sold; the large conservatory was converted into a vinery; many duplicate fruit trees, and many unimportant varieties of fruits, were disposed of and the ground put to better use. And in February 1859 it was 'ordered that an extensive series of experiments be instituted on the comparative value of the various esculents now advertised by the Trade, and that the Fruit and Vegetable Committee be requested to examine the results from time to time, inserting them in their reports for the information of the public'. Systematic trials as then visualized still continue to play an important role—some would argue the most important role—in the work of the Society's Garden.

All this on fifteen pounds a week? Optimistic though the Council may have been, the future of its Garden was really very much in jeopardy.

CHAPTER ELEVEN

ALL IS IN JEOPARDY

In 1840, BENTHAM, WHO WAS THEN COMPLETING HIS ELEVENTH year as Secretary, was also contemplating relinquishing his office and, probably at his suggestion, a committee, consisting of himself, Dr. Henderson (a Vice-President), and Lindley, was appointed to draw up a report on the progress of the Society since 1 May 1830. The report, an account of Bentham's stewardship, was submitted to the Anniversary Meeting in 1840, and published in the *Transactions*.[1] It was an encouraging one. At the beginning of 1830 the affairs of the Society had fallen into a state of irregularity and confusion; in view of the large debt, it had been necessary in the first instance to restore the Society's credit and every subject of expenditure not of the most urgent necessity was unsparingly cut off. As a result, the Fellows could now congratulate themselves on the fact that a reduction of the debt from £20,293 to £12,904 had been effected. Many plants raised from seed collected by David Douglas in 1831 and 1832 had been propagated and distributed. In 1836 Theodore Hartweg had been sent out to Mexico, and since his arrival there the Society had received numerous consignments which had enriched its Garden and made it possible to distribute hundreds of plants and thousands of packets of seeds. The number of foreign and Foreign Corresponding Members had been increased to a total of 237, and the lists were believed to include 'nearly every name of distinction in Horticulture in every part of the Globe'. The exchanges with these gentlemen had resulted in the receipt of much useful information and numerous plants new to Great Britain. In the Garden the collection of fruits and ornamental plants had been greatly increased, as had the area of the glass.

Bentham was able to look back over the years of his secretaryship with considerable satisfaction, for the Society's prestige had been restored. It was now well organized and free from warring factions, though not without well-meaning critics; and, although still carrying a considerable interest-bearing debt, it was not likely to be financially embarrassed so long as it continued to ensure that expenditure was kept

[1] 2nd Series, 2 (1842), pp. 373–458.

within its income. At the Anniversary Meeting on 1 May 1841, Bentham retired and was succeeded by Dr. Alexander Henderson, a medical man who first joined the Council as early as 1823, and who held the post of Secretary until the Anniversary Meeting in 1845, when he in turn was succeeded by James Robert Gowen, an amateur gardener of independent means interested in rhododendrons and orchids.

As befitted 'the greatest encourager of gardening in England' and the successor as President to Knight, the experimentalist, the Duke of Devonshire was anxious that experimental work be undertaken at the Garden, and in 1841 suggested that the Society should appoint a competent person 'to conduct some experiments in Horticultural Chemistry, more especially for the purpose of investigating the exact nature of the influence produced upon garden plants by soil, and by the substances employed as manures'. Moreover, he offered to contribute fifty pounds per annum for three or four years towards the cost of such experiments. The Society accepted the offer, appointed a 'Chemical Committee' to give effect to the proposal, and in 1842 Mr. Edward Solly, F.R.S., became the committee's officer. He was the brother-in-law of John Forbes Royle, who was to be the Society's Secretary from 1851 to 1858, and his duties included the giving of five or six lectures on 'Chemistry applied to the arts of cultivation'. The reports of the experimental work carried out under the auspices of the committee were embodied in articles entitled 'Experiments on the inorganic constituents of plants', 'On the exhaustion of soils' and 'On seed steeping', published in the *Transactions*. The committee continued in being until 1846, when it was dissolved, but the Council, desirous of preserving the Society's connection with Mr. Solly, appointed him Honorary Professor of Chemistry to the Society.

Although by 1840 the Society's debt had been considerably reduced, it was still very necessary for the Treasurer to maintain a watchful eye on financial matters, with the object not only of reducing the debt still further but also of increasing income. His task, and that of the committee appointed to assist him in these matters, was by no means easy; sometimes the bank account was overdrawn; sometimes bills had to be dealt with by means of a temporary loan from the bank or ordered to be 'paid as funds will permit'. Moreover, considerable expense was being incurred at the Garden by the completion of the Conservatory, the improvement of the rest of the glass, and by the acquisition of new tents and staging for the Exhibitions. There was expense also at Regent Street, where a new roof for the Meeting Room was necessary. As these items amounted to almost £5,000, the reduction of the debt was by no means as rapid as had been anticipated and at the Anniversary Meeting in May it stood at over £9,500.

One of the Society's extravagances had always been the production of its luxurious *Transactions* with their excellent quality of paper, generous margins and size of type, and fine colour plates. By 1830, when the first seven volumes had been produced, the cost had risen to £25,250. Small wonder that there had been a gap of five years, from 1830 to 1835, between the end of the first and the beginning of the second series. Obviously in 1845 their production was consuming far too disproportionate a share of the Society's slender finances. In any case they were not now fulfilling to the same extent their splendid function of earlier days when there was no horticultural press. Even though the monthly *Gardener's Magazine*, edited by Loudon, which had been vigorously informing the public of horticultural matters throughout Britain, including those of the Society, since 1826, had ceased publication in 1843, the weekly *Gardener's Chronicle* had been functioning since 1841 and was a much more suitable vehicle for articles on cultural experiences written by, and of particular interest to, professional gardeners, than were the *Transactions*.

Thus it was that in 1845 Council decided to discontinue the publication of the *Transactions* after the completion of the third volume of the second series. The Society's official publication from 1 January 1846 would be the *Journal*.

It is not inappropriate at this point to discuss briefly the association of Lindley and the *Gardener's Chronicle* with the Society, or Lindley and the Society with the *Chronicle*, for from this time the paper figures largely in the Society's history; certainly the history of the Society figures regularly in its pages. From the *Chronicle*'s inception, Lindley, its horticultural editor, strove to make the paper 'a weekly record of everything that bears upon Horticulture or Garden Botany, and to introduce such Natural History as has a relation to Gardening, together with Notices and Criticisms of every work of importance on the subject which may appear'.[1] In his prospectus to the first number, on 2 January 1841, Lindley continued:

Gardening is in many respects the art of creating an Artificial Climate, similar to that in which plants are naturally found: evidence, however, regarding the real nature of climate, as concerns vegetation, is greatly wanting. Physiological inquiries, and all those interesting topics which elucidate the harmony of nature, and the dependence of the various parts of the creation each on the other, will also form a subject of discussion. Another peculiar feature will be the introduction of information relating to Foresting, or Arboriculture. This is one of the most important horticultural subjects to which the attention of the public can be directed; for it is often little understood by those who have occasion to practise it, although the amount of property affected by the management of timber stands second only to that of land. The natural laws

[1] *Gdnr's Chron.* (1841), p. 1.

which govern the production of timber and regulate its growth, the value of it, the extent to which it is influenced by soil, and consequently to what circumstances are to be ascribed the great inferiority in quality of the same species grown in different places, are all points to which attention will be given. We shall endeavour to collect information upon that very important but much neglected subject, the diseases of trees, and the cause of their decay, whether natural or accidental, as well as to convey the earliest notices of the introduction of new species, which promise to increase either the beauty or value of woodland property. When to plant, to prune, and to fell, will be stated weekly in the Calendar, together with the weekly garden operations. . . . To the Florist our Miscellany will have much interest, not only because everything relating to those rare and beautiful productions which are his particular care will be constantly treated of in such a manner as to make him thoroughly acquainted with the merits or demerits of new varieties, and with their best modes of cultivation, but also because we shall take care that such opinions as may be given are the results of an honest examination by competent judges unbiased by personal interest.

The paper's aims in large measure were the Society's aims; the paper's horticultural editor was the Society's Vice-Secretary; both editor and Vice-Secretary were to prove staunch allies of the Society during the difficult years which lay ahead. And to implement the *Chronicle*'s objectives, Lindley provided himself with a remarkable team of collaborators and correspondents, including the Professors of Botany at Oxford, Cambridge, Glasgow, Edinburgh, and King's College, London, curators of botanic gardens, many of the finest private gardeners of the day, as well as some of those who were intimately connected with the affairs of the Society, including the Secretary, George Bentham.

Mr. Gowen's first year of office was not very encouraging. The summer of 1845 was very wet and consequently the receipts from the Exhibitions in the Garden declined, while the expenses were considerably heavier. Moreover, the cost of expeditions—Fortune's to China, and Hartweg's to South America—had already amounted to about £900. As a result, by the following year, at the Anniversary Meeting, the debt had increased by nearly £450 to a little over £10,000. The report presented at that Meeting stated that 'the number of Fellows elected continues to be smaller than that of those who die or for various reasons quit the Society; the number of Fellows at the present time being 1,233, which is 19 fewer than at the Anniversary in 1845'.

By the time of the Anniversary Meeting in 1847 there had been a little improvement and the debt had been reduced by nearly £600 to under £9,500. The Exhibitions in the Garden had been more successful. Prince Albert had been an early visitor to the one held on 9 May 1846, and the total number of visitors for the three events had reached the record figure of 24,362.

And in this same year the Regent Street office staff had to be re-organized. Presumably there had been some poor time-keeping, for the Council 'Resolved that a book be procured and the officers of the Society be required to enter in such book their hours of arrival and departure.' In view of his long service, James Scott, the Librarian, resented this new rule and, possibly believing that the Council would retract, tendered his resignation. But Council was adamant and the resignation was accepted. Joseph Davis, the accountant clerk, who had been in the Society's service for twenty-six years, also objected, but upon reflection agreed to comply.

Thus it was that the Secretary and Vice-Secretary were asked to prepare, with the assistance of the auditors, recommendations on the future staffing of the office and to define the duties of each officer. The report, which was adopted, provided for a staff of Vice-Secretary, librarian sub-accountant, professional accountant, office-keeper, outdoor porter, and collector of money.

Dr. Lindley, the Vice-Secretary, whose salary was to continue to be £450 per annum with a yearly travelling allowance of fifty pounds, was usually to spend Mondays at the Garden, but on other week-days to be at Regent Street during the ordinary office hours from 10.45 a.m. to 4.15 p.m. His duties were to conduct all special correspondence, edit the *Journal*, take charge of the Garden and the Exhibitions there, prepare the business for all councils and committees, attend all public meetings of the Society, receive visitors, and be responsible for the orders of the Council being executed by the persons under him. Quite obviously there were to be precious few Society matters on which Lindley was not to have information and considerable authority.

The librarian sub-accountant's chief duties, apart from the care of the books, were to receive all money paid in at the office, to keep the accounts under the orders of the professional accountant, to conduct routine correspondence, and to deal with inquiries in Lindley's absence.

The professional accountant was to be a part-time official, attending only as often as might be necessary to supervise the keeping of the accounts and preparing a quarterly balance sheet for the auditors; he was to provide a confidential clerk to check the accounts and to leave with the Vice-Secretary a balance sheet on the last Tuesday in every month.

The resident office-keeper, among other things, was to act as an extra clerk when called upon to do so, and the collector of money 'to apply personally to all Members of the Society in arrear of their subscriptions, who may be in London or the vicinity', and to pay over those subscriptions to the Treasurer or the sub-accountant whenever they amounted to more than twenty pounds.

It was believed that not only would the reorganization be more efficient than the previous practice, but that it would also save £120 per annum. And in this belief, in February 1848, William Brailsford was appointed librarian and sub-accountant at a salary of £120 per annum.

Under the Bye-Laws a Fellow was legally liable for any subscription due at the date of his resignation or death. When a Fellow who tendered his resignation refused to pay his arrears, unless there were exceptional circumstances, steps were taken to recover the sum through the courts. But many who lost interest in the Society did not tender their resignations, but merely allowed their subscriptions to lapse, and when a Fellow died his executors often failed to meet his liability to the Society. In yet other cases the Fellows became bankrupt and unable to pay. The Society was loath to relinquish its claim to arrears which were legally due to it, and after some years the books carried a large sum in arrears of subscriptions which, apart from mistakes due to carelessness or misunderstandings, was a very doubtful asset. In March 1848 the Finance Committee, having gone systematically into 315 cases, came to the conclusion that in 209 of these, involving £1,493. 12s. 0d., the entries should be expunged, as the Society had no legal claim or only such as it did not appear advisable to proceed upon. In sixty-two other cases, involving £2,491. 17s. 0d., the Society appeared to have a claim, but no present means of securing payment because of insolvency or no known address; it was decided that these cases should be listed separately for record purposes, but not as representing available resources. A third group consisted of forty-four Fellows who were clearly indebted to the Society, and from whom letters applying for payment had already yielded £710. 13s. 6d.

The Exhibitions in the Garden, on the financial success of which the welfare of the Garden so much depended, were a great disappointment in 1848. Not only were expenses heavier, but because of inclement weather the receipts were less; the result was a net income of only £1,322. 15s. 2d. as compared with £1,733. 3s. 5d. in 1847. Lindley was therefore asked to consider the subject of Exhibitions generally with a view to rendering them more attractive and less expensive. His report could only recommend savings amounting to about £350, to be effected chiefly by reducing the number of competitive classes, which, he said, 'will probably be attended by some diminution of the quantity of plants produced, but that would be an advantage rather than the contrary, for the mass of plants has now become almost unmanageable in May and June'. Notwithstanding a late spring, under Lindley's revised schedule the Garden Exhibitions yielded a larger net income than those of the preceding year.

Presumably because the small Shows held in Regent Street conflicted in May, June, and July with the Exhibitions held in the Garden, in 1849 the former were discontinued and at those Meetings six lectures by Dr. Lindley were substituted, lectures wherein he discussed the structure and functions of roots, stems, leaves, and flowers, as well as plant diseases.

In the history of gardening interest in plants has always fluctuated, and the Chiswick Exhibitions were certainly reflecting the changing interests of the 1850s. Probably the most remarkable of these was the loss of interest in heaths. Of the July Exhibition of 1849 the *Gardener's Chronicle* wrote:

. . . indifference is manifested yearly towards Heaths. They are in themselves among the most beautiful objects in the greenhouse; great success in growing them shows great horticultural skill; and the detached branches, or solitary bushes amidst other plants excite everybody's admiration. Nevertheless the Heath tents are generally almost empty. This we take to be caused by the monotony of the forms of Heaths and the entire absence of a graceful mode of growth. Groups of them have no picturesque effect. The flowers indeed display all tints of red and yellow and white; the foliage is of the purest green; the blossoms are of greatly varied shape; and yet the plants have an un-inviting sameness. The flowers are all tubes, the leaves are all narrow and the general form of the bushes is so round that a person ignorant of their nature might imagine them to be relics of the clipped hedges of our ancestors. In fact a row of finely-grown Hottentot Heaths is like a line of Hottentot Kraals. This is fatal to masses of such plants exciting pleasurable emotions in a crowd of lookers on.

It is because they are so entirely the reverse of this that the Orchids fascinate everybody. Where they are, and where Roses are, the crowd is greatest; it is thither that the earliest visitors invariably resort, and there linger. You never find the tent of Orchids deserted. Men say that it is because of their singular forms, and their aromatic fragrance; but we believe that the explanation is chiefly to be found in their graceful outlines and infinitely varied aspects. It is as difficult to give sameness to a bank of highly cultivated Orchids as it is to throw variety into a line of Cape Heaths.[1]

Neither the writer of this leader, nor anyone else at that time, could have foreseen that a century later exhibits of orchids would still command wide interest, though not wide culture, and that heaths of another kind would be in universal demand.

At the Anniversary Meeting in 1850 J. R. Gowen resigned the secretaryship to become Treasurer, and was succeeded by Dr. Daniel. However, the latter did not find favour with the Fellows, and at the Anniversary Meeting in 1851 they took the unprecedented course of rejecting two of Council's nominations. Lord Ashburton was re-elected to the Council in the place of Dr. Daniel, and, by twenty-two votes to eight, Dr. J. F. Royle to the post of Secretary.

[1] *Gdnr's Chron.* (1849), p. 435.

Royle (1799–1858), surgeon and naturalist, after an education in Edinburgh had gone to India in 1819 on the medical staff of the Bengal Army. In 1823 he had been appointed Superintendent of the garden at Saharanpur and had quickly wrought great reforms in its administration. He had employed collectors and gradually built up a valuable collection of economic plants, and become an authority on drug plants. In 1831 he had returned to England, with his collections, and between 1833 and 1840 had published his *Illustrations of the Botany and other Branches of the Natural History of the Himalayan Mountains*, a two-volume work which was a model of research into a branch of natural history then little pursued. In it he recommended the introduction of *Cinchona* plants into India, a recommendation which the Governor-General of India approved in 1852. He had also been the first to bring to the attention of the Indian Government the suitability of certain parts of the Himalayas for the cultivation of the Chinese Tea plant. In 1837 he had been elected Professor of Materia Medica at King's College, London.

Royle's appointment to the post of Secretary was a remarkable one. In the first place, Royle did not know that his name had been put forward for the post, for no one had approached him on the matter; he was simply told that he had been elected. And in the second place he certainly did not know that Lindley had been a candidate for the post.

Why Lindley was passed over it is difficult to understand. Since his appointment as Garden Assistant Secretary at Chiswick in 1822 he had served the Society with loyalty and devotion; he was more familiar with the affairs of the Society than anyone; and as Vice-Secretary he had undertaken a major share of the secretarial duties in Bentham's period of office. He was Professor of Botany at University College, London, and *Praefectus horti* at the Chelsea Physic Garden. He was a renowned scientist. He was horticultural editor of the *Gardener's Chronicle*. He was most certainly an excellent administrator, otherwise he could not have successfully undertaken, simultaneously, the work which his various appointments entailed. Surely no one was better equipped for the post of Secretary than he? But obviously there were influences in the Society who did not support him. He was a masterful outspoken man who had been involved in controversial matters and he had clearly offended some Council members, for, once convinced of the rectitude of his purpose, it mattered not who or what opposed him.

Throughout the Society's history the Council has been repeatedly obliged to check a recurring tendency on the part of judges to lower the standard of awards for exhibits by the too free bestowal of medals. In the ten years ending in 1852 the intrinsic value of the medals awarded at the Exhibitions in the Garden had increased by about seventy per cent and, if only on the ground of economy, the Council felt it necessary to put a stop to the continued increase in expense. It decided therefore that fewer high-grade medals should be offered for all classes of plants, except stove and greenhouse plants of which the transport of large specimens involved exhibitors in considerable expense. The Council was also of the opinion that, as the early difficulties attending the cultivation of orchids had been largely overcome, and as they were now extremely popular plants, they no longer demanded the encouragement they had formerly received.

Mrs. Lawrence, who for many years had been a prominent exhibitor of, among other things, orchids, did not agree. She joined forces with Charles Henry Bellenden Ker, another critic of long standing, and in a letter of protest threatened to cease exhibiting. An acrimonious correspondence with Lindley ended in 1854 with a letter announcing her intention of selling her orchids and of taking no further part in Exhibitions at the Garden. In point of fact she did not intend to sell all her orchids; a note in the *Gardener's Chronicle* revealed that she still intended to grow a few extremely choice ones, as well as similar stove, greenhouse, and variegated plants. But she was in failing health and had decided greatly to reduce her collection, so that, instead of occupying twenty-three greenhouses, it would now occupy but thirteen. Even this was not to be, for in August of the following year she died and the entire collection was disposed of.

The year 1854, the Society's jubilee, was far from being one of jubilation. At the Anniversary Meeting on 1 May the Council had to report that the debt had increased. Although the Garden Exhibitions had been good from a horticultural point of view, owing to a variety of causes, including the counter-attractions of Kew and the reconstructed Crystal Palace at Sydenham, attendances had declined, and in July 1854 it was estimated that, instead of being a source of revenue as they used to be, the three Exhibitions held that year had resulted in a deficit of £1,311; at the end of the year the Society's debt would be increased by about £1,720. In view of the seriousness of the situation, Lindley was asked to consider how the expenditure could be reduced and to report to the Council at a meeting specially summoned for 1 August.

The largest single saving which Lindley could suggest would be made by the abolition of his office of Vice-Secretary, with its salary of £500 per annum. He said that he hoped that the Council would consider that proposal 'without reference to my own position, or to the long period of more than 32 years during which I have rooted myself in the service of the Society'. Such a statement could hardly make it an easy matter for Council to accept his proposition, and indeed 'having considered the very generous and disinterested proposal of Dr. Lindley' the Council felt 'that it would not be consistent with the best interests of the Society to accept his unremunerated services'. Instead, it was decided to abolish the office of librarian, to discontinue the *Journal*, to ask the Duke of Devonshire to reduce the rent of the Garden, to make application to the Government for apartments in the new building to be constructed on the site of Burlington House (with a view to vacating the Society's Regent Street premises), and to reduce the cost of labour in the Garden.

The Duke of Devonshire readily agreed to reduce the rent of the Garden from £300 to £200, but the application for offices in Burlington House was not successful.

At the Anniversary Meeting in 1855 J. R. Gowen resigned the treasurership, which he had held since he ceased to be Secretary in 1850, and was succeeded by Dr. A. R. Jackson, who died in the following July, and was in turn succeeded by W. Wilson Saunders (1809–79), an enthusiastic naturalist who had spent a brief period in India, was now in business as an underwriter at Lloyds, and was living at Wandsworth. His real name was William Saunders, but as there were other people of this name in Wandsworth he thought it desirable to add Wilson to his after seeking the permission of his old friend Mr. Wilson, the father of Mr. George Ferguson Wilson, who enters into our history later.

Wilson Saunders came to the post of Treasurer at a most desperate time, for the Society was now in severe financial straits, and neither the bank nor either of the two insurance companies to whom the bank suggested the Council should apply were prepared to advance a large sum on such security as the Society could offer. In October it was decided to sell by auction the stove plants and the Herbarium at the Garden, the stock of the *Transactions* and of the *Journal*, and all books in the Library which were regarded as of no importance to the Society. Accordingly in November 1855 a sale of orchids, tree ferns, palms, and other greenhouse plants was held. Among them were the plant of *Phalaenopsis amabilis* which Fortune had sent home from the Philippines and which was considered the finest specimen of its kind ever seen; a plant of *Dendrobium speciosum*, 4½ feet in diameter, with 124 pseudo-bulbs; and a specimen of *Laelia superbiens* (now known as *Schomburgkia superbiens*), 17 feet in circumference, with 220 pseudo-bulbs, still attached to the wood on which it had been found in Guatemala, and probably the finest specimen of a living orchid in Europe at the time. These three specimens fetched £68. 5s., £10, and £36. 15s. respectively, and the whole sale realized only £569. In January 1856 the collections of dried plants formed from specimens sent home by the Society's own collectors and correspondents from various parts of the world realized £225. The old stock of the *Transactions* was sold for £250.

A little over £1,000 could do little more than meet the Society's more pressing needs. Nothing now could conceal the hard facts that the

Society had a large and rapidly growing debt. Expenditure was about £4,662, while income was only about £2,710, of which the Garden at present absorbed about £2,600, leaving practically nothing to meet the unavoidable expenses of the London establishment, which included interest on debt, rent, rates, taxes, salaries, wages, cost of publications and meetings, etc., amounting in all to about £2,000.

After long and anxious consideration the Council came to the conclusion that the Garden Exhibitions would not be profitable in future; the counter-attractions of Kew and the distance from the metropolis would deter visitors from repairing to the Chiswick Garden as formerly. In these circumstances the Council felt that there was 'no alternative but to reduce the latter establishment within very narrow limits, if not relinquish it altogether', and they embodied their solution of the problem, somewhat optimistically, in a printed circular letter, dated 24 December 1855, which was sent to all Fellows:

. . . now that the Garden Exhibitions have ceased to furnish funds for the maintenance of the present Garden establishment, . . . the Council have arrived at the conclusion, that although the means of the Society no longer permit it to maintain a large and costly Garden, yet by some alteration in the existing arrangements, and by giving the action of the Society a new direction, it may be found possible to carry out the objects of the charter with unimpaired utility. This they propose to effect by the adoption of a system of exhibition, instruction, distribution, scientific investigation and publication embodied, in the following proposals.

There followed seventeen proposals, of which the following were the most important: that in place of the Garden Exhibitions, London Exhibitions be held yearly in spring and autumn in some spacious place hired for the purpose; that monthly Meetings be held as heretofore in Regent Street for the dispatch of business, reading papers, the exhibition of horticultural produce, and illustrated lectures followed by discussions; that seeds be distributed as usual; that by means of a collector or otherwise, seeds and roots be obtained from foreign countries for distribution; that only a very small Garden be maintained, and that it be for the purpose of raising such seeds as may not arrive in sufficient quantity for distribution, for restoring the health of imported plants and for experimental purposes; that a regular system of inquiry into subjects of horticultural importance be established by means of special committees; that the *Journal* become a monthly publication, not sold, but printed solely for the use of Fellows and sent to them regularly by post; that the existing rate of subscription for Fellows (viz. an admission fee of five guineas and an annual subscription of four guineas, paid retrospectively) be retained, but that a new class of *subscribers* be established, paying not an admission fee but an annual subscription of two guineas paid in advance and having free admission to Meetings and Exhibitions, but not voting nor receiving the *Journal* and not participating in the distribution of seeds or plants.

The proposals were discussed at a Special General Meeting in February 1856, at which sixty-eight Fellows were present, and at the Council's request the Marquis of Salisbury, although not a member of Council, presided. Lindley read a lengthy statement during which he described the Garden, not for the first time, in very sympathetic terms.

The Garden has been the great scene of the labours of the Society; it was there and through it that the utility of the Society had been demonstrated to the whole world; it was the field in which it had gained a reputation that was acknowledged wherever the name of horticulture was known; and moreover it was the place upon which what may be almost called the affection of a large body of its Fellows had been fixed. That such a place should be relinquished was a conclusion to which nothing but the most imperious necessity could have conducted the Council; but the necessity seems to exist, and it is in part for the purpose of obtaining the authority of the Society to make so great a sacrifice, or of hearing what other course the Fellows may have to propose, that this Meeting is convened.

After considering Lindley's statement, Lord Grey proposed 'That the Council be authorized to terminate the tenancy of the Garden at Chiswick as soon as the lease will permit and that the property therein be sold.' However, this resolution was not adopted; instead, on a proposal from Mr. S. H. Godson, one of the Society's oldest Fellows and a trenchant critic of its financial proceedings, a committee of nine Fellows, of which he became chairman, was appointed 'to investigate the whole of the accounts and consider what is best to be done as to the continuance of this Society; such Committee to report to an adjourned Special General Meeting of the Society on the 11th of March'.

Lord Salisbury presided at the adjourned Meeting, at which sixty-six Fellows were present, and Mr. Godson read the report of his committee. It appeared that they were opposed to the giving up of the Garden as 'a horticultural society without a garden would be like a crew of sailors without a ship'. As to the proposal that a part of the Garden should be retained, that was impossible, as 'The Duke of Devonshire has signified . . . through his agent that the Society must have all or none.' In order to reduce the cost of the Garden the committee recommended that the ornamental and fruit departments be placed under one Superintendent who should replace the two old and faithful head gardeners, George Gordon and Robert Thompson, who had done so much to make Chiswick famous. The committee noted that a further saving of £500 might be effected by accepting Lindley's generous offer to give up his salary. They suggested that the monthly Meetings in Regent Street should be continued; that two Garden Exhibitions should be held each year; and that an appeal should be made to Fellows for contributions to a fund to repay the £2,400 of the loan on which interest was being paid at six per cent. Altogether the Committee seems to have been far more optimistic than the circumstances warranted: 'We venture to exhort the Fellows not to be faint-hearted, but to trust to such a reinforcement of their numbers, by increasing the popularity and celebrity of the Society, as may carry it through all its difficulties to triumph.' The Fellows were a little sceptical, but by twenty-four votes to eleven they recommended the report to the Council's considerations.

The Council was by no means convinced by Godson's report. Though they agreed that the Garden should, if possible, be preserved, they expressed the view that in spite of the proposed reorganization the heavy expenditure would continue. In the past they had not thought it proper to accept Lindley's offer to forgo his salary, and did not think it would be in the best interest of the Society to do so now, especially as the proposed changes would augment rather than diminish his burden. Moreover, they believed that the holding of the proposed two Exhibitions in the Garden probably would result in an additional loss. However, they would be willing to do their utmost to carry out the committee's recommendations, provided that the Fellows came forward with the necessary funds.

After discussion, on a motion from Lord Grey, it was resolved unanimously 'That the Council be authorized to terminate the tenancy of the Garden at Chiswick as soon as the lease will permit, and that the property therein be sold, unless such a sum as the Council may require for maintaining the Garden shall have been subscribed before May 1.'

In the following week an appeal was sent to all Fellows and enclosed with a note to newspapers throughout the United Kingdom. The circular quoted Lord Grey's motion and expressed the hope that all persons interested in horticultural pursuits would respond, and that by donations amounting to at least £5,000, and the introduction of new Members, the Society's funds would be placed in a position which would enable it to carry out with renewed vigour the objects for which it was incorporated. A list of twenty-eight sums, totalling £585, already subscribed, was appended, headed by £100 each from the Dukes of Devonshire and Northumberland, and including twenty-five pounds from Sir Joseph Paxton and twenty guineas from Professor Lindley.

Some idea of the esteem in which the Society was held on the Continent may be judged from a letter from a non-Fellow:

To Professor Lindley.

Sir,—I have anxiously attended to all that has been published regarding the question of relinquishing the garden of the Horticultural Society. Being a foreigner and no Fellow of the Society, I am perfectly aware that I am as little entitled to meddle with English affairs as the poet in Shakespeare's Julius Caesar with the grudge of the generals, and that I may perhaps risk a similar treatment. Nevertheless, the lively interest I take in everything concerning Horticulture, and the thorough conviction that there is no institution in Europe, the discontinuance of which would be in a higher degree deplorable for all friends of gardening than the London Horticultural Society in its full and unabated efficiency, are too strong in me, not to give them way and make me bold to offer £100 on the same terms as will be fixed for other subscribers of funds to be collected for the conservation of the Chiswick Horticultural Gardens. Sir, I know very well that £100 is a trifling sum in England; but I am no man of large pecuniary means, and I think a good will does not fail to find a good place. Directions for payment will be given upon notice.

HEIN. BEHRENS

Travemunde, near Lubeck,
April 9, 1856.

As a mark of the Society's appreciation of Herr Behrens's generosity, he was elected an Honorary Fellow in 1857.

When the Society held its Anniversary Meeting on 1 May 1856 the requisite £5,000 had not been subscribed, but the position looked sufficiently favourable for the General Meeting to adopt the Council's recommendation that the list be kept open until midsummer day. On 24 June it was intimated that £3,267 had been promised by 200 of the 750 Fellows and by twenty-nine non-Fellows. Although the specified £5,000 had not been forthcoming, the Council 'felt bound to exhaust all other resources' before surrendering the lease of the Garden and suggested that the Regent Street house be sold and the Government persuaded to allot the Society rooms at Burlington House or elsewhere. It was also suggested that the number of Fellows might be more than doubled if the subscription were reduced from four to two guineas. The General Meeting authorized the Council 'to take such measures for the reorganization of the Society as they may consider advisable, even though those measures should involve the relinquishment of the Garden at Chiswick and the realization of the property, or any part of the property, therein'.

The Council immediately took steps to sell the Regent Street house. It was put up for auction in August 1856, but failed to reach the reserve figure of £4,500. At another auction in June 1857 it was again withdrawn because the reserve of £3,990 was not reached. This was the first disappointment, quickly to be followed by another.

A two-guinea form of fellowship was introduced, those subscribing at that rate being entitled to a share of the seeds and cuttings distributed at the Meetings in London, but not to plants distributed from the Garden. Fellows who continued to subscribe at the old rate of four guineas were entitled to participate in the distribution of plants, seeds, and cuttings, and also to have an ivory ticket entitling the person presenting it to have most of the privileges of a Fellow other than a vote or a share of plants or seeds. The introduction of the two-guinea rate of subscription led to an influx of new Fellows in 1857, but this did not continue.

The new year began disastrously, for on 2 January the Secretary, Dr. Royle, suddenly died. Lindley, who on two previous occasions at least had offered to resign his salaried post of Vice-Secretary in order to ease the Society's financial position, now repeated his offer. The Council expressed their appreciation of his 'disinterested and liberal conduct' and their hope that he would allow himself to be proposed as a Member of Council and Secretary to the Society. His great friend Sir William Hooker had been effectively canvassing on his behalf. As a result, at a Special General Meeting held on 2 March 1858, he was elected to the Council and to the office of Secretary, and at the Anniversary Meeting held on the following 1 May the appointment was unanimously confirmed, the Chairman, the Rev. L. Vernon Harcourt, declaring that the appointment would be better for Lindley in that it would relieve him from attending to a multitude of minute details that were essential to the working of the Society, and allow him to devote more of his time and talents to his scientific pursuits; and better, too, for the Society, which would now have him, and the benefit of his advice and long experience, as a member of its Council.

On 12 March William Beattie Booth, who whilst acting as Garden clerk at Chiswick had made a valuable contribution to the *Transactions* on camellias and was later librarian in Regent Street, was now appointed Assistant Secretary, and became responsible for much of the routine work hitherto done by Lindley. In April 1859 his salary as 'Assistant Secretary and Accountant' was fixed at £200 per annum 'for the present'.

In accordance with the real or fancied experience that troubles seldom come alone, on 18 January 1858, only a fortnight after Royle's decease, the Society suffered another loss in the death of the Duke of Devonshire, who had been its President for twenty years. It would appear that the only record of his having attended a Council Meeting referred to one held in the Garden adjoining the grounds of his residence, Chiswick House. However, although he did not take part in the management of the Society, it would seem that Fellows were happy to have him as a figurehead. Some, no doubt remembering his expensive trip to Russia, and the cost of his magnificent conservatory and of his great glass-house built especially for the cultivation of the Giant Victoria Water Lily, at Chatsworth, at the same time wondered why he himself did not solve the Society's financial problems, as he so easily could have done.

On 29 January 1858 the Council asked one of their number, Charles Wentworth Dilke,[1] to inquire privately whether His Royal Highness the Prince Consort or His Royal Highness the Prince of Wales would consent to be elected President. A fortnight later Dilke reported that he had seen the Prince Consort, who had said that he would allow himself to be nominated if approached formally. A deputation of five members of the Council headed by the Bishop of Winchester accordingly waited on the Prince, and, his consent having been obtained, on 2 March he was duly elected President of the Society. (Plate 4.)

The first Exhibition in 1858 was held on 21 and 22 April in St. James's Hall, then a new building in Piccadilly, and the Prince Consort presided at a General Meeting held on the first day. In June there was a two-day Exhibition in the Garden, and in November a two-day Fruit and Chrysanthemum Show at St. James's. In spite of the fact that two of these events were held in the heart of London, were freely advertised, and had royal patronage, instead of being a source of revenue they produced altogether a deficit of £455; not a very auspicious beginning for the new President.

As the position had not improved by the end of the year, the annual income from subscribers and from other sources being £2,602, and the annual expenditure £3,233 (£2,027 on the Garden and the rest on Regent Street, including interest on loan), and as loans and other liabilities amounted to £9,810, action of some kind clearly had to be taken.

Some members of Council despaired of the Society's survival, and in December 1858 Mr. James Veitch, the father of Sir Harry Veitch, who figures later in this story, gave notice of his intention 'to bring under consideration the propriety of winding up the affairs of the present Society, with a view to the formation of another Society with a Charter on an enlarged basis, better adapted to the present state of Horticulture'.

For the second time the Society was near dissolution.

In January 1859, having again reviewed the situation, the Council agreed:

(1) That the financial position of the Society is so unsatisfactory as to render it indispensable that every head of expenditure be immediately reduced to the lowest possible point consistent with the existence of the Society.

[1] Charles Wentworth Dilke (1810–69). Son of Charles Wentworth Dilke, who was sometime editor of the *Athenaeum*. A member of Council from 1857 onwards. One of the Commissioners for the Exhibition of 1851. Created a baronet in 1862. One of the founders of the *Gardener's Chronicle*.

(2) That the House in Regent Street be immediately sold for whatever it will produce.
(3) That the Library be sold.
(4) That an office for the transaction of business be hired in London in some convenient situation.

Thus, on 1 March 1859, the Society moved from the ideal premises in Lower Regent Street which had been its home for forty years into miserably cramped quarters, consisting of one room and a lobby, on the first floor over Messrs. Grindley's offices at 8 St. Martin's Place, Trafalgar Square, for which the annual rent was eighty pounds. The house in Regent Street was sold a few days later for £2,960, over £1,500 less than the reserve price placed on it in 1856. And perhaps saddest of all, the magnificent library, together with over 1,500 original drawings, was sold at Sotheby's for £1,112. The unequalled collection of drawings included many made for the Society by such famous artists as Hooker, Bauer, Curtis, and Mrs. Withers. There were also portfolios of drawings executed for the Society by Chinese artists or purchased in China for the Society by John Reeves. Fortunately some of these treasures were later to return to the Society's possession once again, but at prices very different from those for which they were sold in 1859.

During these dark days an event of far-reaching significance occurred. For many years it had been the practice for the Council to appoint committees for finance, the Garden, and Exhibitions, but none to deal with particular classes of plants. However, chiefly at the instigation of James Veitch, in May 1858, because it was thought desirable to interest as many Fellows as possible in the management of the Society's affairs without infringing the Charter, the Council appointed a Fruit Committee, to meet on the first Monday in every month. In the first instance it consisted of thirty-three members, with the Rev. L. Vernon Harcourt, a member of Council, as chairman, and Robert Thompson, the fruit specialist on the Garden staff, as secretary. A fortnight later the committee's province was extended, for they were asked 'to examine and report upon all new esculent vegetables'. In July 1858 it was decided

That the business of the Fruit Committee consists in examining and reporting upon all fruits or esculents brought under their notice, collecting information concerning the qualities of the Fruits grown in different parts of the United Kingdom, and advising the Council generally as to the best modes of increasing the Society's power of promoting the improvement of Fruits and Esculents cultivated in Great Britain and Ireland.

Thus began the first of the series of standing committees which now play such an important part in the Society's work. Of this particular committee, the *Gardener's Chronicle* wrote:

Of late years the gardening world has been overwhelmed with an incredible quantity of new Apples, Pears, Strawberries, Vines, Peaches, Nectarines and Plums, pouring in from Germany, Belgium, France, United States, and strongly reinforced by multitudes of home raised productions of the same kind. All these are of the greatest value in the eyes of the producers, who assure the public, each for himself, that his new seedlings possess the most wonderful qualities. Among them many sorts of very great value are certainly to be found, and it is of the first importance that their qualities should be made known upon evidence that no one can dispute; but there are others in favour of which nothing can be honestly said, and against which buyers should be guarded. Some are new and not good; some are good and not new; some are neither new nor good. It is only by the joint action of good judges having no personal interest in any decision that may be arrived at that in this case a separation of the sound grain from the chaff and tail corn can be effected in a manner deserving the confidence of the public. This was one of the plans of the Council in 1855, and we rejoice to see the present Council making preparations to carry it out with vigour.[1]

An important part of the Society's present work is to endeavour to guide Fellows and the public in their choice of the best species and varieties of plants, flowers, fruits, and vegetables to grow. This is done by the Council making awards to those plants which, in the opinion of committees of specialists, are the most meritorious and deserving of extended cultivation. It is therefore curious that this policy is very different from that adopted during the first fifty years of the Society's life, when an announcement, headed 'Advertisement', was given prominence in the *Transactions* published between 1805 and 1838: 'It is likewise necessary, on this occasion, to remark, that it is an established rule of this Society, to which they will always adhere, never to give their opinion, as a body, upon any subject either of Nature or Art, that comes before them.'

The statement 'to which they will always adhere' is an example of the unwisdom of attempting to say what one's successors shall or will do, for from 1858 onwards the Society, acting through its Council, has systematically made awards to all different kinds of plants. At first two awards were available for meritorious new plants, viz. the 'First Class Certificate of Merit' (F.C.C.) and 'Commended' (C.). Later, an intermediate award, the 'Second Class Certificate' (S.C.C.) was introduced, but it failed to serve the intended purpose, because, as it appeared to disparage rather than praise, it was seldom awarded. So in 1888 the S.C.C. was discontinued and its place taken by the 'Award of Merit' (A.M.).

[1] *Gdnr's Chron.* (1858), p. 171.

Interlude
to Parts Three and Four

EVEN THOUGH PAXTON'S 'COLOSSAL NEW CONSERVATORY' AT CHATS-worth—with the Palm Stove at Edinburgh—ushered in an era of great conservatories, it was really of less significance than another of his Chatsworth glass-houses—his 'Victoria Regia House' which was built principally to accommodate one plant. Seeds of the Giant Victoria Water Lily had been introduced to Kew in 1846; the seeds had germinated, but, as with the *Amherstia* at Chatsworth, the plants refused to flower. Early in August 1849, Sir William Hooker presented one of his plants to Chatsworth, where Paxton planted it on five loads of earth in the centre of a water tank specially designed for the purpose. The tank was 12 feet square and a little over 3 feet deep, the water was heated, and was maintained in gentle motion by a little water-wheel in one corner. Victoria began to grow; by the middle of September the leaves were $3\frac{1}{2}$ feet across and close on 11 feet in circumference—and the tank had to be doubled; by 15 October the leaves had increased in diameter by another foot; and on 9 November Paxton wrote to Hooker, 'Victoria is now in full flower. . . . The sight is worth a journey of a thousand miles.' By September of the following year the famous plant had produced 140 leaves and 112 flower buds; it had also produced seeds and many young plants had been raised. But it had twice outgrown its tank and Paxton had to devise a house more fitted for so magnificent a subject. And at a cost of £800 he produced a quite novel building, 61 feet by 49 feet, enclosing a circular tank 33 feet in diameter.

Built entirely of glass and iron, with the roof on the ridge-and-furrow principle, the Victoria House incorporated several new and special features. Perfect drainage and ventilation were required; thus the roof must not only be a roof but a light and heat adjuster as well; the iron supporting columns must also act as drainpipes and rafters and sash bars must serve the same purpose; the floor must serve as a ventilator and as a dust trap.

While he was building his Victoria House, Paxton learned that the Royal Commission which had been appointed to consider designs for the building which was to be erected in Hyde Park to house the Great

Exhibition of 1851 had rejected all the designs, nearly 250 in all, which had been submitted. He at once decided to submit designs of his own based on the same principles as his Victoria House, and in this lies the real significance of his Chatsworth building.

His first rough sketch was made on a sheet of blotting-paper as he sat at a board meeting of the Midland Railway Company at Derby. In ten days' time more detailed plans were laid before the Commissioners and three weeks later his plans were accepted, the village bells at Chatsworth ringing most merrily all the day of 15 July. Paxton told how both the Victoria House and the plant itself had influenced his plans. In describing his design to the Fine Arts Society on 13 November 1850, he used one of the great leaves, 5 feet in diameter, of the Victoria. He pointed out that the lower surface with its main ribs like cantilevers radiating from the centre, with large bottom flanges, and very thin middle ribs with cross girders between each pair to keep them from buckling, was a beautiful example of natural engineering. 'Nature was the engineer,' said Paxton; 'Nature has provided the leaf with longitudinal and transverse girders and supports that I, borrowing from it, have adopted in this building.' This is how he described the building:

The building will be 2,100 ft. long by 400 ft. broad. The centre aisle will be 120 ft. broad, or 10 ft. wider than the conservatory at Chatsworth. The glass and its iron supports comprise the whole structure. The columns are precisely the same throughout the building and will fit every part; the same may be said of each of the bars; and every piece of glass will be of the same size, namely 4 ft. No numbering or marking will be required, and the whole will be put together like a perfect piece of machinery. The water is brought down valleys on the roof, and thence down the columns; the water in no instance has further than 12 ft. to run, before it is delivered into the valleys or gutters; and the whole is so constructed so as to carry the water outside, and the condensed water inside. The building is divided into broad and narrow compartments, and by tying these together there is little for the cross-ties of the centre to carry. The building is entirely divided into 24 places—in short everything runs to 24, so that the work is made to square and fit, without any small detail being left to carry out. The number of columns 15 ft. long is 6,024; there are 3,000 gallery bearers; 1,245 wrought iron girders; 45 miles of sash bars; and 1,073,760 ft. of glass to cover the whole. The site will occupy upwards of 20 acres of ground, but the available space which may be afforded by galleries can be extended to about 30 acres, if necessary.[1]

Such was the building which was to receive the products of industry of all nations in 1851 and which was, in fact, officially opened by the Queen on 1 May 1851, less than eleven months after the plans had been accepted.

[1] *Gdnr's Chron.* (1850), p. 548.

The erection of the new Palm House at Kew was but one token of the tremendous developments which had been taking place there since the Horticultural Society had come to its aid and since Sir William Hooker had become the first Director officially appointed by Government, in 1841. Then the Garden was about fifteen acres in extent. In less than five years it had increased to over 250 acres, and William Andrews Nesfield, who was later to advise on the Society's Kensington Garden, was planning the layout of the great Arboretum and many of the avenues and vistas so characteristic of Kew today. The Decimus Burton Palm House, begun in 1844 and completed in 1848, cost about £30,000. It is 363 feet long, 100 feet wide at the centre, and 62 feet at its greatest height to the lantern. In 1848 the first Museum of Economic Botany was opened and in 1853 the Herbarium and Library were founded. By 1861 the lake was completed and the material resulting from the excavation was used to build the terrace on which was constructed another Decimus Burton house, the Temperate House, in 1862.[1]

Kew's most important contribution to horticulture during this period resulted from the travels to India of Sir William's son, Joseph Hooker, from 1848 to 1851. During this period he discovered forty-three rhododendrons in the Sikkim Himalaya, the vast majority of them being far more beautiful in leaf and in flower than any previously known. Of most of them seeds reached Kew in a viable state; seeds were distributed from Kew, and at Kew and in several establishments throughout the country, the new Sikkim rhododendrons were raised, and when once they began to flower they were hybridized. None was more successful in this than Messrs. Standish & Noble of the Sunningdale Nurseries; they induced some of the new introductions to flower long before they could normally have been expected to, by grafting on to old standard rhododendrons. This was certainly the case with *Rhododendron thomsonii*, which, grafted in this way, flowered for the first time at Sunningdale in 1857 and by 1861 had produced the wonderful hybrid 'Ascot Brilliant'. In 1855 Standish & Noble were able to write in the *Gardener's Chronicle*:

In the Sikkim Rhododendrons we have the material for giving new features to succeeding crosses. In fact we now possess a large number of plants, the result of hybridising between our best hardy hybrids and *edgeworthii, dalhousiae, ciliatum, glaucum* etc., amongst which we believe there will be found some very remarkable kinds. Then from *fulgens* and *thomsonii* we shall obtain brilliancy of colour, rivalling even *arboreum* itself; while *wightii* will contribute a yellow tint, and *hodgsonii* the beautiful form of its individual flowers, as well as that of its fine compact truss.

In 1858 this nursery for the first time offered *R. griffithianum*, the species

[1] This house was not completed until 1899, when the two wings were added.

which as a parent was to prove to be a turning-point in the history of hardy hybrid rhododendrons; today close on a hundred named rhododendron hybrids can claim to have *R. griffithianum* as one parent. And the most famous of these are the numerous cultivars of *R.* x *loderi* whose other parent is *R. fortunei*, which Robert Fortune introduced from China in 1855 when employed by the East India Company. Hooker was generous in the distribution of the seeds of his Sikkim rhododendrons, sending them particularly to those of his friends who, living in favoured parts of the country, would best be able to grow his new introductions. By so doing he was to lay the foundations of some of the first of the woodland gardens which were to become so popular at the close of the nineteenth and during the twentieth centuries. The Campbells of Stonefield, Tarbert, Argyll, were such friends, and at Stonefield today rhododendrons grown from Hooker's original seeds can still be seen. The MacGregors of Glenarn, Rhu, Dunbartonshire, were other friends to whom Hooker sent his seeds. The plants thus raised, as well as some of the first rhododendron hybrids, showed how amazingly well rhododendrons were suited to this garden, though it was not until the 1920s that A. C. and J. F. A. Gibson, with the collections of Wilson, Forrest, and Ward, and, later, of Ludlow and Sherriff, were to create at Glenarn one of the finest rhododendron gardens in Britain.

In 1839, when the fate of Kew was very much in the balance, the Royal Botanic Society of London was established 'for the promotion of botany in all its branches and its application to medicine, arts, and manufactures, and also for the formation of botanical and ornamental gardens within the immediate vicinity of the metropolis'.[1] The Duke of Richmond was the first president. Within a year the Society had leased from Her Majesty's Commissioners for Woods and Forests the whole of the inner circle of Regent's Park, a little over eighteen acres of rather flat land gently falling from the centre. Plans for the laying out of a garden on this area were put to open competition and in 1840 Mr. Robert Marnock—who was recommended by Loudon—was appointed to lay out the Garden and to be the first Curator. Marnock had previously laid out the Botanic Garden at Sheffield, and been the first Curator of this Garden, and was, in fact, to be a practising landscape gardener until 1879. He appears to have been successful in making the Regent's Park Garden ornamental and park-like in appearance. For thirty years, 1839–69, James De Carle Sowerby, the eldest son of James Sowerby, the author of *English Botany*, acted as Secretary to the Society and was, in fact, its mainstay during this period. Although the Society functioned, sometimes highly successfully, for over ninety years, it was gradually overshadowed by the Royal Horticultural Society and the

[1] Nathan Cole, *The Royal Parks and Gardens of London* (1877), p. 15.

Royal Botanic Gardens at Kew, and, having outlived its usefulness, the lease was terminated in 1931 and the plants sold.

For a time a much more serious rival of the Royal Horticultural Society was the South London Floricultural Society—granted a Royal Charter in 1838—with its origin and location in Lambeth. At its Shows, over a number of years, it was able to offer between fifty and 100 silver medals, as well as a few in gold, for exhibits of flowers, fruits, and vegetables, at least twice a year. However, its association with the Royal Surrey Zoological Gardens was not really conducive to the advancement of horticulture, and, with the gradual industrialization of the South London area, by 1850 the Society had declined to extinction.

As at the Royal Botanic Gardens at Kew, so at the Royal Botanic Garden at Edinburgh, the erection of the Tropical Palm House in 1834 was symptomatic of the great progress being made in Edinburgh at this time, when the House was the largest of its kind in Britain. From 1820 to 1823 the Edinburgh Garden had been transferred from an inadequate site in Leith Walk on which it had stood since 1767 to its present situation at Inverleith, at that time only fourteen acres in extent. From 1810, on the old site, William McNab, the principal gardener, had introduced many rare plants not previously cultivated in Edinburgh, and by 1820 the collection was so large that it could not be adequately accommodated in the five-acre garden. The work of transporting and successfully transplanting the collection, including many old well-established trees and shrubs, was entrusted to McNab, who invented a machine specially for the purpose. The results of this great transplanting experience McNab later embodied into an important paper—*The Planting and General Treatment of Hardy Evergreens*—which was published in 1830. His other valuable contribution to botanical and horticultural literature was his paper of 1832 on the *Propagation, Cultivation and General Treatment of Cape Heaths*, a group of plants which he grew with remarkable success in the new Garden.

At this time McNab was among the foremost horticulturists in the land. He had come to Edinburgh from Kew in 1810, on the recommendation of Sir Joseph Banks, at a salary of fifty pounds a year (he refused to come for the forty pounds salary originally offered to him), and is an example of the way the fortunes of the Botanic Gardens of Kew, Edinburgh, and Glasgow, and of the Horticultural Society were closely bound. McNab had come to Edinburgh from Kew in 1810. Robert Graham, Professor of Botany in Edinburgh and Keeper of the Botanic Garden, had come to Edinburgh in 1820, from Glasgow, where he had occupied the first Regius Chair of Botany since its inception in 1818, the year in which was established, by Royal Charter, the Botanic Garden in Glasgow. After succeeding Graham in Glasgow, William Hooker had vastly improved and developed the Garden, and been knighted, before being appointed to the directorship of Kew in 1841. Hooker's son, Joseph, was to act as assistant to Graham in Edinburgh, from 1843 to 1845, before undertaking his Himalayan journeys and becoming assistant to his father at Kew in 1855. Hooker was succeeded in Glasgow by John Hutton Balfour, who moved to Edinburgh when Graham retired in 1845. In 1839 Robert Fortune had begun to train in Edinburgh under McNab before joining the Horticultural Society in 1842, and David Douglas had worked in the Glasgow Garden under Hooker before being sent by the Horticultural Society to America in 1823. The Society has always maintained those strong links with these institutions, as with others such as the Botanic Gardens of Oxford and Cambridge.

The work of the Society and of Douglas gave a tremendous stimulus to the growing of conifers in Britain. Even so, the noteworthy efforts of Edinburgh and of John Jeffrey in the same field must not be forgotten. In 1850 an association of Scotsmen, mostly from Edinburgh, called the Oregon Association, with Professor J. H. Balfour as its Chairman, was formed with the object of sending a collector to the Pacific Coast of America to collect, chiefly, seeds of conifers.[1] John Jeffrey, from Fife, was the young collector chosen. He had been employed in the Edinburgh Botanic Garden and was recommended to the Association by both Balfour and McNab. He left in June 1850 for York Factory in Hudson's Bay, accompanied the Company's 'despatch brigade' across the continent in the following winter, and was on the Pacific coast in the Mount Baker region by the spring of 1851, sending home seeds of *Tsuga mertensiana*, the Mountain Hemlock; *Pseudotsuga menziesii*, the Douglas Fir; *Picea sitchensis*, the Sitka Spruce; *Abies lowiana*, the White Fir; and *Pinus contorta*, the Beach Pine. In 1852 Jeffrey journeyed further south, doubtless along the Willamette River, the route taken by Douglas twenty-seven years earlier, reached the Siskiyou Mountains which divide south Oregon from California, and further explored the forests on the flanks of Mount Shasta. He sent home seeds of *Tsuga heterophylla*, the Western Hemlock; *Abies procera*, the Noble Fir; *A. amabilis*, the Red Silver Fir; *Pinus contorta* var. *latifolia*, the Lodgepole Pine; *P. balfouriana* and the pine which Dr. Greville named after him, *P. jeffreyi*. Whether this tree is given specific rank, or regarded as a form of the widely distributed *P. ponderosa*, it is a fine monument to the name of the young collector who in the following year disappeared in San Francisco and was never heard of again. Time has shown, though, that his most important introduction was the Western Hemlock.

The nurseries also were playing their part in the introduction of new conifers. The Edinburgh firm of Peter Lawson & Son had introduced

---

[1] *Notes from the Royal Botanic Garden, Edinburgh*, XX (1939), p. 1.

the Austrian Pine, *Pinus nigra* f. *austriaca*, in 1835, and in 1854 had received the first consignment of seeds of Lawson's Cypress, *Chamaecyparis lawsoniana*, collected by William Murray, a member of the Oregon Association, from the valley of the Sacramento River in California. Murray was the brother of Andrew Murray, who was to write *The Book of the Royal Horticultural Society*, and Lawson's Cypress, in its innumerable forms, is now the most popular of garden conifers.

No nursery played a more important role in the introduction of conifers than the firm of James Veitch & Son and their collectors. They sent William Lobb to Chile from 1845 to 1848 and there he found *Fitzroya cupressoides*, *Libocedrus tetragona* the Alerce, *Podocarpus nubigenus*, and Prince Albert's Yew *Saxegothaea conspicua*. Lobb sailed for the Pacific a second time and landed at San Francisco in 1849. During 1850 and 1851 he sent home seeds of *Abies venusta*, the Santa Lucia Fir; *Pinus radiata*, the Monterey Pine; *P. muricata*, the Bishop Pine; *P. sabiniana*, the Digger Pine; *P. coulteri*, the Big Cone Pine, and *P. attenuata*, the Knobcone Pine, and by so doing supplemented the sendings of David Douglas. Later, seeds arrived of *P. lambertiana*, the Sugar Pine; *P. monticola*, the Western White Pine, and *Sequoia sempervirens*, the Californian Redwood, of which Hartweg had already sent seeds to Britain in 1846. In 1852 Lobb was on the Columbia River, whence came seeds of the Douglas Fir, the Noble Fir, and the Western Arbor-vitae, *Thuja plicata*. From further south seeds were received of the Giant Fir, *Abies grandis*; the Colorado White Fir, *A. concolor*; Low's White Fir, *A. lowiana*; the Californian Red Fir, *A. magnifica*, and the Western Yellow Pine, *Pinus ponderosa*. And in 1853, on an expedition into the Sierra Nevada, he secured cones of *Sequoiadendron giganteum*.

A few years later the Veitch firm was distributing most of the hardy conifers of Japan, through the activities of John Gould Veitch, who was in Japan from July 1860 to July 1861; the Hinoki Cypress, *Chamaecyparis obtusa* and its many forms; the Japanese Fir, *Abies firma*; the Japanese Cedar, *Cryptomeria japonica* which Fortune had previously introduced; Alcock's Spruce, *Picea bicolor*—previously known as *P. alcockiana*; the Yezo or Hondo Spruce, *P. jesoensis*; the Tiger-tail Spruce, *P. polita*; the Japanese Red, White and Black Pine, *Pinus densiflora*, *P. parviflora and P. thunbergii* respectively; the Korean Pine, *P. koraiensis*; the Japanese Larch, *Larix leptolepis* (which among all these is the only one of any silvicultural importance); and two plants which Thomas Lobb had previously introduced for Veitch from the Buitenzorg Botanic Garden in Java, but which had died, *Sciadopitys verticillata*, the Japanese Umbrella Pine, and *Thujopsis dolabrata*, the Hiba Arbor-vitae.

This great firm of Veitch employed not only remarkable plant collectors but also remarkable cultivators whose job it was to grow the

(*above left*)
Sir Harry Veitch

(*above right*) Baron
Sir Henry Schröder

(*left*)
Sir Thomas Hanbury

Plate 11.
BENEFACTORS OF
THE SOCIETY

The Rev. William Wilks (Secretary 1888–1912)

Frederick J. Chittenden (Director at Wisley, technical adviser and keeper of the Library at Vincent Square, editor of the Society, and editor of the R.H.S. *Dictionary of Gardening*

new plant introductions, as well as to develop new plants from them by hybridization. One such was John Dominy, who was employed by Veitch in one or other nursery for over forty years. He was an excellent cultivator of stove and greenhouse plants as well as a skilful hybridizer of nepenthes and of orchids. No doubt it was as the raiser of the first orchid hybrid that he was most famed. He crossed *Calanthe musaca* with the pollen of *C. furcata* and two years later, in 1856, the first seedling flowered and was named *Calanthe* x *dominii*. This was the first of the many thousands of orchid hybrids which have since been raised, and gardeners were enthusiastic. Not so Lindley: 'You will drive the botanists mad,' he exclaimed. What would he say today?

The hybridists were also at work with other plants. The first *Gladiolus* hybrid, *Gladiolus* x *colvillii*, had been raised about 1823—a hybrid between the scarlet-flowered *G. cardinalis* and the yellowish-white *G. tristis*. It was the forerunner of a race of early-flowering gladioli which are now grouped under the name of *Nanus* hybrids. In 1841 Van Houtte distributed the first hybrid of a larger flowered type under the name of *G.* x *gandavensis*, and, though there appears to be some doubt as to its origin, *G. cardinalis* and *G. psittacinus* were the stated parents. Be this as it may, *G.* x *gandavensis* has since been very much used in hybridization work. Few were to be as successful in the hybridization of gladioli as James Kelway, who, even as a young working gardener, had been greatly attracted to the scarlet-and-yellow-flowered South African *G. psittacinus*. In 1850 he started his own business at Langport, Somerset, devoted himself to gladiolus culture, and in 1861 distributed the first of the modern florists' hybrids. No new impetus to gladiolus breeding was given until 1889, when *G. primulinus* was introduced from, so it was said, south-east Tropical Africa—the Victoria Falls of the Zambezi. The identity of this plant has been questioned on the grounds that the true *G. primulinus* is a native of Tanganyika, and the name *G. nebulicola* has been proposed for it. But whatever its true name, its introduction into cultivation and its behaviour in the hands of the hybridists has given rise to an entirely new race of gladioli with refined hooded flowers of soft colours, characters which have been carried into the large flowered types, so that the range of colour and variety in this group of garden plants has been enormously increased.

Up to this time the Horticultural Society had done much to popularize the chrysanthemum and, chiefly through its activities, in 1826 more than fifty different cultivars were in cultivation. Their renown as colourful autumn flowering plants was spreading throughout the country and special chrysanthemum societies were being formed. In 1829 the Norwich and Norfolk Chrysanthemum Society was born and, shortly afterwards, similar societies at Birmingham and Swansea. The most progressive society seems to have been formed at Stoke Newington in 1846, for it ultimately became the National Chrysanthemum Society. The societies, of course, held their shows and the types of chrysanthemum exhibited were all of Chinese origin; even the Pompon types which had still to be developed were to be bred from Fortune's Chinese introductions of 1845. But Fortune was to change all this. In 1860 he was in Japan, employed by the East India Company, and near Tokyo saw famous collections of Japanese chrysanthemums. They were quite different from anything he had seen before. He wrote of them:

At the time of our visit they were in full bloom, and most certainly would have delighted the eyes of our English florists had they found themselves so far away from Hammersmith, The Temple, or Stoke Newington. I procured some extraordinary varieties, most peculiar in form and in colouring, and quite distinct from any of the kinds at present known in Europe. One had petals like long thick hairs, of a red colour, but tipped with yellow, looking like the fringe of a shawl or curtain; another had broad white petals striped with red like a carnation or camellia; while others were remarkable for their great size and brilliant colouring. If I can succeed in introducing these varieties into Europe, they may create as great a change among chrysanthemums as my old protege the modest Chusan Daisy did when she became the parent of the present race of pompons.

Fortune certainly succeeded in introducing them, but they did not at once find favour with English growers, who had become accustomed to varieties with incurved blooms of perfect formation. Some of the large reflexed Japanese types with the florets twisting in all directions were too much of a contrast. However, one or two growers such as Mr. John Salter of Hammersmith, who had done much to raise the Chinese incurved type of flower to its peak of perfection, welcomed this new Japanese blood for their breeding work and, twenty years later, the Japanese types were to be more popular than the Chinese and from them the first of the early-flowering outdoor types was bred. Without doubt the introduction of these cultivated Japanese types was the most important event in chrysanthemum cultivation.

During these years camellias still enjoyed great popularity and three important works on them were published. In 1838 the Abbé Berlèse's *Monographie du genre Camellia*, first published in Paris in 1837, was translated into English and German, and from 1841 to 1843 appeared the three volumes of his *Iconographie du genre Camellia*, a most sumptuous work which illustrated in colour 300 different camellias, most of them grown from seeds. Then, from 1848 to 1860, 623 camellias were illustrated in *Nouvelle Iconographie des Camellias*. The work was begun by Alexandre Verschaffelt of Ghent; when he died in 1850 it was continued by his son

Ambroise and his grandson of the same name. It figures and describes the camellias assessed as the most rare, the most beautiful and the most modern during the twelve years of the book's publication. The authors considered that only the double forms were worthy of illustration, and, unlike Berlèse, omitted all single and semi-double forms. It was remarkable that the production of these splendid works did nothing to stimulate further interest in camellia cultivation. On the contrary camellias gradually fell out of favour and remained so for more than half a century, only regaining universal popularity as a result of the introductions from western China during the first twenty years or so of the present century.

In 1843, on the death of Loudon, the *Gardener's Magazine* ceased publication.[1] Since 1826 it had recorded the progress of horticulture both at home and abroad and had been an outspoken critic of the Horticultural Society. Now its place was taken by the *Gardener's Chronicle*—founded in 1841 by Paxton and by Bradley, the editor of *Punch*—the first weekly gardening newspaper. Its first horticultural editor was John Lindley and from this time forth all matters of interest relating to gardening and horticulture in Britain, and especially to the affairs of the Society, were to be faithfully recorded in its pages.

[1] Though another *Gardener's Magazine*, in a different format, was published later in the century and continued until the First World War; it was edited for many years by George Gordon, one of the original recipients of the V.M.H. in 1897 (*see* p. 242).

Part Four

The Kensington Adventure—and Disaster
(1858 - 1885)

CHAPTER TWELVE

THE PRINCE CONSORT

THE SOCIETY STRUGGLED ON WITH ITS ADMINISTRATIVE WORK IN the small office in St. Martin's Place, held its monthly Meetings in a large room in the Adelphi kindly lent by the Society of Arts, and continued to stage its Exhibitions. Three of these were arranged for 1859, for May, June, and December. For the first, in St. James's Hall, in addition to advertisements in newspapers and placards at all the railway stations within twenty miles of London, fifty boys with boards were hired as placard-bearers on each day of the Exhibition.

Horticulturally, the Show was a triumph. In front of the great organ, on raised stages, was a splendid exhibit from the Chiswick Garden of flowering plants, ferns, and palms; in those days, even as today, the Garden had to come to the rescue of the Society's Shows. Close to the Chiswick exhibit, Messrs. Fraser had arranged a large handsome display of azaleas. There was also a row of standard azaleas running the whole length of the hall. Messrs. Veitch were present, of course, with some remarkable new plants; two specimens of *Sequoiadendron giganteum* which William Lobb had introduced for them from California in 1853, and an even more recent introduction, in 1856, from Japan, by Thomas Lobb, the holly-like evergreen with clusters of white flowers in the axils of the leaves, and with oblong blue fruits, *Osmanthus ilicifolius*. There were orchids, rhododendrons, and foliage plants. There was a magnificent exhibit of roses from Messrs. Lane, and, most impressive of all, a display of a wide range of fruits which excited great interest. This was from M. Webber of Covent Garden market and contained coconuts; sapucaia nuts from Demerara, and the groundnuts of commerce; litchis from China; shaddocks from the West Indies; blood oranges from Malta, mandarins from Palermo, and a large rough-skinned kind called the navel orange from Adelaide, S. Australia; pommeloes from the West Indies; pineapples; pears and apples; sweetwater and Hamburgh grapes; strawberries; May Duke cherries.

Unfortunately the Show was not a financial success and resulted in a deficit of £112. The date clashed with a Show at the Crystal Palace and the exhibitors disliked St. James's Hall. They objected to the labour involved in carrying plants into it and maintained that the plants and flowers sustained damage while there because the building was lighted by gas. So the June Show was cancelled, and the Fruit Show which was to be held elsewhere, in December, was abandoned because the fruit crops were poor.

In 1858 a Committee for Fruit and Vegetables had been set up; it was now the turn of the flowers, and in May 1859 a Floral Committee was formed for the purpose of reporting on all flowers or flowering plants submitted for consideration. The committee consisted in the first instance of twenty-eight members, with Professor Henfrey as chairman, Thomas Moore, Curator of Chelsea Botanic Garden, as secretary, and Dr. Lindley as botanical adviser.

Henfrey's services to the committee were unfortunately of brief duration, for he died the same year, at the age of thirty-nine. Trained in medicine and surgery at St. Bartholomew's, because of poor health and an asthmatic condition he had never been able to practise medicine and had turned his attentions to botany, being appointed to the chair of botany at King's College in 1853. He was among the first to try to make known in Britain the new aspects of the great renaissance in botany in Germany and, had he lived longer, he would undoubtedly have played a greater role in establishing the 'New Botany' in Britain; and a greater role, too, in the affairs of the Society.

Moore was fairly deeply involved in Society matters, for he was a friend of Lindley, whose influence had placed him at Chelsea as Curator, in succession to Robert Fortune. He was an authority on ferns, with a very wide acquaintance with garden plants and a flair for the organization and administration of flower shows, his work as one of the Secretaries contributing to the great success of the International Show of 1866.

No doubt because of Henfrey's frail health, the first chairman to function on the Floral Committee appears to have been the Rev. Joshua Dix, who presided at the first meeting on 7 July 1859, and from then on devoted himself heart and soul to the committee's work, presiding over its deliberations 'with an impartiality, a geniality, and tact which secured for him the cordial good will and respect of the large and somewhat heterogeneous body'.[1] Professor Henfrey had also agreed to attend to the production of a monthly *Journal* of one sheet 8vo which would be posted to all Fellows and which would 'contain all such notices of whatever kind as the Society may have occasion to issue, reports of Committees, Anniversary Reports, and miscellaneous information'.

When, at the beginning of 1859, James Veitch and others were talking

---

[1] *Gdnr's Chron.* (1871), p. 1202.

of the Society being disbanded, there were others who were determined that this should not be. Among these were the Treasurer, Wilson Saunders, who had met some of the Society's liabilities with cheques drawn on his own bankers, and Lindley, who had given thirty-six years of his life to the Society. They considered that, in view of its distance from London, the Chiswick Garden should be used in future simply as an experimental station, and that for a show garden and for flower shows, another site should be sought somewhere in London as accessible as Regent's Park and the Crystal Palace. Accordingly, on 25 January 1859, 'It was moved by the Treasurer, seconded by the Secretary, and resolved—That a letter be addressed to Her Majesty's Commissioners for [the Exhibition of] 1851[1] enquiring whether the Horticultural Society can have about 20 acres of land in the middle of the block of ground lying between Kensington, Cromwell, Exhibition and Prince Albert roads—and if so, on what terms.'

In June the Council met at Buckingham Palace at the invitation of the President, who explained his views respecting the terms upon which the land at Kensington Gore might be leased by the Royal Commissioners. The terms, which in general appeared acceptable, were formally communicated to the Society by letter dated 4 July, and on 7 July a General Meeting of the Society unanimously approved the project and authorized the Council to negotiate with the Commissioners. With extraordinary promptitude, on the following day a circular was distributed to all Fellows, outlining the proposals and seeking financial support for them. The circular stated:

(1) That the Commissioners will surround the whole ground with beautiful Italian Arcades open to the Garden, and execute extensive ground works at a cost of Fifty thousand pounds, granting the Society a lease of the ground for 31 years, provided that the Society would at an equal cost lay out the Gardens and erect a Winter Garden at the north end.

(2) That the Commissioners are willing to accept a rental entirely contingent on profits, first providing for the necessary expenditure in keeping up the Gardens at Chiswick as well as Kensington Gore, and next for the payment of interest on any money borrowed by the Horticultural Society and afterwards for payment of interest on the Fifty thousand pounds to be borrowed by the Commissioners for the Arcades and ground work

[1] The Great Exhibition of 1851 was held in the Crystal Palace, erected specially for the purpose in Hyde Park. The building was subsequently moved to Sydenham. The Exhibition made a profit, out of which the Commissioners purchased Gore House Kensington (on the site of which the Albert Hall was later erected) and the adjoining land to provide sites for buildings for the promotion of art and science. After letting off parts of the estate on building leases, the Commissioners reserved the rest for the purposes of the corporation.

All surplus to be then divided between the Commissioners and the Horticultural Society.

(3) The Council being anxious to be placed as soon as possible in a position to confer further with Her Majesty's Commissioners, and to know whether sufficient means will be placed at their disposal, I am to inform the Fellows of the Society that it is proposed to raise the money by Donation, by Life Memberships of 40 Guineas and 20 Guineas, and by Debentures carrying 5 per cent interest with probably contingent adjustment at the expiration of the lease.

(4) That Queen Victoria had promised a donation of £1,000, and that the Prince Consort would contribute £500 and, if necessary, take Debentures to the value of £1,000.

(5) That several Members of Council had intimated that in addition to taking Debentures they would arrange for members of their families to become Life Fellows.

The appeal met with a good response and by 21 October the position was as follows:

Donations	£1,926 2.	0.
93 Life Members at 40 guineas	3,906 0.	0.
73 ,, ,, ,, 20 ,, ...	1,533 0.	0.
95 ,, ,, supposed at 25 guineas	2,493 15.	0.
Debentures	35,500 0.	0.
	£45,358 17.	0.

A month later the necessary £50,000 had been subscribed, and arrangements were made to execute the lease of the new Garden at Kensington Gore.

With the Society's apparently reviving fortunes, new Fellows rolled in. On 20 January 1860 no fewer than 335 were elected. The idea of making members of one's family Life Fellows appealed to the Queen, and at the Meeting on 31 January 'The Chairman announced that Her Majesty The Queen had been graciously pleased to lay her commands on the Horticultural Society to admit the following Members of the Royal Family as Fellows'. There followed the names of twelve princes and princesses, headed by the Prince of Wales and including Princess Frederick William of Prussia, Princess Royal of England.

Meanwhile, on 25 October 1859, the Prince Consort had presided at a Meeting of the Council held at Windsor Castle to consider the best means of obtaining designs for the new Garden, which occupied twenty-two and a half acres just south of the site now occupied by the Royal Albert Hall and which all agreed should be on a geometrical plan, and of obtaining a suitable superintendent for the charge of both the Gardens at Kensington Gore and at Chiswick. Commenting on this proposed appointment, the *Gardener's Chronicle* wrote:

So much will depend upon the conduct and skill of this officer that the selection of a fitting person is one of the most important duties the Council have now to fulfil. He must be a thoroughly practical gardener, versed in every department of horticulture, and known to be so by his works; not a fine gentleman who imagines that fruit growing is the great art and whole duty of man. He must be a skilled ground workman, an experienced manager of men, young enough and active enough to bear the strain which the work of such a Superintendent must render inevitable for at least the few first years. Nor is this all; he must be popular with his brother gardeners, familiar with the management of public exhibitions, and with such an appearance and address as will enable him to receive visitors of all ranks in a manner becoming the magnitude of his charge. With no lower qualifications than these ought the Council to be satisfied. If they can command a higher standard so much the better.

George Eyles, who had been on Paxton's staff, first at Chatsworth and later at the Crystal Palace at Sydenham, should have been very proud indeed, and possibly a little apprehensive, when he was appointed the following month. He had the responsibility for the two Gardens until 1865, became prominent as a landscape gardener at the same time, and had the charge of Kensington until 1871 when he left the Society's service.

The Anniversary Meeting on 1 May 1860 was held in the Museum of Science and Art at South Kensington. Detailed drawings of the design for the Garden, prepared by Mr. W. A. Nesfield, were exhibited, and Fellows had the chance to see for themselves how the work on the ground was progressing. It was reported that the total liabilities of the Society, which in 1859 had been £10,752, were now reduced to £4,296, and that since the beginning of the year 601 new Fellows had enrolled. In the meantime numbers of new and uncommon plants were being distributed by ballot from Chiswick, where the large conservatory was converted into a vinery and housed the biggest collection of vines in the United Kingdom. The collection of hardy fruits was being overhauled and increased with the assistance of Robert Hogg,[1] who had succeeded Thompson as secretary of the Fruit and Vegetable Committee. Exten-

[1] Robert Hogg (1818–97), LL.D., horticultural journalist and pomologist. Editor of the *Journal of Horticulture* and author of the *Fruit Manual*. Sometime Secretary of the Society. Commemorated by the Hogg Medal.

sive trials of vegetables, including no fewer than 140 kinds of cucumber, were also being undertaken. There were also trials of fuchsias, achimenes, begonias, and gloxinias under glass, and, in the open, of phlox, China asters, and other plants. Altogether the prospect was pleasing and 'The Council entertain the confident belief that the Society is now entering upon a career of utility and prosperity such as it has never before experienced.'

Unfortunately, in October, William Beattie Booth, the Assistant Secretary, had to retire because of failing health and, although in retirement he continued to serve the Society as a member of the Floral Committee, his loss to the Society was great. He had entered into its service, as a labourer in the arboretum department at Chiswick, in 1824, the year in which his friend David Douglas departed on his second expedition to America. They were both natives of Scone and both had worked in the gardens at Scone Palace. At Chiswick he had been privileged to assist Lindley in the laying out of the Garden and in planting the Arboretum and in 1825 had been appointed garden clerk. The year 1830 was a momentous one for him, for he began a remarkable association with Alfred Chandler, the nurseryman and floral artist, which was to result, the following year, in the publication of *Illustrations of the Camellieae*—the drawings by Chandler, the descriptions by Booth—of which the *Gardener's Magazine* wrote:

It is highly creditable to the gardening profession that there should be found two young men, the one an assistant in his father's nursery, and the other with no pretensions beyond those of a good gardener—and who, we understand, has actually accepted the situation of a head gardener to a gentleman—capable of producing such a work. It is true that the one, from having been born in a nursery famous for its camellias, and the other from having had an excellent school education in Scotland, having been bred up under one of the best kitchen gardeners in that country, Mr. Beattie of Scone, and having long been first gardener and afterwards clerk in the Horticultural Society's Garden, have had extraordinary advantages; but how frequently are such advantages comparatively neglected. We are proud to see such young men growing up to succeed us in the world, and think we feel almost as much interest in them as if they were our own sons.

The situation of 'head gardener to a gentleman' was that at Carclew, near Penryn, the home of Sir Charles Lemon. Here for some years he grew a wide range of interesting plants of many of which he wrote descriptions which he sent to Lindley for the *Botanical Register*.

On retirement he lived for another fourteen years—'one of the most refined and talented of the gardeners of the present age, one of the kindest and gentlest of men, and one who was endowed with intellectual qualities of no common order'. That was the judgement of the *Gardener's Chronicle* when Booth died in 1874.

Andrew Murray succeeded Booth to the post of Assistant Secretary in January 1861. Only the year before had he come to live in London from Edinburgh, where he was born in 1812, where he had been educated for the law and had become a Writer to the Signet, where he had been president of the Botanical Society and of the Physical Society in 1858–9, and where he had been a member of the committee of the Oregon Association (see p. 179).

In 1863 he was to edit *The Book of the Royal Horticultural Society* and in the following year, to resign the Assistant Secretary post to become a member of Council, where 'his kindness, his quaint originality, his varied knowledge, and his willingness to impart it, gave him a title to respect and esteem which all who knew him . . . involuntarily accorded'.[1]

Unfortunately again, the year 1860 was 'unprecedentedly wet', and the earthworks on the new Garden were delayed; long-continued frost hindered the bricklayers and masons; and there was a strike of the builders' men. However, in February 1861 the small office in St. Martin's Place was vacated, the Society's address became 'South Kensington', and in spite of set-backs, by 19 March the work was sufficiently far advanced to allow of a General Meeting being held in the new Council Room. It was then reported that the cost of the Garden would probably be not much less than £70,000, and the Council was authorized to increase the sum to be raised by debentures from £40,000 to £50,000.

At the Anniversary Meeting held on 1 May an incident, unparalleled before or since, occurred during the election of officers and new members of Council. Mr. Henry G. Bohn, the well known publisher of York Street, Covent Garden, made some observations on those nominated by the Council for the three vacant seats, advocated his own claim to one of them, and invited the Fellows present to substitute his name for that of one of the Council's nominees. But when a ballot was taken he received only ten votes compared with sixty-one, sixty, and fifty-nine received by the Council's nominees.

A week later, on 8 May 1861, a new Royal Charter for which, in view of the arrangements at Kensington Gore, the Council had applied, was sealed. This document, which incorporated the agreement between the Royal Commissioners for the Exhibition of 1851 and the Horticultural Society of London, stated that it was Her Majesty's 'will and pleasure that such Society shall henceforth be called "The Royal Horticultural Society" '. Under the new Charter the arrangements by which Officers and new members of Council were elected at the 'Anniversary Meeting'

[1] *Gdnr's Chron.* (1878), p. 86.

on 1 May (or on 2 May if 1 May should be a Sunday) was discontinued, and it was stipulated that from 1862 onwards the elections should take place at a meeting to be called the 'Annual Meeting' which was to be held on the second Tuesday in February.

In the meantime the Prince Consort was taking great interest in the construction of the Garden and frequently visited the site as the work proceeded. Nothing in any part relating to art was done without his personal inspection and approval, and in at least one instance, being dissatisfied with what had been done, he ordered it to be altered at his own cost. Some months in advance, the date for the formal opening of the Garden had been fixed for 5 June 1861, and although the Garden was not likely to be finished, the date could not be altered, as Queen Victoria had graciously signified her intention to perform the ceremony. Sadly, when the time came, Her Majesty was unable to attend any public function of this kind, for, since March, the Court had been in mourning for the death of her mother, the Duchess of Kent. However, early in the morning of 5 June, in the strictest privacy and accompanied by the Prince Consort and the King of the Belgians, Her Majesty visited the grounds and inspected the collection of flowers and fruit which were still in process of arrangement.

The formal ceremony was performed by the Prince Consort, who was accompanied by all the junior members of the Royal Family, and the large gathering included many public figures of the time, among them Lord Palmerston, Gladstone, and Disraeli. In the course of his speech the Prince referred to the layout of the Garden and its surrounding arcades as 'a valuable attempt . . . to reunite the science and art of gardening to the sister arts of Architecture, Sculpture and Painting', and went on to say, 'Unrivalled opportunities are here offered for the display of works of art and for the erection of monuments as tributes to great men.'

While the purpose of the Garden as conceived by the Prince was doubtless laudable, it had little in common with John Wedgwood's ideas, and even less with those of Thomas Andrew Knight. Banks and Greville had also been deeply interested in works of art, but they had not attempted to combine these interests with their devotion to horti-culture. However, no one appears to have protested that the Society was going astray, and if in 1861 there were any critics of the current policy, publicity seems not to have been given to their views.

Even so, horticulture pure and simple was not entirely forgotten during the opening proceedings.

. . . the great Conservatory glowed with the brilliant colours of Azaleas, Orchids, Roses, and other distinguished members of the floral nation, relieved by superb groups of Ferns—wonderfully beautiful things—and all manner of parti-coloured or gracefully fashioned exotics, among which were exquisite specimens of the goldsmith's art in the form of vases, statuettes, and racing cups, contributed by Messrs. Hancock. Beneath the long colonnades, in endless profusion, extending many hundred feet on either side, were ranged superb masses of Pelargoniums and innumerable groups of other ornamental plants. Towards one end of the colonnade that leads to the entrance, fruit, the admiration of the spectator and the pride of the gardener, was piled in gracefully arranged confusion—in which disorder there was none. On the other side of the Garden, under the corresponding colonnade, stood an extraordinary and very brilliant assemblage of flowers and fruit prepared for table decoration.[1]

The opening ceremony included the planting of a *Sequoiadendron giganteum*, the Wellingtonia or Big Tree of California.

His Royal Highness, having received a spade from a bystander, threw some shovelfuls of earth over the roots for himself and the Princesses his daughters. The Princes acted for themselves, not the least skilful among them being Prince Arthur [later to become a member of Council], who handled the spade with a vigour that showed him to have used well the experience gained in his own little garden at Osborne.[2]

His love of gardening remained with him throughout his life and for many years as Duke of Connaught he was one of the Society's patrons.

The crowning ceremony of the Garden's inauguration took place later in the month when the Queen, still in deep mourning, planted a companion tree to Prince Albert's.

The nature of the Kensington Garden was described in considerable detail by Andrew Murray in *The Book of the Royal Horticultural Society* (1863), and an excellent idea of the layout may be obtained from the drawing reproduced as Plate 8, which shows the view from what is now the site of the Natural History Museum, looking towards Hyde Park and Kensington Gardens, which may be seen in the distance. The Conservatory and Winter Garden, which was 270 feet long, 100 feet wide, and 75 feet high, is shown at the northern end. The Royal Albert Hall now stands between the site of the Conservatory and Kensington Gore, the thoroughfare which at that point forms the southern boundary of Kensington Gardens. The arcades enclosing the Garden may also be seen and considerable lengths of them still exist and constitute parts of the eastern and western galleries of the Imperial Institute.

One of the features of the Garden was the memorial of the Great Exhibition of 1851, the international exhibition which had been held in the Crystal Palace in Hyde Park. The memorial was originally intended

---

[1] *Proceedings of the Royal Horticultural Society*, I (1861), p. 597.   [2] ibid., p. 607.

to be surmounted by a statue of Queen Victoria, and the Prince Consort took a great interest in the selection of the site. A water-colour in the possession of the Society shows the Prince inspecting a model which had been erected for his approval. He died before the work was completed and it was then decided that a statue of him, presented by the Prince of Wales, should be substituted for that of Her Majesty. The memorial was unveiled on 10 June 1863 by H.R.H. the Prince of Wales, later King Edward VII. When the Garden was demolished the memorial was moved on to the site which the Conservatory had occupied and it still stands in that position behind the Royal Albert Hall. Another feature of the Garden was a great cascade flowing into a large rectangular basin in front of the memorial. The water was supplied by a pump from what was then the largest artesian well in London.

The formal opening of the Garden by the Prince, in the presence of so many other royal and distinguished persons, led to a great influx of new Fellows. By the end of 1861 the total number was 2,774, no fewer than 1,752 being elected between 1 May 1861 and February 1862. It was now becoming fashionable to belong to the Society and about a third of the new Fellows were women. No doubt they were especially appreciative of the Shows, with their great banks of colour, as well as recently introduced plants which were always exhibited. The September Dahlia Show of 1861 was especially noteworthy not only for the splendid dahlias, and the playing of the two best bands in London—the Royal Artillery and the London Engineers—but also for a superb pot-grown specimen of *Lapageria rosea*, the Chilean plant which had been introduced in 1847 and 1848, first by Kew and then by Messrs. Veitch, and was now shown by the Dowager Duchess of Northumberland. The plant covered 36 square feet of a flat trellis and, although carrying only thirty-six open flowers, was covered with countless flower buds.

Meanwhile the embellishment of the Garden proceeded. The Society's Fine Arts Committee, which at the suggestion of the Prince had been appointed to advise on such matters, was authorized to expend £500 in each of three years 'on the purchase of one or more works of high art', on the understanding that the Commissioners would pay half.

Simultaneously considerable expense was being incurred at Chiswick, certainly in the cause of true horticulture and not of 'high art', and Eyles was asked to find ways and means of running the Garden on £1,000 a year. He and a subcommittee recommended that not less than fourteen acres of the Chiswick Garden should be surrendered to the landlord. Already some were willing to sacrifice horticulture on the altar of 'high art'.

Possibly the President would have ensured the striking of a happy balance between the two, but towards the end of the year, after a short illness, the Prince Consort, who had done so much to bring the Society from near bankruptcy to comparative prosperity, died of typhoid fever on 14 December. Some indication of the interest which both he and the Queen had taken in the Society's affairs may be gauged from the letter written only ten days later by Sir Charles Phipps to Sir Wentworth Dilke, one of the Vice-Presidents:

Osborne,
December 24, 1861.

My dear Dilke,

The Queen has directed me to inform you that it is Her Majesty's wish that the Horticultural Gardens should be considered as under her peculiar and personal patronage and protection.

The only consolation that Her Majesty can hope to find for the rest of her life, under her bitter and hopeless bereavement, is to endeavour to carry out the wishes and intentions of her beloved husband.

The Queen well knows the deep interest that he took in this undertaking, and would wish to have periodical reports sent to Her Majesty of the progress and proceedings of the Society.

Sincerely yours,
C. B. Phipps

When the question of a successor to the Prince in the office of President arose, the Council took steps to ascertain Her Majesty's feelings and wishes in the matter, and in due course learned that the Queen 'had intimated her desire that during her lifetime the office of President should be held in abeyance, and that she, herself, would endeavour to fulfil so far as practicable the actual duties of President which had been transacted by H.R.H., her deeply lamented husband'. However, three weeks later Sir Wentworth Dilke reported that, 'after some further communication with Her Majesty and the Crown officers, it had been found that it was inconsistent with Her Majesty's royal position to occupy that of President of the Society, and in consequence that idea had been abandoned'. Sir Wentworth added that he 'had reason to believe that the election of His Grace the Duke of Buccleuch would be acceptable to Her Majesty', and the Duke, the owner of two of the finest garden establishments in Scotland—Dalkeith Palace and Drumlanrig Castle—was elected President at the Annual Meeting in February 1862. (Plate 4.)

The outstanding event during his first year of office was a Great International Exhibition which was organized by the Royal Commissioners on somewhat similar lines to the Great Exhibition of 1851. It was held in a new building specially constructed for the purpose at the southern end of the Garden, with an overflow in the adjacent arcades.

Satisfactory arrangements were made with the Commissioners for visitors to the Exhibition to be able to see the Garden and the horticultural Shows, and the result was a considerable addition to the Society's revenue. Fellowship continued to rise and by the end of December had reached a total of 3,313. However, much of the revenue was consumed by taxes, interest on debentures, and rent to the Commissioners, while most of the balance was spent on improvements to the Garden and by the Society's Fine Arts Committee on *objets d'art* for the Garden's embellishment. A subscription list was opened to obtain funds for the purchase of two fountains, but as the £800 thus raised was insufficient for the purpose, with the consent of the subscribers, most of the money was used to purchase for the Garden about a dozen of the best bronzes which had been exhibited.

In the meantime, of course, horticultural Shows were staged. Seven such were arranged for 1863 when the Garden was opened to the public, on payment, for a series of Promenades, on Wednesdays and Saturdays from the middle of May to the end of July. Music was provided during these occasions—and the Horticultural Society now had its 'Musical Committee'. Not unnaturally, the feeling was growing that the 'high arts' were receiving the greater consideration, especially when an exhibition of sculpture, arranged in co-operation with the Sculptors' Institute, was inaugurated, and the Fine Arts Committee, which continued for some years after the Prince Consort's death, commissioned an artist to reproduce for £500 a statue entitled 'Youth at the Stream'. Fortunately the Council was not called upon to pay the bill until the work was delivered eight years later, by which time financial stringency was being exercised and the Council of the day, having no difficulty in finding a better use for £500, promptly decided to sell the work. But, in fact, they did not do so and in the end the Commissioners took possession of it. Council was not so fortunate in another matter. On 10 June 1863 the Prince of Wales, accompanied by his new bride, Princess (later Queen) Alexandra, unveiled the memorial of the 1851 Exhibition which was surmounted by a statue of the late Prince Consort. The Society's share of the cost of installation was £800.

At the Annual Meeting in February 1863 the Council announced with great regret that Dr. Lindley, who had so ably and faithfully served the Society in one capacity or another for forty-one years—and during that period, to use his own words, had 'endeavoured to the best of my ability to promote its true interests as a great English association for the advancement of horticultural knowledge, until, through many changes and some adversity, it has at length gained a position of high eminence, and may be regarded as standing on a secure foundation' (here he was unduly optimistic)—wished to retire from the secretaryship because of failing health. In the previous year, in response to the wish of many friends, he had consented to sit for his portrait. The commission was executed by E. U. Eddis, and the picture now hangs very appropriately in the Lindley Library of the Society's headquarters at Vincent Square. A subscription list for a testimonial was opened and in due course Lindley was presented with a handsome silver épergne on which were represented orchids and other flowers in which he had been especially interested, and on which he had written in the *Transactions* and elsewhere.

William Wilson Saunders, who had been Treasurer since 1855, succeeded Lindley as Secretary, and responsibility for the Society's funds was taken over by John Clutton.

CHAPTER THIRTEEN

KENSINGTON

THE BEGINNING OF BUCCLEUCH'S PRESIDENCY WAS NOT VERY encouraging, for there was a lull in horticultural activities. The attendances at the Shows were poor and, although a good number of people joined the Society in 1863, owing to resignations and failure to keep up subscriptions the net increase during the year was only twenty-three. Many of those elected since it had become fashionable to belong to the Society were not really interested in horticulture. Presumably it was such people the Council had in mind when it decided to utilize the Council Chamber as a reading room, for, of the twenty-one publications with which it was furnished, only five dealt with horticulture or botany, the rest being five daily papers and such periodicals as *Punch*, the *Illustrated London News*, the *Mark Lane Express*, the *Athenaeum*, and the *Edinburgh Review*. It seems likely that the reason why, in November 1863, James Veitch of Chelsea and Lord Ducie took the unusual course of resigning from the Council was because they did not approve of the drift away from things horticultural.

No more approving were some of the more horticulturally minded Fellows who did not hesitate to voice their disapproval in the horticultural Press. On 2 July 1864, one of these, signing himself 'Eboracensis', wrote:

I find *inter alia* in the New Charter of this Society, the following introductory clause. (1) 'Whereas the Horticultural Society of London, hereinafter referred to as "the said Society", was incorporated by Royal Letters Patent under the great Seal of our said United Kingdom, bearing the date at Westminster the 17th day of April, in the 49th year of the reign of his late Majesty King George the Third, *for the purpose of the Improvement of Horticulture in all its branches, ornamental as well as useful.*' I am curious to hear how the Council reconciles with this declaration, on which the Charter of the Corporation rests, the feats of Mumbo Jumbos, tight rope dancers, blazing Burgees, Brigands, and all the other vulgar absurdities which have so intensely disgusted of late that public which has really at heart the improvement of Horticulture. I suppose there can be little doubt that the Charter of the Society will by these acts be declared to be forfeited, whenever any Fellow chooses to bring the matter before the Law Courts.[1]

[1] *Gdnr's Chron.* (1864), p. 628.

But even things non-horticultural were not prospering at the Garden; since the death of the Prince Consort, work on the surrounding arcades, for instance, had much slowed down. Consequently, in January 1864 the Council complained to the Commissioners that the Garden had 'an air of poverty and hesitation' which was injurious to the Society, and asked the Commissioners to authorize the Society with the spending of between £2,000 and £3,000 to make the Garden more attractive horticulturally, and to provide more grass, shade, and exhibition space under cover. The Commissioners did not dispute the criticism, and sanctioned a further expenditure of £13,000, including the Society's part, on the understanding that the money should be disbursed by a joint 'Expenses Committee'. The Commissioners stated that the money so advanced brought the total to £60,000; that no similar appeal for money would be entertained; and that the interest on the total sum would now be £2,400 per annum. Without delay the Council decided to spend up to £900 on a large single-spanned tent, 300 feet by 120 feet, with only two poles supporting the ridge, to house an exhibition of rhododendrons to be staged by Messrs. Waterer & Godfrey. A further £800 was to be spent on planting the Garden, and £500 on improving the entrances and general decoration.

At the Annual Meeting, when these proposed further expenditures on the Kensington premises became known, Dr. Hogg, the backbone of the Society where fruit was concerned, having concluded 'that some other object than the advancement of horticulture is what the ruling majority of the . . . Council have in view', resigned from the Secretaryship of the Fruit and Vegetable Committee. Great difficulty was experienced in replacing him, and five months later he was persuaded to resume the appointment.

A series of Shows was held during 1864 and Meetings with 'lecturettes' like those held in Regent Street before 1858 were resumed; for instance, William Paul talked for twenty minutes on hyacinths; James Bateman talked on the cultivation of the dwarf banana, *Musa cavendishii*—and distributed a large bunch of fruit among the audience—as well as on orchids for the cool house; Thomas Moore talked on ferns, the Rev. E. Bayley on London cottage window gardens, Wilson Saunders on pelargoniums, and Andrew Murray on conifers. Successful though they may have been, no doubt the lecturettes were not so popular as the afternoon 'promenades' on Wednesdays and Thursdays, with their military bands. Nor were the promenades so well patronized as the Fête held on 24 May, the Queen's birthday, when 10,000 persons visited the Garden and saw a display of floral arrangements and attended an evening *conversazione* at which Fellows were received by the President, the Duke of Buccleuch. But these numbers were as nothing compared to an occasion in August.

In July the Queen had visited the Garden and expressed pleasure at the work which was being done. Her Majesty subsequently suggested that in future 26 August, the Prince Consort's birthday, should be regarded by the Society as a holiday on which the public should be given free admission to the Garden. The suggestion was enthusiastically adopted and arrangements were made for a special display of new, rare or very beautiful plants in the Conservatory. Bands were provided at the Society's expense. On 26 August 1864,

The day was delightfully fine and during the course of it, as nearly as can be ascertained, about 153,000 persons were admitted . . . no material damage beyond the unavoidable trampling of the turf slopes, was sustained, notwithstanding the densely crowded condition of the Garden throughout the day. The Conservatory, orchard houses, arcades, and maze were all open, and the cascades and Minton's fountain played. Bands were stationed at various parts, and played at intervals. Towards evening the Old Hundredth Psalm, with a hymn composed by the Prince Consort, and the National Anthem were sung by the assembled visitors on the upper terrace, the singing being led by the trumpeters.[1]

The Council appears to have forgotten that its Garden policy was alienating the purely horticulturally minded, the likes of Dr. Hogg, and, towards the end of the year, decided to purchase three pieces of sculpture for £233 and also some terracotta busts 'to aid in decorating the Garden'. However, this was probably not the reason why, in December, Andrew Murray, the Assistant Secretary, who had held office since 1860, 'again tendered his resignation', otherwise he would not have allowed himself to be elected to the Council at the Annual Meeting in 1865. His post was not filled until March 1865, when Captain John Cockerell was appointed at a salary of £240 per annum 'with an increase of 5 per cent on all receipts above £13,000 up to £20,000'.

A noteworthy newcomer to the Council in 1865 was George Ferguson Wilson. He had joined the Fruit and Vegetable Committee in 1862 and became its chairman in 1865. In the following year he was elected Treasurer and held office for two years.

In 1865 Wilson had recently retired from the position of managing director of Price's Patent Candle Company, a flourishing business which had developed from the candle-making firm of E. Price & Son which his father had founded. A gifted scientist with a special interest in chemistry, he had discovered in 1854 a method of manufacturing pure glycerine, the glycerine being first separated from fats and oils at high temperatures and then purified in an atmosphere of steam. He had lived originally at Wandsworth, but later acquired Gishurst Cottage at Weybridge, where

[1] *Gdnr's Chron.* (1864), p. 842.

he developed his interests in horticulture; herbaceous plants, and particularly lilies, commanded his attention, whilst his orchard house was a tremendous success. 'Gishurst' means 'pigwood', and many of Wilson's friends were surprised at the name. Wilson forecast that soon the word would become so common as to surprise no one. He was right—he produced the valuable insecticide, Gishurst Compound, which for many years was widely used by gardeners.

Later he built a large house, 'Heatherbank', on Weybridge Heath and pursued his gardening interests on a wider scale, always bringing a scientific mind to these interests. 'Laboratory training teaches careful observation and close watching,' he preached. Still later, whilst living at Weybridge, he was to acquire some sixty acres a few miles away—at Wisley, Surrey, make a clearance in a woodland, and there develop an informal garden which was to become famous throughout the horticultural world.

Lindley, who had been unwell for some time, died on 1 November 1865. In the following month the Council decided to institute a medal in his memory, and on the same day made the first award of a Lindley Medal to Messrs. Veitch, of Chelsea, for an exhibit of over fifty magnificently-grown specimens of the lovely white and rose flowered orchid, *Lycaste skinneri*, which James Bateman had introduced from Guatemala. However, the preparation of the die presented exceptional difficulty, and seven years later, 'It proving hopeless to obtain a good likeness of the late Dr. Lindley', the Council decided to substitute some species of plant closely identified with him. But in the end the difficulty was surmounted, and the medal, which was struck in 1874, bears what appears to be a very good reproduction of Lindley's head, complete with his spectacles. (Lindley lost the sight of one eye in infancy, but managed to see with one eye more than most see with two.) Nowadays the Lindley Medal is one of the Society's most coveted awards, being made for 'an exhibit of a plant or plants of special interest or beauty, or showing exceptional skill in cultivation, and for educational exhibits'.

A few weeks after Lindley's death it became known that his library was to be sold and the Council decided to take steps to acquire it and then raise the necessary money, £600, by opening a subscription list, for the Society certainly had not the money to spare for this purpose. Meanwhile, in May 1866, an International Horticultural Exhibition and Botanical Congress, organized by an *ad hoc* committee under the chairmanship of Sir Wentworth Dilke, with Dr. Masters as congress secretary, was held at South Kensington, partly in the Society's Gardens, and made a profit of over £1,850. The committee decided to contribute £1,000 to the Gardeners' Royal Benevolent Institution and to use the balance to enable the Royal Horticultural Society to re-establish a library with Lindley's library as the nucleus. At the same time Dr. Maxwell Masters, now part-editor of the *Gardener's Chronicle*, and other members of the committee, remembering only too well that some years earlier the Society had disposed of its own magnificent library to liquidate debts, were anxious to prevent a similar disaster in the future. To this effect, on 5 May 1868 the Lindley Library Trust was established, consisting of Dr. Masters, Dr. Robert Hogg, the pomologist, and Thomas Moore, the Curator of the Chelsea Physic Garden; three representatives of the Society—John Clutton, the Treasurer, Lieut.-Col. H. Y. D. Scott,[1] the Hon. Secretary, William Wilson Saunders, one of the Vice-Presidents, and a seventh member elected by the other six, Sir Wentworth Dilke. The committee reimbursed the Society for the £600 which it had advanced, and the Lindley Library trustees took over Lindley's books and provided book-cases to allow of their being suitably housed in the Council Room of the Society for the use of Fellows and other students of horticulture under regulations prescribed by the trustees. The trustees made an appeal for funds and for additional books, and one of the first to respond with a gift was H.M. the Queen, who sent two handsomely bound botanical works.

Although since its acquisition in 1866 the Lindley Library has always been housed on the Society's premises, first in Kensington, then in Victoria Street, and finally in Vincent Square, the trustees have been free to move it elsewhere had they so desired. Under a Trust Deed prepared in 1910 the original trustees retired and the Society, acting through its Council, became the trustee. At the same time the whole of the Society's own library, which by that time had again become considerable, was handed over to the Trust. Consequently the Council now has the power to decide where the Lindley Library shall be housed and, though unwanted books may be sold, the proceeds may be used for no other purpose than the Library. The books, pictures, and other property of the Trust are now valued at about £150,000. The Trust has received many gifts of books, but apart from the steady market appreciation in the value of old and rare books, the increase in value of the Library is largely due to purchases made over many years by the Society and immediately presented to the Trust.

[1] Lieut.-Col. (later Maj.-Gen. Sir) Henry Young Darracott Scott (1822–83). Soldier. From 1840 held commission in the Royal Engineers, retiring in 1871 with rank of major-general and a knighthood. Succeeded Sir Henry Cole as secretary to the Commissioners for the Great Exhibition of 1851, in which capacity he had much to do with the design and construction of the Royal Albert Hall. His position with R.H.S. was difficult and became untenable, so that he resigned with all his colleagues in 1873. Though a favourite with the horticulturists, his connection with the Commissioners involved on his part a divided allegiance which must have been as distasteful to him as it was unsatisfactory to the Horticultural Society.

During the year 1865 the increase in the number of Fellows was only nine and clearly the Society was needing some kind of stimulus. In Lindley's time the Meetings in Regent Street were made interesting and instructive not only by the reading of one or more papers but also by the comments which Lindley made on the day's exhibits. In 1865 the chairmen of the standing committees assumed Lindley's role, as may be gathered from a typical minute of that year.

The Rev. Joshua Dix, Chairman of the Floral Committee, and Mr. Geo. F. Wilson, Chairman of the Fruit Committee, pointed out the plants and fruits to which Certificates had been awarded by the Committees and remarked on some of the chief points of horticultural interest on which certain of the awards had been made. The Rev. M. J. Berkeley [who soon was to be instrumental in forming the Society's Scientific Committee] made some observations on the various plants exhibited, calling attention to many botanical peculiarities of interest to the Fellows. Mr. Bateman made a few remarks on orchids. Mr. William Paul then delivered a lecture on the cultivation of spring flowers.

Most of these had worked intimately with Lindley, both in the affairs of the Society and in those of the *Gardener's Chronicle* and were determined to carry on the Lindley tradition.

The Rev. M. J. Berkeley, Mr. Bateman, and Mr. William Paul were all remarkable men—though there were many more like them, all striving to steer the Society on the lines laid down by Knight, and all disciples of Lindley. Miles Joseph Berkeley—the initials 'M.J.B.' are very frequent in the weekly issues of the *Gardener's Chronicle* of this period —had an encyclopaedic knowledge of plants and put this knowledge to the service of botany and horticulture. His chief reputation as a botanist lay in the realm of cryptogamic botany and especially in the study of fungi. It was in his knowledge of these plants and particularly of the diseases they produced in plants that he contributed most to horticulture. After Lindley's death, he acted for several years as botanical referee and general councillor to the Society. 'His straightforward and unpretentious simplicity, yet strength of character, was combined, not only with caution, vast knowledge, and sagacity, but with personal qualities and considerateness towards others which endeared him to his associates, and caused him to be venerated by them.' This was the verdict of the *Gardener's Chronicle* when Berkeley died in 1889 in his eighty-seventh year.

And when James Bateman died in 1897 in his eighty-eighth year this same publication, to which he too had often contributed, proclaimed him as 'one of the most remarkable men in the horticultural world that the century had seen'. In his youth he had been much of a dandy; even so Lindley, who hated the type but who also humorously said, 'I am a dandy in my herbarium,' had become attracted to him and had quickened in him an interest in orchids which he was never to lose. In fact, he became one of the first and most enthusiastic cultivators of orchids, writing, and issuing in parts, between 1837 and 1843, one of the largest books that ever has been published—*The Orchidaceae of Mexico and Guatemala*, with forty superb colour plates of double crown, the work of Mrs. Withers and Miss Drake, and with half a dozen humorous woodcuts by Cruikshank and Lady Grey of Groby. Each plate cost over £200 and only 125 copies of the work were issued—at a cost of 20 guineas each. The copy in the Lindley Library measures 2 feet 6 inches in height by 1 foot 9 inches in width by nearly 3 inches in thickness—and weighs 38 pounds. It is the largest and heaviest book in the Library. The Lindley Library's duplicate copy was sold in 1963 for £650.

Orchids were by no means Bateman's only interest. He had been much engrossed in tropical fruits, even before orchids. Moreover, he was to create two of the most remarkable gardens of the century, one at Knypersley on the bleak Biddulph moorland, which took five articles in the *Gardener's Chronicle* of 1862 to describe, and the other, a smaller one, at Worthing. And it was in one of the houses at Biddulph Grange that he succeeded in producing the golden acid fruits, for the first time in England, on the tropical carambola, *Averrhoa carambola*.

In 1833 he had been enterprising enough to employ his own collector, one named Colley, who was sent to Demerara and Berbice, British Guiana. Although Bateman afterwards described the results of the expedition in the *Gardener's Magazine*, Colley's collection was a poor one, and whilst the undistinguished orchid of unpleasant odour which Lindley named *Batemannia colleyi* may have been not entirely inappropriate for the collector, it did scant justice to the name of the remarkable patron. Bateman was much more successful in his relationship with George Ure Skinner, a Leeds merchant who travelled in Guatemala and who obtained many orchids for the houses at Knypersley, where they were grown for painting by Mrs. Withers and Miss Drake. Later in life he came to live chiefly in Kensington, and thus close to the Society in which he took immense interest.

William Paul had been associated with the *Gardener's Chronicle* since its institution in 1841 and continued to be so until a short time before he died in 1905 in his eighty-third year. His talent for writing had been discovered by Loudon, to whom Paul often lent his aid. When Loudon died in 1843, ever quick to recognize and utilize ability, Lindley seized on the services of Paul for the *Chronicle*; and in 1843 came the first of his contributions—on 'Pot Roses'. He was best known as a rosarian and in 1848 had published *The Rose Garden*, whose many editions and supplements prove that it was a popular success; 'few, if any, knew roses as he did, few could more truly gauge the public taste in regard to them; few could grow them better; few knew better how to display them to advantage' was the verdict of the *Gardener's Chronicle* in 1905. However, his sympathies were not with roses alone; they ranged over almost the whole field of horticulture, except possibly that of orchids. Hollyhocks, hyacinths, camellias, hollies, irises, pelargoniums, decorative shrubs, fruit trees—in all these, and in more, he specialized; all these he grew in his Royal Nursery at Waltham Cross, which he had acquired in 1860 when he parted company with his brother George and with their joint nursery of A. Paul & Son which had been founded at Cheshunt in 1806, and all these he exhibited at the Society's Shows.

At the Annual Meeting in 1866 W. Wilson Saunders retired from the secretaryship and was succeeded by Lieut.-Col. Henry Scott, R.E., who had been active in the Society's affairs and was to take an equally active part in those of the Commissioners. The outstanding horticultural event of the year was the International Horticultural Exhibition, organized at Kensington with the Society's co-operation by an *ad hoc* committee of which Thomas Moore of the Chelsea Physic Garden was secretary. The Show was intended to be held on 22–5 May, but was prolonged until 31 May. Visitors to it had automatic free admission to the Society's Garden and there was a dispute between the Society and the organizing committee about the sharing of the admission fees.

In spite of the International Exhibition, a rather large number of Fellows resigned during the year and a good many others allowed their subscriptions to lapse. By July it was clear that the year's income would be down and equally clear that a saving in labour and other expenses of about £250 should be made. The saving obviously was not to be made on publications. After the cessation of the first series of the *Journal* in 1855 the *Proceedings* had become the Society's official record. Now, when economy was needed, it was perversely decided that the publication of some of the papers read to the Society should be resumed, and in 1866 the first of a 'New Series' of the *Journal*, edited by the Rev. M. J. Berkeley, began.

Until 1867 the Society's Shows had always been held in London or its neighbourhood, but in July of this year, with the co-operation of a local committee, a Show was held at Bury St. Edmunds in conjunction with the Royal Agricultural Society's Annual Show. The local committee guaranteed £600 towards the cost on the understanding that the committee and the Society should have equal shares of any profit; the arrangement proved satisfactory to both parties. Thus began a series of annual provincial Shows—at Leicester in 1868, Manchester in 1869, Oxford in 1870, Nottingham in 1871, and Birmingham in 1872—though the last two were held independently of the Royal Agricultural Society's Show. The financial results varied. At Manchester, where a horticultural congress was held on two of the six days, the gate was disappointing, partly because the site at Old Trafford was rather remote. On the other hand, the Show at Birmingham produced a profit of over £1,000, although 'more thoroughly wet days than the first two could hardly be imagined'.

At the Bath Show of 1873 the first award of the Veitch Memorial Medal was made. James Veitch, by virtue of his skill as a cultivator, his genius as an organizer, and his enterprise in sending forth plant collectors to various parts of the world, as well as by his generosity to horticultural charities, had made the name of the nursery of Messrs. James Veitch & Son famous the world over. On his death in 1869 the horticultural community desired to raise a memorial to his memory. Towards this end a committee was appointed under the chairmanship of James Bateman and numerous meetings were held, chiefly in the Society's Council Room at South Kensington. All manner of suggestions for a fitting memorial were forthcoming: a Veitch club, Veitch almshouses, a Veitch pension for disabled collectors, a Veitch pension for aged gardeners, a Veitch plantation, a Veitch portrait, a Veitch medal, Veitch prizes; and all were considered. On 21 October 1870 a well-attended meeting of subscribers was held at which T. Moore, who had acted as the committee's secretary, reported that £1,012. 12s. 9d. had been subscribed to the Veitch Memorial Fund and that when advertising, printing and postage costs amounting to £121. 14s. 5d. had been deducted, £890. 18s. 4d. remained. The committee recommended that the proposals to have painted a portrait of James Veitch and to establish certain Veitch prizes should be adopted. Fortunately the committee was also able to report that an excellent likeness of Veitch, painted specially to meet the objects of the memorial, had been presented by Robert Crawshay of Cyfarthfa Castle—the portrait which is now at the Society's headquarters at Vincent Square. Thus the sum of £890. 18s. 4d. was invested and from the interest first accruing the die for the Veitch Memorial Medal was furnished.

About this time arrangements were made for any Fellow, who was willing to pay a fee and out-of-pocket expenses, to have his garden inspected by the Superintendent of the Society's Garden, and the practice was continued until the demand for the service became so great that, in 1912, it was found necessary to appoint a garden adviser primarily to visit and advise Fellows on the cultivation and maintenance of their gardens.

The activities of the Fruit and Vegetable Committee and of the Floral Committee had done much valuable work towards maintaining the prestige of the Society and the support of those Fellows who were interested in plants as distinct from 'high art' and musical promenades and tea parties at the Garden. Berkeley, and Dr. Maxwell Masters, who had succeeded Lindley as scientific editor of the *Gardener's Chronicle* and who was always a most loyal supporter of the Society, and indeed was to prove to be one of its saviours, now pressed for a more scientific approach to gardening. Thus, in 1868, the Scientific Committee was instituted, with the President, the Duke of Buccleuch, as its first chairman and Berkeley its secretary. At its first meeting Berkeley stated that the object of the committee was 'to promote and encourage the application of physiology and botany to purposes of practical culture, . . . to originate experiments which may assist in the elucidation of such questions', and to help in connection with the frequent 'complaints that plants in collections are so badly named'. And Council resolved 'that the payment made to Mr. Berkeley for lectures at the general meetings, attendances at Chiswick, for editing the Journal, and as Secretary of the Scientific Committee be £300 per annum'.

Meanwhile the finishing of the Kensington Garden, with its fountains, canals, and statuary, had proved more costly than estimated. The opening of the Garden to the public, free on some days, and at a very small charge on others, together with the arrangements under which visitors to the exhibitions in the adjacent buildings had access to the Garden, caused many Fellows to feel that they were being shouldered out by mere sightseers who were not in the least interested in plants and in gardening. Moreover, after meeting unavoidable expenses, the Society's income, including its share of the gate money, was insufficient to enable the Council to comply with the financial clauses of their agreement with the Commissioners. As a measure of economy some of the glass-houses at Chiswick were demolished and, by arrangement with the Duke of Devonshire, the Garden there was reduced to about one-third of its original size.

The crisis in the Society's affairs which had been building up for some years had to come to a head some time. And to a head it came at the Annual General Meeting in 1873 when Fellows declined to adopt the Council's report which contained proposals for certain arrangements with the Commissioners of which the Meeting did not approve. One of the most prominent speakers was Sir Alfred Slade, who opposed the adoption of the report and asked the Meeting 'to express their opinion that the policy of the Council was *not* wise and ought *not* to be persisted in. (Cheers.)' In the end, having re-elected the President, Treasurer, and Secretary, and elected the recommended new Council members to replace the three retiring ones, on a proposal from Sir Alfred Slade, consideration of the report was postponed and the Meeting adjourned until the following week.

There seems no doubt that the Council had made every effort to work harmoniously with the Commissioners. Possibly it was towards this end that Maj.-Gen. Henry Scott, the secretary of the Commissioners and responsible for the design and execution of the Albert Hall on a site between the northern end of the Garden and Hyde Park, had been appointed Secretary to the Society; that Mr. Henry Cole (Sir Henry in 1875), one of the Royal Commissioners, had been appointed to the Society's Council and was a Vice-President. But in spite of these appointments, some would argue because of them, many Fellows took the view of William Paul that

the Commissioners and the Royal Horticultural Society go hand in hand, much as the giant and the dwarf did in the fable, and that while the giant (the Commissioners) will get all the credit of the work accomplished, the dwarf (the Royal Horticultural Society) will get all the blows. Or, in other words, it will be a sort of joint-stock enterprise, in which the R.H.S. is a working partner so placed that he must work to the point of slavery to obtain a bare maintenance. This certainly is hardly a dignified or proper position for the R.H.S. to accept.[1]

Many Fellows firmly believed that the relationship was one of exaction and oppression on the one hand and of abject concession on the other. But the oppressed can revolt and many were now goaded into indignant rebellion by some of the Commissioners' new proposals, especially those whereby the Commissioners undertook the horticultural management of the Gardens and gave themselves the power, but not the Society also, of determining the arrangement at twelve months's notice. The suspicion gained ground that a cunningly conceived design was afoot to absorb the Society completely into the South Kensington System; and Mr. Henry Cole seems to have been suspect.

At the adjourned General Meeting, on 18 February, Wilson Saunders presided and 'The Council Room was densely crowded, many country Fellows being present.' It was reported that the Council had made counter-proposals to those contained in the letter from the Commissioners which had been read at the Meeting of the preceding week, but that these counter-proposals were not acceptable to the Commissioners. Thus the proposition was still that set forth in the Council's annual report. Once again Sir Alfred Slade was prominent in the very long discussions and finally moved 'that the Report of the Council as it at present stands cannot be received . . . and that it be not adopted'. The motion was carried by a large majority, and the Chairman announced that the Council would meet at the earliest possible date to consider

[1] *Gdnr's Chron.* (1873), p. 216.

what steps should be taken, but that he, personally, believed that they should all resign. It is easy to understand the *Gardener's Chronicle* comment: 'It is not in our power adequately to convey an idea of the excitement manifested.'

The Council shared Mr. Wilson Saunders's views, but on seeking legal advice found that under the existing Bye-Laws they could not resign in a body, but would have to carry on until the next Annual General Meeting in 1874. Thus it was decided that a Special General Meeting should be assembled on 26 March for the purpose of amending the Bye-Laws to allow Council to resign and be replaced at any time. Lord Alfred Churchill presided at what the *Gardener's Chronicle* described as a 'disgracefully noisy meeting', where the reporter observed 'gross impropriety and unfairness which led to a certain number of Fellows present to drown with noise and clamour the utterance of any whose opinions might be distasteful to the clamourers'. However, the proposed Bye-Law was adopted by ninety-three votes to twenty-three, and the whole Council, except Andrew Murray, who was on his way to America, tendered their resignations.

Under the new Bye-Law the outgoing Council members were required to call a General Meeting as soon as possible to fill their places, and until such a meeting was called the resigning members had to continue to act as a Council. Accordingly a fourth General Meeting was held on 4 April to elect a new Council. In the absence of the Duke of Buccleuch, who played no part in these unfortunate happenings, the Chair was again taken by Lord Alfred Churchill. Fellows were in an argumentative mood, the meeting developed into a stormy one, and for a time no progress was made. But presently a Fellow occupied the floor, proposed that the resignations of the Council be accepted—except those of the Duke of Buccleuch, H.R.H. Prince Arthur, H.S.H. the Duke of Teck, and Lord Londesborough. This proposal was carried almost unanimously. The Fellow then further proposed that the eleven vacant seats should be filled by the election of ten new members, whom he named, and Mr. Andrew Murray. The subsequent proposal was carried by eighty-five votes to twenty-three and the result was 'greeted with applause'. A resolution expressing confidence in the Duke of Buccleuch was then carried unanimously and Mr. W. A. Lindsay was elected Secretary in place of Maj.-Gen. Henry Scott.

The Fellow who proposed this popular temporary solution to the Society's troubles was the Earl of Strathmore, whose grandson, Mr. David Bowes Lyon, was one day to be one of the Society's most farsighted and popular Presidents. Thus the flames of the rebellion were extinguished.

One of the first actions of the new Council, sitting under the chairmanship of Viscount Bury,[1] was to report the recent happenings to the Queen, seek her approval of the changes in its membership, and 'express a hope that Her Majesty will be graciously pleased to continue to give to the Society that countenance and support Her Majesty has ever been pleased to bestow upon it'. Presumably the Queen's advisers were not impressed, for the Council minutes contain no reference to any reply from Her Majesty. Moreover, the Duke of Buccleuch, the Duke of Teck, and Lord Londesborough all resigned from the Council, as did Andrew Murray, who addressed his resignation from San Francisco.

Lord Bury (Plate 9), with no horticultural pretensions, succeeded Buccleuch as President, but held the post only until 1875, to be succeeded by Lord Aberdare, who had become a rich man when coal was discovered on the family estate in Glamorganshire. Moreover, he was an accomplished scholar, an excellent man of business, and was gifted with great tact and amiability. No doubt it was for the latter reasons that Her Majesty expressed her desire that he assume the presidency of the Society at this time, when it was in sore straits and when its relationships with the Commissioners were by no means agreeable. But like his predecessor he had no knowledge of the requirements of horticulture or of the proper work of a scientific society. Even so, he and Council tried to come to a more satisfactory working agreement with the Commissioners, as well as to increase the Society's income. Towards this end, in 1874, Lord Bury and his Council had proposed to allow the construction of a skating-rink in the Kensington Garden, in return for a rent of £1,100, but even the Commissioners withheld their consent to this project on the ground that it was not horticultural. In 1879, however, in Aberdare's régime, the Commissioners took quite a different view of lawn tennis, thought it was permissible and allowed it to be played; it became very popular with Fellows living at Kensington. Council did draw the line at rounders, though, and also declined to sanction tennis at Chiswick.

Aberdare was able to effect little in the resuscitation of the Society, for its whole relationship with the Commissioners was fundamentally unsound. Statuary, skating-rinks, and tennis courts were all very well for the 'Kensingtonians', but they were certainly not what the horticulturally minded Fellows were requiring. And in spite of the crowds of non-Fellows, which were very large on days when the charge for admission was as little as twopence, the Society's share of the gate money was not sufficient to enable it to meet its obligations either to the Commissioners or to the debenture-holders.

[1] William Coutts Keppel (1832–94), known throughout the greater part of his life as Viscount Bury, the second title of his father, the sixth Earl of Albemarle, whom he succeeded in 1881. Sometime M.P., Treasurer of the Household and Under-Secretary for War. Raised to the peerage in 1876 as Baron Ashford. President of the Society, 1873–5.

Thus in 1879 the Commissioners gave notice that they proposed to exercise their powers of re-entry at the end of the year. On the other hand, Council believed that the Society's obligations to the debenture holders compelled it to refuse to vacate the Kensington premises unless ejected by legal process. Consequently, in June the Commissioners served an ejection notice on the Society and commenced an action in Chancery against it. The Council accordingly engaged counsel to defend the Society's case. In 1881 judgement was given in favour of the Society and the debenture-holders. However, the Commissioners took the matter to the Court of Appeal, where, in March the following year, the decision was reversed, the view being taken that the parties were not partners, but landlord and tenant. The Commissioners were given their costs and power to take possession of the Kensington Garden in four months. The Society was relieved of all claims in respect of £49,700 debentures and to that extent fared not badly; but the cost of the litigation was nearly £1,000.

The Commissioners were in no hurry to take over the maintenance of the Garden (possibly because if this idea *had* first stemmed from Sir Henry Cole he had now retired), and were content to continue for the next few years to make year-to-year arrangements for a series of international exhibitions, occupying most of the adjacent buildings, with displays dealing with such matters as medicine and sanitation, health, fisheries, inventions. The Society, on the other hand, continued to have the use of offices, the Council Room and Conservatory for its fortnightly Meetings, the limited area being supplemented by a tent for the shows when space was needed for kindred societies' exhibits such as roses, primulas and auriculas, pelargoniums, carnations and picotees. No doubt the apparently generous attitude of the Commissioners at this time was influenced by the fact that, on learning of the result of the litigation, the Queen expressed the hope that some amicable arrangement between the Commissioners and the Society would yet be reached.

Even so, for the third time the fortunes of the Society were at a very low ebb; there were many resignations and many failures to pay subscriptions. And for the third time the principal cause was unwise expenditure, in one way or another, on the Garden; on *one* Garden anyway.

CHAPTER FOURTEEN

CHISWICK

WHEN, IN 1859, LINDLEY WAS ADVOCATING THE NEED FOR A SHOW
Garden and for a site for flower shows and that the Chiswick Garden, to
which he had given so much of his time and devotion, should be used as
an experimental station, he was well aware of the splendid work—work
of a purely *horticultural* nature—which the keen and energetic Chiswick
staff was undertaking there. No longer was it the scene of brilliant
exhibitions and fashionable promenades; and for this many Fellows
rejoiced. It was now, or shortly was to be, devoted to the raising of
thousands of plants for the Kensington Garden, and to the supplying of
vast quantities of material for distribution to Fellows. Even more important, it was actively engaged in the testing of fruits, flowers, and
vegetables, and thus already was functioning, to some extent, as an experimental garden. In fact, the Council had distributed a circular letter
among the trade, inviting co-operation in the trial of every kind of new,
or supposedly new, vegetable, and the Fruit and Vegetable Committee
had undertaken to examine and report on the results of such trials. If
Kensington was to be the seat of 'high art', Chiswick must be the seat of
practical horticulture; and so it was.

In 1857 the great Conservatory had been emptied of its ornamental
plants, and had been planted with vines which were intended to cover
the inside of the roof—as well as to produce a profitable return, all in the
cause of making the Garden as self-supporting as possible. The vines, of
twenty-five distinct types, were planted partly in an outside, and partly
in an inside, border, and in 1859 covered three-quarters of the roof,
which was nearly 30 feet high. Moreover, they, mostly Black Hamburgh,
were fruiting well, averaging ten bunches per vine, each bunch weighing
upwards of 2 pounds. There were also good crops on the vines in the curvilinear vinery. Grapes apart (there were 170 different kinds), there were
many other splendid collections of fruits both out of doors as well as
under glass; in fact, except for a few orchids and ferns, practically all the
glass-houses were now devoted to fruit growing. There were in all over
600 different kinds of apples; a new cherry garden of about 130 sorts and
a new plum garden of 150 sorts; nearly 30 apricots; about 25 nectarines

211

and 50 peaches; about 35 currants, 20 raspberries, 80 gooseberries; about 30 different figs; over 100 strawberries. In the kitchen garden were collections of peas, beans—French, haricots and runners—Chinese vegetable seeds, broccoli, and borecole. Of trials there was one of cucumbers—137 different kinds grown in frames with bottom heat; one of broccoli of 70 kinds and another of 116 so-called different sorts of peas, reduced, after trial, to 70 really distinct kinds. As for flowers, there were trials of 300 kinds of annuals, 74 achimenes, 40 begonias, 150 pelargoniums, 23 heliotropes, as well as petunias, fuchsias, verbenas, and geraniums.

Clearly there was great justification for the statement in the *Gardener's Chronicle* in 1860 that 'This great trial ground for the proving of Fruits, Flowers and Vegetables, is every day acquiring additional interest.'

Unfortunately, this great trial ground was also incurring considerable expense; though Kensington was incurring much more. And Lindley, who knew only too well what the fruits of reckless expenditure had been, was disturbed. At a meeting of Council in August 1861 he issued a statement impressing the importance of economy in the adjustment of regular yearly expenditure, and concluded with the motion, which was unanimously agreed, 'That Mr. Eyles [the Superintendent of the Garden] be called upon to report how the annual sum of £1,000 can be made to suffice for the expenses of Chiswick—not including the cost of distribution and preparing plants for the Garden at Kensington.' Eyles, and the subcommittee appointed to assist him, recommended that not less than fourteen acres of the Garden should be surrendered to the landlord.

Rather illogically the Council now thought it desirable to send a collector to Brazil. Clearly they could not afford to do so, but they were possibly influenced by the knowledge that the prestige of Chiswick had been built on the renown of its plant collectors and of the new plants which had been introduced to, and distributed from, the Garden. John Weir, a member of the Scientific Committee, was chosen for the task of introducing new plants from Brazil and left in the spring of 1861. His first consignment of plants, in excellent condition, arrived in July. He stayed in Brazil for two years, before proceeding to New Grenada. Here his active career was ended in 1864 by an attack of fever which completely paralysed him. He was befriended by the British Consul at Santa Martha and arrived home, in a hopeless condition, in the autumn of 1865, never to work again. An appeal was made to Fellows of the Society, for subscriptions for a fund for Weir and his wife, an appeal strongly supported by the *Gardener's Chronicle* in 1865 and again in 1866; the result was an annuity on the lives of Mr. and Mrs. Weir of a little over fifty pounds a year. 'His honourable connection with the Scientific

Plate 13. The opening of the Old Hall, 22 July 1904, by King Edward VII. Sir Trevor Lawrence, the President, stands at the front of the platform holding the cord, with the Rev. W. Wilks, the Secretary, below him.

David Douglas   Robert Fortune

F. Kingdon Ward   George Forrest

Plate 14. PLANT COLLECTORS

Committee of the Society will be one of the treasured memories of his widow and children,' Mrs. Weir wrote to the Society. Until 1898, when he died, the Weirs lived quietly in New Barnet, he taking great joy from his garden and from his hobby of bookbinding, she scarcely leaving his side.

Weir introduced for the Society many beautiful plants, especially orchids and ferns. They were mostly of a tender nature and, of course, they had to be raised at Chiswick, where there was little enough glass for their accommodation. And at Chiswick they had to be propagated and distributed to those Fellows who were anxious to grow them, for the Council was still of the opinion that the Garden should be effective as a centre in which to introduce and from which to distribute rare plants. At the same time the Council was beginning to realize that, if Chiswick was to continue to function in this way, the emphasis must be on hardy plants, for circumstances were becoming such that tender plants were only for the enjoyment of the few and the Society would not be justified in spending much money to procure them. And soon the realization was to come to the Council that, because the principal nurserymen in the country were now spending large sums of money in employing their own collectors in various parts of the world, the Society's splendid pioneer work in this direction need not continue.

There seemed little hope of maintaining the annual expenses of Chiswick within the sum of the £1,000 which Lindley had suggested. Although £435 had been received from sales of fruit and the reimbursement of Garden charges, expenses for 1862–3 were £2,354. The money had not been extravagantly spent, unless the raising of 50,000 plants for bedding out at Kensington was an extravagance. These apart, large quantities of material had been distributed to Fellows; over 3,000 packages of cuttings of vines and other fruit trees, 11,000 plants, nearly 170 packages of bulbs, nearly 3,000 packets of seeds. The trials of fruits, vegetables, and flowers had continued under the supervision of Berkeley, Moore, and Hogg, and had been judged by the Fruit and Vegetable Committee and the Floral Committee.

Quite obviously Chiswick was serving a useful and important horticultural function, and many Fellows were appreciative. Since the opening of the Kensington Garden attendances at Chiswick had fallen. However, as more Fellows gradually became disillusioned with the Kensington adventure, more began to visit Chiswick once again, and in 1864 close on 9,000 signed the Chiswick visitors' book—more than four times as many as in any of the previous three years. On one day, 27 August—a highlight for Chiswick—between 200 and 300 Fellows and their friends attended a musical promenade and inspected various matters of horticultural interest; the great Conservatory of grapes, the house of muscats, demonstrations of hardy fruits and of fruit tree pruning and training, the collection of half-hardy plants in a new trial ground at the east end of the Conservatory. For the horticulturally minded there was always much of interest to be seen, including, in 1865, an entirely new race of golden-leaved caladiums which Bausé, the foreman in the floral department, had developed.

Not only did the Chiswick Garden thus provide for the horticultural interests of the Fellows; even more so did it offer scope for the horticultural education of its gardeners. For many years the Council had endeavoured to promote the education of the young workmen employed in the Society's Garden. A small library had been gradually formed for their use and for their encouragement an examination had been held and a certificate of proficiency awarded. During the first twenty-five years of the Garden's history, 244 young gardeners had been employed. Of these, 41 had been discharged for various reasons; 13 had deserted shortly after their arrival on finding the discipline distasteful to them; 3 had resigned and 13 had died or had left due to poor health. For the rest, 62 had found situations for themselves, whilst 112 had been recommended to posts by the Society. In 1846, as a further step in the education of its workmen, a reading-room for them was established at the Garden; they could attend lectures on the art and science of gardening, and take examinations in arithmetic, the Definitions and first twenty Propositions in the first book of Euclid, physical geography, systematic and structural botany, physiology, and the art of horticulture. Unfortunately, though the scheme promised well, it gradually fell into desuetude.

In 1864 the matter of horticultural education at Chiswick was raised once again through correspondence in the *Gardener's Chronicle*. On 31 February 'A Very Old F.H.S.' wrote

Gardeners at present are educated in the gardens of the nobility and gentry— the head gardener, in some instances, receiving a premium with every youth he receives. This arrangement need not be changed. It is beneficial as far as it goes, but we all know that in such gardens only one routine is followed, so that a youth on leaving a garden perfect in all its appliances, becomes as it were at sea on leaving it; he requires finishing by learning the horticulture of the world, to be taught at Chiswick, which should be the University of Horticulture. Every youth on the termination of his apprenticeship in the provinces, should serve one year at least at Chiswick, and at the end of that term receive a certificate of ability—he should in fact take his degree. As far as I can see, no great expense would attend the opening of the doors of our school. Two or three professors, i.e. good gardeners, would be required to attend to the pupils, who should do the work of the garden, be instructed in pruning and training and general culture, and hear lectures in the different branches of horticulture, as is now the practice in the public gardens of France. No premium need be paid, but the pupils should give their work for one year's finishing.

And two weeks later, in its leader, the *Chronicle* exclaimed: 'Chiswick, a School of Horticulture! The very idea is refreshing and the sound of the exclamation musical'; and Sir Wentworth Dilke, a Councillor and closely associated with the *Chronicle*, gave notice that he would raise the question of Chiswick becoming 'a school of horticulture for the whole empire'. And in December, at the Council's request, the Society of Arts nominated three representatives to serve on a joint committee 'for the purpose of carrying out a system of examination of Gardeners'.

The Committee on the Improved Education of Gardeners, under the chairmanship of Wilson Saunders, met several times and finally produced a comprehensive report in 1865. Towards the establishment of an efficient school of horticulture for the training of gardeners at Chiswick many recommendations were made. The Garden should include comprehensive collections of tender fruits—pineapples, grapes, melons, cucumbers, orchard house fruits; hardy fruits; vegetables of all kinds; tender plants—stove and greenhouse ornamental plants, orchids, fuchsias, pelargoniums, etc.; hardy plants and out-of-doors flowers of all kinds; hardy trees; demonstrations to illustrate such processes as continental systems of pruning, training etc.; facilities for hybridization. The Garden should be in the charge of a Chief Superintendent and should be divided into three departments, each in charge of a foreman—kitchen garden foreman, plant foreman, fruit foreman. The foremen's staff should consist for the most part of students who should be recommended by a Fellow, be at least twenty years of age, be in good health, have had at least three years' experience in good private gardens, 'have a good hand, spell well, and have a competent knowledge of arithmetic', and have paid a premium of five pounds. Students making satisfactory progress should be systematically transferred from one department to another and be paid thirteen shillings a week for the first year, fourteen shillings for the second and fifteen shillings for the third. Instruction should be given to all students in the theory and practice of horticulture and the facilities of a library and reading-room should be provided for them. Students should pass proficiency examinations twice each year—and candidates twice failing to pass should be discharged—as well as a final examination the passing of which would entitle a student to the Society's Certificate. The final examination should be a test of general knowledge as well as of the theory and practice of horticulture and should be conducted by examiners appointed by the Society.

To most of these recommendations Council agreed and proposed gradually to put into effect. In 1865 arrangements were made for student-gardeners at Chiswick, as well as young men in other gardens and nurseries throughout the country, to be able to sit for two examinations; a preliminary written test in general education conducted by the Society of Arts or other public examining body, and a practical examination in horticulture conducted at Chiswick by the Royal Horticultural Society. Being unable to find a resident Chief Superintendent combining great practical skill in gardening with scientific attainment, Council decided that Eyles, who had had charge of both Kensington and Chiswick, should be relieved of the latter charge, and on 1 January 1866, Archibald Barron, the senior foreman, was made Superintendent. Council further decided to spend £500 on additional glass at Chiswick, to improve the library there, as well as to provide living accommodation for the students. Towards this latter end, in March 1866

It was resolved . . . that the sheds adjoining the carpenter's shop should be fitted as a lodging for the students . . .; a boarded partition being put between the beds—the students to pay the sum of 2/- per week if they avail themselves of the accommodation offered. It was also resolved that, in consideration of the social condition of the young men who are now working in the Garden and the recent rise in the price of labour, the students' wages be 14/-.

Although, by present-day standards, certainly by present-day Wisley standards, the cubicles could hardly have been less attractive, presumably they were all occupied, for in the following year, when the East Gate Lodge was made suitable for the Superintendent, it was decided that his old house should 'be converted into lodgings for students who are to pay at the usual rate for the accommodation'.

Gradually the students' instruction course was broadened; with the co-operation of the Royal Society of Arts, the instruction was supplemented by courses in surveying, freehand and geometrical drawing, garden design, plant physiology, and chemistry. Better facilities were also provided in the form of an orchard house for fruits previously grown on walls—peaches, nectarines, apricots, cherries. Classes were held between 6 and 8 p.m. and, although intended primarily for Chiswick students, young men from Kew, Regent's Park, and elsewhere were admitted. The examinations were now attracting some of the young men who were to become the experts of the future. For instance, among the successful candidates in 1868 was R. Irwin Lynch (1850–1924), then a student at Kew and destined to become the Curator of the Cambridge Botanic Garden and to reign as such for forty years, from 1879 to 1919, making the Cambridge Garden famous for its interesting plants and for the skill with which they were grown and bringing renown to himself by writing the first popular and accurate book on irises in 1904, by his work on hybrid cinerarias, and by his new classification of the genus *Paeonia*—for all of which, and very much more, he received the Victoria Medal of Honour in 1906. In 1869 a young man named James Hudson (1846–1932), employed as a foreman in the garden at Deepdene, Dorking, distinguished himself by being the first candidate to receive 100 per cent of the examination marks. Ultimately he became head gardener to Mr. Leopold de Rothschild at Gunnersbury from 1889 to 1919, making this establishment one of the show-places of the country, renowned especially for its fruits of all classes, and receiving the Victoria Medal of Honour when it was established in 1897. For about twenty years he was to serve on the Council and for many years on the Society's Board of Examiners.

Such was Chiswick in 1870, when at the Annual General Meeting the Chairman, James Bateman, opened the proceedings by making some observations on the report of the Council for the past year which had not arrived from the printers, and 'completely took the Meeting by surprise' by stating that the Council had been considering abandoning the Garden at Chiswick, chiefly, so he said, because of the difficulty in growing plants within the smoke of London, but also partly because of the increasing cost, and partly because the lease had only eleven years to run. An obstacle which would have seriously hampered the change to a new locality—the expense involved in establishing a new Garden— had, he believed, been removed by a valuable bequest to the Society from their late Fellow, Mr. Alfred Davis.

Naturally many of the real horticulturists among the Fellows were astonished at the idea of abandoning the Garden which had done so much for horticulture by the dissemination of new plants, work on the nomenclature of fruits, flowers, and vegetables, and the trials of these, as well as for horticultural education; so much to make the Society the leading organization of its kind in the world. Many Fellows were no doubt of the same mind as Mr. J. R. Pearson, of Chilwell:

I cannot help thinking that when Chiswick is given up, the Royal Horticultural Society may be considered defunct. To members living in the country the vast expenditure on the Kensington Garden is no advantage. They will hardly continue to pay two or four guineas that the inhabitants of Kensington may have a garden to walk about in, or a reading room to lounge in. To be able themselves to see once or twice a year a garden that strongly reminds them of a tea garden on a large scale, will hardly appear a valuable privilege. To anyone really interested in horticulture, a few hours spent in discussing and comparing new fruits and flowers with Mr. Barron was really worth a subscription, and the large and valuable collection of trees and plants was always worth looking over carefully. Then to many a cutting of a plant new to them, or a packet of seeds they could not otherwise procure, was an advantage. The meetings of the Fruit and Floral Committees had always an interest for the lovers of a garden. An experimental garden, like Chiswick, and a large room to hold the committee meetings in, with a really intelligent, enthusiastic gardener, like Mr. Barron, have always appeared to us the necessities of a horticultural society. When Chiswick is given up what shall we members get who do not live near Kensington?[1]

And no doubt there were many Fellows of the same mind as 'Opus':

The news so unexpectedly and so suddenly forced upon us regarding the abandonment of all that horticulturists understand by the simple word—'Chiswick' will ill accord with the sentiments of those who wish the gardeners' art God-speed. . . . Let the new Garden be formed where it may, it should bear the name of 'New', or 'Modern Chiswick' as a daily remembrance of the glorious past.[2]

At a Council Meeting held about this time Mr. G. F. Wilson produced a plan of a garden in the neighbourhood of Weybridge which it seemed to him 'presented some advantages to the Society, having reference to the contemplated change from Chiswick'. A committee was appointed to visit the garden and to report on it—but no further mention of the matter occurs in the Council minutes. It is unlikely that the property in question was at Wisley, for Wilson did not acquire land in that village until 1878. When he did so he lost no time in forming what he called his 'Oakwood experimental garden', in which his aim was 'to make difficult plants grow successfully'. By 1883 the garden was attracting the attention of leading horticulturists, because, in addition to other difficult plants, it contained 'many thousands of lilies planted in all sorts of situations and soils'.[3]

When the time came to implement the decision to vacate Chiswick for a more favoured site it was realized that the funds necessary for the establishment of a new Garden were not available. Council had been misled by the bequest from Alfred Davis which turned out to be one of £2,000 (£1,800 net) 'to be held as a permanent fund' of which only the income was expendable—on the provision of annual prizes or similar purposes. Even so, though the Garden had to remain at Chiswick its expenditure needed to be cut down. Thus the Duke of Devonshire's agents were approached about the possibility of cancelling the existing lease of thirty-two acres and replacing it with one for a much smaller area. The Duke generously agreed and granted a new lease for between ten and eleven acres, at a rental of ten pounds per acre, for a period of twenty-one years, renewable at the Society's option. To bring the Gar-

---

[1] *Gdnr's Chron.* (1870), p. 313.   [2] *Gdnr's Chron.* (1870), p. 247.
[3] *Gdnr's Chron.* (1883), p. 178, fig. 27.

den to its reduced size two glasshouses were demolished, the least valuable fruit trees were discarded, and surplus plants were sold. The hardy perennials were removed to the part of the Garden to be retained, and planted into new borders flanking the great Conservatory. Likewise was the collection of bedding pelargoniums preserved. The Arboretum, not now so essential as it was when designed in 1824, in view of the magnificent one at Kew, was lost. The changes were not without their debit side, however. It was estimated that trenching and clearing ground, 400 yards of new boundary wall, a house for the Superintendent, etc., would cost over £770, and as such money was not readily available it was resolved 'that such portions of the above be made as the proceeds of the forthcoming sale of surplus stock at Chiswick might warrant'.

To one man in particular, the curtailment—the mutilation—of the Garden was disappointing and distasteful; he was Archibald Barron, Chiswick's Superintendent, and one of the Society's most valued and valuable employees. An Aberdonian, he had received his first training as a gardener from his father at Crathes Castle. From Crathes he had moved south to Oxton, near Peterborough, playing his part in the formation of the celebrated pinetum there, before proceeding to Arundel Castle to work under McEwan, the renowned fruit grower. When McEwan was appointed Superintendent at Chiswick he called his former pupil to his aid. Thus Barron came to Chiswick, soon to have charge of the great vines which had recently been planted and to learn from the knowledge and experience of such men as Lindley, Robert Thompson, Robert Hogg, and Thomas Moore—and henceforth to work devotedly for the cause of the Society.

So distressed was he by the curtailment of Chiswick that he decided to leave the services of the Society. He obtained the post of superintendent of Victoria and Greenwich Parks and tendered his resignation. But the Council would have none of this. Eyles, the Superintendent at Kensington, was now devoting much of his time to private practice as a landscape gardener and so the Council offered Barron the post of 'Gardener-in-Chief at Kensington and Chiswick' at a salary of £250 a year. Having devoted so much of his life to the Society's service, one can well imagine that it would have been a severe wrench for him to have left Chiswick, and no doubt this quiet, retiring man who gained the admiration and esteem of his fellow workers and Fellows—'To anyone really interested in horticulture, a few hours spent in discussing and comparing new fruits and flowers with Mr. Barron was really worth a subscription,' one Fellow had said—was sincere when he wrote, very simply, that he had much pleasure in accepting the offer.

Partly to aid Barron in his work at Chiswick, a Professor of Botany to the Society was appointed in 1872. The Professor's duties were 'to conduct the scientific business of the Society, both horticultural and botanical, and, where Chiswick was concerned, to give lectures to the Students, to supervise the experimental work and to attend to the correct naming of plants'. The holder of this new post, at a salary of £250 per annum, was Professor (later Sir) William Turner Thiselton Dyer, who for the past two years had been Professor of Botany at the Royal College of Science, Dublin, and who later was to be Director of Kew and a Vice-President of the Society.

In 1881, shortly after the Royal Commissioners had served the Society with an ejectment notice for Kensington, Chiswick was *en fête*; at the Garden, on a blazing day in July, the Chiswick, Turnham Green and District Horticultural Society held an exhibition in the great Conservatory, inadequately screened from the sun by the vines and a veil of canvas. The exhibition did not rival the grand scenes and associations of a previous generation, but it did recall the time when the Chiswick Shows and Fêtes were the pride of horticulture, and the greatest attraction of the fashionable world. This Fête was not dominated by the wealthy upper classes, but by the residents of the countless villas and houses that had grown up for miles around Turnham Green. It was these people who 'filled the gardens decked out in all the fashion of the hour, lounged in the exceeding heat with all the dignity they could command, and bore their part in the popular gathering in a manner which showed their taste and their appreciation'.[1] It was these people, and their kind, who were to carry the Society to the crest of the wave.

On this July day Barron had the Garden in splendid condition and the results of the labours of the Garden staff were for all to see and appreciate; the fine old Conservatory—the noblest feature of the Garden; the conversion of the great orchard house into a rose house; the house of begonias, a great collection superbly grown by Hemsley, the foreman, containing many seedlings raised at Chiswick, and in the opinion of many judges 'one of the finest displays of the flowering Begonia yet seen'; the houses aglow with double- and single-flowered ivy-leaved and zonal pelargoniums; the gloxinia house; the palm and fern houses; the vegetable department; the floral department, including the rock garden which seemed 'to present, both geologically and florally, a natural phenomenon'; on the walls and in the open ground the large collection of fruit trees; the various trials and the work of the various committees; the facilities for horticultural education.

Well done, Chiswick! There at least is real loyalty to the fundamental aim of the Royal Horticultural Society, and most satisfactory efforts are found in force to promote its true work. Let the Fellows of the Society show their

[1] *Gdnr's Chron.* (1881), p. 101.

interest in this work by visiting the Garden, and by their countenance strengthen the hands and encourage the heart of their superintendent. Then shall practical horticulture be once more the leading feature in the operations of the Society, and gardeners everywhere will have much cause to rejoice and be glad.[1]

That judgement of 1878 was even more appropriate in 1882, when the Society's lease at Kensington was terminated by the Royal Commissioners.

[1] *Gdnr's Chron.* (1878), p. 529.

Interlude
to Parts Four and Five

BETWEEN 1856 AND 1874 GREGOR MENDEL, WORKING IN HIS LITTLE garden at the Monastery of St. Thomas in Brunn, was making those discoveries of the laws of inheritance with which his name is now associated and was laying the foundation of the science of genetics. His famous paper wherein he describes his great discovery of the segregation of characters was published in 1865, but it was not until its rediscovery in 1900, and its publication in the Royal Horticultural Society's *Journal*, that it became really known and accepted as one of the most fundamental and important discoveries ever to be made in biology. Strangely enough, there were others who were working along lines similar to Mendel. In a paper published in 1866 in *The Report of the International Horticultural Exhibition and Botanical Congress*, Thomas Laxton independently and clearly described the phenomenon of dominance and other facts on which Mendel based his discovery. Six years later, in 1872, he published in the Society's *Journal*, 'Notes on some changes and variations in the Offspring of Cross-fertilised Peas'. This paper, one of the most valuable the Society has ever published, dealt with the transmittable characters in peas. He used 'Ringleader', a white pea three feet high, to cross with the purple-flowered Maple Pea, and described the results of the first, second, and third generations arising from the cross, showing, as Mendel had done, the proportions of the various characters in each generation.

Laxton's cross-breeding of peas was by no means the only activity of this remarkably scientific horticulturist—a true disciple of Thomas Andrew Knight; he also cross-bred strawberries, potatoes, roses, and pelargoniums and other plants. Among peas the best cultivars he raised were probably 'Gradus'—the first large-podded early wrinkled marrow pea and an advance of great economic value—and 'Thomas Laxton'; among strawberries, 'King of the Earlies' and 'Noble'—the parents of 'Royal Sovereign', which was introduced in 1892; among the potatoes, 'Early Laxton', 'Bouncey', and 'Bedfordshire Hero'—all now superseded. Many of the zonal pelargoniums and hybrid perpetual roses that he raised were highly popular by the turn of the century. Laxton died in

1890, at the age of sixty, and his great work was continued by his sons, Edward and William, the well-known Laxton Brothers, at Bedford, who later turned their attention to apples, pears, and plums. By 1930 the Laxtons had raised 170 new cultivars of plants, many of them of great economic value, including forty-six which had received the First Class Certificate and twenty-eight the Award of Merit, from the Royal Horticultural Society. Among them are well-known names; of strawberries, 'Royal Sovereign'; of apples, 'Laxton's Superb', 'Laxton's Fortune', 'Laxton's Epicure', 'Lord Lambourne'; of pears, 'Laxton's Superb', 'Laxton's Satisfaction', 'Beurré Bedford'; of plums, 'Early Laxton', 'Laxton's Gage', 'Laxton's Bountiful'.

There were other disciples of Knight, experimentalists imbued with the desire to improve plants by hybridization for the benefit of their fellow men, and fit to rank with Laxton was Thomas Rivers, born at Sawbridgeworth in 1798, where he lived and worked until he died in 1877. He contributed to the science of gardening by his work on the root pruning of fruit trees, double grafting, orchard houses, cordon training, the introduction of the Manetti stock, the cheap construction of houses for fruit culture, and on the cross-breeding and selection of fruits and other plants. After making his name as a rose grower he turned his attention to fruits, and it is as a pomologist that he is now most renowned, and especially as a hybridist and the raiser and introducer of new cultivars of, chiefly, peaches and nectarines, of which he bred early-fruiting kinds and thus extended the season by several weeks. At his death he had raised and fruited some 1,500 peach trees, all under glass. Of these only a handful were worth naming—but some of the names can still be found in catalogues. The son, T. Francis Rivers, had assisted his father in his experimental work for several years and carried on as the head of the great nursery when Thomas Rivers died. As with the Laxtons, it is difficult to separate the work of the sons from that of the father, but it is clear that Francis had more success with apples and pears than had his father, for he it was who bred 'Conference' and 'Dr. Hogg' pears and 'Thomas Rivers', 'Early Rivers', and 'Rivers' Early Peach' apples. For his splendid work he was the recipient of the first Hogg Medal. Hogg was the foremost pomologist of his day, who took a leading part in founding the British Pomological Society in 1854, produced his famous *Fruit Manual* in 1860, and was very active in the affairs of the Horticultural Society and especially in the affairs of the Society's Fruit and Vegetable Committee.

At the Society's Shows all the new productions of Laxton, Rivers, and others were shown. 'Cox's Orange Pippin' apple was a prize-winner at the Society's Grand Fruit Exhibition in 1857, although it had been bred in 1830 by Richard Cox, a retired brewer who distributed scions in 1836.

'Worcester Pearmain' received a First Class Certificate in 1874, when exhibited by Richard Smith, a nurseryman of Worcester. And easily the most successful of these Shows was the one staged at Chiswick in 1883 for the National Apple Congress with the objects of examining and comparing the merits of as many varieties as possible and—as always with the Society—of correcting nomenclature. The 236 exhibitors showed 10,150 lots of apples, some nurserymen each displaying over 200 varieties, whilst the Society itself exhibited 328 varieties.

One of the outstanding exhibits at the Congress was that of Messrs. G. Bunyard & Co. of Maidstone. George Bunyard had entered the family nursery business, which had been founded in 1796, in 1855. In 1869 the firm moved to another three-acre Maidstone site at Allington, a name later to be widely known through the introduction of the apple 'Allington Pippin'. As the site proved favourable for the growth of fruit trees, Bunyard naturally concentrated on fruit culture and by the turn of the century some 165 acres were under cultivation. In 1871 he introduced 'Gascoyne's Scarlet', raised by a Mr. Gascoyne of Sittingbourne, and in 1885 'Lady Sudeley', raised by a Mr. Jacobs at Petworth. At the National Apple Congress, Bunyard impressed all by his expert knowledge of fruit to the extent that he was appointed chairman of the Fruit Conference held in Edinburgh in 1886. He was the driving force behind the organization of the City Exhibition of Fruit, held in the Guildhall, London, in 1890, and for this work the Fruiterers' Company made him a Freeman of the City. For thirty-four years he served on the Fruit Committee of the Horticultural Society, and on the Council for some ten years.

The breeding of new plants during these years was, of course, not confined to fruit. There were, in fact, several remarkable gardeners who had the feeling for the cultivation of a very wide range of plants and were equally successful in hybridizing such diverse subjects as fruits, orchids, begonias, insectivorous plants, stove plants, ferns, etc. One such was John Seden, who, employed by Veitch, was initiated into the practice of hybridization by John Dominy. In his later years, when he was transferred to Veitch's Langley Nursery in 1889, he turned his attention to the improvement of hardy fruits and raised new cultivars of strawberry, raspberry, gooseberry, apple, and crab which were distributed by Veitch. Before this time he had been a well-known raiser of new orchids, hippeastrums, gloxinias, begonias, working with the new material which his firm had introduced through the medium of its own special collectors, as well as with the new material the Horticultural Society, and others, had introduced.

In 1873 his first orchid hybrid, *Cypripedium* x *sedenii*, flowered. Thereafter he raised 150 hybrid cypripediums, 140 laelio-cattleyas, 65 cattleyas, 40 dendrobiums, 25 laelias, 16 phalaenopsis, 20 epidendrums, 12 masdevallias, 9 calanthes, 6 disas, 4 zygopetalums, and many others. The first bigeneric hybrid was flowered by him in 1887 from seeds raised in 1882; it was x *Zygocolax veitchii*, a cross between *Zygopetalum crinitum* and *Colax jugosus*, and the forerunner of many similar hybrids with increasingly complex parentage. In 1864-5 Richard Pearce, collecting for Veitch in Bolivia and Peru, had introduced *Begonia boliviensis*, *B. pearcei*, and *B. veitchii*. Seden took these in hand and laid the foundations of the race of tuberous begonias which are so much in favour today for pot growing and for bedding out. The first cultivar with pure white flowers originated in a batch of seedlings of *Begonia rosaeflora* and the first double-flowered type was obtained by fertilizing a flower of *Begonia* x *sedenii* (*B. boliviensis* crossed with an unnamed parent) with its own pollen.

Still another of Veitch's hybridists, John Heal, further developed the begonia. By crossing *Begonia socotrana*, which had been introduced in 1880 from the island of Socotra by Professor Bayley Balfour of Edinburgh, with varieties of summer-flowering tuberous-rooted begonias, he evolved the winter-flowering begonias, the first of which, 'John Heal', was raised in 1883. Other workers were to follow his lead, so that within less than ten years, in 1892, Messrs. Lemoine & Son of Nancy produced the most useful and beautiful of the winter-flowering types— 'Gloire de Lorraine', of which there are now numerous derivatives.

Begonias apart, Heal immensely improved the *Hippeastrum* or Amaryllis, being awarded numerous certificates from the Society for his meritorious forms. Among *Streptocarpus* hybrids, which were first produced by W. Watson, the Curator of Kew, Heal bred entirely new forms and colours of which the *achimeniflorus* forms are noteworthy examples. New forms and colours were also bred into the gorgeous-flowered epiphyllums, at that time known as phyllocacti, and with greenhouse rhododendrons he developed an entirely new race. The Veitch collectors Thomas Lobb and Charles Curtis had introduced half a dozen species of rhododendron from Java, Malaya, and adjacent islands, including *Rhododendron teysmannii*, *R. javanicum*, *R. jasminiflorum*, and *R. brookeanum*. Using this material for hybridization, Heal extended the colour range and size of flower and truss. One of his seedlings showed a tendency to petaloidy in the stamens. A flower of this he self-pollinated and by so doing produced the *balsaminaeflorum* hybrids, a race with double flowers of great substance and with the same rich colours as the *javanico-jasminiflorum* hybrids.

The firm of Veitch also had a hand in the cultivation of lilies, John Gould Veitch introducing from Japan in 1860 *Lilium auratum*, the Golden Rayed Lily. At that time there were, of course, many species of lily in cultivation. *Lilium candidum* had been in cultivation since beyond recall; *L. pyrenaicum* from the Pyrenees and *L. martagon* from Europe and Asia had arrived in Britain in 1596; *L. chalcedonicum* from Greece about 1600; *L. canadense* from eastern North America in 1620; *L. pomponium* from northern Italy and southern France in 1689; *L. superbum* from eastern North America in 1738; *L. dauricum* from North-East Asia in 1745; *L. tigrinum* from China, Japan, and Korea, and *L. monadelphum* from the Caucasus in 1804; *L. concolor* from China in 1806; *L. bulbiferum* from Central Europe in 1820; *L. speciosum* from Japan in 1832, *L. brownii* from China in 1835. Only two hybrids were in cultivation and they were not known to be hybrids. Plants for long cultivated in Japan had been introduced into European gardens in 1830 as forms of *L. dauricum*; they are now thought to be hybrids between *L. dauricum* and *L. concolor* and are now grouped under the name of *L.* x *maculatum*. The other hybrid was *L.* x *testaceum*, which was in cultivation in Britain before 1842 under this name, but was thought to be a species from Japan; it is a hybrid between *L. candidum* and *L. chalcedonicum*.

The magnificent *L. auratum* was in flower by 1862 and when exhibited by Veitch before the Horticultural Society, where 'ten thousand eyes beheld it', as Lindley wrote, it created a horticultural sensation—and, some years later, was to be the parent of the most sensational of all lily hybrids. This hybrid was raised by the great American historian Francis Parkman, at that time President of the Massachusetts Horticultural Society; he pollinated a deep-coloured form of *L. speciosum* with pollen from *L. auratum* and obtained about fifty seedlings. When these flowered in 1869 all but one were indistinguishable from the mother parent. The exception had a flower much like a crimson *auratum*, about twelve inches in diameter and very fragrant. Parkman increased this stock to about fifty bulbs, all of which he sold to Anthony Waterer of Knaphill Nursery. Waterer exhibited flowers before the Royal Horticultural Society in 1879 under the name of *L.* x *parkmannii*. The hybrid was painted by Fitch for the *Florist and Pomologist* of 1876, and for Elwes's magnificent *Monograph of the Genus Lilium* of 1880. Unfortunately Waterer's bulbs became infected with mosaic and were eventually lost. Since that time, of course, the same cross, but using different forms, has been made more than once.

Among the lily breeders at this time was George Ferguson Wilson, who was to play an important role in the affairs of the Horticultural Society. Henry John Elwes was another and, later, Mrs. Backhouse, who is now remembered by her series of lily hybrids between *L. hansonii* and forms of *L. martagon* which she began to make about 1890. And there was the practising physician, Dr. Alexander Wallace of Colchester, who was importing bulbs from Kramer & Co. of Japan and who, in 1871, offered his bulbs for sale to the public, thus linking the name of Wallace to that of lilies—a link which continues to the present day.

After the introduction of *L. auratum* several other species were to be brought from Japan, China, and California before the turn of the century and the great era of lily cultivation still lay ahead.

During this period the development of the narcissus began and the man mostly responsible was Peter Barr, a Scotsman who in 1862 founded, with a partner, the firm of Barr & Sugden (later known as Barr & Sons), of King Street, Covent Garden. The firm specialized in bulbs and especially in daffodils. Long before this, Barr's imagination had been stirred by reading Parkinson's statement of 1629, that there had been in cultivation nearly one hundred sorts of daffodils which had vanished from gardens. Barr refused to believe that so large a number had been lost and began to tour the country in search of them. Many he found; he also found two important collections which he eventually procured. William Backhouse, a banker of Wolsingham, Durham, and Edward Leeds of Manchester had been cultivating daffodils for a quarter of a century. When Peter Barr secured their collections he classified the varieties according to their parentage and structural characters. The Leeds collection became the Leedsii daffodils and the Backhouse collection the Barrii daffodils. Barr's classification was discussed and, in the main, accepted at the Daffodil Conference which the Royal Horticultural Society sponsored in 1884 and which gave great stimulus to daffodil cultivation, and especially to the work of such men as the Rev. G. H. Engleheart, then vicar of Chute Forest in Wiltshire, who had just begun his experiments which were to transform the daffodil. The conference also gave great stimulus to the Society, for a resolution proposed by Henry John Elwes and seconded by John Gilbert Baker was adopted as follows: 'That in the opinion of this Conference uniformity of nomenclature is most desirable, and that garden varieties of Narcissi, whether known hybrids or natural seedlings, should be named or numbered in the manner adopted by florists, and not in the manner adopted by botanists.' To carry this resolution into effect and to assist the Society's Scientific Committee in its investigations in the doubling of daffodils, a Narcissus Committee was formed under the auspices of the Scientific Committee. Through the activities of the new committee a trial of daffodils was begun in 1887, at Kew, the soil at Chiswick not being considered suitable; two years later the committee was empowered with the recommending of First Class Certificates and Awards of Merit; and in 1890 a Conference on Daffodils was held at Chiswick. Later the Narcissus Committee was to function independently of the Scientific Committee and in 1902 it took tulips under its wing.

In the meantime F. W. Burbidge published *The Narcissus: Its History and Culture* (1875), the first important study of the daffodil since Dean Herbert's *Amaryllidaceae* of 1837, in which a few daffodils are discussed, and which was the forerunner of the first really scientific study of this group of plants, J. G. Baker's *Handbook of the Amaryllidaceae* (1888).

The years under discussion also saw the beginning of the evolution of the modern sweet pea. *Lathyrus odoratus*, the sweet pea, is a native of southern Italy and Sicily and was introduced to England in 1699 when Father Cupani sent seeds from Sicily to Dr. Uvedale at Enfield. The flowers were mostly purple, pale purple, and red, with hooded standards and close wings and keel—and of wonderful fragrance. Chiefly because of the fragrance, the popularity of the sweet pea gradually spread. Nearly a century later, in 1793, Mason, a seedsman of Fleet Street, was listing several distinct colours, black, crimson, purple, and white, and a pink and white bicolor, 'Painted Lady'. James Carter of Holborn, the founder of the firm which today bears his name, was concerned with the introduction of a few more named forms. But progress in the development of the sweet pea was slow. Not until 1860 was the first edged type raised—by Major Trevor Clarke—'Blue Hybrid', which over twenty years later was to receive the First Class Certificate from the Society. And not until 1865 did the Society make any award to a sweet pea; then it was to 'Scarlet Invincible'.

Then occurred one of the great milestones in sweet pea history; Henry Eckford, a Scot, who had shown his breeding skill with verbenas and cinerarias whilst working in Gloucestershire, turned his attention to sweet peas in 1870. With great intuition he crossed his several promising seedlings and by 1882 had introduced the first-named seedling of his raising—'Bronze Prince'. Six years later he started his own small nursery at Wem, in Shropshire, which by the turn of the century was famous throughout the horticultural world. Most of the thirty-one awards which the Society made to sweet peas between 1870 and 1900 were to varieties of Eckford's raising. His flowers were larger, with erect standards, a much greater colour range, but they still retained the old fragrance. They became known generally as the giant or grandiflora types and were widely grown for cutting as well as for garden decoration. Whereas before 1880 sweet peas were grown as mixtures and bunches of mixed colours were bought at Covent Garden, by 1900 they were being grown more or less true, and Covent Garden was selling bunches of one colour. And then, in 1900, 'Countess Spencer' arrived on the scene.

Nothing could impede progress in the development of the rose with such enthusiasts as the Pauls, Rivers, the Rev. Samuel Reynolds Hole (later Dean Hole) and the Rev. Henry Honywood D'Ombrian fighting the cause. These enthusiasts were the driving force behind the first

National Rose Show, held at St. James's Hall, London, in 1858. Two years later when the Rose Show was held at Crystal Palace, 16,000 people attended. Thereafter the organization of the Show came under the supervision of the Horticultural Society, under whose auspices it was held until 1876, when the National Rose Society was formed, thanks principally to the initiative of D'Ombrian, who was its first Secretary, with Mr. Edward Mawley as Joint Honorary Secretary; Canon Hole was the first President. The three of them dominated the affairs of the Society for the next thirty years.

In the meantime the Hybrid Tea group was first distinguished about 1884 from crosses between the Hybrid Perpetuals and the tea-scented roses which were so popular at this time, and in 1886 *Rosa multiflora*, one of the parents of the Polyantha roses, was introduced from Korea and Japan.

In 1889 the National Rose Conference was held at Chiswick. Hybrid Perpetuals, Teas, hybrids of all sorts, climbing roses, and old-fashioned roses were largely shown, whilst never before had so interesting a series of species and curiosities been assembled.

There are about sixty species of Roses at the disposal of hybridists. These species do not merely exist on paper, nor within the seclusion of herbaria, for a large number of them were to be seen, smelt, and studied at Chiswick. Had the Rose Conference at which the Royal Horticultural Society and the National Rose Society loyally co-operated, done nothing more nor better than bring together so many Rose species, and almost extinct varieties, they would yet have given more impetus to Rose Culture and progressive improvement than has been effected by any Rose Show of the ordinary character that has yet been held.

Such was the enlightened comment of the *Gardener's Chronicle*,[1] then edited by Dr. Maxwell Masters.

Another gardening weekly had this to say:

Such a show as this recalls the memories of years gone by, when the Ayrshire, the Boursault, and Noisette Roses were as much thought of as the exhibition blooms at the present day. The old fashioned type of Rose was here in its prime side by side with the latest addition to the Hybrid Perpetual and Tea-scented sections. It was a time for making comparisons between the old and new-comers, and a pang of regret must have been felt that many of these long-introduced types are not more thought of. These are the kinds that when properly used give real delight, not so much from their comparative novelty as from the intrinsic beauty in themselves. If this conference does no more than further the cultivation of the many climbing and other old fashioned Roses, it will have achieved a great object that will be reflected in an improved condition of our gardens.

[1] (1889), p. 16.

This was the opinion of *The Garden: An Illustrated Weekly Journal of Horticulture in All Its Branches*,[1] founded in 1871 by William Robinson, who in 1879 launched *Gardening*, another weekly journal which was to be re-titled *Gardening Illustrated*, and who, using much material previously printed in *The Garden*, published, in 1883, *The English Flower Garden*, the most popular and influential of his works. This came to be known over the years as the 'gardeners' bible', and was constantly revised and reissued, the fifteenth edition appearing in 1933, two years before the author died at the great age of ninety-six.

The son of Irish peasant parents, Robinson came to London in 1861 and was employed as under-gardener in the Royal Botanic Society's Gardens in Regent's Park. Here he stayed until 1866, for three of these years being foreman of the herbaceous department and forming a close friendship with Robert Marnock, the Garden's first Curator and a well-known landscape gardener. Through Marnock he met influential people, including the proprietors of *The Times*, who commissioned him to report on the horticultural aspects of the Paris Exhibition of 1867 for that paper. (Later he was to publish *Parks, Promenades and Gardens of Paris*.) From this time forth he never ceased writing about plants and gardens until shortly before he died, and his pen exercised a profound influence on the planning and planting of flower gardens. By advocating the doctrine of simplicity and the use of hardy plants from the temperate regions of the world he most materially broadened the scope and the interest of outdoor gardening, and by so doing helped to overthrow the carpet-bedding forms of gardening of Paxton's day. The opening sentence of the first edition of *The English Flower Garden* reads: 'One purpose of this book is to help to uproot the common notion that a flower garden is necessarily of set pattern—usually geometrical—placed on one side of the house,' and the preface states: '. . . the aim for the first time [is] . . . to make each place at various seasons and in every available situation an epitome of the great flower garden of the world itself. The old and the general plan is to repeat in the garden, and usually in the best position in it, the lifeless and offensive formality of wall-paper or carpet. How to destroy this miserable conventionality, is, it is hoped, clearly shown, and that too, not by diminishing the number of flowers, but, on the contrary, by increasing them.'

In his crusade against 'the horticultural shams and artificialities of the time', two circumstances helped him enormously. The first was his meeting with Miss Gertrude Jekyll, who visited him at *The Garden* office in Covent Garden in 1875 and became a contributor to this paper. A friend of Ruskin, an artist by instinct and training—she had studied in Paris, Venice and Rome—and a natural lover of flowers, she was

[1] XXXVI (1889), p. 14.

immediately sympathetic to Robinson's views on hardy-plant gardening, recognizing that colours in the garden could be used much as an artist uses them on canvas. In the 1880s she began to design gardens in the Robinsonian 'natural' manner, blending and contrasting plant form and colour marvellously. Later she was to meet Edwin Landseer Lutyens, the architect who in 1896 designed her house, Munstead Wood. The pair had much in common, and the partnership developed into a fruitful one; over the years they worked together on many projects—'a Lutyens house with a Jekyll garden'.

The other circumstance which came to Robinson's aid—as well as to Miss Jekyll's—was the opening up of China, especially to British plant collectors, and the consequent arrival in Britain of all manner of new and hardy plant material which lent itself to Robinson's methods of treatment and was to change greatly the face of gardening; *Aucuba*, *Ligustrum*, Holly, and Yew were to give place to *Rhododendron*, *Magnolia*, *Camellia*, and much else besides.

Part Five

Recovery: Sir Trevor Lawrence
and the Rev. William Wilks
(1885 - 1919)

CHAPTER FIFTEEN
NEW HEADQUARTERS

LORD ABERDARE HAD RESIGNED THE PRESIDENCY IN 1885 BECAUSE he was overburdened by the weight of public and official duties. Claiming no special merit as a horticulturist, he had been elected to the leadership of the Society at a time when it was in debt and in difficulty. By his courtesy, tact and business management he had guided the Society through its disastrous lawsuits and had more or less freed it from debt and from the incubus of the Kensington Garden. Even so, in 1885 the Society was still in a perilous state and its existence now depended upon the choice of the right man to guide it. Fortunately the right man was at hand in the person of Sir Trevor Lawrence, who for some years had been a member of Council and a noted exhibitor of orchids. He was unanimously elected President at the Annual General Meeting of 1885.

Sir Trevor was the son of Sir William Lawrence, the celebrated surgeon and physiologist to whom Sir Trevor had succeeded in 1867. His mother was the well-known Mrs. Lawrence of Ealing Park, whose specimen plants at the Society's Shows in the 1830s had been the envy of all rivals and had won so many awards, and whose parties were famous in their day. Sir Trevor emulated both his parents; he studied medicine at St. Bartholomew's Hospital before spending ten years in India on the Army Medical Staff; and he took up orchid growing with a zest that resulted in the possession of one of the finest and best-cultivated collections in the country.

The new President (Plates 9–10) realized that the Society's perilous state was a result of wandering from its proper course—the improvement of horticulture. Thus he set to work to guide the Society back and to turn its attention 'to horticulture pure and simple' instead of to public entertainment. And for the first time the President began to take the Chair at the Council Meetings. He quickly saw that only the most drastic treatment would prevail and that the Society must cut loose from the expenses of Kensington.

In 1885 the Government was approached—to no effect—about the possibility of providing the Society with a site on which to erect a building for its own use. A committee was appointed to draw up a statement of the Society's work with a view to enlisting larger public interest. Most of the Council members were of the opinion that for the successful undertaking of the Society's work the appointment of an Assistant Secretary was essential. However, the Treasurer was opposed to such an appointment because the necessary salary—£200 a year, he estimated—could not be spared. So Sir Trevor and five other members jointly guaranteed £135 a year for four years to enable an appointment to be made. In June, Henry R. Newport was appointed, but, proving unsatisfactory, he was dismissed in November and replaced by Captain E. L. Bax.

During the year 1886 the Kensington premises were occupied by a Colonial and India Exhibition, and the Society maintained the care of the plants which had been sent to illustrate the vegetation of the various colonies. For this, the Society was remunerated by the appropriate colonial governments. Unfortunately the Commissioners would not allow Fellows to have transferable tickets and the resulting dissatisfaction led to some two hundred resignations. Meanwhile the Council still explored the possibility of the Society's finding a home of its own and at the Annual General Meeting in 1887 there was a generally expressed desire that this should be done.

Accordingly a memorial was transmitted to the Queen 'setting forth the present position of the Society, and the circumstances which have led to it, and praying Her Majesty, as patron of the Society, to take into her favourable consideration the claim of the Society to encouragement and support in its endeavours to establish itself at South Kensington on a permanent and independent basis'. The Queen's secretary replied that, while Her Majesty hoped that the Society would be able to come to an agreement with the Royal Albert Hall Corporation, it was feared that the Commissioners would not be able to provide a gratuitous site for the Society's offices. As might have been expected, such offers as were received from the Commissioners were quite unacceptable to the majority of the Council and, during 1887, a search was made for premises elsewhere. The search was expedited by the activities of a committee composed partly of Fellows who were not on the Council. As a result, at the Annual General Meeting in 1888 the Fellows approved a proposal that the Society should sever its connection with South Kensington and move to offices at No. 111 Victoria Street, Westminster, as well as make arrangements for its shows to be held in the Drill Hall of the London Scottish Volunteers, Buckingham Gate, Westminster.

The offices, which were on the first floor of No. 111 Victoria Street (later called No. 117), consisted of two rooms, the larger of which would house the Lindley Library and be used by the Council; the rent, inclusive of rates and taxes, would be £120. The main part of the premises in

Buckingham Gate consisted of a hall 135 feet by 75 feet and the rent for its use for twenty meetings each year would be £100 per annum.

The proposed move was rather revolutionary and not all members of Council approved of it. Those who did not approve resigned and were replaced by Fellows who did. Sir Trevor and his new team at once set the Society on its true course and, by so doing, inaugurated a period of steady progress and prosperity which has continued to the present day.

The Treasurer was Dr. Daniel Morris, later Sir Daniel. He had had a brilliant career at Cheltenham, the Royal College of Science, and Trinity College, Dublin. In 1877 he had become Assistant Director of the Botanical Garden at Peradeniya, Ceylon, and had made a name for himself by his studies of the disease which was ravaging the coffee plantations of the island. After two years in Ceylon he had been appointed Director of the Public Gardens and Plantations of Jamaica and thus commenced a long, happy and useful association with the West Indies. In 1886 he had moved to Kew as Assistant Director and here his wide knowledge of colonial agricultural problems brought him renown and further service as a special commissioner to the West Indies to study and report on the fibre, sugar, and banana industries on behalf of the Colonial Office. It was during his service at Kew that he became closely associated with the Society and with the Society's Garden at Chiswick. He was forty-four years old when he became Treasurer and, although he held the post only for three years, he did much to restore the Society's fortunes. After his retirement from the Treasurership he became a Vice-President of the Society, a member of the governing body of the John Innes Horticultural Institute and of the Imperial Institutes of Mycology and of Entomology; and for his services to horticulture he was awarded the Victoria Medal of Honour when this order was founded in 1897.

W. Lee of Downside, Leatherhead, a noted orchid grower, resigned from the secretaryship at the first Council Meeting after the Annual General Meeting of 1888 and the Council unanimously appointed the Rev. William Wilks (Plate 12) to his vacant office. This office Wilks continued to fill for the next thirty-two years, and to his energy, singleness of purpose, and wisdom the Society's transition from poverty to prosperity was largely due. His name must surely rank in the annals of the Society with those of Wedgwood, Banks, Knight, and Lindley. Educated at a school in Clapham, and at Pembroke College, Cambridge, where he took his degree in 1864, he studied at Wells Theological College for two years before being ordained to the curacy of Croydon in 1866. Thirteen years later he became vicar of Shirley, Croydon, where he spent the rest of his life and where he made and maintained a garden.

The rest of the team who strongly supported the President in his new policy were all outstanding horticulturists. There was W. T. Thiselton Dyer, a man of tremendous drive and enthusiasm, who had been the Society's Professor of Botany and was now Director of Kew and in the process of making Kew the botanical centre of the Empire, only the year previously (1887) having initiated the *Kew Bulletin of Miscellaneous Information*, primarily to record the work done at Kew in connection with the economic botany of the Empire. There was Dr. Robert Hogg, the Berwickshire man who had learned his horticulture in the establishment of Peter Lawson & Son of Edinburgh, who had become a great authority on fruit, secretary of the Society's Fruit Committee, and active in the affairs of the Chiswick Garden, superintending the selection of the plants for the replanting of the fruit garden. He was, moreover, a trustee of the Lindley Library. There was George Ferguson Wilson, strong advocator of the Society's guinea subscription and whose garden at Wisley was to become the Garden of the Society. There was George Paul, the rosarian, for many years vice-chairman of the Society's Floral Committee, for well over sixty years intimately and closely associated with the Society's exhibitions and one of the original sixty horticulturists to be awarded the Victoria Medal of Honour. There was George Paul's great friend Harry (later Sir Harry) James Veitch, a member, and for a long time the head, of the foremost nursery in the land, James Veitch & Son; probably the most outstanding horticulturist of his day, he was able to assume the role of Treasurer to the Society in 1918, when in his seventy-eighth year; his portrait, by Rivière, now hangs in the Council Room at Vincent Square (Plate 11). There was A. H. Smee, an enthusiastic orchid grower and active member of the Society's Orchid Committee, an accomplished chemist interested in the chemical constituents of orchids, and one with a sympathetic understanding of the working classes, among which he endeavoured to spread a knowledge of horticulture, especially in reference to allotment gardens. There was Sydney Courtauld, of 'amiable disposition, uniform courtesy, benevolence', also sympathetic to the welfare of his fellow men to the extent that he and his wife presented a garden, and a considerable endowment for its maintenance, for the enjoyment of the inhabitants of Braintree, his home. There was Professor, later Sir, Michael Foster, Professor of Physiology at Cambridge and Secretary of the Royal Society, celebrated in the horticultural world for his work on the cultivation and breeding of irises. There was Colonel R. H. Beddome, who had joined the Indian Army in 1848, had become head of the forest department in southern India in 1860 and had retained this post until he retired in 1882. There was E. G. (later Sir Edmund) Loder, the creator of the great garden at Leonardslee. And there was Baron Henry Schröder, another great orchid grower, who helped greatly to popularize these plants in Britain and soon proved to be one of the greatest of all benefactors to the Society, well deserving his appellation 'The Father of the Hall' (Plate 11).

It was with such a Council to guide its affairs that, on 25 March 1888, the Society moved from South Kensington, where it had spent £80,000 without any permanent benefit, to Victoria Street, Westminster, its address for the next sixteen years. Two days later the first of a continuous series of fortnightly meetings was held in the Drill Hall. Moreover, with a speed which seems remarkable, arrangements were made with the Treasurer and Benchers of the Inner Temple for a Show to be held in their gardens on the Embankment, on 17 and 18 May.

In appalling weather a magnificent Temple Show was staged in two spacious tents. 'That a Society supposed to be under a cloud should yet be able . . . to command such splendid service from the exhibitors, is a proof of vitality for which the best auguries may fitly be drawn,' was the view of the *Gardener's Chronicle*.[1] 'On entering the long tent with its fine display of herbaceous plants and "market stuff", the visitor could scarcely refrain from an exclamation of delight and surprise.' The paeonies, the cut tulips, the lilies, the lilies of the valley, the calceolarias, and other herbaceous plants, had all been grown to perfection. Apples from Nova Scotia and Australia, mangoes, oranges and grapes from Australia, market produce from the Channel Islands—all rejoiced the eye and whetted the appetite. And in the large tent there were palms, decorative foliage plants, cinerarias, azaleas, tree paeonies, Japanese maples, and an abundance of orchids of all kinds, shown by the trade as well as by the President and some of his friends on the Council and other amateur orchid growers. The *Chronicle* concluded its notice:

We are aware that we have not been so sparing of adjectives as it is our duty to be on ordinary occasions, but this new departure . . . is so remarkable, and the circumstances are so peculiar, that a few superlatives are more than admissible. Altogether the display is one which shows convincingly that the Society is amply worthy of that extended support which we heartily hope it will get in the shape of new subscribers.

In spite of heavy rain on both days, and notwithstanding the fact that expenses exceeded receipts by ninety-one pounds, the event was regarded as a success. Thus began the famous annual Temple Show—the forerunner of Chelsea.

Exactly thirty years before, the practice had begun of making awards to plants, and now, in 1888, the Council was not at all happy about the prevailing system. Experience had shown that the First Class Certificate had been, and was being, recommended far too freely. The Second Class

[1] Vol. 3 (1888), p. 624.

Certificate, on the other hand, had seldom been used, presumably because it appeared to denigrate, rather than to commend, the plant to which it was applied. Thus the Council now instituted a new order of commendation—the Award of Merit—'in the hope that the Committees will be able by its use to discriminate between what is really a First Class introduction or novelty, and what is simply a meritorious advance on, or variation of, some well-known and established plant'.

Whilst the departure from Kensington resulted in the resignations of many Fellows who lived in the neighbourhood but were not really interested in gardening, the return of the Society to the paths of true horticulture led to an influx of new Fellows from the rest of the country, and during 1888 there was a net increase of 528, bringing the total membership of Fellows to 1,636. At the same time the financial position improved; at the beginning of the year there was a debt of £1,152, at the end a credit balance of about £200.

Thus the year 1888 was the turning-point in the Society's fortunes and the beginning of a long period of unabated prosperity. At first the pace was slow, understandably, and probably the better for it; the good horticulturist prefers steady, well-matured growth rather than speedy, sporadic lush development followed by set-backs.

Although the arrangement whereby the Society's offices were in Victoria Street, whilst the Shows and General Meetings were held in Buckingham Gate, was serving its purpose, no one thought it was ideal. The Drill Hall especially was unsuitable for the Society's purpose, for it was too small and the lighting was poor. Baron Henry Schröder was the prime mover for something better. He had in mind a large specially constructed building somewhere in Westminster, and started a fund against the day when that dream should become practicable. The scheme was mentioned in the President's address to the Prince of Wales (later King Edward VII) when the Prince opened the Temple Show in 1890:

The Royal Horticultural Society, in addition to its ordinary work, is now devoting its energies to the provision of a great national want—a Central Metropolitan Hall or Home for the Horticulturists of the United Kingdom. Such buildings exist in the chief European capitals and in the United States of America, and the Council have ample evidence from amateurs and the very important trade engaged in Horticulture that they are urgently required in London.

And in replying, His Royal Highness said: 'You have alluded to a great want—that of a Central Metropolitan Hall. I sincerely hope your labours in that respect may be successful, for I feel sure that such a Hall will be of the greatest use and advantage.'

At the Annual General Meeting of 1890 Daniel Morris felt compelled to resign from the treasurership and was succeeded by Philip Crowley, a great student of natural history, the possessor of one of the finest and largest collections of birds' eggs in the world, as well as one of the most complete collections of butterflies. He was also a very fine gardener who tried many experiments in growing fruit at his home at Waddon House, Croydon, as well as being a keen cultivator of chrysanthemums, orchids, and foliage plants. For several years he was chairman of the Fruit and Vegetable Committee and was to be the Society's Treasurer until 1899.

As Treasurer . . . he had paid unremitting attention to the finances of the Society, whose prosperity is in no small measure due to his thorough business aptitude and knowledge, and his constant and watchful care; and as Chairman of the Fruit and Vegetable Committee he has made himself equally respected and beloved by every member of the Committee, by his firm but gentle rule, and his unvarying courtesy and cordiality to all; and in both offices alike he has been remarkable for the ungrudging and unwearying amount of personal work he has bestowed, and for the almost infinitesimal amount of credit which he has been willing to accept—he has ever been one of those most kind of all helpers, viz., those who work their best and hardest and then make light of it. May the Royal Horticultural Society never be without such a Treasurer.

This was written of him in the Society's *Journal* of 1900. He had died shortly before the end of the year, and his great friend and colleague, Wilks—the Society's Honorary Secretary—as vicar at Shirley, near Croydon, where Crowley was buried, officiated at his funeral on Christmas Eve.

He was succeeded in the office of Treasurer by Joseph Gurney Fowler, senior partner in a well-known firm of accountants. Fowler was an amateur orchid grower and from 1905 to 1916 was chairman of the Orchid Committee. He was Treasurer until 1916.

In the spring of 1892 Wilks asked to be relieved of his honorary post because he had received an offer of literary work which he did not feel justified in refusing. The Council, however, was anxious to retain his services and persuaded him to decline his lucrative offer and to remain in the service of the Society, as the salaried Secretary, at £250 a year. Unfortunately under the existing Bye-Laws his acceptance of remuneration necessitated his relinquishing his seat on the Council.

The Bye-Laws, in fact, were in need of amendment, and on two occasions, at this time, were amended. For some years, because of the uncertainty of the Society's continued existence, no Life Fellows had been admitted. Thus, in 1894, the Bye-Laws were changed to allow an annual subscription to be commuted for life by a single payment. Since it was now realized that some Fellows were at a disadvantage in being unable to visit the Shows regularly, it was decided that Fellows living more than thirty-five miles from London should be eligible for a double share of the plants and seeds distributed annually from Chiswick. As Fellows have always set great store on receiving plants and seeds from the Society's Gardens, this action alone was bound to result in increased Society membership. However, not until 1899 were the existing Bye-Laws critically and thoroughly examined, and then the matter of their legality was raised. As the 1860 Charter was so encumbered with matters relating solely to the South Kensington lease, how could one separate the rest of the Charter from what had become irrelevant and obsolete? It was impossible. Thus a petition for a new Charter was made and on 14 November 1899 the Queen duly granted a Supplementary Charter.

In 1897, in common with every other organization in the country, the Society was anxious to celebrate, in the most appropriate way, the sixtieth anniversary of Queen Victoria's accession to the throne. For many years the Queen had been the patron of the Society and many members of the Royal Family were Fellows; the late Prince Consort had for some years been the Society's President; it was but fitting that the Society should celebrate the remarkable occasion of the Queen's sixty years' reign. But how? Many projects were carefully considered before the Secretary's proposal was adopted for the establishment of the Victoria Medal of Honour in Horticulture, to be awarded from time to time to those deserving of special honour at the hands of the Society. The Queen's permission to establish the medal was sought and, although Her Majesty scrupulously abstained from taking any prominent part in choosing the methods of celebrating her Jubilee, she intimated her assent to the Society's proposal.

It was thought right in making the award of the medal that every department connected with the art and science of gardening should be represented. Moreover, it was also thought appropriate that the number of recipients of the medal, at any one time, should be limited to sixty, to correspond with the number of years of Her Majesty's reign. Thus a tentative list of sixty names to be so honoured was compiled, and after it had been amended, at the President's suggestion, by the withdrawal of the names of all members of the Council, and the substitution of other names, the list was finally approved. 'It would not have been at all becoming if the Council, who had the selection of the names, should have distributed the medals among its own members,' said the President.

It so happened that the list of proposed recipients of the medal, sent to one of the gardening papers for publication, contained a mistake. As a result, John Weathers, the Assistant Secretary, who had previously been criticized for mistakes in the recently published *List of Awards to Plants* and the *Catalogue of the Lindley Library*, was asked to resign.

The medal is of fine gold and was designed by Miss Giles and executed under her immediate supervision by Mr. Pinches. The obverse (Plate 22) represents Flora, in a kneeling attitude, drawing a flower towards her, and inhaling its perfume. Over her head are the letters V.R.I. (*Victoria Regina Imperatrix*); below are the letters R.H.S. (the Society's initials); and on either side the dates 1837 and 1897. On the reverse is displayed a reproduction of the Society's badge of a tree; a band across the centre bears the words 'Victoria Medal', and round the edge the superscription 'Royal Horticultural Society'.

And so, on 26 October 1897, the President and the Council invited the sixty recipients of the medal to luncheon at the Hotel Windsor, Victoria Street, Westminster. After luncheon the company adjourned to the Drill Hall, where many people had assembled to witness the historic ceremony of the presenting of the medals. The Secretary called out the names of the recipients, each one stepping forward to receive the medal from the President's hands.

John Gilbert Baker, keeper of the Herbarium and Library at the Royal Botanic Gardens, Kew, was a great botanist and an authority on ferns as well as on many groups of bulbous plants.

Professor (later Sir) Isaac Bayley Balfour had held the chair of botany in the Universities of Glasgow and Oxford, was now Professor of Botany and keeper of the Royal Botanic Garden at Edinburgh and, through his work on *Primula* and *Rhododendron* and other groups of plants, was yet to make his greatest contribution to horticulture.

Peter Barr, founder of the firm of Barr & Sugden, later Barr & Sons, and one of the greatest of daffodil breeders, had retired the year before at the age of seventy-four.

Archibald F. Barron, the Society's wonderfully steadfast servant at Chiswick, had retired at the end of 1895.

Edward John Beale, senior partner in the seed firm of James Carter & Co., of High Holborn, London, had been closely concerned with the passing of the Seed Adulteration Act.

William Boxall was a well-known collector and grower of orchids; he had travelled the world in search of orchids—Burma, China, Borneo, Java, Brazil, Central and South America—as a collector for Messrs. Hugh Low & Co., of Clapton, and for Messrs. James Veitch & Son, of Chelsea.

William Bull of King's Road, Chelsea, was the well-known nurseryman, and new and rare plant merchant, who specialized in decorative warm-house plants.

A fruit specialist and fruit nurseryman, George Bunyard had played a prominent role in the great Apple Conference of 1883 and was to serve on the Fruit and Vegetable Committee for thirty-four years and on the Council for close on ten years.

An old Chiswick servant, Frederick William Burbidge, was a distinguished botanist-gardener; he had been appointed to the curatorship of Trinity College Botanic Garden, Dublin, in 1879, and in 1894 he became keeper of Trinity College Park; during all these years he had greatly encouraged gardening pursuits in Ireland.

William Crump was in the service of the Earl of Beauchamp at Madresfield Court near Malvern; in fact, he was to spend forty years with the Earls of Beauchamp—and give splendid service to the Society as an examiner for its Diploma in Horticulture; a highly successful grower of fruits, he crossed 'Cox's Orange Pippin' with 'Worcester Pearmain' and raised the apple 'William Crump'.

Secretary of the National Chrysanthemum Society and one of the founders of the Royal Gardeners' Orphan Fund, Richard Dean specialized in florists' flowers and for many years was a member of the Floral Committee.

Another honour to fall to George Dickson, head of the firm of Messrs. Dickson, Nurserymen, Chester, in this year of the Diamond Jubilee, was the Freedom of the City of Chester.

The Rev. Henry Honywood D'Ombrian was an eminent rosarian who had been the moving spirit behind the formation of the National Rose Society in 1876 and was to be its secretary for the next twenty-five years; in 1876 also he had formed the Horticultural Club, which still exists, whilst from 1860 until 1876 he had edited the *Floral Magazine*, the periodical devoted to florists' flowers.

A noted authority on ferns, cultivating many which received awards from the Society, and for many years president and secretary of the British Pteridological Society, Charles Thomas Druery secured recognition from contemporary botanists by the discovery of the botanical phenomenon known as apospory.

A Scotsman who had served his gardening apprenticeship in England and held important posts in England and in Ireland before returning to Scotland in 1871 as head gardener to the Duke of Buccleuch at Dalkeith Palace, was Malcolm Dunn; he was a pomologist, a fine grower of grapes, a landscape gardener, a great lover of trees, a strong advocate of the Scottish Arboricultural Society and an enthusiastic supporter of the scheme for a forestry school in Scotland; unfortunately he died only two years later.

Canon Ellacombe made his Gloucester garden at Bitton, his home for sixty years, famous throughout the horticultural world, by the plants he cultivated and by his writings about them; he was a truly great gardener who, in his *A Gloucester Garden* (p. 293) wrote: 'I was long ago taught and have always held that it is impossible to get or keep a large collection [of plants] except by constant liberality in giving; there is that scattereth and yet increaseth, was Solomon's experience, and it certainly is so in gardening.'

Henry John Elwes was regarded as the greatest living authority on European trees, and on lilies.

Professor (later Sir) Michael Foster was an outstanding authority on irises who had made important contributions to iris breeding.

John Fraser, with his brother, had succeeded to the famous business in Lea Bridge Road noted for its hardy woody, and stove and greenhouse, plants, and was at this time head of a nursery at South Woodford which specialized in such diverse subjects as heathers, vines, and ivies; he was a great exhibitor and competitor at the Society's shows and exhibitions, and on one occasion that fine gardener and exhibitor, Mrs. Lawrence, having been beaten by the Lea Bridge firm at one of the great Chiswick shows, bought the whole of the exhibit—and took over May, the grower, as well.

For twenty-five years George Gordon was to be editor of the *Gardener's Magazine*; a great lover of all plants, he was active in his work on behalf of the National Chrysanthemum Society, the National Rose Society, the National Sweet Pea Society, and the National Dahlia Society.

John Heal served the firm of Messrs. James Veitch & Son for more than half a century—until the firm ceased to be, in 1914; he was a renowned plant breeder who raised hybrid rhododendrons of the *javanicum* type, developed an improved race of *Streptocarpus*, as well as a race of winter-flowering begonias by crossing tuberous-rooted types with *Begonia socotrana* which Professor Bayley Balfour had introduced.

The Rev. Prof. George Henslow for many years was Honorary Professor to the Society and a frequent, and popular, speaker at the Society's meetings.

One-time Director of the Botanic Garden in Rio de Janeiro, Hermann Herbst was a pioneer in the development of forced lily of the valley culture and in the introduction of many exotics on a commercial scale—especially palms and adiantums.

Dean Hole—the Rev. Samuel Reynolds Hole—was primarily a rosarian; he was the author of the highly successful *Book about Roses* and had helped to found the National Rose Society in 1876, being its first president and, until he died in 1904, its only president; he was also closely associated with *The Garden*.

Sir Joseph Dalton Hooker, Director of Kew for thirty years, was one of the outstanding men of his day.

An authority on auriculas and carnations, the Rev. F. D. Horner was secretary of the Northern Auricula Society as well as of the Northern Carnation Society for over twenty years.

James Hudson was the head gardener at Gunnersbury House; in fact, he was to spend most of his working life—forty-three years (he died in 1932)—in that establishment, which was famous for its collections of hardy and indoor fruits; and he was to serve on the Council for some twenty years as well as acting as one of the Society's examiners.

Miss Gertrude Jekyll was one of two women to be honoured; an artist with paints as well as with plants, she was a designer of gardens— a disciple of William Robinson—using her artistic sense of colour to great advantage.

Peter Kay was a nurseryman, the owner of Claigmar Vineries, Church End, Finchley, one of the first to take up the cultivation of the Canon Hall Muscat, and marketing on a large scale not only grapes but tomatoes and cucumbers.

One-time partner of the firm of Downie, Laird & Laing, of Edinburgh, for many years John Laing had been head of the firm of John Laing & Sons of Forest Hill; he was a successful hybridizer and raiser of florists' flowers—penstemons, clivias, streptocarpus, gloxinias—and he completely revolutionized the tuberous begonia.

'McIndoe's Best of All' melon commemorated the name of James McIndoe, gardener to Sir Joseph Pease at Hutton Hall, Guisborough, and well known as a grower and exhibitor of fruit, especially of grapes and melons.

Charles Maries at the time of the presentation was in India; he will always be remembered as the collector who, when employed by Veitch, introduced so many fine plants from China and Japan.

Henry Ernest Milner was a landscape gardener who had done much for the Earl's Court Exhibition of 1892.

A great grower of every kind of plant, but especially of chrysanthemums, which he did so much to improve, Edwin Molyneux was a gardener at Swanmore Park, Bishops Waltham.

In 1871 George Monro had founded the great Covent Garden firm and, throughout his professional life, was a generous supporter of all gardeners' charities.

Internationally famous as a horticulturist, Fred. W. Moore (knighted in 1911) was in charge of the Royal Botanic Gardens, Glasnevin, from 1878 until he retired in 1912.

Dr. Daniel Morris was an ex-Treasurer of the Society, and Assistant Director of Kew, who was taking an active part in Society affairs and later in those of the John Innes Horticultural Institute and the Imperial Institutes of Mycology and of Entomology.

George Nicholson was writing the five-volume *Illustrated Dictionary of Gardening*, which was published between 1885 and 1900; Curator at Kew from 1886 until he retired in 1901, he ranked with Elwes in his knowledge of trees and shrubs—especially of oaks and maples.

James O'Brien had been secretary of the Orchid Committee from its institution in 1889 and remained so until a few years before he died in 1930; he was renowned as an orchid grower, first with Messrs. Hugh Low & Co. at the famous Clapton Nurseries, then with Sir George Holford at Westonbirt, and finally with Messrs. E. G. Henderson & Son of Wellington Road, St. John's Wood, and the Pineapple Nurseries, Maida Vale, London.

George Paul had been intimately and continuously associated with the Society for over forty years and was to continue so for another twenty years; primarily a rosarian, he was also interested in the hybridizing of philadelphus, weigelias, rhododendrons, and lilacs.

William Paul, his brother, was also a rosarian, an industrious contributor to the *Gardener's Chronicle* and a frequent speaker at the Society's meetings.

Head of the celebrated fruit nursery firm of T. Rivers & Son, T. Francis Rivers was also to receive the first Hogg Medal, commemorating the great pomologist, in 1898—the year before he died.

The Hon. Walter Rothschild, with a wide knowledge of plants, especially of orchids, had created his splendid garden at Tring in Hertfordshire.

Henry F. C. Sander was senior partner of the firm of Sanders, St. Albans, whose great orchid establishment enjoyed a world-wide reputation; at one time no fewer than twenty-three collectors were employed in various parts of the world.

Another with a great orchid collection, certainly the finest private collection in Britain, was Baron Henry Schröder, of the Dell, Egham; he was soon to be the driving force in securing the Society's new premises at Vincent Square.

John Seden, of the firm of J. Veitch & Son, was a great hybridizer of orchids, nepenthes, caladiums, gloxinias, and begonias—in fact, he raised the first tuberous-rooted begonia; after receiving the V.M.H. he turned his attention to the raising of fruits—strawberries, gooseberries, apples.

Nathaniel Newman Sherwood, head of the firm of wholesale seedsmen, Messrs. Hursts, of which he had become the sole proprietor in 1890, was always a great benefactor of gardeners' charities and was to be a liberal subscriber to the Purchase Fund of the Society's Hall.

At Crathes, in Aberdeenshire, James Smith had been an apprentice gardener with Archibald Barron and, like Barron, had come to England;

dward Augustus Bowles, a noted gardener and active Member of the Society
for nearly fifty years

At the Society's sesquicentenary in 1954 Phylis, Lady Moore, hands the
congratulatory address from the Royal Horticultural Society of Ireland to
the Hon. David Bowes-Lyon.

Plate 15

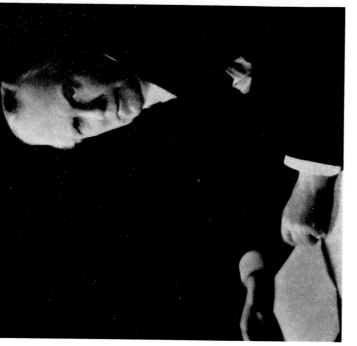

(*above*) G. W. E. Loder, later Lord Wakehurst (1929–1931)
(*right*) Sir David Bowes Lyon (1953–1961)

Plate 16 PRESIDENTS OF THE SOCIETY

he was head gardener to the Earl of Rosebery at Mentmore, Leighton Buzzard, for twenty-eight years and had worked indefatigably towards the formation of the Royal Gardeners' Orphan Fund in 1887.

Martin Ridley Smith had a world-wide reputation as a raiser of new carnations and for many years served the National Carnation and Picotee Society as its president.

A specialist in the cultivation of all kinds of plants, Walter Speed was head gardener to Lord Penrhyn at Penrhyn Castle; in fact, he was to serve three Lord Penrhyns over a period of nearly fifty-eight years.

One who had done much to maintain the seed firm of Messrs. Sutton & Sons of Reading in its proud and pre-eminent position was Arthur Warwick Sutton; he was to serve on the Council.

Owen Thomas was Queen Victoria's head gardener at Windsor, and a member of the Society's Fruit and Vegetable Committee.

Generally known as 'Thompson of Ipswich', William Thompson was manager, with Mr. Morgan, of the commercial establishment at Ipswich which was famous for its introduction and distribution of seeds of new and interesting plants.

David Thompson was a Scotsman who, having received his early gardening training in Scotland before moving to England, returned to Scotland in 1858, ten years later became gardener to the Duke of Buccleuch at Drumlanrig, and for thirty years maintained Drumlanrig in the forefront of British horticulture.

Harry Turner was the son of the renowned Charles Turner of the Royal Nurseries, Slough; he was always a loyal exhibitor at the Society's exhibitions and a strong supporter of the National Carnation and Picotee Society and of the National Auricula Society.

The second woman to receive the award was Ellen Ann Willmott, possibly the foremost authority on roses; she had still to write her great work, *The Genus Rosa*, which was issued in parts between 1910 and 1914, the species she described being illustrated in colour by Alfred Parsons.

George Ferguson Wilson had already done much for the Society and for horticulture in many capacities; in a few years his garden at Wisley was to become the Society's Garden.

Once an Eton master, the Rev. Charles Wolley-Dod was now a distinguished amateur botanist and horticulturist in Cheshire and a great stickler for accurate nomenclature.

An industrious worker on behalf of horticultural education and school gardening, John Wright had been associated with the *Journal of Horticulture* for nearly twenty years as sub-editor before succeeding Dr. Hogg as editor.

George Wythes was gardener to the Duke of Northumberland at Syon House, Brentford, a frequent exhibitor of fruits, vegetables, and all manner of other plants at the Society's shows and meetings, for over twenty-five years a member of the Fruit and Vegetable Committee, and a hard-working member of the Gardeners' Royal Benevolent Institution for something like thirty years.

These were the first sixty to receive the now much coveted V.M.H., and of them the *Gardener's Chronicle*[1] wrote:

We are proud to think a hundred more equally worthy (with one or two exceptions) could easily have been found, hence those on whom the honour was conferred will, of course, look on themselves in the light of representatives of others. It is difficult to see how, on the whole, the selection could have been better made, and it is equally difficult to see how the list could have been improved when many of those who, by universal verdict, would have found a place therein, felt themselves debarred, from one cause or another, from being nominated.

When the Queen died three years later, the number of possible holders of the V.M.H. was increased to sixty-three. Thus in 1901, because there was a vacancy due to the death of Malcolm Dunn, the award of the V.M.H. was made to Sir George King, the distinguished botanist who had recently retired from the post of director of the Botanical Survey of India and had done so much for the cinchona and quinine industry of India; to George Norman, gardener to the Marquis of Salisbury at Hatfield House with its renowned kitchen garden; to Eleanor A. Ormerod, the economic entomologist who had long been acting as intermediary between the scientists and the practical growers; and to James Sweet, of Messrs. J. Sweet & Sons Ltd., of Whetstone, a market nurseryman specializing in ericas.

The name of Dr. Robert Hogg was missing from the list of the names of the original sixty to receive the V.M.H. only because he had died earlier in the year—on 14 March. No one could have been more deserving of the honour; author of the encyclopaedic *Fruit Manual*, one of the editors, latterly the sole editor, of the *Journal of Horticulture*, joint secretary for several years, with Sir Joseph Paxton as president, of the British Pomological Society, which he had helped to institute in 1854 and which later was merged into the Society's Fruit Committee when this was formed in 1858, one of the Directors, with Berkeley and Moore, of the Society's Garden at Chiswick, and in this connection responsible for the superintending of the replanting of the fruit garden, one-time Secretary to the Society, one of the trustees of the Lindley Library, and one of those foremost in the organization of the notable International

[1] Vol. 22 (1897), p. 310.

Horticultural Exhibition and Botanical Congress of 1866, Hogg had served horticulture and the Society for half a century. Wilks eulogistically said of him:

He was not like any other man. He had a very marked individuality; a sort of solidity and terseness of expression, both in word and manner, which was reflected on the picturesque ruggedness of his outward form, reminding one not a little of the massive, open, wind-swept heather clad hills of his own Scotland. No one who ever saw him could possibly forget him, or mistake him for any other; and no one who really knew him but now feels he has one staunch and true friend the less.[1]

There were many who shared Wilks's feelings, and one of them, Harrison Weir, wrote in the *Gardener's Chronicle* of 27 March:

Grand as the exhibitions of fruit often are at the present time the Royal Horticultural Society has no special medal to offer as the highest award for fruit. It has its Flora, its Banksian, Veitch, etc., but no special fruit medal. May I, therefore, suggest this. Is there not now unusual and highly fitting opportunity to have such a medal, and let it be in the honour of one whom to know was to love, and to associate with was indeed a privilege.

Thus it was that in 1898 the Hogg Medal was introduced, and the dies were presented to the Society by Hogg's friends and admirers.

One other medal was struck during the same year. The steady increase in the number of exhibits meriting the highest award necessitated a review of the cost of the Society's Gold Medal. Thus a smaller Gold Medal was instituted to take the place of the original one, which had been in use since 1811; the new medal was again redesigned in 1929.

The Society's Shows, of course, continued, and gained in popularity. Many conferences were held. The Garden was taking on a new lease of life and the various committees were actively judging and reporting on the trials there. No committee was more serious in its endeavours than the Orchid Committee, and in 1897 it was decided that in future any orchid which received a First Class Certificate should be painted and the paintings used for future reference. Miss Nellie Roberts was 'appointed the artist for six months', though, in fact, she continued to paint orchids for the Society's records for the next fifty-six years, and in 1953 was awarded the Veitch Memorial Medal.

During these years the Society was extending its influence throughout the country. It was sending deputations of the Council to shows of local horticultural societies—Newcastle, Truro, York, and Chester, for instance, and, moreover, was striving to ensure as uniform a system of judging as possible at these shows. Towards this end, in 1895 *The Code*

[1] *Jl R. hort. Soc.*, XXI (1897), p. xlviii.

of Rules and Suggestions for Judges, Schedule-makers and Exhibitors was published. This booklet, compiled by an *ad hoc* committee, ran into eight editions and during the next thirty years came to be regarded throughout the country as a sort of bible for those concerned with the organization of horticultural shows; it was the forerunner of the *Horticultural Show Handbook*.

The years 1898 and 1899 were historic ones, not only for the Society but, even more important, in the field of plant genetics. In 1894, at the suggestion of Sir Francis Galton, the Royal Society had appointed a committee for conducting statistical enquiries into the measurable characters of animals and plants. Three years later the committee was reconstituted as the Evolution Committee and W. Bateson, who had been made a Fellow of the Royal Society in recognition of his studies on variation, was appointed secretary. Believing that the practical horticulturists had the greatest experience and knowledge in plant breeding, he now sought to form an alliance with the Horticultural Society in pursuance of this work on the study of evolution. On 9 February 1898 Bateson explained to the Council, and to Dr. Masters, chairman of the Scientific Committee, his ideas; accurate observations on variation, heredity, selection, and other phenomena connected with evolution were necessary if outstanding problems were to be solved; practical plant breeders were constantly working on material of the utmost scientific importance; would the Society endeavour to induce all such breeders to maintain complete and accurate accounts of all hybridizations, the failures as well as the successes?

Later in the day Masters met his Scientific Committee and explained Bateson's ideas. Probably this meeting was the most important and historic in the whole of the committee's existence. It rose magnificently to the occasion and gave its blessing to the work of Bateson's Evolution Committee. The Society at once set up a subcommittee to deal with the matter and an appeal was sent out to all horticulturists. From this time forth the Society was firmly linked with all the new researches and through all the exciting times at the beginning of the twentieth century was the mainstay of the early experimenters.

No one was more enthusiastic towards, and in sympathy with, the new ideas than Wilks. He conceived the idea of an international conference on hybridization, writing to C. C. Hurst: 'I am glad you take kindly to my latest baby just sprung upon the world—an infant of only as yet a few days. It is so encouraging when one's efforts and plans are cordially seconded. Please do all you can to help me on and get the Conference to go down. Blow the trumpet whenever you can.'

Many trumpets were, in fact, blown and the Conference on Hybridization was held on 11 and 12 July 1899, beginning with a luncheon at

Chiswick and closing with a banquet in the Whitehall Rooms of the Hotel Metropole in honour of the distinguished foreign guests. The proceedings were opened with a paper by Bateson on 'Hybridisation as a Method of Scientific Investigation', in which he stressed the two problems of the origin of species and the possible magnitude of variations, pointing out that it was only by the fullest examination of particular individuals and their progeny that the real truths of variation could be discovered. He urged the necessity for the crossing of variants with their nearest allies and for the careful statistical analyses of the results, treating each character separately. C. C. Hurst, in a second important paper, spoke of his hybridization work with orchids, insisting that, by analysing each character separately, he had discovered that they behaved as distinct units, and that some were dominant whilst others were recessive, only reappearing in the second or later generations. The third significant paper was given by the Dutch botanist Hugo de Vries, soon to become famous for his mutation theory; 'Hybridisation as a means of Pangenetic Infection' followed much the same theme as the paper by Hurst.

The 1899 conference is undoubtedly the most significant and important in the Society's history, and the report of it, published in 1900, occupies no fewer than 348 pages of the Society's *Journal*. Recalling the event on the occasion of the International Conference on Hybridization and Plant-Breeding, in 1906, Bateson said:

It is just eight years since, on the hottest day of a very hot summer, the first Conference devoted to Hybridisation and Plant Breeding assembled at Chiswick. Looking back on that occasion, we realise what some of us even then suspected, that we were concerned in a remarkable enterprise. No such conference had taken place before, and our proceedings were of the nature of an experiment. That definite results might come from that beginning we naturally hoped, but of those who endured the heat of that stifling marquee, or inspected the plants exhibited in that tropical vinery, not one, I suppose, anticipated that in less than a decade we should have such extraordinary progress to record. The predominant note of our deliberations in 1899 was mystery. In 1906 we speak less of mystery than of order.[1]

The papers by Bateson, Hurst, and de Vries at the 1899 conference together contained the essence of the Mendelian principles which were to be made known a year later and which were to throw so clear a light on the new experiments. De Vries in Holland and Correns and Tschermak in Germany simultaneously unearthed the long-disregarded paper, written in 1866 by Gregor Mendel, the Abbot of Brunn, concerning his experiments with peas. Mendel had clearly seen the necessity of each character being treated separately and had discovered the fact of the

[1] *Gdnr's Chron.*, vol. 40 (1906), p. 81.

segregation of characters as units, some being 'dominant', others 'recessive', with an inheritance ratio of dominants over recessives of 3:1.

On 8 May 1900 Bateson left his home near Grantchester to lecture to the Society on 'Problems of Heredity as a subject for Horticultural Investigation'. In the train he read Mendel's paper, which he had just received from de Vries, for the first time. Immediately he realized that the paper contained what all had been seeking and incorporated its substance into his lecture later in the day. Those who listened to Bateson on this historic day were therefore the first in Britain to hear of Mendel's epoch-making discovery. Soon, however, all Fellows were to learn of it, for Wilks, realizing the enormous importance of the work, had Mendel's paper translated and published in the Society's *Journal* for 1901.

The 1906 conference, the third on these matters—the second having been organized in America in 1902—was announced as an 'International Conference on Hybridisation and Plant Breeding', was under the presidency of Professor Bateson, and was another important milestone in the history of the Society. In his opening speech Bateson pointed out that the newly born science they were to discuss was still nameless, and said:

To meet this difficulty I suggest for the consideration of this Congress the term *Genetics*, which sufficiently indicates that our labours are devoted to the elucidation of the phenomena of heredity and variation: in other words, the physiology of descent, with the implied bearing on the theoretical problems of the evolutionist and the systematist, and application to the practical problems of breeders, whether animals or plants.

The conference occupied three days and was attended by a great number of scientists from many countries—and Wilks was more than happy. Writing joyfully to Hurst on 7 August, he said: 'The Conference was admitted on all sides to be a record success' and, two days later, 'I am resolved to get the Report out by Christmas. To do this I am postponing my holiday a month or six weeks so as to enable me to set the printers going before I leave.' On 23 August he wrote again: 'I want to make this Report (the last of my Editorship) a fine thing.'

And a fine thing it was—under the title of *Report of the Third International Congress 1906 on Genetics*—an octavo volume of 481 pages, full of important papers, which had a far-reaching influence on future plant breeding. Thus the Society well and truly launched the new science of genetics. Wilks's 'latest baby' did indeed grow and prosper beyond any conception he could have had at the time, to the extent that over the years a series of genetical congresses has been held and geneticists are now numerous throughout the world.

At the turn of the century the Council could look back with satisfaction on the twelve years of steady progress under the leadership of

Sir Trevor Lawrence and the Rev. William Wilks. At the end of 1887 the total number of Fellows had been 1,329, of whom 556 were Life Fellows whose commuted subscriptions had already been spent; there were thus only 773 paying subscribers. By 1900 the total membership was 4,750, of whom only 250 were Life Fellows of the old régime; there were thus 4,500 active subscribers. At the end of 1887 the Society had no investments but a debt of £1,152. By 1900 the debt had been wiped out and the investments amounted to £10,239—not including the Davis and Parry trust funds which were valued at £2,122. The Society was now in a position to contemplate such projects as the acquisition and maintenance of a large garden and a home of its own, and these important developments outshone all others during the first four years of the new century.

Since the appointment in 1896 of S. T. Wright as Superintendent, a good deal of money had been spent, and many improvements made, at Chiswick. Even so, the Garden still left something to be desired, partly, of course, because of its limited size, and there was a growing feeling that a larger Garden, with better glass, in a less smoky atmosphere, was required. In April 1899 Messrs. Veitch, Lloyd, Gurney Fowler, and Hudson were appointed as a committee to collect information regarding sites for the future Garden of the Society, and in the following November Mr. Veitch reported on the Committee's findings. On 24 January 1900 the Council inspected the most promising site, at Limpsfield in Surrey, and their report, presented to the Annual General Meeting in February, stated that

The subject of the approaching Centenary of the Society in March 1904, is naturally attracting considerable attention. After consideration of various excellent projects . . . the Council have decided to recommend the acquisition of a new Garden . . . as being, under all the circumstances, the best and most practical method of celebrating the Centenary. . . . It is therefore proposed to issue an appeal to all the Fellows, and to raise a Fund for the purchase of a more suitable site for a Garden, in memory of the first hundred years of the Society's existence. The Council fully recognise the advantage of the Society's possessing a hall of its own in which plants, flowers and fruits can be seen by the Fellows under more favourable conditions as regards light and space than are possible in the building at present used for the meetings. They do not, however, see their way to its attainment, but will be happy to consider any suggestion concerning it.

The report was formally adopted without any dissentient vote and Council assumed that they were therefore free to proceed with the acquisition of the Limpsfield site. However, the views of many silent Fellows were voiced by the *Gardener's Chronicle*, which, on 10 March, said: 'We protest most earnestly against the view taken that the adoption of the Report of necessity carries with it acquiescence in the details of a scheme which were not, and have not been up till now, laid before the Fellows. How can the Fellows acquiesce in anything which is unknown to them?'

However, notwithstanding growing opposition, the Council called a Special General Meeting for 25 April 1900, the printed notice of which stated that it would be proposed that the Meeting 'adopts the proposal of the Council to purchase a freehold site in the parish of Limpsfield, in Surrey, and authorizes the Council to take the necessary steps for acquiring the said site, and for developing new gardens thereon'. At the Meeting there was considerable opposition, led by Mr. H. J. Elwes and supported by Sir William Thiselton Dyer and Sir Michael Foster. It transpired that Mr. Arthur Sutton, who had been elected to the Council in February, had resigned, as he was very strongly opposed to the proposal, because, among other things, he considered the land in question to be too heavy, waterlogged, and quite unsuitable for the purpose in view. In the end, on a proposal from Mr. H. J. Pearson, a member of the Council who in addition to being a horticulturist was also an authority on the birds of northern Europe, it was resolved 'That the Centenary of the Society be celebrated by removing the Gardens from Chiswick, subject to the Council being able to find a new site [but not necessarily that at Limpsfield] which commends itself to the majority of the Fellows'. Although the resolution was carried by a large majority, it was clear that by no means everyone thought that the acquisition of a new Garden was the best means of celebrating the centenary; but thanks to the conciliatory and impartial attitude of the President, what might have become an embittered Meeting was brought to a fairly satisfactory close, at least from the Council's point of view.

Examination and consideration of possible sites was continued throughout 1900 and in November it was decided that the following advertisement should be inserted in several papers:

The Royal Horticultural Society, having decided to remove the Experimental Gardens from Chiswick into the country beyond the radius of the London smoke, would be willing to hear of any freehold agricultural land of about 40 acres suitable for their purpose.

A few weeks after the Annual Meeting of 1901 the Council summoned a Special General Meeting to be held in the Drill Hall on 23 April, 'to consider, and if approved, to adopt the proposal of the Council to purchase, on behalf of the Society for the purpose of its new Gardens, forty-eight acres of land in the County of Kent, forming part of Rabbits'

Farm, and adjoining the Little Boys' Home at South Darenth', and the notice invited Fellows to meet some members of Council on the site on 18 April. The receipt of the notice led numerous Fellows, including Mr. Arthur Sutton, to write to the *Gardener's Chronicle*[1] expressing opposition to the scheme, and their letters occupied six columns of small type. 'The Meeting was very largely attended, the corridors and staircases even being filled by those who could not find space in the room.'

In his opening speech Sir Trevor Lawrence made it clear that the proposal before the Meeting was the result of the instruction given to the Council by the Special General Meeting held on 25 April 1900, and that he himself had repeatedly given it as his personal opinion 'that by far the best way of celebrating the centenary of the Society would be the provision of a Hall for its Meetings, and offices for its work, if any arrangement to carry that out could possibly be come to', but in spite of his having taken a great deal of trouble to find a suitable site he was bound to say he had entirely failed.

Mr. Harry Veitch, chairman of the Exploratory Committee, explained the Council's proposal, 'but the scheme had no chance against the torrent of criticism poured upon it,' first by Mr. Sutton and then by Dr. Masters, editor of the *Gardener's Chronicle*, who read extracts from a long and detailed argument against the proposal which he had received from Sir William Thiselton Dyer. After a lively discussion the President put the following amendment proposed by Mr. Sutton and seconded by Dr. Masters: 'While thanking the Council for the trouble they have taken in seeking a site for a new Garden, this Meeting is of opinion that the proposed site is *not* the best means of celebrating the forthcoming Centenary of the Society.' The amendment was 'carried by a very large majority amid enthusiasm', and Dr. Masters subsequently received a letter from Mr. Henry Cannell, the well-known nurseryman of Swanley, inquiring whether the offices of the *Gardener's Chronicle* were illuminated on the evening following the Meeting.

In the course of the Meeting several speakers stated that in their view a hall was to be preferred to a new Garden, and despite the fact that the Chairman had to rule that that question was not on the agenda, Mr. H. J. Elwes, Mr. A. Sutton, and Mr. N. N. Sherwood all intimated their willingness to contribute £1,000 towards the cost of a hall, and 'Baron Schröder, who was sitting next to the President, whispered that he would give £5,000'.

A rather curious difference of opinion subsequently arose in connection with one of these offers. In 1903 Mr. Elwes declined to implement his 'promise', contending that it was governed by a letter which he wrote to the President. As the latter was adamant that the offer was

[1] Vol. 29 (1901), p. 254.

unconditional, the matter was referred to arbitration, and Sir Edward Fry, an eminent lawyer, decided 'that Mr. Elwes was bound to pay the Society £1,000'.

On 4 June 1901 the Council appointed a committee consisting of Baron Schröder (chairman), Sir Trevor Lawrence, Dr. M. Masters, Messrs. N. N. Sherwood and H. J. Veitch, with the Rev. W. Wilks as secretary, with power to add to their number, 'to consider the question of a Hall and to report thereupon to the Council'. On 28 January 1902 Lord Ilchester and Mr. H. B. May were added to the committee. At the Annual General Meeting on 11 February 1902 the President reported that the committee had examined four sites and were engaged in negotiations about a fifth, and that it was hoped that it would soon be possible to call a Special General Meeting to consider the matter. Mr. Arthur Sutton moved and Surgeon-Major Ince seconded the following resolution: 'That this Meeting is glad to learn from the President that steps are being taken to secure a site for a new Hall, and pledges itself to give its most favourable consideration to any proposal which the Council shall in due course lay before it.' The resolution was carried with only three dissentients in a large and crowded meeting.

About three weeks later, on 7 March 1902, Baron Schröder reported to the Council that his committee recommended the acquisition of a site in Vincent Square, Westminster, belonging to the Ecclesiastical Commissioners, who were prepared to give a lease of 999 years at a rental of £690 per annum. The report met with a mixed reception and it was only carried by six votes to five. However, it was decided that a Special General Meeting should be held at the Drill Hall on Friday 21 March 1902, 'to receive from the Council and, if approved, to adopt a report recommending a proposed site for a horticultural hall and offices.' Two members of Council, Messrs. C. E. Shay and J. T. Bennett-Poë, who had always felt very strongly that a new Garden should have preference over a hall and offices, resigned from the Council.

The report of Baron Schröder's committee, together with a memorandum expressing the Council's view on the matter, was printed and circulated during the intervening fortnight, and about 300 Fellows attended the meeting on 21 March 1902. The memorandum stated that the Council was 'fully aware that a considerable number of Fellows desire that a garden better than Chiswick should be secured as a memorial of the Centenary of the Society', but that 'The policy of the existing Council is to endeavour to secure, first a suitable Hall and offices, . . . and when that is done, to devote attention at once to the acquisition of a site for a new garden'.

In the course of a long speech in support of the Council's proposal Sir Trevor Lawrence paid tribute to Baron Schröder, who, unfortunately, had had to go to the South of France for his health. The Baron, said Sir Trevor, was one of the best friends the Society had ever had. As chairman of the committee charged with the task of finding a site for a hall he had been indefatigable, and he had not only promised £5,000 towards the cost of the hall but, having found what appeared to be an ideal site, and fearing that the opportunity to acquire it might be lost while the Society was making up its mind, he had taken a lease of the site for 999 years and was prepared to transfer the lease to the Society at a moment's notice. Continuing, Sir Trevor said that pre-liminary plans had been prepared, and that it was estimated that the cost of a building and offices would be about £25,000. As £8,000 had already been promised, although no formal appeal had yet been launched, he was confident that Fellows could be relied upon to produce the balance for a purpose so essential for the Society's well-being. He then proposed

That the Fellows of The Royal Horticultural Society, in General Meeting assembled, accept the principle of building a new Hall in celebration of the Centenary of the Society and hereby adopt the report laid before them this day by the Council. They also desire to record their appreciation of Baron Schröder's public-spirited conduct in securing a site, which they hereby adopt, and they authorize the Council to take the necessary steps to enable the building to be opened in the year 1904.

The proposal was seconded and strongly supported by Sir William Thiselton Dyer, but Mr. C. E. Shay moved the following amendment: 'That this Meeting stand adjourned to this day fortnight, at the same time and place if possible, and that in the meantime copies of the Report be sent to every Fellow of the Society.' Another ex-Member of Council, Mr. J. T. Bennett-Poë, seconded the amendment, and Sir Alexander Ar-buthnot and Mr. George Gordon, the editor of the *Journal of Horticulture*, spoke in support of it. On the other hand, Sir Michael Foster, Dr. Masters, Mr. Arthur Sutton, and Dean Hole (the rosarian, then in his eighty-third year) all supported the President's proposal. The majority of those present were against the possibility of having their votes swamped by those of absentees who had not taken a close interest in the Society's activities and were not familiar with the ins and outs of the problem. Moreover, the Meeting became impatient at what, at best, appeared to be merely delaying tactics, and there were cries of 'Vote! Vote!' The President therefore put the amendment and all but eleven voted against it. 'On the original resolution being put, the President, amid much cheering, declared it carried with three dissentients.'[1]

In the following week, on 25 March, Baron Schröder, who had been a

[1] *Gdnr's Chron.*, vol. 31 (1902), p. 218.

member of Council from 1886 to 1893, and who since 1887 had persistently advocated the need for the Society to have 'a home of its own', was re-elected to the council in the place of Mr. C. E. Shay, who had resigned. On 8 July Baron Schröder's committee recommended the Council to adopt plans prepared by the architect, Mr. Edwin J. Stubbs, and he was instructed by the Council to submit them to the ground landlords (the Ecclesiastical Commissioners) and to the London County Council. The approval of the Commissioners having been obtained, the site in Vincent Square was formally leased on 22 July 1902, for 999 years. Meanwhile the appeal for contributions to the hall building fund was launched and Mr. G. J. Ingram was appointed as the collector on the understanding that his remuneration would be five per cent of the donations he secured. Impetus was given to the appeal by a letter received by Capt. (later Sir) George Holford, a member of Council, from His Majesty King Edward VII, which was published in *The Times*. In sending a donation of one hundred guineas, 'by way of showing the interest he takes in The Royal Horticultural Society', His Majesty referred to the speech he made at the Temple Show in 1890 and said that he wished to repeat 'if possible with a stronger feeling than ever, not only the desirability, but the actual necessity of such a building as it is proposed by the Society to erect'. His Royal Highness the Prince of Wales (later King George V) also showed his interest by sending a donation of fifty guineas. The encouragement thus given by the Royal Family was particularly welcome because, on going into detail, the Council now estimated that the cost of the hall and offices, including furniture and equipment, would be about £40,000, a much higher figure than that originally mentioned. However, the prospect gave no cause for alarm, as during the year no fewer than 1,400 new Fellows were elected, the largest number in any one year since the formation of the Society. By 18 November the architect was able to report that the London County Council had approved the plans subject to some small modifications, and steps were taken to obtain tenders for the work.

On 24 March 1903 a tender for the excavations and foundations of the hall was accepted, and the contract for the building itself was signed on 19 May. Work proceeded apace and the most common question at the fortnightly Meetings at the Drill Hall was 'How is the hall getting on?' By November things were sufficiently well advanced for it to be announced that the first Show in the hall would be held in July 1904. On 27 November 1903 the donations to the building fund received or promised amounted to £23,000 and an appeal for further contributions, towards the balance of the estimated cost, £17,000, signed at the Council's request by Baron Schröder, 'the father of the Hall', was issued on 7 December.

For some years the Society had been using on its stationery and other printed matter a device (see figure below) consisting of a tree enclosed in a garter bearing the words 'Royal Horticultural Society', surmounted by a crown. Several versions, depending on the die-maker employed, appeared over the years, and in no two were the trees identical. During the construction of the hall the architect proposed to incorporate the device in the paved floor of the entrance and he inquired which tree was represented. Whereupon 'it was unanimously decided that an oak tree was intended', though the answer should have been 'an apple tree'. A

(*left*) An early device of the Society, used from 1899; (*centre*) the device in use from 1908 until about 1927, representing an oak tree; (*right*) the current device, an apple tree, used from 1928 onwards

representation of an oak tree was incorporated in the floor and remained there for about fifty years, when the design of the paving was changed and the Society's new device as approved by the College of Arms was embodied in it.

Although, naturally, the hall was foremost in the Council's thoughts during the early part of 1903, the need for a new Garden had not been forgotten, and on 27 January it was decided 'that Messrs. Hudson, Marshall, May and Veitch be requested to act as a committee to look for a suitable site for a new Garden'; and no doubt they did so, but if they found anything both suitable and within the means of the Society in view of its mounting commitments in connection with the hall, there does not appear to be any record of it. But presently something came out of the blue! On 4 August 1903 Sir Thomas Hanbury[1] attended the Council and offered to present to the Society sixty acres of freehold land at Wisley, formerly the property of the late G. F. Wilson. Sir Thomas

---

[1] Sir Thomas Hanbury, K.C.V.O. (1832–1907), then the owner of the famous garden at La Mortola, Ventimiglia, Italy. The estate had been acquired in 1866, when there was a scanty olive grove on it. He and his brother Daniel, a botanist and pharmacologist of eminence, established an experimental botanic garden in the generally favourable though sometimes trying climate of the Genoese Riviera. By 1889 there were some 3,600 different plants growing there.

explained that he would vest it in the hands of three trustees[1] for the use of the Society for the purpose of a Garden, but leaving the Society free to let such part as farm land as the late Mr. Wilson had hitherto done.

Miss Willmott also attended the Council and explained various points connected with the Garden.

Sir Trevor Lawrence proposed, and Baron Schröder seconded the proposal, 'that the most grateful thanks of the Society be tendered to Sir Thomas Hanbury for his most generous offer.' (Plate 11.)

Of course, everyone was delighted; now there was no longer any need for dispute about the relative importance of a hall and a new Garden; and notwithstanding the cost of the hall the Society would be able to celebrate its centenary with both a new hall *and* a new Garden. The position was at least equal to anyone's wildest dreams, and one can quite understand why, for almost the first time in ninety-nine years, the Council broke into 'Applause'.

The President enjoined the Council to treat the matter as confidential until the conveyance was signed, so as not to hamper Sir Thomas in negotiating the purchase of the property. But negotiations must already have been well advanced, for on 15 August the *Gardener's Chronicle* announced the gift, and as the news led to many inquiries from Fellows anxious to see the Society's new Garden, the next issue of that journal carried a note from the Secretary of the Society to the effect that it would probably not be possible to open the Garden to Fellows for some months. A few weeks later the Secretary reported to the Council that the property had been formally handed over to him as the Society's representative on 9 September 1903. A committee of the Council met at Wisley in the following week to deal with the tenants of the farm land, to decide when Mr. Wright (the Superintendent of the Gardens) should go to live at Wisley, to make recommendations about a water supply, the fencing of the public footpath through the property, and the number and size of the glass-houses which should be built, and to report generally on the requirements at Wisley. Meanwhile the solicitor was instructed to endeavour to complete the surrender of the Chiswick lease by Christmas, reserving the right to retain until May 1904 such parts of the ground as were necessary for the annual distribution of plants.

The report of the Council for 1903, the Society's hundredth year, was eminently satisfactory. The construction of the hall and offices was well advanced; upwards of £24,000 had been given or promised as the result of an appeal made by Baron Schröder, and, while about £16,000 was still required to meet the cost, the Council had no reason to doubt

---

[1] The first trustees were Mr. Cecil Hanbury, Miss Ellen Willmott, and Mr. John Thomas Bennett-Poë. In 1938 the Hanbury trust land was vested in the Official Trustee of Charity Lands.

that that sum would be found by one means or another. A new Garden had been acquired through the generosity of Sir Thomas Hanbury, whose handsome gift had come 'as a complete surprise' to both the Council and the general body of Fellows. It was, of course, obvious that, apart from the cost of the Hall, money would have to be found for the establishment of the new Garden, e.g. for the provision of glass-houses and dwellings for the staff, and some, though not all, members of the Council felt that a new source of revenue must be found. Others were more concerned about the rapidly growing crowds at the fortnightly Shows at the Drill Hall, where it was becoming very difficult to see the exhibits properly. So, for one reason or another, the majority agreed that the Fellows should be consulted about the advisability of raising the minimum subscription from one to two guineas per annum. In this connection it is as well to note that, in spite of the greater value which money had at that time, the public was accustomed to pay £1. 2s. 6d. for admission on the first day to the Society's spring and summer Shows at the Temple Gardens and Holland House, compared with the charge of one pound for admission on the first day at the present Chelsea Show. Thus, at the Annual General Meeting in 1904 it was proposed that the Bye-Laws be altered to raise the minimum annual subscription to two guineas; but when putting the proposal to the Meeting the Treasurer intimated that the Council had an open mind and understood that an amendment was likely to be proposed. An amendment to retain the existing minimum subscription of one guinea, but to require new one-guinea Fellows to pay an entrance fee of one guinea, was, in fact, proposed by Mr. Harry Veitch and carried 'by practically the whole Meeting'. The resulting practice was continued until the end of 1931.

Seldom can any society, in spite of great vicissitudes, have been in such a satisfactory position at the end of its first hundred years as that enjoyed by the Royal Horticultural Society. Appropriately, it was proposed to celebrate the fact with a dinner at the Hotel Metropole, at which the Rt. Hon. Joseph Chamberlain, M.P., a Vice-President of the Society and a keen grower of orchids, was to take the Chair. However, the idea did not catch on, possibly because, owing to the limited size of the available rooms, the gathering had to be confined to men, and, apart from seventy invited persons, only thirteen applied for tickets. Consequently the proposal was abandoned and it was announced that 'owing to unforeseen circumstances' the dinner was 'unavoidable postponed'.

The great occasion of 1904 was the formal opening of the hall on Friday, 22 July, by His Majesty King Edward VII, accompanied by H.M. Queen Alexandra and H.R.H. Princess Victoria. The royal party were received at the entrance by the President and Council, and proceeded to a raised dais erected in the centre of one side of the building. 'Save for palms at the back of the platform, nothing in the way of decoration was attempted, but the fine proportions, spacious area and light appearance of the Hall produced a favourable impression.' (Plate 13.) The President, Sir Trevor Lawrence, read an address, and in replying His Majesty said:

I am very glad that you have at length obtained a suitable Hall for your beautiful and interesting shows, and adequate accommodation for your library and for the performance of the official work of the Society, and it is with great pleasure that The Queen and I are here today to declare these new buildings open. We are also pleased to be able to congratulate the Society on having acquired the garden to which you allude and for which you are indebted to the goodness of Sir Thomas Hanbury. The Queen and myself wish that every success may attend the opening of this new Hall and its adjoining premises, and that the Centenary which we are celebrating this year may prove to be the occasion of an accession of prosperity to the Royal Horticultural Society. I have much pleasure in declaring this Royal Horticultural Hall—this magnificent Hall—open.

Before leaving the hall the Queen accepted a bouquet of orchids from Lady Lawrence, and Princess Victoria a bouquet of Souvenir de la Malmaison carnations from Miss Lawrence. That favourite orchid, *Odontoglossum crispum*, for long known as *O. alexandrae*, discovered by Hartweg, and introduced to cultivation by Weir, two of the Society's collectors, was appropriately included in the Queen's bouquet.

The first fortnightly Show in the new hall was held four days after the formal opening. In conjunction with it the National Carnation and Picotee Society held its annual competitions. Although the exhibition as a whole was disappointing, especially the carnations, the exhibits of fruits were good—particularly Veitch's gooseberries. This magnificent exhibit consisted of a basket of fruits of each of no fewer than eighty-seven varieties, backed by fifty cordon-trained trees 3–5 feet in height, and all wreathed with berries. All the best dessert and culinary varieties were included, among them the new cultivars 'Langley Gage' (white), 'Langley Beauty' (pale yellow) and 'Golden Gem'. This exhibit, for which a Hogg Medal was awarded, was typical of the comprehensive displays which Messrs. Veitch sent to the Society's shows for many years.

When the hall was formally opened in July a good deal of work still remained to be done on the offices, lecture-room, and library. However, it was completed before the end of the year. Baron Schröder, although he had already contributed £5,000 to the building fund, with his usual generosity, undertook to pay the cost of the fittings and furniture of the library and for the removal of the Lindley Library books to their new home. At the end of 1904 the Council reported that Fellows had subscribed £25,178, leaving a balance of £8,989 still to be found. However, the prospect was pleasing, for during the first year of the Society's second century the number of new Fellows and Associates elected was 1,337, only forty less than in the preceding record year.

Although eclipsed by such epoch-making developments as the acquisition of a hall and a new Garden, there were several other noteworthy events during the years 1901–4. Following the death of Queen Victoria in January 1901, Queen Alexandra became the Society's patron, and in March 1904 His Majesty King Edward VII graciously acceded to a request that he should become joint patron with the Queen. During 1901 the Affiliated Societies Medal was struck to provide local horticultural societies with a means of recognizing particularly meritorious exhibits at their shows. And because the steady increase in the number of Fellows, Associates, and affiliated societies naturally added to the work in the office, and in order to lighten the Secretary's task, in 1901 an Assistant Secretary was appointed in the person of the Rev. J. C. Eyre-Kidson. He held the office for three years only and then was succeeded by Mr. T. H. Sedgwick.

In June 1902, by the kindness of the Earl of Ilchester, a member of Council, a Coronation Rose Show and a Conference on Roses were held at Holland House, Kensington. The Show was a disappointment, for two main reasons. In the first place, owing to the exceptionally bad weather, the roses were the weakest feature of the Show. But of a quite different and much more serious nature, owing to the serious illness of the King, the Coronation, with all its attendant festivities, had to be postponed. Under these circumstances, not unnaturally, considerable gloom attended the Show—the first of a series of Holland House Shows.

At the end of 1904, the hundredth year of the Society's existence, the total number of subscribers was 8,360.

By February 1906 Sir Trevor Lawrence had held the office of President for twenty-one years and, to commemorate his fine work throughout that long period, the Council decided that a gold medal, to be designed by Alfred Gilbert, should be struck and awarded annually 'for exhibits of a specially meritorious character'. As the negotiations with Gilbert proved abortive, in 1908 the design was entrusted to Bertram Mac-Kennal. The first specimen, struck in 1909, was presented to Sir Trevor. Today the Lawrence Medal is awarded by the Council annually for the most outstanding exhibit shown to the Society during the year; no exhibitor may receive this medal more than once in three years and it is one of the Society's most treasured awards. But apart from this medal, the Council was anxious that Sir Trevor's portrait should be painted by Sir Hubert Herkomer, and hung in the Council Room alongside that of Sir Joseph Banks. The universal popularity of the President, whose courteous and conciliatory attitude in the Chair was greatly appreciated, was such that Fellows promptly subscribed over one thousand guineas towards the cost of the portrait. Herkomer's sympathetic study is one of the most successful of the Society's portraits. (Plate 9.)

Baron Sir Henry Schröder had also sat for Sir Hubert Herkomer. In 1909 the Council, believing it desirable that the Society should also possess a portrait of the Baron, 'one of the greatest benefactors of the Society', obtained his permission for Herkomer to supervise the copying of his portrait. Equally appropriate was it for the Society to have a portrait of the late Sir Thomas Hanbury, the donor of the Wisley estate, and Mr. Percy Bigland was commissioned to make a copy of his portrait of Sir Thomas which was at La Mortola. Both copies are now in the Council Room. (Plate 11.)

During these years horticulture and the Society lost two great personalities. Dr. Maxwell Masters, chairman of the Scientific Committee and editor of the *Gardener's Chronicle*, died in 1907. A memorial fund was raised and the following year the Society consented to become the trustee of the fund on the understanding that the income be used to provide one or two lectures each year. The first Masters Memorial Lectures were appropriately given in 1909 by Professor Hugo de Vries, on Masters's *Vegetable Teratology* and 'The Production of Horticultural Varieties'. The Masters Memorial Lectures are still an important event in the Society's calendar and over the years have formed impressive scientific contributions to the Society's *Journal*.

In a somewhat similar way the Society undertook to be the custodian of a fund raised in 1908 in memory of George Nicholson, the Curator of the Royal Botanic Gardens, Kew, and author of *The Illustrated Dictionary of Gardening*, which was the forerunner of the Society's *Dictionary*; Nicholson had died in 1908. The income from the fund is used to provide a prize, the Nicholson Prize, for the leading student in the Wisley diploma examination.

Throughout its history the Society has always been conscious of the need to make every endeavour to tidy up the nomenclature and classification of groups of cultivated plants. From this point of view splendid work had been done at Chiswick and was now being done at Wisley. In the early 1900s, owing to the rapid increase in the number of named daffodils and due to the inter-crossing of hitherto fairly distinct groups, there was great scope for such work on the genus *Narcissus*. And towards this end, in 1908 a Committee was appointed to draw up a scheme of classification for daffodils for garden and for show purposes. This classification, which has been emended from time to time, is now in use throughout the world. At the same time, in order to reduce the possibility of a given name being used for more than one cultivar, a scheme was introduced for the registration of daffodil cultivar names, and the *Classified List of Daffodil Names*, now in its seventeenth edition, became the forerunner of the checklists of cultivar names in use today. In this the Society was anticipating events by close on half a century, and today the Society has a special registration centre and acts as the international registration authority for several great groups of horticultural plants.

In July 1910 the Lindley Library Trust was transferred from the original trustees to the Society, acting through its Council, and such books as the Society had acquired since its first library was sold in 1859 were presented to the Lindley Library Trust. Thereafter the Society conducted the library in much the same way as if it were the Society's own property, meeting the cost of maintenance and improvements. Thus in 1911 the Society purchased, among other works, Sibthorp's *Flora Graeca* and Redouté's *Les Liliacées*, which cost £200 and £120 respectively; and in this same year some 370 volumes were received as gifts. The library had now grown so extensive that more bookcases were urgently needed. The need for these came to the knowledge of Baron Bruno Schröder, nephew of the late Baron, who had so generously supplied the original fittings, and he took it upon himself to provide the necessary new fittings, so that the whole of the cost of furnishing the library might continue to be associated with the name of Schröder.

The great horticultural event of 1912 was the Royal International Horticultural Exhibition held in the grounds of the Royal Hospital, Chelsea, on 22–30 May. Although the Exhibition owed its inception to the Society, for several reasons it was thought wise that the Society should act as a benevolent godparent, rather than as the responsible promoter, of the Exhibition, which was accordingly organized by a small public company of which the Duke of Portland was the president, Mr. J. Gurney Fowler, the Society's Treasurer, the chairman, Sir Jeremiah Colman the treasurer, and Mr. Edward White, a member of the firm of landscape gardeners Messrs. Milner, Son, & White, the managing director. The Society contributed £1,000 to the expenses and guaranteed a further £4,000 should this be required. The Society's standing committees met at the Exhibition and the awards which were made to meritorious new plants were those of the Society. The Council gave a banquet in the hall at Vincent Square, to which over eight hundred guests were invited, and Sir Trevor Lawrence gave an al fresco lunch to the foreign visitors and others at his home at Burford. From all points of view the Exhibition was a great success—and none of the guaranteed money was required.

The Exhibition tent was the largest ever erected up to that time, for its 40,000 square yards of canvas covered about 3½ acres of ground. Its five spans were each 36 feet high and 52 feet wide; they varied slightly in length, the longest being 280 feet. The wire guys weighed 40 tons and the ridge-wires 7½ tons. It was lit by electricity. There were special tents for the exhibits from France, Belgium, and Holland, and these were the biggest single-spanned tents available in London, each 140 feet long and 85 feet wide. The orchid tent was 250 feet long, 70 feet wide, and 46 feet high, and was heated by hot-water pipes in an endeavour to maintain the temperature at 60°F. A special system of ventilation was installed in the cut-flower tent—600 feet long by 40 feet—in the hope of prolonging the life of the flowers.

Some of the exhibits were enormous. For instance, that of Mr. Leopold de Rothschild required some twenty vans to transport the plants from Gunnersbury House, Acton, to the show ground. This wonderful display of fruit trees in pots occupied 1,380 square feet and in it thirteen different fruits in fifty different varieties were represented. The highest award, the King's Cup, was given to Sir George Holford for an exhibit of orchids occupying 1,100 square feet, which, said the *Gardener's Chronicle*, 'a generation ago would have been considered a miracle.' The orchid exhibits were the outstanding feature of the Exhibition. They provided the finest display of orchids ever assembled, and splendidly illustrated, as did the exhibits of other plants, the progress of horticulture since the International Exhibition of 1866. Orchids exhibited in 1866 were in large measure species; at the Orchid Conference in 1885 the work of the hybridist was beginning to show and, by 1912, hybrids were greatly in the majority, illustrating how hybridization had vastly extended the range of form and colour.

At the judges' luncheon there were some who had attended the Exhibition of 1866. One such was Mr. Harry Veitch, who responded to many calls from the assembly for him to speak. He said that the occasion was a very solemn one for him, for he remembered very well the Exhibition of 1866 and was thankful that he had been spared to take part in this present one; he could not hope to be present at the next Exhibition, but if he happened to be he would give his best services. Mr. Veitch had thrown himself, heart and soul, into the preparations for this Exhibition and, to the great happiness of everyone, in honour of the occasion, His Majesty King George V (who had succeeded to the throne in 1910) conferred upon him a knighthood. (Plate 11.)

Thanks to the foresight of Mr. R. C. Cory, a wealthy and tremendously interested amateur gardener who was later to become a great benefactor to the Society, the Exhibition was fully documented. Realizing the need for such, he persuaded Mr. R. Hooper Pearson, the editor of the *Gardener's Chronicle*, to undertake the compilation and editing of a book *The Horticultural Record*, on the production of which he spared neither time nor money and which, published in 1914, with an abundance of coloured plates, is a fitting record of the great Exhibition.

Partly because of the annual increase in the number of Fellows, and partly because of the increase in the number and size of the exhibits, for some years the Temple Gardens had been too small for the Society's Great Spring Show. Now the International Exhibition had shown that crowds of people were quite prepared to flock to Chelsea, where a larger site was available, even though Charing Cross was more central. So the Society forsook the Temple and in 1913 held the first of its long series of Chelsea Shows. Compared with those of recent years, the first Chelsea Show was a small one; it was confined to the area between Monument Road and Eastern Avenue; no part of Ranelagh Gardens was occupied; and the marquee was less than half the size of that now used. Even so, much more space than formerly was available for visitors and exhibits, including exhibits of horticultural sundries, and the Show was an unqualified success.

At the Annual General Meeting in 1913, Wilks completed twenty-five years of service to the Society in the office of Secretary. During these twenty-five years the number of Fellows had increased to close on 13,500; from a state of bankruptcy the Society had progressed until now it had invested funds to the amount of £67,258. It possessed a home in Vincent Square of which every Fellow was proud, and a Garden at Wisley of great beauty and interest. Such vast improvements in the Society's fortunes were in no small measure due to the wisdom and work of the Secretary and, in appreciation of this fact, the Council decided that his portrait should be painted at the Society's expense and that a circular letter should be sent to all Fellows inviting subscriptions to a testimonial to take the form of silver plate and a cheque. Wilks's portrait, unfortunately, is one of the least successful of those which now hang in the Council Room. (Plate 12.)

On 1 April 1913, to universal regret, the President resigned. Aged eighty-one and in failing health, having held the reins for almost twenty-nine years, Sir Trevor died in December. Of him *The Times* wrote that he was a generous and broad-minded but

unostentatious supporter of charities, a popular and delightful host, and a singularly handsome man, who seemed till he reached four-score years to have learnt the secret of perpetual youth and health. He was on terms of close friendship with leaders in science, literature and other walks, such as Lister, Kelvin, Paget, Virchow, Pasteur, Browning, Meredith, Herbert Spencer, Russell Lowell, Lecky, and Wolseley.

At the International Horticultural Banquet of 1912, Monsieur Maurice de Vilmorin, one of the world's foremost horticulturists, said: 'Your President has very quickly conquered all who have ever had the good fortune to be brought into personal contact with him—conquered them by the only force worth conquering with, the amiability and good grace of his charming personality.' Wilks, and the Society, had 'lost one of the kindest of friends and one of the wisest of counsellors'.

Sir Trevor had suggested that Field-Marshal Lord Grenfell (Plate 10) would make an admirable President, and this distinguished soldier was duly elected on the day Lawrence resigned. Unfortunately he held the office for a comparatively short time—only until 1919. It was a desperately important time, however, for most of it coincided with the years of the war, when the President's influence was able to smooth away many difficulties. Although he placed the services of his country first, gardeners, and especially those connected with the trade, were to owe him a deep debt of gratitude for the way he looked after their interests.

The outbreak of war on 4 August 1914 naturally had an adverse effect on the growth of the Society during the next four years. At the end of 1914 the numerical strength, which had consistently risen annually for many years, stood at 14,404, but during 1915 it fell to 13,937. Although throughout the war the losses from resignations and other causes were heavy, there continued to be a counteracting annual intake of about 800 new Fellows, Associates and affiliated societies, and in December 1918 the total number stood at 12,914. The tide then turned, bringing in no fewer than 1,661 new Fellows and Associates in 1919, and by the end of 1920 all the lost ground had been recovered and the total numerical strength had risen above the prewar figure to the record total of 15,280.

The comparatively small extent to which the numerical strength of the Society suffered from the war was largely due to the fact that, in spite of bombs, the Society's programme of Meetings and Shows was continued with the minimum of disturbance. During the first two years both the fortnightly Shows and Chelsea Show were continued, and when in 1917 the hall was requisitioned by the War Office for the use of the Australian Forces, the Society carried on its fortnightly Meetings in the London Scottish Drill Hall in Buckingham Gate, where they had been held for many years before the Old Hall was built. Naturally the exhibits were on a small scale. The Vincent Square hall was formally returned to the Society in October 1919. Meantime Chelsea Show had been revived in May of that year.

Among other activities during the war, the Society raised funds and secured gifts of fruit trees and vegetable seeds for the assistance of horticulturists in allied countries which had suffered from enemy action. It assisted the Government's food production campaign by publications and by organizing a panel of lecturers who spoke on the cultivation of vegetables. It also raised funds for the Red Cross by the sale of plants, seeds, books, and horticultural sundries, and sent bulbs and seeds to prisoners of war in German camps.

In 1919 still another medal was instituted, the Grenfell Medal, to commemorate the services to the Society of the President, who, owing to pressure of other work, had to resign from his office in that year. The medal is awarded for exhibits of pictures, photographs, or objects of a similar nature, of horticultural or botanical interest; it was designed by one who had been a member of Council since 1908—and who was to be continuously associated with the Council for the next forty-five years—Mr. E. A. Bowles, one of the greatest gardeners of his, or any other, generation, with an encyclopaedic knowledge of all plants, and a recognized authority on *Crocus, Colchicum, Galanthus,* and *Narcissus.* He was also a talented artist, served the Society for many years not only as a Councillor and as a Vice-President, but as chairman of the Narcissus and Tulip Committee and of the Library and of the Scientific Committees, the activities of all of which he guided with great wisdom and knowledge.

Lord Lambourne (Plate 10), who, as Lieut.-Col. Mark Lockwood, had taken his seat on the Council in 1914, succeeded Grenfell as President, and in the following year Wilks, then aged seventy-six, and Secretary for thirty-two years, resigned. The Society did not entirely lose the benefit of his great experience and ability, for he was elected to a seat on the Council. But his stay on the Council was all too short, for he died, very suddenly, on 2 March 1923.

'When in one man wisdom is added to knowledge, tact to firm handling of affairs, patience to tenacity of purpose, singleness of aim to ability, knowledge of man to love of nature and simple natural things, the cause to which that man attaches himself is bound to be well served. Such a man was the Rev. William Wilks,' said the writer of the obituary notice in the Society's *Journal.*

He came to the secretary's chair with the Society burdened with debt, and until that debt was disposed of he took no recompense for his services. From his appointment by the Council in 1888 until his retirement in 1920 his ungrudging services were always at the disposal of the Society, and he saw it rise from poverty to prosperity, its Fellowship increase from 1,108 to nearly 16,000, its hired rooms replaced by a magnificent hall and offices wholly free from debt; its old outworn grounds at Chiswick exchanged for the new garden at Wisley and the growth of that garden in size, value, and importance; and the establishment of a school of horticulture and a station for the investigation of horticultural problems; he saw the *Journal,* which had been a very uncertain publication, become a useful one sought by all horticultural stations the world over; and he saw the growth of the Society in importance, power, prestige, and responsibility, until it is by far the most important horticultural Society in the world.[1]

Apart from his tremendous work for the Society and the making of his own garden at Shirley, Croydon ('The Wilderness' he called it), Wilks's greatest contribution to horticulture was the development of the Shirley Poppy. From a white-edged variant of the field poppy, *Papaver rhoeas*, by careful selection from year to year, he finally developed a race of delicate colouring with no trace of the black patch so characteristic of the wild plant, and widely and generously distributed seeds so that all might share their beauty.

At Wisley today there is a permanent memorial to Wilks and to his work—the handsome wrought-iron gates at the main entrance to the Garden. (Plate 18.) They were designed by Mr. Edward White and the design incorporates the initials 'W.W.' and the flowers of the Shirley Poppy.

[1] *Jl R. hort. Soc.*, XLVIII (1923), pp. 157–60.

CHAPTER SIXTEEN

CHISWICK—WISLEY

ALTHOUGH SPLENDID WORK HAD BEEN DONE AT CHISWICK DURING the period of the Kensington adventure, because of the expenses the latter had incurred the Garden was in by no means as satisfactory a condition as Sir Trevor Lawrence and his excellent team of Councillors required. For instance, everyone deplored the condition of the glass and very soon extensive repairs had to be carried out. Even more important, the Council were of one mind that the Garden must be a school of scientific and practical horticulture—'ornamental as well as useful'— and laid down a scheme for the Garden's better future utilization. It should be devoted to the cultivation of such fruits, vegetables, and decorative plants and flowers as it might seem expedient to draw the attention of Fellows to at any given time; to the trials of new cultivars of all kinds of plants side by side with existing well-tried kinds; to the experimentation into the culture of plants; to the trials of horticultural appliances and materials. As all such trials and experiments would be of little general value or interest unless they were made known to all the Fellows, the publication of the Society's *Journal* should be recommenced immediately. And so the *Journal* was revived in 1889, a fact which was particularly appreciated by Fellows in the provinces and no doubt helped to enrol the 173 new Fellows of that year.

Under the superintendence of Barron, trials were undertaken with renewed vigour. During the 1900–1 session trials were made of 104 cultivars of lettuce, 25 of endive, 33 of celery, 36 of leeks and 30 of broad beans; 34 new cultivars of potato, 23 new peas, and 30 new tomatoes were tested. In the floral department 415 cultivars of carnations and picotees, 354 of dahlias, 58 of ivy-leaved pelargoniums, 70 of violas and bedding pansies, 112 different strains of China asters, and 32 of stocks were tried. Moreover, a very large collection of michaelmas daisies and sunflowers was being grown especially for a conference on these plants which was due to be held in the autumn and which, it was hoped, would serve to clear away the great existing confusion in the nomenclature of these plants obtaining in different parts of the country. This has always been one of the main aims of the Society and it has never been more vigorously pursued than during these years which constituted a great era of conferences in Chiswick's history.

Three months after being appointed President, Sir Trevor Lawrence had taken the Chair at an Orchid Conference at Kensington when the largest and most varied collection of orchids ever seen up to that time was staged. Sir Trevor, Baron Schröder, the Duke of Devonshire, and many other private growers exhibited, as well as such members of the trade as Messrs. J. Veitch & Son, Hugh Low & Co., and Messrs. F. Sander & Co. There was a full programme on orchid nomenclature, the reading of several papers, including two particularly fine ones by Mr. Veitch on hybridization and by Mr. J. O'Brien on cultivation. And three Veitch Memorial Medals were awarded to people who in various ways had been instrumental in promoting a knowledge of orchids: Professor Reichenbach, Professor of Botany at Hamburg and the most distinguished orchid authority of his day; the Rev. Charles Parish, who had collected orchids in Burma and elsewhere; and Mr. John Seden, a leading orchid cultivator.

The Orchid Conference of 1885 was followed in 1886 by one on orchid nomenclature held in conjunction with a provincial show at Liverpool. Again Sir Trevor took the chair. The main speaker was Dr. Ridley of the Department of Botany of the British Museum. Professor Reichenbach should also have spoken, but he was unable to be present. However, in October there appeared in the *Gardener's Chronicle*[1] an extract from one of Reichenbach's papers in *Reichenbachia*, and his words have a very familiar ring today.

There has been a great deal of controversy respecting the nomenclature of Orchids both by those who are versed in the matter as well as by those who are not. No one seems to have been successful in formulating a plan on the subject worthy to be followed. Those who are able to perceive the difference between garden and botanical nomenclature will doubtless arrive at the conclusion, that it is not possible to bring both into harmony, for so long as the botanist has to serve garden interests he will have to study the ideas as well as the tastes of amateurs. This was Lindley's view and it is also mine. Of course, science ought not to stand still for the sake of amateurs; on the other hand these cannot be expected to follow every change in the views of scientific men, as these are often founded upon circumstances which to an amateur are unfathomable.

One of the last plant conferences to be held at Kensington was the one devoted to primulas in April 1886. It was dominated by the Florists' Auricula—then an extraordinarily popular flower—whose origin and history was discussed by Shirley Hibberd. Even so, species also were

[1] (1886), p. 466.

represented: the Canadian *Primula mistassinica*, today a very rare plant in cultivation; *P. rusbyi* from New Mexico; *P. rosea* in several splendid forms, the variable *P. denticulata*, *P. floribunda* and *P. involucrata*, and others, from the Himalayas; *P. japonica*, *P. sieboldii* and *P. obconica* from Japan; *P. verticillata* subsp. *sinensis* from Abyssinia; *P. kaufmanniana* from Turkestan; and, of course, many of the European species. Clearly at that time *P. sinensis* and *P. obconica* had not begun to exhibit the remarkable degree of variation which was to be so striking a feature of the next Primula Conference—in 1913—where, too, many new Chinese species were to be so much in evidence. At the 1886 conference, Sir John Llewellyn occupied the Chair and Miss Gertrude Jekyll exhibited 'a hill of moss dotted over with border Primroses in white, crimson, yellow and red that had a pretty effect in their uncommon setting'. In 1913, Sir John again presided and Miss Jekyll discussed primulas in the garden.

Thereafter, for the next few years, the Chiswick Garden became the scene of the Society's conferences. Though all of them no doubt severely taxed the resources of the Superintendent and his staff, and may not have been entirely satisfactory financially, all were enormously rewarding scientifically and educationally. At the Rose Conference in 1889, though many hybrids—Hybrid Perpetuals, Hybrid Teas—were shown, the main features were the collections of species and of old-fashioned types. At that time there were some sixty rose species at the disposal of the hybridist; chiefly two—and certainly not more than half a dozen—had been used in hybridization, and with, even at that time, remarkable results. 'How much may we not expect in the future when our great rosarians and our botanical establishments turn their attention to the number of untried species?' asked the *Gardener's Chronicle*.[1] With equal justification the same question could well be asked today when hardly more than eight species have been exploited by our rose breeders.

The main objects of these conferences were admirably stated by Mr. Harry Veitch, chairman of the Vegetable Conference of 1889; 'the promotion of the profitable cultivation, uses, and improvements of all kinds of roots, tubers, bulbs, leaves, flowers, and seeds, by the reading of papers, discussion of propositions, and demonstrations of practice, and to bring together, for the purpose of reciprocal information and fellowship, all those interested in the growth of vegetables.' At this particular conference there were no competitive classes; different varieties of vegetables had been assembled chiefly for purposes of comparison and identification.

The Chrysanthemum Conference and Exhibition of the same year was held in the great Chiswick Vinery,

[1] Vol. 6 (1889), p. 16.

with great banks of soft glowing colour, the varied shapes, from the formal balls admired by the old school of florists to the more elegant 'Japs', the neat Pompons, and the correct Anemone-flowered varieties. All sections were represented to please all tastes so that a large and most instructive display was got together under a covering than which nothing could be more beautiful or more fitting, for the roof of the huge building, from end to end, was clad with the foliage of the vines in all the loveliness of their autumn tints, enhanced by the rays of the sun that would have done credit to June. But so many were the people and so constant the hum of voices that the speakers had difficulty in being heard.[1]

Whether the speakers could be heard or not, they all had occasion to revert to the history of the chrysanthemum in terms of the work of the Society. Parks, Reeves, Fortune, all in the service of the Society in China or in Japan, had furnished the material which at that time was, and still is, the basis of our modern chrysanthemums. Sabine, the old Secretary who had enriched the *Transactions* with several contributions on this particular flower, no doubt would have been proud of this conference.

The history and development in cultivation of certain plants was one of the main themes of the conferences at Chiswick in 1890. For instance, at the Dahlia Conference, held jointly with a Grape Conference, Cannell, the nurseryman of Swanley, who had done much to develop the Cactus dahlia, exhibited many cultivars which showed the stages through which the dahlia flower had passed to its then present form. At the Daffodil Conference, Burbidge read an important paper on the history of the daffodil and Professor Michael Foster another on the progress made in daffodil breeding and cultivation since the last conference of 1884. Both Foster and Mr. Scrase-Dickins alluded to the work of the Society's Narcissus Committee, which until 1886 had been associated with the Scientific Committee, in adjusting the nomenclature of daffodils, and of the Society's *Daffodil Register*, which, at that time, contained the names of fifty-four cultivars recognized by the committee as the best of their class in constitution and other characteristics. In some measure Foster spoke with the voice of prophesy when he counselled that only those forms which are really distinct should receive distinguishing, separate names and that the names given should be such as could easily be written and pronounced and, if possible, have some relation to the things signified. In some form or another, all Foster's counsel is incorporated in the articles and recommendations for the naming of new cultivars in the 1961 edition of the International Code of Nomenclature for Cultivated Plants. 'Though it is our duty to strive to attain this virtue in a name, the task is a very hard one,' said Foster.

[1] *Gdnr's Chron.*, Vol. 6 (1889), p. 532.

Those who have this task today are finding it very much more difficult than it was in 1890.

Polystichum angulare var. *divisilobum* sub-var. *plumosum* sub-sub-var. *densum* was the name given to one fern at the Fern and Carnation Conference of 1900; and the *Gardener's Chronicle*, whilst describing the plant in question thus: 'The plumage of an ostrich or a bird-of-paradise is the only thing we can think of at all comparable to the infinitely minute sub-divisions and graceful appearance of this fern', very rightly protested against the name. At this conference the ferns stole all the thunder from the carnations and picotees. They 'were something, extraordinary; the variety and interest they provided was indeed marvellous'. The scolopendriums from Dr. Lowe were 'almost stupefying in their wonderful variety'—all having proceeded from the old Harts'-tongue.[1]

By 1890 many of the conifers introduced earlier in the century by Douglas and Hartweg, Messrs. Veitch, and others, had attained a considerable size; it was high time that a judgement was made on their value, either for decorative or utilitarian purposes. It was also high time, therefore, that the Society held a Conifer Conference; and this was done in 1891, when information was gained about the hardiness and rate of growth of many species, their value for shelter, timber, or decoration, their requirements as to soil and aspect. Never before had there been brought together such an array of home-grown specimens. From almost every part of the British Isles came fruiting and vegetative branches, as well as specimens of woods of European, Asiatic, and American species; for the introduction into cultivation of many of these species the Society had been responsible. Specimens from Scotland, especially those from Perthshire and adjoining counties, were outstanding. Branches and cones of species rarely seen in cultivation were sent from Fota Island in south-west Ireland, as well as from England. The Queen sent specimens from Balmoral and from Osborne; more than 300 specimens were sent by the Royal Botanic Gardens at Kew. In fact, so many specimens arrived at Chiswick that there was not sufficient space for them to be clearly exhibited. In spite of the detestable October weather, the Conference was a grand success and splendidly illustrated the great contribution the Society had made to horticulture, arboriculture, and silviculture.

In August of the following year, 1892, Chiswick was flooded with begonias, for there was a Begonia Conference—in association with plums and apricots. The begonias were not so much a testimony to the Society as to Messrs. Veitch, who had introduced most of the original types and had been responsible for hybridizing them. Harry Veitch

[1] *Gdnr's Chron.*, vol. 8 (1890), p. 102.

himself spoke of the work done in this direction by the great Chelsea firm.

All these conferences, as well as the trials of fruits, flowers, and vegetables, must have made severe demands on the resources of Barron, the Superintendent, and his staff, and no doubt the general condition of the Garden left something to be desired. At any rate, such was the judgement of the Council, even though they had spent money in an attempt to repair the result of neglect during the years when all available funds were expended at Kensington. Accordingly a committee was appointed to recommend on the best uses to which the Garden and its facilities should be put. The resulting report was rather a severe one—too severe, in fact, in view of what had been accomplished by the small loyal staff; in the committee's opinion the Gardens were 'not, either in condition or in the objects carried out and work done, calculated to sustain the reputation of the R.H.S.', and the cause was the 'absence of sufficient order, method, and energy in the detailed management of the Gardens'. Consequently, Archibald Barron, who had been Superintendent at Chiswick for the preceding thirty years, retired at the end of 1895.

He was not a very old man; in fact, he was only sixty. But he had worked hard and constantly and his health was beginning to fail. Even so, the news of his retirement caused considerable disquiet in the horticultural Press and some Fellows were of the opinion that the Society had treated him badly. Quite clearly this was not so. He only lived for another seven years; during much of this time he was very frail, and for a considerable period towards the end was as helpless as a child, before he died on 15 April 1903. The Society has always behaved honourably towards its old servants and Barron retired on a pension of two-thirds of his salary and was elected a Life Fellow in recognition of his past services.

Barron had been honoured by the Society on several occasions; by the award of the first large silver Veitch Memorial Medal ever offered to any individual, and by the award of the V.M.H. in 1897. On his retirement many of his lifelong friends honoured him. The Barron Testimonial Committee was established with Dr. Masters as chairman and Mr. Harry Veitch as treasurer, and on 21 April 1896, at a luncheon in the Hotel Windsor, at Westminster, Barron received a cheque for £500 in recognition of his services to horticulture and of his integrity and loyalty over a long series of years—years marked by prolonged circumstances of depression and uncertainty at the Garden.

His successor was a Derbyshire man, Mr. S. T. Wright, who had learned his gardening at the famous gardens of Alton Towers, where he had gone in 1875 at the age of seventeen. Later he was to be head gardener at Ednaston Lodge, Brailsford, and at Glewston Court, Ross, where he exhibited fruits, flowers, and vegetables, and won over 700 prizes in England, Scotland, and Wales. His success as a cultivator and exhibitor, as well as his writings to the horticultural Press, brought him before the horti ..ural public. And his membership of the Fruit and Veg...' ...mmittee, as well as his winning in 1896 the Society's prize .or an admirable essay on 'Hardy Fruit Culture', brought him to the notice of the Society. He was to be at Chiswick only until 1903, when in March of that year most of the movable plants in the Garden were sold, the lease disposed of for £4,700, and the Garden closed in May. He himself was transferred to the new Garden at Wisley on 23 April— eight days after Barron's death.

On 3 October the *Gardener's Chronicle* leader summed up the feelings of many on the closing of Chiswick.

The time has gone by for lamenting the abandonment of Chiswick or grieving *r* the long neglected opportunities of that establishment. Sir Thomas Hanbury, V.M.H., has altered that, and we can only hope that the glories of the old garden may shine with enhanced splendour at Wisley. Still, although it would be childish to indulge in useless lamentations, we may surely find a useful stimulus in recalling the time when Chiswick was a live force in horticulture—the time of Knight, of Sabine, of Douglas, of Bentham, of Royle, of Lindley, of Paxton, of Robert Thompson, of George Gordon, of Archibald Barron. What giants these men were in their several departments! Wisley will have its work cut out to produce an equally imposing array; but there need be no reasonable doubt that the men will be forthcoming if the governing body is wise enough not only to consider the necessities of the moment, but to look forward to those possibilities which the association of science with practical horticulture is certain to beget.

There are not many left now who remember Chiswick as it was in its so-called 'palmy' days, when, on occasion, it was the resort of the fashion of the day, when the block of carriages, whose occupants were wending their way to the Garden, began soon after leaving Hyde Park Corner and extended the whole way through Kensington and Hammersmith to Turnham Green. Then the area of the Garden was three or four times greater than it is now. 'Wild Gardens' existed there before the name had been brought into popularity. An arboretum was formed of which a few remnants may still be seen in the adjacent villa gardens; and it can never be forgotten by the most indifferent of cultivators how important were the introductions of Douglas among Conifers, nor what a profusion of flowering plants from various parts of the world were gathered together by him and by other of the Society's collectors and dispersed from Chiswick. Truly Chiswick has had a noble past.[1]

Truly Wisley was to have a noble future!

[1] *Gdnr's Chron.*, vol. 34 (1903), p. 240.

In 1903 the Wisley estate consisted of the late George F. Wilson's renowned woodland garden—nineteen acres of garden ground and water—an entirely delightful informal grouping of all manner of interesting plants; eighteen acres utilized as grassland and about twenty-two acres of arable land. There were two residences on the property. The Hanbury trust deed permitted 'the Society to use and occupy the Wisley Estate or such portion thereof as the Society may require for the purpose of an Experimental Garden and the Encouragement and the Improvement of Scientific and Practical Horticulture in all its branches'.

Wright arrived at Wisley in the springtime of 1903 and must have been greatly impressed by the trilliums, erythroniums, primroses, *Narcissus cyclamineus*, *Cornus canadensis*, *Schizocodon*, *Shortia*, *Galax*, *Epigaea*, covering the woodland floor; by the camellias and rhododendrons in their winter shelters; and, as the months passed, by the vigour of the lilies, especially *Lilium rubellum* and *Cardiocrinum giganteum* (one clump of *L. rubellum* was still there fifty years later), the vacciniums, *Gaultheria shallon* and *G. procumbens*, *Phormium tenax*, *Daphniphyllum macropodum*, splendid specimens of such conifers as *Sciadopitys verticillata*, *Cedrus atlantica* 'Glauca', *Chamaecyparis pisifera* 'Squarrosa', and the brilliant October colouring of *Liquidambar styraciflua*. Little wonder that the Council insisted that this woodland garden 'be carefully preserved and continued'. Near by were a series of ponds in which water lilies bloomed magnificently and on the margins of which *Iris kaempferi*, *Peltiphyllum peltatum*, spiraeas, and osmundas found the conditions greatly to their liking. And there was a rustic bridge almost covered in spring with the long tassels of *Wisteria floribunda* 'Macrobotrys'.

Almost immediately the Chiswick meteorological station, where records had been kept since 1825, was transferred to Wisley, the instruments being supplemented with a sunshine recorder. Although there was not a bus service, and few Fellows at that time owned motor cars, the fame of Wilson's wild garden and interest in the Society's plans for Wisley led to over 6,000 people visiting the Garden during the first full year of the Society's occupancy.

Immediately Wisley was the scene of great activity. Part of this lovely wild garden, which since G. F. Wilson's death had become overgrown with brambles, birch, and *Rhododendron ponticum*, was cleared, and because the old winter shelters for the camellias and some of the rhododendrons were thought to be unnecessary, they were destroyed. In 1905 a range of glass-houses and frames was completed, together with dwellings for the Superintendent and one of the two foremen, the other occupying what is now called Weather Hill Cottage. The glass was designed to accommodate peaches, trials, collections of vines and figs, the cultivation of melons, and the propagation of plants. Numerous trees and

(*above*) Exhibits and visitors outside the marquee
(*below*) A view of some of the exhibits inside the marquee
Plate III SCENES AT CHELSEA SHOW

shrubs, and a collection of fruit trees, all largely the gift of the leading nurserymen, were planted, and a Mr. Todd presented a collection of vines for an outdoor vineyard which, although patiently continued for many years, failed to convince anyone but the donor that the production of grapes for wine was really worth while at Wisley. The soil from the excavation of the houses was used to form a bank to the north on which ornamental trees and shrubs were planted; some of these, such as *Parrotia* and *Poncirus*, were still growing splendidly fifty years later. An old hedge of *Prunus cerasifera* was removed and replaced by a planting of bamboos—the Bamboo Walk. The approach to the Garden from the Portsmouth Road was much improved and a new entrance to the Garden was made beside the Superintendent's house. Handsome oak gates were erected and from these a drive, twelve feet wide, led to Weather Hill Cottage; the drive was bordered by wide cultivated beds, in which hybrid Tea Roses, with climbing roses on tripods, were subsequently planted, and the borders were backed by the hornbeam hedges which are so familiar a feature today. The land to the south of the hornbeam hedge was partly planted with a collection of fruits and partly used as a vegetable trial ground.

The area now known as Seven Acres was then rough pastureland abutting on the western side of the woodland garden. Between 1905 and 1907 a good number of ornamental trees were planted there, but unfortunately none made satisfactory growth—and for some years it was regarded as useless for garden purposes. Likewise in 1907 the first plantings in the Pinetum were made.

The sloping land between the new drive and the glass-houses showed a tendency to slide. In an endeavour to prevent this, between 1907 and 1910 it was planted with conifers, some of them straight out of small pots, and hollies, whilst stone slabs of various sizes were placed along its base to a height of eight feet or so and the spaces between were planted with various rock-garden plants. This bank of stones remained unaltered until 1922, when it was moved back several feet to give better access to the houses and to allow of a wider path to the wild garden.

In 1903 there were a few alpine plants contained in a little rockery at the northern corner of the grassy slope above Wilson's water-lily ponds and rustic bridge. But this was not enough, for at this time the cultivation of alpine plants was becoming very popular and great stimulus was given to rock gardening by Reginald Farrer, who, in 1907, published *My Rock Garden*. So the Council decided that another rock garden should be constructed at Wisley, and in 1911, from designs by Mr. Edward White the landscape architect, Messrs. Pulham, using Sussex sandstone, created the splendid Rock Garden, which, except for some slight changes, is structurally virtually the same today as it was then. On the grassy bank site a number of scattered trees had been planted. The group of conifers at the western end of the ponds, the *Cryptomeria japonica* 'Elegans' half-way up the slope, and the oaks and firs on the higher parts were all brought into the scheme. Water was provided partly by a natural spring near the top of the slope and partly from a large hidden tank which obtained its supplies by a pump from the lower part of the ground. A small moraine, as well as a bog garden, was incorporated into the scheme. Construction began in January and planting in August. *Juniperus communis* 'Compressa' in the moraine and *Prunus subhirtella* 'Pendula' near the top of the garden were the first plants to be placed in position. A special foreman, Mr. D. Sarsons, rock gardener at Wretham Hall, Norfolk, was placed in charge and at once received gifts of suitable plants from Sir Frank Crisp, who had created a celebrated alpine garden at Friar Park, near Henley, and from Mr. E. A. Bowles, who continued to give plants for the next forty-three years. Immediately Fellows showed great interest in this fine new feature and, to stimulate further this interest an alpine house and a number of frames were erected.

During the time the Rock Garden was being built, so was a new bothy, potting-shed, seed-room, and the wall of the frame-yard. In 1911 a start was made on the planting of that part of the Garden now known as Howard's Field as an orchard for the conduct of experiments on pollination, and Mr. A. N. Rawes began his work as assistant for fruit experiments. Thus the Garden was developing and expanding, the Garden staff had to be increased and additional accommodation for them had to be found. In 1915, therefore, five acres of land at the northern end of the Garden were purchased and six cottages were built on what is now called 'The Square' in Wisley Village.

From the beginning of the Society's occupation of Wisley, the Scientific Committee, no doubt much influenced by its association with Bateson and the Royal Society's Evolution Committee, as well as by the success of the first Hybridization Conference, was making recurring demands that research should be undertaken at the Garden. Council had very naturally replied that, desirable as research admittedly was, it must await the settlement of the bills for the hall and the essential buildings at Wisley. Even so, in 1905 it was agreed that George Massee, the plant pathologist at Kew, should conduct an investigation at Wisley into the big-bud disease of blackcurrants in return for an honorarium of £25 per annum. However, more ambitious plans were maturing, and in 1906 the building of a small laboratory was begun and the Council advertised for a director. In January of the following year Mr. F. J. Chittenden of the Essex County Council's Biological Laboratory at Chelmsford, who in 1905 had succeeded the Rev. G. Henslow as secretary of the Scientific Committee, was appointed director of the Laboratory. Then a man of thirty-three, he was to spend the next forty-four years in the Society's service in one capacity or another, and to become—to use the words of another wonderful servant of the Society, E. A. Bowles—'the most efficient and accomplished member of its staff since the days of Lindley and Wilks'.[1] (Plate 12.)

The Laboratory, later to be incorporated into a larger building, was formally opened on 19 July 1907 by Lord Avebury, perhaps better known as Sir John Lubbock. Built of brick, with a tiled roof, it consisted in the main of three chief rooms opening from the entrance hall. One room was designed as a research laboratory which, at the back, opened into a dark room for photographic purposes; on the south side was a glass-house for experimental work. Another room served as an office to which was attached a store-room. Over these rooms and the hall was a boarded loft, reached by a trap door from the ceiling of the hall, which provided further storage space. The main room or students' laboratory was immediately opposite the main entrance, 36 feet long and 21 feet broad, with table accommodation for the students.

The students' course of instruction in the principles underlying practical horticulture was commenced in September, and before long Chittenden began research on the partial sterilization of soil and on the effect of etherization on dormant plants about to be forced. When G. S. Saunders had to retire because of ill health, Chittenden, in 1908, combined the work of editing the *Journal* with his other duties.

A student applying to work at the Garden had not to be more than twenty-two years old, 'not so much below average height as to interfere with his prospects as gardener', and had to provide two character references. Once accepted, he paid an admission fee of £5. 5s., which covered all charges for the two-year course of instruction except for books, stationery, notebooks, etc. He did not receive wages. The instruction consisted of an elementary first-year course and an advanced second-year. Each course included laboratory instruction in elementary science as applied to horticulture, together with field work and garden instruction in the practical operations of horticulture. The practical work was supplemented by lectures and all students had the opportunity of studying the trials and the experimental work and of attending some of the Society's shows and lectures in London. At the end of the two years' course diplomas were granted to those students who had passed written and practical examinations in the principles and operations of horticulture, who had presented an essay on some approved horticultural or scientific subject, who had submitted a collection of at least 200 dried, named, and localized plant specimens collected outside the Wisley

[1] *Jl R. hort. Soc.*, LXXV (1950), p. 424.

Gardens, as well as a collection of insects either injurious or helpful to horticulture. The curriculum received the approval of the Board of Agriculture, of the Science and Art Department, South Kensington, and of the Surrey County Council, and the Laboratory was recognized by the Board of Education as a Technical School for Grant. Reporting on the Wisley School of Horticulture in 1908, H.M. Inspector said: 'The Royal Horticultural Society is to be congratulated on the step it has taken to encourage the educational side of the craft.'

The Wisley School of Horticulture soon became widely recognized and very popular. For instance, in 1911, forty-three students attended, and seven completed their two years' course and sat for the diploma. Chittenden was busily employed in the teaching as well as with his experimental work and was working very long hours in the Garden, as well as on the *Journal* in the evenings. It was thus necessary to give him aid in the teaching programme, and in 1911 Mr. Arthur S. Horne was appointed assistant lecturer. Furthermore, since Chittenden had to spend all the day and half the night at the Garden, it was only reasonable that he should occupy accommodation there. Thus in 1911 a house was built for the director of the Laboratory—as well as a new bothy for the journeyman gardeners.

During this time Wright, the Superintendent, and his staff were fully occupied growing material for the Society's trials and in developing the Garden; 1906–7 were typical years for trials. In the spring of 1906, 271 stocks of cannas had been received for trial from growers and raisers in Europe and America. With twenty-six other stocks they occupied two greenhouses and, with their brilliant flowers and handsome foliage, provided a splendid sight in 1907, during the months of July to October. The Floral Committee examined them three times, made various awards and concluded that 220 distinct cultivars were represented. In conjunction with the National Dahlia Society, a trial of 197 stocks of Cactus dahlias, representing 170 distinct cultivars, was judged by the Joint Committee of the Society and the National Dahlia Society. From mid-April to the end of May the trials were brilliant with the flowers of 1,390 stocks, comprising 895 distinct cultivars, of tulips—singles, doubles, Parrots, Rembrandts, Darwins. Fifty-three stocks of melons filled one span-roofed house and a frame 100 feet long; they were so well grown that the Superintendent received the compliments of the Fruit and Vegetable Committee. This committee also examined trials of 35 stocks of strawberries, 66 of french beans, 54 of kale, 66 of spring-sown onions, 128 of potatoes, 86 of outdoor tomatoes.

In 1908, to meet the possibility of criticism for partiality, all plants under trial were labelled with indicative numbers until the trial had been reported on.

In addition to supervising the trials and the many developments in the Garden, numerous requests for his services as the Society's garden inspector necessitated Wright's frequent absence from Wisley. It was too much, and in 1912 arrangements were made for the advisory inspections to be carried out by Miss Ellen Willmott's gardener, Mr. C. R. Fielder.

During 1913–15 Wisley was the scene of two special trials. The growing diversity of 'horticultural sundries', such as tools and appliances, especially those relating to the control of pests and diseases, led to a demand, from Fellows, for guidance in their choice. Thus in 1913 it was decided that awards should be made to sundries, after trial at Wisley, that the awards should be valid only for ten years and that a start should be made with an invited trial of spraying machines. It was a worthy object and the plan was pursued for some years, but gradually it was found to be impracticable, among other things, to make awards of limited duration, and in the end the practice was discontinued.

The other trial—of tulips—was much more satisfactory. During the early years of the century self-coloured tulips had become exceedingly popular—in large measure owing to the introduction of the fine race now known as Darwins—and the nomenclature was much confused. In an endeavour to remedy this confusion, in 1914–15 extensive plantings of tulips, received under about 4,000 cultivar names, were made and examined by a joint committee of British and Dutch experts who were able to revise the tulip classification, clear up questions of nomenclature and synonymy and prepare a valuable report on tulip nomenclature which was published in 1917 and constituted the standard work on this subject for many years.

In spite of all these developments in the Garden—the testing of fruits, flowers and vegetables, the sorting out of nomenclature problems, the training of students and the research work in the Laboratory—some members of Council, especially the more scientifically minded, were not quite satisfied; Wisley should be more of a scientific establishment. Consequently, in July 1913, a Research Committee was appointed 'to enquire into and report on any reasonable ways in which the Society might assist and advance the more scientific aspects of Horticulture'. Its findings were considered by the Council on 9 December, when, 'subject to a satisfactory arrangement as regards tenure of the Garden', the Council was unanimous in adopting certain recommendations contained in the memorandum prepared by two of the co-opted members, Professor Isaac Bayley Balfour of the Royal Botanic Garden, Edinburgh, and Professor Frederick Keeble of Reading University.

The main recommendations were that the Wisley staff be enlarged; that the entire establishment be placed under the charge of a Director whose staff should consist of an Assistant Director, responsible, among other things, for the education of the students, a Superintendent of the Gardens, a mycologist, a chemist, an entomologist, and a trials' officer; and that a laboratory with the requisite accommodation for educational work and research should be built.

Accordingly, in January 1914, Keeble was appointed Director of the Gardens and no doubt Chittenden was somewhat disappointed. In addition to editing the *Journal*, he was making a great success of the School of Horticulture and already several scientific papers ('Contributions from the Wisley Laboratory') had come from his pen—papers on pollination in the orchards, on the azalea gall, on the narcissus fly, on leaf spot of celery, on American gooseberry mildew, on the inoculation of leguminous crops. He was certainly well qualified for the post of Director, but too loyal and devoted an employee of the Society to complain when passed over. In any case his chance was soon to come, for in 1917, when the war was at its height, Keeble was released from his duties to become head of the Ministry of Agriculture's Food Production Department and in 1919 resigned from the Society's service to become Sherardian Professor of Botany at Oxford, and Chittenden succeeded him as Director of the Gardens. But in 1914 Chittenden was made director of the Laboratory and head of the School of Horticulture; Professor H. Maxwell Lefroy, lecturer at the Imperial College of Science, was appointed part-time entomologist, with Mr. George Fox Wilson as his practical assistant, and Mr. Harold J. Page from University College, London, and the Pasteur Institute, Paris, was appointed to the post of chemist, though he did not take up his duties for some time.

Although a start was made on the additional laboratory accommodation in 1914, the war naturally interfered with its completion and with the appointment of further staff. Even so, the building was finished in 1916 and a fine and beautiful building it was. An extension to the laboratory of 1907, it was constructed to the designs of Messrs. Pine-Coffin, Imrie & Angell of London by the Norwich firm of Messrs. Young & Son, and is of narrow purple-pink brick and oak half-timbering, roofed with tiles collected from old country houses. By the time of its completion, national war requirements had claimed the services of all the members of the staff, either wholly or in part, and much of the contemplated work was brought to a standstill. Not until 1918 could any advance be made, and then Dr. F. V. Darbishire commenced work on certain chemical analyses, largely in connection with wartime foods. By this time the services of Dr. Horne, who had assisted Chittenden, and Lefroy, were no longer available, but in 1919 George Fox Wilson became entomologist, Page took up his duties as chief chemist, to be succeeded by Darbishire the following year, when W. J. Dowson was appointed mycologist. And in 1921 N. K. Gould was made assistant botanist and was concerned, in the main, with teaching.

These were the members of the scientific staff for the next few years.

It was, however, a research student at Wisley who made the most important scientific contribution from the Wisley Laboratory during this period. For years daffodil growers had been losing their stocks through eelworm attack; one well-known hybridizer, Mr. Alec Wilson, had had his stocks valued for income-tax purposes at £12,000, and in two years' time had less than £200 worth left. By 1916 the situation had become so critical that the Society's Narcissus and Tulip Committee requested the Council to have investigated the life history of the daffodil eelworm with the object of discovering the best means of killing the pest without harming the infested bulb. Council agreed to the request and invited James Kirkham Ramsbottom to undertake the investigation.

Coming to Wisley in 1911, after a period at the Chelsea Physic Garden, Ramsbottom had gained first place in the Society's diploma examination, won the Society's Gold Medal and scholarship and become research student at Wisley in 1913. After investigating the iris leaf-blotch disease he had accepted an invitation to become assistant editor of the *Gardener's Magazine* and then returned to Wisley to work on the daffodil eelworm problem in 1916. In this same year he gained the National Diploma in Horticulture. By the following year Ramsbottom had discovered that hot-water treatment of the bulbs of sufficient duration could control eelworm in infested narcissus bulbs. And the method he used was an elaboration of one which had been used since 1880 in Scotland, on Lord Lamington's estate, for the treatment of eucharis or tarsonemid mite in *Eucharis grandiflora*. Ramsbottom's work opened up a new era in the commercial production of daffodils, and gained him the award of the Barr Memorial Cup in 1924. By this time he was assistant managing editor of the *Gardener's Chronicle*, and held an advisory post with George Monro of Covent Garden. But he had never enjoyed good health and in 1925 died in the United States, while on a lecturing tour, at the age of thirty-three.

James's brother, Dr. John Ramsbottom, was to have a distinguished scientific career, gaining a world-wide reputation as a mycologist and an expert on the larger and edible fungi, and for over twenty years acting as Keeper of Botany of the British Museum (Natural History). For his services to the R.H.S. he was made an Honorary Fellow and awarded the Gold Veitch Memorial Medal in 1944, and the V.M.H. in 1949.

CHAPTER SEVENTEEN

MORE HORTICULTURAL EDUCATION

Since 1836 the society had been concerning itself, sometimes vigorously, sometimes rather lethargically, with examinations in horticulture. In the main the examinations had been arranged for those 'labourers', or students, employed by the Society in its Garden. However, in 1865, in association with the Royal Society of Arts, the Society had begun to organize examinations, not only for its own student gardeners but also for young men in other gardens and nurseries throughout the country; a written test was conducted by the Society of Arts or some other public examining body, and a practical test by the Society, at the Chiswick Garden.

Around 1890 several county councils in various parts of the country were arranging short courses of lectures on gardening and horticulture for young gardeners. Likewise many technical institutes, schools, gardeners' mutual improvement societies, and other bodies were endeavouring to promote instruction in practical horticulture by means of lectures and demonstrations. Many of these bodies had been in touch with the Society with a view to its undertaking to conduct examinations on their behalf. The Society was sympathetic to the idea, and agreed to hold examinations simultaneously in as many parts of the country as circumstances demanded. The examinations would be based on the outline syllabus of *Elementary Principles and Horticultural Operation and Practice*, and two sets of questions would be set; one of an elementary standard called the Lower Grade, and one of a more advanced standard —the Higher Grade. In entering for the examination, candidates would state the grade for which they intended to sit. Those passing the examination would be awarded a certificate and, to the candidate in each grade obtaining the highest number of marks, the Society would award a silver-gilt medal. Before the first examination could be held the Worshipful Company of Gardeners had agreed to offer a scholarship to the value of twenty-six pounds a year, tenable for two years, to the most successful candidate, and Sir Trevor Lawrence a second scholarship to the same value. Scholarship holders would study at Chiswick for at least one year, and either at Chiswick or some other approved establishment for the rest of the time.

On 4 May 1893, 204 candidates presented themselves at various centres in the British Isles wherever a magistrate, a clergyman, a schoolmaster, or some responsible person accustomed to examinations, had consented to superintend on the Society's behalf and in accordance with the rules laid down for the conduct of the examination. These centres were as wide apart as West Clare and Kent, Aberdeen and Cornwall. No limit was imposed on the age, position, or previous training of the candidates and the examination was open to both men and women. Seventy-six entered for the Higher Grade; six were placed in the first class (200–300 marks); twenty in the second class (150–200 marks); thirty-six in the third class (100–150 marks); the fourteen who failed to obtain 100 marks were not classed. The 128 remaining candidates entered for the Lower Grade; six reached first class standard, sixteen the second class and thirty-eight the third; sixty-eight were not classed. Maxwell T. Masters and James Douglas were the examiners.

Year by year candidates continued to exhibit a better knowledge of practical horticulture. Even so, the *practical* value of the examination was soon in doubt. Even the examiners were agreed that, as far as the examination was a test of practical experience in the garden, it was so only to a very limited degree; the main value of the examination lay in the *mental training* it gave to those who worked for it.

In later years the two grades were abolished and the examination became known as the General Examination, an examination which, though not necessarily being a great test of practical knowledge, has been the first step in the technical educational ladder for many thousands of horticulturists. Today there are almost sixty centres in Great Britain and Eire where the examination can be taken.

When the Society's General Examination in Horticulture was in its twelfth year, Council decided to supplement it, in 1904, with another—an examination in Cottage and Allotment Gardening for Teachers. The examination was intended for, and was confined to, elementary-school teachers, and was undertaken in response to the increasing demand in country districts that the schoolmaster should be competent to teach the elements of cottage-gardening, and to fill the need for such a test. The general conduct of the examination was on similar lines to that of the General Examination. A certificate was awarded to each successful candidate and a silver-gilt Flora Medal to the best one. Alexander Dean and James Hudson, both eventually holders of the V.M.H., were the examiners, and after the first examination in 1904 had to report that, in general, the practical knowledge of candidates was somewhat crude; that most candidates showed that such knowledge as they had acquired had been gathered from books rather than from actual practice. Even so, the results were rather better than the examiners had anticipated.

At the second examination in 1905 it was obvious that candidates had heeded the criticism of the examiners. The standard was much higher and showed that the better candidates had indeed furnished themselves with practical experience by working in allotments and in gardens. Even so, there were many howlers: for example, 'early peas should be raised from roots saved over from the previous year'; 'raspberries should be propagated from cuttings'. Still, this second examination proved that it was quite possible for children in elementary schools to be well instructed in practical gardening. The results were also significant in showing the extent to which certain schools, specializing in gardening, figured high in the merit list—schools such as Swanley College, Stafford County Technical School, and the Essex and Middlesex Schools of Horticulture; between them these four schools had 9 out of 46 places in the first class, 15 out of 58 in the second, and 17 out of 52 in the third, thus securing 41 passes out of the 156.

This teachers' examination was, of course, the forerunner of the present-day examination for the Teacher's Diploma in School Gardening.

In January 1906 the Society ventured on yet another examination, this time at the suggestion of certain public authorities charged with the administration of the public parks and gardens of the country, who desired to obtain some independent and competent test of the relative knowledge possessed by the men they employed. The examination was thus specially intended for gardeners employed in public parks and gardens belonging to county councils, city corporations, and similar bodies. Partly written, and partly oral, the examination occupied three hours and twenty minutes and was held in the Society's hall at Vincent Square, Westminster. In 1906, eighty-nine candidates were examined by a distinguished company of horticulturists—William Crump, C. R. Fielder, George Nicholson, Owen Thomas, Edward White, and W. Wilks—who reported that, generally speaking, the candidates revealed 'a distinctly remarkable absence of observation and thought, combined with by no means too high a degree of ordinary education. Most of the candidates appeared to possess a rough and elementary knowledge of the subjects inquired of, but were unable to give expression to their ideas in coherent and intelligent language . . . many of them showed evidence of a quite unnecessary degree of nervousness.' Forty-three candidates passed the examination—and one was disqualified for copying.

Commenting on the examination, the leader writer in the *Gardener's Chronicle* told of an experience of his own. He was examining a practical gardener of middle age and much experience. The examination was partly written, partly oral; the oral section was conducted at a table covered with plants, seedlings, fruits, vegetables, grafts, etc., which formed the subjects on which the candidate was to be questioned and which he must have been in the habit of handling in his daily work for years. Even so, his answers were most unsatisfactory. Finally, wearied by his negative attempts to elicit information, the examiner asked the difference, from a cultural point of view, between a cauliflower and a broccoli. Still no answer was forthcoming. On the examiners suggesting that one might be hardier than the other, the examinee then replied: 'Yes, didn't you know that?' Much experienced, and believed to be a good all-round practical gardener, the candidate was utterly unable to express his ideas in an examination room.

Thus it has always been.

Although the various examinations of the Society were a means of training gardeners to express themselves and of raising their intellectual and social condition, they were, nevertheless, the subject of criticism in the horticultural Press. On 17 February 1906 the *Gardener's Chronicle* published, from William Watson, the Curator of Kew, the following letter:

It is doubtful whether such examinations as those held by the Royal Horticultural Society are of much value as a means of training in professional horticulture, or even as a test of knowledge of the principles and practice of the art. Would any practical gardener attach any importance to the success or failure of a young man at an examination in which he is asked to explain or describe the structure and growth of cells, the process of impregnation of the ovule and similar academic questions? And even the more practical questions, such as the description and use of implements, manures and their application, are worthless as tests of anything except perhaps memory. This sort of thing has about the same bearing on gardening as questions on the varieties and special uses of saucepans, the origin and chemical constituents of salt, or the effects of heat on vegetable and animal tissue have on cooking. Of course the college students who know little or nothing of gardening do well at the Royal Horticultural Society's examinations, whilst intelligent, experienced young men of proved ability in the garden rarely get into the first class. Take, for example, the result of the 1905 examination. Of the 160 candidates 76 were from horticultural schools, and the whole of the 20 that obtained firsts were school-students. chiefly from Swanley and Studley, which are for girl students only. This class-room gardening may be of some use, but it is no proof of real gardening ability, or even aptitude. It is impossible to devise a scheme of examination to be conducted in a class-room that would be a satisfactory test, and I rather fancy the examiners know that as well as I do. A gardener requires just that kind of knowledge of his art, and skill in its practice, as will enable him to obtain the best results as a cultivator. He may not be able to give satisfactory answers to any of the 24 questions asked and yet be a champion gardener. I am only concerned to protect the gardener from the imputation of ignorance or want of skill in his profession because he fails in class-room questions, and that things are tending in that direction is to be seen in the action of the London County Council in making the Royal Horticultural Society examinations a test for promotion among its gardeners. Would any responsible gardener or nurseryman select the members of his staff on such lines? I have had many years experience in sorting men for all kinds of positions in horticulture, and I know the danger of being too much influenced by tongue or pen work. In horticulture we want men who are able to *do* things, and if we are going to prefer the training of the schoolmaster and lecturer to that of the gardener we shall get into the same mess as those military leaders found themselves in when well-schooled officers were pitted against field-made men in the Boer war. If we are to have tests in horticultural training they should be real and not sham. The horticultural colleges may be doing useful work, though one wonders where it reveals itself; so far as I can see it is not in any practical field; still, the training they give may be at least as useful as other things taught in schools; but this output should not be confused with the genuine article, much less considered superior, and that is the danger which I see.

There were many who agreed with the general trend of Mr. Watson's remarks—there are many who would agree even today—and one, at any rate, who had constructive suggestions to make. Mr. A. E. T. Rogers, gardener at Sudeley Castle, Gloucester, replied to Mr. Watson on 3 March:

Although I agree with Mr. Watson in the main points of his note regarding examinations in horticulture, yet I do not think it would be wise to disparage horticultural examinations altogether. 'Theory without practice' may be useless in any profession, yet 'theory' combined with 'practice', in gardening, as in other professions, no doubt, is as great a boon as any man can possibly have. I am a 'third-class' man myself, and have been a gardener all my life, but the study necessary to gain the third-class certificate more than compensated me for my trouble, by helping me to understand things more clearly, and making me think more about my work than I otherwise should have done. The R.H.S. examinations are too severe for an ordinary young gardener, who starts his career in the bothy, and who has only had a day-school education. Botany may not be absolutely necessary for a gardener, but a knowledge of elementary botany helps him to understand the particular needs of a plant, and makes plain the reason why they require particular treatment. I would like to suggest that the British Gardeners' Association should institute examinations in horticulture, and *only allow young gardeners to enter.* There should not be one severe examination only, but two or three extending over several years. As a boy enters a garden as a garden boy, let him prepare himself for the first examination to take place when he is about 17 years old, the second examination when he is 20, and the last when he is about 23 years old. At that age he ought to be able to take his first foreman's place, and have three or more years as foreman before becoming 'head'. The first examination need not be severe, but one that should encourage study in elementary botany and the first principles of horticulture, and the others should be gradually more severe. I think by this means the standard of the British gardener might be raised considerably above the present level, and in years to come the gardener would be in a position to hold his own. All successful candidates should be entered on a special register of the British Gardeners' Association, or the B.G.A. might work in conjunction with the R.H.S. in such a matter.

'. . . Not . . . one severe examination only, but two or three extending over several years' was exactly what the Society in a few years' time proposed to sponsor.

In the meantime the feeling was spreading that those engaged in horticulture and gardening required an examination involving not only written tests but practical tests also—tests involving a higher standard of knowledge and technical skill than was required for the purely written General Examination. The matter was discussed at the sixth annual general meeting of the Horticultural Education Association held at Leeds University on 15 September 1911, when Mr. W. B. Little read a paper entitled 'Suggestions for a National Diploma in Horticulture'. This idea gained the support of the Association and Little's paper was published by the Association as a special pamphlet. The chairman of the Association was Mr. F. J. Chittenden, the director of the School of Horticulture, and of the Laboratory, at Wisley.

Two months later, on 21 November, a brief minute of the Society's Council states that 'The Society considered communications from the International Educational Conference Committee [one of the many Committees of the International Exhibition of 1912] and from the Horticultural [Education] Association requesting the Council to appoint a Committee to consider a report on the desirability of establishing for garden workers a National Diploma in Horticulture'. The R.H.S. Council rightly believed that the request was an important one and accordingly, on 5 December, appointed a committee of thirteen members—the Diploma Committee—to consider the matter of a national diploma and to report on its desirability and practicability. The committee was presided over by the Rt. Hon. A. H. Dyke Acland, and amongst well-known botanists and horticulturists serving on it were F. J. Chittenden, E. A. Bowles, and Sir Harry Veitch. The committee met several times, consulted many people whose opinions they considered would be of value, and soon agreed that a national diploma was desirable and, in the report to the Council, urged the Council to accept the proposal and to act as quickly as possible. This the Council did; at its April meeting in 1912 it directed that a copy of the committee's report be sent to the President of the Board (now Ministry) of Agriculture for his opinion and suggested that the Board take up the matter either with or without the co-operation of the Society.

The Board did not hesitate to co-operate, and during 1912 meetings between the Board and the Society were held, so that by the end of the year a decision had been reached. The Board would be willing to give assistance and co-operation in framing a scheme for the issue of a national diploma which might state that it was a National Diploma awarded by the Society under a scheme approved by the Board; the Board would not accept any financial responsibility in connection with the award and it was understood that the Society would be willing to repay the expenses of the examinations for the diploma. The original thirteen-man Diploma Committee was disbanded, and another one—a joint committee of the Society and the Board—was set up for the task of framing a scheme for issuing the new diploma. The Rt. Hon. A. H. Dyke Acland also acted as chairman of this smaller committee, which had as its members Professor Keeble, F. J. Chittenden, W. P. Wright, and J. Hudson, representing the Society, and Professor J. B. Farmer and A. G. L. Rogers representing the Board.

The joint committee presented its report to the Council in June 1913; the report was accepted and sent to the Board of Agriculture for approval, and by August the National Diploma in Horticulture was in being. It was intended for professional horticulturists—florists, fruit growers, gardeners, horticultural inspectors and instructors, landscape gardeners, market gardeners, public park gardeners, nurserymen, seedsmen. Candidates of either sex would be eligible to take the examination for the diploma provided they had attained the required age and could produce evidence of a satisfactory educational background such as having gained the certificate of the College of Preceptors, the Oxford and Cambridge Local Examinations Boards, matriculation at any British university or any similar certificate which from time to time might be approved by the Council. Candidates unable to produce such a certificate would be required to pass a qualifying test established by the Society; in this, candidates would show their ability to write an essay on some subject of general knowledge, as a test of their ability to spell and to express themselves clearly, an acquaintance with arithmetic up to and including decimals and elementary mensuration, and a knowledge of elementary geography.

There would be two examinations for the diploma, a preliminary and a final. Having registered, having reached the age of twenty-one, having had at least four years of horticultural experience in a public or private garden or nursery or in an approved horticultural institution, and having received a satisfactory report on his conduct and work from his employer, a candidate would be eligible for the preliminary examination. This would be of two days' duration, one day of written and the other of practical work, and would be based on the general principles of horticulture, involving an elementary knowledge of biology, chemistry and physics, as far as these are essential to an understanding of horticultural practice; candidates would be required to prove their ability to perform the operations of gardening with proper skill. It would be absolutely necessary for candidates to have passed the preliminary examination, and subsequently to have been engaged in horticultural practice for at least two years, before being eligible to take the final.

The syllabus for the final examination would be divided into the following sections, each dealing with a particular branch of horticulture, and each candidate would be able to enter for the section in which he felt himself most proficient: General Horticulture, Fruit Growing for Market, Hardy Fruit Growing for Market, Market Gardening in the Open, Horticultural Inspection, Horticultural Instruction.

It was emphasized in 1913, and it has always been emphasized since, that in both examinations the principal aim would be to test the candidates' practical acquaintance with plants and general garden work and their practical knowledge of horticulture. The practical tests would be conducted in a suitable garden or nursery and would be supplemented by *viva voce* questions and written papers. Candidates would be required to satisfy the examiners in all three parts of the examinations—practical, written and oral—and no amount of excellence in the written part of the examination would qualify for a pass in either examination if they were to fail in the practical.

The joint committee for framing the scheme for the N.D.H. had done a most splendid job of work, as the next fifty years were to show. During this half-century few major changes in the framework of the examinations have been found necessary. Men and women still compete on equal terms; the age of entry has been lowered to seventeen, though four years in practical work are still essential before a candidate can enter for the diploma examinations; an educational standard is still required. As proof that he had attained the latter, from 1952 until 1966 a candidate was required to pass an examination of three papers—English, Arithmetic and General Science—but exemption from this examination was granted to a candidate who produced evidence of his general education to an approved equivalent standard. As this educational examination was called the preliminary, it became necessary, in 1952, to introduce the name intermediate for the examination previously known as the preliminary. The final examination still has six sections, although these have changed somewhat since 1915 and now comprise General Horticulture, General Commercial Horticulture, Fruit Crop Husbandry, Vegetable Crop Husbandry, Glass-house Crop Husbandry, and Horticulture in Public Parks.

The first preliminary examination was held in 1914 and sixty-three candidates were examined. The practical tests were held in five centres—Wisley, Edinburgh, Cardiff, Manchester, Peterborough—and each candidate was required to perform a full day's work in the garden in the presence of the examiners. Forty-three candidates passed the examination and the examiners arranged the forty-three names in order of merit, six in Division A, thirty-seven in Division B. Mr. A. Simmonds headed the list. He had been at Wisley from 1907 to 1911, first as a student and then as a demonstrator, and in 1922 was to be appointed Assistant Director at Wisley. He was transferred, three years later, to Vincent Square, where he became Assistant Secretary. And there he was to remain for the next thirty-seven years, acting as Assistant Secretary, Deputy Secretary in 1946, and finally as Secretary from 1956 until he retired in 1962.

During June of 1915 the first final examination for the N.D.H. was held. The practical work occupied two full days and was tested in the Society's Garden at Wisley, in order that the conditions under which the work was done should, as nearly as possible, be the same for everyone. Likewise in 1915 Wisley was the venue for the practical work of the preliminary examination. It might have been expected that the forty-three successful preliminary candidates—provided they had completed six years of practical work—would have taken this final examination. And under normal circumstances they possibly would. But in August 1914 Britain had entered the First World War and many of the younger men had temporarily abandoned horticulture for military service. As it was, twenty-two of the original forty-three entered for the final and, of these, seventeen became the first to hold the N.D.H. qualification and could be congratulated on having passed through a really stiff ordeal and on having proved themselves worthy to receive the high mark of distinction which the National Diploma in Horticulture confers.

Over the years nearly 5,000 men and women have entered for the preliminary, or intermediate, and some 2,000 for the final. Less than 800 have eventually gained the diploma. Of those who have journeyed to Wisley to be examined on the important central core of the examination—the practical work in the garden—are there any who would not assent to the feelings and experiences of William C. Crisp, one of the original seventeen holders of the N.D.H., as recounted by him in the *Gardener's Chronicle*[1]—even though in recent years candidates may not have had the freedom of the Garden between one examination day and the other which apparently obtained at that time?

. . . As is usual at examinations, candidates are more or less nervous, yet when we met at Wisley we were apparently a very happy party, although each

[1] Vol. 53 (1915), p. 123.

candidate no doubt had his own fears as to what would be the result of the examination in his own case. At the very commencement the examiners tried to set the candidates at their ease, and by luncheon on the first day all nervousness seemed to have been dispelled, and all had settled down to work, resolved to give a good account of themselves, at the same time determined to derive as much pleasure and knowledge as possible from the various tests, the afternoon—being taken up by very interesting tests of knowledge—passing quickly enough. The tests finished for the day, our ride to Ripley was interesting, as we were enabled to exchange experiences of the day. After tea, the majority being determined to make the most of the spare evening hours, we again returned to the R.H.S. Gardens, for a visit of inspection and study. The alpine gardens being visited, and many plants of interest criticised and brought to the notice of all, rain interfering with further studies in the open, we adjourned to the glass department, where, dividing into parties, we made acquaintance with many interesting subjects, darkness putting an end to our study. We reluctantly left the gardens, the walk to Ripley giving us opportunity for helpful discussions of various items of interest to horticulturists. Meeting at 9.50 a.m. on the 2nd, each candidate again seemed determined to do his best. Having been given our papers of various operations to be performed, we soon settled down to the work allotted to us, each individual having little time to spare if he was to perform the tests in a satisfactory manner. The luncheon interval gave us a brief space for rest and refreshment, enabling us to feel ready for the afternoon's work, which again proved very interesting, the time passing very quickly, and at 5.15 p.m. we were en route for Byfleet, where we entrained for our various destinations. Having to wait a few minutes at Byfleet, each candidate appeared to regret not having done justice to himself in one or more of the tests, but all were agreed that the visit would be long remembered, as having given us much pleasure and helpful association, and, whatever the result as to individual success or failure, we were all confident that by the preparatory study and the tests of knowledge we should be better fitted to meet the requirements of our various positions in horticulture. May I be allowed to express the thanks of all to the examiners for their kindly interest shown to us, the opinions given expression to by the candidates being that the examiners had acted with justice and kindness to all concerned, each candidate being sure that everything possible had been done to enable him to perform the work of the examinations so as to give satisfaction to himself and to the examiners.

At its inception the horticultural Press maintained that the diploma would become a charter for those who learnt their gardening by working as apprentices under head gardeners and that the examination would provide a valuable qualification for those employed in private gardens. But this was not to be realized. Over the years, chiefly owing to the effects of two world wars, private gardening has changed enormously and today it is unusual to find a private gardener with an N.D.H. qualification. Such people are now mostly holding responsible jobs in the horticultural advisory services of the country—both local and government, on the staffs of botanic gardens, in public parks, in seed firms, nursery firms, fertilizer and insecticide companies, as lecturers in horticultural institutes, colleges, and universities, as writers for the horticultural press, and as broadcasters on radio and television. They are all, by general consent, possessed of sound horticultural knowledge combined with practical experience and skill, and the fact that they are holding key posts everywhere is a measure of the enormous influence the Society has had on horticultural education during the twentieth century.

Though it is outside the span of years under discussion, it is appropriate, at this point, to comment on the National Certificate in Elementary Horticultural Practice. The 1930s saw a considerable increase in the number of institutions, especially farm institutes, offering an elementary vocational course in horticulture. In some instances the course was a general one; in others more specialized along a certain branch of horticulture. In any case it was desirable that those having taken such courses should possess a certificate to this effect. A consideration of the syllabuses of various institutions led to the conclusion that a certificate from an institution, stating that a student had qualified in horticulture, sometimes meant a good deal and sometimes practically nothing; a prospective employer was not to know the difference and could very easily be misled. The obvious requirement was a certificate awarded after passing an examination common to the whole country and organized by a body having no special connection with any one institution. The N.D.H. examination was too severe. The Society's General Examination was held at a time of year inconvenient for students attending farm-institute courses, and in any case, provided no real test of skill in practical work. Quite obviously a new examination and a new certificate were necessary for candidates attending such institutions.

The Horticultural Education Association laid these considerations before the Council of the Society and requested its assistance in overcoming the difficulty. As always in matters educational, this assistance was readily given and, in consultation with members of the H.E.A. concerned with the organization of institutional courses, a scheme was prepared for the new National Certificate in Elementary Horticultural Practice, which was established in 1937.

Interlude
to Parts Five and Six

SHORTLY AFTER THE WAR OF 1860 BETWEEN THE ALLIED POWER of Britain and France and the Chinese the French missionaries were in the Chinese field. Armand David arrived just after the end of the war, Jean Marie Delavay and Paul Guillaume Farges about 1867, and Jean André Soulié in 1886. All were naturalists as well as missionaries. All were fine plant collectors, especially Delavay. All discovered many new plants of great horticultural merit. And all, whenever possible, sent home seeds. Though the seeds germinated, the seedlings were invariably treated as hot-house subjects and grown in far too much heat, whereas, in point of fact, the vast majority should have been treated as hardy plants. The number to survive such treatment was comparatively small. Even so, the herbarium specimens of these collectors offered abundant evidence of the vast floral richness of the provinces of western China. So did the collections of Dr. Augustine Henry, who was later to collaborate with H. J. Elwes, from 1906 until 1913, in the seven-volume work *The Trees of Great Britain and Ireland*. Henry entered the Chinese Maritime Customs in 1881, was sent to Ichang, in Hupeh, the following year as Assistant Medical Officer, stayed there until 1889, and sent his first collection to Kew in 1886. After some leave in England, where he saw at Kew the excitement his specimens had caused, he returned to China in 1891 as an official of the Customs Department—and there he stayed until 1900. His introductions were few; but he had discovered many beautiful species new to science which other collectors were induced to seek and bring into cultivation.

Not the first (A. F. Pratt had preceded him in 1887), but certainly the most important and successful of these was E. H. Wilson, who was sent to China by the firm of Veitch in 1899 with the main object of introducing the Dove Tree, *Davidia involucrata*. He was successful in this, as well as in the introduction of *Abies fargesii, Magnolia delavayi, Rhododendron fargesii* and *R. discolor, Stranvaesia davidiana, Viburnum rhytidophyllum, Clematis armandii, Acer griseum* and *A. davidii, Senecio clivorum*, and others, all fine garden plants. In 1903 he departed once again for China, again for Veitch, this time with the express purpose of introducing *Meconopsis integrifolia.* Not only was *M. integrifolia* introduced, but a very rich harvest of *Meconopsis punicea, Thalictrum dipterocarpum, Primula cockburniana, P. veitchii* (now *P. polyneura*), *P. vittata, Rheum alexandrae, Populus lasiocarpa, Rosa moyesii, R. willmottiae, Viburnum davidii, Rhododendron souliei, R. sargentianum, R. orbiculare, R. intricatum, R. lutescens,* and *R. calophytum,* and, most important of all, *Lilium regale.* In the autumn of 1904 Wilson sent about 300 bulbs of this grand trumpet lily to Messrs. Veitch, who flowered them in 1905 and distributed them under the name of *L. myriophyllum,* a species which Delavay had previously discovered and which had been so named by the French botanist Franchet. Not until 1912 was Wilson's find recognized as a new species and authoritatively named *L. regale.* Its ease of culture, especially the ease with which it can be raised from seeds, led to the great revival in the growing of lilies both in Britain and America.

Wilson made two more expeditions to China, in 1907 and in 1910, and two to Japan, in 1914 and in 1918, all on behalf of the Arnold Arboretum in the United States, and all were splendidly successful. It was on his last trip that Wilson was taken to the city of Kurume on the island of Kyushu and for the first time saw the Kurume azaleas there. He wrote:

I went prepared to see a display of blossoms, but the entrancing beauty of myriad delicately coloured flowers clothing a multitude of shapely grown plants surpassed my most sanguine expectations. Most of the plants were trained into low standards, each about 20" high with flattened or convex crowns some 24" through and were monuments to the patience and skill of the Japanese gardener.

Most of the types Wilson introduced were 'delicately coloured'. Others which have been introduced since are not so delicate. Fortunately the patience and skill of the British gardener has not as yet been sufficiently monumental as to have trained the plants into standards.

The impact of Wilson's introductions was naturally considerable; that of the Forrest introductions was even more so. Between 1904 and 1932 George Forrest (Plate 14) undertook seven expeditions to western China. The first was financed almost entirely by A. K. Bulley of Ness, in Cheshire whose garden is now the Botanic Garden of the University of Liverpool. The others were financed by various syndicates, usually headed by J. C. Williams of Caerhays Castle, Cornwall, and comprising great gardeners all active in the affairs of the Horticultural Society; and usually the Royal Horticultural Society subscribed to them. By these expeditions Forrest enriched British and many overseas gardens with many hundreds of new plants of all kinds, trees, shrubs, herbaceous and alpine. It is true, as has been often said, that, as many of Forrest's subscribers were especially interested in rhododendrons, and as Forrest was paid a bonus for every new rhododendron species he found, he tended to concentrate on this genus, possibly to the neglect of others. At the same time it is also true to say that he himself was fascinated by these plants, and that by the encouragement which he received from his sponsors and from botanists at home, especially from botanists at the Royal Botanic Garden, Edinburgh, notably Bayley Balfour, Wright Smith, and H. F. Tagg, his rhododendron collections, as well as those of Kingdon Ward, Farrer, Wilson, Cooper, Rock, and others, were to enable much of the taxonomy of this great genus to be unravelled.

Of rhododendrons Forrest made nearly 5,500 gatherings containing over 300 new species, including *R. griersonianum*, which was to prove to be so valuable a plant for hybridization that, at the time of the publication of the Society's *Rhododendron Handbook*, in 1964, it had entered into the parentage of over 150 named cultivars. Of primulas, by which Forrest was also fascinated, he collected over 150 species, about a third of them new, including *Primula malacoides*, beyond all debate Forrest's most important introduction. It flowered for the first time in Britain in 1908, and most probably the entire European garden stock today is derived from Forrest's first sending of seeds. The first plants were slender and small-flowered. Within a few years phenomenal changes were achieved by the plant breeders, professional and amateur, in several directions; increase in size of corolla and in habit and vigour, fimbriation of the petals and sometimes of the calyx, fragrance, and intensity and range of flower colour. And in all these changes there is no sign or record of hybridization having played a part. Messrs. Sutton of Reading and Messrs. Carter of Raynes Park, Surrey, are two firms responsible for the development of Forrest's 'Fairy Primrose'. Forrest always maintained that his finest introduction was *Gentiana sino-ornata*, which he found in 1904, but did not introduce until 1910. Certainly its discovery awakened in him a keen interest in this genus, of which he collected several hundreds of specimens containing many new species. And certainly its arrival in cultivation stimulated renewed interest in gentian growing.

In the same way, his introduction of *Camellia saluenensis*, its hybridization at the hands of J. C. Williams at Caerhays, the publicity given to the Williams hybrids by Lord Aberconway and the scientific description of them by Sir William Wright Smith at the Royal Botanic Garden, Edinburgh, under the name of *Camellia* x *williamsii* ('one of the best shrubs ever introduced to our gardens', Lord Aberconway described it) gave a tremendous impetus to camellia growing both in Britain and in America. And again, in Cornish gardens particularly, the arrival of *Magnolia mollicomata* from Forrest caused great excitement, especially when it was realized that it could be flowered in half the time it takes

M. campbellii to flower. Since that time it has also been realized that, in some northern gardens where *M. campbellii* is useless out of doors, *M. mollicomata* can be grown very satisfactorily.

The several species of *Nomocharis* which Forrest introduced widened the field of those interested in lilies and gave a great challenge to lily growers. Though the challenge was accepted, few have had success with these beautiful plants. For a time Mr. Andrew Harley, who was awarded the Reginald Cory Memorial Cup in 1936 for his hybrid *Gentiana* 'Devonhall' and who was awarded the Victoria Medal of Honour shortly before he died in 1950, grew them well in his garden at Devonhall in Perthshire. In more recent years Major and Mrs. Knox Finlay have grown them magnificently at Keillour Castle, near Perth, and have exhibited them at the Society's Shows at Vincent Square, their beautiful and remarkable exhibit of species and hybrids being awarded the Society's Holford Medal for 1956—the medal awarded to the year's most outstanding exhibit from an amateur.

A. K. Bulley, who had first sponsored Forrest, was the first to sponsor Captain Frank Kingdon Ward (Plate 14), in 1911. At this time Bulley was the owner of the nursery firm of Bees Ltd. of Liverpool and was chiefly interested in alpine and herbaceous plants. From this time forth, until his death in 1958, Kingdon Ward was to spend his life travelling and collecting in the Sino-Himalayan regions, and, much as with Forrest, rhododendrons, primulas, lilies, meconopsis, and gentians were the plants in which he was most interested. *Rhododendron wardii*, with its pale lemon-yellow saucer-shaped flowers and orange-flushed buds, the parent of many distinguished hybrids; *Rhododendron macabeanum*, also yellow of flower and the finest of all the large-leaved rhododendrons for most gardens; the Blue Himalayan Poppy, *Meconopsis betonicifolia*; the yellow-flowered *Primula florindae*, so prone to produce interesting orange- or bronze-flowered hybrids; the orange-flowered *Primula bulleyana* and *P. chungensis*; the white, pink-flushed-flowered *Lilium mackliniae*, bridging the gap between lily and nomocharis, all these—and hundreds more, are his introductions.

After sponsoring Forrest and Ward in 1913, A. K. Bulley engaged R. E. Cooper as his personal collector and for three years Cooper travelled in Sikkim and Bhutan. He, too, introduced new rhododendrons and primulas, but unquestionably his most important introduction was to be the pale or deep-rose-flowered *Viburnum grandiflorum*. At Bodnant, this splendid deciduous shrub was to be crossed with *Viburnum fragrans* (now to be called *V. farreri*), which Farrer had introduced in 1914, and the resulting hybrid, *V.* x *bodnantense*, or at any rate, one seedling of it, 'Dawn', was to gain for Lord Aberconway the award of the Reginald Cory Memorial Cup from the Society in 1947.

Reginald Farrer, and William Purdom who had travelled for Veitch and the Arnold Arboretum, collected in Kansu and North China in 1914 and 1915 and, as a result, not only did *Viburnum farreri (fragrans)* come into our gardens, first through Purdom in 1909, and then again through Farrer in 1914, but *Buddleia alternifolia, Gentiana farreri* and *G. hexaphylla, Geranium farreri,* and the Hairbell Poppy, *Meconopsis quintuplinervia.* In 1919, this time with E. H. M. Cox as his companion, Farrer visited Upper Burma and in this way introduced several rhododendrons, the lovely *Nomocharis pardanthina* var. *farreri,* and *Juniperus recurva* var. *coxii.*

During these years Joseph Rock was holding the dual post of Professor of Botany and Professor of Chinese in the College of Hawaii. In 1920 he began to travel, first to Burma and Siam, and then to western China, and continued to journey in south-eastern Asia for the next thirty years, although he did little serious plant collecting after 1934. He covered much of the ground previously collected by Forrest, and reintroduced many of Forrest's plants, as well as much else that was new.

This great wealth of new material arrived in Britain during the years when formal gardening was giving place to a more natural form of planting, much of it in the form of woodlands, and when gardeners were showing a much greater interest in the character of individual plants. The plants from the Sino-Himalaya were excellent for this purpose— and helped to change completely the character of many gardens, especially those with acid soils.

The Royal Botanic Garden, Edinburgh, is a case in point. Sir Isaac Bayley Balfour and later Sir William Wright Smith and members of their staffs endeavoured to grow as much of this material as possible. Hundreds of rhododendrons were planted, and great drifts of primulas, meconopsis, and lilies were grown in their shelter. Not only were these plants *grown* at Edinburgh, but at Edinburgh their taxonomy was in large measure established. Thus it was with rhododendron, primula, lily, gentian, and meconopsis. The enthusiasm of the staff even affected some of the students in botany at Edinburgh. George Taylor, for instance (now Sir George, the Director of Kew, and a splendid servant of the Society), whilst a student at Edinburgh became interested in meconopsis to the extent that he was to monograph the genus. Later he was to become interested in many other Sino-Himalayan genera and to accompany Mr. Frank Ludlow and Major George Sherriff on an expedition to south-east Tibet and Bhutan. It was much the same at Kew, under the régimes of Sir David Prain and, later, of Sir Arthur Hill, and of their Curators of the Gardens, William Watson, and William Jackson Bean whose *Trees and Shrubs Hardy in the British Isles,* gradually incorporating the new material, was to go through several editions and exercise a powerful influence on twentieth-century practice.

299

The influence of the Sino-Himalayan material on certain private gardeners and gardens was even more remarkable—the gardens of Lord Aberconway, Lieut.-Col. Stephenson Clarke, Sir John Ramsden, Mr. Lionel de Rothschild, Mr. J. B. Stevenson, Mr. Armytage-Moore, Mr. Charles Eley, Sir John Stirling Maxwell, Mr. G. H. Wilding, Mr. Gerald Loder, Lieut.-Col. J. G. Millais, Lord Headfort, Lord Stair, Mr. Kenneth McDouall, Mr. P. D. Williams, and, of course, Mr. J. C. Williams. These, and others, formed themselves into the Rhododendron Society. Mr. J. C. Williams at Caerhays Castle in Cornwall, as well as at Werrington, near Launceston, which he also bought and which later passed to his son Alfred, had been growing rhododendrons from 1885 and was quick to realize the importance of the Wilson introductions for Veitch. In the Caerhays garden book, under the date October 1903, there is the entry: 'Bought Chinese rhododendrons, 25 sorts, from Veitch'; and a little later in the year, 'Some Chinese plants from Veitch'. In January 1906 is the entry 'Have agreed with Veitch for the right to select 15 of Wilson's second Rhododendrons [from Wilson's second journey] in which are several yellows' and on 14 March, 'The second lot of Chinamen arrived and were planted: all were *very* small'. It was at Caerhays that a number of the plants introduced by Wilson flowered for the first time in Europe: *Rhododendron fargesii* and *R. sutchuenense* in 1911, *R. auriculatum* in 1912, *R. calophytum* in 1915, *R. orbiculare* in 1920. In the meantime Williams was raising the Forrest introductions; by 1917 he had hundreds of plants of some forty-seven of Forrest's species, so many, in fact, that he made the 'Chinese' garden at Werrington across the valley from the house, to accommodate the surplus; not only surplus rhododendrons, but also magnolias and camellias. Today, many of J. C. Williams's plants have grown to an immense size.

It was much the same story in other Cornish gardens into which the new material was distributed—for Cornish gardeners have always been generous to each other: Carclew, Heligan, Tremough, Menabilly, Tregothnan, Scorrier, Penjerrick, Lanarth, Lamellen, in all of which there were already great Himalayan rhododendron species and hybrids, as well as many of the introductions of the Lobb brothers and others. They were followed a little later by Trewithen and finally Trengwainton. At Trewithen Mr. George Johnstone, descendant of the Mr. Hawkins who was one of the founders of the Horticultural Society, was to make a special study of his magnolias, which resulted, in 1955, in the publication by the R.H.S. of his book *Asiatic Magnolias in Cultivation*.

By no means all great gardeners and gardens succumbed to the fascination of rhododendrons, camellias, magnolias, and the numerous other Sino-Himalayan introductions. In Northern Ireland Mr. Armytage-Moore at Rowallane certainly did. Most owners of large gardens in southern Ireland, however, remained content in large measure to grow supremely well plants from the southern hemisphere, although Mr. Bryce on Garinish Island in the Bay of Glengariff, after having commissioned the distinguished architect H. A. Peto to design an italianate garden, surrounded it with a splendid collection of both southern hemisphere and Sino-Himalayan plants. Gardens with soil rich in lime were simply unable to grow many of the western Chinese and Himalayan plants; the Botanic Garden at Glasnevin, under Frederick Moore, couldn't; the University Botanic Garden at Cambridge under the curatorship of the famous Richard Irwin Lynch couldn't. And some gardeners had little desire to grow this material, even if they could have done. It is unlikely that Henry Nicholson Ellacombe, at Bitton, where the soil was limy, would have grown many of the new peat-loving introductions, had his soil been suitable. Certainly his father, Henry T., who had been at Bitton before him, wouldn't; Bitton, he claimed, 'remained unchanged through all the caprices of fashion'. After all, not all roads led the plant collectors to western China. The mountains of Europe and the Balkans were searched for plants; Asia Minor, North Africa, South America were visited, and some gardeners enjoyed most growing the plants they themselves had collected.

Such was the case with E. A. Bowles, who travelled frequently on the Continent. Crocuses, daffodils, hardy cyclamens, snowdrops, anemones, irises; monstrous forms of plants, which he called his 'lunatic asylum': these were the plants he most loved to grow and loved to study and on which he wrote with such authority in the *Handbook of Crocus and Colchicum* of 1924, a worthy successor to George Maw's *Monograph of the Genus Crocus* of 1886, and in the *Handbook of Narcissus* (1934). It was possible to be a great gardener, and to enjoy being one, from 1900 onwards, without being unduly influenced by the trees and shrubs of the north-west Himalaya and western China, as Bowles's three books—*My Garden in Spring* (1914), *My Garden in Summer* (1914), and *My Garden in Autumn and Winter* (1915)—amply illustrate. It still is.

But it was not easy to remain indifferent to the introduction of the alpine treasures from the Sino-Himalaya, as well as from Europe, and elsewhere; nor to remain indifferent to writings on rock gardens and on rock-garden plants as forceful and picturesque as those of Reginald Farrer—or of Clarence Elliott. Of course, there were rock gardens before Farrer published his first book on the subject, *My Rock Garden*, in 1907. The firm of Backhouse of York had been building them for years; there had been one at the University Botanic Garden, Cambridge, since the mid-1860s; there had been one at Kew since 1882, when G. C. Joad had left to the Gardens his collection of over 2,500 alpine plants; there had been one at St. John's College, Oxford, since the mid-1890s, built by a young fellow of the College, H. J. Bidder. Also in the 1890s E. A. Bowles had begun to build *his* rock garden—a labour of love which occupied him for many years and on which he grew so many of his precious bulbs; and there was the rock garden of Sir Frank Crisp, at Friar Park, near Henley, described in the *Gardener's Chronicle*[1] in 1909:

The mountain top appears clothed in snow, the effect being obtained by the use of some alabaster. Appropriate plants are disposed at suitable spots, and the visitor can imagine himself to be in the midst of the Alps. Some idea of the extent of the rockery may be obtained from the fact that 7,000 tons of stone (from near Leeds) have been used in its construction, whilst it is furnished with 4,000 distinct plants.

There were the rock gardens at the Royal Botanic Garden, Edinburgh, and at Glasnevin, described by Farrer in *My Rock Garden* (1907)[2] as the finest specimens of the style he called 'The Devil's Lapful'. 'The plan is simplicity itself. You take a hundred or a thousand cartloads of bald square-faced boulders. You next drop them all about absolutely any-how; and you then plant things amongst them. The chaotic hideousness of the result is something to be remembered with shudders ever after.' At Edinburgh, 'The Devil's Lapful' of 1907 was replaced during 1908–14 by a large four-acre rock garden—basically the one of today. There was the imposing rock garden at Brockhurst, East Grinstead, made by F. J. Hanbury, and hewn, as it were, out of the side of a sandstone hill, and supporting, marvellously well, not only a large and unusual collection of choice shrubs and alpine plants from abroad, but a unique collection of British plants as well. And in 1911 there was the Rock Garden at Wisley.

Possibly Farrer's writings had more influence on the cultivation of alpine plants than on the construction of rock gardens, for today many fine plants are grown on rock gardens of hideous construction, or not grown on rock gardens at all. And thus it was and has been during and since the Farrer era. At Abbotswood, for instance, the rock garden was not of great significance, and yet Mr. Mark Fenwick grew a superb collection of alpine plants, many in an alpine house, with which he de-lighted those who attended the shows of the Alpine Garden Society. But unquestionably Farrer's *The English Rock Garden*, written in 1913 but not published until 1919, gave a tremendous stimulus to the growing of the plants he described so vividly in the various editions of his classic work. Clarence Elliott was another who, by his agreeable writings, his collect-ing, and his growing of alpines at his Six Hills Nursery at Stevenage in Hertfordshire—the nursery which his writings and plants made famous throughout the alpine plant world—exercised considerable influence on

[1] Vol. 46 (1909), p. 281.　　[2] p. 8.

alpine plant culture. And in 1917 Mr. W. E. Th. Ingwersen took charge of the Rock Garden at Wisley. He possessed a vast knowledge of alpines, and was a great gentleman, qualities which he retained when developing his own Birch Farm Nursery, Gravetye, East Grinstead, founded in 1925.

In these ways gardens and gardening were changing—and, naturally, so were the nurseries. Some nurseries, some of the most renowned in the annals of British horticulture, ceased to be: Lee of Hammersmith in 1899; Veitch in 1914; Turner of the Royal Nurseries, Slough, in 1921. Other nurseries, destined for fame, were taking their place in the horticultural world.

The firm of L. R. Russell was still dealing on a considerable scale in stove and greenhouse plants, for which they were to receive many Gold Medals at R.H.S. Shows and elsewhere. But the times, and horticulture, were changing, and this long-established firm realized this and gradually moved its production towards ornamental trees and shrubs, climbing plants and fuchsias. It had been founded around 1850 by John Russell, as Devonshire Nurseries, at Haverstock Hill, London. Three of Russell's sons—David, Louis, and William—joined their father in business, and expanded by starting a new business, in 1883, on Lord Petre's estate at Brentwood, Essex, and by taking over the nurseries of an old-established firm at Richmond, Surrey, in the early 1880s. In 1902 the three brothers dissolved partnership and Louis, or 'L.R.' as he became known amongst his trade friends, continued with the direction of the Richmond group of nurseries. He enlarged his business by taking over the Wood Lane Nurseries, Isleworth, from Lee of Hammersmith, began to grow a wide range of ericaceous plants at Milford, at what he called his American nurseries, and in 1912 took possession of the nurseries of Messrs. Thomas Cripps & Sons, of Tunbridge Wells. But the 1914–18 war was financially to hit him badly, to the extent that when the war was over he had to part with all his nurseries save those at Richmond. 'L.R.' continued exhibiting at the R.H.S.—he received Gold Medals for stove and greenhouse plants, ivies, *Azalea indica*, bamboos, fuchsias—and in 1929 he was awarded the V.M.H. By 1936 expansion was inevitable and the firm moved to its present headquarters at the thirty-five-acre Richmond Nurseries, Windlesham. On the death of 'L.R.' in 1942, his son John L. Russell assumed control, received the V.M.H. in 1957, and is now ably supported by his own son, the second 'L.R.', who, in 1965, was to stage the wonderful exhibit of ornamental trees and shrubs which received the Lawrence Medal at Chelsea.

There had been another nursery at Windlesham since 1847, when Standish & Noble had established the Sunningdale Nurseries, where a splendidly wide collection of trees, shrubs, roses, and other plants was grown. In 1898, on the death of Charles Noble, Harry White became manager and pioneered the growing and hybridizing of many of the new rhododendrons arriving from the Himalayas and western China, making the Sunningdale Nursery famous for these plants. In 1927 he was awarded the V.M.H. and, in 1932, the Loder Rhododendron Cup, for his work on the propagation and cultivation of rhododendrons.

In 1885 the nursery of over fifty acres which William Jackman had founded at St. John's, Woking, in 1810 was moved to another site of nearly sixty acres between Woking and Mayford. Many fine plants were raised in the nursery, but much the most widely known, of course, is *Clematis* x *jackmanii*, which was raised during the time George Jackman was in charge of the nursery and which received the First Class Certificate from the R.H.S. in 1863. There is some doubt about the actual cross, but it is thought to have been *Clematis lanuginosa* x *C. hendersonii* or *C. viticella*. George Jackman & Son (Woking Nurseries) Ltd., now under the personal direction of Mr. G. Rowland Jackman, is one of the finest tree and shrub nurseries in the country, and its catalogue, the *Planters Handbook*, is a splendidly factual publication.

There had been a Goldsworth Nursery at Woking in Loudon's day—and an eminent nursery it was. By 1877, when Walter Charles Slocock took it over, it had lost much of its former eminence—and had dwindled to rather less than twenty-five acres. By the turn of the century Slocock had built up the Goldsworth Old Nursery into a fine business, concentrating in the main on conifers and rhododendron hybrids, and exporting on a considerable scale to Australia, New Zealand, and the United States. Walter Slocock was awarded the V.M.H. in 1916, and almost half a century later, in 1964, his son, Oliver C. A. Slocock, was similarly honoured.

In Woking, Surrey, there was another nursery—Knaphill, founded by Michael Waterer in 1790, and the Waterers have been associated with it ever since. The name of Waterer has been closely connected with azaleas, particularly since the middle of the last century, and especially with that group known as the Knaphill azaleas. In 1870 Anthony Waterer crossed the Chinese *Rhododendron molle* with the American *R. calendulaceum*. His hybrids were later bred with hybrids of *R. molle* and another American species, *R. occidentale*; later the North American *R. arborescens* was added to the parentage. In this fashion were the Knaphill azaleas bred by the two Anthony Waterers—father and son. The flowers had great size and substance and a fine colour range. In the *Rhododendron Society Notes* in 1924, Mr. P. D. Williams wrote of them:

The colours have always been remarkable; the crimsons deep and solid, the scarlets brilliant as a new hunting coat, the yellows attaining the colour of rich Guernsey butter, the oranges bright with crimson filaments to the anthers, and of course there were beautiful pinks and whites. Bronze foliage, which harmonises so well in azaleas, was also carefully developed.

But there was scope for further development, which was done at Knap-hill, at the neighbouring Goldsworth Old Nursery by the Slococks, at Lanarth by Mr. P. D. Williams, at Exbury by Mr. Lionel de Rothschild, as well as by Mr. Gogar Stead at Christchurch, New Zealand.

Michael Waterer had also established a nursery at Bagshot, and after his death trading was carried on at the two nurseries under the name of H. & J. Waterer. However, about 1844, and by mutual consent, Hosea Waterer took over the Knaphill Nursery and John Waterer the Bagshot Nursery—and thus it was for over forty years. Then in 1890 a company was formed to acquire the assets of John Waterer, and traded under the name of John Waterer & Sons. Early in the 1900s the Bagshot nurseries were commonly known as the American nurseries, for they shipped enormous quantities of rhododendrons and evergreens of all kinds to the United States. In 1914, when the Wargrave Hardy Plant Farm Ltd. amalgamated with the Bagshot Nursery, the name of the company was changed to John Waterer, Sons & Crisp Ltd. Since then the company has continued to grow both in stature and in acreage and many are the splendid exhibits of rhododendrons and flowering trees and shrubs which it has staged at the Society's shows. In recent years it has established two thriving garden centres and now owns a 140-acre apple farm with a fully equipped gas storage and packing station.

The firm of Rochford's was established by Thomas Rochford in 1877, on a site in Tottenham near the present Tottenham Hotspur Football Club. Owing to the expansion of London, in 1881 he was forced to move to Turnford, where he soon established three acres of glass-houses. So quickly did his business develop that by 1896 he had built thirty-nine houses along Turnford High Road to accommodate his main employees as well as a social club, with hostel, for the accommodation of single men. Hostel and houses are still in use today. When Rochford died in 1901 twenty-two acres were under glass and devoted mainly to pot-plants and forced flowers. The second Thomas Rochford continued the business until he died at the early age of forty-one, in 1918, to be suc-ceeded by the third Thomas Rochford, the present chairman and managing director, who, mostly in the last twenty years, has developed the house-plant business of Thomas Rochford & Sons Ltd. to the extent that it is unrivalled in the world. Twice since 1963 the firm's marvellous exhibits at Chelsea, designed in the main by Mrs. Rochford, have been awarded the Society's Lawrence Medal, and in 1964 Mr. Rochford was the recipient of the V.M.H.

At the turn of the century the firm of Hillier of Winchester was flourishing exceedingly. In 1864 Edwin Hillier had bought a small nurseryman's and florist's business in Winchester, trading under the name of Farthing. The business prospered, and in the 1870s the now famous West Hill Nursery was purchased. Edwin's two sons inherited from him; Edwin Lawrence built up the collection of trees and shrubs for which the name of Hillier is now justly noted, whilst Arthur Richard acted as the administrative head. Unfortunately, in 1913 the 130-acre Shroner Wood Nursery which Edwin Lawrence had developed into one of the finest pinetums in the country, had to be sold. It is now the private estate of Lord Amherst of Hackney, who is creating a garden around many of the original trees of the Hillier pinetum. However, before the sale, Hillier had bought a new piece of land on the west side of Winchester where a wide range of trees and shrubs, roses and fruit trees was being grown. Edwin Lawrence died in 1944, having been awarded the V.M.H. in 1941; his brother Arthur retired in 1946—and died in 1963—and the great business continued to develop under its present head, Harold G. Hillier—son of Edwin—who has a world-wide reputation as a plantsman, whose fine catalogue of trees and shrubs is an essential reference work, and who, in an age when economic pressures force more and more nurserymen to concentrate on growing more and more of fewer and fewer popular garden plants, continues to grow an enormously wide range of plant material. A regular exhibitor at all the Society's Shows, Harold Hillier was to receive the V.M.H. in 1957 and the Lawrence Medal in 1960 and in 1964 for exhibits of conifers.

In 1901 C. F. Langdon entered into partnership with J. B. Blackmore, an enthusiastic cultivator of begonias and carnations, and thus was formed the Bath firm which in 1904 began seriously to breed delphiniums. Over the years Blackmore & Langdon's have achieved world-wide fame as raisers, cultivators, and exhibitors of tuberous begonias, delphiniums, cyclamen, polyanthus, phlox, and many are the Gold Medals they have received from the Royal Horticultural Society, at shows the length and breadth of the country—as well as in exhibitions overseas.

In 1899 Amos Perry founded his nursery at Winchmore Hill and specialized in hardy plants, and in the next thirty years was to receive close on a hundred awards from the R.H.S. for plants he had introduced or bred—including a number of bearded irises, hybrids between Californian and Chinese species of the *sibirica* group, as well as new forms of the oriental poppy, lily, trillium, and, latterly, *Hemerocallis*. At the International Flower Show at Chelsea in 1912 he showed the first white-flowered oriental poppy—'Silver Queen'—and, two years later, he produced a second, 'Perry's White'. He and his firm also specialized in water plants and in the construction of water gardens of all kinds, and in the 1930s he published his splendid *Water, Bog and Moisture Loving Plants*. To this day the exhibits of such plants at Chelsea Flower Show from Perry's Hardy Plant Farm are a joy to behold.

Perry was by no means the only one to contribute to the popularity and the development of the iris. Sir Michael Foster, who had been the pioneer in the breeding of the modern bearded iris, had died in 1907. His mantle had fallen on to W. R. Dykes, who was appointed Secretary to the R.H.S. in 1920, and made important contributions to iris literature, and who, in his breeding of new types of bearded iris, strove for pale colours in large flowers. Dykes died, tragically, in 1925, and the following year the finest iris of his raising flowered for the first time; the flower, large and yellow, was named 'W. R. Dykes', and has had a great influence on the breeding of yellow irises. Mrs. Dykes continued the work of her husband and bred the white-flowered 'Gudrun' which was to have as much influence on the breeding of white-flowered bearded irises as had 'W. R. Dykes' on the yellows.

Two others were also extending Foster's pioneer work. One was Sir Arthur Hort, who had been connected with Harrow School for over thirty years, and had been much influenced by Foster. He raised his fine white-flowered, golden-reticulated 'Theseus' and wrote charming essays on irises and other matters in *My Garden, New Flora and Sylva, Gardening Illustrated*, essays which were published in Hort's *The Unconventional Garden* (1928) and *Garden Variety* (1935). The other was George Yeld, a master for fifty-two years at St. Peter's, York, who after Foster's death made available some of Foster's seedlings, as well as some of his own, such as 'Sir Michael' and 'Lord of June', which remained firm favourites for a long time. Yeld became the first president of the Iris Society when it was founded in 1924; since 1952 it has been the British Iris Society.

However, it was left to a mining engineer, Mr. A. J. Bliss, to make the greatest contribution to iris breeding in this period. In 1910 he raised the first iris to have velvety-textured falls—'Dominion'—which, when introduced in 1917, and selling at seven guineas a tuber, was a landmark in iris history.

It was also a landmark in the history of the gladiolus when, in 1902, Mr. S. F. Townsend, the resident engineer working on the construction of the railway bridge across the Zambezi river, sent four corms of what was called *Gladiolus primulinus* to Sir Douglas Fox. These grew and flowered on 1 December 1903, plants about 2 feet high and with hooded primrose and red flowers no more than 2 inches across. Sir Douglas asked for more corms, which he distributed to the Botanic Gardens at Kew, Edinburgh, and Cambridge, and to leading growers in Britain and abroad. For the Zambezi plant the name *G. nebulicola* has been proposed. By 1908 William Kelway had hybridized it with some of the existing hybrids and had produced some of the first of the new *Primulinus* hybrids with thin wiry stems and with rather small hooded, ruffled, or laciniated flowers with a very great range in colour.

The year 1900 is an important one in the history of the sweet pea, for not only was the National Sweet Pea Society formed but the 'Countess Spencer' was raised by Silas Cole, gardener to the Earl Spencer, Althorp Park, Northampton. Cole bred it from seeds of Henry Eckford's 'Prima Donna' and its shell-pink flowers with waved and frilled standard and wings caused a sensation; the fact that it was almost lacking in fragrance was overlooked in the excitement caused by the first of the 'waved Spencers'. 'Countess Spencer' did not breed true; fortunately 'Gladys Unwin', with smaller and paler pink flowers—still waved and frilled—did. From these two seedlings a whole range of colours in the waved-flower type has since been developed.

Almost as sensational was the production in 1904 of a yellow Malmaison carnation by Hugh Low & Co. It encouraged James Douglas, the gardener and florist, to revive the breeding of hardy perpetual-flowering types, which, with the introduction of the American carnation, led hybridists to evolve the perpetual-flowering carnation with which the names of Allwood, Dutton, and Engelmann must always be associated. In 1910 Montagu Allwood, of Wivelsfield, Sussex, began his attempts to cross the perpetual-flowering carnation with the old white, pink-fringed *Dianthus plumarius*, attempts which ultimately were to lead to the establishment of the Allwoodii Pinks.

Peter Barr had rescued the narcissus collections of Leeds and Backhouse and now the Rev. G. H. Engleheart was leading the race in the breeding of the modern superb-quality daffodil. In 1898 his 'Will Scarlett' astonished everyone by its orange-red cup; it was awarded the F.C.C.; three bulbs, half the stock, were sold for £100, and it was to have a great influence on daffodil breeding. Today Engleheart is probably best remembered for his great white-trumpeted 'Beersheba', which was first shown in 1923, the year in which Mr. and Mrs. R. O. Backhouse showed the first pink daffodil of any consequence, 'Mrs. R. O. Backhouse'. And in this same year the most sensational daffodil that had appeared for many years was first shown, the single bulb being valued at £500; it was 'Fortune', bred by Messrs. Walter T. Ware Ltd. of Bath and the receiver of the First Class Certificate in 1924. It is still a favourite and first-class flower, as indeed are such flowers as 'Carlton', 'Havelock', and others with large yellow and deep-gold cups bred by P. D. Williams, who was also the first to raise the shallow-crowned jonquil hybrids such as the outstanding 'Trevithian'. From 1898 until he died in 1943 the Brodie of Brodie was raising daffodils at Brodie Castle at Forres, Morayshire, raising fine hybrids in almost all sections, such as the yellow-trumpeted 'Cromarty', the large-cupped red and white 'Red Hackle' and the small-cupped creamy-yellow 'Seraglio'.

And working in Ireland, Mr. Guy L. Wilson in Ballymena and Mr. J. Lionel Richardson in Waterford were the leading daffodil breeders for many years, the former specializing in white and pale-coloured flowers of which the giant white trumpet 'Broughshane' is probably the most remarkable, and 'Empress of Ireland' and 'Panache' the most beautiful. The latter concentrated mostly on red cups; 'Bahram', 'Ceylon', 'Narvik', all of his breeding, were some of the material from which the outstanding red-cups of the 1960s were to be developed. Guy Wilson died in 1962 and Lionel Richardson in the previous year. Richardson was probably the greatest breeder and exhibitor of daffodils of all time, for he was awarded sixty R.H.S. Gold Medals, twenty First Class Certificates, and seventy-one Awards of Merit. Happily Mrs. Richardson still continues her husband's marvellous work.

These years also saw tremendous advances in the breeding of two other groups of plants. One was the work of a great plantsman, the other of an allotment-holder. Ernest Ballard was the great plantsman—of the calibre of those of the Veitch era. He grew ramondas and haberleas superbly, developing a strain of *Ramonda myconii* which threw more pure white and pink forms than pale blue; he developed fine strains of *Nerine*, and of the double-flowered *Iberis*; he produced the first double-flowered *Aubrieta*; he vastly improved the *Rudbeckia*; and in 1938 the R.H.S. awarded him the Cory Cup for his remarkable and outstandingly fine *Hepatica* x *media* 'Ballardii'. But much more important than these are his contributions to the development of the michaelmas daisy. He began working on these plants about the turn of the century and received his first award from the R.H.S. in 1907 for his 'Beauty of Colwall' (at Colwall were his nursery and trial garden), the first of nearly fifty Awards of Merit and several First Class Certificates he was to receive. Year after year he brightened the Society's Autumn Shows with new cultivars of his raising, sturdy hardy plants with flowers of a wide colour range—whites, lilacs, pinks, crimsons, purples. By his work he greatly changed the face of the garden in autumn.

And the allotment-holder of York, the working gardener George Russell, greatly added to the attractions of the garden in late spring and early summer. He began experimenting with lupins in 1911, worked steadfastly on them twenty years, and then, in 1937, Messrs. Baker Ltd. sensationally showed the public the results of his work by exhibiting a great display of Russell lupins at an R.H.S. Show in June. In describing the exhibit in *My Garden*, Mr. D. W. Simmonds wrote:

My first impression was indescribable. Never before have I seen such mar-vellous colouring, or been thrilled by such exotic blendings, and I can safely claim to have seen every worth while plant or race of plants introduced during the past forty years; I have praised some and condemned many; but with the exception of the Spencer Sweet Peas I have seen nothing to come within a mile of the new Russell Lupins as staged . . . by Messrs. Baker in scores of shades and colours; self colours in rich pink, orange-yellow, strawberry-red; bicolors of royal purple and gold, apricot and sky-blue, rose-pink and amethyst, and dozens of intermediate shades and combinations, on hundreds of massive spikes. The highest possible Royal Horticultural Society's Award, the Gold Medal, was never more richly deserved.

Even so, it was an exhibit of British ferns from Mr. Robert Bolton which, in that year, was awarded the Society's Lawrence Medal for the best exhibit shown during the year! Over 70,000 people visited Baker's Floral Farm (in 1935 this firm had secured both Mr. Russell and his plants) to see the Russell lupins growing in the fields, and by the time the first catalogue was published over half the named varieties had been sold out.

In the meantime the flower-seed firms such as Messrs. Sutton & Sons of Reading, Messrs. Carter & Co. of Raynes Park, Messrs. Webb & Sons of Stourbridge, and others, were developing and staging great exhibits of calceolarias, gloxinias, *Schizanthus*, cinerarias, *Nicotiana*, *Nemesia*, *Primula obconica*, *Primula sinensis*, and from 1908 *Primula malacoides*.

To what extent the R.H.S.'s endeavours in the field of horticultural education and research affected such work elsewhere it is difficult to say. It is obvious, however, that this thirty-year period is a most impor-tant one from this particular point of view.

At the South Eastern Agricultural College, founded in 1894, the first principal Mr. A. D. Hall, later Sir Daniel Hall, who was to be active in the service of the R.H.S., was interested in many phases of horticulture, as well as in agriculture. It was largely through his en-deavours that the South Eastern College gained further status as the Wye Agricultural College. And it was at Wye that Hall began his work on tulips which ultimately the R.H.S. was to publish. J. M. R. Dunstan succeeded Hall as principal, and his interest in fruit growing was to lead to the foundation of the East Malling Research Station in 1912. Gradu-ally courses in fruit growing and in market gardening were established at Wye, though there were none in ornamental horticulture. If, just before and shortly after the turn of the century, any of the men of Wye wished to increase their knowledge of ornamental horticulture, they had to attend the Women's Horticultural College at Swanley.

Swanley Horticultural College had been opened for the training of men in 1889, but seven years later thirty-nine women were in residence

—and only a few men. By 1903 the men had been entirely replaced by women. Both Wye and Swanley prepared students for their own diplomas, but when in 1916 London University introduced its degree in horticulture the two colleges began to cater for the London degree. In the meantime, in 1898 Evelyn, Countess of Warwick, founded Warwick Hostel in Reading to provide horticultural training for women. In five years' time the premises had been outgrown and the college moved to Studley Castle in Warwickshire and took the name of Studley College. As at Wye and Swanley, Studley trained its students for its own diploma and for the London degree, and does so to this day.[1] Swanley, unfortunately, was destroyed by the bombs of 1945, and is now part of the horticultural department of Wye College.

In 1932 Miss Beatrix Havergal, who for five years had been running a small horticultural training establishment for young women, moved to Waterperry, near Wheatley, Oxford, and there founded the Waterperry Horticultural School (for women) which has since gone from strength to strength and is now well known not only for its course of horticultural instruction but also for its Gold Medal exhibits of strawberries at the Chelsea Flower Shows.

Shortly before 1889 Sir John Bennet Lawes bequeathed to the nation, with an endowment of £100,000, his experimental station at Rothamsted. In 1889 trustees were appointed, the necessary trust deed was executed, and a committee of management was formed. Sir John—then Mr. J. B. Lawes—had begun experiments with various manuring substances, first with plants in pots, and later in the field, shortly after entering into possession of his hereditary property at Rothamsted, in Hertfordshire, in 1834. In 1843 he had begun the long-term practical experiments which continue to this day and which truly laid the foundation of the Rothamsted Experimental Station. It is the oldest research station in Britain concerned with agricultural and horticultural research.

Although the Duke of Bedford at Woburn had set up an experimental fruit farm in 1894, it was not until 1903 that another research station was established, and then it was at Long Ashton, mainly on the initiative of the Bath and West and Southern Counties Society. It was the National Fruit and Cider Institute, and its object was to place on a firm basis experiments which had been conducted in cider-making. And with a small grant of £300 from the Board of Agriculture this was, in fact, done, until 1912. Then the Institute became associated with the University of Bristol, received greatly increased grants from the Board of Agriculture, and as the Long Ashton Research Station, under the directorship of Professor B. T. P. Barker, widened its scope to include problems of fruit culture and the practical control of pests and diseases of fruit trees. From

[1] Studley is due to close in 1969.

1924 until 1958, as research chemist, deputy director, and finally director, Professor T. Wallace was to do much important work on plant nutrient requirements and deficiencies which has helped to make the name of the station renowned throughout the horticultural and agricultural worlds.

The John Innes Horticultural Institute was founded in 1909. John Innes, a Scotsman of an old and distinguished family, had acquired the Manor House at Merton in Surrey, had farmed on a considerable scale and had planted his estate with a fine selection of trees. On his death in 1904 he had left his estate and fortune 'for the study of the growth of trees and for the improvement of horticulture by experiment and research'. These rather vague terms of reference were given more concrete form by the work of the first director, William Bateson, who only the year previously, 1908, had been appointed to the Chair of Biology at Cambridge. He had christened the new science of genetics, and genetics and chromosome studies would be practised at the new station. Bateson was succeeded by Daniel Hall, who before he retired in 1939 was to widen the scope of the research work and to make famous the 'J. I.' series of standardized sterilized potting and seed composts. The work of M. B. Crane on orchard pollination and of W. J. C. Lawrence on the conditions required by seedling plants was to influence, respectively, practice in orchards and in glass-houses all over the country; both Crane and Lawrence were to receive the V.M.H.

At the insistence of the commercial fruit grower, the Wye College experimental station was started on twenty-two acres of land at East Malling in 1912. Thus was born the research station which was to revolutionize fruit growing, first by the studies of Mr. Ronald Hatton (Sir Ronald in 1949), who, in the years immediately before, and during the war of 1914–18, experimented with the effects of apple stocks and the growth of scions, work which was to lead to the standardization of stocks to produce fruit bushes and trees of well-defined type. Hatton was appointed director of East Malling Research Station in 1918 and was to remain there until he retired in 1949. In 1930 he delivered to the R.H.S. the Masters Memorial Lecture, and was awarded the V.M.H., while in 1952 he was elected a Vice-President of the Society.

From small beginnings in 1913 the Cheshunt Experimental and Research Station, under the directorship of Dr. W. F. Bewley from 1921, was to make a major contribution to solving the problems of glass-house growers, especially those in the Lea Valley (Dr. Bewley was to receive the V.M.H. in 1938), before being transferred to a new and enlarged home near Toddington, Littlehampton, as the Glass-house Crops Research Unit, still under Dr. Bewley's direction.

In such ways has horticultural education and research progressed.

Part Six
From One War to the Other
(1919 - 1945)

CHAPTER EIGHTEEN

THE NEW HALL

LORD LAMBOURNE, THE NEW PRESIDENT, WAS PRIMARILY A SOLDIER and a politician. Born in 1847 and schooled at Eton, he had served in the Coldstream Guards from 1866 to 1883 before retiring from the Army with the rank of Lieutenant-Colonel. Then he turned to politics; in 1892 he was returned as Conservative Member for the Epping Division of Essex and represented that constituency in Parliament for twenty-five years. In 1917 he was raised to the peerage and in 1919, the year in which he succeeded Grenfell as the Society's President, he was appointed Lord Lieutenant of the county. By no means a great horticulturist, he had however a fine eye for a good florists' flower and, although in later years he cultivated some rhododendrons and magnolias, it was dahlias, hippeastrums, carnations, and other richly coloured garden plants which appealed most to him. During the five years he had sat on the Council of the Society he had shown immense interest in all its affairs and had become a personality in the horticultural world. As he regarded his election to the Presidency of the Society as the greatest honour that had come to him and as he had the rare gift of being 'get-at-able by all, and hail-fellow-well-met to peer and peasant, gardener and king',[1] it was inevitable that he should prove to be a highly popular and successful leader of the Society.

At the start he could not have found his office an easy one to fill, for a few months after his appointment he lost the services of Wilks, the great and wise Secretary, who resigned. Two years later, in 1921, A. J. Gaskell, who had been Assistant Secretary since 1906, who had worked closely with Wilks and who, like Wilks, was steeped in the affairs of the Society, also resigned. Difficult though it may have been for Lambourne, it was much more so for the new Secretary, William Rickatson Dykes, who came to the Society in 1920 from Charterhouse, where he had been a master since 1903 and where he had made a name for himself as an authority on the genus *Iris*, the Cambridge University Press having published his splendid monograph in 1913—a beautiful work which for many years remained the standard authority on the botany, the history,

---

[1] *Gdnr's Chron.*, vol. 85 (1929), p.18.

and the cultivation of irises. Dykes had indeed assumed the mantle of the late Sir Michael Foster—and had done so with considerable ease. To assume the mantle of Wilks was a very different story and an immensely more difficult task, for Dykes had no real knowledge of the Society's history, no real experience of working with committees, and no real knowledge of the administration of a great Society such as the R.H.S. But he had great courage, knew no fear, was blessed with unlimited energy and enthusiasm, and quickly adapted himself to the Vincent Square environment. Though his reign as Secretary was to be a comparatively brief one, it was none the less a noteworthy one.

For some months after the resignation of Gaskell in April 1921, Dykes managed with the assistance of a woman, until the appointment, in November 1922, of R. W. Ascroft as Assistant Secretary. Gaskell's was not the only resignation of 1921; in July, Charles G. A. Nix, the Treasurer, also resigned. Nix was an amateur gardener and keen forester, planting at his estate at Tilgate many unusual trees, not only for their ornamental value but also for their potential timber qualities. He was, however, best known as an authority on fruits, especially on apples and pears, and, apart from his treasurership, his best work for the Society related to its Fruit Committee, of which for many years he was chairman. He was awarded the V.M.H. in 1923, and thereafter periodically served on the Council until finally retiring in 1934 at the early age of sixty. He was to live in retirement at his home at Warninglid, Sussex, for another twenty-two years.

As Treasurer he was succeeded by C. T. Musgrave, a lawyer and Land Registry official and clever amateur gardener who grew many rare and difficult plants at Hascombe in Surrey. This was the first of three occasions on which he was to be elected to the treasurership. His first term of office ended in 1924, when Sir William Lawrence, son of Sir Trevor and a newcomer to the Council in 1923, was elected in his stead. Sir William was a worthy successor to his father by reason both of his kindly and courteous nature and of his knowledge and love of plants. Whilst Sir Trevor's interests had been, in the main, with orchids, Sir William's were in hardy and half-hardy plants, with the cultivation of which he loved to experiment, reporting the results of his experiments to the horticultural Press, especially to the pages of the *Gardener's Chronicle* and of *Gardening*. To the Society he gave much of his time, serving on many committees—the Floral, the Wisley Advisory, the Publications, the Lily, and the Joint Iris. The Society has indeed good cause to remember the services of the Lawrence family over three generations.

Sir William it was who was responsible for the formation of the Alpine Garden Society, of which he was an inspiring president. On 29 October

1929 a meeting was held in one of the Society's committee rooms to discuss his proposal to form a society with the objects of offering advice on the making of rock gardens and the growing of alpine plants, of organizing discussions on the cultivation of particular plants, of exchanging plants among members, of arranging lectures, and of publishing a bulletin. From this meeting the Alpine Garden Society was born, a society which has admirably fulfilled its objectives, and whose *Bulletin*, from the time of the appearance of the first number in April 1930, has been an outstanding publication. Undoubtedly the Society stimulated the formation of the Scottish Rock Garden Club in 1933.

One of Lord Lambourne's first suggestions was that a committee be appointed to consider the matter of the making of awards to plants and to exhibits with a view to assuring greater consistency. The committee made several recommendations which were adopted by Council, but not all of them proved satisfactory. For instance, there was the recommendation that in addition to the award of a Gold Medal, the Council should mark its appreciation of an exhibit of outstanding merit by sending to the exhibitor a special form of congratulation. In theory this was a splendid idea; but in practice it proved not very satisfactory simply because some exhibitors became disgruntled if they did not invariably receive the Council's congratulations each time they were awarded Gold Medals. Thus after some years 'the Congratulations of the Council' was discontinued and the Society reverted to the position wherein the highest available award was the Gold Medal. Again, there was the recommendation that, on the suggestion of any of the committees, the Council should consider the award of a Lindley Medal in silver-gilt, silver or bronze, for an exhibit of a plant or plants of special interest or beauty, or showing exceptional skill in cultivation, irrespective of any other award the exhibit might have received. In practice it was found desirable to make the Lindley Medal available for an award instead of, and not in addition to, any other of the Society's Medals. And again, there was the recommendation that a number of silver cups be purchased for award at the Chelsea and the Great Autumn Shows to exhibits which were just below Gold Medal standard. Unfortunately the practice proved misleading to the majority of Fellows and to the public, who rather naturally, though erroneously, concluded that an exhibit on which a silver cup was displayed had been adjudged superior to one on which there was only a card with the representation of a Gold Medal. Consequently, after some years the use of what became known as 'Standard Cups' was discontinued.

Of the wisdom of one recommendation there could be no doubt: that a new award, the R.H.S. Award of Garden Merit, should be made on the advice of the Wisley Garden Committee, to plants of proved and outstanding excellence for garden use; generally, but not necessarily so, the plants should have been thoroughly tried at Wisley; and the award should be given to plants long grown in our gardens as well as to more recent introductions, provided that they were of outstanding merit in their class and did not require any very special treatment in order to prove their excellence. The first Award of Garden Merit was given on 31 January 1922 to *Hamamelis mollis*, while on 22 February of the same year, two species of crocus received the award, the spring-flowering *C. tomasinianus* and the autumn-flowering *C. speciosus*. It is to wonderful plants of this nature that the Award of Garden Merit is still given, and has been since 1922.

In 1920, Messrs. Lovell, Reeves & Co., in whose possession the copyright of the *Botanical Magazine* had been since they purchased it from the Curtis family in 1845, decided that, as the *Magazine* was no longer an economic proposition, they could not continue publication after the end of 1920. The *Botanical Magazine* was founded in 1787 and is, today, the oldest illustrated periodical in the world devoted to plants. Moreover, it has always been the most authoritative periodical, chiefly because the responsibility for the letterpress and plates has for so long been in the hands of the Directors of Kew. The Society, and the horticultural Press, firmly believed that, if production should cease, the 'event would be a disaster to horticulture all over the world, and would undoubtedly diminish the prestige of British horticulture'.[1] This view was shared by three great and enlightened gardeners, Messrs. H. J. Elwes, L. de Rothschild, and R. Cory, who promptly acquired the copyright. Very naturally they offered the copyright to Kew, doubtless in the hope that the Ministry of Agriculture, to which department of state Kew is attached, would be able to find the resources necessary for the *Magazine*'s publication. However, as the Ministry did not accept the offer, the copyright and goodwill were presented to the Society, who in 1921 purchased the old stock and made arrangements for the publication of the *Magazine* to be resumed in 1922, so that, with its detailed descriptions and accurate coloured plates, it might continue to provide botanists and horticulturists throughout the world with a valuable aid to the identification of plants. At the same time Reginald Cory undertook to produce the volume which should have appeared in the intervening two years.

Believing that it was desirable that the Society should maintain, as a record, a painting of any plant to which an award had been made, Mr. Cory presented to the Council, of which he had recently become a member, a set of such paintings he himself had had prepared during 1922. As a result of his generous action it was decided to continue on the same lines at the Society's expense in 1923. In fact, the practice was

[1] *Gdnr's Chron.*, vol. 70 (1921), p. 267,

continued for a good many years, but eventually discontinued, except for orchids, when it was realized that the paintings were seldom consulted and that the cost of their production was steadily increasing.

The Cory Cup is another instance of Cory's goodwill and generosity to the Society. Instituted in 1923, and presented annually by him to the Society, its purpose was to encourage the production of hardy hybrids of garden origin, and it was to be awarded only to the raiser of a plant shown at an R.H.S. Show that is the result of an intentional cross and has a true species or subspecies as one parent. During his lifetime, the cup was awarded, among others, to the raisers of *Eucryphia* x *nymansay*, *Rosa* x *highdownensis*, *Ceanothus* x *burkwoodii*, *Gentiana* x *hascombensis*, and *Lilium* x '*Maxwill*'. On Cory's death in 1934, at the early age of sixty-two, the purpose of his cup was continued in the Reginald Cory Memorial Cup, which now is won outright. And also on his death his valuable collection of horticultural and botanical books was bequeathed to the Lindley Library. Quiet, kindly, courteous, generous, widely read, well informed, Cory also served the Society as a member of Council, of the Narcissus and Tulip Committee, Floral Committee B, Publications Committee, Library Committee, Wisley Advisory Committee, and the Joint Iris Committee. He made his own garden at Duffryn, near Cardiff, famous throughout horticultural circles, cultivating extensively trees and shrubs, cacti and succulents, and especially dahlias for their decorative value in the garden.

In 1922, at the request of Sir Harry Veitch, the trusteeship of the Veitch Memorial Fund, which had been established in 1870 in memory of James Veitch of Chelsea the founder of the firm, was vested in the Council of the Society. The object of the trust was, and still is, annually to award medals and prizes to those who have helped in the advancement and improvement of the science and practice of horticulture and for special exhibits. The first two Veitch Memorial Medals under the new trusteeship, in 1922, were awarded to Mr. W. J. Bean, Curator at Kew, and to Dr. Lloyd Praeger, the eminent Irish botanist. Both received Silver Medals and prizes of fifty pounds, the former for his work on trees and shrubs—his *Trees and Shrubs Hardy in the British Isles* had been published in 1914, and a third and supplementary volume was to appear in 1923—and the latter for his monograph, *The Genus Sedum*, which had been published in the Society's *Journal* in 1921.

Two years after making his request to Council, on 6 June 1924, Sir Harry Veitch died. For half a century he had been the most outstanding figure in British horticulture, exercising more influence on all things pertaining to horticulture than any other. He, and James his father, had been members of the Committee of the International Horticultural Exhibition and Botanical Congress, held in London in 1866—the

Exhibition from the profits of which the Lindley Library had been purchased and vested in the Society. At the second great International Exhibition, in 1912, he had again played a leading role, and for his efforts had received his knighthood. He had also received the Order of the Crown from the King of the Belgians, the French Legion of Honour, the French Isidore St. Hilaire Medal, and the United States's George R. White Gold Medal, all for his eminent services to horticulture. And proud though he was of all these, apart from his knighthood the award of the Society's V.M.H. in 1906 pleased him most. With the Society he had had a long and most loyal association, as a member of Council, for many years as chairman of the Orchid Committee, and in 1918, at the ripe age of seventy-eight, as Treasurer. His portrait, painted by Sir H. Rivière, presented to him in 1910, now hangs in the Society's Council Room. The work of the Veitch firm in the introduction of new plants and in the hybridization of plants has been briefly sketched elsewhere. In 1914, Sir Harry retired from business and, as there was no successor in the family, rather than risk losing the pre-eminent position the firm had won, he decided not to sell the goodwill, but disposed of the nursery and the land for building purposes. By so doing he closed a remarkable era in the history of British horticulture.

Always, throughout its history, much of the immensely valuable work of the Society has been done through the medium of its various committees; and the success of the committees in large measure has rested in the hands of the chairmen and secretaries, who, almost without exception, have given unceasingly and unsparingly of their time and talents. The remarkable examples of James O'Brien and of Alfred Gurney Wilson amply illustrate the point. O'Brien, one of the country's greatest orchidologists, had been secretary of the Society's Orchid Committee from 1889, the year of its institution. In 1924 he thought fit to resign his honorary post, for he was over eighty years old. Even so, he remained an interested member of the committee until he died in 1930, at the age of eighty-nine, when he was its oldest member. Gurney Wilson succeeded him as secretary and secretary he remained until 1942, when he succeeded Sir Jeremiah Colman as chairman. He, too, had a vast knowledge of orchids and of orchid literature. Having founded, in 1910, and edited until 1916, the *Orchid World*, he was editor, from 1921 until 1932, of the *Orchid Review*. For fifty years he was hardly to miss a Society Show and in the end was to become one of the Society's greatest benefactors.

In 1924 an important change was made in the composition of the Society's Floral Committee. At this time many of the ornamental tree and shrub introductions of Wilson, Forrest, and others had reached the flowering and fruiting stages, were causing increasing interest, and were being exhibited at the Society's meetings. Because of the shortage of time it was difficult for the Floral Committee, when judging these exhibits, to give them the care and consideration they merited. Thus, in order to expedite the judging of novelties, the Floral Committee was divided into two; Floral Committee A was allocated all the florists' flowers and Floral Committee B all trees and shrubs and botanical species, other than orchids and daffodils, for which already there were Committees.

Floral A was under the chairmanship of the tall and handsome, gentlemanly and gracious H. B. May, then in his seventy-ninth year. Presiding at the dinner in May's honour on 20 June 1925, on the occasion of his eightieth birthday, Lord Lambourne said: 'You have had a long life, fairly full of happiness; you have weathered its storms, and I hope you will sail down the remainder of the stream of life on the smooth waters of love and affection.' The wish was fulfilled; May, who had been for many years a member of Council and chairman of the Narcissus and Tulip Committee as well as Chairman of the Floral Committee, survived Lord Lambourne, living to pass his ninety-first birthday and to enjoy the affection and esteem of all. On his committee in 1924 was a man who had become a member of the Narcissus and Tulip Committee as long ago as 1906, and a member of the Floral Committee in 1920, and was to succeed to the chairmanship of Floral A in 1938, filling the office with distinction for twenty years—George William Leak.

Over Floral Committee B, in 1924, G. W. E. Loder presided, and he, in a few years' time, was to be the Society's President.

Although it was only twenty years since the Exhibition Hall at Vincent Square had been built, the report submitted to the Annual General Meeting in 1924 stated that 'At times the number of visitors has been so great that the Council realizes that the greatest problem with which it is faced is to provide adequate accommodation for the groups staged by exhibitors and for their inspection by the Fellows. The problem . . . has been and is receiving very serious attention.'

In fact, the Council, for various reasons, already had rejected a suggestion that the Society should transfer lock, stock, and barrel to the site of the Royal Botanic Society's Gardens in Regent's Park. Moreover, it had been looking into the possibility of acquiring the school playground at the back of the hall, as an extension to the hall, and had concluded that its acquisition was out of the question. Now the Council was examining the possibilities of a site in Elverton Street, the site, in fact, occupied by the present New Hall. The approval of the General Meeting was sought, and obtained, for the continuation of the negotiations. Having ascertained that the site would be available, and since the Council were satisfied of its suitability for the Society's needs, in December 1925 the lease of the land for 999 years was duly signed.

Contrary to the situation twenty years before, the Society was not now worried financially. There was an income of nearly £30,000 from annual subscriptions, and invested funds and assets amounted to over £60,000. Membership during the past year had increased by over one thousand and the total membership on 15 November 1923 was over nineteen thousand. It was hoped that the erection of the new hall would not only provide adequate accommodation for all the Society's Shows, including the Autumn Show which in 1923 had suffered a loss of over £800, though not including Chelsea Show but that it would also be capable of accommodating such important Shows as those of the National Rose Society.

While designs for the new hall were still being discussed, and before the contract was signed and let, disaster hit the Society, for on 1 December 1925 Dykes, the Secretary, died when only forty-eight years of age and in the prime of life. On 27 November whilst motoring with his wife on a road slippery with snow, his car skidded and collided with a lorry. Mrs. Dykes escaped with a few bruises, but her husband was thrown out, lost his right ear and suffered such severe damage to his right arm that, a few days afterwards, it had to be amputated. Death followed speedily on the operation. Two of his close colleagues, F. J. Chittenden and C. T. Musgrave, wrote of him:[1]

With all his occupation in the Society's affairs and his interest in his plants he never lost a certain boyish delight in a merry tale, and it was perhaps to this youthfulness in him that his character owed its charm. Like a boy, too, he was almost impetuous in his desire to carry out some new scheme which he had evolved and which he thought would be beneficial to the Society; and by adopting the blunt straightforwardness of the soldier, he has been known to fail to convince his hearers when he might have succeeded had he been prepared to use the tact and skill of the diplomat. After all, this straightforwardness was one of the finest traits in a very attractive character, remarkable for its strength and its sincerity. His one idea in life was to promote the best interests of the Society, and in this he succeeded to an extent far greater than is generally appreciated.

All iris gardeners had unbounded appreciation for his work on these plants. His *Irises* of 1911 was the first book adequately to deal with the species and their cultivation. His monograph, *The Genus Iris* (1913), was written primarily from the botanical point of view. His *Handbook of Garden Irises* (1924) was intended for gardeners and sums up twenty years of work with these plants.

The Council appointed Lieut.-Col. F. R. Durham to succeed Dykes as Secretary. Unlike his predecessor he was not a horticulturist; by

[1] *Jl R. hort. Soc.*, LI (1926), p. 178,

training and experience he was a civil engineer. Council did not, however, regard his lack of gardening knowledge as disadvantageous. The Society's work was expanding and extending in many directions in an endeavour to keep pace with the rapidly growing interest in horticulture throughout the country. More room for exhibitions was only one of the Society's problems. Its offices could no longer accommodate the necessarily increased staff. The Lindley Library could no longer adequately accommodate all its books. Not so much a horticulturist but rather a man with administrative experience, organizing ability, and the equable temperament to enable him to work with all the varied interests represented in the complex constitution of the Society was now required for the Secretary's chair which Durham was to fill for nearly twenty years.

The first major operation needing his attention was the building of the new hall. In considering designs particular attention was given to lighting and ventilation. It was known only too well that a building with a semicircular 'St. Pancras Station' type of roof could become too hot for a flower show; therefore what was called the 'Swedish' type of roof, with concrete flats and vertical windows, was favoured although it was a novelty in Britain. The contract was signed in August 1926 and the foundation stone formally laid by Lord Lambourne on 19 October, a metal box containing specimens of the Society's medals in silver being placed in the stone. Building work continued throughout 1927 and, in spite of some delays, except for minor details it was completed according to schedule in time for the formal opening, on 26 June 1928, by H.R.H. Princess Mary, Viscountess Lascelles, who, earlier in the year, had graciously accepted an invitation to become one of the Society's patrons. The new building contained not only the finest exhibition hall in central London, but administrative offices as well; a lecture theatre on the first floor and, on the second and third floors, committee rooms enabling the various committees to judge and report on plants, flowers, fruits, and vegetables under the favourable conditions of top north lighting. In the basement a restaurant, kitchens, and cloakrooms were provided. (Plate 21.)

The Great Autumn Show of September was the first to be held in the new building (it also occupied the Old Hall) and gave exhibitors and Fellows the chance to criticize: the lighting was splendid, except on the dais; the great height tended to dwarf the exhibits and, had the roof been lowered by twenty-five feet or so, there would still have been an abundance of light, the exhibits would not have been dwarfed and many thousands of pounds would have been saved; the great height, as well as the pillars, tended to reduce the apparent width of the hall. Even so, the hall was a splendid one, and had it been half as large again, many would have been much better pleased.

The other outstanding horticultural event in 1928 was the International Exhibition of Garden Design and Conference on Garden Planning which was held in both halls from 17 to 24 October. In opening the Exhibition, the Earl of Crawford and Balcarres said:

I believe this is a unique effort to display in this country the relations of sculpture, of garden ornament, and of decoration with horticulture itself. Here we have illustrations of garden planning, of garden design, of garden decoration, and we may say that it is a pioneer Exhibition and, as such, important both for the fine arts in this country and for that to which the Society has long directed its strenuous and successful efforts, viz. the cultivation and beautification of our countryside.

Although Lord Crawford was winning for himself a reputation as an art critic, it is doubtful if he was very familiar with much of the Society's history. At any rate, it appears that he knew little about that historic day of 5 June 1861, when, opening the Society's new Kensington Garden, the Prince Consort had described the Garden as 'a valuable attempt . . . to reunite the science and art of gardening to the sister arts of Architecture, Sculpture and Painting', and had emphasized that 'Unrivalled opportunities are here offered for the display of works of art and for the erection of monuments as tributes to great men'. Anyone attending the 1928 Exhibition, and knowing something of the history of the disastrous Kensington days, must have had cause to wonder.

The object of the Conference and Exhibition was a most worthy one; to raise the standard of garden planning by bringing it more prominently to public notice by means of illustrations, drawings, photographs, and models of different styles of garden planning adopted to various countries, suited to varying conditions of site and soil, and, at the same time, to emphasize the true functions of sculpture in gardens. The Exhibition was divided into four sections. One was historical and retrospective—a rare and comprehensive collection of valuable pictures, plans, tapestries, photographs, and books illustrating the development of gardens in Britain from 1500 to 1850, and of gardens in France, Italy, and Spain. Another section was devoted to garden planning for town and country. Plans, designs, and models, illustrating garden design, were arranged in two groups, the east side of the hall being given over to Britain and the Dominions, the west side to Belgium, France, Germany, Holland, Sweden, and the United States. A third section—public parks and gardens—contained exhibits from over thirty of the most important public bodies in Great Britain; the object was to provide an opportunity to the public and to municipal authorities to examine plans, models, and photographs of public parks and gardens, embracing a wide range of modes of treatment of open spaces. The fourth section attempted to display sculpture in the true garden setting and occupied the entire central portion of the hall—150 feet by 70 feet—and was arranged as a formal garden designed by Mr. Reynolds-Stephens, president of the Royal Society of British Sculptors. His garden did not please everyone. Though Sir William Lawrence described it as 'an inspired layout', the *Gardener's Chronicle* criticized it as being 'an architect's garden, which differs greatly from that of the landscape gardener's, to whom the garden is of supreme importance and not merely an adjunct of the house to contain lay figures'.[1]

Of the importance of the Exhibition—one of the most ambitious that has ever been staged and one which attracted many overseas visitors—and of the scholarly nature of many of the papers read at the Conference and published in the Society's *Journal*, none could doubt. *Gardening*, the paper William Robinson had founded, regarded the project chiefly as a challenge to municipal authorities.

It is especially to be hoped . . . that members of Town Councils and public men generally may have taken note of what they saw and heard. To such an extent is the future of town and landscape, and thus the environment which posterity will have to live in and be influenced by, in the hands of these men, that it is obviously of the highest importance that they should not only appreciate good work, but should make a point of getting it, whenever they have a park, a public garden, a cemetery, a building estate, or even an area of playing fields to lay out for the community. The public aspect of landscape architecture has received far too little attention in the past. Many corporations, it is true, have secured the services of men who considered parks from the aesthetic as well as from the strictly practical standpoint, and who have been fully qualified to translate their ideals into actualities, but far too many others have allowed results to be produced that seem to belie the possibility of their having ever had such services behind them. After such an exhibition as this, however, there can at least not be the excuse of ignorance for the repetition of such Victorian atrocities as one meets with all too frequently today. . . . A park should not be only a place of recreation, it should be a thing of beauty as well, it should enable the industrial worker to get a breath of the country, it should give the town dweller the benefits of a restful garden, and it should be capable of an ennobling influence on everyone.[2]

Forty years later there are not so many 'Victorian atrocities', but the words of *Gardening* assume still greater significance.

At Wisley, in 1919, George Fox Wilson had been appointed the Society's entomologist and Felix Cuthbert Brown the Society's trials recorder, and both were to render loyal service for over thirty years. The opportunity had been taken to acquire two small farms of about 160

[1] *Gdnr's Chron.*, vol. 84 (1928), p. 338.
[2] *Gardening*, L (1928), p. 681.

acres in all, adjacent to the northern end of the Garden, together with several cottages. The old village school house had also been purchased subject to a life interest of the then tenant. As the work and collections at Wisley were expanding rapidly, the additional land would be necessary for extensions to the Garden and for accommodation for the additional staff; and in 1924 six cottages were, in fact, built on the new land.

The propagation department at the Garden was especially busy. The Society had contributed to the expeditions of Reginald Farrer and George Forrest and, as a result, vast amounts of seeds were arriving at the Garden from China and Tibet and many thousands of plants were being raised and distributed. In addition, of course, there was the usual propagation necessary for the various trials. The Council was anxious to have a trial of roses in co-operation with the National Rose Society, but failing to secure this co-operation, decided to hold its own trial, and in 1922 a start was made on part of the land of the newly-acquired Deers Farm—and the work was continued for some years.

In 1922 the Society also entered into a scheme under which a plantation of fruit on part of Deers Farm was to become a central station for a national trial of fruits for commercial purposes. The scheme was administered by a joint committee on which the Ministry of Agriculture and the Society were equally represented, and the work was supported by an annual government grant on an acreage basis, beginning with five-and-a-half acres exclusive of the area to be planted with a collection of standard varieties. This work, which eventually extended to twenty-six acres under trial, and nineteen under standard collections, was continued until 1960, by which time the National Fruit Trials, under its director, Mr. J. M. S. Potter, had been transferred to Brogdale, near Faversham, because of Wisley's liability to spring frosts.

In April 1922 the genial and popular Superintendent of the Garden, S. T. Wright, died. He had been in the service of the Society since 1896 and the first Superintendent at Wisley. For nearly twenty years he had enthusiastically used his wide knowledge and appreciation of plants, and his facility for imparting this knowledge and enthusiasm to others, into transforming what, in 1903, was mostly rough corn land surrounding a charming woodland, into a great garden of scientific and amenity value worthy of the Society. And during the years he acted as the Society's garden adviser he was the means of transforming many a Fellow's garden. Typical of the great gardeners of his day, he was interested in all garden plants, although it was for fruits that he probably had greatest regard. How could it have been otherwise when, in 1896, he had won the R.H.S. prize for a splendid essay on hardy fruit culture and when, for twenty-five years, he had acted as secretary of the Fruit and Vegetable Committee? The members of this committee subscribed to a memorial sundial placed just inside the main gate at Wisley and opposite the house he had occupied for eighteen years.

The Council was divided on the matter of Wright's successor, but fell in with the views of F. J. Chittenden, the Director of the Garden, who, wishing to be relieved of some of the lectures to students, and to avoid a continuance of something like dual control of the Garden staff, believed that the vacancy should be filled by the appointment of an Assistant Director. So, with effect from 1 January 1923, A. Simmonds, who had been at Wisley from 1907 until 1911, first as a student and then as a demonstrator, was appointed Assistant Director, a post which he occupied until 1925, when he was transferred to the Vincent Square office and became Assistant Secretary in succession to R. W. Ascroft. At Vincent Square he was to remain until 1962.

In December 1923 the Council appointed a commission consisting of Dr. W. Bateson, the director of the John Innes Horticultural Institute, Professor J. B. Farmer, Professor of Botany and director of the biological laboratories at the Imperial College of Science and Technology, and Mr. A. D. Cotton, keeper of the Herbarium at the Royal Botanic Gardens at Kew, 'to enquire into the character and efficiency of the scientific and educational work which is being carried on at Wisley'. The report, made in the following May, was indefinite, but a committee appointed to consider it recommended the appointment of two new officers—a keeper of the Laboratory and a keeper of the Garden, acting under the Director, and that a new type of paid student-gardener be employed.

Accordingly, in 1925 Mr. R. Findlay took up the duties of keeper of the Garden. Robert Findlay's earlier experience had been gained in gardens in Scotland and, although he had been head gardener at Wiverton Hall, Norfolk, from 1904, he had returned to Scotland in 1908 as head gardener to the brothers McDouall at Logan in Wigtownshire, where he was able to make extensive improvements in a garden of outstanding interest. Volunteering for active service in 1915, he returned after the war, not to Logan, but to the near-by estate of Lord Stair at Castle Kennedy, and there remained until 1922, when he left Scotland to become superintendent of the Royal Park at Greenwich. Not for another two years was the Laboratory appointment made, and then, in 1927, Mr. M. A. H. Tincker was appointed keeper. Trained in Cambridge and London, he had been a plant physiologist at the Welsh Plant Breeding Station, and for close on twenty years was to undertake similar work at Wisley, work concerned with the effect on plant growth of light, hormones, and growth substances, soil conditions—as well as soilless cultivation. In 1928 Dr. Dowson accepted a mycological post with the government of Tasmania, resigned from the Society's service and was succeeded by D. E. Green. With Findlay's appointment, and the transference of Simmonds to Vincent Square, the office of Assistant Director was discontinued.

Hitherto the Gardens had been closed on Sundays, but in 1925 the Council took the unprecedented course of inviting Fellows to return postcards intimating whether they wished the Gardens to be opened on Sunday afternoons. The voting was 2,391 in favour of Sunday opening and 569 against. Consequently the Gardens were opened to those presenting Fellows' or Associates' tickets on Sundays from 2 p.m. to 6 p.m. from May to September inclusive and, in the following year, the opening period was extended to the second Sunday in October. Some thirty-five years later the Gardens were to be open on Sunday the whole year round.

Sunday opening rendered the erection of a gate-house necessary; it was built by the garden staff from designs by Messrs. Imrie & Angell, the architects for the Laboratory. Likewise the enlargement of the Laboratory made necessary, when labour was available after the end of the war, the terracing of the ground, on the Garden side of the Laboratory, to correspond with the varied heights of the building. Sussex sandstone was used for the retaining walls, which were planted with rock plants and capped with slabs of York stone. The ground was levelled, sown with grass, and two water-lily ponds were constructed, one of them heated to accommodate the blue *Nymphaea stellata*. Later the road in front of the Laboratory was also terraced and similar walls made; the main entrance was changed, with, in 1925, the erection of a wall and the wrought-iron gates to commemorate the Rev. W. Wilks.

In the meantime, round about 1920, the rough pasture known as Seven Acres which previously had proved unsatisfactory for the growth of trees and shrubs was developed to accommodate many of the introductions from the Farrer and Forrest expeditions. The sharp eye of Chittenden noticed small plants of ling growing here and there in the grass, and this discovery prompted him to make a heath garden; at the same time he decided to convert a large gravel pit in the middle of the field into a pond. Digging showed that there was no real fault in the soil. The former apparent infertility had been due to an iron pan which had to be broken before roots could penetrate below or water rise above its surface. How abundantly justified Chittenden's faith in this field has been.

The laying out of Seven Acres brought the Pinetum, which had been planted with some conifers in 1909, more into the Garden, and in 1927 a broad walk was made through it, the public right of way being bridged. Later birches and maples were planted among the conifers. A collection of old-fashioned roses and rose species was sited, in 1909, just beyond the little wood of Scots pine which G. F. Wilson had planted about 1898 and on the edge of Howard's Field, where in 1911 an orchard of apples for experimental purposes had been made, but which was later superseded by ornamental trees and shrubs.

In these ways, and in others, the Garden was gradually developing and becoming very popular with the Fellows. The staff was encouraged by the visits of committees to judge the trials and to see the scientific work, and especially by the visits of the President, who unfortunately was now in failing health. It had been doubtful whether or not Lord Lambourne would be able to be present at the International Exhibition of Garden Design. But he managed to be there, and to introduce Lord Crawford; and this was almost his last appearance among his colleagues on the Council, for he died on 26 December 1928. As his portrait, by W. G. M. Glehn, which hangs in the Council Room at Vincent Square excellently suggests, he had proved himself a genial, kindly President who had happily guided the Society along the road of continued prosperity. He, and his carnation buttonhole, had been popular with everyone. At any rate, it was a carnation until 1923; then his wife died and thereafter a sprig of myrtle took its place, cut from the plant in his garden raised from a sprig in Lady Lambourne's wedding bouquet. The wreath of carnations and myrtle which was the Council's floral tribute at his funeral was altogether appropriate.

In 1920 Mr. Gerald W. E. Loder had joined the Council. He was living at Wakehurst Place, near Ardingly, climatically a very favoured part of Sussex, where since 1903 he had been collecting, and growing with astonishing success, trees and shrubs, especially conifers and rhododendrons and New Zealand plants which he frequently brought to the Society's Shows. No doubt the success of his brother, Sir Edmund Loder, at Leonardslee, in growing and hybridizing rhododendrons had been a great incentive to him. In 1921 he had presented to the Society the Loder Rhododendron Cup to commemorate his brother's name. On the Council, his wide horticultural knowledge and business ability were greatly respected. As he was also a man of immense personal charm, and as in 1926–7 he had been president of the Royal Arboricultural Society, his colleagues on the Council persuaded him to succeed Lord Lambourne as the new President. (Plate 16.)

Loder was a scholar with a fine historical sense and sympathetic to the idea of a memorial to the late President. As the most important event during Lambourne's term of office had been the erection of the New Hall, a memorial bas-relief portrait of him by Reid Dick was placed on the centre of the inside wall of the dais of the hall, and this simple, impressive work of art was unveiled by Loder in 1930. Four years later, at his suggestion, tablets recording the names of past Presi-

327

dents, Treasurers and Secretaries were placed on the flanks of the memorial. Again, it was at his suggestion that, in 1930, Council commissioned Mr. Frank Hodges to make a portrait of John Wedgwood, who had convened the inaugural meeting of the Society in 1804, from a miniature lent for the purpose by Miss Allen, the founder's granddaughter. This portrait now hangs in the President's Room at Vincent Square. Loder was also the moving spirit behind three other similar matters. In 1931 a memorial to Sir Thomas Hanbury was unveiled, by Mr. Cecil Hanbury, Sir Thomas's son, in the hall of the Wisley Laboratory, recording the fact that through Sir Thomas's generosity the sixty acres which constituted the nucleus of the Gardens had been held in trust since 1903 for use for the encouragement and improvement of horticulture. Next, on the 128th anniversary of the Society's formation, an illuminated record was unveiled in the bookshop of Messrs. Hatchard at 187 Piccadilly, London, stating that 'in a house on this site the Royal Horticultural Society was founded on 7 March 1804', and a bronze commemorative plaque was placed on the front of the building, which faces Burlington House. The unveiler on this occasion was the Hon. Henry D. McLaren. Honolulu was the scene of the third memorial tablet. In 1929 the Council, having heard that a memorial to the Society's famous collector, David Douglas, outside the old Kawaiahao Church, was decaying, arranged for its re-erection within the Church, together with a bronze tablet recording, with a translation, the original Latin inscription.

Under the third Royal Charter, that of 1899, the Society was empowered, notwithstanding the Statutes of Mortmain, to hold lands not exceeding an annual value of £5,000. In view of the lease of the Elverton Street site it was now decided that an application should be made to the Crown for a new Charter authorizing the Society to hold property up to the annual value of £30,000. It was also decided to revise the Bye-Laws to provide that, in future, the office of Secretary should not be filled by election by the Fellows, but be occupied by a paid official appointed by the Council. It was also thought wise that the Bye-Laws should, in future, provide that members of Council automatically retiring after five years' service should not, as a rule, be eligible for re-election until the expiration of a year. The approval of the Fellows to these changes was obtained at the Annual General Meeting in 1928, an appropriate application was lodged, and the Society's fourth Royal Charter and amended Bye-Laws came into force on 9 July 1928.

When the site of the New Hall was acquired there was, among other proposals, one that in due course the Society should endeavour to obtain the adjoining property occupied by the Express Lift Company, construct new offices there, and then evacuate the Vincent Square premises. However, in 1929 all such schemes were abandoned. It was decided to increase the accommodation in the Vincent Square building by constructing a third floor over the offices, and by moving the Library on to it. As a result of these operations the present Council Chamber and the Secretary's Room are now practically the only parts of the office section remaining as they were in 1904, though the front elevation in Vincent Square has very much the same appearance in spite of the insertion of the additional floor. A few years later still more office accommodation was found to be necessary and it was obtained by constructing rooms over what was the musicians' gallery at the southern end of the exhibition hall. The Society received a grant of £1,250 from the Carnegie United Kingdom Trust towards the cost of refitting the Lindley Library in its new home.

In the autumn of 1929 Mr. William Cuthbertson, a member of Council and one of the three partners—Mr. W. Fife and Mr. Birnie were the others—who had formed the firm of Messrs. Dobbie & Co., suggested that means should be found whereby the Society might confer honour on persons who had rendered distinguished service to horticulture whilst employed in gardens, nurseries or seed establishments. The Council cordially approved the proposal, and at the Annual General Meeting in 1930 Bye-Laws were made empowering the Council to elect as Associates of Honour persons of British nationality who have rendered distinguished service to horticulture in the course of their employment, the number of such Associates not to exceed 100 at any time. The first thirty recipients of this much-appreciated honour were presented with their diplomas and badges at Chelsea Show in 1930. Subsequent presentations have been made at the Society's Annual General Meetings.

At this time one of Cuthbertson's colleagues on the Council was Mr. Thomas Hay, the Superintendent of the Central Parks, London, who had astonishingly departed from custom by lavishly planting thousands and thousands of meconopsis and primulas in the London parks and who had had Volume CLV (1929) of the *Botanical Magazine* dedicated to him. This honour had stimulated Hay to collect portraits of the eminent botanists and horticulturists to whom the *Botanical Magazine* had been dedicated during the last hundred years. It occurred to both Cuthbertson and Hay that the hundred portraits, accompanied with bibliographical notes, would form an interesting supplementary volume to the *Botanical Magazine*. Thus Cuthbertson decided to make himself responsible for the volume, which, with the assistance of Ernest Nelmes of Kew in the preparation of the bibliographies, he published in 1931, arranging that any profits which might accrue from sales should be placed to the credit of the *Botanical Magazine*.

The outstanding horticultural event in 1930 was the Ninth International Horticultural Congress, which was held by the Society's invitation in London on 8–15 August, rooms at the Caxton Hall being hired to supplement those available for meetings at the Society's halls. The Congress was attended by 668 people representing fifty-one countries, and on one evening the Society entertained 300 delegates and representatives at a banquet in the New Hall. Also in the New Hall an Exhibition unique among British flower shows was held; the leading nurserymen and seedsmen, instead of staging their own individual displays, combined their resources and staged co-operative groups of carnations, dahlias, gladioli, roses, sweet peas and herbaceous plants, stove and greenhouse plants, ornamental trees and shrubs, plants from seeds, and fruits, all of which allowed Mr. Edward White to design a balanced and an agreeably laid out Exhibition.

The Congress was important from the point of view of the nomenclature of cultivated plants. In 1927, at the Eighth International Horticultural Congress, an international Committee for Horticultural Nomenclature had been set up with A. B. Rendle, Keeper of Botany, British Museum (Natural History), as chairman, and F. J. Chittenden, the Director of the Society's Gardens, as secretary. Both had helped to prepare, as had E. A. Bowles, on behalf of the Society, a long memorandum on horticultural nomenclature, which had been included in a report on the subject submitted to the International Congress of Brussels in 1910. The immediate task of this committee had been to supplement the *International Rules of Botanical Nomenclature* with rules for the naming of garden plants. At this Ninth International Horticultural Congress the Committee drew up a new set of rules which were presented as resolutions to the Congress and were duly passed. A month later, at the Fifth International Botanical Congress in Cambridge, Rendle called attention to the work of the London Horticultural Congress committee, pointing out that its rules contained nothing contrary to the *International Rules of Botanical Nomenclature*, and proposed that they should be added to the third edition of the 'Botanical Rules' as an Appendix. Rendle's proposition was accepted and, as Appendix VII—*Nomenclature of Garden Plants*, by A. B. Rendle—rules for naming garden plants appeared in the 1935 edition of the *Rules for Botanical Nomenclature*. The nomenclature of cultivated plants was now the joint concern of both horticulturists and botanists, and the intimate connection between the Society and horticultural nomenclature holds to this day.

In his opening speech to the 1930 Congress, Mr. Loder referred to the Society's work on Pritzel's *Index Iconum Botanicarum*, a guide to figures and pictures of plants which had been published in 1855, with a supplement in 1866. The Society had realized the necessity of bringing Pritzel's *Index* up to date and had undertaken the publication of a new work, with the active co-operation of the Director of Kew, and under the editorship of Dr. Otto Stapf, who in 1922 had retired from the keeper-ship of the Kew Herbarium and Library. The work was published under the new title of *Iconum Botanicarum Index Londinensis*; by the end of 1930 the first four volumes had been issued and two others were to follow during 1931. Ten years later two supplementary volumes were pub-lished, and another is in active preparation.

Loder, owing to pressure of other work, found it necessary to resign from the President's chair at the Annual General Meeting in 1931, though he remained on the Council. He was, and always had been, a very busy man, leading an active political life (he had represented Brighton in Parliament from 1890 to 1906) and an active business life with the Southern Railway, becoming joint deputy chairman of the new combination of Southern lines in 1923, and chairman in 1932. In 1934, for his good works in many spheres, he was raised to the peerage, but died, as Lord Wakehurst, two years later at the age of seventy-one. His term as President had been a brief one—but one of great distinction.

CHAPTER NINETEEN

PROGRESS MAINTAINED

SINCE THE INSTITUTION OF THE VICTORIA MEDAL OF HONOUR IN 1897, when Miss Gertrude Jekyll and Miss Ellen Willmott had been awarded it, and since the time when the number of recipients who could hold the award had been increased to sixty-three, in 1901, when Miss Eleanor Ormerod had been honoured, no other lady received the award until 1931; then Lady Aberconway was honoured for her great interest in the advancement of horticulture and in the cultivation of new and rare plants in the garden she had done much to make at Bodnant in North Wales. Originally the grounds at Bodnant had been laid out by Lady Aberconway's father, Mr. Henry Pochin, in 1875 and succeeding years, sometimes with the assistance of a landscape gardener. After her father's death in 1895 Lady Aberconway devoted special attention to increasing the collection of flowering plants, especially shrubs, made splendid herbaceous borders and planted countless bulbs. Quick to recognize great gardening talent in her son, the Hon. H. D. McLaren, she entrusted the care of the large garden to him in around 1903, and from this time onwards their joint exhibits of rare and choice plants were frequently to be seen at Vincent Square.

McLaren (Plate 17) had been elected to the Council in 1923. In accordance with the provisions of the Bye-Laws he had vacated his seat in 1928, but was re-elected in 1929. Two years later, on the resignation of Loder, he was appointed President, and it would have been a unique occasion in the history of the Society had the President been able to present the V.M.H. to his mother at the Annual General Meeting in 1932. Unfortunately Lady Aberconway was unable to be present, but the President spoke for her and for himself:

Lady Aberconway desires me to say that she appreciates most deeply this honour which the Society has conferred upon her. I can only say that it would have been a very great personal pleasure to me to have handed to her, on behalf of the Society, this recognition of her work, because it is from her and from her garden that I have learned all that I know of gardening.

In 1934 he himself was to receive the same award.

Like his predecessor, the new President was a politician. He had entered the House of Commons in 1906 as the Liberal Member for West Staffordshire and had been Parliamentary Private Secretary to the Chancellor of the Exchequer from 1908 until 1910. From 1910, in succession to his father, until 1922, he had represented the Bosworth division of Leicestershire, and in 1918 had been made C.B.E. in recognition of his work in connection with the Ministry of Munitions. Like his predecessor, he also took an active part in industry, becoming chairman of the great shipbuilding firm of John Brown & Company, which was to build the *Queen Mary*, *Queen Elizabeth*, and *Queen Elizabeth II*, and of Thomas Firth and John Brown Limited. To the Council table of the Society he brought the same tremendous energy, initiative and determination which he showed in business, and many of the far-reaching changes in the affairs of the Society which were to be made during his presidency were the direct result of his powerful advocacy and influence. And to the Council table he brought his great love and knowledge of plants. For thirty years he had been developing his garden at Bodnant, planting it extensively with rhododendrons, magnolias, camellias, primulas, gentians, meconopsis, and collecting under glass hippeastrums, clivias, streptocarpus, cypripediums, so that it was now one of the finest in the world. He was one of the first to recognize the significance of the new material introduced from the expeditions of Wilson, Farrer, Forrest, Ward, and others, and constantly encouraged the Society to support such expeditions, always with the object of making Wisley, as he would so often say, 'the finest Garden in the world'.

The staffing at Wisley, and at Vincent Square, was one of the first matters to engage his attention. At the end of 1930 the Council had considered the report of a committee which had been deliberating for twelve months on the remodelling of the School of Horticulture and the work of the Laboratory. At the same time the Council was assessing the staff complement at Vincent Square in relation to the increased work. As a result of long deliberations it was decided to create a new post at Vincent Square, that of technical adviser and keeper of the Library, with duties to include the editing of the *Journal* and the supervision of the Society's other publications. Chittenden had undertaken to edit the *Journal* in 1908—and was still doing so. He was a scientist with an international reputation, having published papers on mosses and fungi in scientific journals, and papers on plant diseases, pollination in orchards, and many other technical subjects, in the Society's *Journal* and elsewhere; the first edition of *Some Good Garden Plants* (1929) was also his work. Moreover, he had represented the Society at international botanical and horticultural congresses in New York, Berlin, Vienna, and Cambridge. Understandably therefore the new post at Vincent Square

333

was offered to him. He accepted it, thus vacating the directorship of the Gardens which he had filled with such distinction since 1919. He took up his Vincent Square duties in 1931 and in October of this year Mr. R. L. Harrow, who was retiring from his post of Curator of the Royal Botanic Garden, Edinburgh, succeeded Chittenden as Director at Wisley.

Harrow was an Englishman who had made his horticultural reputation in Scotland. He had been trained by Lynch in Cambridge, had moved to Kew, and in 1891 to Edinburgh, where he was to remain for forty years. In Edinburgh he had the marvellous opportunity of growing the enormously rich collections, many of them new species, sent home by Forrest, Ward, and others, and was able to demonstrate his skill as a cultivator of rare and difficult plants. The newly introduced material had transformed the character of the Edinburgh Garden—and many other gardens—and Harrow and his chiefs, first Professor Bayley Balfour and later Professor Wright Smith, had been responsible for extensive alterations and improvements.

In 1935 Harrow was given the assistance of Mr. B. O. Mulligan, an ex-Wisley horticultural student. Mulligan acted as assistant to the Director from 1935 to 1941, then again for a short time in 1946, before leaving for Seattle, where, for some years, he has been director of the Arboretum of the University of Washington.

Apart from the change in the directorship, the Wisley staff was enlarged by the addition of a number of journeymen. Moreover, the decision, made as long ago as 1924, gradually to introduce a new type of paid student-gardener, was now implemented; student-gardeners would now work under arrangements similar to those in operation at the Botanic Gardens at Kew and Edinburgh, the whole of the day being devoted to work in the garden, with certain evenings given to lectures and laboratory work. Moreover, in order to provide more student accommodation, 'The Lilacs', one of the houses in Wisley village, acquired with Deers Farm, was converted into a hostel.

Horticulturally, the first important event under the régime of the new President was the holding of a Conifer Conference and Exhibition in November 1931—and a most remarkable event it was. It was the first conference of its kind to have been held since 1891, and Colonel F. R. S. Balfour, the fine gardener and arboriculturist of Dawyck, Peeblesshire, was responsible for the suggestion that, because so much new coniferous material had been introduced during the last forty years, the time was opportune for a second conference. Thus, with the principal objects of collecting experiences on the growing of the new Chinese, Burmese, and Tibetan conifers, of revising nomenclature, and of collecting statistics on the growth of conifers in the British Isles and of comparing these statistics with those of forty years ago, a series of papers was read and a vast collection of growing trees and cone-bearing branches was exhibited. Especially noteworthy were the exhibits of Lord Headfort of Kells, Ireland, Mr. Gerald Loder of Wakehurst Place, Sussex, Lieut.-Col. L. C. R. Messel of Nymans, Sussex, and the Director of Kew. On behalf of the conference, Colonel Balfour, Mr. Murray Hornibrook, and Mr. W. Dallimore of Kew worked immensely hard and all three contributed important papers. (And in his opening address to the conference, the President, inadvertently it would seem, coined the word 'hortanical'.) The report of the Conference was published in 1932 under the title *Conifers in Cultivation*, and is one of the finest of the Society's many fine publications.

The early years of the twentieth century had seen a revival of interest in the genus *Lilium*, an interest sparked off in 1905 by the recent introduction of *Lilium regale* from China, and by the knowledge of the ease with which this lovely species could be flowered from seeds. Inspired by that great lily enthusiast Arthur Grove, who at this time was deeply involved in the production of the Supplement to Elwes's famous *Monograph* of 1880 on the genus, Major F. C. Stern (later Sir Frederick) took up the cultivation of these beautiful plants. In 1931, at his suggestion, the Council established the Lily Committee, which advocated the formation of a Lily Group to encourage the cultivation of lilies and of the allied plants, *Fritillaria* and *Nomocharis*. Two of the first results of this activity were the publication in 1932 of the first issue of the *Lily Year Book* and the holding, the following year, of a highly successful Lily Conference.

How successful the conference was can be judged from the letter which Miss E. Willmott wrote to the *Gardener's Chronicle*, describing the reactions of a distinguished visitor.

Although the Lily Conference itself has passed, the recollection of Major Stern's enthusiastic initiative, and the admirable organisation, crowned by the glorious display in the hall, will never be effaced from the memories of those who had the good fortune to be present. The tributes from far and wide must be very gratifying to those who worked so hard to make the Conference and Show successful. In a letter from the Abbé Souillet, he writes full of appreciation, not only of the kind welcome he received, but of the courtesy of one and all towards him and the generous hospitality he met with on every side. His one regret is that he was unable to express his thanks in English. He cannot understand how England could ever have been called *perfide Albion*, as he found it the reverse. He was amazed by the magnificent display of lilies in the hall, the beauty of the blossoms and the superb cultivation of the plants. The assiduity with which the lectures were attended every day and by such a large number of persons, surprised him. Were it not that the Lily week had made such an indelible impression he would have thought it the 'dream of a Terrestrial Paradise'.[1]

The last conference on lilies had been held in 1901 in the great Vinery at Chiswick, and in the report of the conference published in the Society's *Journal* particular mention was made of the collection of lilies staged by Messrs. Wallace, then of Colchester; 'probably more species and varieties were represented than have ever, anywhere or at any time before, been brought together.'[2] The same words could with truth have been spoken at this 1933 conference.

Since the time of its formation the Lily Group has served a splendid function. Its membership is open to all Fellows and Associates, without additional subscriptions, and it has enabled lovers of lilies and allied plants to secure all the advantages which might accrue from the formation of a separate society without any corresponding disadvantages. Its lead was soon to be followed by those interested in fruit and in rhododendrons.

For some years the numerical strength of the Society had been showing a steady annual increase. However, in 1931, a decline in the prosperity of the country as a whole was reflected in the Society; the total numerical strength fell from 28,026 to 27,612, and there was a corresponding fall in the number of visitors attending the fortnightly Meetings. The downward trend continued in 1932, when the membership fell by a further 693. However, by the end of 1933 prosperity had begun to return, the total membership rose again to 28,397 and thereafter there was a steady increase until the outbreak of the Second World War.

Though the depression lasted only for two years, it disturbed the Council for all that. At the first sign of the set-back in 1931, a committee was appointed to advise as to how the intake of new Fellows and the attendances at the fortnightly Meetings could be increased. Various recommendations were made—and some were put into practice. For example, arrangements were made with some of the leading nurserymen and seedsmen to enclose fellowship proposal forms with their catalogues, and for a time this method of bringing the Society and its work to the notice of non-Fellows had some, though never a marked, effect. Again, on the assumption that neither the Society nor its fortnightly Shows were known to a vast number of people working in London but living in the country and that many such people would join the Society if they knew of its existence, complimentary tickets giving admission to the Shows were freely made available to the staffs of some of the large business houses in London; the Shows remained open until 9 p.m. and the

---

[1] *Gdnr's Chron.*, vol. 94 (1933), p. 92.
[2] *Jl R. hort. Soc.*, XXVI (1901), p. 332.

charge for admission after office hours was reduced to a shilling. However, few cheap tickets were issued and many of the free ones were not used. Moreover, the extension of the hours of opening was most unpopular with exhibitors as well as their staffs. By far the most effective measure was the abolition of the entrance fee which a prospective new Fellow, who wished to subscribe one guinea a year, had been required to pay; immediately there was a greatly increased intake of new Fellows.

At the Annual General Meeting in 1932, Mr. R. D. Trotter, who had acted as Treasurer since 1929, now had to give up these duties, as he was not this year a member of the Council. Mr. C. T. Musgrave stepped into the breach for a year, for the third—and last—time. He was then approaching seventy years of age, having been, as he still was, a wonderful and tireless supporter of the Society, as Treasurer, Councillor, chairman of Floral Committee B, chairman of the committee for the building of the New Hall, vice-chairman of the Wisley Committee. At his home at Hascombe, Godalming, he grew a fine collection of trees and shrubs and alpine plants and was interested particularly in gentians. Undoubtedly his most important horticultural achievement was the raising of his hybrid *Gentiana* x *hascombensis*, which won for him the Cory Cup. And undoubtedly that which pleased him most was the dedication to him of the volume of the *Botanical Magazine* for 1936: 'A prudent and valued Treasurer of the Society, eminent as a cultivator of rare and beautiful plants in two renowned gardens at Hascombe, both of them created by him and instinct with his spirit, a friend as generous of his knowledge of plants as of his experience of the law.' Until the day he died, 30 January 1949, at the age of eighty-six, he was to remain intensely interested in the diverse affairs of the Society. In 1933 Mr. Trotter was again returned to the Council, and to the treasurership, and so continued until 1938, then to be succeeded by Mr. George Monro. Like Musgrave, Trotter was to have still one other term as Treasurer, making three in all.

In 1933 the Government was anxious to encourage the home-production of early vegetables, flowers and fruits, and, at the suggestion of Mr. F. A. Secrett who had recently joined the Society's Fruit and Vegetable Committee, the Society held the first of a series of seven annual Early Market Produce Shows, which did much to increase the production and attractive presentation of early vegetables by market gardeners. Mr. Secrett's exhibit of vegetables and flowers in market packages at this Show in 1934 was judged to be the finest exhibit shown to the Society in that year and consequently gained him the Lawrence Medal. He was to have a close association with the Society lasting for nearly forty years. Joining the Narcissus and Tulip Committee in 1927, he was its chairman from 1959 to 1962. In this capacity he succeeded Mr. G. W. Leak, who had been a member of the committee since 1906, and, after serving as a vice-chairman for many years, eventually became chairman in 1955. When Secrett was elected to the Council in 1939, Leak had been serving there since 1925. And together they served on the Council until 1960, when Leak retired at the age of ninety-two, having been awarded a gold Veitch Memorial Medal the year before and having been a Vice-President since 1957. Leak died in 1963, the year in which Secrett was appointed a Vice-President and awarded a gold Veitch Memorial Medal. Both were also members of the Shows Committee and of the Wisley Advisory Committee. And both loved to visit Wisley, the former blissfully happy examining the daffodils, tulips, gladioli, paeonies, roses, sweet peas, delphiniums and other hardy herbaceous plants, the latter more at home in the vegetable trials. For duration and importance their records of participation in the Society's affairs have seldom been equalled.

One very cold day in the autumn of 1954 Leak and Secrett, with other members of the Wisley Advisory Committee, were at the Garden. Leak, aged eighty-six, was wearing a raincoat of the lightest weight. One of his colleagues on the committee said, 'Look at that old man! He must be cold; he should be wearing a heavy coat.' The colleague in question was Mr. Frank Jordan, at that time eighty-nine years old—and he was not even wearing a lightweight raincoat. He was another wonderful servant of the Society; a great judge of greenhouse and hardy fruits, who as a young man in various employments in Britain had harvested 300 pine-apples a year, had raised bananas of excellent quality and forced 10,000 strawberry plants in pots—before the days of 'Royal Sovereign'; he had also been one of the Society's examiners for many years and a member of the Society's Fruit and Vegetable Committee for over forty years—in fact, until shortly before he died in 1958, aged ninety-three.

Although from time to time the Council had sent deputations to important Continental shows, it was not until 1933 that the Society exhibited abroad. In that year, as the Royal Agricultural and Botanical Society of Ghent was celebrating its 125th anniversary, a co-operative British exhibit, under the auspices of the Society, was staged at the Ghent Floralies. Towards this exhibit the Society, the Royal Botanic Gardens at Kew and Edinburgh, the President, the Marquis of Head-fort, Sir William Lawrence, Mr. T. Hay, Mr. G. W. E. Loder, Mr. J. B. Stevenson, and several nurseries all contributed. The exhibit was not a spectacular one, but it consisted in the main of new and rare plants—new primulas, lilies, meconopsis, many new trees and shrubs, which had been introduced during the past thirty years by British plant collectors, and as such it attracted the attention of Continental horticulturists. Not for over twenty years did the Society stage another exhibit on the Continent.

The Society's Spring Show at Chelsea raised no accommodation problems. Not so the Autumn Show. Although the opening of the New Hall in 1928 had more than doubled the exhibition space, it was still felt that the two halls together did not afford sufficient room for an Autumn Show corresponding with the Spring Show. However, it was not until 1933 that the Council was able to hire a sufficiently large building, and in September of this year a Great Autumn Show was held at the National Hall, Olympia. In 1934 Olympia was not available and the corresponding Show was held at the Crystal Palace, returning to Olympia in 1935 and 1937. As no suitable building was available in 1936 and in 1938, exhibitors had to be content with the Society's halls.

In conjunction with the 1934 Autumn Show, a conference on apples and pears was held which did much to highlight the value of the work being done in the commercial fruit trials at Wisley, and especially the work on the testing of new varieties. Mr. A. N. Rawes, in charge of the trials, recounted that since 1922 more than 100 varieties of apple and pear had been planted for trial; that certain of them, after a suitable period of testing, had been discarded as not being up to standard; that others had not yet reached the stage when a true judgement could be made of their value. So far only seven apples had shown sufficient promise to justify planting at substations for further trial and Mr. Rawes believed that one or two of these would prove superior to some of the older varieties. He mentioned particularly 'Laxton's Superb', 'Laxton's Epicure', and 'Lord Lambourne' apples, and 'Laxton's Superb' and 'Beurré Bedford' pears—all products of the Laxton Brothers of Bedford.

There were further conferences during the next few years: one on daffodils and one on cherries and soft fruits in 1935; another, in co-operation with the Alpine Garden Society, on alpine plants, in 1936; and a three-day conference on ornamental flowering trees and shrubs in 1938. In view of the many flowering trees and shrubs which had been introduced in living memory from China, the Andes, Tasmania, and elsewhere, such a conference was almost inevitable and very desirable, if only to gather together those who had pioneered the growing of the new introductions, for an exchange of views. One important paper was given by one of the younger generation of horticulturists, Mr. F. P. Knight, who had been fortunate enough to gain experience in the propagation of much of this new material, and who in less than twenty years' time was to be Director of the Society's Gardens. And another, on magnolias and camellias, was given by the President himself, who forecast that the return of the camellia to almost universal popularity was soon to come; popularity not as a greenhouse and conservatory plant, but as a hardy outdoor plant. His prophecy was to be fulfilled and to him, as much as to anyone, is due the present-day vogue for these plants. Forrest had introduced several camellias, and one of them, *C. saluenensis*, had been growing magnificently in the garden of Mr. J. C. Williams at Caerhays Castle in Cornwall. Mr. Williams crossed a pale form of this species with pollen of *C. japonica* which he had grown from seeds obtained from Japan shortly after the turn of the century. As a result of the cross, many seedlings were raised; many Mr. Williams retained at Caerhays, and one of them was given the First Class Certificate in 1942; and many he distributed to his gardening friends—including the President, who by this time was Lord Aberconway. The President was most enthusiastic, justifiably describing the hybrid as 'one of the best shrubs that has ever been introduced to our gardens', and moreover persuading the Society's Professor of Botany, Sir William Wright Smith, Regius Keeper of the Royal Botanic Garden, Edinburgh, to describe the hybrid under the name of *Camellia* x *williamsii*. The First Class Certificate form is now known, of course, as 'J. C. Williams', and there are many more named clones. Undoubtedly Mr. Williams's foresight in originally making the cross and Lord Aberconway's enterprise in publicizing the virtues of the cross were the main impulses behind the tremendous revival in interest in these plants.

In 1937 Lord Aberconway, who was a very keen competitor, had won a Gold Medal at Chelsea Flower Show for his exhibit of primulas and hybrid rhododendrons made at Bodnant. Disappointingly for him, he had not won the premier amateur award at the Show; this, the Cain Challenge Cup, had been won by his great competitor, Mr. Lionel de Rothschild of Exbury, for his exhibit of azalea hybrids. Incidentally, an exhibit of carnations and pinks had gained the Sherwood Challenge Cup which was offered for the most meritorious exhibit in the Show. The exhibitors, of course, were Messrs. Allwood Bros., who, at the 1920 Chelsea Show, had introduced *Dianthus* x *allwoodii*, the hybrid between the carnation and the pink. The Allwood exhibits have always been appreciated by royal visitors to Chelsea.

The Chelsea Show of 1937 was very much of a celebration of the Coronation of Their Majesties the King and Queen, patrons of the Society, with the staging of a remarkable Empire Exhibit, under the general supervision of Mr. J. Coutts, the Curator of Kew. For the first time anywhere in the world, under one roof, albeit a canvas one, one was able to see plants from the arctic as well as from the tropics, with others from temperate climates; plants from India, Ceylon, Canada, New Zealand, Australia, South West and East Africa, Palestine, the West Indies, Fiji, the Seychelles, the Falkland Islands, Newfoundland, and many more from colonial dependencies and mandated territories. The Exhibit covered an area of 1,800 square feet, and was designed to give some indication of the contribution the various parts of the Empire

Henry, Lord Aberconway (1931–1953)   Lord Aberconway (1961–   )

Plate 17. PRESIDENTS OF THE SOCIETY

The entrance to the Garden, with the wrought-iron
gates erected in memory of the Rev. W. Wilks

The alpine meadow in spring. *Narcissus bulbocodium*
in flower

Plate 18. WISLEY

have made to our gardens; it may not have been as colourful, and thus as attractive, to the general public as the Bodnant rhododendrons, the Exbury azaleas, the Allwood carnations, or many other exhibits, but it was of very great educational value and did much to justify the comment in the *Gardener's Chronicle* that this particular Chelsea Show undoubtedly 'is the finest of the series of Chelsea Shows, and far exceeds the International Show of 1912 in its extent, variety, elegance and colouring'.[1]

The outbreak of war on 3 September 1939 had a far-reaching effect on the Society in a variety of ways. The Great Autumn Show which was to have been held at Earl's Court in September was cancelled. A Show was held in the halls in October, but lighting restrictions prevented the holding of any more Shows during the remainder of that year. During the greater part of the war, Shows were held at monthly intervals except during January, August, November, and December, but Chelsea Show was discontinued until 1947. Throughout the war the Society encouraged Fellows to give the nursery trade such support as was possible in order that nurserymen would find it worth while to continue to maintain a nucleus of any rare plants which might otherwise be lost to cultivation.

In order to assist in a campaign to supplement the supply of imported food by increasing the production of vegetables in gardens and on allotments, the Society organized a panel of advisers and lecturers throughout the country. In this connection the Society began to build a library of lantern slides illustrating cultural operations for loan to lecturers and horticultural societies, and a model allotment was laid out at Wisley. This work also enabled the Society to assist the Ministry of Information in the production of a film on the subject. Demonstrations of cultural operations were also given at Wisley. Photographs taken at Wisley primarily for the lantern-slide library were also used to illustrate in great detail a publication entitled *The Vegetable Garden Displayed*, which was reprinted again and again and became the most widely sold book which the Society has ever produced.

At Wisley the staff of male employees and student-gardeners of military age was greatly depleted, the latter being replaced by inexperienced young men. Despite this, however, the Gardens continued to be generally well maintained, and extensive trials of vegetables were carried out to assist the Government in the selection of the most desirable of the restricted stocks of vegetable seeds available for importation. Up to 1942 a list of plants and seeds available for distribution to Fellows was published each year, but in 1943 it was quite impossible to distribute plants, and from that time onwards the annual distribution has been confined to seeds.

[1] *Gdnr's Chron.*, vol. 101 (1937), p. 366.

In view of the risk of damage from enemy action, many of the most valuable books in the Lindley Library were transferred for the duration of the war to Aberystwyth and Wisley. The Society's *Journal* continued to be issued almost as regularly as usual. Until 1939 it had been edited by Chittenden. Then, when he began work on the Society's new *Dictionary of Gardening*, responsibility for the *Journal* was given to Sir Daniel Hall, assisted by Mr. R. E. Hay. When Sir Daniel died, in 1942, Mrs. Vera Higgins, who had replaced Mr. Hay as assistant in 1941, took over the editorship and valiantly carried on until the end of 1945, when she retired and was replaced by Mr. P. M. Synge, the present editor. And in spite of the war, Sir Daniel's monograph of *The Genus Tulipa*, which at the beginning of 1940 was well advanced, was published the same year, a quarto volume with forty plates in colour, still the standard work on the genus and a remarkable publication for the times.

As the Government found it necessary to economize in the use of fuel for heating glass-houses for anything but food crops, and as at the same time it was desirable in the national interest to preserve exceptionally valuable ornamental plants, at the request of the Ministry of Fuel and Power, and with the approval of the Ministry of Agriculture, the Society appointed a Fuel Advisory Committee to issue certificates in respect of collections of glass-house plants deemed to be worth preserving.

Among the Society's other wartime activities were the organization of sales of gardening books, bulbs, plants, seeds and horticultural sundries in aid of the Red Cross, and the dispatch of vegetable and flower seeds, donated by the trade, to British personnel in German camps for prisoners of war.

As might be expected, the large number of persons who joined the armed forces, or were engaged in making munitions or in other work of national importance, reduced the number who were able to avail themselves of the privileges which the Society could continue to offer. At the end of 1938 the total numerical strength of the Society stood at the then record figure of 36,577, the average net increase per annum during the preceding five years having been 1,636. In 1940, the first full year of the war, there was a net loss by resignation and death of no fewer than 7,187, and while during the last three years of the war the intake of new subscribers exceeded the continuing loss by resignation and death, at the end of 1945 the total numerical strength stood at 27,629. The total set-back due to the war was 8,948. As so many Fellows during these difficult years were unable to receive any personal benefit from their membership apart from the monthly *Journal*, the loyalty with which they continued to subscribe to, and support, the Society was quite remarkable.

The times were especially difficult for the Treasurers. Mr. R. D.

Trotter had served from 1933 to 1938 and then was succeeded by Mr. George Monro, who held the post until 1943. Mr. Monro was head of the well-known firm of Messrs. George Monro Ltd., of Covent Garden and Waltham Cross, Hertfordshire, the firm which his father of the same name had founded, and had a vast knowledge of the wholesale handling of fruits, flowers, and vegetables. He had been almost continuously on the Council since 1924 and had been chairman of the Joint Dianthus Committee, the Joint Perpetual-Flowering Carnation Committee, and the Joint Dahlia Committee, as well as vice-chairman of the Narcissus and Tulip Committee. In 1921 he and his two brothers had presented to the Society a cup in memory of their father, the George Monro Memorial Cup, which up to 1938 had been awarded for the best exhibit of grapes shown by an amateur at the Fruit and Vegetable Show. From 1939 to 1949 the cup was not offered. Now it is awarded for the best exhibit of vegetables shown by an amateur during the year, and since 1953 has been in the almost continuous possession of Col. E. J. S. Ward.

In 1943 Mr. Trotter entered his third period in the office of Treasurer and guided the Society on sound financial lines during five critical years before and after the end of the Second World War. Mr. Trotter had succeeded to the family estate at The Bush on the outskirts of Edinburgh in 1932. He was an enthusiastic plantsman, landscape gardener, and forester, and at The Bush had developed a delectable heather and pine garden. In 1946 he sold the estate to the University of Edinburgh and now it is administered as the Edinburgh Centre of Rural Economy, the woodlands and plantations and the garden being utilized by the University students in forestry and horticulture. All this apart, Mr. Trotter made one unique contribution to horticulture. For years, in his garden in Inverness-shire, he cultivated with astonishing success, and with the ease with which others grow lettuces, *Meconopsis delavayi*, introduced by George Forrest in 1913. Everyone who has attempted to cultivate the plant has found it most obdurate, except Mr. Trotter, who, over the years, distributed many ounces of seeds in the hope that someone, somewhere, might stumble on the happy knack of growing the plant as he did. So far no one has. Mr. Trotter died in 1968, aged eighty.

Interlude
to Parts Six and Seven

In 1930 E. H. WILSON, WHO FOR THE PAST THREE YEARS HAD BEEN keeper of the Arnold Arboretum, and Mrs. Wilson, were killed in a motor accident in Massachusetts. 'Chinese' Wilson, as he was known in the States, had enriched gardens in Britain and the States with many splendid plants about which he wrote, sometimes scientifically, as in *The Lilies of Eastern Asia* (1925), and, in association with Alfred Rehder, in *The Monograph of Azaleas* (1921); and sometimes popularly, as in *Aristocrats of the Garden* (1926). He had received the V.M.H. in 1912.

George Forrest, who for his services to horticulture had been awarded the V.M.H. in 1921, died in 1932 in western China when he had all but completed his seventh, and which was to have been his last, plant-hunting expedition. 'If all goes well,' he had written shortly before his death, 'I shall have made a rather glorious and satisfactory finish to all my past years of labour.' It was indeed a glorious and satisfactory finish, as the same letter testified:

Of seed, such an abundance, that I scarce know where to commence, nearly everything I wished for and that means a lot. Primulas in profusion, seed of some of them as much as 3–5 lbs., same with Meconopsis, Nomocharis, Lilium, as well as bulbs of the latter. When all are dealt with and packed I expect to have nearly, if not more than two mule-loads of good clean seed, representing some 4–500 species, and a mule-load means 130–150 lbs. That is something like 300 lbs. of seed. . . .

For a short time after Forrest's death Lord Aberconway (then the Hon. H. D. McLaren) employed the collectors Forrest had so wonderfully trained to collect material on his own behalf, and of course on behalf of all his gardening friends and thus horticulture in general.

Since 1923 Joseph Rock had been assiduously covering the ground on which Wilson, Farrer, and Forrest had collected. Always on the look-out for particularly good forms of plants, he collected and introduced many such from south-east Tibet in 1923–4, Kansu in 1925–6, and from north-west Yunnan in 1929–33. Most of his expeditions were undertaken on behalf of the National Geographical Society of Washington, although he was also partly sponsored by a syndicate of gardeners in Britain, as well as on the Pacific coast of America. By 1934 he considered himself too old for plant exploration (he was by that time fifty), and though he returned to China again in 1934 it was to continue his studies of the Na-Khi peoples begun two years before.

During these years Kingdon Ward was introducing new, as well as previously tried, plants from the Sino-Himalayan region: from Tibet and Bhutan in 1924–5; from Burma and Assam in 1926–8 and in 1933; from north-east Upper Burma and the Tibetan frontier in 1931; from Tibet, Assam, Burma in 1935–9. His collecting activities were to be partly interrupted by the war of 1939, but in 1946 he was back in Assam again and for the next four years collected there and on the frontier of Tibet. His last expedition was to Upper Burma in 1953. Unlike Forrest and Rock, Kingdon Ward was a prolific writer about his journeys and the plants he saw and collected. And he wrote with a style which vividly conveyed the excitement and wonder of the great forests, meadows, and high mountains which he loved and in which he had spent his life.

Rhododendrons in the wild, lashed by the mountain gales, caressed by the sun and stung by the driven rain, in winter buried under 10 or 20 feet of snow, are unforgettable. Man can assemble in close embrace a far greater range of rhododendrons than nature ever knew; but never can he reproduce the drama of living plants on the high and lonely passes of Sino-Himalaya.

This was one of his last written statements, in Mrs. Urquhart's book *The Rhododendron* (1958). His fine services to horticulture and gardening were recognized when he was awarded the V.M.H. in 1932 and when he was installed as an Honorary Freeman of the Worshipful Company of Gardeners in 1957.

The years of the war likewise interrupted the magnificent work in the field of plant exploration and plant introduction—mostly in Bhutan and south-east Tibet, and in Kashmir, of Maj. George Sherriff and Mr. Frank Ludlow. From 1933 until 1938, in the latter year accompanied by Dr. George (now Sir George) Taylor in south-east Tibet, they introduced many splendid plants which had been in cultivation previously, but which had long since been lost, many others which were still in our gardens though sparingly, and others which had never been in culture and were, in fact, unknown to science—rhododendrons, primulas, gentians, meconopsis, lilies, and many subjects suitable for the rock garden. Once the war was over Ludlow and Sherriff returned again to their labours for four more years, and in 1949 brought their most fruitful years of collecting to a climax by sending to Britain by air a large collection of living plants. Individual plants had been introduced in this way previously, but never before nor since has so much living material been flown home. This is not surprising, for the expenses of air transport are heavy. The Ludlow and Sherriff plants were collected in Bhutan, personally transported to Calcutta, placed on the plane, and received by Taylor at London airport. The air-lift operation was abundantly worth while, for a number of plants became successfully established in cultivation which otherwise would have remained unknown to gardens. Since Ludlow and Sherriff ended their collecting careers their impressive contributions to horticulture have become more apparent with the approaching maturity of many trees and shrubs—especially rhododendrons. For their great services to horticulture the R.H.S. made Mr. Ludlow an Honorary Fellow and awarded Maj. Sherriff the V.M.H.

After the war, most of the Sino-Himalayan region became closed to European travellers, who perforce had to concentrate on Nepal, which became the scene of several plant-collecting expeditions: the expeditions of Polunin in 1949; of Lowndes in 1950; of Polunin, Sykes, and Williams in 1952; of Stainton, Sykes, and Williams in 1954; of Stainton in 1956. The 1952 and 1954 expeditions were sponsored jointly by the R.H.S. and the British Museum, and Sykes, in 1952, had just completed his two-year course as a horticultural student at Wisley. From all these expeditions new plants, as well as new forms of other plants previously introduced, were brought into cultivation.

However, in prewar and postwar years by no means all the new plant introductions were to come from western China and the Himalayas. The southern hemisphere was not ignored, for H. F. Comber took part in two expeditions there. Comber had been reared in the fine garden of Nymans, in large measure the handiwork of Lieut.-Col. L. C. R. Messel, where his father J. Comber was head gardener and had been since 1894, after having served in several establishments, including that of James Veitch & Son, where he had acquired a knowledge of the rare plants for which this firm was famous. At Nymans J. Comber carried through many improvements, planted a pinetum, a rock garden, and a heather garden as well as many rare trees and shrubs. At Nymans, too, he hybridized, and, as was usual at this period, worked particularly with rhododendrons. *Eucryphia* x *nymansay*, the hybrid for which the garden is especially renowned, is not of his making, however. This was a chance hybrid between the two Chilean species, *Eucryphia cordifolia* and *E. glutinosa*. The R.H.S. recognized Comber's services to horticulture by making him an Associate of Honour in 1930 and by awarding him the V.M.H. in 1936.

Harold Comber was already familiar with the plants from the Andes and Tasmania growing at Nymans before he visited these parts of the world. From 1925–7, financed by a syndicate in which the Hon. H. D. McLaren was prominent, he explored the Andes of Chile and the

346

Argentine and collected seeds of plants from the higher altitudes, thereby hoping to introduce hardier forms of some plants which had proved to be somewhat tender in cultivation except in the most favoured and sheltered gardens. Then from 1929–30 Comber collected in Tasmania on behalf of another syndicate, which this time was formed by Mr. Lionel de Rothschild. From these expeditions, Nymans, and many other gardens, were enriched by embothriums, eucryphias, nothofagus, and much else.

Dr. Balfour Gourlay also visited Chile and the Andes, first with Mr. Clarence Elliott and then with Mr. E. K. Balls—and once again new plant material for cultivation resulted. Mr. E. K. Balls also travelled in the Near East, as also did Dr. P. H. Davis. The latter has, in fact, spent some twenty years botanizing from Greece to Persia, during which time he has collected nearly 50,000 beautiful herbarium specimens as well as ample seeds of plants chiefly of interest to rock-garden enthusiasts.

So vast an amount of material, mostly from the Sino-Himalaya, had been grown and propagated during the years before the war that the great gardens of the country, which were, in the main, woodland or semi-woodland gardens on a grand scale, with the emphasis mostly on rhododendrons, azaleas, camellias, and magnolias, tended to become overplanted, or the owners found it necessary to extend the garden boundaries. Thus it was in botanic gardens as well as in private gardens. Thus it was particularly at the Royal Botanic Gardens at Kew and Edinburgh. In 1924 Kew decided to establish a Pinetum at Bedgebury in Kent, under the joint auspices of the Gardens and the Forestry Commission. In 1925 Mr. George Harry Younger endowed his estate at Benmore in Argyll and gifted it to the nation as a demonstration school for forestry and horticulture; the forests came under the aegis of the Forestry Commission and the actual garden of close on 100 acres under the Regius Keeper of the Royal Botanic Garden, Edinburgh. In both instances the decision to take over the additional property was influenced by the atmospheric pollution at both Kew and Edinburgh. Bedgebury was to be essentially a pinetum devoted to the cultivation of conifers. Benmore, on the other hand, was to be a great woodland garden for the cultivation of rhododendrons and other shrubs as well as of conifers, in a climate of over 90 inches of rain in the year.

Unquestionably the rhododendrons of the Sino-Himalaya had caught the imagination of gardeners with many acres of land at their disposal. These men entered into friendly rivalry, germinating their seeds, nurturing their young plants, planting their many acres and holding week-end house-parties, at which they discussed their plants with their gardening friends. Never before was there such enthusiasm for any one group of plants. Moreover, they organized themselves wonderfully well.

In 1915 these great rhododendron enthusiasts formed themselves into the Rhododendron Society, and in 1926 organized their first show which filled the Old Hall at Vincent Square and was highly successful. The show became an annual event until the outbreak of war. To spread knowledge of the behaviour of rhododendrons in cultivation, *The Rhododendron Society Notes* were published, in annual parts, forming three volumes containing much information, botanical as well as horticultural. The society's most important publication, however, was that of 1930, *The Species of Rhododendron*: . . . 'the lasting monument to the Rhododendron Society, as also it will be to those who compiled, Mr. H. F. Tagg for the lepidote rhododendrons, Mr. J. Hutchinson for the elepidote, and Dr. Rehder for the Azalea series', as G. Johnstone described it in the R.H.S.'s 1958 *Rhododendron and Camellia Year Book*. The aim of the book, which J. B. Stevenson edited, was to provide a single-page description of each species and to attempt to group the species into series. The grouping was admittedly tentative and has had to be revised, but the book is still an immensely important one for the student of rhododendrons.

After its Annual General Meeting of 1931, the Rhododendron Society became absorbed into the Rhododendron Association, which had been formed at a meeting in May 1927 in the Lecture Theatre of the R.H.S. Mr. Lionel de Rothschild, who presided, had referred to the existing Rhododendron Society of twenty-five members and had suggested that the time had come to invite a large number of interested people to take part in the organization of the shows and in the promotion of the cultivation of the rhododendron. And so the Rhododendron Association came into being, with Mr. de Rothschild the president, Admiral Walker-Heneage-Vivian vice-president, and Mr. J. B. Stevenson treasurer. From 1929 until 1939 the association published an annual *Rhododendron Year Book*, containing annotated lists of species, and collectors' expedition numbers in addition to the Stud Book of hybrids. In 1945 the affairs of this splendid association were wound up and in the association's place a group of the R.H.S., on the lines of the existing Lily Group, was formed. The members of the Association who were also Fellows of the R.H.S. became members of the Group, other Fellows of the R.H.S. also being eligible for membership. The joint committee which met regularly to adjudicate upon exhibits at Vincent Square is now one of the standing committees of the R.H.S. and has taken camellias under its wing. The old *Year Book* is now the R.H.S. *Rhododendron and Camellia Year Book*.

The cult of the rhododendron even spread to Tresco Abbey garden in the Isles of Scilly, but fortunately, in this instance, not to any large extent. The Lord Proprietors of the Isles of Scilly were, and still are, wise enough to cultivate plants which it is almost impossible to cultivate out of doors elsewhere in Britain; thus the garden was gradually stocked with plants from the Cape, Australia, New Zealand, Tasmania, South America, and thus was made into the unique garden and botanist's paradise of today.

To a much greater degree the rhododendron influenced the Mc-Douall brothers at Logan in Wigtownshire, whose garden was, and to some extent still is, the Scottish equivalent of Tresco, although never in its history has Logan been able to grow in the open the enormous range of tender plants which are so much at home at Tresco. Even so, the owners of Tresco, who regularly came to Wigtown to shoot, persuaded and encouraged the owners of Logan to build a garden on the Tresco lines. So keen and enthusiastic did the McDouall brothers become that all interest was lost in the shooting and all the money from the estate was poured into the garden, at that time a formal walled and terraced garden. Then came the rhododendron; hundreds of rhododendrons from the amateur growers in the south, and twenty acres or so of land surrounding the walled garden, had to be given over to them. It was not necessary for Lord Stair at the near-by gardens of Lochinch to take in more land, for already there were hundreds of acres available for the rhododendrons which all his friends in the south were growing and which he decided he must also try; by so doing he completely transformed the gardens which originally had been laid out in the seventeenth century and restored in 1847. As with all his gardening friends, Lord Stair was to become a keen hybridizer of his favourite plants.

Fortunately the cult of the rhododendron spread, on a very big scale, to the Royal Park at Windsor. In 1931, when Mr. Eric Savill (now Sir Eric) was appointed to the post of deputy surveyor of Windsor Parks and Woods, there was no garden in the whole of the Windsor Great Park. In 1932 he selected a site for a small woodland garden, was given plants by friends such as Lord Aberconway, Mr. Lionel de Rothschild, Mr. J. B. Stevenson, Sir John Stirling Maxwell, the Earl of Stair, Mr. F. R. S. Balfour, Sir John Ramsden, Mr. George Johnstone and others, was encouraged by various members of the Royal Family, and, using his own genius for placing plants and the cultivation skills of his staff, created the superb garden which today is known as the Savill Garden.

All such gardening activities everywhere were more or less abandoned with the coming of the war in 1939 and gardens were turned to food production. The great collections of rhododendrons, azaleas, magnolias, camellias, and the rest were mostly left to take care of themselves. But it is impossible for ornamental horticulture to flourish in wartime and some of the great prewar gardens by 1945 were sadly neglected and overgrown

349

and some were never to recover. Fortunately, to some of the others the National Trusts came to the rescue.

The National Trust had been established in 1895 'to preserve places of historic interest and natural beauty'. It had concerned itself with the preservation of certain areas of beautiful land in the Lake District, the Peak District, and stretches of the coastline, as well as with the preservation of certain great houses of historic importance and of the gardens attached to such houses. To advise the Trust on matters of architecture, works of art, etc., the Historic Buildings Committee came into being, while for advice on the management of the gardens attached to houses already in their hands, the Trust turned to the R.H.S. In 1948 a joint committee of the National Trust and the R.H.S. was set up and very soon was to be concerned with the acquisition of more great gardens, not necessarily associated with historic houses. By public subscription a Garden Fund was organized. The Hon. V. Sackville-West and the Earl of Rosse approached the Queen's Institute of District Nursing, which had been running the National Gardens Scheme since 1927. As a result of this approach it was agreed that as from 1949 a percentage of the takings from the opening of gardens in aid of that charity be allocated to the Gardens Committee.

Not until 1931 was the National Trust for Scotland established—with the very same objectives; and for advice on the gardens under its control the Trust set up in 1950 its own Gardens Committee under the chairmanship of Lady Elphinstone, sister of Mr. David Bowes Lyon, Treasurer of the R.H.S. and a few years later its President. And, as in England, a valuable link between the Scottish Trust and Scotland's Gardens Scheme was forged when the county organizers of the latter body agreed that there should be a permanent alliance between the Scheme and the Gardens Committee of the Trust.

In this way some of Britain's finest gardens have been saved, when, because of high rates of taxation and death duties, they might otherwise have been lost.

Hidcote Manor garden in Gloucester was the first garden to come under the aegis of the National Trust; begun in 1903 by Maj. Lawrence Johnston, it is of most intriguing design and has a justly renowned collection of shrubs and of other plants. Then followed Bodnant, the Aberconway garden in Denbighshire, one of the most magnificent gardens—some would say *the* most magnificent—in the country; then Nymans, the Messel garden in Sussex. Now the Trust has the control of Stourhead in Wiltshire, one of the first (it was begun about 1740) and perhaps the finest of our landscape gardens; Sheffield Park in Sussex, a 'Capability' Brown landscape garden around a vista of five lakes, with some modification by Repton, and its collection of trees and shrubs, mostly the work of A. G. Soames from about 1910; the hillside arboretum of Winkworth in Surrey; Trengwainton in Cornwall, the creation since about 1920 of Sir Edward Bolitho; the valley garden of Glendurgan, also in Cornwall; two other modern gardens in the grand manner in Northern Ireland—Mount Stewart, near Newtownards, in large measure the work of the seventh Marchioness of Londonderry, and Rowallane, south-east of Belfast, the beautiful and magnificent creation of H. Armytage-Moore; and many more besides.

In Scotland, one of the most renowned, most beautiful and most vulnerable gardens of all came to the Trust—the garden at Inverewe in Wester Ross, begun by Osgood Mackenzie in 1864 on a barren, utterly treeless peninsula and now a luxuriant collection of plants from Asia, Australia, New Zealand, Chile and South Africa. There are others: the castle and garden of Brodick on the Isle of Arran, the formal garden dating from 1710 and the woodland garden from the early 1920's, the latter entirely the creation of the late Duchess of Montrose, daughter of the twelfth Duke of Hamilton, and of her son-in-law, Maj. J. P. T. Boscawen; Culzean Castle and garden in Ayrshire, with terraces, fountain garden, an early nineteenth-century camellia house, woodland, and a walled garden of 1783; Falkland Palace and garden in Fife, the palace the residence of Stuart kings for centuries, the garden a modern one on the site of the early Stuart original; Crathes Castle and garden in Kincardineshire, the castle dating from 1553, part of the garden from the very early years of the eighteenth century, and the comprehensive collection of trees, shrubs, and herbaceous plants the work of the late Sir James and Lady Burnett in this century; Pitmedden at Udney in Aberdeenshire, the seventeenth-century formal 'great garden' which the National Trust for Scotland recently has restored; these and others.

Not only is the National Trust for Scotland maintaining these important gardens, it is also creating a new one—and thereby training young horticulturists in practical gardening. At the Threave School of Practical Gardening in Kirkcudbrightshire, the Trust is accommodating young men between the ages of sixteen and twenty-one, teaching them the practical side of gardening against a theoretical background, and by so doing is creating on sixty acres of land an entirely new garden consisting in the main of an arboretum and rock and peat gardens.

To the postwar rescue of the magnificent collection of trees and shrubs in the Westonbirt Arboretum came, not the National Trust, but the Forestry Commission. The Arboretum had been founded in 1829 by R. S. Holford and developed by him until his death in 1892. It had then been in the care of Sir George Holford from 1892 until 1926, during which time the collections of trees and shrubs, especially of rhododendrons and acers, had been vastly increased. From 1926 until 1951 the Arboretum had been the responsibility of the fourth Earl of Morley— and of his curator, Mr. W. J. Mitchell. The Second World War had brought grave burdens to the estate and, largely because of shortage of labour, the Arboretum had declined. Thus it was when, in 1956, the Forestry Commission acquired from the fifth Earl of Morley the Arboretum of some 116 acres, the area known as Silkwood which is 370 acres in extent, together with 117 acres of parkland. The Commission appointed an advisory committee of distinguished arboriculturists and botanists, under the chairmanship of the Hon. Lewis Palmer, at that time Treasurer of the R.H.S., and this committee, with local Forestry Commission supervision, has given Westonbirt a new lease of life.

After the war, in spite of crippling taxation, it was still occasionally possible for large new gardens to be created. Sir Eric Savill at Windsor has not only maintained and developed the Savill Garden but has created on a scale of over 200 acres the immense woodland gardens known as the Valley Gardens, where is now growing the rhododendron collection of species, each under the original collector's number, originally built up by Mr. J. B. Stevenson at Tower Court, Ascot, together with hybrids of these, as well as many of the hardy plant introductions of all kinds, of this and previous centuries. The creation of the gardens in the Royal Park at Windsor is unquestionably the greatest development in ornamental horticulture of this century and is fit to rank with that of any other century. The large woodland garden at Knightshayes Court to the north of Tiverton, Devon, is entirely the postwar creation of Sir John and Lady Heathcoat-Amory. So is Mr. L. Maurice Mason's garden at Fincham, King's Lynn, Norfolk; here is one of the finest botanical gardens of the country, containing an immensely interesting collection of trees and shrubs, and a vast collection of plants under glass, most of which Mr. Mason has himself collected in the wild on his annual expeditions to various parts of the world.

At Crarae on Lochfyneside in Argyll there was a garden before the war, but the developments of recent years made by the late Sir George Campbell have so transformed the place that Crarae, with the unique Forest Garden, can be counted a postwar garden. It is the same with the island garden of Kiloran, on the Isle of Colonsay; although Lord Strathcona started the garden about 1930, the garden of today, with its rhododendrons and tender plants, is essentially the work of the last twenty-five years. Much the finest entirely postwar garden in Scotland is that made by Sir James Horlick on the windy island of Gigha, in Argyll. On a flat unpromising site, Sir James, with great ingenuity and wisdom, has planted extensive shelter belts within which he has assembled a large collection of choice rhododendrons, camellias, embothriums, and many other flowering shrubs, as well as herbaceous plants, in the creation of yet another splendid woodland garden.

By no means all postwar horticultural developments have centred round rhododendron and woodland gardens and the National Trusts. Ornamental horticulture in general has received a great boost, where it was very much required, by the development of the gardens of the Northern Horticultural Society at Harlow Car, Harrogate. In 1911 the North of England Horticultural Society had been formed and, from the start, had endeavoured to organize its affairs very much on the lines of the R.H.S. Monthly meetings were held and there were splendid shows at which such well-known firms as Messrs. Sutton & Sons, Reading, Messrs. Bath Ltd.—and others—exhibited. It is this Society which now sponsors the Harrogate Spring Show, which, organized by W. V. Bishop, the Parks Superintendent of Harrogate and an Associate of Honour of the R.H.S., ranks in Britain second only to Chelsea as a spring show. During the First World War the society pursued the possibility of emulating the R.H.S. by establishing a trial garden in the north, a northern equivalent of Wisley, where new plants could be tested under conditions of soil and climate rather different from those of Wisley. However, nothing came of the idea.

In the meantime many local horticultural societies had been formed in the north—and indeed all over Britain—and in 1946 was born the Northern Horticultural Society with the object of co-ordinating many of the activities of the local societies, of providing a focal point for education and discussion—and, ultimately, of providing a trial garden. The garden materialized long before many people anticipated, in large measure thanks to the energy of the society's first chairman, Lieut.-Col. C. H. Grey, whose three-volume work, *Hardy Bulbs*, had been published in 1937-8, and the initiative of Mr. Bishop. Thus the gardens of the Northern Horticultural Society were established at Harlow Car, Harrogate. Today the gardens occupy some sixty acres and, thanks to the endeavours of their directors, Lieut-Col. Grey, Sir William Milner, and now Mr. A. Sigston Thompson, and of their superintendents, Mr. J. R. Hare and now especially Mr. G. Smith, the gardens can boast their woodlands, stream, arboretum, herbaceous garden, rose garden, rock garden, trials ground, and nursery.

Such postwar developments were exceptional, however, and almost certainly they are the last of their type. For economic reasons it is now almost impossible for new large private gardens to be developed. Many which still exist do so by endeavouring to cut down on labour costs, by using unskilled labour—even this is expensive—and by commercializing to help pay maintenance costs. A few gardens have succeeded magnificently in this, but most gardens are unequipped to enter the commercial field and can hardly hope to succeed. Once they have failed and been more or less abandoned, as some one-time great gardens have been, the land will be used for building purposes and what once was a great establishment and garden will be replaced by countless smaller houses and gardens.

This trend has gradually been gaining momentum since the end of the Second World War and constitutes one of the most remarkable in postwar horticulture. Bungalows of smaller and smaller size have sprung up all over the country, each with its own small garden, and the owner, or his wife, is the gardener. Thus a new race of amateur gardeners has arisen, thirsting for more knowledge—and radio and television have come to their aid. To the aid of thousands the R.H.S. has also come, for during the first thirteen years after the end of the Second World War the Society's membership more than doubled, so that in 1960 it was more than 58,000. By 1966 it was to be almost 75,000.

In the field of research postwar horticultural engineering received a great fillip when the National Institute of Agricultural Engineering settled into its new permanent home at Wrest Park in Bedfordshire, there to investigate problems in glass-house heating, irrigation, and other engineering matters. Impetus to vegetable research was given in 1949, when, at Wellesbourne in Warwickshire, the National Vegetable Research Station was established to study fundamental problems in the vegetable-growing industry. Horticultural research and training have been organized and expanded at the University departments of horticulture at Reading, Wye, and Sutton Bonnington. Experimental horticultural research stations have been set up in various parts of the country and some, such as the Plant Protection Station at Fernhurst, have made major contributions to the development of fungicides, insecticides, and chemical weed-killers. And the National Agricultural Advisory Service has been established in England and Wales, its purpose in Scotland being filled by the horticultural departments of the colleges of agriculture. The establishment of the N.A.A.S. was partly the result of the activities of the Horticultural Education Association, whose pre- and postwar publication—from 1932 to 1933 the *Year Book* and from 1935 *Scientific Horticulture*—excellently summarizes contemporary developments in most aspects of horticulture.

Part Seven

On the Crest of the Wave
(1945 - 1968)

CHAPTER TWENTY

LORD ABERCONWAY

As a result of the war the society's expenditure on salaries, wages, printing, fuel, postage—in fact, expenditure on practically everything—had risen considerably; at the same time its income from subscriptions, hall-lettings, etc., was much below prewar level. It was evident that the Society must either curtail its activities or increase its income. In 'A Message from the President', sent to Fellows in the September number of the *Journal* in 1945, Lord Aberconway reviewed the position and made it clear that the Council considered that a reduction of the Society's activities would be unwise, and that it had decided, and decided very reluctantly, to raise the subscription rate from one guinea to two and from two guineas to three. 'I hope and believe', he said, 'that the great majority of subscribers will continue to support the Society in spite of the increased subscriptions and that the Society will thus be enabled, in the future, as in the past, to hold, by merit and not only by members, its distinguished position as the leading Horticultural Society in the world.' The horticultural Press fully backed the President and Council, the leader writer in the *Gardener's Chronicle* saying:

The R.H.S. has many and large commitments, and in the near future will need a new Director at Wisley and a new Secretary at Vincent Square and such positions will not be filled by the best men available unless the salaries are attractive. The beauty and usefulness of Wisley would suffer under financial stringency, and the educational work of the Society—publications, examinations, trials, etc.—would decline if the charge for Fellowship remained at the pre-war level. Much of the work of the Society is done gratuitously by Standing Committees, but by far the major portion is conducted by paid and able staff; moreover, the upkeep of the two halls involves a considerable annual outlay, while Wisley has to be financed from Westminster. We think that very few Fellows will cease to subscribe, or grumble at the new charges, as the great majority wish to see the Society's activities maintained and the Council unembarrassed by financial difficulties. We remember when the Society was in a parlous condition and the glory had departed from its famous Gardens at Chiswick. We do not wish to see a return of those bad old days and,

355

therefore, will willingly 'pay-up' to assist the Society in holding its position as the premier horticultural Society in the world.[1]

The Council's action, and the encouragement of the horticultural Press, were fully justified. There were, not unnaturally, a good many resignations; but the total numerical strength only fell by 271, and that loss was more than recovered in the following year. Moreover, many who had resigned subsequently sought readmission, and there was a steady intake of new Fellows. By 1950 the total numerical strength had risen to 38,268, thus surpassing the prewar total of 36,577.

The changes in staff which the *Chronicle* had forecast quickly came about. Lieut.-Col. F. R. Durham retired in March 1946, having been Secretary for almost twenty years and having amply justified the Council's view that at the time of his appointment, an able administrator, rather than a horticulturist, was necessary to handle the Society's complex affairs. His years in office had been exciting and strenuous ones. The increased accommodation of the New Hall had allowed for larger Shows which had achieved new heights of excellence, as well as for the revival of conferences, the organization of which called for an enormous amount of detailed work. One of the largest, and the most successful, had been the International Horticultural Congress of 1930, at which the standardization of colour nomenclature for plants had been discussed. Durham had taken especial interest in this work, which was to result in the collaboration between the Society and the British Colour Council in the production of the *Horticultural Colour Chart*, the first volume being published in December 1938, and the second in February 1942. To this *Colour Chart*, as well as to the *Gardener's Diary*, Durham gave much of his time. During his régime membership of the Society increased and the scope of the Society's activities both at Vincent Square and at Wisley was much enlarged, and the burden on the Secretary correspondingly heavier. On his retirement his health was causing considerable anxiety, and he died, suddenly, the following year, at the age of seventy-four.

In 1946 there were three retirements at Wisley. Mr. Harrow had been Director there since 1931 and though during the war years the staff had been depleted, the Garden had, nevertheless, been well maintained; extensive trials, especially of vegetables, had been carried out, and Battleston Hill, a piece of rising ground carrying a mixture of pine and broad-leaved trees, between the Garden and the Portsmouth road, had been purchased. More adjoining land consisting of four acres of woodland and an arable field of fourteen acres between the trust land and the Portsmouth road had also been acquired, whilst a house had been built on the fruit trial ground for the assistant for fruit experiments. Harrow

[1] *Gdnr's Chron.*, vol. 117 (1945), p. 113.

continued to enjoy his retirement at Godalming until 1954, when he died at the age of eighty-seven.

Dr. Tincker resigned from the keepership of the Laboratory to take up a short-term appointment in the Bahamas and London with the 21st Century Corporation, before being appointed, in 1948, to the staff of the North of Scotland College of Agriculture. At Wisley he had accomplished much research, had co-ordinated the work of the various departments in the Laboratory, and had been responsible for the supervision of the Society's practical examinations.

The other Wisley retirement was that of Mr. J. W. Blakey, the keeper of the Garden. Though he had been keeper only since 1938, when he succeeded Robert Findlay, John William Blakey had, in fact, been employed in the Society's Gardens for the past thirty-eight years, during which time he endeared himself not only to staff and students but to countless yearly visitors as well. During all this time he had hardly ever taken more than a very few continuous days of holiday. In fact, he could hardly afford the time to take a holiday; he was too busy raising many thousands of plants from the seeds sent home by Forrest and others, for growing in the Garden as well as for the annual distribution to Fellows. In recognition of his services to horticulture and of his wonderful loyalty to the Society he was awarded the Society's Associateship of Honour in 1938. He never married and on retirement lived in Yorkshire, where he died in 1954 aged seventy-five. He knew the collection of plants in the Garden intimately, saw the possibilities for hybridizing in many of them (not unnaturally, since he had worked for James Veitch & Son), and was, in fact, the raiser of several new plants, especially some well-known *Berberis* hybrids of which *B.* x *rubrostilla* is probably the most noteworthy, as well as a fine strain of *Primula japonica*.

Durham's successor at Vincent Square was Brigadier C. V. L. Lycett, who again was appointed by virtue of his administrative ability and experience. 'I have not asked him the difference between a Schizanthus, a Schizostylis, a Schizophragma, and a Schizocodon,' said the President at the Annual General Meeting in 1946, '. . . but that is the kind of thing I am sure he will pick up as he takes up his duties of Secretary.'[1] Until this time, since 1925, Simmonds had acted as Assistant Secretary. Now he was given the post of Deputy Secretary with the special task of organizing the Society's Shows.

Mr. J. S. L. Gilmour, who had been Assistant Director at the Royal Botanic Gardens, Kew, since 1931, succeeded Mr. Harrow at Wisley. At Kew he had proved an able administrator and had been immensely interested in the education and welfare of the student-gardeners.

[1] *Jl R. hort. Soc.*, LXXI (1946), p. xxv.

Biological classification and British botany were his main interests, and he had published *British Botanists* in 1944, whilst his *Wild Flowers on Chalk* was to appear in 1946. (Plate 20.)

The vacant keepership of the Garden was filled, with the title of Curator, by Mr. F. E. W. Hanger, who since 1927 had been employed at Exbury. At first he had served there under the head gardener, Mr. Bedford, whom he succeeded in 1934. In 1940 Mr. Lionel de Rothschild appointed him agent of the estate. Francis Hanger was a great cultivator of plants and had full scope in the exercise of his gifts in the growing of the many hybrids of Mr. Rothschild's breeding, especially rhododendrons and azaleas. He was also a great exhibitor, staging at the Society's Shows many fine exhibits from Exbury and entering into keen, though friendly, rivalry with the President and his wonderful gardener, Mr. F. C. Puddle, who was also a breeder of rhododendrons, as well as of hippeastrums, clivias, and cypripediums, and who did much to make Bodnant the great garden it is today.

Hanger immediately applied himself with enthusiasm to the improvement of the Garden, especially to the development of Battleston Hill, planting it with magnolias, rhododendrons, azaleas, camellias, and a wide range of other trees and shrubs. The rose-borders which flanked the main walk from near to the Garden entrance and in the direction of the Rock Garden, were replaced by finely kept grass, with beds for spring and summer bedding.

In view of the great and growing attention being paid by local authorities to the horticultural treatment of public parks and gardens, in September of 1947 an Exhibition of Municipal Horticulture was held in the Old Hall. It was sponsored by the Society, was organized by a special committee which had the co-operation of the Institute of Park Administration, the Royal Botanic Gardens, Kew, the London County Council, and many other local authorities and was the first municipal horticultural show ever to be staged in Great Britain and created a great deal of interest and discussion.

Almost for the first time since he had become President in 1931, Lord Aberconway was meeting with some opposition at Vincent Square—over the question of the desirability of reviving the Chelsea Show in 1947. During the war the need for nurserymen to devote much of their land to food production had led to a drastic reduction of ornamental nursery stock. Now many of them, especially those accustomed to staging large exhibits at Chelsea, contended that they needed at least another year to restore their stocks, that large rock gardens would be far too costly to stage, that greenhouse plants would be too few, and that the chance of late frosts would make rhododendrons and camellias, which alone could provide a display of colour, an unknown quantity.

On the other hand, the President and some—by no means all—of his colleagues on the Council held the view that not to hold a Show in 1947 would probably result in the Society's being deprived of the site altogether. Moreover, the Society had its responsibility to its Fellows and to the public. 'Whatever else we do without, we should not go without a Chelsea Flower Show next year,' the President said in October 1946. The President won his point and subsequent events vindicated his optimism. Although the Show was only two-thirds the size of that staged in 1939, and despite a belated winter of unusual severity, its success surpassed the dreams even of the President. No one foresaw so great a gathering of Fellows, who formed long queues in the streets before the Show opened. The *Gardener's Chronicle* reported that no matter how many new Fellows were enrolled and how much profit was made,

no account will ever be given of the happy friendships, torn apart by the catastrophe from which we have emerged, that were restored: yet the delighted faces that characterised this great occasion bore their testimony, reflecting the pageant for which they had assembled. In a few acres was arranged a display of the finest of our Spring-time gardens for which we had waited almost a whole decade.[1]

The Show was a further triumph for the President in that his exhibit of rhododendrons, most of them hybrids raised at Bodnant and beautifully exhibited by Mr. Puddle, was awarded the Society's Gold Medal.

By 1949 nurseries had so far recovered as to allow of Chelsea Show being held on a prewar scale. The Show covered about eleven and a half acres, with nearly three acres under canvas; even so it was difficult to provide the space for all who wished to exhibit plants, flowers, and fruits, and some of the exhibitors of horticultural sundries had to be disappointed. In the great marquees there were 220 exhibitors of magnificent orchids, sweet peas, begonias, irises, lilies, paeonies, fuchsias, carnations, cacti, rhododendrons, roses, aquatics, and other plants. In addition there were 177 exhibitors of a bewildering array of horticultural sundries, whilst out of doors were the rock gardens and formal and informal gardens. For the first time the coveted Lawrence Medal was won by the Crown Estate Commissioners, their exhibit of a woodland garden of rhododendrons, azaleas, trees and shrubs, with primulas, expertly and tastefully arranged by Mr. E. Savill and Mr. T. H. Findlay, being considered by many with long experience of Chelsea to be the most beautiful of its kind they had ever seen. Since 1949 the Crown Estate Commissioners have won the Lawrence Medal on three other occasions, a record shared only with Messrs. Sutton & Sons Ltd. Since 1931 this great seed firm has been awarded the Lawrence Medal on seven occasions, sometimes for

[1] *Gdnr's Chron.*, vol. 121 (1947), 195.

exhibits of vegetables, sometimes for annual and greenhouse flowers from seeds.

Rhododendrons were now such dominating plants at Chelsea—and other shows—and were so much in demand by the public that the Society sponsored a Rhododendron Conference in 1949. And the popularity of camellias, which the President had forecast some few years before, demanded that in 1950 the Society should organize a Camellia Conference, in association with magnolias. It was the first conference of its kind in Britain, and the exhibits, lectures, and discussions all served to stimulate an interest in growing the species and cultivars of both genera—but especially of *Camellia*. Almost for the first time it was realized how wide was the range of the cultivars of *C. japonica*. And almost for the first time it was realized how much the United States was able to teach Britain about these plants. Soon after 1940 the Southern California Camellia Society had set itself the task of elucidating the tangled nomenclature of camellia cultivars, for it had been estimated that in the States there were at least five separate names in common use for every camellia cultivar. Though the American checklist had been able to reduce these synonyms to manageable proportions, a great deal of similar work still needed to be done. The great outcome of the Society's conference was that it led to the immediate co-operation of camellia growers in Britain, the United States, and elsewhere and, in 1962, to the formation of the International Camellia Society, with Mr. E. G. Waterhouse, the well-known Australian camellia authority, as its first president, and Mr. Charles Puddle, the head gardener at Bodnant, where he had succeeded his father, the society's first secretary.

Three months after the highly successful Camellia and Magnolia Conference that great servant of the Society, Frederick Chittenden, died in his seventy-eighth year. In a splendid obituary notice in the *Journal* for 1950, E. A. Bowles wrote:

The death . . . deprives the horticultural world of one of the most eminent of its botanists, teachers and practical gardeners. The R.H.S. in particular has lost the most efficient and accomplished member of its staff since the days of Lindley and Wilks. As one who worked happily with him for very nearly 50 years, I recall with pleasure and gratitude the blessing of his friendship and the benefit of contact with such a lovable and Christian character and the stimulation resulting from the unfailing flow of information so generously imparted to me from his encyclopaedic knowledge.[1]

At the time of his death he was a member of the Society's Examinations Board and of its Library and Publications Committee. For his outstanding services to the Society and to horticultural education and

[1] *Jl R. hort. Soc.*, LXXV (1950), p. 424.

literature, the Society had honoured him with the Victoria Medal of Honour in 1917 and the Veitch Memorial Gold Medal in 1947. Moreover, the 1948 volume of the *Botanical Magazine* had been dedicated to him by 'The President and Council to express their gratitude for the beneficent influence of his wise and skilful teaching on so many horticulturists of the present day'. Certainly from a national point of view Chittenden's most valuable work lay in the field of horticultural education and particularly in connection with the establishment and conduct of the examinations for the National Diploma in Horticulture. When he died he was editing a new index of the *Botanical Magazine* as well as the Society's *Dictionary of Gardening*, the four volumes of which, unfortunately, were not published until the following year, and then only because of the time and energy devoted to the task of preparing the last two volumes by the Society's editor, P. M. Synge, and librarian, W. T. Stearn.

Bowles further wrote of Chittenden:

Among his natural qualities he was remarkable for his great capacity for work; meticulous accuracy in all he wrote; remarkable eyesight which enabled him to write a small but exceptionally legible hand without glasses up to his death. He was temperate to the point of austerity and had remarkable powers of self control, possessing iron nerves and he apparently knew no fear. He bore no ill-will even when he might have considered that he had just cause; having decided what he considered to be the right course, he pursued it unperturbed by criticism and, even when that was groundless, disdained self-defence.

At Wisley, the year after his death, the building of more cottages was completed, and the group was named 'Chittenden Close'.

And in 1951, at Wisley and throughout the Society, the deaths of two of Chittenden's old friends and colleagues were mourned, for both had given wonderful service to horticulture for over thirty years. George Fox Wilson had entered Wisley as a student in 1911, had been awarded the Worshipful Company of Gardeners' Scholarship, and had assisted Professor Maxwell Lefroy in the entomological department before leaving for military service. After the war he returned to Wisley, in 1919, to the post of entomologist, the post he still held at the time of his death, when he was the senior member of the Wisley scientific staff. He had published many research papers in the Society's *Journal* and elsewhere —papers on the treatment of eelworm in chrysanthemum, phlox and in other garden plants, on the pests of stored seeds, the pollination by insects of fruit trees, the introduction and spread of foreign pests, the fumigation of glass-houses, the uses and effects of the recently developed systemic insecticides—and on much else. He was well known to a host of Fellows through his advisory work and to the students at Wisley as a brilliant teacher who took great interest in their careers. 'The students at Wisley have lost more than a tutor of entomology,' wrote the 1951 students to the *Gardener's Chronicle*. 'His unassuming manner, quiet efficiency and constant readiness to help won the respect of all those whose privilege it was to attend his lectures.'

Within a few weeks of the passing of Fox Wilson, Felix Cuthbert Brown, who had also been a student at Wisley, in 1915 and again after the war, and had been appointed to the staff in the same year as Fox Wilson—1919—to the post of trials officer, also died, The post was, and indeed still is, one of great responsibility, involving the layout of the trial grounds, the raising, transplanting and after-treatment of the actual trial plants, the recording of all relevant growth data, the inspection of the trials at certain times by the appropriate committees, and the preparation of detailed reports for publication in the Society's *Journal*. To these tasks Brown always gave tireless energy and great practical skill; and from them he ultimately acquired an encyclopaedic knowledge of the cultivars of garden flowers and vegetables. He also acquired some considerable knowledge of the whims and idiosyncrasies of members of his various committees which enabled him to handle with tact some of the more difficult characters on the Iris, Border Carnation, Joint Perpetual Flowering Carnation, Early Flowering Chrysanthemum, Delphinium, Dianthus and Sweet Pea Committees, for all of which he acted as secretary. 'His colleagues and many Fellows will remember his direct gaze and ready smile, and not less the innate kindliness and good humour which made every contact with him a happy occasion,' wrote his friend and colleague, Mr. N. K. Gould.

Just as Brown had accepted the onerous task of trials officer on completing the students' course at Wisley, so did J. B. Paton accept the post of trials recorder from 1951 until 1957, when he left the service of the Society to take up an appointment with the Commonwealth War Graves Commission. Paton recorded the floral and vegetable trials at Wisley, and for most of this time contributed the monthly 'Notes from Wisley' to the Society's *Journal*.

The passing of Fox Wilson and Brown, aged fifty-four and fifty-six respectively, did not cause the only staff changes at Wisley in 1951. Mr. Gilmour, who had been Director during the past five years, resigned on being appointed director of the University Botanic Garden at Cambridge. Much had happened at Wisley during Gilmour's term of office. Many changes in the Garden had been made, including the development of Battleston Hill into a beautiful woodland garden; much scientific work had been done, including work on the cytology of plants by Dr. E. K. Janaki Ammal of the cytological department; and a horticultural training scheme for ex-servicemen had been instituted and courses of instruction organized and put into effect. To succeed Mr. Gilmour, Dr. H. R. Fletcher resigned from the scientific staff at the Royal Botanic Garden, Edinburgh, where he had worked in close collaboration with Sir William Wright Smith, the Regius Keeper of the Garden and the Society's Professor of Botany. (Plate 20.)

Wisley reacted to these changes by staging at the Chelsea Show of 1951 an exhibit of a mossy glade of primulas, meconopsis, lilies, and rhododendrons which was described as the finest that had ever been provided from the Society's Gardens. But then during the next few years all the Chelsea exhibits from Wisley could have been thus described, thanks, in the main, to the genius of Francis Hanger, the Curator, in growing and staging the plant material. The 1951 Chelsea Show was rather a special one in that it was the Society's contribution to the Festival of Britain. Extensive alterations were made in the layout of the floral part of the Show, notably by the erection of an additional span of canvas over Monument Road, thereby bringing the whole area occupied by the floral exhibits under one canopy. The great marquee therefore covered over three acres and was believed to be the largest continuous stretch of canvas ever erected in the world. Their Majesties the King and Queen and many other members of the Royal Family visited the Show and were immensely pleased to see the magnificent display of woodland plants from Windsor Great Park, an exhibit which deservedly won the Lawrence Medal for the Commissioners of Crown Lands—for the second time in three years. The organization of this wonderful Show was a great triumph for the Vincent Square staff.

At Chelsea over the years the general standard of presentation of exhibits of all kinds has risen enormously. Gardens in the open show much more finish. A large proportion of the displays under canvas, instead of being staged on tables, are now placed on the ground, where they are seen to greater advantage. Backgrounds are seldom used except against the marquee walls, thus improving not only the individual exhibits but also the view of the marquee as a whole. The exhibits of sundries, i.e. garden furniture, glass-houses, frames, tools, and horticultural requisites of all sorts and sizes, have increased to an even greater extent than have those of plants and flowers, and the standard of presentation is now very high. At the early Chelsea Shows there was no attempt at grouping similar displays, and a stack of potting loam might be exhibited on the ground, while the next site might be occupied by a canvas structure containing tools and implements, for exhibitors of sundries were free to use tents or wooden structures of any design they thought fit, or to display their products in the open if they so wished. It was not until 1949 that all exhibits of sundries were housed in stands of uniform design, in Eastern Avenue.

The Chelsea Show of 1951 was the last King George VI was to see, for he died in February of the following year and the horticultural world was saddened by the death of one who was a knowledgeable amateur gardener and keenly interested in the Society's activities. He it was, with the Queen, who had fostered Sir Eric Savill's magnificent conception in the Windsor Great Park, and by his interest, knowledge, and encouragement had helped Sir Eric to create these remarkable gardens. He it was who was instrumental in procuring for the gardens the vast collection of rhododendron species which the late Mr. J. B. Stevenson and Mrs. Stevenson had assembled at Tower Court, Ascot, and had retained under the original collectors' numbers, so that now this collection is the most important scientific rhododendron material in cultivation anywhere.

Mr. L. G. Pavey, who had been for many years in the Society's employ in the cashier's office and for the past five years had acted as chief cashier, was now the Assistant Secretary, an appointment which had been necessary because of the increased amount of work now falling to the Secretary and his deputy.

Shortly after her accession, Her Majesty Queen Elizabeth II was graciously pleased to follow the tradition started by George III and extended her patronage to the Society. In May, accompanied by H.R.H. the Duke of Edinburgh, Her Majesty honoured Chelsea with her presence.

The outstanding horticultural event in 1952 was the holding of the Thirteenth International Horticultural Congress in London, in September. The Society undertook the secretarial work for the National Organizing Committee, which included representatives of the Ministry of Agriculture, the Department of Agriculture for Scotland, the Ministry of Agriculture for Northern Ireland, the Horticultural Education Association, and the Horticultural Trades Association, and which was under the chairmanship of Dr. H. V. Taylor, for many years a member of Council and chairman of the Examinations Board and author of *The Apples of England* and *The Plums of England*. At the conference 150 papers were read by representatives of twenty-seven countries. Some of the most important sessions were those devoted to horticultural nomenclature, with which matter Chittenden and other members of the Society's staff had for long been associated. At the closing session of the Congress, at which Dr. H. V. Taylor presided, the report of the International Committee on Horticultural Nomenclature, of which the Society's Librarian, Mr. W. T. Stearn, was secretary, was adopted. This report contained the recommendation to adopt provisionally the proposed *International Code of Nomenclature for Cultivated Plants*, the full text of which Stearn, as editor, had prepared, and also conceded the necessity of setting up an international registration organization for the names of cultivated plants. Action on the matter of registration was, however, deferred until the next Congress to give time for the preliminary work of preparation. From this time onwards the Society was to be deeply involved in the international registration of the names of cultivars of cultivated plants.

In May 1953 the Society suffered a great loss in the death of Lord Aberconway, its President since 1931. Possessed of extraordinary initiative and drive, he eschewed delay in reaching decisions or hesitation in giving effect to them. Many times during his years of office immensely important decisions had to be taken—the doubling of the subscription rates immediately after the war and the revival of Chelsea as early as 1947, for instance; at all times they were taken with uncompromising courage. Under his régime every single one of the Society's activities was broadened and benefited. Throughout his long association with the Society he was a strong advocate and supporter of plant exploration, especially in countries likely to yield new plants which would be hardy in the British Isles. Thus he induced the Society to give encouragement and financial support to such collectors as Forrest, Kingdon Ward, Ludlow and Sherriff and their associates, members of the staff of the British Museum in the Sino-Himalayan region, to Comber in South America and Tasmania and to Balls and Davis in the Near East. He supported such causes because all his life he had been a truly great gardener. Not content simply to collect and grow choice plants, he desired, if possible, to improve them, and thus devoted much time, knowledge, and skill to hybridization. During the last twenty years of his life a steady stream of hybrids poured from Bodnant, and of hybrid rhododendrons alone forty-four received the Award of Merit and fifteen the First Class Certificate.

Some weeks before he died, speaking to me, when I was the Wisley Director, at Vincent Square, he said: 'You probably know that I was much opposed to you or to any other scientist being appointed to the directorship at Wisley. I want to tell you that I was wrong and I am happy to be able to tell you so.' Whenever I see the portrait of Lord Aberconway, painted by Sir Oswald Birley, in the Society's Council Room, I remember these, for me, moving words.

CHAPTER TWENTY-ONE

SESQUICENTENARY

The Hon. David Bowes Lyon accepted the Council's invitation to succeed the late Lord Aberconway as President. He was the sixth son of the fourteenth Earl of Strathmore, the brother of Queen Elizabeth the Queen Mother, uncle of the Queen, and a grandson of the Earl of Strathmore who had suggested a temporary solution to the Society's problems in 1873. Like his predecessor in the President's chair, he was a great natural gardener and had been so from his youth. He had never enjoyed very robust health, in consequence of which his doctors had ordered him a period of open-air occupation. This 'open-air' period he had spent at the Royal Botanic Gardens at Kew, where his foreman had been Mr. Frank Knight, soon to be the Director of Wisley. At Kew he had gained an insight into the way of life of those who take up horticulture as a career, an experience which was to be of inestimable value to him during his years as President. His fine garden, St. Paul's Walden Bury in Hertfordshire, laid out originally in the style of Le Nôtre, came to him by inheritance and he devoted all his spare time to working in it himself, restoring many of its original features and cultivating many beautiful plants, especially roses, which were always his chief joy and which grew so well in his heavy clay. (Plate 16.)

David Bowes Lyon was a very busy man: Lord Lieutenant of Hertfordshire, an active working banker, a director of half a dozen important companies, a trustee of the British Museum, chairman of the Joint Gardens Committee of the Society and the National Trust. Even so, his greatest interest was in horticulture and in the affairs of the Society. He had first joined the Council of the Society in 1934. After an interval during the war, when he served his country in the United States, he resumed his activities on the Council and succeeded Richard Trotter as Treasurer in 1948. On becoming President his place as Treasurer was filled by the Hon. Lewis Palmer, a very keen botanist and gardener, greatly interested in South African plants and *Agapanthus* in particular.

The year 1953 was important in the history of Wisley, for great progress was made in the construction of a modern hostel for the accommodation of thirty-six horticultural students, whilst work was begun on an adjoining restaurant for the use of Fellows and other visitors to the Gardens. Moreover, the old School House in Wisley village was converted into two flats for members of the Wisley staff. But the main significance of 1953 was that it was the year in which the Council was formulating its plans for the forthcoming celebration of the 150th anniversary of the Society's foundation on 7 March 1804.

The sesquicentenary celebrations were held on 27 and 28 July. On the evening of Monday, 26 July, a banquet was held at the Savoy Hotel, London, where the guests were received by the President and the Hon. Mrs. David Bowes Lyon. The company included the Rt. Hon. Sir Thomas Dugdale, Minister of Agriculture, as well as numerous distinguished guests representing horticultural organizations in Australia, New Zealand, North America, South Africa, Denmark, Finland, France, and Holland. In his speech of welcome the President referred to the famous Anniversary Dinners held during the Society's early years and recalled that history has it that they were 'convivial affairs'. The guests brought their own dessert and vied with each other in bringing the best fruits, especially pineapples. In those days ladies were not invited to the dinners, but were permitted to view the dessert before dinner. 'I do not think such an arrangement would meet with much approval today,' said the President, 'particularly as so many of our Fellows are ladies, and indeed so many ladies hold places of great responsibility in horticulture today. So, although I must apologize for the absence of any pineapples on our tables tonight, I am sure . . . that you will agree with our decision not to follow the policy of our predecessors and to welcome the ladies at this dinner tonight.' Professor Dr. E. van Slogteren, the grand old man of Dutch horticultural plant pathology, replied to the President on behalf of the foreign guests—and did so with the President's friendly informal manner which pervaded the entire sesquicentenary proceedings.

'It may seem a little strange', the Professor said,

that at the celebrations of so healthy a society as The Royal Horticultural Society a plant doctor should be invited to address you. But perhaps the explanation is not so very complicated, for just as the medical care of the human being is something that goes from the cradle to the grave, so the plant doctor has to care for plants from sowing to fruition and has to study the life processes of the plants, those that are healthy as well as those that are diseased.

You may sometimes hear complaints that the number of plant diseases increases alarmingly with the number of plant doctors, and you may form the opinion that a plant doctor is more delighted to see a sick plant than a beautiful healthy plant! I cannot deny that sometimes these complaints may seem justified, but in general I think they are wrong.

You will understand, of course, that a plant doctor would be very unwise if he only cured diseases, for by doing so he would simply be digging his own grave, and would be obliged to join the army of unemployed and live on the dole. Therefore, he not only tries to find cures for some of the diseases, but at the same time he does his utmost to promote the growing and flowering capacity and the beauty of the plants.

And doing so he will meet the sympathy and get full co-operation of all those who love the plants. And where could the plant doctor for this be in better company than among the Fellows of this famous Society in which have been united for 150 years all those who love plants?

I am very glad to be here, and I want, on behalf of all the foreign guests, to express our appreciation and gratitude. I only regret that in this expression of my feelings I am handicapped by the fact that I have to speak a language that is not my own. No doubt there are some present who will realize how big a handicap this is. Some of us, in trying to speak English, often get the impression that you English either spell or pronounce wrongly. Perhaps you will realize our difficulties the better if you will permit me to quote a few lines from a textbook which, in verse, shows us foreigners how some words in English are pronounced differently although their spelling is the same:

> 'Oh dearest creature in creation,
> Studying English pronunciation,
> I will teach you in my verse,
> Sounds like corpse, corps, horse and worse.
> I will keep you, Susie, busy,
> Make your head with heat grow dizzy;
> Tear in your eye, your dress you'll tear,
> So shall I!—Oh hear my prayer:
> Pray console your loving poet,
> Make my coat look new, dear—sew it!'

It ends: 'Hiccough has the sound of cup—
> My advice is, "Give it up!"'

Of course, in speaking about our difficulties in your language, I recognize that your difficulties in our language might be even greater! I am reminded of the story of a person who went to Paris and whose friend, knowing that he knew only a few words of French, asked him whether he had had any difficulty with his French. 'No', he said, 'not at all—only the French had!' But I think that in the near future things will be better. We have been promised that you will make things easier for us—first, by making your language easier; secondly, by accepting the decimal system; and thirdly, by keeping to the right of the road!

But in spite of these things, all of us love to be in England, with its beautiful downs, its many beautiful parks and its splendid gardens—too often concealed behind the hedgerows. We are grateful to you not only for allowing us to be at this banquet and for your other hospitalities, but above all for allowing us to be present at this wonderful celebration of your famous Society which we all admire so much. Science is international and can best be advanced by international co-operation. So it is with horticulture. Your Society, the most illustrious Horticultural Society in the world, has already served international horticulture for 150 years.

We admire very much your Gardens at Wisley, your buildings and your institutions, your *Journal*, your *Year Books* in which your able experts render such a great service to international horticulture. Above all, time is the best critic, and after existing so long, your splendid Society can only be praised.

We know that no nation is so flower-minded as the English. We realize that this is due to the co-operation and efforts of your large number of Fellows, all of them united by the common love of plants, this love of plants that brings happiness to your lives.

I wish to express from the bottom of my heart the hope that The Royal Horticultural Society may during the coming ages continue its growth and its prosperity and above all I hope that for a long number of years it may continue to be guided by its eminent President.

On 27 July there was a brilliant show of flowers, especially of roses and carnations, in the New Hall, and in the Old Hall a wealth of rare books was displayed, together with the original Charters of the Society. 'It was easy at this exhibition', reported the *Gardener's Chronicle*,

to feel oneself slipping back through time as one thought of the 150 years of the Society's history. This week of celebration came at a fitting moment in the life of such a thriving body, and those of the Fellows who were able to visit Vincent Square might well have felt proud as they walked through this quiet hall and enjoyed the priceless volumes, the portraits of many past notables of the Society, the ancient Charters, and the superb collection of Royal autographs preserved on beautifully illuminated vellum pages.[1]

The representatives of no fewer than thirty-seven learned societies and organizations, on the afternoon of the 27th, delivered addresses of congratulation and the ceremony of presentation was a moving and impressive one. Proceeding in chronological order of the foundation of their organizations, those in the United Kingdom preceding those from overseas, each representative handed his society's address to the President: The Worshipful Company of Gardeners (1605), The Royal Society of London (1660), The Trustees of the British Museum (Natural History) (1753), The Royal Society of Arts (1754), The Royal Society of Edinburgh (1783), The Linnean Society of London (1788), The Geological Society of London (1807), The Royal Caledonian Horticultural Society (1809), The Zoological Society of London (1826), The Royal Geographical Society (1830), The British Association for the Advancement of Science (1831), The Royal Entomological Society of London (1833), The Botanical Society of Edinburgh (1836), The Botanical Society of the

[1] *Gdnr's Chron.*, vol. 136 (1954), p. 56.

British Isles (1836), The Royal Agricultural Society of England (1838), The Royal Microscopical Society (1839), The Chemical Society (1841), The Pharmaceutical Society of Great Britain (1841), The National Chrysanthemum Society (1846), The Royal Photographic Society of Great Britain (1853), The Royal Scottish Forestry Society (1854), The Shropshire Horticultural Society (1875), The City and Guilds of London Institute (1878), The Royal Forestry Society of England and Wales (1882), The British Mycological Society (1896), The Institute of Landscape Architects (1929); and from overseas, The University of Utrecht Botanical Garden (1725), La Société Nationale d'Horticulture de France (1827), The Massachusetts Horticultural Society (1829), The Royal Horticultural Society of Ireland (1830), Det Kongelige Danske Haveselskab (1830), The Royal Horticultural Society of Victoria (1849), Koninklijke Algemeene Vereeniging voor Bloembollencultuur (1860), Koninklijke Nederlandsche Maatschappij voor Tuinbouw en Plantkunde (1873), The Botanical Society of South Africa (1913), The Royal New Zealand Institute of Horticulture (1923), Puutarhaviljelijäin Liitto (the Association of Finnish Horticultural Societies) (1925), The Finnish Horticultural Producers Association, and The American Horticultural Society, Inc. (1926). (Plate 15.)

The President announced that on this great occasion in the history of the Society he and the Council had sent a loyal message to Her Majesty the Queen, the Society's patron, and that Her Majesty had been graciously pleased to reply as follows:

I sincerely thank you and the Council of the Royal Horticultural Society for your kind and loyal message. As your Patron, it gives me the greatest pleasure to congratulate the Society on its one hundred and fiftieth anniversary and I trust that for many years to come it may continue to flourish and prosper.

ELIZABETH R.

After the presentation of the addresses, Mr. Palmer, the Society's Treasurer and Vice-Chairman of the Council, addressed the distinguished gathering with great charm and wit:

I believe that it is customary, when referring to learned societies in a gathering such as this, to assign to them the feminine gender. While I have no doubt that many of you will readily realize the reasons that have prompted that classification, yet I have always thought that there was one respect in which the reactions of learned Societies were essentially unfeminine. Take birthdays, for instance. The older learned societies get, the more they seem to enjoy their birthdays and even positively to parade them!

I have been reading recently in the press about the proceedings of the gerontologists—if that is the right word. That their society is not represented here today I must assume to be a tribute to the continued juvenility of The

Royal Horticultural Society. But I was struck by one theory which was propounded in their proceedings and which I came across in my reading. In so far as I was able to comprehend it, it was that those factors in an organism which operate to halt the growth of that organism at or near the maximum size compatible with the environment in which that organism has to exist will also operate to produce the onset of senescence. Well, far be it from me to venture to hold an opinion on the truth or otherwise of this theory in the biological field, but I could not help being struck by its plausibility in so far as it refers to human societies. Unless there is active life and growth, surely a society must tend to decay.

May we not assume, therefore, that the continued youthful vigour of The Royal Horticultural Society, even at the age of 150 years, is perhaps due to the fact that it is still growing?

While I have watched this ordered procession of representatives of learned societies, I could not help reflecting that even in the field of science we have suffered some loss of the spaciousness of other days. The first learned societies to be founded took as their field of study almost the whole of science. Then later, with the onset of the nineteenth century, perhaps, came the age of specialization, and with it the segmentation of science. There were founded innumerable specialist societies, each specializing and taking as its field of study one particular facet of knowledge.

If I may be permitted in this company to use such a frivolous metaphor, I might liken it to this—that the minuet which was danced by the older learned societies in the spacious days of the seventeenth century has now perhaps, more in keeping with the spirit of the age, become (I am not an expert in these things, but I believe it is called) a conga, where each one hangs on to the coat-tails of the other and weaves in and out among the intricacies of modern research. And so long as we maintain the cohesion of a conga and do not give way to the ever-present, pressing temptation that besets us all to perform a *pas seul* in our own restricted field, so long shall we continue to perform the function for which we were founded, that is, to seek out knowledge, to correlate it with other knowledge and to disseminate it as widely as possible.

But even knowledge will obey the natural laws. The more widely it is disseminated, the more it tends to become diluted. Thus there are societies of great concentration of knowledge—I see the representatives of many ranged in front of me—but there are also societies of considerable dilution of knowledge; and The Royal Horticultural Society, with its 45,000 Fellows, must claim to belong to the latter category. Therefore, I must, with all due humility and modesty, express the great feeling of honour which we have that so many of our more learned sisters have seen fit to come here today to present their congratulations on the occasion of this anniversary.

Nor can I conclude, Mr. President, without expressing our appreciation of the presence of so many representatives from our sister societies overseas, who have taken the trouble and borne the expense of coming here today—an outstanding testimony to the fact that horticulture, like art, is one of the links that transcends the historical and geographical divisions of the human race.

After the ceremony the company adjourned to the Lecture Room, where the President presided at a lecture given by the Deputy Secretary, on the history of the Society. The lecture was followed by a showing of coloured lantern slides of the Wisley Garden throughout the year, with a running commentary by the Wisley Director.

In the Old Hall, on the evening of 27 July, the President and Mrs. Bowes Lyon received over 800 guests who were interested to see the Society's historical documents and possessions as well as the congratulatory addresses which had been received in the afternoon. In the New Hall there was the magnificent Flower Show to be seen, as well as a collection of Reginald Farrer's original drawings. And at 9 p.m. the lucky people who crowded into the Lecture Room saw one of Maj. George Sherriff's films illustrating the vegetation of the Eastern Himalayas, and another film, by Mr. Oleg Polunin, of one of his expeditions to Nepal.

The culminating ceremony of the celebrations was held at Wisley, on the afternoon of 28 July, when Her Majesty Queen Elizabeth the Queen Mother flew from Norfolk to Wisley aerodrome in an aircraft of the Queen's Flight and thence drove to the Gardens to open the new students' hostel, named Aberconway House, in memory of the immediate past President. The Queen Mother was greeted by the members of the Council, the Society's senior staff and nearly 5,000 Fellows. She presented gold watches to two of the Society's employees who had given long and faithful service: to Mr. G. Hilderley, an expert on fruit growing; and to Mr. E. Smithers, who throughout his fifty years of service at Wisley had worked in no part of the Garden but in Wilson's original wild garden.

Then, in opening the new hostel, the Queen Mother felicitously said:

It is a particular pleasure to be here today on an occasion of great significance in the life of The Royal Horticultural Society, whose activities have long claimed my admiration and interest.

One hundred and fifty years of steady progress and unfailing service constitutes a record of which you must be proud, and I think that the Society, especially during the last few decades, has done more to bring pleasure to an ever-increasing number of people than any other association that I can recall.

It is encouraging to know that this increase in appreciation reflects a prosperity, for this has made possible continuing extensions of the service of the Society to horticulture, and it is one of these which we are celebrating today.

If ever there was a nation of gardeners, I think that we in this country can claim that distinction, and I am glad to think that the great work of The Horticultural Society during its 150 years of life has extended its influence far beyond our shores to the advantage of horticulture throughout the world.

The cherry field in spring

Wisley exhibit at Chelsea Show (1953)

Plate 19. WISLEY

(*left to right*) J. M. S. Potter, R. Adams, J. S. L. Gilmour (Director),
I. C. Enoch, G. Fox Wilson, N. K. Gould, Dr E. K. Janaki Ammal,
D. E. Green; a photograph taken in October 1950

A. Simmonds (Assistant Director at
Wisley, Assistant and Deputy Secretary, Secretary 1922–1962)

Dr H. R. Fletcher (Director of the
Garden at Wisley 1951–1954,
the author)

Plate 20. STAFF AT WISLEY

Your President has recalled that one of the earliest purposes of the founders was the training of young gardeners, and this need is certainly much greater today even than it was a generation ago. Then there were up and down the country countless large gardens, each under the direction of a skilled head gardener from whom beginners might learn the science and craft of this most delightful pursuit, horticulture. Changing conditions have put an end to all but a few of them, but though gardens are smaller, they are certainly far more numerous. It is, I am sure, largely due to The Horticultural Society, for it is by their skill in growing and display both here at Wisley and in Vincent Square that countless new doors have been opened wide.

The membership of the Royal Horticultural Society provides the best testimony to the intense and immense new interest that it has done so much to promote, and if gardens are to increase in beauty and science to assist discovery, opportunity must be provided for those who seek knowledge and experience. This splendid hostel will most admirably fill this great need, and I do not doubt the welcome it will receive. It is very fitting that it should bear the name of one whose contribution to The Royal Horticultural Society and to gardening was immeasurable.

I wish to all the students who pass through this place success and happiness, and I have now great pleasure in declaring the hostel open.

After the ceremony of opening, Her Majesty unveiled a stone tablet in the wall of the hostel commemorating the occasion and planted a tulip tree on the lawn in front of it.

These wonderfully happy celebrations were touched with sadness, for two months earlier E. A. Bowles, the greatest amateur gardener of this century and the most distinguished botanist and horticulturist serving the Society, had died in his eighty-ninth year. The Society and the horticultural world were still mourning his loss. As recently as 16 February he had attended the Society's Annual General Meeting, and had moved everyone, some to tears, when he had presented the President with the Victoria Medal of Honour, with these words:

I feel very unworthy to present this, our highest honour, to one so eminent and so kind as he has always been. Perhaps I might be likened to the skull or the mummy at the feast which the ancients had placed beside their good food to remind them that they were getting on in years. I need no such reminder. You have only to look at me. I am almost ashamed to come and hobble about among you as I do, and if it were not for the kindness of all that I meet here at the R.H.S., who are always ready to give me a hand and keep my feet from stumbling, I do not know that I should be able to carry on. But if I give up the R.H.S. and the pleasure I get from it, what will become of me? I do not think life would be worth living.

Now that I know that we have such an able President to look after our affairs it does not much matter if I get even a little older and am no longer able to come here.

373

Mr. President, I have great pleasure in presenting to you the Victoria Medal of Honour.

In making this presentation I doubt whether my technique is correct. For instance, ought I to place it in the President's left hand and ask *him* to transfer it to his right hand for the presentation to himself?

Anyway I thank you all for conferring upon me the great honour of presenting this Medal to one of the kindest and best friends that I have.

Bowles had himself received the V.M.H. as long ago as 1916; the Veitch Memorial Medal in gold for his work on *Crocus*, *Colchicum* and other garden plants, in 1923; the Peter Barr Memorial Cup for his work on *Narcissus* in 1934, and a Grenfell Medal in Gold for his flower paintings. For raising the lovely *Crocus chrysanthus* 'Snow Bunting', he had been awarded the Reginald Cory Cup in 1925. He had been a member of Council with a break of only one year since 1908, a Vice-President since 1926, and chairman for many years of several committees—the Library, the Scientific, the Narcissus and Tulip. His association with these three committees had been a long one. He had joined the Scientific in 1902, when Sir Joseph Hooker was chairman; he became vice-chairman in 1907 and chairman in 1933, succeeding Sir David Prain. In 1907 he had become a trustee of the Lindley Library; in 1910, when the Council of the Society took over the duties of the trustees, he became a member of the newly formed Library Committee and in 1939 succeeded E. A. Bunyard as its chairman. In 1904 he had become a member of the Narcissus and Tulip Committee and its chairman in 1911. (Plate 15.)

As he had forgotten more than most members of his committees ever were to know, it was but natural that at times he would be impatient with certain of his colleagues and with their suggestions. And if provoked he could be devastating. Once at a meeting of the Joint Narcissus Committee a particular daffodil was proposed for an award. For some reason Bowles took a very unfavourable view of the flower and strenuously opposed the proposal. Finally a vote was taken, the vote went against him and the award to the daffodil was recommended. As the meeting was dispersing a colleague said to him, in most friendly fashion, 'Well, Mr. Bowles, I think that was a very popular decision, don't you?' 'Yes,' Bowles replied, 'and so was the release of Barabbas!'

In the *Gardener's Chronicle*, the President wrote:

The passing of E. A. Bowles will be widely mourned, for few will dispute the estimate that, taking all in all, he was the greatest amateur gardener of the past half-century. His knowledge of garden plants was wide and deep, and both scientific and practical. Throughout his long life (in a week he would have entered his 90th year) he had lived at Myddelton House and had grown there most plants of any merit which will survive out of doors in the Home Counties, and also many greenhouse plants. And about each plant he knew not only practically everything which is to be found in literature, but also those things which are learned only by those who garden with their own hands. He could, and did, talk about plants in a most entertaining manner, and it was virtually impossible for anyone, however knowledgeable, to spend many minutes with Bowles in his garden without being impressed by the vastness of his knowledge, and without acquiring some interesting and worthwhile information.

As might be expected, his garden at Myddelton House was full of choice and uncommon plants, and nothing gave Bowles greater pleasure than to share them with others who would appreciate their worth. He was accustomed to greet an expected visitor with, 'I hope you've brought a basket', for he did not like any fellow gardener to go away empty-handed. Then, with his visitor, he would set out on a tour of the garden armed with an old digging fork which had been cut down to two prongs to adapt it for lifting pieces of plants without causing undue disturbance. Countless amateur gardeners, scattered throughout the length and breadth of the country, will treasure for many years to come choice plants which were given them by the generous owner of Myddelton House. And they will also treasure other plants, often equally attractive and sometimes rare, which came up in the soil attached to the gifts, for the soil in some parts of Bowles's garden was literally full of seedlings of the smaller bulbous plants.[1]

The Treasurer, a close friend, admirably and movingly wrote of him in the Society's *Journal*:[2]

He was nearly the last of a generation of great gardeners which included the late Lord Aberconway, Sir Edmund Loder and his brother Lord Wakehurst, Mr. H. J. Elwes, Mr. Reginald Farrer, Messrs. J. C. and P. D. Williams and many others of equal fame, and in some ways he was the greatest of them all. His interest in plants embraced not only all plants from the humblest weed to the most sophisticated Orchid—with something of a bias in favour of the weed —but everything connected with Botany as a living science. He would always put great emphasis on the word 'living'; with herbarium specimens he was inclined to be impatient—'mummies' he called them.

Those who have read his delightful books on *My Garden in Spring, Summer* and *Autumn* will remember that he came of French Huguenot stock, and that his family were connected with the 'New River' of which a loop, subsequently by-passed by the Metropolitan Water Board, flowed through the gardens of Myddelton House. He was brought up and educated with a view to taking orders in the Church of England, and, although the onset of severe attacks of asthma frustrated this intention, he remained a duly licensed lay reader, and to the end of his long life took part of the duty at his parish church. It was

---

[1] *Gdnr's Chron.*, vol. 135 (1954), p. 194.
[2] *Jl R. hort. Soc.*, LXXIX (1954), p. 290.

these severe attacks of asthma that first drove him to the high Alps and started him on the annual exiles in late spring from which he never returned without a heavy cargo of plants which he had himself collected in the wild, and which were duly ensconced in the garden at Myddelton House, whence they have been carried far and wide by all those friends, and even strangers, who visited his garden. In middle age these attacks of asthma diminished in severity and finally ceased altogether.

Bowles always used to say that it was Canon Ellacombe who had first aroused his enthusiasm for gardening. The garden at Bitton he maintained was the most interesting garden he had ever seen, and many of the more uncommon plants at Myddelton House came originally from that garden. For all his learning and astounding knowledge, Bowles was first and foremost a gardener and not a scientist. He had all the artist's delight in form and colour. Those who have seen the garden at Myddelton House when *Crocus speciosus* and *Cyclamen neapolitanum* are in flower will know that he could use colour lavishly, but it is debatable whether he himself did not lay even more stress on form. He would spend infinite care in pruning the Ivies and the conifers that were planted by the front door to the exact form that satisfied his sense of beauty. His instinct was to be restrained in the use of colour, but he loved leaf form and all sorts of variegations and used them to great effect. His bed of Acanthus and another one entirely composed of grasses and sedges, some gold, some silver, some glaucous and some green, were good examples of his genius in this direction. For Bowles was an artist. His flower paintings were of no mean order. He used to refer to what he called 'the early Bowles's' which hung rather like a stamp collection all over the wall of the staircase at Myddelton House, and the series of pictures which he made of Crocus and Galanthus are among the best flower illustrations of the present day. It is to be hoped that means will be found one day of reproducing them in colour. It was a great deprivation to him when increasing blindness finally put an end to his own painting, though, as Chairman of the Picture Committee of the R.H.S., he continued to take an active interest in the work of others up to the end.

His own personal habits were of the most Spartan sort. A lifelong bachelor, he lived in Myddelton House just as his parents had left it to him. Although so near to London it boasted neither central heating, electric light nor the telephone, and when, as some concession to modern luxury, he installed gas in the kitchen, he berated the workmen who laid the pipe for their lack of care in digging up his lawn. There are vivid recollections of staying with him one February during the war, when his house was without window panes, and the evening was spent in looking up in his very good private library, some recondite points in the nomenclature of Cyclamen, in greatcoats by the light of one oil lamp over a minute wood fire, to the accompaniment of occasional explosions of V-bombs which shook the house. He would work in the garden in all temperatures and all weathers making only minor concessions to the elements in the matter of dress and nearly always in a stiff collar. When he came to London he invariably donned the same blue suit and bowler hat which made him such a familiar figure at Chelsea and at the fortnightly shows of the R.H.S.

Bowles was a man of profound learning. Throughout a long life he had studied to acquire knowledge on those subjects that interested him. He was a recognized authority on certain genera of plants, notably Crocus, Colchicum, Galanthus, Narcissus, Anemone and his general knowledge of plants was encyclopaedic; and he was very rarely wrong in his facts. He had too a very good knowledge of botanical and horticultural literature from classical times down to the present day. In early life he had collected together a wonderful library full of rare books and early herbals, with all of which he was thoroughly acquainted. In his writings and speech he was most particular in his choice of words and had in a marked degree the scholar's desire to find the precise word that expressed his meaning.

But it was in his garden or those of his friends that the human quality of his learning came out, learning absorbed not only from books but from his observations made in continually working with his hands among his plants. Plants were almost personalities to him. He seemed always to know all about them and to be able to recognize them not only by taste on which he frequently relied, but by some sort of sixth sense. Long after his eyesight had begun to fail he had an uncanny power of recognizing plants at a distance when those with perfect sight were at fault. In his own garden he knew to a nicety where his plants were, whether they were flowering or dormant. Pointing with his two-pronged fork he would indicate exactly where a bulb was to be found, and even whether it was in the first, second or third layer—for his bulbs frequently grew one on top of the other two or three deep.

It was a rich education to go round with him and absorb, now a piece of botanical information, and now an historical anecdote, then a culinary recipe —for he was somewhat of an epicure—or even a fascinating trick like making the pig-squeak on the leaves of Bergenia, which was a joy to old and young alike. And there were many young visitors to his garden. Until he reached a very advanced age he had regularly taken the boys of his parish in Sunday School, and if their tastes were so inclined they were always welcome in his garden of an evening or at the weekend, and when one used to visit him, it was unusual if one or two boys did not turn up during the course of the visit. The only visitor who was not welcome was the person, male or female, who cared not at all for plants but chattered about something else all the way round the garden. He would suffer fools, or what passed with him for fools, with only a very moderate amount of gladness. In human beings the qualities he most valued were accuracy, sincerity and humility, and people who failed to come up to his rather exacting standards in this respect sometimes found that he had a very acid side to his tongue. Those who experienced it, however, were conscious that it was seldom unjustly applied. At his passing a large church was filled to capacity with all sorts and conditions who had come to his funeral. There can be few near-nonagenarians—or 'octogeraniums' as he himself would always call them—to whom such a tribute is paid.

There are, however, many who would pay to this great man the tribute he himself had paid to Chittenden in 1950 and who would say: 'I recall with pleasure and gratitude the blessing of his friendship and the benefit of contact with such a lovable and Christian character and the stimulation resulting from the unfailing flow of information so generously imparted to me from his encyclopaedic knowledge.'

It was appropriate that a memorial fund should be established to perpetuate Bowles's memory and to assist young gardeners to travel or to embark upon special studies.

Shortly before the sesquicentenary celebrations Mr. W. D. Cartwright, who had been on the Society's staff for forty-six years and was a familiar figure at Vincent Square and especially at Wisley, where he had been a friend to many past students, retired. In 1908 he had enrolled at Wisley as a student-gardener, had gained the Wisley Diploma in Horticulture in 1910 and in that same year had been appointed chief clerk at Wisley and secretary of the Society's Floral Committee. Except for one very short period, he held the latter office continuously until 1924, when the Floral Committee was divided into A and B, and he took over the secretaryship of Floral A—the florists' flowers committee. On his retirement he did not relinquish this secretaryship; he carried on until he had been secretary of this committee for fifty-four years. He is but one of many who have given a lifetime of service to the affairs of the Society, and in 1964 he was deservedly awarded the Veitch Memorial Medal in silver for all his good works.

In the same year as Mr. Cartwright retired from Wisley, Dr. Fletcher resigned from the directorship to return to Edinburgh to become assistant keeper of the Royal Botanic Garden, and subsequently, in 1956, Regius Keeper. Mr. F. P. Knight succeeded Fletcher and was at once plunged into the administration of developments in the Gardens and Wisley village. In 1955 the Society bought the land between the Gardens and the road to the village and converted part of it into a much-needed car park. Two years later an implement shed and workshop were erected in the field west of Battleston Hill, and in the following year the first floor of the old hostel by the frame-yard was converted into a flat, the ground floor being adapted for use in connection with the distribution of seeds. Two more cottages were built in the village in 1956, to be followed by two more and four bungalows in 1961; these allowed for the demolition of three sub-standard cottages.

In 1956 there were changes in the personnel at Vincent Square. Brigadier C. V. L. Lycett retired; he had acted as Secretary since just after the war and by his energy, tact and administrative abilities had played a most important part in the Society's great postwar expansion. It was utterly appropriate that Mr. Simmonds, the Deputy Secretary, who had spent the whole of his career with the Society, should at this stage be promoted to Secretary. (Plate 20.)

Sir David Bowes Lyon (he had been knighted in 1959) was an enthusiastic supporter of international horticultural shows, and through his influence the Society upheld the prestige of British horticulture by staging an exhibit in the form of a woodland garden at the quinquennial shows at Ghent in 1955 and 1960. At the Floralies Internationales held in Paris in 1959, the Society not only exhibited another woodland garden but, with the co-operation of some amateurs and horticultural traders, staged three other exhibits. And again in 1963 the Society exhibited at the International Horticultural Show at Hamburg. To most of these exhibits, so different from those usually seen on the Continent, Wisley, and especially Francis Hanger, the Curator, contributed much.

From time to time the Society has received various bequests, but much the most generous was that received in 1957 under the will of Alfred Gurney Wilson, who bequeathed to the Society his library, his paintings of orchids, and the residue of his estate amounting in all to over £25,000, 'For the purpose of constituting a trust fund (to be known as the "Gurney Wilson Trust Fund"), the income arising therefrom to be used for furthering the horticultural work of the said Society in such manner as the Council of the said Society shall in their absolute discretion deem fit'. Not content with that which he had done for the Society during his long life—and he had given unsparingly of his time and knowledge—he had been anxious to do all in his power to assist in the continuation of that work in perpetuity.

At the Annual General Meeting in 1958 the President intimated that the Society proposed to create a Long Service Medal for gardeners who had spent the whole of their working lives in one single garden, nursery or horticultural establishment—and the announcement was greeted with tremendous applause. Thus, instituted in 1958, the Society's Long Service Medal is awarded to any man or woman of British nationality, resident in the United Kingdom, who has completed forty years' continuous satisfactory employment as a gardener or in some other horticultural capacity in a private, commercial, public or botanical garden, nursery, market garden, fruit plantation or seed trial-ground with one employer or family, or in one place. Bars are awarded for fifty or sixty years' service. By the time of the Annual General Meeting in 1959, 201 Medals had been awarded, sixty-one with one bar and thirteen with two bars.

In announcing the Long Service Medal, the President spoke of long service of another kind.

The Chairman of our Orchid Committee, Mr. Curtis (I do not think he is here today) has just completed fifty years on that Committee, and he has com-

379

pleted fifty-four years on the Narcissus and Tulip Committee. He only just beats that other great stalwart, Mr. Leak, the Chairman of the Narcissus and Tulip Committee who has been fifty-two years a member of the Committee. Both Mr. Curtis and Mr. Leak are still going strong.

In point of fact this was not quite true—for only Mr. Leak was 'still going strong'. Less than two months after the Annual General Meeting, Charles H. Curtis, the doyen of British horticultural journalists, passed away at the age of eighty-eight. He had joined the staff of the *Gardener's Chronicle* in 1918 and been appointed managing editor the following year, a position which he held until he retired in 1950, after thirty-one years of service, years during which he reported the affairs of the Society with great accuracy and sympathy. He had edited *The Orchid Review* from 1933 until his death. He had been a founder-member of the National Sweet Pea Society in 1900, its honorary secretary, its honorary treasurer, its president, and had edited many of its publications. To the National Chrysanthemum Society he had also acted for some years as secretary and to the British Florists' Federation he had been founder-secretary. Since 1912 he had been a judge at Chelsea Flower Show and, because of his wide knowledge of plants, had been greatly in demand as a judge at shows in Paris, Rotterdam, Amsterdam, Haarlem, Boskoop, Genoa, Rome. Passionately interested in the welfare of those employed in horticulture, for close on sixty years he was chairman of the United Benefit and Provident Society, as well as chairman for many years of the Gardeners' Royal Benevolent Institution.

Curtis retired at the age of eighty, and, though he was still to be a contributor to the *Chronicle*, he wrote his last leader on 24 June 1950.[1]

Any man who has become what Dean Hole's gardening friend described as an 'Octogeranium' has much cause to be thankful and particularly so if a kindly Providence has blessed him with good health and the energy that usually accompanies it. Such a blessing has been mine and it has permitted me to engage, for more than half a century, in an occupation that has never ceased to be enthrallingly interesting, always entertainingly varied and always congenial. . . . On many occasions I have said I would not willingly change my occupation and the passing of the years has not altered my opinion.

This is surely the testimony of all who have given their lives, unselfishly and unsparingly, to the cause of horticulture.

Curtis, more than anyone, would have enjoyed the friendly association and appreciated the significance of the Third World Orchid Conference of 1960. This conference, sponsored jointly by the Society

[1] p. 243.

and the American Orchid Society, was held in London. Nearly 550 members, representing twenty-one countries, countries as far apart as Australia, Japan, Hawaii, held their meetings at Vincent Square from 30 May to 5 June—immediately after the Chelsea Show where had been staged the greatest display of orchids since the International Exhibition of 1912, a display occupying an area of 5,000 square feet. The Old Hall was hardly to be recognized, divided as it was into two sections. One was used as a lounge, decorated in midnight blue and yellow, to display paintings of orchids which had received awards from the Society and which showed the evolution of orchid hybrids throughout a century of hybridization. The other served as a lecture theatre where, for four days, speakers from fifteen countries and internationally renowned in the orchid world covered all facets of orchid interest.

Thus, during these four days, the Society united into one world all orchid-growing countries with bonds of friendship. At the Chelsea Show many of those attending the conference had met for the first time for several years and the orchid enthusiasts had made Chelsea a very invigorating and somewhat light-hearted affair. Not inappropriately, therefore, the conference was launched on the same gay, rather flippant, note, when, after Sir David Bowes Lyon had opened the proceedings, Dr. W. T. Stearn of the Department of Botany, the British Museum (Natural History), London, and formerly the Society's Librarian, described orchids as being full of wickedness, deceit, and immorality; their numbers excessive; their flowers upside-down to confuse the botanists; as being capitalists, living on the sweated labour of the fungi in their roots; as immoral, promiscuous, producing bi, tri-, and quadri-generic hybrids; as practising deceit with their floral structures, the classic example being *Orchis apifera*, the British Bee Orchid.

The males of certain bees and wasps emerge before the females and, looking about for a mate, what do they see but an apparent female sitting on top of a stalk. But this isn't really a female—it is the bee orchid impersonating one, giving out the same scent as the female insect. How was a poor celibate wasp or bee to know it was being deceived? It was attracted to the bee orchid, and contact affected pollination, but the deceitful orchid never even offered the insect a drink!

After four days of meetings, the conference ended on a more sober note, with the recommendation that the Society assume the duties of international registration authority for the cultivar names of orchid hybrids, an important and valuable work which had been undertaken in the past by Messrs. Sander & Sons of St. Albans. In 1895 this firm of orchid growers instituted a system for the registration of the names of orchid hybrids and in 1906 published the first issue of *Sander's List of Orchid*

Hybrids. In subsequent years several addenda were published and orchid hybridists throughout the world have been greatly indebted to the enlightenment and initiative of the Sander family. However, by 1960 the great increase in the number of hybridists and consequently the great increase in the number of hybrids had rendered the task of registration a rather arduous one, and Messrs. David Sander's Orchids Ltd. were anxious to be relieved of the work. Thus as from 1 January 1961 the Society took over the duties of International Registration Authority for Orchid Cultivars and agreed to publish from time to time new registrations and so keep up to date *Sander's List of Orchid Hybrids*.

The Orchid Conference was the last outstanding event during the Presidency of Sir David Bowes Lyon. The hope of Professor Dr. E. van Slogteren, expressed at the time of the sesquicentenary, 'that for a long number of years [the Society] may continue to be guided by its eminent President', was not to be fulfilled, for Sir David died suddenly and prematurely on 13 September 1961, at the age of fifty-nine. Once again the horticultural world grieved the loss of one who, in the words of Mr. Palmer, the Treasurer and a close friend, 'touched life at so many points that his passing will leave a gap in the lives of innumerable people, great and small. For with all his great connections and important activities, he would talk to anyone on level terms and with a touch of gaiety and humour that always warmed the heart.'[1]

The Council, acting under the Bye-Laws of the Society, elected Lord Aberconway as President *ad interim* until the next Annual General Meeting. (Plate 17.)

Although Lord Aberconway had been a member of Council only since 1958, he had impressed all his colleagues by his tremendous energy and drive, his great business sense, his high intelligence, his ability quickly to see to the heart of a matter, no matter how complex, his steadfastness of purpose, and his kind and generous nature. Moreover, he had surprised many of his colleagues by his knowledge of the Society and of horticulture. However, such knowledge was but natural, for Lord Aberconway had had the highest regard—almost reverence—for the work of his father, which he knew intimately, both in business and in horticulture. He was fully aware of the great demands which the affairs of the Society had made on his father—and the nature of these affairs. His knowledge of plants had been mostly gained from the great collection in the family garden at Bodnant. Long before he was appointed to the Council he had become an authority on rhododendrons, camellias, magnolias, and other plants. His few years on the Council and his attendances at the Society's Shows had brought him into contact with a wide spectrum of plants and of horticultural problems, all of which his keen

[1] *Jl R. hort. Soc.*, LXXXVI (1961), p. 422.

mind had easily and eagerly absorbed. Such qualities, combined with the courage to reach, and implement, a decision which may not prove popular, are required of the ideal President. It was indeed fortunate for the Society that Lord Aberconway, in spite of countless other commitments, acceded to the Council's unanimous request that he succeed his great friend in the office of President.

CHAPTER TWENTY-TWO

WISLEY IN THE 1960s

THE 1962 ANNUAL GENERAL MEETING, THE FIRST AT WHICH LORD Aberconway presided, was a memorable one. The new President spoke in most moving terms of his predecessor:

It is with hearts still heavy from the death of our late much-beloved President that your Council appears before you today. Sir David Bowes Lyon was a wonderful President. He was all that a President should or could be. He was unsparing in the service of the Society. Nothing was too much trouble for him. He was personally known to, and indeed was a friend of, very many Fellows in all walks of life. I think I would be voicing the opinion of those of you, probably the great majority who regularly attend our Annual Meetings, if I say that you too share that sense of very personal loss which your Council feels. You will remember the charm and the friendliness that came from him at those meetings, and the wisdom and wit of his words. But his service to the Society went far deeper than that; far deeper than I could hope to express. I will only say that his personality and enthusiasm established a spirit of trust and friendly co-operation among members of the Council, on the Committees, among the staff at Vincent Square, and at Wisley, which is a very great asset to your Society.

I think, ladies and gentlemen, that you would wish to stand for a moment in grateful and affectionate remembrance of our late President.

One outcome of Sir David Bowes Lyon's death was that a vacancy was made in the ranks of the holders of the Victoria Medal of Honour, a vacancy which was most appropriately filled by the gracious acceptance of the Society's highest honour by Her Majesty Queen Elizabeth the Queen Mother, the sister of Sir David. Thus for the first time in the Society's history the V.M.H. was received by a brother and sister.

History was made again at this 1962 A.G.M. when the Treasurer, the Hon. Lewis Palmer, presented the V.M.H. to Lord Aberconway. This was the first time the award had been given to the third generation of any family; Lord Aberconway's father had received it in 1934 and his grandmother in 1931.

The death of Sir David Bowes Lyon was not the only one Lord Aberconway had to report. Some five weeks after Sir David died, Francis

Hanger, the Curator at Wisley, also passed away, at the early age of sixty-one. Since his appointment to Wisley in 1946 he had done much to advance the prestige of the Society, by far-reaching developments in the Garden, by the great exhibits which he had staged at Vincent Square and at Chelsea—as well as on the Continent—by his writings in the Society's *Journal* and *Year Books*, and by his appearances on television in 'Gardening Club'. Undoubtedly his greatest achievement was the planting of the Wisley woodland garden on Battleston Hill and the breeding of certain hybrid rhododendrons and azaleas, including the splendid hardy yellow-flowered hybrids of *Rhododendron litiense* and 'Adriaan Koster' parentage—the 'Moonshine' group. Several of these have received the Award of Merit, as indeed have other of Hanger's hybrids of different parentage such as 'Lady Bowes Lyon', 'Billy Budd', and 'Beefeater'—the latter, a *Rhododendron elliottii* hybrid, having been awarded the Society's F.C.C. Hanger's contributions to horticulture were deservedly rewarded; in 1939 he became an Associate of Honour of the Society, at the age of thirty-nine the youngest recipient ever to be so honoured, and in 1953 he was awarded the V.M.H.

On the death of Francis Hanger the post of Curator at Wisley was not filled. Council believed, very rightly, that the Director, Mr. Knight, was perfectly qualified to bear the duties of Curator, for he was a fine gardener and plantsman with considerable experience of organization. As a youth he had gained a sound knowledge of plants even before entering on any organized training, for he had worked at Werrington Park in Cornwall, where there was a splendid collection of plants, especially of rhododendrons—the introductions of E. H. Wilson, G. Forrest, and F. Kingdon Ward. From 1919 to 1923 he had been a probationer-gardener at the Royal Botanic Garden, Edinburgh, where he developed an intense interest in plant propagation, and then for six years had worked at Kew, first as a student-gardener, and later in charge of the Arboretum nurseries. His apprenticeship over, he had gained further experience, with Messrs. Bakers' Nurseries Ltd., with Knaphill Nursery as general manager, and finally with Messrs. R. C. Notcutt, as general manager and managing director. Thus throughout his career he had had the opportunity of cultivating almost every kind of plant and had gained much administrative experience. It was only natural therefore that Council, rather than fill the vacant post of Curator, should ask the Director to play a more direct role in the maintenance and development of the Garden. To this end he was relieved of much of the administrative work, which then fell on the shoulders of Mr. M. D. Burge, the administrative officer, who had succeeded Mr. Cartwright as chief clerk.

A year before Hanger died, on 19 September 1960, the Society had suffered another grave loss through the death, at the age of sixty-three, of its botanist at Wisley, Norman Kenneth Gould. He had arrived at Wisley as a student in 1914 and had joined the Royal Garrison Artillery in 1916. Not until 1920 did he return to Wisley, and then to gain the Wisley diploma and to be appointed assistant botanist, responsible in the main for teaching, under Chittenden, the following year. Thus Gould worked at Wisley for forty-six years without the slightest desire to work elsewhere, even though tempting offers were made to him. From 1925 until 1959 he was secretary of Floral Committee B and, for some years, secretary of the Rhododendron Committee, the Scientific Committee and the Rhododendron Group.

With an undoubted flair for plant taxonomy, it was inevitable that, over the years, he should accumulate a vast store of information on the taxonomy of cultivated plants; in fact, during this century few can have been his equals in this; this, at any rate, was the opinion of many, including E. A. Bowles. For nearly forty years he imparted his knowledge to the students at Wisley and to the many Fellows of the Society who not only corresponded with him but also visited him at the Garden. Not a very fluent speaker, he was nevertheless a splendid teacher. He was, too, a fine photographer, being responsible, with James Wilson, for all the photographs for the *Vegetable Garden Displayed*, for illustrations for articles, and for scores of lantern slides. Because of his quiet and unassuming, often retiring, nature, much of his work was not always recognized, though this did not worry him. Even so he was deeply moved when in 1950 the Society conferred on him the Associateship of Honour. Splendid botanist and teacher, and truly great gentleman that he was, he as much as anyone deserved this honour. At Wisley he will never be forgotten, for his name is commemorated in the Norman Gould Prize awarded annually to the two Wisley students who make the best herbarium collections of British plants from outside the Garden, and submit them for the Wisley diploma examination.

Gould's post of botanist was filled by his assistant, Mr. C. D. Brickell, who four years later was to become the Society's senior scientific officer in succession to Mr. D. E. Green, who retired on 31 March 1964, after thirty-six years of service with the Society, and was succeeded by Miss A. V. Brooks.

Green, after graduating in science at the University College of North Wales, Bangor, and after working for a time in the plant pathology section of the Department of Agriculture at Leeds University, came to Wisley in 1928 as mycologist to the Society. For the next thirty-six years he was to advise Fellows of the Society on all matters pertaining to the diseases of their plants, was to lecture to the Wisley students—as well as to those at Kew—on horticultural mycology, and at the same time undertake research work on various plant-disease problems, such as antirrhinum rust and parsnip canker. Some twenty-five years of experience are embodied in his book *Diseases of Vegetables*, published in 1942. Always a popular member of the Wisley staff and a great favourite with the Wisley students, he was presented on his retirement with a cheque for £190 from former students and present colleagues, at the Annual General Meeting of the R.H.S. Garden Club in 1964.

This meeting of the Society's Garden Club—and the attendant cricket match—was not quite the happy occasion which many of those who look forward with keen anticipation to these annual meetings had envisaged. One personality, popular with his Wisley colleagues, with the Vincent Square staff, and with a vast number of Fellows, was not present; Percy James Dykes had died on 4 April at the early age of fifty-five, and his countless friends were still sad at heart. First employed at Wisley for four years—from 1929 onwards—he returned once again to Wisley in January 1946, eventually to be appointed foreman, and then superintendent, of the glass-house department. This highly exacting post, which carries the responsibility for producing large quantities of a very wide range of plants for the trials, teaching and examinations, Dykes held until he died, and at all times filled with great success and even greater modesty. For his splendid services to the Society the Associateship of Honour was conferred on him in 1963.

Yet another member of the Wisley staff was to sever his services with the Society. In 1965 Mr. R. E. Adams, who had entered Wisley in 1941 as a student and who had later acted as assistant to three Directors, resigned to take up an appointment with the Department of Agriculture and Fisheries for Scotland.

In spite of the loss of long-serving and experienced members of the Wisley staff, the 1960s have been years of immense progress in every direction. New turnstiles have been installed at the main entrance gate, the gate-house has been extended, new stone walls have been constructed as well as a new tarmac approach apron; Chittenden's outstanding creation in Seven Acres, the heather garden, has been almost entirely replanted; in the Pinetum many decrepit conifers, mostly spruces, have been grubbed and replaced by more suitable subjects; in the famous Wilson wild garden, some old trees, long past their best, have been removed to allow for more light, old paths renewed and new ones made to connect more easily this part of the Garden with the Rock Garden, where, at the foot, old conifers have been cut down and the area thus cleared blended into the existing Rock Garden by the addition of new paths and rocks; in the region of the Alpine House splendid new frames have been built to accommodate newly introduced plants, chiefly from the eastern Mediterranean region.

This part of the world is particularly rich in bulbs and the alpine department already possessed a selection from the expeditions of Dr. Peter Davis and Mr. Oleg Polunin. In 1960 Rear-Admiral J. P. W. Furse retired from a distinguished career in the Navy and celebrated by undertaking with the Society's editor a short two months' plant-collecting expedition across Turkey and Iran. This was in the nature of a reconnaissance for his future, longer expeditions. Quite a large collection of bulbs and tubers of such genera as iris, particularly of the Juno, Oncocyclus, and Reticulata sections, cyclamen, fritillaria, tulips, and lilies was brought back and duly planted in pots in frames by the Alpine House at Wisley. Paul Furse had long been a keen student of fritillaries and was also known for his extensive paintings of flowers.

In 1962 he ventured forth again, this time with his intrepid wife, and spent seven months travelling in Turkey and Iran, climbing high into the Zagros mountains in the south, the home of some of the rare Dionysias, and sleeping in his much-loved Land Rover, the 'Rose of Persia', in places ranging from 'deep snowdrifts to hot deserts', to use his own words. This expedition yielded a tremendous collection, increased by further material from Turkey, Iran, and Afghanistan in 1964, when they penetrated into Badakshan, the north-eastern province of Afghanistan near the Russian border. Here they found many fascinating plants, links between the bulbs of the Pamir-Alai ranges of Russian Turkestan and these areas. They brought back many colour forms previously unrecorded and unseen in cultivation of Juno and other irises and also of tulips.

In 1966 they were again in Afghanistan, but floods prevented them from reaching the Badakshan region again. Furse's articles in the *Journal* have proved among the most popular features.

In 1963 another collecting expedition, largely of Wisley inspiration, visited Iran and Turkey. It was organized by Brian Mathew, one of the Wisley students, who took with him three others, David Baxter, Stuart Baker, and David Pycraft. The party was awarded the Bowles Memorial Scholarship. They had wanted to explore in the Caucasus, but permission was withheld by the Russians. Even so, they found Iran a rich field, arranging with Furse to cover different areas from those he had visited.

Mathew had become enthusiastic about the Middle East flora and in 1965 went to Turkey and south-east Europe, this time accompanied by Margaret Briggs and Dr. A. J. and Mrs. Tomlinson, enthusiastic members of the Alpine Garden Society. David Baxter joined him again for part of the time and so did Paul Miles, another Wisley student.

All this collecting activity gave the alpine department at Wisley a huge collection of bulbs, and it was found that these not only grew much better, but also saved much labour, when planted out in raised metal frames where they could be dried out but not desiccated in the summer as in their native country. Thus two long frames have been built and these form a source of great interest to visitors in the spring. Probably never before has such a large and varied collection of Middle East bulbs been assembled.

Between the Alpine House and the Rock Garden at Wisley a new peat garden has been created, whilst the peat garden on Battleston Hill has been extended; on this hill more paths have been constructed, more primulas, meconopsis, and lilies have been planted and, in some areas, many shrubs removed to allow more space for the development of others; the rose borders on Weather Hill have been entirely replanted and much of the poor sandy soil replaced by new loam; the annual borders, for so long a conspicuous and popular feature on Weather Hill, have been moved to a new position opposite the dahlia trials; the old examination plots, so familiar to many hundreds of students, are now the site for the trial of deciduous azaleas, and new examination plots are sited on the fruit field; new glass-house accommodation has been provided mainly for forcing plants for early flower shows, whilst the former Peach House has been adapted for the production of large quantities of young plants in the spring and for display purposes later in the year; new vistas have been opened up, one of the most impressive being that from the restaurant area into Seven Acres.

Much the most important developments centre round water and sewage. An additional water supply to the Garden has been installed involving the laying of a new water main and the provision of two additional pumps, new pump houses and a storage tank to hold about 60,000 gallons of water; and, of even greater importance for the Garden and for the staff living at Wisley, a main sewage system has been installed. In the village much new living accommodation for the staff has been provided, while on the site the National Fruit Trials vacated in 1960 a new sports field and sports pavilion have been constructed.

One addition to the Garden has not met with universal approval— the Bowes Lyon Memorial Pavilion. Inevitably it is condemned by those who hold the view that any building alien to its environment is wrong; inevitably it is much admired by those who approve of contemporary design and the use of contemporary materials. The Society held a competition for designs for the Pavilion open to registered architects and qualified members of the Institute of Landscape Architects. Ninety-eight entries were received and considered by a Board of Assessors, the members of which were Lord Aberconway, Sir William Holford, Mr. Geoffrey Jellicoe, Mr. Peter Shepheard, and Mr. Peter Youngman, the President of the Institute of Landscape Architects. Their report, together with photographs of the winning design, submitted by Mr. D. Lees, A.R.I.B.A., was published in the *Journal* in July 1963 and models of the design, and plans of others, highly commended by the assessors, were exhibited at Chelsea Flower Show in that year.

The pavilion is sited on Weather Hill at the western end of the broad grass paths which run between the long rose borders. On the design of a building which has caused so much discussion as this one it is only fair to allow the architect, Mr. Derrick Lees, to speak:

The design is contemporary, involving materials, techniques and ideas prevalent in this age. There are some classical elements in the design, which is formal and embodies a geometrical system of order that is carried through in three dimensions. Thus the measurements have their own inevitability. The aim has been to bring all parts of the Pavilion together in one theme so that a sense of harmony and unity is created for the whole building. New materials have made possible new opportunities.

The Pavilion is approached up a slight gradient between two wide beds of roses which are about 150 yards long. The visitor gradually comes up, under and into the Pavilion. Just beyond and flanking it are two fine Dawyck Beech trees and beyond them a grove of Silver Birch, all of which are important elements in the composition. Yew hedges have recently been planted to shield the Pavilion and to form a back-cloth behind the Silver Birch. Two spaces are created by the planting, one in and around the Pavilion and the other in the Silver Birch grove from where there is a fine view through the centre of the Pavilion and down the concourse of roses.

The basic idea for the design came to me very shortly after reading the conditions of the Competition. I envisaged an undulating timber roof apparently floating over the Memorial stone in its site at the top of the rose borders. The two faceted roof lights of perspex are unusual and perhaps the first of their kind while the deeply recessed aluminium mouldings round the pillars, which give strong vertical reflections and shadows, provide some of the qualities of classical pillars. The structure is steel with timber framing and a teak ceiling finish. The paving is formed of reconstructed York stone. In the centre of the floor of the Pavilion is the Memorial stone of black marble, the inscription of which is beautifully carved by Mr. David Kindersley.[1]

The inscription on the memorial stone reads:

THIS PAVILION
STANDS IN GRATEFUL AND
AFFECTIONATE MEMORY OF
THE HONOURABLE
SIR DAVID BOWES LYON
K.C.V.O.
PRESIDENT OF THE SOCIETY
FROM 1953
UNTIL HIS DEATH IN 1961

JULY 1964

[1] *Jl R. hort. Soc.*, LXXXIX (1964), p. 363.

The Wisley staff cleared and levelled the site, laid the foundations, the paving and memorial stone and carried out the necessary landscape work in the surrounding area. On 2 July 1964 Her Majesty the Queen Mother, with Lady Bowes Lyon, Lord Elphinstone, and several of Sir David's personal friends, paid an informal visit to the Garden, where they were received by the President and Lady Aberconway with members of the Council, and where they met Mr. Lees, Mr. Kindersley, and the members of the Garden staff who had helped in the construction.

In contrast to the Memorial Pavilion, the extension to the restaurant has won universal approval, and it is, indeed, a most elegant building utterly appropriate to its surroundings.

The responsibilities of the Director and his staff for growing an enormous amount of plant material for trial, exhibition, and show purposes, in addition to the maintenance of the Garden and the Wisley estate, which now consists of about 300 acres, are very great even under ideal climatic conditions. How much more so, therefore, when the valuable plant material is subject to such hazards as winter damage by birds, snow, late spring frosts, gales, storms, all of which are liable to strike the Garden, and very often do, during any year. Fortunately only very occasionally is real havoc caused, as during the ninety-minute storm, with its attendant $4\frac{1}{4}$ inches of rain, which hit Wisley on 16 July 1947, when Seven Acres was covered with 3 inches of water; when one great torrent of water swept from Battleston Hill, through the nursery, the delphinium, iris, and other trial grounds, and the Curator's garden, and poured into the car park and over the walls and steps near the Laboratory; when an even greater torrent swept from Weather Hill, uprooting roses and much else in its path and carrying tons of soil into the frameyard; when glass-houses and stoke-hole were flooded; when paths in the line of the torrents were scoured into crevices in some instances measuring 9 feet by 6 feet by 4 feet; when labels and plants were found 500 yards away from their true homes; when the annual border was ruined and the trial of annuals had to be cancelled; and when, miraculously, the Rock Garden escaped severe damage. Mercifully such destruction is infrequent. Even so it *may* happen more than once in a lifetime—as it did at Wisley in 1965, again in July.

On 21 July at 1540 G.M.T. a small tornado passed over an area of the Garden only some 60 yards in diameter and lasted only for a few minutes, but left immense destruction behind it, chiefly in the region of the fruit field. The Society's fruit officer, Mr. E. G. Gilbert, described the devastation wrought:

The damage was both frightening and heartbreaking on the fruit field. No description can adequately convey the utter mess and devastation that confronted one. The whole floor of the apple orchard was so strewn with half-grown apples that it was impossible to walk without treading on them. Whole trees lay with much of their root system in the air and in the plum orchard full grown trees were smashed to pieces. The subsequent count of casualties showed:

Trees completely or partially uprooted—174 (127 apples, 43 plums, 4 peaches)

Trees badly damaged and/or leaning—58 (30 apples, 26 plums, 2 peaches)

In addition to the obvious casualties many other trees certainly suffered considerable root damage and could be rocked by hand quite easily.

The whole of the fruit field area was littered with twigs of willow, cedar and ornamental oak which had presumably been carried a quarter of a mile or more from the garden at Ockham Mill and the river bank nearby.

Perhaps the most frightening damage was to be seen among the large forest trees bordering the Portsmouth Road. Specimens of nearly 6 feet girth had been snapped in half and several large trees fell right across the road. Two vehicles were trapped though no one was more than slightly hurt.

But it was the chaos in the fruit field that one inevitably turned to. Offers of help were immediate and generous and the Meteorological Office, who had been contacted as soon as the tornado was sighted, undertook a full survey of the damage, including aerial photographs. From it all interesting, often puzzling, facts kept emerging. Invariably damage increased proportionally with the size of tree (of nearly 200 two-year-old pear trees only three were damaged); a full grown peach tree, broken from its stock at ground level, had landed upside down in the head of an apple tree some 40 feet distant; most of the uprooted apples had suffered no branch or crotch breakage, whereas many of the plum trees were smashed to pieces or snapped off half way up the trunk; the changing, yet progressive, direction in which groups of trees had fallen showed clearly the cyclonic nature of the winds. Yet there was no clearly defined track of damage. Rather were there several large areas of real devastation, the remainder of the orchards being strewn with smaller ones. Individual isolated trees were often found with roots in the air but with no apparent damage to neighbouring specimens. It is often characteristic of this type of tornado that it appears to bounce along and only comes into violent contact with the ground at irregular intervals.

Undoubtedly, one of the most remarkable effects the storm had was on a particular apple tree. Much of its root system had been snatched from the soil only to be found neatly lying on the surrounding grass. The nature and suddenness of the force that struck the tree must have been sufficient to pull the roots upwards clean from their anchorage yet with a bare minimum of disturbance to the soil and with the tree still perfectly upright and unmoved from its correct station. This is consistent with the centre of the storm passing directly over this tree.

Naturally, an immense amount of work was entailed in clearing up the damage. After careful and detailed inspection by independent experts most of the uprooted and/or leaning apple trees were pulled upright, staked and replanted; the majority of damaged plums were too smashed to attempt similar treatment and, in any case, it is known that plums do not possess the same power of recovery that apples seem to have. . . .[1]

By 1967 about 120 apple trees set upright or replanted after the tornado had recovered remarkably, and no doubt the new irrigation system, as well as Mr. Gilbert's expert and close attention, were responsible.

Now that the National Fruit Trials are no longer at Wisley, the Society's collection of fruit, in a sixteen-acre field to the west of the Bowes Lyon Memorial Pavilion, assumes considerable importance. The collection includes eight acres of apples comprising over 500 cultivars, all on Malling VII stock. Plums occupy approximately four acres, and the 175 or so cultivars are on Brompton rootstock. However, the plum collection was so badly damaged by the tornado that it is planned to propagate a new collection with the trees on St. Julien A rootstock and planted as pyramids rather than as the existing half-standards. Of pears, about eighty of the leading cultivars are all on Quince A rootstock. On fences are fan-trained specimen trees of apple, pear, plum, peach, nectarine, morello and sweet cherry. There are also collections of blackberries, loganberries, strawberries and fruit-tree stocks.

Fellows still interested in growing their own fruit can find much to learn in the near-by model fruit gardens. These were planted in 1947 at the suggestion of the Society's Fruit Group, and their layout is designed to show how small areas can best be used for the production of hardy fruits and to stress the advantage of growing them in one self-contained plot where their requirements do not conflict with those of other crops. The layout of each garden illustrates the grouping of the various fruits, their recommended planting distances, the type of plant best suited to the private garden—cordon, dwarf pyramid, and dwarf bush. The large garden, 48 feet by 90 feet, is suitable for supplying a large private household with fruit for the greater part of the year; apples and pears are grown as cordons, plums as half-standards, and bushes of black, red, and white currants, gooseberries and raspberries are included. The medium garden, 48 feet by 60 feet, contains the same range of fruit, but on a smaller scale, and, except for one row of cordon pears, apples and pears are grown as dwarf pyramids. In the small garden, 30 feet by 60 feet, there is a row of cordon pears, nine dwarf bushes of apples on Malling VII stock, as well as currants, gooseberries, and raspberries.

Today, more Fellows are more concerned with growing their own vegetables, and thus no doubt will find the model vegetable gardens of even greater interest. The largest is 90 feet long and 30 feet wide and is cropped in accordance with the plan given in the Society's *Vegetable Garden Displayed*. Properly cropped and maintained, this size of plot can

[1] *Jl R. hort. Soc.*, XCI (1966), p.102.

supply all the vegetables needed by the average family, except for such items as mushrooms and asparagus. For smaller families, the plot measuring 48 feet by 16½ feet demonstrates ways of growing a wide variety of the smaller type of vegetable in a limited space, whilst a third plot, 48 feet by 36 feet, is cropped with vegetables occupying the ground for a number of years, or with those which are normally propagated by vegetative means, such as sea-kale, globe artichokes, rhubarb, and asparagus.

The trials of ornamental plants and of vegetables, the latter in Wisley village, so fascinating to Fellows and in some ways the most important aspect of the work in the Society's Garden, epitomize over one hundred years of the Society's endeavour to show to the public the best kinds of plants to grow. In the report of the Floral Committee of 9 February 1860 there is this statement:

The arrangements to be made for carrying out the experimental trials of New Flowers and Plants at Chiswick, which the Council had entrusted to the Committee, having been discussed, it was agreed, that during the present season, trial collections should be obtained, as complete as possible, of all the following kinds of flowers: Verbenas, Bedding Pelargoniums of all kinds, Petunias, Bedding Lobelias, Heliotropes, Fuchsias, Tydaeas and Achimenes, Bouvardias and Variegated Begonias; and that Fellows of the Society, and others, should be invited to contribute plants, etc. for this purpose.[1]

And the Garden Superintendent's report to the Council of 16 April 1860 states:

Since my last report, we have had several presents of plants, from the principal Nurserymen in the neighbourhood of London; consisting of Achimenes, Begonias, Pelargoniums, Petunias, Fuchsias, Verbenas, Geraniums and Azaleas; all of which, excepting the Azaleas, are for trial; and will be brought in due time before the Floral Committee. I have also sown upwards of 300 kinds of annuals in pots, to be eventually planted out in the Experimental Flower Garden, for the purpose of having their merits tested by the Committee.[2]

The first inspection of flower trials took place, apparently at Chiswick on 2 August 1860, 'to inspect Trials of various annuals, achimenes and variegated begonias', and the first detailed report on a flower trial, signed by Joshua Dix and Thomas Moore, chairman and secretary respectively of the Floral Committee, is dated 13 September 1860.

[1] *Proceedings Roy. hort. Soc.*, 1 (1860), pp. 162–3.
[2] *Proc. R. hort. Soc.*, 1 (1860), pp. 176–7.

In the meantime, in the report of the Fruit Committee of 7 February 1860, 'The Secretary reported that preparations had been made at Chiswick for the trial of the different varieties of Garden Vegetables . . . according to a plan adopted by the Council; and suggested that during the present season comparative trials should be made of the different varieties of Peas, Beans, Kidney Beans, Broccolis, Savoys, Borecoles, and Cucumbers, which was agreed to.'[1] This appears to be the first reference to a trial of vegetables by the Society.

Thus for over a century the Society has conducted its floral and vegetable trials and over the years many hundreds of thousands of stocks have been tested; of ornamental plants alone, from 1946 to 1963, there were over 34,500.

Today there are two groups of floral trials, the permanent and the invited. The permanent trials are continued from year to year. Plants for these trials are selected by the appropriate specialist committees and are grown beside a collection of standard cultivars maintained largely for purposes of comparison. If, after a number of years, plants are not recommended for an award, they are deleted from the trial. Thus herbaceous plants are normally removed after three years, and rhododendrons after ten years. The following permanent trials are at present in being, after having been selected by the appropriate committees, who are also engaged in the judging of them (in most cases by the appropriate subcommittee). Floral Committee A deals with the gladioli, hemerocallis, paeony, perennial phlox, and pyrethrum trials; the Rhododendron and Camellia Committee has care of the rhododendrons, and the Narcissus and Tulip Committee of the daffodils; the Joint Border Carnation and Picotee Committee is concerned with border carnations and the Joint Dianthus Committee with pinks; other joint committees deal with trials of dahlias, delphiniums, early flowering chrysanthemums, and iris. The joint committees are formed of representatives of the R.H.S. and outside specialists, whilst other committees are composed entirely of R.H.S. members.

The invited floral trials are those to which Fellows and the public are invited to send plants or seeds in an appointed year. Such trials are usually of short duration and are repeated at intervals of a few years in accordance with a programme known as the trials calendar. This calendar is reviewed annually, the Council reserving the right to delete projected trials, insert new ones, and alter the arrangements in any way which seems in the best interests of the Society. These trials include many types of annuals, a wide range of bedding plants, greenhouse and pot plants, bulbs, corms, small shrubs, heathers, and, in this case each year, sweet peas.

[1] *Proc. R. hort. Soc.*, 1 (1860), p. 155.

None of the vegetable trials is permanent—they are all short-term invited ones and are judged by a subcommittee of the Fruit and Vegetable Committee, which also decides which plants shall be accepted for trial, and which standard cultivars shall be grown; the subcommittee also plans the three-year trials programme. At fairly regular intervals the vegetable trials include brussels sprouts, carrots, cauliflower, onion, cabbages, peas, lettuce, leeks, broad beans, runner beans, and beet.

Up to the time of judging, cultivars in a particular trial are, as a rule, labelled only with indicative numbers; only after judging are the plants labelled with their names and with the names of their senders. However, when a collection of well-tried, well-known, standard cultivars is included in a trial, for purposes of comparison, these are labelled with their names from the commencement of flowering.

To be present at the judging of any trial by the appropriate committee or subcommittee, as, for instance, the Director of the Garden is privileged to be (Fellows and the general public are not so privileged), is a humbling and an enriching experience. Most of the judges are specialists in the particular plant they are judging; they have a lifetime of experience in the cultivation of the flower or vegetable in question; many can look back on twenty or thirty or more years of judging and can remember accurately and vividly the cultivars which were given awards many years ago; they can see differences in seedling type, in habit, in flower, which the untutored and inexperienced eye cannot detect; and those with the greatest knowledge and wisdom are the most unassuming.

The awards available for plants grown in trials are: First Class Certificate—to plants of great excellence; Award of Merit—to plants which are meritorious; Highly Commended and Commended; and the awards are given to plants for garden decoration, for general garden use, for the open border, or for the rock garden.

The responsibility of growing the material for the trials is, of course, great, as is the responsibility of recording the trials. The trials recorder's duties are onerous and demand great meticulousness. Invitations to participate in the trials have to be sent out; entry forms and labels have to be checked carefully; notes made of dates of seed sowing, of planting, of inspection, and of growth throughout the trial; and finally, detailed descriptions of all plants on trial must be prepared, including measurements of the various parts of the plant and the careful matching of the colour of the flower with the Horticultural Colour Chart. Such duties extend well beyond the normal working day. When J. B. Paton left the service of the Society in 1957, the duties of trials recorder were undertaken by Mr. P. Walker, who at that time was foreman of the vegetable trials. He was appointed trials recorder and vegetable trials superintendent, Mr. O. J. Clayton being made the superintendent of the floral department. It was but appropriate that in 1965 Mr. Walker, for his great services in his most exacting post, should have had the Society's Associateship of Honour conferred on him. At the Annual General Meeting in 1966 great applause greeted the President's citation:

[At Wisley] he does a wonderful job in ensuring that the trials are real trials, that all entries get equal growing conditions and equal treatment, namely, the best. The Vegetable Trials are of course his real love, and his enthusiasm is such that he has more than once almost persuaded me that size is not in fact the main criterion on which vegetables are judged. Your knowledge, Mr. Walker, your unswerving devotion to work, your skill as an instructor, your readiness to help others, and the service you have thereby rendered to horticulture, make this award entirely suitable.

I have received today a very nice gesture from our Wisley students, who have cabled me: 'Please convey our congratulations to Mr. Walker on his award.' I do so with great pleasure.

In the final analysis, of course, it is the Director who carries ultimate responsibility for all the trials; responsibility, too, for the organization and supervision of the Society's examinations, the horticultural instruction course to thirty-six students, in fact for the entire administration of the Society's affairs at Wisley.

The administrative staff, the botanist, the entomologist (entomologists have stayed but a short time at Wisley in recent years, though Miss J. Maynard has acted as assistant to the entomologist—and, for a period, assistant to the mycologist—for more than twenty years), the plant pathologist, the trials recorder, the fruit officer and the Laboratory steward and librarian (in this capacity Mr. R. P. Scase has completed almost twenty years of service) all have their headquarters in the Laboratory. Very many Fellows avail themselves of the services of the staff, seeking information on the diseases and pests of garden plants and on methods of control. Requests for the identification of flowers and of fruits and for guidance in their cultivation and propagation amount to several thousands every year, whilst questions relating to the characteristics of soils and fertilizers are also very numerous. Research is also undertaken on specially selected problems in pest and disease control. Members of the staff conduct courses of lectures to the horticultural students and demonstrations to Fellows, as well as certain outside lectures. Other important activities of the Laboratory and outdoor staffs are the preparation and staging of exhibits at the Society's Shows, contributing to, and otherwise assisting in the production of, the Society's many publications, acting as secretaries for various committees meeting fortnightly at Vincent Square, and helping to organize the

397

practical work for the National Diploma in Horticulture and other examinations held annually at Wisley. For the use of staff and students a library comprised mainly of reference works and scientific periodicals is maintained and with the library is associated a small herbarium of garden plants and specimens representative of the British flora.

The portraits hanging in the Laboratory are a visual commentary on much of the Society's history: Thomas Andrew Knight, great scientist and the Society's outstanding President from 1811 to 1838; John Lindley, as Assistant Secretary, Vice-Secretary, and Secretary 'the greatest servant the Society has ever had'; Archibald Barron, for thirty years the Superintendent of the Society's Gardens at Chiswick; George Ferguson Wilson, one-time owner of the Wisley estate and creator of the present wild garden at Wisley; Sir Thomas Hanbury, who presented to the Society, in trust, some sixty acres of G. F. Wilson's estate, including the wild garden, in 1903; Samuel T. Wright, the first Superintendent at Wisley and great exhibitor of flowers, fruits, and vegetables; George Fox Wilson, entomologist at Wisley for over thirty years; Francis Vernon Darbishire, the chemist at Wisley from 1918 to 1932; William R. Dykes, Secretary of the Society from 1920 to 1925 and a great authority on irises; Frank Reader, the courteous chief cashier of the Society from 1892 to 1927; Sir Harry Veitch, for fifty years, until his death in 1924, the outstanding horticultural figure of his day and for many years a member of Council; other past members of Council, William Cuthbertson, Henry B. May, who for many years was chairman of the Narcissus and Tulip Committee and of the Floral Committee, and George William Leak, who was also a Vice-President of the Society and a great lover of the Garden; and the most outstanding figure in the history of Wisley Gardens, and great servant of the Society in almost every capacity for forty-five years, Frederick James Chittenden.

It is not possible to work at Wisley without being continually reminded of the loyal and lasting services to horticulture which all these, and countless others in the employment of the Society, or in any way concerned with the affairs of the Society, have given. There are many students who come to Wisley and react in the same manner as did J. B. Paton, who, in an account of Wisley Gardens at the time of the Society's sesquicentenary, wrote:

In 1907 there was but a small laboratory called the Botany Room, an office, a working laboratory and a dark-room. It was in this small building that Mr. F. J. Chittenden began his work for the Society and initiated many of the developments which have since materialised. When the writer arrived at Wisley as a student gardener, having heard a great deal about this remarkable man, and realised for the first time that so much of his work had originated in this small part of the present laboratory, it fired the imagination of the impressionable student and thrilled him much more than the whole of the rest of the building.[1]

Two plaques in the Laboratory no doubt have also fired the imagination of students and will continue to do so. One commemorates the name of J. K. Ramsbottom, who, within a year or two of being a Wisley student, discovered the hot-water treatment for narcissus eelworm and thus saved from peril the daffodil industry, and the other the name of Frank Kingdon Ward, who, within a year or two of being a student at Cambridge, began a lifetime of work in the field of plant introduction and enriched our gardens with countless good plants.

Certainly those in training at Wisley live in a remarkable horticultural atmosphere and certainly, too, Chittenden, who did so much for horticultural education, would have approved of the present-day training. The teaching facilities in the Laboratory have been vastly improved and the two-year course of instruction in the theory and practice of horticulture provides a very sound grounding in almost every aspect of the profession. Students work in the various departments of the Garden during the day, under the supervision of the superintendent or the foreman in charge, all of whom are expert in their various subjects. Who more expert, for instance, than the superintendent of the Rock Garden, Mr. W. K. Aslet? His wide knowledge of alpine and rock-garden plants and of their cultivation is hardly to be rivalled, as the wonderful pans he displays in the Alpine House well show. The practical work in the Garden is supplemented by a series of some seventy practical demonstrations concerned with the growing of shrubs, trees, flowers, fruits, and vegetables, as well as by regular tests on the naming of plants, pests, and diseases. Thus for two years students have the opportunity to familiarize themselves with the rich collections in the Garden, so many of the plants, especially those in the trials, being comparatively new to horticulture. Moreover, students are allowed to visit some of the Society's Shows, some to assist, from time to time, the secretaries of the committees which meet at Vincent Square and at Chelsea Flower Show. This in itself is a splendid opportunity for the young horticulturist.

In the afternoons the students attend lectures in the Laboratory given by members of the Wisley staff and by outside specialists; lectures in elementary and systematic botany, plant physiology, plant breeding, plant pathology, horticultural chemistry, entomology, fruit and vegetable cultivation, commercial glass-house crops, machinery, draughtsmanship, garden design and layout, surveying and levelling, meteorology, bookkeeping. On completion of the course students sit the examinations of the Wisley diploma.

[1] *Jl R. hort. Soc.*, LXXIX (1954), p. 496.

Whilst undergoing this intensive training in this remarkable environment, students are given over four pounds a week for pocket money and
free board and lodging in the very modern, well-equippped hostel,
Aberconway House. Those who are accepted for training at Wisley are
indeed fortunate.

CHAPTER TWENTY-THREE

VINCENT SQUARE IN THE 1960s

AT THE ANNUAL GENERAL MEETING OF 1962, LORD ABERCONWAY announced the retirement from the office of Secretary of Mr. A. Simmonds.

He has spent the whole of his working life—and I mean working—in the service of the Society and is unequalled in his knowledge of its history, its ramifications and the personalities of those who worked for it and with it. In short, he is the fount of great knowledge and the source of great wisdom. The affairs of the Society grow continually more complex, and Mr. Simmonds, as our chief executive, has been a tower of strength to everyone. Certainly I am confident that my colleagues on the Council, past and present, will agree with my view that Mr. Simmonds is one of the most distinguished Secretaries that this Society has ever been fortunate enough to have.

We wish him a long and happy retirement from his executive duties. But we shall not let him lead an idle existence; indeed, that would be quite out of character. He will sit on various of our Committees; we shall put to him various conundrums for him to solve, and we hope he may be persuaded to apply his great knowledge of the Society and its past to writing its history.

And later in the meeting, when presenting Mr. Simmonds with a gold Veitch Memorial Medal, the President further said:

Mr. Simmonds, beneath his modest exterior, is really a very modest person. And I shall get into fearful trouble with him if I let myself go and say publicly what he knows I think of him; so I will content myself with saying that this Medal is a token of the esteem in which you, Mr. Simmonds, are held by members of Council, past and present, by your staff, and, by all the Fellows, even those you may have put in their place from time to time, with words courteous but said with an expressiveness not quite so gentle. Well done, thou good and faithful servant!

Good and faithful indeed; and none more so. How could it have been otherwise when at the age of fifteen or sixteen he had come under the influence of Chittenden at Wisley and, one feels, for the rest of his life had always maintained the image of Chittenden before him? It is an odd coincidence that their handwriting was so similar. Moreover, one also feels that, throughout his long professional life with the Society, the image of John Lindley was also constantly before him. Their professional careers with the Society ran remarkably close parallel courses. Lindley, at the age of twenty-three, had been appointed Assistant Secretary at the Chiswick Garden in 1822 and in 1826 had been given the additional post of Assistant Secretary at the Society's headquarters in London. For twenty years, from 1838 until 1858, he held the post of Vice-Secretary to the Society before being finally appointed Secretary. When he retired from the secretaryship in 1863 he had served forty-one years with the Society. Simmonds, after being at Wisley from 1907 to 1911, first as a student and then as a demonstrator (and gaining most marks in the first examination for the National Diploma in Horticulture), after serving in the First World War, and attaining the rank of major in the machine gun corps, being twice mentioned in dispatches and receiving the Military Cross, and after spending three years as assistant horticultural superintendent in Kent, was appointed Assistant Director at Wisley on 1 January 1923, at the age of thirty. From 1925 for twenty-one years he acted as Assistant Secretary to the Society at Vincent Square, was Deputy Secretary from 1946 until 1956 before being appointed Secretary. On retiring in 1962 he had served the Society in an executive position for forty years.

Simmonds has described Lindley as the greatest of all the Society's servants. This statement may be argued. It should not be forgotten that Lindley had other commitments apart from those with the Society; whilst employed by the Society, for over thirty years (1829–60) he was also Professor of Botany at University College, London, and for over twenty years (1841–65) helped to edit the *Gardener's Chronicle*. Moreover, in Lindley's day the Society was not the vast organization it was later to be; membership was never more than a few thousands and its affairs were fairly simple compared with what they were to become under the régime of Wilks, for instance. It may be argued that Wilks rendered the Society the greatest service, for, during the thirty-two years he was in the Secretary's chair (1888–1920), the Society rose from poverty to prosperity, its membership increasing fifteenfold. But for twenty-four of these thirty-two years Wilks had other outside work to occupy him, for he had been trained for the Church and held the living of Shirley (1879–1912). It may also be argued that in his many varied capacities none worked more steadfastly and more successfully *entirely* in the interests of the Society, which was his whole life, than did F. J. Chittenden; as researcher, teacher, and landscape designer at Wisley; as the initiator at Wisley of the trials which were to develop into the National Fruit Trials; as one of the pioneers in modern horticultural education; at

Vincent Square as technical adviser, editor of the Society's publications, especially the *Dictionary of Gardening*, and as keeper of the Lindley Library; as representative of the Society at international botanical and horticultural congresses, where he ensured that, henceforth, the Society should be intimately concerned with the nomenclature of cultivated plants.

These matters may be argued. But none may argue the fact that the quadrumvirate of Lindley, Wilks, Chittenden, and Simmonds stands supreme in the annals of the Royal Horticultural Society.

Apart from carrying many of the Society's administrative burdens, especially those in connection with the Shows—Chelsea Show particularly—probably Simmonds's best work was done in connection with the Society's Narcissus and Tulip Committee and with international plant registration. In 1926 he succeeded C. H. Curtis as secretary of this committee and took over responsibility for the *Classified List of Daffodil Names*, which had been first published in 1908. Simmonds found that the list was far from complete, that many cultivars in commerce both in Britain and in Holland had not been registered. By convincing raisers and stockholders of the desirability of using only registered names, he soon established a state of affairs in which it was very rare to find a daffodil in commerce in Europe under an unregistered name.

The work on narcissus so impressed the Dutch that the General Bulb Growers' Society of Haarlem sought the Society's co-operation in an endeavour to straighten out the nomenclature of tulips in the same fashion as had been done for daffodils. An enormous number of new tulips, especially of the Mendel and Triumph groups, had been indiscriminately named and tulip nomenclature was in a state of chaos. To determine questions of synonymy, tulip trials were held in Holland for several years, and examined by a joint committee of the R.H.S. and the Dutch society. The results of the work were published in 1939 in *A Classified List of Tulip Names*, in a foreword to which Mr. E. A. Bowles wrote:

It seems to me only right that the gardening world . . . should know to whose zeal, skill and indefatigable labour they owe the high standard of completeness and accuracy attained in this List. Therefore, as Chairman of the Narcissus and Tulip Committee . . . I have taken upon myself to thank Mr. A. Simmonds . . . in the name of the President and Council of the Royal Horticultural Society, for the unremitting care he has bestowed on this complicated and difficult task. I prophesy that all interested in tulips will thank him for many years to come as they discover for themselves the usefulness and value of so complete a list of recognised tulip names.

Since that time the list has been taken over and maintained up to date by the Royal General Bulb Growers' Society, and adopted as the international register of tulip names.

As Mr. G. W. Leak wrote in the Society's *Daffodil and Tulip Year Book* for 1959:

The usefulness of a system of registration of cultivar names, as exemplified in Mr. Simmonds's work with daffodils and tulips, was recognised at the International Horticultural Congress in 1952, and he may well be proud that his work has been regarded as the pilot scheme for the system of international registration of cultivar names which is being gradually adopted for all genera of which large numbers of cultivars exist.

Writing today, Mr. Leak would no doubt have added the clause 'and in which the Society is now so deeply involved'—or words to this effect.

Simmonds's two predecessors in office, Durham and Lycett, had not been horticulturists; they had been essentially administrators. The Council, even in 1925, had rightly taken the view that the work of the Society was expanding so rapidly and its varied affairs becoming so complex that one with administrative experience and organizing ability, rather than a horticulturist, was necessary in the Secretary's chair. Simmonds, on the other hand, had been unique in that he had great knowledge of horticultural matters as well as an intimate knowledge of every single aspect of the Society's work. Obviously on his retirement it was desirable that a trained administrator once again be appointed as his successor, and Mr. John Hamer, who had been on the Society's staff for a year, assumed the role of Secretary in 1962.

A graduate of the University of Leeds, Hamer's wide administrative experience had been acquired in the later war and postwar years in Malaya. In 1946 he had joined the Malayan Civil Service and during the period 1948–55 had served as a district officer in Malacca, then as District Officer, Klang, Selangor, where he had established the first financially autonomous town council in the Federation. He had also planned and established a model 200-house urban rehousing scheme for working-class families and had set up a successful adult education scheme. In 1955, having been accepted as British Adviser by the Rajah of Perlis, he had prepared proposals for the reorganization of the state administration in anticipation of independence, together with plans, which were adopted in detail, for the introduction of autonomous local government. Early in 1957, when British Advisers were withdrawn from all states, he had become deputy chairman and chief executive officer of the Rural and Industrial Development Authority, which had as its aim the encouragement and economic development of existing rural industries, and the introduction of new ones, by way of grants, loans, training courses, managed prototypes and the provision of improved

The Alpine House in spring   Dry wall at main entrance in spring

Plate IV THE GARDENS AT WISLEY

roads, water supplies, drainage and other rural necessities. Promoted from this post to that of secretary to the Ministry of Agriculture, he had been responsible for the implementation of policy and its integration throughout the seven departments controlled by the Ministry. From this post he had joined the Federal Treasury as Controller of Supply—and thus had been responsible for the supervision and control of expenditure, and for the preparation, for presentation to Cabinet, of examined expenditure estimates for all departments.

In October 1958 he had become State Secretary, Penang, and thus in charge of the administration and state head of the Civil Service. In this capacity he was a member of the Executive Council—the State Cabinet—and responsible for the preparation of all matters tabled in the Council. In addition, the preparation of government-inspired addresses in the Legislative Council became his responsibility. Further, as head of the Civil Service in the state he was responsible for the supervision and control of all state departments, for promotions and discipline and for staff recruitment, training and service negotiations. Thus Hamer's experience included particularly the economic and financial aspects of administration at many levels, together with an interest in social and educational developments and continuous practice in problems of personnel recruitment, training, and welfare.

Experience of this nature is, of course, quite invaluable to the secretary of a Society such as the R.H.S., for the Secretary must make many objective judgements untrammelled by gardening and horticultural considerations. The lack of horticultural training and knowledge is of little consequence, especially when the President and Treasurer are renowned horticulturists—let alone all the Council members and the Society's Wisley staff. The President, Lord Aberconway, has spent his life in the horticultural atmosphere of Bodnant and is an expert on many groups of trees and shrubs. Until the Annual General Meeting of 1965 the Hon. Lewis Palmer had continued to occupy the Treasurer's chair and, in this capacity, gave great service to the Society for twelve years. Mr. Palmer is a great gardener who until recently gardened on chalk in Winchester and is particularly authoritative on South African plants. In the office of Treasurer he was succeeded by Mr. Oliver E. P. Wyatt, a headmaster by profession and another very fine gardener, the horticultural godchild of Mr. E. A. Bowles and Sir Frederick Stern, and an immensely successful grower and breeder of lilies, being awarded the Lyttel Lily Cup in 1953. One of his many hybrids, 'Oliver Wyatt'—of *Lilium parryi* parentage—was given the Award of Merit in 1965—the same year in which he himself was awarded the V.M.H.

Mr. Hamer is ably assisted by two Assistant Secretaries, one of whom, Mr. L. G. Pavey, joined the Society forty years ago, in 1927, as subscriptions clerk. Pavey is a native of Shirley and one of several members of the Vincent Square staff who have been employed by the Society as a result of the direct, or indirect, influence of Wilks. Frank Reader, the Society's chief cashier from 1890 to 1927, was a teacher at Shirley and churchwarden at Wilks's church, before being induced by Wilks to work for the Society. Fred Streeter, who, after being clerk, and assistant cashier, succeeded Reader, was also a native of Shirley. So was J. Thornton, who was appointed subscriptions clerk in 1929, and is now in charge of the subscriptions department; he was induced to come to the Society by Streeter. H. A. B. Coppard, who joined the staff of the Society in 1910 and retired from the post of chief clerk on 31 August 1961—after over fifty years of service—though not a native of Shirley, certainly lived there for a considerable time during his employment with the Society. Pavey arrived at Vincent Square because his father was a friend of both Streeter and Coppard. He was closely associated with the organization of the Thirteenth International Horticultural Congress in 1952, the Society's sesquicentenary celebrations of 1954, and with the Third World Orchid Conference of 1960. Today he is in large measure concerned with such financial matters as the oversight of the subscriptions department, hall lettings, *Journal* advertisements, insurance, and deputizing for the Secretary on the Finance and General Purposes Committee.

The Secretary's other assistant is Mr. J. Cowell, who has been with the Society only since the end of 1958. He is largely involved in the organization of the Society's Shows and competitions, the lecture programme and the important registration work for daffodils, delphiniums, dahlias, orchids, and dwarf conifers. When necessary he must deputize for the Secretary at Meetings of the Council. In the organization of the Shows he is assisted by Mr. R. F. Sargent, who has been in charge of the Shows office since 1951, when he succeeded Mr. Blampied. In fact, Sargent has been in this office since 1934 (he joined the staff in 1929) and has played his part in the organization of over thirty Chelsea Flower Shows.

Anyone holding a post of great responsibility with the Society, and especially at Vincent Square, must be deeply conscious of the devoted work of others in the same sphere in the past. And none more so than he who is in charge of the Society's publications, which, throughout the Society's history, have maintained an extraordinarily high standard of excellence. No R.H.S. publication has surpassed the somewhat luxurious—and, in view of the Society's limited financial resources of the time, certainly too expensive and too extravagant—first publication, the two series of ten quarto volumes of the *Transactions*. These were published between 1807 and 1848 and contain not only splendid practical papers and a record of some of the Society's activities but fine colour plates as well, the latter mostly the work of William Hooker and Mrs. Withers, many of which are coloured, or partly coloured, by hand, and then sometimes varnished. The *Proceedings*, issued as an octavo volume, separate from the *Transactions*, between 1838 and 1843, and sold as a single volume in 1844, were printed in small type and for the most part contain accounts of the Society's meetings. It is now a very rare work and the Society possesses only one copy. Further issues of the *Proceedings* were bound up with the *Journal*, the first octavo volume of which was issued in 1846. This series of the *Journal* was continued for nine volumes through 1854, by which time the Society's financial affairs were in such dire straits that its library was sold in 1859. No further issue of the *Journal* was made until 1866, when a new series was started and, at first, issued at irregular intervals.

The new series of the *Journal* was the first to name an editor—the Rev. M. J. Berkeley, mainly responsible for the founding of the Scientific Committee, who edited the first four volumes, in 1866, 1870, 1872, and 1877. Samuel Jennings, the Assistant Secretary, was the editor of Volume V (1879) and the Rev. George Henslow, secretary of the Scientific Committee, of Volume VI (1880). Volumes VII—X, which contain the reports of conferences and of frost damage, do not carry the names of the editors. D. Morris, the Treasurer, and W. Wilks, the Secretary, edited Volumes XI and XII (1889–90), whilst John Weathers, Assistant Secretary, was co-editor with Wilks of Volumes XIII–XX (1891–7). Wilks, unassisted, edited the next nine volumes (1897–1905) and in 1905 retired from the editorship after nearly twenty years of service. George S. Saunders took over from Wilks during 1906–8 and was responsible for Volumes XXX, XXXI, XXXII, and the first part of Volume XXXIII. The second part of this volume was taken over by Chittenden, who then continued to act as editor until 1939 and thus was responsible for Volumes XXXIV–LXIV. Sir Daniel Hall, assisted by Mr. R. E. Hay, accepted responsibility of the editing from Chittenden; Mrs. Vera Higgins replaced Hay as assistant in 1941 and became editor when Sir Daniel died in the latter half of 1942. When Mrs. Higgins retired at the end of 1945 the present editor, Mr. P. M. Synge, was appointed and thus has been responsible for all the volumes from LXXI.

Mr. Synge is a graduate of Cambridge, where he took an honours degree in Natural Sciences, including botany. While at Cambridge he undertook his first plant-hunting and botanical expedition with the Oxford Exploration Club to the mountains of Sarawak in Borneo, and later spent nearly a year collecting plants in the Equatorial mountains of East Africa, where he saw many of the fantastic giant senecios and lobelias which unfortunately have refused to settle down to conditions in most British gardens. Synge, moreover, has had experience of book publishing and is himself the author of several books, including *Mountains of the Moon, Plants with Personality, A Diversity of Plants, Flowers in Winter*, and the *Collins Guide to Bulbs*. He is an exceedingly keen gardener, interested particularly in trees and shrubs, especially magnolias and rhododendrons, as well as in bulbous plants, especially lilies. His success as a cultivator of lilies and his knowledge of these plants is such that, in 1965, he was awarded the Lyttel Lily Cup.

As the *Journal* is circulated monthly to all Fellows in many countries, it must, and does, provide interest to all grades of gardener, from the specialist downwards. In its pages a deep and rich mine of information is contained, information, moreover, which is readily accessible, for each volume is carefully indexed and every ten years the indices are consolidated into a ten-year volume. Thus anyone interested in a particular plant can readily trace all the *Journal* references to it over a long period of years, back, in fact, to the time when the first consolidated index began. There are few garden plants of merit which are not written about with authority somewhere in the pages of the *Journal*. Even cultivars are described in detail, especially the newly introduced ones which have received an award after trial at Wisley or at the Vincent Square Shows. Details of the former are published in the *Proceedings* of Committees, which are sent only to those Fellows and institutions who request them. Not only new plants—and old—but new advances in horticultural science and technology, the texts of lectures delivered to the Society and accounts of plant-collecting expeditions—all this, and much more, is chronicled in the pages of the *Journal*.

It is appreciated that, for anyone starting in gardening, the *Journal* contains much that is rather too advanced. However, for the novice the Society provides more elementary publications. *The Vegetable Garden Displayed* and *The Fruit Garden Displayed*, with their numerous illustrations, are really visual aids to garden operations concerned with fruit and vegetables. The series of *Gardening Handbooks* prepared with the help of the Society's editorial staff and published by Penguin Books in conjunction with the Society treat in a simple fashion, and at a small price, groups of flowering plants and command a wide sale, the volume on roses, for instance, having sold well over 100,000 copies. Such publications, rather elementary though they may be, are completely authoritative; they are not written, as is so much horticultural literature today, by journalists who often have little practical experience about the matters on which they write, but by the most knowledgeable and expert gardeners, amateur or professional, whom the Society can command.

For the specialist or enthusiast for a particular group, the Society publishes a series of three *Year Books*—the Daffodil and Tulip, the Lily, and the Rhododendron and Camellia. These, intentionally, are more up to date than the *Journal* with information on new cultivars, often describing many plants not yet available to the public. The same applies to new techniques. In fact, the *Year Books* include articles which would be regarded as too technical or too botanical and too limited in appeal for the *Journal*. At the same time the enthusiastic beginner is not neglected. The interests of enthusiasts for other groups of plants are covered by publications of their particular specialist society, such as the *Rose Annual* of the Royal National Rose Society, or the *Iris Year Book* of the British Iris Society.

As the Society is a scientific one, it naturally publishes works of a more scientific nature which make it advisable for the editor to be either a scientist or one with a strong scientific bent. The *Dictionary of Gardening* is an encyclopaedia, with brief descriptions and cultural requirements, of all the main species of flowering plants likely to be found in cultivation in the temperate regions—with a good many tropical ones as well—together with longer articles on other aspects of horticulture. The *Dictionary* consists of four large quarto volumes and a Supplement. A new Supplement is to be published in 1969.

Another publication which caters for the scientist, especially for the plant taxonomist, is the *Botanical Magazine*, the oldest illustrated scientific plant periodical, with coloured plates, in the world. The plates of the *Magazine* were hand-coloured until the end of Volume 165, published in 1947, since when the plates have been mechanically reproduced, although great care is still taken to ensure as high a standard as possible. Since 1922 this unique magazine has been published by the Society; in fact, as Mr. Synge has said, 'the Fellows of the Society are the owners of the *Magazine*, and through members of the Council, the trustees of a notable and great tradition'.[1]

And again for the more scientific gardener, from time to time the Society has published monographs of particular genera. Some, such as H. W. Pugsley's *Monograph of Narcissus, sub-genus Ajax*, and R. Lloyd Praeger's *Monograph of Sedum*, have been printed in the *Journal*. Others the Society has published separately: Sir Daniel Hall's *The Genus Tulipa* (1940), Sir Frederick Stern's *Study of the Genus Paeonia* (1946), and *Snowdrops and Snowflakes* (with a chapter by E. A. Bowles) (1956), G. H. Johnstone's *Asiatic Magnolias in Cultivation* (1955), and Mr. J. R. Sealy's *Revision of the Genus Camellia* (1958)—all of them splendidly illustrated.

These monographs are obviously among the most important contributions to horticultural knowledge as well as to systematic botany that

[1] *Jl R. hort. Soc.*, LXXIII (1948), p. 5.

the Society has made and they do help in the stabilizing of plant names, since they must rest on many years of both study and growing of plants. In this field lie perhaps the best possibilities of combining the work of botanist and gardener, but, as Synge has said in a talk at a recent International Horticultural Congress,

There is considerable difficulty . . . in combining satisfactorily in one volume of a monographic calibre the views of the systematic botanist working in a national herbarium and the knowledgeable grower of the plants, sometimes an amateur scientist but rarely with the same conceptions and language. The grower tends to be obsessed by the merits of the outstanding individual and so may become an excessive 'splitter' while the herbarium botanist tends to view the taxon in the light of the population represented by the range of his specimens.

Another major publishing undertaking has been the Society's Horticultural Colour Chart, the first serious attempt in Britain to regulate the description of colour in flowers by comparison with standard colours. The first chart, prepared by Mr. Robert F. Wilson, the secretary of the British Colour Council, was published by the Society, in two volumes, in 1941. Twenty-five years of experience of its use showed how it might be improved, and thus in 1966 the Society published a completely revised chart giving a wider range of colours and printed by a new process of the McCorquodale Colour Display Company by which each colour is mixed separately and is then led down by a separate duct on to the paper. The new chart has 200 leaves of different hues; the leaves are arranged in four fans and each leaf shows four patches of colour of lessening degrees of intensity. Its production represents a major undertaking and the expenditure of much time by several people, especially by Dr. R. H. Stoughton, lately Professor of Horticulture at Reading University and Vice-Chancellor of Ghana University, a member of Council and the recipient of the V.M.H. in 1954.

The history of horticulture in Britain—and beyond—since 1804 is embodied in the Society's publications, especially in its *Transactions*, *Proceedings*, and its *Journal*, and all—and a great deal else—are available for consultation and study in the Society's Library.

To enter the Lindley Library—with its portrait of John Lindley, russet-cheeked, brown-bearded, with moustache trimmed, and side-whiskered, with high forehead and thin steel-framed spectacles, and with a sprig of rose hips in one hand—is to be aware of the fragrance of history and to be reminded of much of the Society's past; of the nucleus of the Society's Library in the rooms of the Linnean Society; of the first recorded acquisition of five French gardening books presented in 1806 by Sims, probably he who edited Curtis's *Botanical Magazine* from 1801 to 1826; of the first purchase of books by the Society, including the first edition of Miller's *Gardeners Dictionary*; of the first book-case to be purchased at the end of 1813; of the appointment of the first Library Committee in 1817; of the transfer of the library to the Society's own house at 21 Regent Street 'to the relief of the Linnean Society'; of the steady growth of the library by gift and purchase until the Society's financial crisis of 1859, when the library had to be sold, by auction, by Messrs. Sotheby & Wilkinson, then of Wellington Street, The Strand, the 985 lots realizing the sum of £1,112. 1s. 6d.; of the rebuilding of the library by purchases, donations, and bequests, soon after the sale, when the Society launched on the disastrous Kensington adventure in 1861; of the Society's purchase of Lindley's library for £600 when Lindley died in 1865, and the vesting of the Lindley books in the Lindley trust; of the housing of the Lindley Library, with the Society's own books, in the Society's premises at South Kensington and in due course of the transference, with the Society's office, first to 117 Victoria Street and then to Vincent Square; of the scheme of 1910, approved by the Charity Commission, whereby it was arranged that 'the body called the Royal Horticultural Society shall be the Trustee of the Charity, provided that the Society shall exercise its powers and duties as such Trustee through the Council for the time being of the Society'; of the arrangement, at the same time, that the Society's own library, which by 1910 was considerable, should become the property of the trust, thereby ensuring that never again would the Society's library be sold; of the furnishing of the Library in a large room at the north-west end of the second floor (now the typists' room) first by Baron Sir Henry Schröder and secondly by Baron Bruno Schröder; of the transference of the Library to the new third floor of Vincent Square; of the evacuation of most of the Library during the years of the war; of various bequests, such as the great Cory bequest of 1934 and the Stoker bequest of 1964; and of the various Librarians—for a short time Mr. W. B. Hemsley; Mr. H. R. Hutchinson from 1911 until 1931; from 1931 until his retirement in 1939 Mr. F. J. Chittenden, who also held the post of technical adviser; from 1939 until 1952 Mr. W. T. Stearn, who had been Assistant Librarian since 1932; from 1953 until 1956 Miss L. D. Whiteley; and since 1957 the present Librarian, Mr. Peter F. Stageman, who was trained at the University Library, Cambridge, where, apart from war service, he remained on the staff for twenty-two years, and who has generously supplied the following account of some of the Lindley Library's treasures.

'The modern history of the Lindley Library may be said to have begun with the appointment in 1932 of Mr. William T. Stearn, whose arrival at Vincent Square heralded an era of development in the

Library's work and an increase in the quality and quantity of the book stock. As with all active and growing libraries, more space soon became an urgent need, and this was remedied by adding to the tops of the wooden cases in the corridor and by fitting extensions above the steel cases in the stack room.

'Over this period Mr. E. A. Bowles presided over the Library Committee, acting as its chairman from 1934 until his death in 1954.

'Mr. Bowles was succeeded in the Chair by Sir George Taylor, and under his guidance many gaps in the Library's resources have been filled and the much-needed extension of accommodation achieved.

'The most important event in the prewar years was the arrival in 1936 of the books bequeathed by Mr. Reginald C. Cory, who had died in May 1934. Mr. Cory was a wealthy industrialist and a generous benefactor to the Society, serving on the Council and on several committees including the Library Committee. The bequest consisted of books on botany and horticulture which Mr. Cory had collected over many years and which included fine copies of the great colour-plate folios of the nineteenth century.

'The research in connection with the cataloguing and collating of the Cory bequest brought the Library international importance for bibliographical reference and by this means it received one of three copies of Miss M. F. Warner's typescript, *Early Horticultural Literature : a check-list of works published in 16th to 18th centuries :* this is one of the most useful bibliographical reference works in the Library.

'Mr. Stearn carried out bibliographical research on many of the more important works and inserted his notes of published reports into the front of relevant books. The prime importance of priority of publication so far as names of plants are concerned has made Mr. Stearn's researches in this field of lasting value.

'Exchanges of publications with institutions, overseas as well as at home, have been established and this has added considerably to the wealth of accumulated knowledge stored in the Library. The Society's *Journal*, which is used for exchange purposes, does much to make the progress of British horticulture known abroad. At the time of writing the *Journal* is sent on exchange to ninety-two societies and institutions abroad and to thirty-nine at home.

'By the time Mr. Stearn left in 1952 the re-cataloguing of the Library's rare and valuable books was well in hand. This work was being carried out mainly by Mrs. F. M. G. Cardew, who had been trained at the Bodleian Library, Oxford, and had managed the Lindley Library during the war years when Mr. Stearn was absent on active service. Mrs. Cardew continued with the cataloguing until her retirement in 1960 and, although her work was incomplete, that which was done was meticulously carried out and has proved of great value. Mrs. Cardew had a few years of retirement before her death in February 1967.

'Nurserymen and seedsmen have for many years sent their catalogues to the Library and as new editions are received the earlier ones are carefully stored for future reference. These lists, recording thousands of cultivar names and descriptions, are filed under the names of firms and are frequently consulted by Fellows and visitors.

'Mr. (now Dr.) Stearn was succeeded by Miss L. D. Whiteley, who remained until the end of 1956. Miss Whiteley established the subject catalogue which, after fifteen years, has grown into a valuable subject bibliography containing a reference to every bound book received by the Library since 1952.

'By 1962 the need for shelf-space had become a matter of urgency and the Library Committee, under the chairmanship of Sir George Taylor, noting that the average annual rate of shelf-run used was 65 feet, drew up a memorandum stating immediate requirements and estimated needs for the next twenty-five years. The report was accepted by the Council, but a suitable site for an extension to the Library proved to be a problem, and after two or three schemes had been proposed and rejected it was finally decided to utilize a part of the basement of the Old Hall. Construction of an enclosure was completed by March 1966 and 1,566 feet of adjustable pressed-steel shelving were erected as well as a series of wide shelves for storing bulky material.

'In 1964 another rich bequest was received in the form of the library of horticultural and botanical books collected by Dr. Fred Stoker, who, like Mr. Cory, had served the Society in many ways. In a survey of the books, printed in the *Journal* for September 1965, the bequest was described as "the library of a scientist and scholar": it included books not already in the Lindley Library and clean copies of others to replace worn volumes.

'Dr. Stoker had a beautiful garden overlooking Epping Forest, at Loughton, Essex, and there is an account of the construction and development of the garden in his book, *A Gardener's Progress* (1938).

'The trust deed relating to the establishment and conduct of the Library permits the sale of duplicates and, as the Cory and other bequests have duplicated some items in the stock, arrangements have been made, from time to time, to offer series of duplicates, carefully inspected by a subcommittee, at auction in London. The first sale was held in 1958. The results were encouraging and another sale took place in 1959. Over the next four years further duplicates, some of great value, were brought to light and in 1963 another sale was held. This realised nearly £11,000, which, after the expenses of the sale were deducted, was placed in the Library fund. In permitting the sale of duplicates the trust deed stipulates that the proceeds of sales must be utilized in purchasing books, prints or drawings wanted for the Library, and may also be applied to binding, repairing or restoring the stock. In accordance with these terms the Committee has acquired further valuable and important books and has had many of the old and broken bindings repaired or renewed.

'Amongst recent purchases must be mentioned a Repton Red Book: this manuscript, dated 1792, relates to Waresley Park, in Huntingdon, and contains water-colour sketches of the estate with overlays showing the estate before the proposed improvements.[1] There is no record of the Library ever before having contained a Repton manuscript. Another rarity is a Swedish periodical entitled *Magasin för blomster-älskare och idkare af trädgards-skotsel*, Stockholm, 1803–9. This volume was bought in London in 1964 and contains 36 fine coloured plates engraved on copper.

'There are so many books of importance in regard to rarity and text content and in beautiful illustrative plates, that it is possible to give only an indication of the scope of the Library's stock.

'Although there are leaves from some fifteenth-century herbals, including *Gart der Gesundheit*, printed by Peter Schöffer at Mainz in 1485, the earliest book in the Lindley Library is the elder Pliny's *Naturalis hystoriae libri xxxvii*, which was printed in Paris in 1514; it is a compilation in Latin from the writings of Greek authors and contains notes on plants, with illustrations copied from the German *Herbarius* and manuscripts. Perhaps the best known of the Library's sixteenth-century books is the *Grete herball*, an octavo volume printed at Southwark in 1526. In scope this book covers a wide field of natural history, and forms an interesting glimpse of the philosophy of medicines in the early sixteenth century. The primitive illustrations were adapted from earlier works and it seems doubtful whether they were of much use in identifying the plants whose virtues were described in the text which they accompanied.

'The earliest known book on horticulture is contained in the Library; it is the *Lustgärten und Pflantzungen*, printed, and possibly compiled, by Christian Egenolph at Strassburg in 1530. On its title-page is a fine woodcut believed to be the first known illustration of a gardener at work.

'The early herbals were illustrated with woodcuts which can only be described as diagrams and were perhaps intended to be helpful to those who could not read. By 1530 a more realistic form of plant drawing had been introduced by Hans Weiditz and other artists. Weiditz was of the same school as Dürer and illustrated the *Herbarum vivae eicones* (1530) of Otto Brunfels.

'The Library has a fine copy of Leonhard Fuchs's *De historia stirpium* (1542) containing splendid illustrations which are both decorative and botanically accurate: copies of these blocks were used by later herbalists,

[1] *Jl. R. hort. Soc.*, XCIII (1968), p. 210.

including our own Turner and Lyte. Fuchs was born in Bavaria and became a prominent physician and scholar and was concerned at his fellow doctors' lack of interest and ignorance in the use of plants.

'This was the era of the great voyages of discovery and many hitherto unknown plants were being introduced and numerous books, many of which are in the Lindley Library, were published to describe and illustrate them.

'By the end of the sixteenth century interest in plants widened to include literature on their decorative qualities. Copper-plate engraving had taken the place of the woodcut and, although this was a costly process, it enabled the artist to be more accurate and to indicate to some degree the texture of his subject. Engraving on copper will occasionally be found on pages of type, usually as head- or tail-pieces, but the plate and type could not be printed simultaneously as could the woodcut and type. It was therefore the practice to print plates and to have them inserted at the appropriate part of the text or to have them gathered in order and bound in at the end. One of the best examples of early line-engraving in the Lindley Library is a Dutch book, *Hortus floridus*, Utrecht, 1614, by Crispin de Passe the younger (1589–1667). This is an oblong quarto depicting flowering plants, many of them bulbous or tuberous, drawn from a low level so that the plants have a living appearance against the sky. The older wood-engravers were somewhat limited by the size of the wood block, but the copper-engravers were less restricted in the dimensions of their designs as the copper plate could be cut to the size of the drawing and if this exceeded the page area of the book, then the print was folded once or twice by the binder. Examples of large-scale copper-engraving will be seen in *Hortus Eystettensis*, published at Eichstatt in 1613: this very large folio is the earliest illustrated catalogue of a garden in the Library: it was compiled by Basil Besler, an apothecary of Nürnberg, for Bishop Konrad of Eichstatt of whose garden Besler had charge.

'In 1958 the Council purchased for the Library the twelve volumes of *Hortus Indicus Malabaricus* (1678–1703) by Heinricus van Rheede tot Draakestein, who was Governor of Malabar. These engravings excited interest, as they showed many beautifully drawn plants hitherto unknown in this country.

'In the last years of the seventeenth century Jan Commelin, joint director of the new physic garden at Amsterdam, compiled a work describing and illustrating the rare plants which had been brought to the garden from the Dutch colonies in South Africa, India and the Far East. He died before the work, of which the Library has a fine copy, was published, and it was completed by his nephew Caspar Commelin and produced by Blaeu, better known as a map-engraver.

'The numerous new plants which poured into England from newly explored regions in the eighteenth century gave great scope to publishers and engravers and the Library has some fine examples. The works of Nicolaus von Jacquin are outstanding books of this period and as many of the plates are folded they demonstrate the advantage of copper-engraving not being restricted as to shape of the design.

'Amongst botanical books the Library's copy of the three volumes of Poiret, *Leçons de flore* (1819–20) came with the Cory bequest, and this copy is said to be one of only two made up of vellum sheets. The illustrations are in the style of the miniaturist and were drawn and coloured by hand by Pierre Turpin (1775–1840), who was a contempory of Redouté and illustrated the works of the travellers, Humboldt, Bonpland, Saint-Hilaire and others. It is believed that the Library's copy in a luxurious green, gold-tooled binding was made for Louis XVIII of France. Sibthorp's *Flora Graeca*, ten folio volumes (1806–40), must also be included amongst the treasures. Only twenty-eight copies of the first edition of this work were produced and each cost 240 guineas: the whole work cost £30,000 to produce. Sibthorp died before it was published and the task of producing it fell to Sir James Edward Smith, first president of the Linnean Society. At his death in 1828 publication was not complete and the final three volumes were issued under the direction of John Lindley. *Le raisin: ses espèces et variétés*, by Johan Simon von Kerner (1775–1830), is another great rarity which may be seen in the Lindley Library: the illustrations are original coloured drawings by the author. The Lindley Library copy is incomplete, consisting of only three parts of the twelve issued. In any account of the Library's treasures mention must be made of James Bateman's *Orchidaceae of Mexico and Guatemala* (1837–43), of which 125 copies were published; besides being a rarity, this work, which weighs 38 pounds, has the distinction of being the heaviest book in the Library. Early in 1957, when he was in Hove, Sussex, listing the books bequeathed by the late Mr. Alfred Gurney Wilson, the Librarian found seven large orchid paintings, some signed by the talented Mrs. Augusta Withers, flower painter to Queen Adelaide. It soon became evident that these drawings were the originals from which some of the plates in Bateman's massive volume were made.

'The Library possesses numerous other important botanical works including florae of widespread regions of the globe and on the systems of classification of plants, including the first edition of Linnaeus' *Genera plantarum* (1753). The importance of many of the older books lies not entirely in their history and antiquarian value but in the fact that they contain first published descriptions of newly discovered plants and the volumes are therefore needed for reference in conjunction with *Index Kewensis*, the bibliography of "first references".

'The whole splendid pageant of plant illustration is fully represented and apart from the artistic qualities of the plates they have value in frequently being more useful to botanists than photographic references.

'Newly introduced plants whose decorative qualities were thought to be worthy of the attention of gardeners were brought to the notice of the public in the form of engraved plates often folio in size, such as the spectacular work by the Nürnberg physician C. J. Trew in his *Plantae Selectae* (1750–3), illustrated by G. D. Ehret (1708–70), one of the greatest and most influential of botanical artists.

'The introduction of lithography to this country made possible the numerous large folio volumes of colour-plate books of the nineteenth century. The process was quick and inexpensive and as limits of size were less restricted than earlier methods, artists were allowed free rein in their designs. The Library has copies of most of the very large books which made their appearance during the first half of the nineteenth century: among these splendid volumes are included Samuel Curtis's *Monograph of the genus Camellia* (1819), and J. D. Hooker's *Rhododendrons of Sikkim-Himalaya* (1849–51).

'Lithography added greatly to the scientific value of botanical and horticultural books until the introduction of colour-printing by mechanical means. The lithographs were often coloured by hand with great skill and the quartos and folios command ever-increasing prices when they come up for sale.

'From its beginning the Society has enjoyed the support of the Royal Family and the official patronage of the reigning Sovereign. Foreign royalties and persons of distinction were also elected Honorary Members or Fellows in early years, and a custom arose of obtaining the autographs of these notabilities on vellum or paper sheets bearing appropriate floral designs. The Society has placed in the care of the Library its collection of thirty-nine royal autographs and selections from the collection are exhibited from time to time at the Flower Shows.

'The Society has always treasured its collection of drawings and in its early days there was a Drawings Committee to superintend their production and care. In the difficult period of 1859, when the library was sold, the drawings brought only a small sum at the sale and the committee's minute book is tantalizing in referring to the works of the gifted artists who had been employed in preparing the drawings. Only ten folios of Hooker drawings and eight volumes of Reeves drawings have found their way back to the Library. It can only be hoped that the other sets of illustrations will come to light and be recognized by the initials H.S. which are probably stamped on the lower corners.

'In 1814 the Society began forming a collection of drawings of plants and fruits for purposes of demonstration and identification. William

Hooker was one of the artists engaged for this work, as he was a highly skilled draughtsman, and between 1815 and 1821 he made 158 drawings of fruits.

'New plants were being discovered in China during the first half of the last century and the Society, anxious to have a record of them, arranged with an officer of the East India Company, John Reeves, to employ local artists to draw native plants. These drawings were sold with the rest of the Library in 1859, but subsequently found their way back to the Society, partly through the Cory bequest and otherwise by purchase.

'The Library has valuable sets of earlier drawings and amongst these must be included the 600 unpublished sepia line-and-wash plant illustrations by Claude Aubriet (1665–1742). There is also a bound volume of eight coloured drawings on vellum by this artist depicting flowering plants and shrubs. Aubriet accompanied the botanist Tournefort to the Levant and in later years Louis XIV engaged him as painter at the Jardin des Plantes.

'The volume of miscellaneous coloured drawings of cultivated plants by Pieter Kouwenhoorn is one of the earliest series in the Library's collection of flower paintings. The paintings are on vellum and are dated about 1630 and depict mainly bulbous plants. Reference has already been made to the artist Pierre Turpin; in the Library's collection there is a volume of twenty-five coloured drawings on vellum by this artist. These drawings are small and exquisitely painted, with the names of the flowers lettered in gold leaf.

'Georg Dionysius Ehret, a German artist, came to England in 1736 and deservedly met with rapid success. The Library has numerous engraved plates from Ehret's designs and there are also original drawings on vellum by this outstanding artist in the collection made by John Stuart, third Earl of Bute, and in a set of small coloured drawings on vellum.

'Twentieth-century artists are represented in the Library and include the coloured drawings made by Alfred Parsons, R.A., for Ellen Willmott's *Genus Rosa* (1914). Each of the original drawings is bound in the book, facing the appropriate coloured reproduction.

'Early in 1950 the Library received a collection of over 300 botanical drawings by Miss Dorothy Martin (1882–1949) who had been art mistress at Roedean School, Brighton. The drawings which depict English plants and trees are in water-colour and are models of technique in this medium.

'In recent years the Society published two further parts to the Supplements to Elwes's *Monograph on the Genus Lilium*; the drawings for these publications (part 8 (1960) and part 9 (1962)) were made by Miss

Margaret Stones and have been placed in the Library's collection together with examples of this artist's work prepared for articles in the *Journal*.

'All these drawings which the Society has acquired for the Library, together with the early herbals, the great colour-plate folios and the succession of garden books of nearly five centuries, are secure for the enlightenment and pleasure of future generations of plant- and garden-lovers.'

Undoubtedly one of the most important developments at Vincent Square, indeed in the multitudinous activities of the Society, during the 1960s, has been concerned with the nomenclature of cultivated plants and especially with plant registration. In these matters the Society has for long been interested and indeed has taken the lead. Appendix VII of the 1935 edition of the *International Rules for Botanical Nomenclature*—'Nomenclature of Garden Plants'—was largely the work of E. A. Bowles and F. J. Chittenden. W. T. Stearn, the Society's Librarian, and J. S. L. Gilmour, who had recently resigned from the directorship of Wisley, were intimately concerned with the formulating of the *International Code of Nomenclature for Cultivated Plants* which was drawn up by the International Committee on Horticultural Nomenclature and Registration of which Gilmour and Stearn were both members, Stearn also being the secretary, and which was published by the Society in 1953. At the Fourteenth International Horticultural Congress held at Scheveningen, Holland, in 1955, the *International Code of Nomenclature for Cultivated Plants* became the responsibility of the International Commission for the Nomenclature of Cultivated Plants of the International Union of Biological Sciences; at first Gilmour acted as rapporteur for the Commission and later was to succeed Dr. R. de Vilmorin as chairman, whilst H. R. Fletcher, who the year previously had left Wisley for Edinburgh, accepted the duties of secretary. Since then several revised editions of the *International Code of Nomenclature for Cultivated Plants* have been published, and all have a section dealing with the international registration of cultivars (varieties) of plants and with international registration authorities.

The primary object of registration is to create and maintain order in the nomenclature of the cultivars of any particular group of plants; registration strives to avoid duplication of a cultivar name when applied to two or more cultivars; it strives to avoid the application of one cultivar name to two or more cultivars. To be efficient, registration must function on the international level, for the rate of interchange of cultivars from one country to another, even from one continent to another, is very speedy. When commerce in an article becomes international, so must the nomenclature of the article concerned; and a stabilized nomenclature for a particular group of cultivars, brought about by the registration of the cultivars concerned, can only operate by international agreement, through international registration author-ities. And an international registration authority for any group of plants can only adequately function when once it has prepared a check-list or register of the names of the cultivars of the group in question. Although the first of such authorities was only appointed at the Sche-veningen Horticultural Congress in 1955, the Society, through the pioneer work of A. Simmonds, had been virtually acting in this capacity for many years. Consequently at the Scheveningen Congress the Society was appointed the international registration authority, not only for the genus *Narcissus*, but for *Rhododendron* and *Delphinium* as well. With *Narcissus* there was no problem, for already the Society had its *Classified List of Daffodil Names*. Since 1955 the list has been revised several times and is now published by the Society as the *Classified List and International Register of Daffodil Names*, the last edition appearing in 1965. Between one edition and another, newly registered names are published in the Society's *Daffodil and Tulip Year Book*. Since Mr. Simmonds's retirement, the responsibility for the *Register of Daffodil Names* has rested with Mr. J. Cowell, assisted by a Daffodil Classification Advisory Committee. Neither had the Society much of a problem in taking on the international registration of the names of *Delphinium* cultivars, for a checklist of such names had been published in 1949, and a short addendum was pub-lished in 1961. The checklist is now out of date and a new edition no doubt will soon be required.

For *Rhododendron* cultivars, however, no checklist of names existed and, before the Society could begin to function as the international authority for these plants, an international register of such names had to be prepared. This was undertaken by H. R. Fletcher, and the Society published the *International Rhododendron Register* in 1958. Since then one supplement has been published, but, as with daffodils, each year a list of new registrations is published in the Society's *Rhododendron and Camellia Year Book*.

At the Fifteenth International Horticultural Congress in Nice in 1958 the Society was appointed the international registration authority for cultivars of the genus *Lilium*. As a result, the *International Lily Register* was compiled by Miss Gillian Peterson, at that time a member of the Society's staff, and published by the Society in 1960. Since then one supplement has been published and newly registered cultivars are listed in each issue of the *Lily Year Book*. The work of lily registration is now undertaken by P. M. Synge, also secretary of the Lily Committee.

The Sixteenth International Horticultural Congress, in Brussels, in 1962, accepted the recommendation of the Third World Orchid Con-ference, held in London in 1960, that the Society take on the duties of international registration authority for orchid names, and so far two addenda to *Sander's List of Orchid Hybrids* have been published by the Society. Orchid registration is undertaken by Mrs. M. Wreford, a member of the Society's staff, assisted by a small advisory committee whose chairman is J. S. L. Gilmour.

International registration authorities are appointed usually only at international horticultural congresses, and by the Council of the International Society for Horticultural Science. However, at the International Botanical Congress in Edinburgh in 1964 the above council accepted a recommendation that the Society take over the international registration of dwarf and other garden conifers and, since that time, the Society has acted as registration authority for this group of plants. Once again the registrar is advised by a small committee under the chairmanship of Gilmour.

Finally, at the Seventeenth International Horticultural Congress held in Maryland in August 1966 an invitation was extended to the Society to become the international registration authority for dahlia cultivars. The invitation was readily accepted and the work of compiling an international checklist has begun. The task is not an easy one, for, even though a simple group classification has been accepted by the national authorities in the United Kingdom, Holland, and America, it is necessary to secure the active co-operation of other national authorities before an international checklist may be published.

There is no doubt that horticulturists the world over are greatly concerned that the names of plants be stabilized, and the establishment of international registration authorities for all the major groups of horticultural plants is an important step towards this stabilization. It is a splendid thing that Lord Aberconway and his colleagues on the Council continue to encourage the Society to extend its activities, and great influence, into this vitally important field of work. Council has decided to establish a special registration department in which records and up-to-date lists of registered cultivars will be brought together with the long-term aim in view that this department, assisted by specialist advisers and small committees, will gradually assume the responsibility for all registration work. In the field of international plant registration the Society continues to lead the world.

And lead the world the Society certainly continues to do in its conduct of examinations. In 1963 the jubilee of the National Diploma in Horticulture was commemorated by a strangely moving ceremony at Vincent Square. On 14 September the large Lecture Hall was filled with horticulturists who had gained the N.D.H. in former years, including eight who had been successful in the first year, and with representatives of the Ministry of Agriculture, Ministry of Education, The Worshipful Company of Gardeners, Royal Botanic Gardens, Kew, National Farmers'

Union, National Council for Technological Awards, Women's Farm and Garden Association, Horticultural Education Association, National Union of Teachers, and other important bodies interested in the educational work of the Society. With the President on the platform were members of Council and the Master of the Worshipful Company of Gardeners, the Hon. Roger Nathan. The President addressed his audience thus:

The Society has many and varied activities. Not the least important in the eyes of Council is the holding of examinations, though that is a branch of our activities of which Fellows may be relatively unaware.

The N.D.H., or National Diploma in Horticulture, is by far the most important of our examinations, and the Diploma is the highest qualification technically that a gardener in Britain can achieve. In conducting this examination each year the Society renders an important service to horticulture by maintaining and certifying for successful candidates a high and constant standard of professional competence. . . .

Before being admitted to the final examination of the N.D.H. a candidate must have satisfied the Society as to his educational standard by passing (or being exempted from) the Preliminary Examination; must have passed the Intermediate Examination, and must have been engaged for at least six years in practical gardening. For the Final Examination a candidate may choose to be examined in the section of Horticulture in which he feels most proficient. The majority choose General Horticulture, but others select General Commercial Horticulture, or Fruit Crop Husbandry, or Vegetable Crop Husbandry, or Glass House Crop Husbandry, or Horticulture in Public Parks. Thus there are six sections. A prize of £10, or the *Dictionary of Gardening*, is generously provided by the Worshipful Company of Gardeners to each student gaining most marks in his section, and the Master, Mr. Roger Nathan, is here to present those prizes [to the successful candidates of 1963]. The Chittenden Prize is awarded annually to the student who gains most marks in the section for General Horticulture, and the Chittenden Award to the student who gains the most marks in the Intermediate Examination.

The tests are severe; about one-third pass the intermediate; and of those who go on to take the final, about one-third pass. . . .

Over the years public recognition of the value of technological qualifications has grown, and such qualifications are more and more keenly sought. Technological colleges abound, with courses for special industries; and many old methods are being changed.

The Society is always eager to move with the times and is anxious that the N.D.H. should be modernised and should give the maximum assistance to students and to the industry. It would indeed be remarkable if the requirements of fifty years ago were still in every particular suitable to present circumstances. Accordingly, the Society has appointed a study group to examine the scheme and to suggest any changes in the regulations that may be necessary at the commencement of the second fifty-year period.

Council is confident that the N.D.H., in entering its second fifty-year period, will continue to play its important part in the horticultural life of this country.[1]

For the better part of two years the N.D.H. study group was unable to make the progress anticipated for the reason that the survey of horticultural education, which a subcommittee of the Pilkington Advisory Committee on Agricultural Education was carrying out, might well have a bearing on the work of the group. Not until the long-awaited Report of the Pilkington Committee had been published in May 1966 was the study group able to resume its work. Although an interim recommendation which had regard to the possible implications of the Advisory Committee's Report, has been adopted by Council, the study group still has much work to do. As far as the Society is concerned, the prime consideration is that, whichever of the Pilkington Committee's recommendations may be adopted by Her Majesty's Government, and whenever they may be implemented, it is the Society's duty to maintain for as long as may be required, the services to horticulture and to young men and women who aspire to horticultural careers, which it has for so many years been happy to provide.

The Society is not concerned, and never has been, in securing a monopoly of examinations in horticulture. The Society accepted responsibility for the establishment, conduct, and administration of the N.D.H. at the invitation of Government over fifty years ago. If now, as the Council's report for 1966 said, it is felt by those who will make use of the services of successfully trained and qualified candidates that some new structure is necessary, the Society will have no hesitation in discontinuing the facilities it now provides as the need for them disappears. The N.D.H. is at present financed from the Society's funds and is supported by the knowledge and experience generously made available by experts in this field. Even so, where any new examination structure proves to be deficient, or where it does not adequately cater for those who wish to achieve a special proficiency, the Society will continue to offer facilities for candidates to acquire the highest possible qualifications.

One change was made in the N.D.H. examination in 1966. The preliminary examination, a purely educational test, was discontinued for it was felt that all N.D.H. candidates should be able to achieve the necessary educational qualifications either before leaving school or by study afterwards.

The N.D.H., of course, is only one of the examinations which the Society admini ers and conducts. There is also the General Examination in Horticulture, an elementary examination open to amateur and professional gardeners; the Teacher's Diploma in School Gardening

[1] *Jl R. hort. Soc.*, LXXXVIII (1963), pp. 517–18.

which caters for the qualified teacher who is required to give instruction in gardening; and the National Certificate in Horticulture, intended for students who have had at least twelve months' experience in practical horticulture and are, at the time of the examination, attending a full-time course in horticulture at a county farm or horticultural institute. The N.C.H. is the 1960 successor to the National Certificate in Elementary Horticultural Practice which was established in 1937 and has rendered a considerable service to horticultural education. However, with the establishment of the examinations of the City and Guilds of London Institute, which examinations have had far-reaching effects upon the world of horticulture education, it has become clear that the N.C.H. in its present form cannot continue to command the support of those institutions for whom it is provided and that some modification of its form is necessary. Although the examination has recently been partly linked to the City and Guilds examinations, to the extent that holders of the N.C.H. are exempt from Stages I and II of these examinations, this matter is still one of the many problems with which the Society's Examinations Board is concerned.

For over thirty years Dr. H. V. Taylor was a member of the Examinations Board, and its chairman from 1940 until he resigned because of ill health in 1964. He died the following year. Dr. R. H. Stoughton, with a long association with the Board, with experience of the Council and fully aware of the requirements of the horticultural industry in terms of training, succeeded Dr. Taylor as chairman.

In accordance with the provisions of the Bye-Laws of the Society, the three members of Council longest in office retire after the Annual General Meeting. Each year, however, the Council may nominate for re-election any one of the retiring members. Very often retired members of Council, who have given long service to the Society and who are familiar with its intricate affairs, are invited to return after a year of absence. But age must take its toll and inevitably the time comes when some Councillors retire and request not to be re-elected for the reason that they no longer have the energy and stamina to stand up to the heavy demands which the Society exacts of its Councillors. Recently such a time came for Sir Frederick Stern and Mr. E. P. F. Sutton. Both had given many years of loyal and wise service to the Society. Both for many years in their various ways had held pre-eminent positions in British horticulture, the former as one of the greatest of amateur gardeners who had demonstrated in remarkable fashion the wide range of plants which can be grown on chalk, the latter, nost kind and modest of gentlemen, as head of the 'House of Sutton', The Royal Seed Establishment at Reading. Both were elected Vice-Presidents of the Society. To horticulture's great loss Sir Frederick died in July 1967.

CHAPTER TWENTY-FOUR

SHOW DAY—AND ANNUAL GENERAL MEETING

THROUGHOUT THE YEAR THE SOCIETY'S SHOWS ARE THE SCENE OF the year's pageant of flowers. At times of special shows and competitions the scene is also one of intense, though friendly, rivalry—the shows and competitions of the Alpine Garden Society, the Royal National Rose Society, the British Iris Society, the Delphinium Society, the British National Carnation Society, the National Sweet Pea Society, the National Dahlia Society and the National Chrysanthemum Society. And invariably every evening before a Show the scene is one of considerable chaos.

Throughout the day before a Show cars, vans, lorries, pantechnicons arrive at the Halls and discharge their crates of flowers everywhere—on the floor, under tables, on the staging and stands, on the stairs, in the vestibule and in any nook and corner available. Exhibitors and friends welcome each other with handshakes and cheerful banter and often, for as long as possible, try not to disclose their finest exhibits. Already these men and women have spent months bringing their plants and flowers to the peak of condition; have spent long hours selecting and packing and have travelled many miles bringing their exhibits to Westminster. They will work on the staging of these throughout the day, and although they ought to be out of the Halls by 10 p.m., it is a common sight to see some still working at midnight; some indeed have been known to work all through the night. At midnight before a Show, the scene in the Halls is usually one of great disorder. Beneath the surface, however, there is clearly organization and planned purpose, for by 10.30 a.m. the following day—the first day of the Show and the day when the exhibits are judged—when some of the exhibitors will have been at work for at least three hours, every exhibit is neat and tidy, the floor cleaned, and all is ready for the Judging Committees.

The Society invites anyone to exhibit, whether they be Fellows of the Society or not. Applications for space for an exhibit must be made to the Secretary, not later than the first post on the Wednesday before the Show in question, and the Secretary must be told the nature of the proposed exhibit and the amount of space it will occupy. No entry fees are charged, nor are there any charges for space or tabling. Even so, most exhibitors at the Society's Shows are involved in considerable expense in exhibiting and the Society is immensely indebted for the support of those who, throughout the years, continue to stage magnificent displays in the Halls, as well as at Chelsea and the Great Autumn Show: Hillier & Sons, L. R. Russell Ltd., John Waterer Sons & Crisp Ltd., R. C. Notcutt Ltd., Sunningdale Nurseries, Burkwood & Skipwith Ltd., Knaphill Nursery Ltd., Walter C. Slocock Ltd., Slieve Donard Nursery Co. Ltd.—all exhibitors of flowering trees and shrubs; Wheatcroft Bros. Ltd., Harry Wheatcroft & Sons Ltd., R. Harkness & Co., Alex Dickson & Sons Ltd., William Lowe & Son (Nurseries) Ltd., C. Gregory & Son Ltd., Samuel McGredy & Son Ltd., Benjamin R. Cant & Son Ltd., Chaplin Bros. (Waltham Cross) Ltd., Messrs. H. Robinson —all exhibitors of roses; Sutton & Sons Ltd., Carters Tested Seeds Ltd., Edward Webb & Sons (Stourbridge) Ltd.—exhibitors of florists' flowers from seed; Suttons and Carters for vegetables; Allwood Bros. Ltd., Lindabruce Nurseries Ltd., C. Engelmann Ltd., carnation growers; W. E. Th. Ingwersen Ltd., Edrom Nurseries, Maurice Prichard & Sons Ltd., always with rock-garden plants, and the latter also with herbaceous plants; George G. Whitelegg Ltd., and Gavin Jones Nurseries Ltd. for rock gardens at Chelsea; Bressingham Gardens, Thomas Carlile (Loddon Nurseries) Ltd., Hillier, Waterer Sons & Crisp, dealers in herbaceous plants; Blackmore & Langdon, wonderful exhibitors of delphiniums, begonias, polyanthus; Robert Bolton & Son, famed for sweet peas; Walter Blom & Son Ltd., for tulips and other bulbs; Mrs. Lionel Richardson of Waterford, Guy Wilson Ltd., Michael Jefferson Brown, Wallace & Barr Ltd., Alec Gray of Camborne, Kelway & Sons Ltd., P. de Jager & Sons—all for daffodils; R. Wallace & Co. for lilies; H. Woolman Ltd., Stephen Treseder & Son Ltd., John Crutchfield Ltd., Wards Nurseries Ltd., Dobbie & Co Ltd., for dahlias; H. Woolman Ltd., Elm House Nurseries, Fox Lane Nursery, Hatfield, Bedenham & Sons, Greenyer Bros. Ltd., Duntrune Nurseries, all for chrysanthemums; Thomas Rochford & Sons Ltd., and certain Parks Departments such as Slough, Liverpool, Brighton, specialists in greenhouse plants; Bees Ltd., Fisk's Clematis Nursery in clematis; Kelway & Sons Ltd., W. J. Unwin Ltd. in gladioli and other flowers; McBean's Orchids Ltd., Stuart Low Orchids, Charlesworth & Co. Ltd., David Sander's Orchids Ltd., all orchid growers.

To all these, and to many others, the gratitude not only of the Society, but of the British gardening public, is very real.

Competition and friendly rivalry at the Shows is by no means confined to the various organized plant societies and to the trade; it is equally keen among the amateurs who take part in the competitions for ornamental plants, rhododendrons, camellias, daffodils, and trees and shrubs in spring, summer, autumn, and winter; Lord Aberconway and the National Trust, Bodnant; The Countess of Rosse and the National Trust, Nymans; The Crown Estate Commissioners, Windsor; Sir Giles Loder, Leonardslee, Horsham; Sir Ralph Clarke, Borde Hill, Haywards Heath; Mr. E. de Rothschild, Exbury; Mr. F. Julian Williams, Caerhays Castle, Cornwall; General Harrison, Bodmin; Mr. R. Strauss, Ardingly; these are some of the amateurs who each year enrich the Shows by exhibiting plants and flowers many of which are not very readily available in the trade.

Though money prizes are not offered, there are many other awards available for competition at particular Shows. At the Daffodil Competition, for instance, the Devonshire Trophy is offered. It was presented in 1958 by Mary, Duchess of Devonshire, in memory of the tenth Duke of Devonshire, a keen daffodil grower, and is offered for the best exhibit of one stem of each of twelve cultivars representing at least three of the eleven divisions of the Society's classification of daffodils. Two cups are available for competition at the Daffodil Show. The Engleheart Cup, which the Society first offered in 1913 and which commemorates the exalted name, in the daffodil world, of the Rev. G. H. Engleheart, is awarded to the best exhibit of one stem of each of twelve cultivars raised by the exhibitor. The fact that between 1935 and 1964 this Cup was won on twenty-five occasions by Mr J. Lionel Richardson is an index of his skill as a daffodil breeder. In 1965 and 1966 the Cup was awarded to Mrs. Richardson. The second cup, the Bowles Cup, was presented by the late Mr. J. L. Richardson in 1949 for award for exhibits of daffodils shown by amateurs.

For the competition of rhododendron-lovers, four cups are available at the Rhododendron Show. All were originally presented to the Rhododendron Association and were transferred to the Society in 1946. The McLaren Cup was given to the Association by the Hon. Henry McLaren (the late Lord Aberconway) and is usually offered for award for the best exhibit of one truss of a species of rhododendron. The Lionel de Rothschild Cup is awarded to the best exhibit of one truss of each of eight species. The Crosfield Cup, presented to the Rhododendron Association by the late J. J. Crosfield, is usually offered for award for the best exhibit of one truss of each of six rhododendron hybrids raised by, or in the garden of, the exhibitor. Between 1946 and 1966, Mr. Edmund de Rothschild has been awarded this cup on fourteen occasions, and he, no doubt, would be the first to acknowledge his father's flair for rhododendron hybridization for much of his success. The fourth cup, the Rothschild Challenge Cup, was given to the Association by the late Mr. Lionel de Rothschild and, though it was not offered until 1964, is now awarded for the best non-competitive group

427

of rhododendrons and azaleas staged by a trade grower. Messrs. W. C. Slocock Ltd. were the winners in 1964, 1965, and 1966.

In 1965 Sir Giles Loder, Bt., presented the Leonardslee Bowl for award at the Late Camellia Competition, for the best exhibit of one bloom of each of twelve camellias, whilst in 1919 the late Sir Francis Burdett, Bt., presented the Foremarke Cup for twenty spikes of gladioli of not less than ten cultivars and not more than two spikes of any one cultivar; Sir Francis's cup is open to competition both to the trade and to amateur growers exhibiting at the Gladiolus Competition. And for those interested in cacti and succulents there is the silver Sherman Hoyt Trophy, provided from Mrs. Sherman Hoyt's prize fund, to be won at the early summer competition for these plants.

By competitors at the Autumn Fruit and Vegetable Show, two cups, offered by the Society, and a trophy, are to be won. The R.H.S. Vegetable Cup, dating from 1910, is offered to the competitor who secures the greatest number of prize points for exhibits of vegetables, whilst the Society's Affiliated Societies Cup of 1908 is offered for the best collection of fruit shown by an affiliated society. The silver Riddell Trophy is provided each year from a fund established in 1931 by Lord Riddell for the encouragement of the cultivation and exhibition of vegetables.

On the morning of a Show the Secretary and his staff are on the scene early to ensure, as far as possible, that all exhibits conform to the Society's regulations. Occasionally the Secretary sees something which does not please him and immediately proceeds to have the matter righted before the President and committees arrive for the judging. Usually the change involves no problems. Occasionally, however, the Secretary is required to exercise considerable tact. Some years ago, during the régime of the late Lord Aberconway, a member of the secretariat entered the hall to see that all was well. The morning was a hot one and one exhibitor had found the temperature too much for him; he had removed his jacket and shirt and was putting the finishing touches to his exhibit wearing only his trousers. The Society's official was not pleased and the exhibitor was asked to wear his shirt at least. But he refused and, in the middle of a heated argument, the President arrived. Instantly he sized up the situation. 'Sir,' he said, 'if you will put on your shirt, I will take off my jacket.' The missing shirt was immediately donned and the President carried his jacket over his arm for the rest of the morning.

Judging is in the hands of several standing committees which are appointed by the Council annually. One Committee stands somewhat apart from the rest, the Scientific Committee, which meets in the afternoon of a Show day and reports upon diseases, pests, newly imported plants which may not have yet been named, and other objects of botanical and horticultural interest. All the other committees, of course, meet in the morning. The Floral Committee, which deals with all ornamental plants other than those within the province of, and dealt with by, the Orchid, Narcissus and Tulip, Rhododendron and Camellia, and Joint Committees, is divided into three sections; Section A deals with cultivars of horticultural origin which are the result of prolonged breeding and selection, or of multiple hybridity, and those which are normally grown for garden decoration; Section B deals with plants collected in the wild, species and their varieties, cultivars and first generation (F.1) hybrids including all trees and most shrubs, and lilies, and again those which are normally grown for garden decoration; Section C deals with ornamental plants usually grown for decorative effect in heated glass-houses or dwelling-houses. Then there is the Fruit and Vegetable Committee; the Narcissus and Tulip Committee; the Orchid Committee, which deals with all orchids except the hardy terrestrial kinds; the Rhododendron and Camellia Committee; the Rock Garden and Alpine Group Committee, dealing with non-competitive group exhibits of rock-garden and alpine plants; and the Picture Committee, adjudicating on exhibits of paintings, drawings and photographs of plants, of flowers, and of gardens.

The following joint committees are also appointed annually by the Council and the governing body of the other society or societies concerned, to examine and report on new plants. The Joint Border Carnation and Picotee Committee (the Joint Committee of the R.H.S. and the British National Carnation Society) reports on all hardy border carnations; the Joint Perpetual-flowering Carnation Committee (R.H.S. and the British National Carnation Society) on all perpetual-flowering carnations; the Joint Dianthus Committee (R.H.S., the Alpine Garden Society and the British National Carnation Society) reports on all members of the genus *Dianthus* except carnations; the Joint Chrysanthemum Committee (R.H.S. and the National Chrysanthemum Society); the Joint Dahlia Committee (R.H.S. and the National Dahlia Society); the Joint Delphinium Committee (R.H.S. and the Delphinium Society); the Joint Iris Committee (R.H.S. and the British Iris Society); the Joint Narcissus Committee (R.H.S. and the Daffodil Society) deals with all narcissi submitted for certificate at the Daffodil Society's annual show; the Joint Rock Garden Plant Committee (R.H.S., Alpine Garden Society and the Scottish Rock Garden Club) deals with rock-garden and alpine-house plants other than dianthi, irises, rhododendrons, narcissi, and tulips; the Joint Sweet Pea Committee (R.H.S. and the National Sweet Pea Society).

In the Society's *Regulations for Exhibitions*, which is sent to all members of committees, the committees' objects are stated in detail:

To encourage the introduction of new species, and the production of improved cultivars of fruits, vegetables, flowers and decorative plants by examining and reporting to the Council upon the merits of such as may be submitted; to report to the Council on fruits, vegetables, flowers and plants grown at Wisley and elsewhere for comparison and experiment; to recommend awards to novelties or other objects of great excellence which have been hitherto over-looked or ignored; to collect and disseminate information respecting the adaptability of particular kinds of fruits, vegetables, flowers and plants to varied conditions of soil, locality, etc.; to refer to the Scientific Committee all objects of special scientific interest which may be brought before them; and to report to the Council upon non-competitive exhibits staged at the Meetings and to recommend awards for exhibits of outstanding merit.

A Joint Committee reports to the Council of the Royal Horticultural Society and to the governing body of the other society concerned on the merits of the plants submitted to the Committee or examined in a trial, and any awards made on the recommendation of a Joint Committee are made jointly by the Societies concerned.

The following medals may be recommended for groups exhibited at the Shows: for exhibits of ornamental plants: the Gold, Silver-gilt Flora, Silver-gilt Banksian, Silver Flora, Silver Banksian, Flora; for exhibits of plants of special interest or beauty or showing exceptional skill in cultivation and for educational exhibits: the Silver-gilt Lindley Medal, Silver Lindley, Lindley; for exhibits of fruit: the Gold Medal, Silver-gilt Hogg, Silver Hogg, the Hogg; for exhibits of vegetables: the Gold, the Silver-gilt Knightian, the Silver Knightian, the Knightian; for exhibits of pictures, photographs or objects of a similar nature of horticultural or botanical interest: the Gold Medal, Silver-gilt Grenfell, Silver Grenfell, Grenfell.

Subject to special regulations governing the work of particular committees, the following awards may be recommended to individual plants: to plants exhibited at the Shows: the First Class Certificate to plants of great excellence, the Award of Merit to plants which are meritorious and the Certificate of Preliminary Commendation to new plants of promise; to plants grown in the trials at Wisley: the First Class Certificate, the Award of Merit, Highly Commended, Commended.

It is with these objects in mind, and with the knowledge of the awards they are empowered to recommend to the Council, that these committees meet some twenty-four times in the year at the Shows—and many other times at Wisley. The chairmen of the standing committees are usually members of the Council; the chairmanship of the joint committees usually alternates annually between a member of Council and a member of the other joint committee. All are aware, indeed all members of all committees are aware, of their responsibilities and of the tradition they have inherited from the past. Always the Society's committees have been comprised of the greatest horticulturists of their day, who, by their endeavours, have contributed so much to the prestige of the Society and to British horticulture.

The members of the committees are, of course, experts and authorities on the particular plants they are judging. Even so, it is unusual for the committees not to find something new, or remarkable, at any one Show; and this is one of the most remarkable aspects of the Shows. Although they are held year after year in the same place (only the Great Autumn Show now seems not to have one particular site), more or less at the same time, and usually comprise exhibits staged largely by the same firms, nurserymen or private establishments, they never fail to be able to offer something new to the gardening public—whether amateur or professional. That is especially the case with Chelsea Show, which is quite unique and about which the *Gardener's Chronicle* wrote in 1965:

. . . over the years . . . it has developed an atmosphere peculiar to itself. Chelsea is unique not just because the focal point is a 3½ acre marquee put up each year just for a four-day flower show, or that at any one time 50,000 people may be present with as many more wishing they were, but rather because it has become a tradition; a shop window for the whole complex which constitutes the horticultural industry of this country; an industry which caters for the nation's first choice in hobbies, on which more than £30 million is spent annually.

When once judging of the groups in the Halls has been done, the various committees assemble in their respective Committee Rooms to adjudicate on any individual plants which may have been sent for the committee's inspection. And then it is time for lunch.

For luncheon the Council meets in the Council Room and the morning's activities are discussed informally; the lunch is, in fact, what has now come to be called 'a working lunch'. Shortly after 1.30 p.m. Council sits to hear the reports of the chairmen of the various committees, to accept, or occasionally change, some of the committees' recommendations and to discuss other Society matters, of which, usually, there are many. Immediately the recommendations of the committees have been confirmed they are sent to the Secretary's office and to the Show office, so that the appropriate medals and awards may adorn the respective exhibits as soon after lunch as possible, and so that the Press may be informed. At his Council Meetings the President occupies a high-backed chair with the Society's crest embossed on the leather back; on his immediate left is the Treasurer, and on his right, the Secretary. And looking down on the proceedings are some of the great figures of the past, portraits of some of those who have given immense service to the Society: the President's immediate predecessor, Sir David Bowes Lyon, rather serious and a little worried, perhaps, with a vase of roses beside him and a book of roses on the table in front of him; the strong features of the President's father, Lord Aberconway, with a vase of rhododendrons and white cypripediums; the jovial Lord Lambourne, white-moustached, blue-eyed, bow-tied, with a sprig of myrtle in his button-hole and, on the table beside him, red carnations; the kind and sensitive face of Sir Trevor Lawrence; the broad strong head of Sir Joseph Banks looking one firmly in the eye and demanding a straight answer to a question; Lord Grenfell in field-marshal's uniform; Sir Thomas Hanbury, mutton-chopped and moustached; the fine generous features of Baron Henry Schröder; Sir Harry Veitch, with brownish-grey beard, grey side whiskers and reddish cheeks, his left hand holding a masdevallia, his right hand a lens; and the Rev. W. Wilks, pink-featured and wigged, and with a glass of daffodils on the table beside him. In the presence of so rich a legacy from the past it is impossible not to treat the day's business with great seriousness.

At the time of the second Show in February, Council sits only for a brief period—usually only for long enough to confirm the day's awards, so that these may be available to the exhibitors and to the Press—for this is the day of the Annual General Meeting when the President presents to the Fellows the report of the Council, including the Society's accounts and balance sheets, of the year that has just passed, when the annual awards are made and when the officials of the Society—the President, the new Vice-Presidents, the Treasurer, new members of Council, and the auditor—are elected for the ensuing year. Though the Council's report has been published in the *Journal* before the Annual General Meeting, the President, in his address, reviews in broad terms the progress the Society has made and the set-backs which have been encountered, both at Vincent Square and at Wisley, begs the adoption of the report, and requests the Treasurer to second his motion. In seconding the adoption of the report the Treasurer reviews the finances of the Society during the past year and invariably draws attention to the steady increase in all the items of regular expenditure.

After the election of the office-bearers, the Society's annual awards for the previous year are presented. The Secretary calls out the names of the individuals concerned; one by one they walk to the platform, and are greeted by the President, who makes an appropriate citation before handing over the award in question:

The Victoria Medal of Honour. Established in 1897 and awarded to British horticulturists resident in the United Kingdom, whom the Council considers deserving of special honour at the hands of the Society. It is the Society's highest award and the number of V.M.H.s may not exceed sixty-three at any one time.

The Associateship of Honour. Established in 1930 and conferred on persons of British nationality who have rendered distinguished service to horticulture in the course of their employment. The number of Associates of Honour may not exceed 100 at any one time.

The Veitch Memorial Medal. In 1922 the Veitch Memorial Trust was vested in the Council of the Society, and awards of medals and prizes are made annually to those who have helped in the advancement and improvement of the science and practice of horticulture and for special exhibits.

The Loder Rhododendron Cup. Presented in 1921 by the late Gerald Loder (Lord Wakehurst) in memory of his brother, Sir Edmund Loder, Bt. Though the cup is awarded annually, it is never awarded more than once in seven years to the same individual.

The A. J. Waley Medal. Instituted in 1937 by the late Alfred J. Waley to provide an annual award to a working gardener who has helped in the cultivation of rhododendrons. The fund was transferred by the Rhododendron Association to the Society in 1946.

The Lawrence Medal. Instituted in 1906 to celebrate the late Sir Trevor Lawrence's twenty-one years' tenure of office as President of the Society. It is struck in gold and awarded for the best exhibit shown to the Society during the year. No exhibitor may receive this medal more than once in three years.

The Williams Memorial Medal. Instituted in 1896 by the trustees of the Williams Memorial Fund in commemoration of B. S. Williams, and redesigned in 1927. It is struck in gold and awarded for a group of plants and/or cut blooms of one genus which show excellence in cultivation, staged at one of the Society's Shows. Fruit and vegetables are excluded.

The Mrs. F. E. Rivis Prize. Provided from a fund presented in 1960 by Miss A. K. Hincks in commemoration of her sister, Mrs. F. E. Rivis, with a view to encouraging excellence in cultivation.

The Holford Medal. Presented by the executors of the late Sir George Holford in 1928. Struck in gold, it is awarded for the best exhibit of plants and/or flowers (fruits and vegetables are excluded) staged during the year by an amateur at one of the Society's Shows other than Chelsea.

The E. H. Trophy. Provided from a fund bequeathed in 1961 by the late W. J. M. Hawkey in memory of his grandmother, mother, and wife, Mrs. Elizabeth, Mrs. Ellen, and Mrs. Emma Hawkey, and so far awarded to the best exhibit in which carnations predominate, shown to the Society during the year.

The George Moore Medal. Instituted in 1926 and presented by the late G. F. Moore, V.M.H. In gold, it is awarded to the exhibitor of the new *Cypripedium* which shows the greatest improvement on those of the same or similar parentage and which was shown to the Society during the year.

433

The Westonbirt Orchid Medal. Provided from a fund presented in 1960 by the late Mr. H. G. Alexander, V.M.H., in commemoration of the collection of orchids made at Westonbirt. Struck in gold, it is awarded annually (*a*) to the exhibitor of the best cultivar of an orchid species or of a hybrid grex which has been shown to the Society for the first time and received an award during the year or which, having received an award during the previous five years, has had the award raised during the year, or (*b*) for the most meritorious group of orchids shown to the Society during the year, or (*c*) for the most finely grown specimen orchid shown to the Society during the year, or (*d*) for any scientific, literary or any other outstanding personal achievements in connection with orchids.

The Farrer Trophy. Instituted in 1959 in commemoration of Reginald Farrer, the plant collector and authority on alpine plants, and offered for award for the best exhibit of plants for the rock garden or alpine house staged during the year at one of the Society's Shows other than Chelsea.

The Gordon-Lennox Cup. Presented by the late Lady Algernon Gordon-Lennox in 1913. Up to 1944 it was usually awarded for the best exhibit of fruit shown by an amateur at the Autumn Fruit and Vegetable Show. From 1945 to 1949 it was not offered. It is now offered for award for the best exhibit of fruit shown by an amateur during the year.

The Jones-Bateman Cup. Presented by Miss L. Jones-Bateman of Cae Glas, Abergele, in 1920, for the encouragement of fruit production and offered triennially for original research in fruit culture which has added to our knowledge of cultivation, genetics, or other relative matters.

The George Monro Memorial Cup. Presented in 1921 by Mr. George Monro and his brothers in memory of their father. Up to 1938 the cup was awarded for the best exhibit of grapes shown by an amateur at the Fruit and Vegetable Show. Now it is offered for award for the best exhibit of vegetables shown by an amateur during the year.

The Reginald Cory Memorial Cup. Continuing the purpose of the earlier Cory Cup, this award is given to encourage the production of new hardy hybrids of garden origin.

The Wigan Cup. Presented by the late Mr. A. L. Wigan in 1911 and offered for an exhibit of roses. Now it is offered for award for the best exhibit shown to the Society during the year by a local authority.

There are Fellows who have been attending the Annual General Meetings of the Society for forty years and more who readily affirm that the President rivals his father in the firm, efficient, and friendly fashion in which he conducts the Meeting and in the fine flair he has for intuitively expressing the most appropriate of sentiments in each of his addresses to the many award winners. This no doubt is the conviction of Mr. Fred Streeter, for instance, who, at the Annual General Meeting of 1946, when he received the V.M.H. at the hands of the President's father, was splendidly addressed thus:

Mr. Streeter, you have served your gardening apprenticeship under some very fine gardeners, including Mr. Bedford. You have been a great cultivator and a great exhibitor of fruits and vegetables. I understand that in your career as head gardener you have won no less than fifty gold medals, not all from the Society, real gold medals, so that if the American Loan fails we shall know where to turn. You have lately begun to broadcast. I would like to congratulate you most sincerely on your broadcasting, Mr. Streeter, because you have fought that very pernicious doctrine that trenching is no good. Of course trenching is no good if you do not put anything at the bottom of the trench, but just scratch up the soil. All good gardeners like you put good stuff at the bottom, and I think you will agree with me that it is the right and proper way to cultivate vegetables and fruits, and those who do not do it generally make a failure of gardening. I am very glad that you have stood up for the old creed of gardeners which is as good today as it was in the days of Adam.

In 1966, when Mr. Streeter received the Gordon-Lennox Cup on behalf of Lord Egremont, there was much more that Lord Aberconway could have said to him on the subject of fruit cultivation. But in this the President refrained; instead, he spoke of other matters:

I see that last year I said that Lord Egremont had won this Cup three times in the last four years; now it is four times in five years, and it includes the last three years running. At cricket, three wickets with successive balls is a hat trick; four in succession, a feat once performed by a Surrey bowler named Peech, is I believe known as a peach trick. We hope, Mr. Streeter, that you and Lord Egremont, by winning the Cup five years in succession, will coin a new phrase, 'a grape trick'.

Every Fellow of the Society, especially every Fellow able to attend an Annual General Meeting, will echo the words of Professor H. W. Miles in his vote of thanks to the President at the end of the Annual General Meeting of 1965:

It falls to few people to be privileged to speak for over 70,000 fellow members of a Society.

Yet that is the privilege I have this afternoon and I rise, my Lord President, to thank you for the gracious and friendly way in which you have held our attention and conducted this our Annual Meeting.

You have made each of us in the audience feel part and parcel of the meeting, and I am sure that many others, reading of it later in the Society's *Journal*, will share our feeling of really belonging to this Society. This I regard as extremely important, with a world-wide scattered membership such as that of our Society. . . .

When they read, as we have heard, your friendly and intimate words of commendation and appreciation of the work of those whom the Society has honoured today, and to those who have given us pleasure by their colourful exhibits, I think they will feel that experience for which we only have a rather inadequate expression, 'heart-warming'.

To me, this has been a heart-warming occasion, made so by the friendliness that you have displayed today, and which reflects your deep personal interest in all the affairs of this great Society. These are attributes that we, as members, value most highly in our President.

And every Fellow will echo the words of Mr. H. J. Randall in his vote of thanks at the 1966 Annual Meeting:

. . . It is I think fitting that I should extend the scope of our thanks to include the President's wife, who shares his enthusiasms, and in a charming way assists at a number of this Society's functions. It is often said that British wives do most of the garden work while their husbands receive most of the credit. That is just as it should be, of course, but we mortals are glad today to pay homage to our senior partners. We all wish Lord and Lady Aberconway many more years of happy gardening life together, and to our President we express both our thanks and our high regard.

The Meeting at an end, the President will retire to the President's room, there possibly to conduct a little more Society business with the Secretary, possibly to take a little well-deserved stimulant, and to collect his belongings. And there he will be confronted with the portraits of John Wedgwood, Sir Joseph Banks, Richard Anthony Salisbury, William Townsend Aiton, Charles Francis Greville—all founders of the Society; of the Earl of Dartmouth, Thomas Andrew Knight, the Duke of Devonshire, Prince Albert, the Duke of Buccleuch, and Lord Bury—the first six Presidents of the Society who encompassed the first seventy years of the Society's history. For anyone with the least sense of history it is not possible to be unmoved by these portraits. For one with a strong feeling for history, as has the President, especially the President who a few moments earlier has been deeply moved by his triumphant Meeting, it is inevitable that he pause for a moment to contemplate the features of those who pioneered this greatest of horticultural societies, for a moment to remember the disasters and triumphs of the past, for a moment to glance to the future—and to wonder.

In his paper on the objects of the Society of 1805, Knight wrote:

In the execution of this plan, the committee feel that the Society have many difficulties to encounter, and, they fear, some prejudices to contend with; but they have long been convinced, as individuals, and their aggregate observations have tended only to increase their conviction, that there scarce exists a

The Old Hall in Vincent Square

The New Hall in Greycoat Street

Plate 21

Long
Service
Medal
with bars
for fifty and
sixty years' service ▶

▲

The first medal of the Society, from a design by Dr. Robert Batty

Plate 22

MEDALS AWARDED BY THE SOCIETY

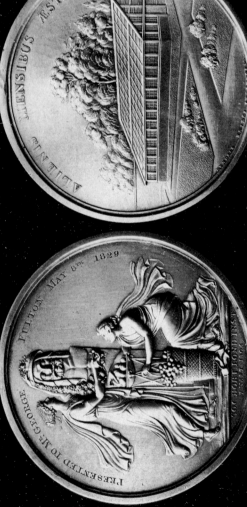

single species of esculent plant or fruit, which (relative to the use of man) has yet attained its utmost state of perfection; nor any branch of practical horticulture which is not still susceptible of essential improvement: and, under these impressions, they hope to receive the support and assistance of those who are interested in, and capable of promoting, the success of their endeavours.

The President realizes that Knight's words are as significant now as then; that the endeavours of the Society then are still the same over 160 years later. The young Horticultural Society did indeed have many difficulties to encounter and many prejudices to contend with. And this must be the future lot of the Royal Horticultural Society, which, in the meantime, most triumphantly rides the crest of the wave.

CALENDAR OF EVENTS

1804   The Horticultural Society is formed with the Earl of Dartmouth the President, John Wedgwood the Treasurer, and the Rev. Alexander Cleeve the Secretary.
Death of William Forsyth, one of the founders of the Society.
J. C. Loudon's *Observations on the Formation and Management of Useful and Ornamental Plantations* published.
William Kerr's first consignment of plants, including *Lilium tigrinum*, from China, arrive at Kew.
Lilium monadelphum introduced from the Caucasus.
Lady Holland sends dahlia seeds from Madrid to Britain.

1805   The Horticultural Society's meetings held in the rooms of the Linnean Society, first at 10 Panton Square and later at 9 Gerrard Street, Soho.
Thomas Andrew Knight writes *Introductory Remarks relative to the Objects which the Horticultural Society have in view*.
R. A. Salisbury appointed Honorary Secretary to the Society.
Benjamin Price engaged as clerk to the Society.
The first recorded exhibit at a Society meeting, 'A Potato, exhibited by Mr. Charles Minier'.
J. C. Loudon engaged in landscape gardening.
Loudon publishes *A short Treatise on some Improvements made in Hot-houses*.
Colvill, of the King's Road Nursery, raises *Rosa lawrenceana* (*R. chinensis* 'Minima').

1806   John Wedgwood retires from the treasurership of the Society and is succeeded by Charles Greville.
Exhibits of vegetables and fruits at the Society's meetings.
The first recorded gift of books to, and the first books purchased by, the Society.
T. A. Knight elected to the Society's Council and his paper *On the Direction of the Radicle and Germen during the Vegetation of Seeds*, published by the Royal Society.
John Sutton founds 'The House of Sutton'.
Paeonia suffruticosa var. *papaveracea* first flowers in cultivation in Britain in garden of Sir Abraham and Lady Amelia Hume, at Wormley Bury, Herts.

1807   First publication of the Society's *Transactions*.
        The last plate of Thornton's *Temple of Flora* published (the first in 1797).

1808   The Society decides to strike its first medal.
        John Veitch founds the Killerton Nursery.

1809   The Society's first Charter granted, establishing the Society's name as
        The Horticultural Society of London.
        Charles Francis Greville, one of the Society's founders, and Treasurer,
        dies.
        John Elliot succeeds Greville as Treasurer.
        Caledonian Horticultural Society formed in Edinburgh.
        A botanic garden founded in Cork.
        Rhododendron catawbiense introduced from North Carolina.
        'Hume's Blush Tea-scented China' Rose introduced from China by
        Sir Abraham Hume.

1810   Death of the Earl of Dartmouth, the Society's first President.
        Joseph Sabine joins the Society.
        William McNab, of Kew, appointed principal gardener at Royal
        Botanic Garden, Edinburgh.
        William Jackman founds the Woking Nurseries.
        'Hume's Blush Tea' Rose flowers for the first time in Colvill's Nursery.
        The first part of W. T. Aiton's *Hortus Kewensis* published.

1811   Thomas Andrew Knight elected the Society's President.
        Benjamin Price promoted from clerk to Assistant Secretary of the
        Society.
        The Society's first Medal in Gold presented to Sir Joseph Banks.
        Rhododendron arboreum introduced from India.

1812   The Society has its first seal.
        Joseph Sabine elected to the Society's Council.
        Robert Fortune born at Blackadder Town, Berwickshire.
        Botanic garden founded at Hull.
        Thomas Hogg publishes *A Concise and Practical Treatise on the Growth
        and Culture of the Carnation, Pink, Auricula, Polyanthus, Ranunculus, Tulip,
        Hyacinth, Rose, and other Flowers*.

1813   The Society purchases the first book-case for its Library.

1814   The Society's Gold Medal awarded to R. A. Salisbury.
        William Anderson appointed Curator of Chelsea Physic Garden.
        Azaleodendron 'Odoratum' in cultivation in Royal Botanic Garden,
        Edinburgh.
        Fully double purple dahlia flowers in garden of Comte Lelieur near
        Paris.
        The last part of W. T. Aiton's *Hortus Kewensis* published.

1815 Benjamin Price dismissed and Thomas Hare appointed the Society's Assistant Secretary in place of Price.

Joseph Sabine made a Vice-President of the Society.

The Society sets up a Drawing Committee and William Hooker is commissioned to draw fruits.

Unsuccessful attempt made by the Society to use part of Chelsea Physic Garden for its own Garden.

James Ridgway launches *The Botanical Register*.

1816 Queen Charlotte becomes the Society's first royal patron.

Joseph Sabine and John Cresswell prepare a report on the affairs of the Society.

R. A. Salisbury resigns from the office of Secretary of the Society and is succeeded by Sabine.

James and Thomas Backhouse of York enter the nursery business.

Wisteria sinensis brought to England from China by Captain Wellbank.

The last part of Redouté's *Les Liliacées* published.

Isaac Emmerton publishes *A Plain and Practical Treatise on the Culture and Management of the Auricula*.

1817 First meeting of the Society's Library Committee.

The Society rents the first floor of 21 Church Street for its Library and other business except its meetings.

The Society accepts an offer from John Reeves in Canton to send to the Society Chinese plants and drawings of plants.

J. C. Loudon joins the Society.

Flower show held in County Cork probably organized by Horticultural Society of Ireland.

The Botanical Cabinet first issued by Conrad Loddiges & Sons.

The first part of Redouté's *Les Roses* published.

1818 Thomas Hare resigns from post of Assistant Secretary and is succeeded by John Turner.

Horticultural sundries first appear at the Society's Shows.

The Society acquires its first Garden at Kensington and Charles Strachan is appointed the first gardener.

The first drawings arrive from John Reeves in China.

The first ball-type dahlias are seen in Britain.

Humphry Repton, landscape architect, dies.

Robert Hogg (future pomologist) born.

1819 The Society purchases a house in Waterloo Street—No. 21 on the west side of what is now Lower Regent Street and three doors down from the entry into Jermyn Street.

Charles Strachan discharged and replaced by William Christie.

John Lindley appointed an assistant in the library of Sir Joseph Banks.

J. C. Loudon begins work on the *Encyclopaedia of Gardening*.

Botanic Garden founded at Bury St. Edmunds.
Sydenham Teast Edwards, botanical artist, dies.
Samuel Reynolds Hole (future rosarian) born.

1820   Donald Munro appointed gardener to the Society.
Twelve named cultivars of chrysanthemum growing in the Society's Garden and Reeves sends ten new kinds.
Death of Sir Joseph Banks and the institution by the Society of the Banksian Medal.
John Lindley commissioned to draw some single roses for the Society, and some larches.
Robert Graham appointed Regius Keeper of Royal Botanic Garden, Edinburgh, and the beginning of the transference of Edinburgh Garden from Leith Walk to a new site at Inverleith.
William Jackson Hooker succeeds Robert Graham in the Chair of Botany in Glasgow.
Camellia reticulata introduced from China, by Captain Rawes.
The first part of Robert Sweet's *Geraniaceae* is published.

1821   The Society leases thirty-three acres at Chiswick, from the Duke of Devonshire, for its Garden.
Joseph Sabine writes on chrysanthemums in the Society's *Transactions*.
The Society sends John Potts to China and George Don to west coast of Africa, east coast of South America and the West Indies, to collect plants.
Primula sinensis introduced from China by Captain Rawes.

1822   John Lindley appointed Assistant Secretary at the Society's Garden.
John Potts dies after introducing seeds of *Primula sinensis* and other plants.
The Society sends John Forbes, as its collector, to Brazil.
James Dickson, one of the Society's founders, dies.
Reeves introduces *Prunus serrulata* to the Society's Garden.
The first edition of Loudon's *Encyclopaedia of Gardening* published.
John (Gregor) Mendel born.
Henry Nicholson Ellacombe born.

1823   The Society gives up the small Kensington Garden.
Joseph Paxton employed in the Society's Chiswick Garden.
John Forbes dies in East Africa.
John Damper Parks sent to China as the Society's collector.
David Douglas sent to America as the Society's collector.
Rhododendron molle introduced from China.
Gladiolus x *colvillii*, the first *Gladiolus* hybrid, raised.
The first part of Sweet's *British Flower Garden* published.
Henry Eckford (future sweet pea breeder) born.

1824   Parks introduces sixteen new cultivars of chrysanthemum from China.
James McRae sent by the Society to collect plants in South America
and introduces seeds of *Araucaria araucana*.
David Douglas leaves on his second mission to America on behalf of
the Society.
Robert Thompson appointed to the Chiswick staff.
Caledonian Horticultural Society receives its first Royal Charter.

1825   *Camellia Britannica* published, with text by E. B. Buckingham and
plates by Alfred Chandler.
The first part of Sweet's *Cistiniae* published.
Sir Henry Steuart's *The Planter's Guide* published.
Peter Barr (future daffodil breeder) born.

1826   Turner, Society's Assistant Secretary, discharged for theft.
The Society awards large silver medals to provincial horticultural
societies.
The first reliable meteorological records are kept at the Society's
Garden.
Forty-eight cultivars of chrysanthemum being grown in the Society's
Garden.
The Society publishes the *Catalogue of Fruits Cultivated in the Garden of the
Horticultural Society at Chiswick*—mostly the work of Robert Thompson.
Paxton leaves the Society's Garden to become head gardener to the
Duke of Devonshire at Chatsworth.
The Duke of Devonshire undertakes a special mission to Russia.
Loudon establishes *The Gardener's Magazine*.
J. R. Gowen makes the cross between *Rhododendron catawbiense* x *R.
ponticum* x *R. arboreum*, which yields the hybrid 'Altaclarense'.
Michael Waterer of Knaphill Nursery hybridizes *Rhododendron arboreum*
with *R. caucasicum* and produces R. 'Nobleanum'.

1827   John Lindley appointed Assistant Secretary to the Society as well as
at the Garden.
The first of a series of 'public breakfasts'—later 'Fêtes'—held at
Chiswick Garden.
The first part of Sweet's *Flora Australasica* published.

1828   John Elliot resigns from the treasurership of the Society and is suc-
ceded by R. H. Jenkinson.
George Gordon appointed a departmental foreman at Chiswick
Garden.
'Mutual Improvement Society' formed for gardeners at Chiswick.
John Lindley elected a Fellow of the Royal Society and the first Profes-
sor of Botany in the University of London.
John Lindley's *Pomological Magazine* appears.
James Edward Smith, founder of the Linnean Society, dies.

1829   David Douglas sails again for N.W. America, on behalf of the Society.
Richard Anthony Salisbury, one of the Society's founders, dies.
R. S. Holford founds the arboretum at Westonbirt.
The Norwich and Norfolk Chrysanthemum Society formed.
The Birmingham Botanical and Horticultural Society formed.
G. W. Johnson's *History of English Gardening* published.

1830   Joseph Sabine resigns from the post of Secretary to the Society and is succeeded by George Bentham.
Alexander Seton appointed the Society's Treasurer in succession to R. H. Jenkinson.
Lady Radnor elected the first lady Fellow of the Society.
The Horticultural Society of Ireland reconstituted.
Illustrations of Orchidaceous Plants published, with text by Lindley and illustrations by Francis Bauer.
Loddiges' *Catalogue of Plants*, fifteenth edition, published.
William McNab's *Planting and General Treatment of Hardy Evergreens* published.
Lilium maculatum introduced from Japan.
Thomas Laxton (future plant breeder) born.

1831   Lindley begins a series of lectures to Fellows at the Society's meetings.
The Society holds its first competitions at its meetings in Regent Street.
John Reeves retires from Canton and becomes active in the affairs of the Society.
Illustrations and Descriptions of the plants which compose the natural order Camellieae and of the varieties of Camellia japonica *cultivated in the Gardens of Great Britain* published, with text by William Beattie Booth and plates by Alfred Chandler.
Hugh Ronald's *Pyrus Malus Brentfordiensis* published.
Thomas Francis Rivers (future plant breeder) born.
Trevor Lawrence (future President of the Society) born.

1832   Douglas resigns from the Society's service.
James Veitch establishes what was to be known as the Exeter Nursery.
Paxton commences publication of *The Horticultural Register*.
William McNab's *Propagation, Cultivation and General Treatment of Cape Heaths* published.
A. L. Lambert's *A Description of the Genus Pinus* published.
Lilium speciosum introduced from Japan and *Rhododendron zeylanicum* from Ceylon.
'Inwoods Springwood Rival'—first ball-type dahlia—flowers in Britain.

1833   The Society's first Shows held under canvas at Chiswick Garden.
The last of the twenty volumes of the *Botanical Cabinet* issued with complete index.

Maxwell Tylden Masters (future editor of the *Gardener's Chronicle*) born.

1834 The Society starts a system of affiliation of societies.
Palm Stove at Royal Botanic Garden, Edinburgh, opened.
Paxton begins publication of *The Magazine of Botany*.
J. B. Lawes experimenting with manures at Rothamstead.
'Lyne's Springwood Rival' ball-type dahlia appears.
Douglas dies in Hawaii.
John Underwood, first Curator of Botanic Garden at Glasnevin (from 1798) dies.

1835 Thomas Edgar succeeds Alexander Seton as the Society's Treasurer.
John Lindley appointed Director of Chelsea Physic Garden.
Rhododendron campanulatum introduced from Himalayas, and *Lilium brownii* from China.
Peter Lawson & Son, Edinburgh, introduce the Austrian pine.

1836 The Society's Regent Street competitions discontinued.
The Society's Knightian and Floral Medals instituted.
The first horticultural examinations for student-gardeners employed at Chiswick are started, in which Robert Fortune distinguishes himself.
Theodore Hartweg sent by the Society to introduce plants from Mexico.
The great new conservatory at Chatsworth, designed by Paxton, is begun.
Catalogue of Roses published by Rivers & Son.
Michael Foster (future iris breeder) born.

1837 Queen Victoria becomes the Society's patron on the death of William IV.
The Duke of Devonshire joins the Council of the Society.
Berlèse's *Monographie du Genre Camellia* first published in Paris.
The first part of James Bateman's *Orchidaceae of Mexico and Guatemala* published.
Dean Herbert's *Amaryllidaceae* published.
Joseph Sabine dies.

1838 Thomas Andrew Knight dies and is succeeded as President by the Duke of Devonshire.
Lindley's 'Kew Committee' formed to inquire into the management of Kew Gardens.
Horticultural Society of Ireland receives its Royal Charter.
South London Floricultural Society given Royal Charter.
Firm of James Veitch & Son founded at Exeter.
David Moore appointed Curator of Glasnevin Botanic Garden.
Loudon's eight-volume *Arboretum et Fruticetum Britannicum* published.
William Robinson, author of *The English Flower Garden*, born.

1839   Robert Fortune joins the staff of the Royal Botanic Garden, Edinburgh, to work under William McNab.

Dr. Nathaniel Bagshaw Ward describes his Wardian Case in the *Gardener's Magazine*.

Royal Botanic Society of London established.

Orchidaceae in the Collection of C. Loddiges & Sons published.

James Ford's *Pinetum Woburnense* published.

J. F. Royle publishes his *Illustrations of the botany and other branches of the natural history of the Himalayan Mountains and of the flora of Cashmere*.

1840   One wing of a new conservatory at the Society's Chiswick Garden finished.

Paxton's Chatsworth conservatory finished.

Kew Gardens transferred to the Commissioners of Woods and Forests.

Robert Marnoch appointed to lay out the grounds of the Royal Botanic Society of London.

William Lobb sails for Brazil to collect for Veitch & Son.

Joseph Knight publishes his *Catalogue of Coniferae*.

1841   George Bentham retires from the post of Secretary of the Society and is succeeded by Dr. Alexander Henderson.

The Society's Chemical Committee set up.

Sir William Hooker appointed Director of Kew.

John Hutton Balfour succeeds William Hooker in the Chair of Botany at Glasgow.

Gladiolus x *gandavensis* raised by Van Houtte and distributed.

The *Gardener's Chronicle* begins publication, with John Lindley as horticultural editor.

The first volume of Berlèse's *Iconographie du Genre Camellia* published.

Lindley's *Pomological Magazine* reissued as *Pomologia Britannica*.

1842   Robert Fortune employed in the Society's Garden at Chiswick.

Edward Solly appointed the Society's chemist.

Captain Everard Hume sends seeds to Kew of *Cryptomeria japonica*.

The Treaty of Nanking signed and a number of Chinese ports opened.

Nathaniel Bagshaw Ward publishes *On the Growth of Plants in Closely Glazed Cases*.

1843   Robert Fortune sails for China to collect plants for the Society.

Thomas Lobb sent to Java by the firm of Veitch to collect plants.

J. B. Lawes begins long-term experiments at Rothamsted.

J. C. Loudon dies and *Gardener's Magazine* ceases publication.

Miss Gertrude Jekyll born.

1844   Fortune introduces *Anemone hupehensis* var. *japonica* and *Jasminum nudiflorum*.

Death of John Wedgwood, one of the Society's founders.

Building of Palm House at Kew, designed by Decimus Burton, begins.

1845   Alexander Henderson retires from post of Secretary of the Society and is succeeded by J. R. Gowen.
Decision to discontinue publication of the Society's *Transactions*.
Robert Graham retires from Royal Botanic Garden, Edinburgh, and is succeeded by Prof. J. Hutton Balfour.
James Veitch & Son send William Lobb to collect in Chile.
George Yeld (future iris breeder) born.

1846   The Society's Chemical Committee dissolved and Solly appointed Honorary Professor of Chemistry to the Society.
The Society's *Journal* begins publication.
Reading Room and Library established at Chiswick for Society's students.
Robert Fortune returns from China and succeeds William Anderson (who dies) as Curator of Chelsea Physic Garden.
Stoke Newington Chrysanthemum Society formed—later to be the National Chrysanthemum Society.
Seeds of the Giant Victoria Water Lily introduced to Kew.
Henry John Elwes born.

1847   The Society's Regent Street office is reorganized and James Scott, the Librarian, resigns.
Standish & Noble establish the Sunningdale Nurseries.
Joseph Dalton Hooker begins his Himalayan journeys.
G. W. Johnson's *Cottage Gardener's Dictionary* published.
Dean Herbert dies, having almost completed his *History of the Species of Crocus*.
George Nicholson (future Curator at Kew) born.

1848   Robert Hutton succeeds Thomas Edgar as the Society's Treasurer.
William Brailsford appointed the Society's Librarian and sub-accountant.
Anemone x *elegans*, the pink 'Japanese Anemone', is raised at Chiswick.
Robert Fortune again goes to China—for East India Company.
Thomas Moore appointed Curator of Chelsea Physic Garden in succession to Robert Fortune.
Decimus Burton Palm House at Kew completed.
The first Museum of Economic Botany at Kew is opened.
The first part of *Nouvelle Iconographie des Camellias* published by Alexandre Verschaffelt.
William Paul's *The Rose Garden* published.
The Cottage Gardener founded by G. W. Johnson.

1849   Small Shows in Regent Street room discontinued and lectures by Lindley substituted.
William Townsend Aiton, one of the Society's founders, dies.
James Veitch & Son send William Lobb a second time to the Pacific coast of America.

James McNab succeeds his father as Curator of Royal Botanic Garden, Edinburgh.

Giant Victoria Water Lily flowers in Britain for the first time—at Chatsworth.

Rhododendron barbatum introduced from Himalayas.

First part of J. D. Hooker's *Rhododendrons of the Sikkim Himalaya* published.

1850   J. R. Gowen resigns from the post of Secretary to the Society and is succeeded by Dr. Daniel.

Gowen appointed Treasurer to the Society.

Donald Munro, the Society's gardener, retires.

Joseph Paxton builds the Victoria Water Lily House at Chatsworth and his designs for the Crystal Palace are accepted.

The Oregon Association formed in Edinburgh and John Jeffrey sent to the west coast of America to collect plants on behalf of the Association.

James Kelway begins business at Langport, Somerset.

Joseph Knight and Thomas A. Perry publish *A Synopsis of Coniferous Plants grown in Great Britain and sold by Knight & Perry*.

1851   Dr. J. F. Royle appointed the Society's Secretary in succession to Dr. Daniel.

Crystal Palace Exhibition opened by the Queen.

Joseph Paxton knighted.

George Herbert Engleheart (future daffodil breeder) born.

1852   Standish & Noble publish Practical Hints on *Ornamental Plants & Planting*.

Wm. Barron publishes *The British Winter Garden; a Practical Treatise on Evergreens*.

1853   The foundation of the Herbarium and Library at Kew begins.

Fortune again in China on behalf of tea and the East India Company.

Charles McIntosh's *The Book of the Garden* published.

1854   The Society's jubilee; the *Journal* discontinued and post of Librarian abolished.

Chamaecyparis lawsoniana introduced by Peter Lawson & Son through William Murray.

The British Pomological Society formed.

1855   J. R. Gowen resigns from the treasurership and is succeeded by Dr. A. R. Jackson.

Dr. Jackson dies and in August is succeeded, as Treasurer, by W. Wilson Saunders.

The Society in financial straits.

The Society sells orchids and other plants at Chiswick.

Robert Fortune introduces *Rhododendron fortunei* from China.

Pritzel's *Index Iconum Botanicarum* published.

William Thompson of Ipswich issues his first seed catalogue.

1856   The Society's subscription rates altered and a two-guinea subscription introduced.

The Society's Regent Street house for sale, but fails to produce the reserve figure of £4,500.

Sale of the Society's herbarium specimens and reserve stock of *Transactions*.

Calanthe x *dominii*, the first orchid hybrid, raised by John Dominy for Veitch.

John Reeves dies.

Gregor Mendel begins his hybridization work in garden of monastery of St. Thomas in Brunn.

1857   The Society's Regent Street house again up for sale and again withdrawn.

The Society's Grand Fruit Exhibition held.

George McEwan appointed Superintendent of the Society's Chiswick Garden.

Robert Thompson appointed fruit inspector at Chiswick.

George Gordon leaves the Chiswick Garden.

Rhododendron thomsonii flowers for the first time in cultivation, at Sunningdale Nurseries.

George Russell (future lupin breeder) born.

1858   The Duke of Devonshire, the Society's President, dies.

The Prince Consort is elected President.

Dr. Royle dies and John Lindley is elected to the Council and to the office of Secretary.

William Beattie Booth appointed Assistant Secretary.

George McEwan, Garden Superintendent, dies and is succeeded by Archibald Henderson, who resigns before the end of the year.

The Society's Fruit Committee established, and with it is merged the British Pomological Society.

The Society's 'First Class Certificate of Merit' and 'Commended' brought into being.

First National Rose Show held at St. James's Hall, London.

Rhododendron griffithianum offered to the public for the first time, by Sunningdale Nurseries.

The Floral World is launched with James Shirley Hibberd as editor.

George Gordon publishes *The Pinetum*.

1859   The Society's Regent Street house sold and the Society moves to cramped quarters at 8 St. Martin's Place.

The Society holds its Monthly Meetings in the Adelphi in a room lent by the Society of Arts.

The Society takes a lease of the new Garden at Kensington Gore.

The Society sells its Library and over 1,500 original drawings.

The Society's Floral Committee established under chairmanship of Rev. Joshua Dix.

Professor Henfrey, the first appointed chairman of the Floral Committee, dies.

George Eyles placed in charge of the Chiswick Garden and the development of the Garden at Kensington Gore.

Veitch sends Richard Pearce to collect plants in Chile, Peru, and Bolivia.

1860   William Beattie Booth retires from post of Assistant Secretary.

16,000 people attend Rose Show at Crystal Palace.

Robert Fortune in Japan sees for the first time famous collections of Japanese chrysanthemums, some of which he later introduced.

John Gould Veitch collecting in Japan and introduces *Lilium auratum*. *Anemone* x *elegans* 'Alba' raised in France.

'Blue Hybrid', the first edged-type sweet pea, raised.

Robert Hogg's *Fruit Manual* published.

Miss Ellen Ann Willmott (future rose specialist) born.

Building begins on Decimus Burton Temperate House at Kew.

1861   Andrew Murray succeeds William B. Booth as Assistant Secretary.

The Society vacates its office in St. Martin's Place and moves to South Kensington.

The Society's new Royal Charter is sealed and the Society now called 'The Royal Horticultural Society'.

The Garden at Kensington Gore opened by the Prince Consort.

The Prince Consort dies on 14 December.

The Society sends John Weir to collect plants in Brazil.

The lake at Kew is completed.

William Robinson is employed as under-gardener in Royal Botanic Society's Garden at Regent's Park.

Rhododendron 'Ascot Brilliant'—a hybrid of *R. thomsonii*—raised at Sunningdale Nurseries.

1862   The Duke of Buccleuch elected President of the Society.

Great International Exhibition at Kensington Gore organized by the Royal Commissioners.

Peter Barr founds the firm of Barr & Sugden—later known as Barr & Sons.

Lilium auratum is first flowered and exhibited at a Society meeting by Veitch.

1863   Lindley retires from post of Secretary to the Society and is succeeded by William Wilson Saunders.

John Clutton succeeds Wilson Saunders as Treasurer.

James Veitch resigns from the Council.

James Veitch, the elder, dies.

Andrew Murray's *Book of the Royal Horticultural Society* published.

Clematis x *jackmanii* receives First Class Certificate from Society.

1864 'Lecturettes' resumed at the Society's meetings.

Committee on the Improved Education of Gardeners formed jointly with the Society and with the Society of Arts.

John Weir paralysed for life.

Edwin Hillier buys a small nurseryman's and florist's business in Winchester—the beginning of the present firm of Hillier & Sons.

Osgood Mackenzie begins to make garden at Inverewe in Wester Ross, Scotland.

Richard Pearce collecting for Veitch in Bolivia.

1865 Captain John Cockerell succeeds Andrew Murray as the Society's Assistant Secretary.

John Kelk succeeds John Clutton as the Society's Treasurer.

George Ferguson Wilson elected to the Council.

The Society holds practical examinations in horticulture at Chiswick.

The Society makes its first award to a sweet pea—'Scarlet Invincible'.

John Lindley dies; Joseph Paxton dies; Sir William Hooker dies and is succeeded by his son Joseph as Director of Kew.

James Dobbie starts a seed and nursery business which later becomes Dobbie & Co. Ltd., Edinburgh.

Maxwell Tylden Masters becomes senior editor of the *Gardener's Chronicle*.

Mendel's famous paper on the segregation of characters is published, but remains unnoticed.

Edward Augustus Bowles (future fine servant of the Society) born.

1866 George Ferguson Wilson succeeds John Kelk as the Society's Treasurer.

Lieut.-Col. Henry Scott succeeds W. Wilson Saunders as the Society's Secretary.

Archibald Barron appointed Superintendent of the Society's Chiswick Garden; Eyles concerned only with Kensington Garden.

The Society purchases Lindley Library for £600 and the Society's Lindley Medal is instituted.

International Horticultural Exhibition and Botanical Congress held at South Kensington.

Thomas Laxton publishes his observations on the dominance of characters in the *Report of the International Exhibition and Botanical Congress*.

1867 The Society holds a Show at Bury St. Edmunds—the first Society Show outside London and the London area.

Robert Thompson retires from the Society after forty-five years of service, most of it as superintendent of the fruit and vegetable section of the Garden and as keeper of the meteorological records at the Garden.

William Robinson reports on the horticultural aspects of the Paris Exhibition for *The Times*.

1868   John Clutton elected Treasurer of the Society for a second time.
The Lindley Library Trust established.
The Society institutes its Scientific Committee with Buccleuch its first chairman and Berkeley its first secretary.
The Society holds a Show at Leicester.

1869   The Society holds a Show at Manchester.
George Bunyard launches out on a national scale in fruit culture at Allington.
Rev. Samuel Reynolds Hole publishes *A Book About Roses*.
James Veitch dies.

1870   The Society holds a Show at Oxford.
Veitch Memorial Medal instituted through Veitch Memorial Fund.
Chiswick Garden reduced from 32 acres to 10 or 11.
Henry Eckford begins to work on sweet peas.
Anthony Waterer at Knaphill begins to develop the Knaphill azaleas.
William Robinson's *Alpine Flowers for English Gardens* and *The Wild Garden* published.
Ernest Ballard (future plant breeder) born.

1871   The Society holds a Show at Nottingham.
George Eyles leaves the service of the Society.
Archibald Barron made gardener in chief at Kensington and Chiswick.
The Garden founded by William Robinson.
George Bunyard introduces 'Gascoyne's Scarlet' apple.
Dr. Alexander Wallace of Colchester first offers his lily bulbs for sale to the public.
Amos Perry (future plant breeder) born.

1872   The Society holds a Show at Birmingham.
W. T. Thiselton Dyer made Professor of Botany to the Society.
Thomas Laxton publishes 'Notes on some changes and variations in the offspring of Cross-fertilised Peas' in the Society's *Journal*.

1873   The Duke of Buccleuch resigns from Presidency of the Society and is succeeded by Lord Bury.
W. A. Lindsay elected the Society's Secretary in place of Henry Scott.
Sir A. Slade elected the Society's Secretary *pro tempore*.
Fellows decline to accept Council's report at Annual General Meeting.

Frederick James Chittenden (fine future servant of the Society) born.
George Forrest (future plant collector) born.

1874 Bonamy Dobrée elected the Society's Treasurer.
The Lindley Medal is struck.

1875 Lord Bury resigns from the Society's Presidency and is succeeded by Lord Aberdare.
F. W. Burbidge publishes *The Narcissus; its History and Culture.*
Henry Pochin begins to lay out the gardens at Bodnant.
Gertrude Jekyll meets William Robinson.

1876 The National Rose Society formed.
Ernest Henry Wilson (future plant hunter) born.

1877 Robert Hogg appointed the Society's Secretary.
Samuel Jennings appointed Assistant Secretary and editor of the Society's *Journal.*
Henry Webb appointed the Society's Treasurer.
Veitch sends Charles Maries to collect in China and Japan.
Walter Charles Slocock takes over the Goldsworth Nursery at Woking and develops a conifer and rhododendron nursery.
Thomas Rivers dies; William Rickatson Dykes (future Society Secretary and iris authority) born.

1878 Sir Trevor Lawrence elected to the Council.
Frederick Moore succeeds his father as Director of Glasnevin Botanic Garden.

1879 *Lilium* x *parkmannii*, the first hybrid lily to be raised in cultivation, exhibited to the Society.
William Robinson launches *Gardening.*
F. W. Burbidge appointed Curator of Botanic Garden of Trinity College, Dublin.
R. I. Lynch appointed Curator of Botanic Garden, Cambridge.

1880 Lawn tennis introduced at the Kensington Garden.
Professor I. Bayley Balfour introduces *Begonia socotrana* from which winter-flowering begonias are evolved.
H. J. Elwes publishes *The Genus Lilium.*
Sam McGredy starts a nursery at Portadown, Co. Armagh.

1881 The Society loses its lawsuit with the Royal Commissioners and has to pay litigation costs.
H. F. C. Sander establishes orchid nursery near St. Albans.
Augustine Henry goes to work in Shanghai.

453

1882 William Haughton elected Treasurer and Maj. F. Mason Secretary of the Society.

The Society's lease at Kensington terminated by the Royal Commissioners.

Henry Eckford names the first of his sweet pea seedlings—'Bronze Prince'.

Augustine Henry goes to Ichang, by the gorges of the Yangtze river.

1883 National Apple Congress held with a Show at the Society's Chiswick Garden.

John Heal of the firm of Veitch raises the first winter-flowering begonia —'John Heal'.

John Russell and three sons start a new nursery at Brentwood, Surrey, and take over the nurseries of an old-established firm at Richmond, Surrey.

William Robinson publishes *The English Flower Garden*.

1884 The Society sponsors Daffodil Conference and the Society's Narcissus Committee formed under auspices of the Scientific Committee.

Hybrid Tea roses first distinguished.

W. Baylor Hartland's *A Little Book of Daffodils* published.

Amateur Gardening begins publication.

Gregor Mendel dies.

William Robinson buys Gravetye Manor near East Grinstead.

1885 Lord Aberdare resigns from the presidency of the Society and is succeeded by Sir Trevor Lawrence.

Orchid Conference held at Kensington, and a National Pear Conference at Chiswick.

George Bunyard introduces 'Lady Sudeley' apple.

The first volume of G. Nicholson's *Illustrated Dictionary of Gardening* published.

Joseph Dalton Hooker retires from post of Director of Kew and is succeeded by W. T. Thiselton Dyer.

J. C. Williams of Caerhays Castle, Cornwall, begins to grow rhododendrons.

Rev. H. T. Ellacombe dies.

1886 Colonial and India Exhibition held at Kensington.

Primula Conference held at Kensington.

Fruit Conference, with George Bunyard the chairman, held in Edinburgh.

Conference on orchid nomenclature held in Liverpool.

Rosa multiflora introduced from Korea and Japan and to be used as one of the parents of the Polyantha roses.

Augustine Henry's first Chinese specimens arrive at Kew.

William Watson appointed Assistant Curator at Kew, under G. Nicholson.

George Maw's *Monograph of the Genus Crocus* published.

1887   The Society sponsors a Conifer Conference and holds a trial of daffodils at Kew.

George Ferguson Wilson buys the estate at Wisley known as Oakwood.

Thomas W. Sanders appointed editor of *Amateur Gardening*.

1888   The Society leaves South Kensington and takes offices at 111, later 117, Victoria Street, Westminster, and holds Shows at Buckingham Gate, Westminster.

Dr. Daniel Morris elected the Society's Treasurer.

Rev. William Wilks elected Honorary Secretary when W. Lee resigns.

The Society's 'Award of Merit' brought into being.

The first Temple Show held in two tents on the Embankment—the forerunner of Chelsea Show.

Apple and Pear Conference held at Chiswick.

Henry Eckford founds his nursery at Wem in Shropshire.

J. G. Baker's *Handbook of the Amaryllidaceae* published.

Isaac Bayley Balfour appointed Regius Keeper, Royal Botanic Garden, Edinburgh.

1889   The Society's *Journal* revived.

National Rose Conference, and a Chrysanthemum Conference and Exhibition, held at Chiswick.

Rothamsted Experimental Station established.

Swanley Horticultural College opened for the training of men.

Gladiolus primulinus introduced.

1890   Daniel Morris resigns from the Society's treasurership and is succeeded by Philip Crowley.

Conferences on daffodils, dahlias and grapes, ferns and carnations held at Chiswick.

City Exhibition of fruit held in the Guildhall and George Bunyard made a Freeman of the City.

A company formed to take over the assets of John Waterer of the Bagshot Nursery trading under the name of John Waterer & Sons.

Augustine Henry retires from China.

Death of Thomas Laxton.

1891   Conferences on conifers, hardy summer-flowering perennials, small hardy fruits, asters and perennial sunflowers held at Chiswick.

1892   William Wilks becomes the Society's salaried Secretary.

The Society's Narcissus and Tulip Committee established.

Conferences on begonias, apricots, and plums held at Chiswick.

Full report of the 1891 Conifer Conference published in the Society's *Journal*.

Formation of English Arboricultural Society—later to become the Royal Forestry Society of England, Wales and Northern Ireland.

'Royal Sovereign' strawberry introduced.
Winter-flowering begonia 'Gloire de Lorraine' introduced by Messrs.
Lemoine & Son of Nancy.
Sir George Holford succeeds to Westonbirt estate.

1893   The Society sponsors the first examination which later is to be known as
the General Examination.

1894   Changes in the Society's Bye-Laws.
Conference on trees at Chiswick.
First Conference on and Exhibition of British-grown fruit held at
Crystal Palace.
Duke of Bedford at Woburn establishes an experimental fruit farm.
South Eastern Agricultural College (later Wye Agricultural College)
founded with Daniel Hall the first principal.

1895   The Society publishes the *Code of Rules and Suggestions for Judges, Schedule
Makers and Exhibitors*.
Archibald Barron retires.
Primula Conference held at Westminster.
The National Trust established.
Messrs. Sander & Sons of St. Albans institute scheme for registration
of names of orchid hybrids.
Henry Nicholson Ellacombe's *In a Gloucestershire Garden* published.
J. C. Williams begins to keep records of his plantings at Caerhays
Castle, Cornwall.

1896   S. T. Wright appointed Superintendent of Society's Chiswick Garden.
Testimonial to Archibald Barron established.
The Williams Memorial Medal instituted by the trustees of the
Williams Memorial Fund.
Edwin Landseer Lutyens designs Gertrude Jekyll's house, Munstead
Wood.

1897   The Society establishes the Victoria Medal of Honour to celebrate the
sixtieth anniversary of Queen Victoria's accession to the throne.
Miss Nellie Roberts begins to paint orchids which receive a First Class
Certificate.
'Evolution Committee' of the Royal Society established with W.
Bateson as secretary.
Robert Hogg and James Bateman die.
The first issue of *Country Life* appears.

1898   The Society's Hogg Medal and small Gold Medal instituted.
The Society agrees to assist Bateson and his 'Evolution Committee'.
John Weir, Society's collector in Brazil 1861–4, dies.
Countess of Warwick founds Warwick Hostel in Reading for horti-
cultural training of women.

Harry White becomes manager of Sunningdale Nursery and pioneers the hybridization of rhododendrons.

Three of the six bulbs of G. H. Engleheart's narcissus 'Will Scarlett' bought by John Pope for £100.

1899 The Queen grants the Society a Supplementary Charter.
The Society sponsors a Conference on Hybridization.
Horticultural Trades Association formed.
E. H. Wilson sent to China by Veitch to introduce *Davidia*.
End of the firm of Lee of Hammersmith.
Amos Perry founds his nursery at Winchmore Hill.

1900 Philip Crowley dies and Joseph Gurney Fowler succeeds him as Treasurer.
Report of the Conference on Hybridization published in the Society's *Journal*.
'Countess Spencer' sweet pea raised by Silas Cole.

1901 The number of holders of Victoria Medal of Honour increased to sixty-three.
The Affiliated Societies Medal struck.
Lily Conference held at Chiswick.
Gregor Mendel's paper of 1866, *Experiments in Plant Hybridisation*, published in Society's *Journal*.
Firm of Blackmore & Langdon established.
Sweet pea 'Countess Spencer' exhibited.

1902 Coronation Rose Show and Conference on Roses held at Holland House, Kensington—the first of a series of Holland House Shows.
L. R. Russell takes over direction of the Richmond Group of Nurseries of John Russell & Sons.

1903 Contract signed for the building of the Society's Hall.
Sir Thomas Hanbury offers to the Society George Ferguson Wilson's garden and land at Wisley for the Society's Garden.
Archibald Barron dies.
S. T. Wright moves from Chiswick to Wisley.
Swanley Horticultural College now entirely for women.
Warwick Hostel moves to Studley Castle in Warwickshire and Studley College is established.
National Fruit and Cider Institute established at Long Ashton.
Gerald W. E. Loder begins to develop the garden at Wakehurst Place, Sussex.
Maj. Lawrence Johnston begins to make the garden at Hidcote Manor, Gloucester.
E. H. Wilson leaves for his second expedition to China for Veitch to introduce *Meconopsis integrifolia*.
William Robinson publishes *Flora and Sylva*.

1904   The Society's centenary.
Opening of the Society's Hall by King Edward VII, who agrees to
become the Society's joint patron with Queen Alexandra.
The Society sponsors an examination in cottage and allotment garden-
ing for teachers—the forerunner of the examination for the Teachers'
Diploma in School Gardening.
E. H. Wilson sends Veitch 300 bulbs of *Lilium regale* from China.
Sponsored by A. K. Bulley, George Forrest leaves for western China
on the first of his seven plant-collecting expeditions.
Blackmore & Langdon begin delphinium breeding.
A yellow Malmaison carnation produced by Hugh Low & Co.
Reginald Farrer's *The Garden of Asia* and R. I. Lynch's *Book of the Iris*
published.
The Rev. Samuel Reynolds Hole, rosarian, dies.

1905   Glass-houses and houses for the Superintendent and a foreman built at
Wisley.
George Massee works at Wisley on big-bud disease of blackcurrants.
F. J. Chittenden succeeds Rev. G. Henslow as secretary of the Scienti-
fic Committee.
The Society sponsors a Conference on Fruit Growing.
Veitch flowers *Lilium regale* for the first time (under the name of *L.
myriophyllum*).
David Prain appointed Director of Kew in succession to W. T.
Thiselton Dyer.
William Robinson's *Flora and Sylva* ceases publication.
Henry Eckford, sweet pea breeder, dies.

1906   A. J. Gaskell appointed Assistant Secretary to the Society.
International Conference on Hybridization and Plant Breeding at
which Bateson coins the word *genetics*.
The Society's Lawrence Medal instituted.
The Society sponsors examinations for those employed in public parks
and gardens belonging to county councils, city corporations, etc.
A small laboratory built at Wisley.
First volume of Elwes and Henry: *The Trees and Shrubs of Great Britain
and Ireland, Sander's List of Orchid Hybrids*, and *Hortus Veitchii* compiled
by J. H. Veitch, all published.

1907   Sir John Lubbock (Lord Avebury) officially opens the Wisley Labora-
tory of which F. J. Chittenden is appointed director.
New students' course at Wisley commences and A. Simmonds (future
Secretary of the Society) enrols as a student.
The first plantings made in the Wisley Pinetum.
Ernest Ballard receives his first award from the Society for a michael-
mas daisy 'Beauty of Colwall'.
Dr. Maxwell Masters and Sir Michael Foster die.
Reginald Farrer's *My Rock Garden* published.

1908   The Society appoints a committee to draw up a scheme of classification of daffodils and the *Classified List of Daffodil Names* is published.
Chittenden undertakes to edit the Society's *Journal*.
The Affiliated Societies Cup founded by the Society.
Conference on the spraying of fruit trees.
E. A. Bowles first elected to the Council.
W. D. Cartwright (long servant of the Society) enrols at Wisley as a student-gardener.
William Bateson appointed to the Chair of Biology at Cambridge.
William Kelway produces some of the first *Gladiolus primulinus* hybrids.
Primula malacoides, from Forrest's seeds, first flowers in Britain.
George Nicholson dies and the Nicholson Prize is instituted.

1909   The first Lawrence Medal presented to Sir Trevor Lawrence.
Professor Hugo de Vries gives the first Masters Memorial Lecture.
John Innes Horticultural Institute founded, with William Bateson the director.
William Purdom collecting in Kansu for Veitch and the Arnold Arboretum.

1910   Lindley Library Trust transferred from the trustees to the Society.
The Society's Vegetable Cup established.
W. D. Cartwright appointed chief clerk at Wisley.
George Forrest introduces *Gentiana sino-ornata*.
A. J. Bliss raises the first iris with velvet-textured falls—'Dominion'.
Montagu Allwood begins his attempts to cross perpetual-flowering carnations with *Dianthus plumarius*—which finally led to the development of Allwoodii Pinks.
Gurney Wilson founds *The Orchid World*.
The first part of Miss E. A. Willmott's *The Genus Rosa* published.

1911   Rock Garden built at Wisley, as well as a new bothy, potting-shed, and seed room; part of Howard's Field at Wisley planted as an orchard.
The Wigan Cup presented to the Society by Mr. A. L. Wigan.
North of England Horticultural Society formed.
Sponsored by A. K. Bulley, Frank Kingdon Ward leaves for north-west Yunnan to collect plants.
George Russell begins experimenting with lupins.
Irises, by W. R. Dykes, published.

1912   The Society appoints a garden adviser.
Royal International Horticultural Exhibition held at Chelsea.
East Malling Research Station and the Long Ashton Research Station (the latter a development of the National Fruit and Cider Institute) established.
The Peter Barr Memorial Cup presented to the Society by the trustees of the Peter Barr Memorial Fund.
Harry James Veitch is knighted.

1913 Sir Trevor Lawrence resigns from the presidency, dies in December, and is succeeded as President by Field-Marshal Lord Grenfell.
The Society holds its first Chelsea Show, and a Primula Conference.
The Society's Research Committee appointed to advise on Wisley.
The Society's *Daffodil Year Book* published, as well as W. R. Dykes's *The Genus Iris*, F. Kingdon Ward's *The Land of the Blue Poppy*, and the seventh and last volume of Elwes and Henry: *The Trees of Great Britain and Ireland*.
The Engleheart Cup founded by the Society and the Gordon-Lennox Cup presented to the Society by Lady Algernon Gordon-Lennox.
Cheshunt Experimental and Research Station established.
A. K. Bulley engages R. E. Cooper (future Curator of Royal Botanic Garden, Edinburgh) as his personal collector in Sikkim and Bhutan.
Augustine Henry appointed Professor of Forestry at Dublin.

1914 Outbreak of war.
Lieut.-Col. Mark Lockwood elected to the Society's Council.
Prof. Frederick Keeble appointed Director of the Gardens and Chittenden director of the Laboratory and head of the School of Horticulture.
George Fox Wilson appointed assistant to the entomologist, Professor H. Maxwell Lefroy.
The Society holds first preliminary examination for the National Diploma in Horticulture.
The Horticultural Record financed and published by R. C. Cory as a record of the International Exhibition of 1912.
E. A. Bowles's *My Garden in Spring* and *My Garden in Summer* published.
W. J. Bean's two-volume *Trees and Shrubs Hardy in the British Isles* published.
The firm of Veitch ceases to function and the name of the firm of John Waterer & Son is changed to John Waterer, Sons & Crisp Ltd.
Reginald Farrer and William Purdom collecting in Kansu and North China.

1915 At Wisley six cottages at 'The Square' built.
First final examinations for the National Diploma in Horticulture held.
The Rhododendron Society formed.
E. A. Bowles's *My Garden in Autumn and Winter* published.

1916 Joseph Gurney Fowler resigns from the treasurership of the Society and is succeeded by Charles G. A. Nix.
The new Wisley Laboratory completed.
J. K. Ramsbottom works at Wisley on daffodil eelworm.
Rhododendron Society publishes its first *Notes*.
London University introduces its degree in horticulture.

1917 J. K. Ramsbottom discovers that daffodil eelworm can be controlled by hot-water treatment.

Iris 'Dominion' marketed by A. J. Bliss at seven guineas per plant.
Farrer's *On the Eaves of the World* published.

1918   Sir Harry Veitch Treasurer of the Society for one year.
E. H. Wilson for the first time sees Kurume azaleas on the island of
Kyushu.
Ronald Hatton appointed Director of East Malling Research Station.

1919   Lord Grenfell retires from presidency of the Society and is succeeded
by Lord Lambourne (Lieut.-Col. Mark Lockwood).
The Society's Grenfell Medal instituted.
The Foremarke Cup presented to the Society by Sir Francis Burdett.
F. J. Chittenden appointed Director, W. J. Dowson the mycologist,
G. Fox Wilson the entomologist, and Felix C. Brown the trials recorder
at Wisley.
C. H. Curtis appointed manager editor of *Gardener's Chronicle*.
R. Farrer and E. H. M. Cox collecting in Upper Burma.
Farrer's *The English Rock Garden* published.
F. G. Preston succeeds R. I. Lynch as Curator of Cambridge Botanic
Garden.

1920   William Wilks resigns from the post of Secretary to the Society and is
elected to the Council.
W. R. Dykes succeeds Wilks as Secretary.
The Jones-Bateman Cup presented to the Society.
Heather garden developed at Wisley, in Seven Acres, and the Lake
is made.
Messrs. Lovell, Reeves & Co. decide that they cannot continue pub-
lication of the *Botanical Magazine* after the end of the year.
Joseph Rock begins his plant-hunting career in the Sino-Himalaya.
E. A. Bunyard's first volume of *Handbook of Hardy Fruits* published.

1921   Charles G. A. Nix retires from the Society's treasurership and is
succeeded by C. T. Musgrave.
A. J. Gaskell, Society's Assistant Secretary, resigns.
The Society institutes the Award of Garden Merit.
N. K. Gould appointed assistant botanist at Wisley.
The Society sponsors a Potato Conference.
The Society publishes Praeger's 'Account of the Genus *Sedum*' in its
Journal.
The copyright of the *Botanical Magazine* presented to the Society.
The Loder Rhododendron Cup and the George Monro Memorial
Cup presented to the Society.
Gurney Wilson edits the *Orchid Review*.
The firm of Turner, of the Royal Nurseries, Slough, ceases to function.
Farrer's *The Rainbow Bridge* published.

1922   R. W. Ascroft appointed Assistant Secretary at the Society's headquarters at Vincent Square.

A. Simmonds appointed Assistant Director at Wisley.

The trusteeship of the Veitch Memorial Fund vested in the Council of the Society.

S. T. Wright, Superintendent at Wisley, dies.

Beginning of the National Fruit Trials at Wisley.

British Iris Society founded.

David Prain retires from the directorship at Kew and is succeeded by A. W. Hill.

William Watson retires from curatorship of Kew and is succeeded by William Jackson Bean.

Isaac Bayley Balfour retires from Regius Keepership of Royal Botanic Garden, Edinburgh, and is succeeded by W. Wright Smith.

Henry John Elwes dies.

1923   Hon. H. D. McLaren elected to the Society's Council.

R. Cory institutes the award of the Cory Cup.

William Wilks dies.

'Mrs. R. O. Backhouse', the first pink-cupped daffodil, exhibited by Robert Ormston Backhouse.

Charles Eley's *Twentieth Century Gardening* published.

1924   C. T. Musgrave retires from the Society's treasurership and is succeeded by Sir William Lawrence.

The Society's Floral Committee divided into 'Floral A' and 'Floral B' Committees.

Six cottages built at Wisley.

National Pinetum set up at Bedgebury under auspices of Royal Botanic Gardens, Kew, and the Forestry Commission.

Iris Society formed with George Yeld the first president.

E. A. Bowles's *Handbook to Crocus and Colchicum* published.

Dykes's *Handbook of Garden Irises* published.

George Forrest introduces *Camellia saluenensis*.

1925   W. R. Dykes, the Society's Secretary, is killed, and succeeded by Lieut.-Col. F. R. Durham.

A. Simmonds leaves Wisley to become Assistant Secretary to the Society at Vincent Square.

The Society leases the land on which now stands the New Hall for 999 years.

R. Findlay appointed keeper of the Wisley Garden under the Director.

Wisley Garden opened to Fellows and Associates of the Society on Sundays.

Wrought-iron gates erected at Wisley to commemorate the Rev. W. Wilks.

G. W. Leak elected to the Society's Council.

J. K. Ramsbottom dies.

Bunyard's second volume of *Handbook of Hardy Fruits* published.

1926   Contract signed for building of the Society's New Hall and foundation stone laid by Lord Lambourne.

E. A. Bowles elected a Vice-President of the Society.

The George Moore Medal instituted and presented to the Society by G. F. Moore.

The British Gladiolus Society is formed and the Rhododendron Society organizes its first show.

A. D. Hall succeeds Wm. Bateson as director of John Innes Horticultural Institute.

A. J. Macself takes over editorship of *Amateur Gardening* on death of T. W. Sanders.

1927   The building of the Society's New Hall begins.

M. A. H. Tincker appointed keeper of the Wisley Laboratory under the Director.

International Committee for Horticultural Nomenclature set up at Eighth International Horticultural Congress.

The Rhododendron Association formed.

Opening of Jealotts Hill, the Agricultural Research Station for the Agricultural Division of I.C.I. which includes Plant Protection Ltd.

1928   The Society's New Hall opened by H.R.H. Princess Mary.

Lord Lambourne dies and is succeeded as Society's President by Mr. Gerald W. E. Loder.

C. T. Musgrave elected Treasurer to the Society for a second time, in succession to Sir William Lawrence.

The Society's fourth Royal Charter granted.

D. E. Green appointed mycologist at Wisley.

International Exhibition of Garden Design and Conference on Gardening Planning held in both the Society's Halls.

The Society sponsors Primula Conference.

Holford Medal presented to the Society by the executors of the late Sir George Holford.

Dr. Wilfrid Fox founds the Roads Beautifying Association.

The first number of *New Flora and Sylva* appears, founded and edited by E. H. M. Cox.

1929   R. D. Trotter succeeds C. T. Musgrave as the Society's Treasurer.

A third floor is built at the Society headquarters at Vincent Square.

The Society arranges for the re-erection of the David Douglas Memorial in Honolulu.

The Society's Gold Medal redesigned.

The Sewell Medal instituted and presented to the Society by A. J. Sewell.

Some Good Garden Plants published, the work of F. J. Chittenden.

Alpine Garden Society formed with Sir William Lawrence the president.

Rhododendron Association publishes its first *Rhododendron Year Book*.
H. Comber collecting in Tasmania.
W. J. Bean retires from the curatorship of Kew and is succeeded by
T. W. Taylor.

1930   Memorial bas-relief portrait of Lord Lambourne unveiled in the
Society's New Hall.
Associateship of Honour instituted by the Society.
Ninth International Horticultural Congress held at Vincent Square;
a new set of rules for naming garden plants is accepted and presented
at the Fifth International Botanical Congress in Cambridge.
The first number of the Bulletin of the Alpine Garden Society pub-
lished.
The first four volumes of *Iconum Botanicarum Index Londinensis* pub-
lished (a new edition of Pritzel's *Index Iconum Botanicarum*).
Rhododendron Society publishes *The Species of Rhododendron*.
E. H. Wilson dies.

1931   G. W. E. Loder resigns from the presidency of the Society and is
succeeded by the Hon. H. D. McLaren.
F. J. Chittenden leaves Wisley for Vincent Square to the post of
technical adviser and keeper of the Library.
R. L. Harrow appointed Director at Wisley.
Memorial to Sir Thomas Hanbury unveiled in Wisley Laboratory.
'The Lilacs' at Wisley converted into a hostel.
The Society holds Conifer Conference and Exhibition.
The Rhododendron Society absorbed into the Rhododendron Associa-
tion.
Fund established by Lord Riddell for a silver trophy to be awarded by
the Society yearly.
Botanical Magazine 'Dedications and Portraits' published by William
Cuthbertson.
Two further volumes of *Index Londinensis* published.
National Trust for Scotland established.
The Society establishes the Lily Committee.

1932   C. T. Musgrave succeeds R. D. Trotter as Treasurer—his third term
in office.
Hon. H. D. McLaren unveils the tablet and illuminated record in the
bookshop of Messrs. Hatchard at 187 Piccadilly, London—the site on
which the R.H.S. was founded in 1804.
The Society establishes the Lily Group and publishes *The Lily Year Book*.
The Society publishes 'Conifers in Cultivation'—the report of the 1931
Conifer Conference—and Lloyd Praeger's 'An Account of the
Sempervivum Group', in its *Journal*.
Miss B. Havergal founds the Waterperry Horticultural School for
Women.

George Forrest dies in China at the end of his seventh expedition there.

J. Coutts succeeds T. W. Taylor as Curator at Kew.

E. Savill begins to develop the Savill Garden.

1933 R. D. Trotter again becomes the Society's Treasurer.

The Society sponsors a Lily Conference and a co-operative British Exhibit at the 125th Anniversary Show of the Royal Agricultural and Botanical Society of Ghent.

The Society's Great Autumn Show held at Olympia.

The Society publishes H. W. Pugsley's 'Monograph of Narcissus, sub-genus Ajax' in its *Journal*.

A. Grove publishes first part of Supplement to Elwes's *The Genus Lilium*.

E. A. Bunyard's *Anatomy of Dessert* published.

F. Ludlow and G. Sherriff collecting in the Himalayas.

Formation of Scottish Rock Garden Club.

1934 H. D. McLaren, President, becomes Lord Aberconway, the second Baron.

Hon. David Bowes Lyon joins the Council of the Society.

Tablets recording the names of past Presidents, Treasurers and Secretaries placed on the flanks of the bas-relief portrait of Lord Lambourne in the Society's New Hall.

The Society holds its Great Autumn Show at Crystal Palace and sponsors a Conference on Apples and Pears.

R. Cory dies, the Cory Cup becomes the Reginald Cory Memorial Cup and Cory's botanical and horticultural books are bequeathed to Lindley Library.

E. A. Bowles's *Handbook of Narcissus* published.

Miss E. A. Willmott dies.

1935 The Society sponsors Conferences on Daffodils and on Cherries and Soft Fruits.

Nomenclature of Garden Plants published as an appendix to the 1935 edition of the *Rules of Botanical Nomenclature*.

F. A. Secrett elected to the Society's Council.

Miss Gertrude Jekyll dies.

E. J. Salisbury's *The Living Garden* published.

1936 The Society's P. D. Williams Medal instituted.

The Society sponsors Conference on Alpine Plants in co-operation with Alpine Garden Society.

The firm of L. R. Russell moves to its present site at Richmond Nurseries, Windlesham.

E. A. Bunyard's *Old Garden Roses* published.
Rev. G. H. Engleheart dies.

1937   New National Certificate in Horticultural Practice established.
Exhibit from the Empire shown at the Society's Chelsea Show.
'Russell Lupins' first shown at Vincent Square, by Messrs. Baker Ltd
The A. J. Waley Medal instituted.
E. A. Bunyard's *Epicure's Companion* published.

1938   R. D. Trotter succeeded as Treasurer by G. Monro.
J. W. Blakey appointed keeper of the Wisley Garden.
The Society sponsors Conference on Ornamental Flowering Trees and
Shrubs.
The Society publishes first volume of *Horticultural Colour Chart*.
Christopher Tunnard's *Gardens in the Modern Landscape* published.
George Yeld (iris breeder) dies.

1939   Outbreak of war.
The Lyttel Lily Cup presented to the Society by the Rev. Professor
E. S. Lyttel.

1940   The Society publishes Sir Daniel Hall's *The Genus Tulipa*.

1941   The Society publishes *The Vegetable Garden Displayed*.
Sir Arthur Hill, Director of Kew, dies; Sir Geoffrey Evans appointed
Acting Director.

1942   Deaths of Sir Daniel Hall, Sir Jeremiah Colman (famous orchid grower), W. H. Divers (for over fifty years a member of the Fruit and Vegetable Committee), Lionel de Rothschild (well-known rhododendron
grower) and L. R. Russell (nurseryman).

1943   R. D. Trotter appointed the Society's Treasurer for third term of office.
Professor E. J. Salisbury appointed Director at Kew.
The Duke of Portland and the Marquis of Headfort (Vice-Presidents
of the Society) and the Brodie of Brodie (famous daffodil breeder) die.

1944   Sir David Prain (Society's Vice-President) and E. S. Lyttel die.

1945   Rhododendron Association wound up and the Rhododendron Group
of the Society formed.
Swanley Horticultural College destroyed by bombs; becomes part of
Wye College.
National Cactus and Succulent Society formed.

1946   Col. F. R. Durham retires from post of Secretary and is succeeded by
Brig. C. V. L. Lycett.

466

A. Simmonds appointed the Society's Deputy Secretary.

R. L. Harrow retires from directorship of Wisley and is succeeded by J. S. L. Gilmour.

M. A. H. Tincker resigns from the keepership of the Wisley Laboratory.

J. W. Blakey retires from post of keeper of Wisley Garden and is succeeded by F. E. W. Hanger, with title of Curator.

The Society publishes *Rhododendron Year Book* and F. C. Stern's *A Study of the Genus Paeonia*.

The Crosfield Cup, the Lionel de Rothschild Cup, the Loder Cup, the McLaren Cup, the Rothschild Challenge Cup—all transferred to the Society by the Rhododendron Association.

The Northern Horticultural Society formed.

1947　The Society revives Chelsea Flower Show.

The Society publishes the *Fruit Year Book.*

Exhibition of Municipal Horticulture held in the Society's Old Hall.

William Jackson Bean, formerly Curator of Kew, dies.

1948　The Hon. D. Bowes Lyon succeeds R. D. Trotter as Treasurer.

Joint Committee of R.H.S. and National Trust established.

Formation of Hull University Botanic Garden.

1949　The Society sponsors Rhododendron Conference.

The Bowles Cup presented to the Society by J. L. Richardson.

National Vegetable Research Station established at Wellesbourne, Warwickshire, and the National Agricultural Advisory Service's Experimental Station at Luddington, Stratford-on-Avon.

Miss A. L. Bulley gives her father's garden at Ness to the University of Liverpool with an endowment of £75,000.

Ludlow and Sherriff send large collections of living plants by air to Britain from Bhutan and south-east Tibet.

O. Polunin collecting in Nepal.

Camellia x *williamsii* (*C. japonica* x *saluenensis*) described.

Sir Ronald Hatton retires from directorship of East Malling.

1950　F. J. Chittenden dies.

The Society sponsors Conference on Camellias and Magnolias.

N.A.A.S. Experimental Stations at Fairfield, near Preston, and at Stockbridge, near Selby, Yorks., established.

C. H. Curtis retires from *Gardener's Chronicle* after thirty-one years' service as managing editor.

Gardens Committee of the National Trust for Scotland established.

D. Lowndes collecting in Nepal.

1951　J. S. L. Gilmour resigns from the directorship of Wisley and is succeeded by H. R. Fletcher.

G. Fox Wilson, Wisley entomologist, and F. C. Brown, Wisley trials recorder, die.

All floral exhibits at Chelsea Show staged under one tent.

The Society publishes *The Fruit Garden Displayed*.

The Geranium Society and the Society of Floristry formed.

N.A.A.S. Experimental Stations at Efford, Lymington, Hants, and at Rosewarne, Camborne, Cornwall, established.

George Russell of 'Russell Lupin' fame, dies.

1952 The Society plays leading role in organization of Thirteenth International Horticultural Congress and becomes involved in the registration of cultivars.

The Society publishes the *Dictionary of Gardening* and *George Forrest; Journeys and Plant Introductions*.

The Iris Society becomes the British Iris Society.

Polunin, Sykes, and Williams collecting in Nepal.

Ernest Ballard, breeder of michaelmas daisies, dies.

1953 Lord Aberconway dies and is succeeded as President by the Hon. David Bowes Lyon.

The Hon. Lewis Palmer succeeds D. Bowes Lyon as Treasurer.

Aberconway House, the new hostel at Wisley, begins to be built.

The Glass-house Crops Research Institute established.

F. Kingdon Ward in Upper Burma on his last expedition.

Amos Perry, plant breeder, dies.

1954 The Society's sesquicentenary.

H. R. Fletcher resigns from the directorship of Wisley and is succeeded by F. P. Knight.

W. D. Cartwright retires from the Society's staff at Wisley.

E. A. Bowles dies.

The *Rhododendron Year Book* renamed the *Rhododendron and Camellia Year Book*.

Stainton, Sykes, and Williams collecting in Nepal.

1955 The Society exhibits at Quinquennial Show at Ghent.

The Society publishes G. H. Johnstone's *Asiatic Magnolias in Cultivation*.

1956 A. Simmonds appointed Secretary to the Society, succeeding Brig. C. V. L. Lycett, who retires.

Two more cottages built at Wisley.

The Society publishes F. C. Stern's *Snowdrops and Snowflakes*.

Sir William Wright Smith, the Society's Professor of Botany, dies.

Parks Apprenticeship Scheme established at Ealing.

Westonbirt Arboretum acquired by the Forestry Commission.

J. D. A. Stainton collecting in Nepal.

Dr. George Taylor succeeds Sir Edward Salisbury as Director of Kew.

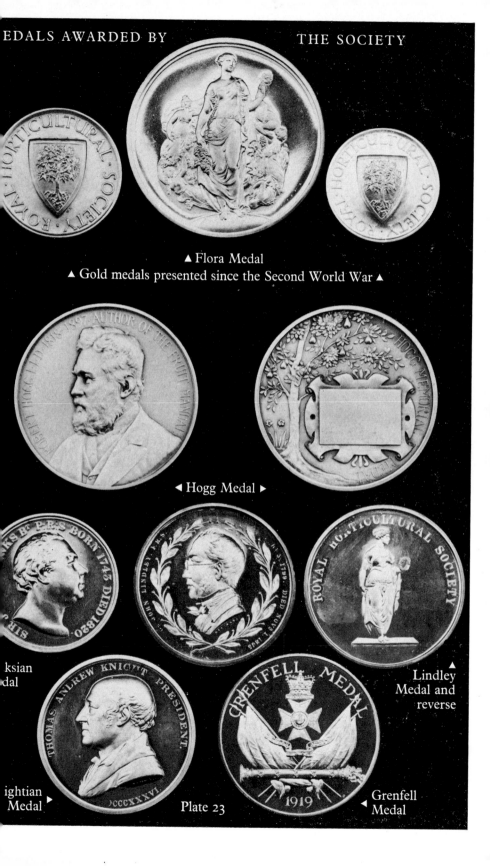

▲ Flora Medal
▲ Gold medals presented since the Second World War ▲

◄ Hogg Medal ►

ksian
dal

ightian
Medal ►

▲
Lindley
Medal and
reverse

Plate 23

Grenfell
Medal ◄

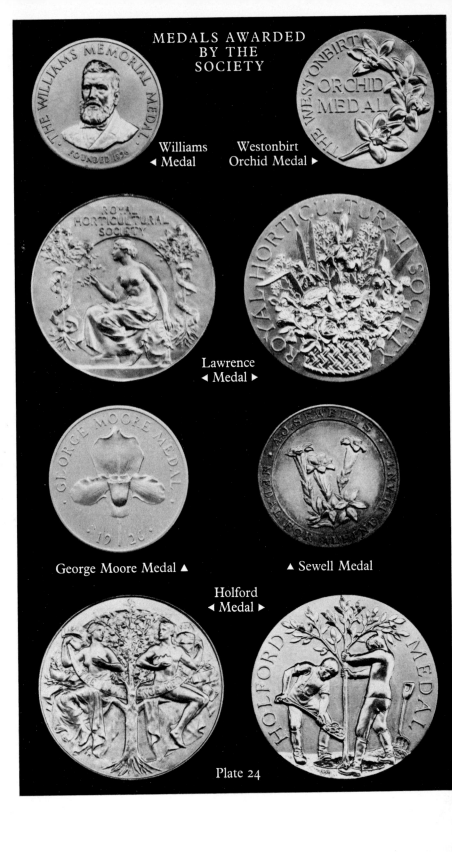

MEDALS AWARDED
BY THE
SOCIETY

Williams
◄ Medal

Westonbirt
Orchid Medal ►

Lawrence
◄ Medal ►

George Moore Medal ▲

▲ Sewell Medal

Holford
◄ Medal ►

Plate 24

1957 The Society receives the Alfred Gurney Wilson bequest.

1958 The Society creates Long Service Medal for Gardeners.
The Devonshire Trophy presented to the Society.
Royal Forestry Society of England, Wales and Northern Ireland institutes a certificate and diploma in arboriculture.
N.A.A.S. Experimental Station at Lea Valley, Hoddesdon, Herts., established.
F. Kingdon Ward, C. H. Curtis, and Montagu Allwood die.

1959 The Society exhibits at Paris Floralies and holds a Lily Conference.
The Farrer Trophy instituted.
National Association of Flower Arrangement Societies formed.

1960 The Society exhibits at Ghent Show.
The Society sponsors the Third World Orchid Conference, in association with American Orchid Society.
G. W. Leak retires from the Society's Council.
National Fruit Trials transferred from Wisley to near Faversham.
Westonbirt Orchid Medal instituted from fund presented to the Society by H. G. Alexander; from fund presented to the Society by Miss A. K. Hincks the Mrs. F. E. Rivis Prize is established.
Sesquicentenary of Jackman & Son (Woking Nurseries) Ltd.

1961 Sir David Bowes Lyon dies and is succeeded as President by Lord Aberconway.
Two cottages and four bungalows built at Wisley.
The Society takes over duties of International Registration Authority for Orchid Cultivars.
The E. H. Trophy provided by the Society from a fund bequeathed by W. J. M. Hawkey.
Federation of British Horticultural Exporters Ltd. formed.
Third International Rock Garden Plant Conference held.

1962 A. Simmonds retires and J. Hamer appointed the Society's Secretary.
International Camellia Society formed.

1963 The Society exhibits at International Horticultural Show at Hamburg.
G. W. Leak dies.
Fourth World Orchid Conference held in Singapore.

1964 First National Chrysanthemum Society Conference held in Society's New Hall.
Association of British Tree Surgeons and Arborists established.
Name of British Geranium Society changed to British Pelargonium and Geranium Society.
The Heather Society formed.

New Botanic Garden founded in Liverpool.
Plant Varieties and Seeds Act set up.
Hillier & Sons celebrate their centenary.
R. Hay resigns as editor-in-chief of *Gardener's Chronicle*.

1965   O. E. P. Wyatt succeeds Hon. Lewis Palmer as the Society's Treasurer.
Tornado at Wisley.
The Society exhibits at the Ghent Floralies.
The Leonardslee Bowl presented to the Society by Sir Giles Loder.
New edition of *Fruit Garden Displayed* published by the Society.
National Rose Society given Royal Charter.
First students enrol for the internal degree in horticulture at the Bristol College of Science and Technology, the University of Bath.
The Garden History Society founded.
Closure of Roads Beautifying Association (founded 1928).
Opening of the Jodrell Laboratory at Royal Botanic Gardens, Kew.
Centenary of the firm of Dobbie & Co. Ltd., Edinburgh.
John Innes Institute becomes part of the University of Norwich.

1966   The Society holds its Great Autumn Show at Alexandra Palace for the first time.
The Society publishes *Fruit—Present and Future*, to mark twenty-first anniversary of the Society's Fruit Group.
Fifth World Orchid Conference at Long Beach, California.
Formation of the Nerine Society.

1967   Sir Frederick Stern, Vice-President, dies.

1968   The Society's membership subscription increased to three pounds and five pounds and Student and Associate Membership abolished.
A. Simmonds, late Secretary, dies.

ORIGINAL CHARTER OF THE HORTICULTURAL
SOCIETY OF LONDON

GEORGE THE THIRD, by the Grace of God, of the United Kingdom of Great Britain and Ireland King, Defender of the Faith, to all to whom these presents shall come, Greeting: Whereas several of our loving Subjects are desirous of forming a Society for the Improvement of Horticulture in all its branches, ornamental as well as useful, and having subscribed considerable sums of money for that purpose, have humbly besought us to grant unto them and such other persons as shall be approved and elected as hereinafter is mentioned, Our Royal Charter of Incorporation for the purposes aforesaid: *Object of the Society*

Know Ye, that We, being desirous to promote such improvement, have, of our especial grace, certain knowledge, and mere motion, Given and Granted, and we do hereby Give and Grant, that Our Right Trusty and Wellbeloved Cousin and Counsellor George Earl of Dartmouth, Knight of the Most Noble Order of the Garter, Our Right Trusty and Wellbeloved Cousin and Counsellor Edward Earl Powis, our Right Reverend and Wellbeloved Father in God Brownlow Lord Bishop of Winchester, Our Right Trusty and Wellbeloved John Lord Selsey, Our Right Trusty and Wellbeloved Counsellor Charles Greville, Our Right Trusty and Wellbeloved Counsellor Sir Joseph Banks, Baronet and Knight of the Most Honourable Order of the Bath, our Trusty and Wellbeloved William Townsend Aiton, John Elliot, Thomas Andrew Knight, Charles Miller, Richard Anthony Salisbury, and John Trevelyan, Esquires, and James Dickson, Thomas Hoy, and William Smith, Gardeners, and such others as shall from time to time be appointed and elected in the manner hereinafter directed, and their Successors, be and shall for ever hereafter continue to be, by virtue of these Presents, one Body Politic and Corporate, by the name of 'THE HORTICULTURAL SOCIETY OF LONDON;' and them and their Successors, for the purposes aforesaid, We do hereby constitute and declare to be one Body Politic and Corporate, and by the same name to have perpetual Succession, and for ever hereafter to be Persons able and capable in the Law, and have power to purchase, receive, and possess any Goods and Chattels whatsoever, and (notwithstanding the *Incorporation*

Corporate Name

Power to purchase Goods and Lands

Statutes of Mortmain), to purchase, hold, and enjoy, to them and their Successors, any Lands, Tenements, and Hereditaments whatsoever, not exceeding, at the time or times of purchasing such Lands, Tenements, and Hereditaments respectively, the yearly value at a Rack Rent of One Thousand Pounds in the whole, without incurring the penalties or forfeitures of the Statutes of *To sue and* Mortmain, or any of them: and by the name aforesaid to sue and *be sued* be sued, plea and be impleaded, answer and be answered unto, defend and be defended in all Courts and places whatsoever, of Us, our Heirs, and Successors, in all Actions, Suits, Causes, and Things whatsoever; and to act and do in all Things relating to the said Corporation in as ample manner and form as any other Liege Subjects, being Persons able and capable in the Law, or any other Body Politic or Corporate, in our said United Kingdom *To use a* of Great Britain and Ireland, may or can act or do: and also to *Common Seal* have and to use a Common Seal, and the same to change and alter from time to time as they shall think fit.

Number of And We do hereby declare and grant that there shall be an in-*Fellows* definite number of Fellows of the said Society; and that they the *indefinite* said George Earl of Dartmouth, Edward Earl Powis, Brownlow Lord Bishop of Winchester, John Lord Selsey, Charles Greville, *First Fellows* Sir Joseph Banks, William Townsend Aiton, John Elliot, Thomas *named* Andrew Knight, Charles Miller, Richard Anthony Salisbury, John Trevelyan, James Dickson, Thomas Hoy, and William Smith, shall be the first Fellows of the said Society, and that any five or more of them, all having been duly summoned to attend the Meetings of the said Fellows, shall and may, on or before the first day of May next ensuing the date of these presents, under their respective hands, in writing, appoint such other persons to be Fellows, Honorary Members, and Foreign Members of the said Society, as they may respectively think fit.

Council and And We do further declare and grant, that, for the better Rule *Officers* and Government of the said Society, and for the better direction, management, and execution of the Business and Concerns thereof, there shall be thenceforth for ever a Council, President, Treasurer, and Secretary of the said Society, to be elected in manner herein-after mentioned; and that such Council shall consist of fifteen Members to be elected from among the Fellows as hereinafter directed, whereof any five shall be a quorum; and We do hereby *First Council* nominate and appoint the said George Earl of Dartmouth, Edward *and Officers* Earl Powis, Brownlow Lord Bishop of Winchester, John Lord *named* Selsey, Charles Greville, Sir Joseph Banks, William Townsend Aiton, John Elliot, Thomas Andrew Knight, Charles Miller, Richard Anthony Salisbury, John Trevelyan, James Dickson, Thomas Hoy, and William Smith, to be the first Council; the said George Earl of Dartmouth to be the first President; the said Charles Greville to be the first Treasurer; and the said Richard

Anthony Salisbury to be the first Secretary to the said Society: all and each of the aforesaid Officers and Counsellors to continue in such their respective Offices until the First day of May One Thousand Eight Hundred and Ten: and that the said George Earl of Dartmouth shall have power to appoint such four Persons from and amongst the Members of the said Council, to be Vice-Presidents of the said Society, as he shall think fit, until some other Persons shall be chosen in their respective rooms, in the manner hereinafter mentioned.

Annual Removal of three Members of Council and Election of three others

And it is Our further Will and Pleasure that the Fellows of the said Society, or any eleven or more of them, shall and may, on the First day of May One Thousand Eight Hundred and Ten, and also shall and may on the First day of May in every succeeding year, unless the same shall happen to be on a Sunday, and then on the day following, assemble together at the then last or other usual place of meeting of the said Society, and proceed, by method of Ballot, to put out and remove any three of the Members who shall have composed the Council of the preceding year, and shall and may in like manner by method of Ballot elect three other discreet Persons from amongst the Fellows of the said Society to supply the places and offices of such three as may have been so put out and removed; it being our Royal Will and Pleasure that one-fifth of the said Council and no more shall be annually changed and removed by the Fellows of the said Society:

Annual Election of Officers

And also that they the said Fellows, or any eleven or more of them, shall and may at the time and in manner aforesaid, by method of Ballot, elect from amongst the Members of the said Council, when formed and elected in manner aforesaid, three fit and proper Persons; one of such Persons to be President, another of such Persons to be Treasurer, and the other of such Persons to be Secretary of the said Society for the year ensuing: And also,

Vacancies occasioned by death

in like manner, shall and may, in case of the death of any of the Members of the Council, or of the President, Treasurer, or Secretary for the time being, within the space of two months next after such death or deaths, in like manner elect other discreet Persons, being Fellows of the said Society, to supply the places and Offices of such Members of the said Council, or of the President, Treasurer, or Secretary so dying: And also shall and may appoint such other

Appointment of other Officers

Persons to be Officers of the said Society for the year ensuing as they may think proper and necessary for the transacting and managing the Business thereof.

Appointment of Vice-Presidents

And it is Our further Will and Pleasure that, so soon after the Elections aforesaid as conveniently may be, the Person who shall at any time hereafter be elected to be President of the said Society, in manner aforesaid, may and shall nominate and appoint four Persons, being Members of the said Council, to be Vice-Presidents of the said Society for the year ensuing.

473

Election and Removal of Members

And We do further declare and grant, that, from and after the first day of May now next ensuing, the Fellows of the said Society, or any seven or more of them, shall and may have power from time to time at the general Meetings of the said Society, to be held at the usual place of meeting of the said Society or at such other place as shall have been in that behalf appointed, by method of Ballot, to elect such Persons to be Fellows, Honorary Members and Foreign Members of the said Society, and all Fellows, Honorary Members, and Foreign Members, to remove from the said Society as they shall think fit. Provided that no such Fellow, Honorary Member, and Foreign Member shall be declared elected or removed, unless it shall appear upon such Ballot that two-thirds of the Fellows present at such Meeting shall have voted for the same.

The Council empowered to make By-Laws

And We do further declare and grant that the Council hereby appointed, and the Council of the said Society for the time being, or any three or more of them (all the Members thereof having been first duly summoned to attend the Meetings thereof), shall and may have power according to the best of their judgment and discretion to make and establish such By-Laws as they shall deem useful and necessary for the Regulation of said Society, and of the Estate, Goods, and Business thereof, and for fixing and determining the times and places of meeting of the said Society, and also the times, place, and manner of electing, appointing, and removing all Fellows, Honorary Members, and Foreign Members of the said Society, and all such Subordinate Officers, Attendants, and Servants as shall be deemed necessary or useful for the said Society; and also for filling up from time to time any vacancies which may happen by death, removal, or otherwise, in any of the Offices or Appointments constituted or established for the execution of the Business and Concerns of the said Society; and also for regulating and ascertaining the qualifications of Persons to become Fellows, Honorary Members, and Foreign Members of the said Society, respectively; and also the Sum and Sums of Money to be paid by them respectively, whether upon admission or otherwise, towards carrying on the purposes of the said Society; and such By-Laws, from time to time, to vary, alter, or revoke, and make such new and other By-Laws as they shall think most useful and expedient, so that the same be not repugnant to these Presents or the Laws of this our Realm.

By-Laws to be confirmed by Ballot at a General Meeting

Provided that no By-Law hereafter to be made, or alteration or repeal of any By-Law which shall hereafter have been established, by the said Council hereby appointed, or by the Council for the time being of the said Society, shall be considered to have passed and be binding on the said Society, until such By-Law or such alteration or repeal of any By-Law shall have been hung up in the Common Meeting-Room of the said Society, and been read by the President, or any one of the Vice-Presidents for the time being, at two successive General Meetings of the said Society, and until the same shall have been confirmed by Ballot by the Fellows at large of the said Society; such Ballot to take place at the ensuing Meeting next after such two Successive General Meetings of the said Society, seven at least of the Fellows of the said Society being then present: and Provided that no such By-Law, or alteration or repeal of any By-Law, shall be deemed or taken to pass in the affirmative, unless it shall appear upon such Ballot that two-thirds of the Fellows present at such Meeting shall have voted for the same.

Witness His Majesty at Westminster, the 17th day of April, in the Forty-ninth year of Our Reign.

By Writ of Privy Seal,

WILMOT

PAST AND PRESENT HOLDERS OF THE
VICTORIA MEDAL OF HONOUR

1961 H.M. QUEEN ELIZABETH THE QUEEN MOTHER, who with her wide knowledge and love of plants and by her interest, encouragement, and enthusiasm has made great contributions to horticulture.

1931 LADY ABERCONWAY (d. 1933 in her eightieth year); for her great interest in the advancement of horticulture and in the cultivation of new and rare plants.

1934 LORD ABERCONWAY (d. 1953, aged 74); son of the above, President of the Royal Horticultural Society 1931–53, and very great gardener.

1961 LORD ABERCONWAY; son of the above and President of the Society 1961–.

1926 ALEXANDER, H. G. (d. 1965, aged 90); orchid grower and raiser to Sir George Holford, Westonbirt, Gloucestershire.

1949 ALLWOOD, M. C. (d. 1958 in his seventy-ninth year); great authority on the genus *Dianthus*, raiser of many *Dianthus* hybrids as well as new perpetual-flowering types, and author of several works on carnations and pinks.

1966 AMORY, SIR JOHN HEATHCOAT-, BT.; amateur gardener and creator of one of the finest gardens of the twentieth century at his home at Knightshayes Court, Tiverton, Devon.

1951 AMSLER, DR. M. (d. 1952, aged 75); a skilful amateur gardener and specialist in the growing of lilies.

1960 ANDERSON, E. B.; well-known amateur gardener and distinguished cultivator of difficult and rare alpine and bulbous plants.

1964 ANLEY, MRS. GWENDOLYN (d. 1968, aged 91); creator of a splendid garden in Surrey and specialist in the cultivation of alpines, irises, and day-lilies.

1942 ARMYTAGE-MOORE, HUGH (d. 1954, aged 81); creator of the great garden of Rowallane in Northern Ireland.

1928 ATKINSON, WM. (d. 1933); managing director of Messrs. Fisher, Son and Sibray, Sheffield, who were the first to exhibit hardy trees and shrubs out of doors at the Temple Shows, and the raisers of *Berberis stenophylla*, the hybrid between *B. darwinii* and *B. empetrifolia*.

1933 BAKER, G. P. (d. 1951, aged 95); amateur gardener, active in the introduction and cultivation of new plants and in his support of the R.H.S.

1897 BAKER, J. G. (d. 1920, aged 86); botanist at Kew from 1866 until he retired in 1899, and great authority on bulbous plants.

1953 BALFOUR, A. P.; an authority on annual and biennial flowers.

1927 BALFOUR, F. R. S. (d. 1945, aged 72); horticulturist and arboriculturist, in large measure the creator of the famous gardens at Dawyck, Peeblesshire; extensive traveller and introducer of several trees from the Pacific coast of North America.

1897 BALFOUR, SIR I. B. (d. 1922, aged 68); Regius Keeper of the Royal Botanic Garden, Edinburgh, Regius Professor of Botany in the University of Edinburgh and great authority on Asiatic plants, especially primulas and rhododendrons.

1907 BALLANTINE, HENRY (d. 1929, aged 95); for nearly half a century gardener and bailiff at the Baron Schröder establishment, at the Dell, Englefield Green, Surrey, and noted authority on orchids.

1949 BALLARD, E. (d. 1952, aged 81); a successful cultivator of many groups of plants, but especially noted for his breeding work with michaelmas daisies.

1965 BARNARD, T. T.; social anthropologist, botanist, and gardener with an especial knowledge of the flora of South Africa, cultivator of many South African plants and raiser of several new South African *Gladiolus* hybrids.

1924 BARNES, NICHOLAS F. (d. 1950, aged 85); for fifty years in charge of the Duke of Westminster's famous gardens at Eaton Hall, Chester.

1897 BARR, PETER (d. 1909 in his eighty-fifth year); famous in the history of horticulture for the part he played in the development of the narcissus.

1931 BARR, PETER RUDOLPH (d. 1944, aged 82); son of the former, head of the firm of Messrs. Barr & Sons, of Covent Garden and Taplow, and an expert on daffodils and tulips.

1897 BARRON, ARCHIBALD F. (d. 1903, aged 68); a wonderfully loyal servant of the Society in its Garden at Chiswick.

1923 BARTHOLOMEW, ARTHUR CHURCHILL (d. 1940, aged 94); noted dahlia grower and the only man to have received the Blue Riband of the British Dahlia Growers' Association more than once; he was awarded the Riband three times.

477

1901 BATESON, WILLIAM (d. 1926, aged 65); Director of the John Innes Horticultural Institute and founder of the modern science of genetics and the *Journal of Genetics*.

1897 BEALE, EDWARD JOHN (d. 1902 in his sixty-sixth year); senior partner in the firm of James Carter & Co., of High Holborn, London, holding a leading position in the seed trade and closely associated with the passing of the Seed Adulteration Act.

1917 BEAN, W. JACKSON (d. 1947, aged 83); for forty-six years on the staff of the Royal Botanic Gardens, Kew, latterly as Curator, and author of *Trees and Shrubs Hardy in the British Isles*.

1906 BECKETT, EDWIN (d. 1935 in his eighty-second year); famous as a grower and exhibitor of vegetables and for his knowledge of trees and shrubs, he was associated from 1884 until he retired soon after 1931, first with Lord Aldenham and then with the Hon. Vicary Gibbs.

1902 BENNETT-POË, JOHN T. (d. 1926); a fine cultivator of uncommon plants, an enthusiast for daffodils, florists' auriculas and Old English tulips, a member of the R.H.S. Council and several R.H.S. committees.

1952 BENTLEY, W. (d. 1953, aged 78); a keen gardener for over half a century, latterly he created a fine garden at Quarry Wood, near Newbury, where he specialized in lilies.

1944 BESANT, W. D. (d. 1946, aged 60); Director of the Parks Department of Glasgow Corporation.

1938 BEWLEY, WILLIAM F.; the author of many contributions to horticultural research and Director of the Cheshunt Research Station.

1922 BILNEY, WILLIAM A. (d. 1939, aged 86); member of the firm of Messrs. Morgan, Veitch & Bilney, for several years a member of the R.H.S. Council and its honorary solicitor, and a keen amateur gardener.

1932 BLISS, DANIEL (d. 1939, aged 68); for thirty-five years Superintendent of Swansea Public Parks and for several years president of the Institute of Parks Administration.

1961 BOLITHO, LIEUT.-COL. SIR EDWARD; Cornish amateur gardener, the creator of a fine Cornish garden, specializing particularly in rhododendrons and magnolias.

1949 BOLTON, ROBERT (d. 1949, aged 80); the sweet pea grower who did much to improve these flowers by raising many new cultivars, and strong supporter for many years of the National Sweet Pea Society.

1922 BOSCAWEN, THE REV. CANON A. T. (d. 1939, aged 77); one of the creators of the Cornish fruit, flower, and vegetable growing industry, the introducer to Cornwall of the anemone, and creator of the gardens at Ludgvan.

1953   BOWES LYON, THE HON. SIR DAVID (d. 1961, aged 59); President of the R.H.S. from 1953 to 1961 and Treasurer from 1948 to 1953.

1916   BOWLES, E. A. (d. 1954 in his eighty-ninth year); one of the most knowledgeable amateur gardeners of the twentieth century, expert on crocuses, colchicums, anemones and snowdrops, a member of Council of the R.H.S. for close on fifty years and a Vice-President for nearly thirty years.

1897   BOXALL, W. (d. 1910 in his sixty-sixth year); collector and grower of orchids for the establishments of Messrs. Hugh Low & Co., Clapton, and of Messrs. James Veitch & Sons, Chelsea.

1942   BRODIE OF BRODIE, THE (d. 1943, aged 75); famous daffodil grower and breeder of many new cultivars.

1897   BULL, WILLIAM (d. 1902, aged 74); the well-known nurseryman of King's Road, Chelsea, who specialized in the cultivation of new and rare plants both of a hardy and of a tender nature.

1897   BUNYARD, GEORGE (d. 1919 in his seventy-eighth year); prominent fruit grower who served for thirty-four years on the Fruit Committee of the R.H.S. and for about ten years on the Council of the R.H.S.

1897   BURBIDGE, FREDERICK WILLIAM (d. 1905, aged 58); distinguished botanist-gardener, for over twenty-six years Curator of Trinity College Botanic Garden.

1957   CAMPBELL, WILLIAM MACDONALD (d. 1964, aged 64); Curator of the Royal Botanic Gardens, Kew, from 1937 until he retired in 1960.

1902   CANNELL, HENRY (d. 1914 in his eighty-second year); noted florist and founder of the firm of H. Cannell & Sons which did much to popularize such flowers as chrysanthemums, pelargoniums, fuchsias, dahlias, violets, heliotropes, cannas, and begonias.

1904   CHALLIS, THOMAS (d. 1923, aged 88); one of the most famous gardeners of his time, for nearly sixty years gardener at Wilton House, near Salisbury, and for many years a member of the R.H.S. Fruit and Vegetable Committee.

1914   CHEAL, JOSEPH (d. 1935, aged 87); senior director and founder of the nursery firm of Messrs. J. Cheal & Sons, Crawley, with an extensive knowledge of fruits, trees, and shrubs.

1917   CHITTENDEN, F. J. (d. 1950, aged 76); great servant of horticulture and of the Society in almost every single capacity.

1936   CLARKE, COL. STEPHENSON R. (d. 1948, aged 86); owner of the magnificent garden at Borde Hill, Sussex, and expert cultivator of trees and shrubs, greenhouse plants and bulbs.

1947   CLARKE, WM. (d. 1963, aged 78); trained in the gardens of some of the great houses of England and Scotland, he later had twenty-nine

479

years' service with Southport Corporation, mainly as Parks and Cemeteries Superintendent, and for many years was ground manager of the great Southport Flower Shows.

1908 COLMAN, SIR JEREMIAH, BT. (d. 1942, aged 82); head of the mustard firm of Colman & Sons, growing in his fine garden at Gatton Park, Reigate, Surrey, an immense collection of orchids from all parts of the world and many hybrids of his own raising, and for upwards of twenty-one years chairman of the R.H.S. Orchid Committee.

1936 COMBER, J. (d. 1953, aged 87); for many years gardener to the Messel family at Nymans, Handcross, Sussex, where he raised the garden to a position of great distinction.

1902 COOKE, MORDECAI CUBITT (d. 1914 in his ninetieth year); mycologist and an energetic writer of scientific mycological works, including the *Fungoid Diseases of Cultivated Plants*, published by the R.H.S.

1959 COOKE, R. B.; distinguished amateur gardener of Corbridge, Northumberland, specializing in the cultivation of difficult alpine plants.

1911 COOMBER, THOMAS (d. 1926); for upwards of forty-seven years gardener at The Hendre, Monmouth, and successful exhibitor of fruits at the shows of the R.H.S., of which for many years he was a member of the Fruit and Vegetable Committee.

1943 COTTON, A. D. (d. 1962, aged 83); for over twenty years keeper of the Herbarium and Library at the Royal Botanic Gardens, Kew, and editor of the *Botanical Magazine*.

1933 COUTTS, JOHN (d. 1952 in his eightieth year); for many years Curator of the Royal Botanic Gardens, Kew, possessing an encyclopaedic knowledge of plants and horticulture.

1958 COWAN, J. MACQUEEN (d. 1960, aged 68); assistant to the Regius Keeper at the Royal Botanic Garden, Edinburgh, 1930–54, and an authority on the genus *Rhododendron*.

1947 CRACKNELL, J. S. W. (d. 1965, aged 70); managing director of the seed firm of Watkins & Simpson Ltd. from 1949 until 1960, president and a council member of the Seed Trade Association of Great Britain, and for a time a member of the Council of the R.H.S.

1944 CRANE, M. B.; famous for his work on fruit cultivation and on the genetics and origin of garden plants.

1935 CRANFIELD, W. B. (d. 1948 in his ninetieth year); a great cultivator of many types of plant—irises, tulips, paeonies and hardy ferns; his collection of the latter he gave to the R.H.S. Gardens at Wisley.

1918 CRISP, SIR FRANK (d. 1919, aged 76); one of the pioneers of rock gardening and of the cultivation of alpine plants at his garden, Friar Park, in the upper reaches of the Thames.

1897 CRUMP, WILLIAM (d. 1932 in his ninetieth year); served for forty years with the Earls of Beauchamp at Madresfield Court near Malvern, and was noted especially as a fine fruit grower.

1930 CURTIS, C. H. (d. 1958, aged 88); horticulturist and horticultural journalist, managing editor of the *Gardener's Chronicle* for over thirty years, editor of the *Orchid Review* for twenty-five years, and for fifty-eight years chairman of the United Horticultural Benefit and Provident Society.

1914 CUTHBERTSON, WILLIAM (d. 1934, aged 75); partner of Messrs. Dobbie & Co., Edinburgh, and a prominent figure in the seed trade, the R.H.S., the Horticultural Trades Association, and floricultural activities.

1910 CYPHER, JOHN J. (d. 1928); one with a wide knowledge of orchids and indoor plants generally, who introduced the present system of exhibiting large groups of plants in an artistic fashion.

1931 DALLIMORE, W. (d. 1959, aged 88); leading authority on trees and shrubs, for over forty years employed at the Royal Botanic Gardens at Kew, and for eleven years keeper of the Kew Museum.

1938 DARLINGTON, H. R. (d. 1946, aged 83); a well-known cultivator of roses, for many years associated with the National Rose Society, for a time as president.

1904 DEAN, ALEXANDER (d. 1912, aged 80); a remarkable cultivator of a wide range of plants, for twenty years a member of the R.H.S. Fruit and Vegetable Committee, a strong supporter of the National Dahlia and National Potato Societies and instrumental in founding the National Vegetable Society.

1897 DEAN, RICHARD (d. 1905, aged 75); for forty years a trader in seeds, florists' flowers and hardy plants, as well as potatoes, and for many years secretary of the National Chrysanthemum Society, as well as the National Floricultural Society which ultimately was merged into the Floral Committee of the R.H.S.

1925 DICKS, S. B. (d. 1926, aged 80); for about sixty years continuously in the wholesale seed business of Messrs. Cooper, Taber & Co., and a great authority on vegetables.

1939 DICKSON, ALEXANDER (d. 1949 in his ninety-second year); for many years head of the firm of Messrs. Alex. Dickson & Sons, Newtownards and Belfast, and a specialist in roses.

1907 DICKSON, GEORGE (Newtownards) (d. 1914, aged 84); famous rose grower who did much for horticulture in Northern Ireland.

1897 DICKSON, GEORGE A. (Chester) (d. 1909, aged 74); head of the firm of Messrs. Dicksons, Nurserymen, Chester, and for a time mayor and alderman of that city, of which he was given the freedom on the occasion of the Diamond Jubilee Celebrations.

1958 DIGBY, COL. THE LORD (d. 1964, aged 69); a horticulturist and dendrologist of wide interests and an active worker on behalf of the R.H.S., being a Council member for eleven years, chairman of the Orchid Committee and vice-chairman of the Rhododendron and Camellia Committee.

1912 DIVERS, W. H. (d. 1942, aged 87); fine all-round gardener with long distinguished service in the gardens at Belvoir Castle and for fifty years a member of the Society's Fruit and Vegetable Committee.

1897 D'OMBRIAN, THE REV. H. H. (d. 1905, aged 87); the rosarian who for very many years acted as secretary of the National Rose Society, of which he was one of the founders.

1943 DORRIEN-SMITH, MAJOR A. A. (d. 1955, aged 79); the great gardener who further developed the unique gardens at Tresco Abbey with plants from Australia, New Zealand, South Africa and from similar climates.

1899 DOUGLAS, JAMES (d. 1911, aged 73); a remarkable cultivator of many diverse kinds of plants from fruits to auriculas (his exhibits of the latter won many gold medals), and an active worker on behalf of various plant societies and of the R.H.S., on whose Council he for a time served.

1897 DRUERY, CHARLES T. (d. 1917, aged 74); the great authority on British ferns on which he was the author of several works; the discoverer in ferns of the condition known as apospory, and president and honorary secretary of the British Pteridological Society.

1897 DUNN, MALCOLM (d. 1899, aged 61); from 1871 head gardener to the Duke of Buccleuch at Dalkeith Palace, and keenly interested in all things pertaining to horticulture and arboriculture; almost as well known in London as in Edinburgh.

1925 DYKES, WILLIAM RICKATSON (d. 1925, aged 48); well-known breeder of, and writer on, irises, and Secretary of the R.H.S. from 1920 to 1925.

1905 ECKFORD, HENRY (d. 1905, aged 82); world-famous raiser of sweet peas at his business at Wem in Shropshire.

1945 ELEY, C. C. (d. 1960, aged 87); cultivator of a fine garden at East Bergholt Place, Suffolk, and part founder, in 1915, of the Rhododendron Society, of which he was secretary for sixteen years.

1897 ELLACOMBE, THE REV. CANON (d. 1916, aged 94); one of the greatest gardeners of his day, who made the garden at Bitton, Gloucestershire, famous throughout the horticultural world.

1951 ELLIOTT, CLARENCE; noted collector, introducer, and distributor of plants and writer on a wide range of horticultural subjects.

1897 ELWES, HENRY J. (d. 1922, aged 76); regarded as the greatest traveller of his day and foremost authority on the trees of Europe and on lilies.

1900 ENGLEHEART, THE REV. G. H. (d. 1936 in his eighty-fifth year); one of the greatest breeders of daffodils of all time.

1933 FARMER, SIR JOHN (d. 1944 in his seventy-ninth year); Professor of Botany and Director of the Biological Laboratories at the Imperial College of Science and Technology from 1907 to 1929, organizer of the Forest Products Research Board, and a leader in the formation of the Imperial College of Tropical Agriculture at Trinidad.

1903 FENN, ROBERT (d. 1912, aged 96); a smallholder who carried out experiments in the cross-breeding of plants, being most successful with potatoes.

1937 FENWICK, MARK (d. 1945, aged 84); creator of the famous garden at Abbotswood, Stow-on-the-Wold, cultivator of a wide range of plants and especially authoritative on alpine and rock-garden plants.

1910 FIELDER, C. R. (died 1946); renowned as a landscape gardener, plantsman, and fruit grower, and closely associated with the R.H.S. as Horticultural Adviser and as an examiner.

1961 FINDLAY, T. H.; splendid cultivator of all kinds of plants and assistant to Sir Eric Savill in the creation of the gardens in the Great Park at Windsor.

1956 FLETCHER, H. R.; Director of the R.H.S. Garden at Wisley 1951-4, Regius Keeper of the Royal Botanic Garden, Edinburgh from 1956, Queen's Botanist in Scotland from 1966.

1921 FORREST, GEORGE (d. 1932, aged 59); foremost of plant collectors in the Sino-Himalayan region, introducer to cultivation of hundreds of new plants and collector of over 30,000 beautiful herbarium specimens of immense scientific value.

1897 FOSTER, SIR MICHAEL (d. 1907, aged 70); Professor of Physiology in the University of Cambridge, and specialist in the cultivation and breeding of irises.

1948 FOX, DR. WILFRID S. (d. 1962, aged 87); amateur horticulturist, creator of an arboretum in Surrey, with an especial interest in the genus *Sorbus*, and strong in support of the Roads Beautifying Association.

1897 FRASER, JOHN (d. 1900, aged 78); famous as a cultivator of hard-wooded plants and as an exhibitor of stove and greenhouse plants and, during his last years, a Vice-President of the R.H.S.

1922 FRASER, JOHN (d. 1935); botanist, horticulturist, dendrologist and journalist, he was editor of the *Gardening World* from 1895 to 1909 and a regular contributor to the *Gardener's Chronicle* from 1883.

1965 FURSE, REAR-ADMIRAL J. P. W.; active plant collector, mostly in Persia and Turkey, introducer of many alpine and bulbous plants, and excellent botanical illustrator.

1963 GAULT, S. M.; renowned cultivator of every kind of plant from fruits and vegetables to sempervivums, and Park Superintendent at Regent's Park, London.

1916 GIBBS, THE HON. VICARY (d. 1932, aged 79); amateur gardener of diverse and catholic tastes, owner of the garden at Aldenham House, Elstree, where he grew a wide variety of trees and shrubs and a large collection of michaelmas daisies, and where he specialized in the cultivation of vegetables.

1942 GILES, W. F. (d. 1962); authority on the cultivation of vegetables and great worker on behalf of the R.H.S.

1956 GILMOUR, J. S. L.; Director of the R.H.S. Garden at Wisley 1946–51, Director of the University Botanic Garden, Cambridge, from 1951, an authority on plant nomenclature and a member of Council of the R.H.S.

1947 GIUSEPPI, DR. PAUL LEON (d. 1947, aged 66); collector and intro-ducer of alpine plants which he cultivated with great success in his garden at Felixstowe.

1907 GOODACRE, JAMES H. (d. 1922); gardener to the Earl of Harrington at Elvaston Castle and for forty years a highly successful grower and exhibitor of choice fruits.

1897 GORDON, GEORGE (d. 1914, aged 72); a cultivator of a wide range of plants, interested in many plant societies, a well-known judge at flower shows and for twenty-five years editor of the *Gardener's Magazine*.

1924 GROVE, A. (d. 1942, aged 78); for over half a century a student and cultivator of lilies, on which he was the great authority, being the first recipient from the R.H.S. of the Lyttel Lily Cup.

1962 HADDEN, NORMAN G.; clever cultivator of rare and rather tender plants in his Somerset garden.

1934 HALES, W. (d. 1937, aged 64); Curator of the Chelsea Physic Garden from 1899 and active worker in the cause of horticultural education.

1935 HALL, SIR (ALFRED) DANIEL (d. 1942, aged 78); first principal of Wye Agricultural College, head of Rothamsted Experimental Station, head of the John Innes Horticultural Institute, editor of the Society's publications and author of the monograph on the genus *Tulipa*.

1924 HANBURY, F. J. (d. 1938, aged 86); chairman for many years of the company of Allen & Hanbury Ltd., noted botanist and horticulturist, especially orchidologist, and closely associated with the affairs of the R.H.S.

1903 HANBURY, SIR THOMAS (d. 1907, aged 75); fine amateur horticul-turist and great servant of the R.H.S. in that he gave to the Society in 1903 the Wisley estate of the late Mr. George Wilson.

1953   HANGER, FRANCIS E. W. (d. 1961, aged 61); skilled cultivator and expert exhibitor; Curator of the R.H.S. Garden at Wisley from 1946 until he died.

1950   HARLEY, ANDREW (d. 1950, aged 78); amateur gardener who made a fine garden at Glendevon in Perthshire and specialized in the cultivation of nomocharis and gentians and other Sino-Himalayan plants.

1926   HARROW, R. L. (d. 1954, aged 87); Curator of the Royal Botanic Garden, Edinburgh, 1924–31, and Director of the Society's Garden at Wisley 1931–46.

1930   HATTON, SIR RONALD G. (d. 1965, aged 79); Director of East Malling Research Station, who played an important role in the establishment of the National Agricultural Advisory Service, and the National Fruit Trials.

1965   HAVERGAL, MISS B.; creator of the now famous Waterperry School of Horticulture for women in Oxfordshire, and prominent on R.H.S. committees for education and examinations.

1924   HAY, T. (d. 1953, aged 79); for many years Superintendent of the Central Royal Parks; for twenty years a member of the Society's Council and of various R.H.S. committees.

1939   HEADFORT, THE MARQUIS OF (d. 1943, aged 64); main creator of the famous garden at Kells, Ireland, noted especially for its conifers, a Vice-President of the R.H.S. and president of the Royal Horticultural and Agricultural Society of Ireland.

1897   HEAL, JOHN (d. 1925, aged 84); gave a lifetime of service as a hybridizer for the firm of Veitch; originator of many new plants.

1967   HELLYER, A. G. L.; horticultural journalist, for many years editor of *Amateur Gardening* and the author of many gardening books and articles.

1909   HEMSLEY, WILLIAM BOTTING (d. 1924 in his eighty-first year); for many years a distinguished botanist on the staff of the Royal Botanic Gardens, Kew, and from 1899 to 1908 keeper of the Kew Herbarium and Library.

1906   HENRY, PROF. A. (d. 1930, aged 73); renowned traveller, horticulturist, and arboriculturist, and collaborator with Elwes in the production of *Trees of Great Britain and Ireland*.

1897   HENSLOW, THE REV. PROF. G. (d. 1925 in his ninety-first year); for many years Honorary Professor of Botany for the R.H.S., frequent lecturer to the Society and author of many botanical works.

1897   HERBST, HERMANN (d. 1904, aged 74); pioneer in the development of market horticulture and in the introduction of certain palms, adiantums and similar exotics on a wide commercial scale.

1946   HIGGINS, MRS. VERA; a keen amateur gardener, who made valuable contributions to horticultural literature and was for a time editor of the *Journal* of the R.H.S.

1934   HILL, SIR ARTHUR W. (d. 1941, aged 66); for fifteen years Assistant Director, and from 1922 until he died, Director, of the Royal Botanic Gardens at Kew.

1941   HILLIER, EDWIN LAWRENCE (d. 1944 in his eightieth year); son of the founder of the world-renowned nursery of this name and an authority on trees, shrubs, herbaceous plants, alpines, roses, aquatics, and fruit trees.

1957   HILLIER, H. G.; head of the famous Winchester nursery of this name, great authority on all trees and shrubs and member of Council of R.H.S.

1897   HOLE, THE VERY REV. S. REYNOLDS (d. 1904, aged 85); eminent rosarian and the first, and, whilst he lived, the only, president of the National Rose Society.

1897   HOOKER, SIR JOSEPH DALTON (d. 1911, aged 94); the greatest British botanist and one of the outstanding men of his age.

1963   HORLICK, LIEUT.-COL. SIR JAMES; the creator of one of the finest gardens of the twentieth century on the windswept island of Gigha, Argyll, Scotland.

1897   HORNER, THE REV. F. D. (d. 1912, aged 75); renowned florist specializing particularly in auriculas and tulips, for over twenty years secretary of the Northern Auricula Society and for many years secretary of the Northern Carnation Society.

1930   HORT, SIR ARTHUR (d. 1935, aged 71); a keen amateur gardener and raiser of many well-known irises; a frequent writer on horticultural matters.

1953   HUDSON, C. E.; senior officer of the horticultural section of the National Agricultural Advisory Service and prominent member of the R.H.S. Examinations Board.

1897   HUDSON, JAMES (d. 1932, aged 85); for over forty years head gardener at Gunnersbury House, most of the time under Mr. Leopold de Rothschild, famous as a cultivator of fruits; for about twenty years on the Council of the R.H.S. and for a number of years on the Society's Board of Examiners.

1944   HUTCHINSON, JOHN; famous Kew botanist with particular interests in plant relationships and in the genus *Rhododendron*.

1945   INGAMELLS, DAVID (d. 1946, aged 83); Covent Garden salesman and a prominent member of the National Chrysanthemum Society.

1952   INGRAM, CAPTAIN COLLINGWOOD; great authority on—and raiser of several new—cherries, as well as on other shrubs.

1944 INGWERSEN, W. E. TH. (d. 1960, aged 77); a great plantsman and leading authority on alpine and rock-garden plants, founder of the famed nursery at East Grinstead bearing his name, and founder member of the Alpine Garden Society.

1962 INGWERSEN, WILL; son of the above, alpine and rock plantsman, for some years Chairman of the Horticultural Trades Association, and a member of the Council of the R.H.S. and regular contributor to the horticultural Press.

1953 JAMES, THE HON. ROBERT (d. 1960, aged 87); creator of a fine garden at his home, St. Nicholas, Richmond, Yorkshire, and particularly knowledgeable on lilies.

1949 JANES, E. R. (d. 1958, aged 73); successful grower and exhibitor of flowers and vegetables, especially of sweet peas, cyclamen, cinerarias, gloxinias, streptocarpus, and introducer of new colour forms of *Primula malacoides* and *P. sinensis*.

1897 JEKYLL, MISS GERTRUDE (d. 1932 in her ninetieth year); artist, landscape artist, horticulturist, and very great gardener.

1951 JOHNSTONE, GEORGE HORACE (d. 1960, aged 78); skilful amateur gardener, excelling in the cultivation of many plants, especially camellias, magnolias, and daffodils, and author of *Asiatic Magnolias in Cultivation*.

1925 JONES, H. J. (d. 1928, aged 72); highly successful cultivator, raiser, distributor, and exhibitor of chrysanthemums and hydrangeas, pelargoniums, fuchsias, phloxes, delphiniums, and michaelmas daisies, and winner of no fewer than 107 gold medals and seventy-four silver-gilt.

1930 JORDAN, F. (d. 1958, aged 93); an authority on fruit culture who spent some forty years as head gardener in various large private gardens.

1951 KAY, LIEUT.-COL. P. CRICHTON (d. 1954); a leading authority on the production of flowers for market.

1897 KAY, PETER (d. 1909, aged 56); a successful cultivator of grapes, cucumbers, and tomatoes for market.

1965 KEMP, E. E.; on the staff of the Royal Botanic Garden, Edinburgh, since 1932, for most of the time Curator, and fine all-round plantsman.

1909 KER, R. WILSON (d. 1910, aged 71); senior partner in the firm of Messrs. Ker & Sons, Aigburth Nurseries, Liverpool, famous for the high quality of its plants, especially stove plants, and for its exhibits at R.H.S. and other shows.

1901 KING, SIR G. (d. 1909, aged 69); botanist who gave great service to India as Director of the Botanic Garden, Calcutta, Director of the Botanical Survey of India, and as the leader in the development of the quinine industry.

1932   KINGDON WARD, F. (d. 1958, aged 72); famous explorer and plant collector, and introducer of numerous fine horticultural plants, mostly from the Sino-Himalaya.

1958   KNIGHT, F. P.; Director of the R.H.S. Garden at Wisley from 1954, who trained at the Botanic Gardens at Edinburgh and Kew and who had experience in commercial horticulture, being an authority on plant propagation.

1897   LAING, JOHN (d. 1900 in his seventy-seventh year); head of the firm of John Laing & Sons, of Forest Hill; as a hybridist he completely revolutionized the tuberous begonia and bred new penstemons, clivias, streptocarpus, and gloxinias.

1922   LAMBOURNE, LORD (d. 1928, aged 81); popular President of the R.H.S. from 1917 until his death.

1955   LANGDON, ALLAN G.; well-known nurseryman of Bath, Somerset, and expert cultivator and hybridizer of delphiniums, begonias, gloxinias and other groups.

1935   LANGDON, C. F. (d. 1947, aged 79); partner in the firm of Blackmore & Langdon, specializing in the cultivation of tuberous begonias, delphiniums, cyclamen and polyanthus, and successful exhibitor at R.H.S. Shows.

1942   LAWRENCE, IRIS, LADY (d. 1955, aged 67); a great worker for, and much interested in, horticulture generally; widow of Sir William Lawrence, Bt.

1900   LAWRENCE, SIR TREVOR, BT. (d. 1913 in his eighty-second year); the great President of the R.H.S. (1885–1913); a leading orchidologist.

1950   LAWRENCE, W. J. C.; for many years on the staff of the John Innes Horticultural Institute and researcher on composts and the structure of glass-houses.

1929   LAWRENCE, SIR WILLIAM, BT. (d. 1934, aged 63); son of Sir Trevor, grower of hardy and half-hardy plants, a member of Council of the R.H.S. and Treasurer from 1924 to 1928. President of the Iris Society and of the Alpine Garden Society.

1932   LAXTON, E. A. L.(d. 1951, aged 82); head of the firm of Laxton Bros. (Bedford) Ltd., which has raised and introduced so many noteworthy and valuable cultivars of fruits and vegetables, especially of apples.

1930   LEAK, G. W. (d. 1963, aged 95); spent the greater part of his working life with the firm of R. H. Bath, Ltd., Wisbech, an authority on daffodils, tulips, gladioli, paeonies, sweet peas, delphiniums, for many years a member of Council of the R.H.S., and a Vice-President of the Society.

1907   LLEWELLYN, SIR JOHN DILLWYN (d. 1927 in his ninety-second year); great servant of British horticulture, serving on the R.H.S. Council, a member of its Scientific Committee, vice-president of the National Chrysanthemum Society and the National Carnation and Picotee Society, and patron of the National Dahlia Society.

1932   LOBJOIT, SIR WILLIAM G. (d. 1939, aged 80); chairman of the market garden firm of Messrs. W. J. Lobjoit & Son; for seven years, from 1920, Controller of Horticulture under the Minister of Agriculture, and active in the affairs of the National Farmers' Union and the Ministry of Agriculture.

1967   LODER, SIR GILES, BT.; amateur gardener, the owner of the great garden of Leonardslee, Horsham, Sussex, and for many years a member of Council of the R.H.S.

1923   LOWE, JOSEPH (d. 1929); founder of the firm of Messrs. Lowe & Shawyer, of Uxbridge, at one time the largest cut-flower establishment in the world.

1906   LYNCH, R. IRVIN (d. 1924, aged 74); for forty years Curator of the Cambridge Botanic Garden and a wonderful cultivator of a wide range of plants, many of them of a tender nature.

1920   McHATTIE, J. W. (d. 1923, aged 64); for over twenty years Superintendent of the Parks and Gardens of the City of Edinburgh.

1897   McINDOE, JAMES (d. 1910, aged 73); for some thirty years immensely successful cultivator of all manner of fruits for Sir Joseph Peace at Hutton Hall, Guisborough, Yorkshire, within a short distance of the North Sea.

1909   MacKELLAR, A. C. (d. 1931, aged 77); an outstanding figure in British horticulture for over fifty years as head gardener in some of the finest gardens in Scotland and England, especially in the Royal Gardens at Sandringham and Windsor.

1961   MacKENZIE, W. G.; Curator of the Physic Garden at Chelsea from 1945 and especially interested in alpine plants and rock gardens.

1929   McLEOD, J. F. (d. 1950); actively engaged in horticulture for over thirty years and a prominent member of some of the most important R.H.S. committees.

1950   MacSELF, A. J. (d. 1952, aged 83); well-known editor and author, and for twenty years editor of *Amateur Gardening*.

1928   MALCOLM, ALEXANDER (d. 1945); well-known amateur raiser of sweet peas.

1897   MARIES, CHARLES (d. 1902, aged 51); plant collector in China and Japan for Veitch and introducer of many plants, especially of conifers.

1906   MARSHALL, WILLIAM (d. 1917 in his eighty-second year); great amateur gardener, specializing in orchids and ferns, and a loyal supporter of the R.H.S., acting as a member of Council and, for a quarter of a century, chairman of the Floral Committee.

1960   MASON, L. MAURICE; a most distinguished amateur gardener and the
cultivator and introducer to cultivation of many plants from almost
all parts of the world.

1902   MASSEE, GEORGE (d. 1917, aged 67); a mycologist who contributed
greatly to knowledge of the fungous parasites of cultivated plants and
who from 1893 until 1915 held the post of principal assistant in the
Herbarium at Kew.

1904   MAWLEY, EDWARD (d. 1916, aged 74); the great rosarian who did
much for the National Rose Society as secretary for thirty-seven
years, and was also interested in dahlia cultivation.

1917   MAXWELL, SIR HERBERT E., BT. (d. 1937, aged 92); splendid plantsman and writer on, and painter of, plants, growing in his favoured
garden at Monreith in south-west Scotland a wide range of plants,
many of them of a tender nature.

1910   MAY, HENRY B. (d. 1936, aged 91); founder of a large market-
gardening business, and for many years a member of Council of the
R.H.S., and chairman of the Narcissus and Tulip Committee and the
Floral Committee.

1945   MESSEL, LIEUT.-COL. L. C. R. (d. 1953, aged 81); owner of the fine
garden at Nymans, Sussex, and keen amateur gardener and grower
of rare plants.

1949   MEYER, THE REV. CANON ROLLO (d. 1953, aged 84); a raiser of new
cultivars of daffodils and irises, active member of many R.H.S.
committees and for many years honorary vice-president of the
National Rose Society.

1927   MILLAIS, J. G. (d. 1931 in his sixty-sixth year); naturalist, who
developed a great interest in rhododendrons and magnolias which he
examined in gardens throughout the country and on which he wrote
authoritative works.

1932   MILLARD, F. W. (d. 1944, aged 81); a clever gardener who made a
speciality of alpine plants, especially those of Tasmania and New
Zealand, and of the dwarf rhododendrons from the mountains of Asia.

1897   MILNER, HENRY ERNEST (d. 1906 in his sixty-first year); landscape
gardener who did much work in England, Hungary, and Sweden,
and was closely connected with the Earl's Court Exhibition in 1892.

1947   MITCHELL, W. J. W. (d. 1965, aged 91); outstanding gardener who
spent the greater part of his professional life in the arboretum at
Westonbirt—in large measure the creation of Sir George Holford.

1897   MOLYNEUX, EDWIN (d. 1921, aged 70); gardener and bailiff at
Swanmore Park, Bishop's Waltham, from 1878, and one who did
much to improve the chrysanthemum.

1897 MONRO, GEORGE (d. 1920, aged 75); founder of the Covent Garden firm of Monro, and generous supporter of gardening charities.

1934 MONRO, GEORGE (d. 1951); son of the above and a member of Council of the R.H.S. from 1924 until his death, and Treasurer from 1938 to 1942.

1897 MOORE, SIR FREDERICK W. (d. 1949 in his ninety-second year); in charge of the Royal Botanic Garden, Glasnevin, from 1879, when he succeeded his father, Dr. David Moore, until he retired in 1922; father and son were keepers of the Garden for an unbroken period of eighty-five years.

1925 MOORE, GEORGE F. (d. 1927, aged 71); one of the most successful amateur orchid cultivators of his day, staging fine orchid exhibits at R.H.S. Shows, some of his hybrids receiving the First Class Certificate.

1897 MORRIS, SIR DANIEL (d. 1933, aged 89); distinguished botanist and administrator who did much to develop the agricultural possibilities of our colonies and dependencies; one-time Treasurer of the Society.

1924 MORRIS, SYDNEY (d. 1924, aged 73); creator of a fine garden at Earlham Hall, Norfolk, which was celebrated for its roses and hardy herbaceous plants, and an authority on montbretia, of which he raised many excellent cultivars.

1967 MORTON, THE EARL OF; amateur gardener, chairman of the Society's Picture Committee, and a member of the Library, Publications, and Scientific Committees.

1925 MOUNT, GEORGE (d. 1927, aged 83); famous as a grower and exhibitor first of roses and then of fruit trees, and a strong supporter of the R.H.S. and of the National Rose Society.

1926 MUSGRAVE, C. T. (d. 1949, aged 86); three times Treasurer of the Society, for several years a member of Council and chairman of the Housing Committee.

1953 NEAME, SIR THOMAS; an authority on the commercial cultivation of fruits and a member of Council of the R.H.S.

1965 NELMES, W.; Superintendent of Cardiff Parks Department for over thirty years.

1964 NEWELL, J.; Curator of the John Innes Institute and an authority on the cultivation of lilies.

1897 NICHOLSON, GEORGE (d. 1908, aged 61); in the service of the Royal Botanic Gardens, Kew, from 1873 until he retired in 1901, for fifteen years as Curator; editor of the *Dictionary of Gardening* and a great authority on all matters pertaining to horticulture and arboriculture.

1923 NIX, CHARLES G. A. (d. 1956, aged 82); an authority on fruits, particularly on apples and pears, and for many years chairman of the Fruit Committee of the R.H.S.

1901 NORMAN, GEORGE (d. 1906, aged 55); for thirty years head gardener to the Marquis of Salisbury at Hatfield, Herts., and a wonderful cultivator of every kind of garden plant, also possessing great knowledge of the flora of central China.

1897 O'BRIEN, JAMES (d. 1930 in his eighty-ninth year); renowned grower of orchids, for a time general manager of Messrs. E. G. Henderson & Son, introducer to cultivation of many rare orchids, stove plants, and Cape bulbs, and secretary of the R.H.S. Orchid Committee for some thirty years.

1960 OGG, STUART; expert in the cultivation of dahlias, as well as chrysanthemums and delphiniums, and a member of Council of the R.H.S.

1937 OLDHAM, W. R. (d. 1949 in his seventy-ninth year); for many years one of the leading figures in the nursery trade and controller of the famous firm of Messrs. W. Fromow & Sons of Windlesham, three times president of the Horticultural Trades Association and a member of the R.H.S. Council and several committees.

1901 ORMEROD, MISS E. A. (d. 1901); eminent entomologist who devoted much of her life to the service of agriculturists and horticulturists.

1954 PALMER, THE HON. LEWIS; an expert on South African plants, especially on the genus *Agapanthus*; for a number of years a member of Council as well as Treasurer and Vice-President of the Society.

1943 PAM, MAJOR A. (d. 1955, aged 80); an authority on South American bulbous plants, which he grew at his home at Broxbourne, Hertfordshire, and a member of Council of the R.H.S.

1958 PARK, BERTRAM; an eminent cultivator of, and writer on, roses.

1897 PAUL, GEORGE (d. 1921, aged 80); best known as a rosarian who raised a number of useful cultivars, but was equally interested in the introduction of choice trees and shrubs, especially such handsome flowering ones as rhododendrons, lilacs, philadelphus, and weigelias.

1897 PAUL, WILLIAM (d. 1905 in his eighty-third year); the famous rosarian who raised many new rose cultivars, who also specialized in hollies, ivies, pelargoniums, hyacinths, and hollyhocks, and a regular contributor to the horticultural Press for over sixty years.

1911 PEARSON, ALFRED HETLEY (d. 1930); older brother of the following and the senior of the three brothers who made the firm of J. R. Pearson & Sons famous, a renowned cultivator of fruit and vice-chairman of the R.H.S.'s Fruit and Vegetable Committee.

1924 PEARSON, CHARLES E. (d. 1929, aged 73); founder, and secretary for many years, of the Horticultural Trades Association, one of the three brothers who for many years conducted the business of Messrs. J. R. Pearson & Sons, Lowdham; particularly knowledgeable on florists' flowers and hardy plants.

1935   PERRY, AMOS (d. 1953, aged 82); at the famous nursery at Enfield, the cultivator, propagator, and breeder of a great variety of hardy plants—irises, asters, poppies, as well as ferns, and later of water plants and day-lilies.

1926   PETTIGREW, W. W. (d. 1947, aged 80); Superintendent of the Manchester Corporation Public Parks and Gardens and formerly Superintendent of the Cardiff Parks.

1960   PILKINGTON, G. L.; amateur gardener with interests ranging from irises to conifers, the owner of a fine garden at Haslemere, arduous worker for the R.H.S. and a member of its Council.

1914   PINWILL, CAPTAIN W. S. (d. 1926, aged 95); an unrivalled cultivator of rare hardy plants and fruits at his home at Trehane, Cornwall.

1922   POUPART, WM. (d. 1936 in his ninetieth year); excelling as a grower of vegetables for market, one of the first to grow daffodils extensively for the cut-flower market, for many years a member of the Narcissus and Tulip Committee, and Fruit and Vegetable Committee of the R.H.S., and for thirty years the president of the Market Gardeners', Nurserymen's and Farmers' Association.

1912   PRAIN, LIEUT.-COL. SIR DAVID (d. 1944, aged 86); one-time Director of the Royal Botanic Garden, Calcutta, and responsible for the reorganization of the cinchona industry in India, and later Director of the Royal Botanic Gardens, Kew.

1938   PRESTON, FREDERICK GEORGE (d. 1964, aged 81); on the staff of the Cambridge Botanic Garden from 1909 until he retired in 1947, he was for twenty years Curator of the Garden, and always a strong supporter of the R.H.S.

1962   PUDDLE, C. E.; son of the following, who succeeded his father as head gardener at Bodnant, North Wales, and who did much to establish the International Camellia Society.

1937   PUDDLE, F. C. (d. 1952, aged 75); a great gardener who, after training in the orchid nurseries of Messrs. Sander Ltd., St. Albans, and in Messrs. Veitch's nurseries at Chelsea, ultimately became head gardener at Bodnant, where he bred orchids, hippeastrums—and especially rhododendrons.

1939   RAFFILL, C. P. (d. 1951, aged 75); employed at the Royal Botanic Gardens, Kew, for over fifty years, for most of the time in the post of Assistant Curator, and a leading authority on rhododendrons, lilies, irises, and fuchsias.

1949   RAMSBOTTOM, J.; mycologist and Keeper of Botany, British Museum (Natural History) from 1930 to 1950, when he retired.

1904   REDESDALE, LORD (d. 1916 in his eightieth year); as secretary to the Commissioners of Public Works and Buildings from 1874 to 1886, he was responsible for many improvements in the London parks and at Kew became a renowned cultivator of bamboos and for a time was a member of Council of the R.H.S.

1917 RENDLE, A. B. (d. 1938, aged 73); Keeper of the Department of Botany at the British Museum 1906–30 and for many years Professor of Botany to the R.H.S.

1938 REUTHE, G. (d. 1942, aged 87); founder of the nursery at Keston, Kent, which specialized in rare hardy trees and shrubs, especially in rhododendrons, which he exhibited with great regularity at the Society's Meetings.

1897 RIVERS, T. FRANCIS (d. 1899 in his sixty-ninth year); succeeded his father, Thomas Rivers, as one of the greatest of fruit breeders, and a member of Council of the R.H.S.

1962 ROBINSON, G. W.; one-time Curator of the Chelsea Physic Garden and for twenty years Superintendent of the University Botanic Garden at Oxford, and a great plantsman.

1946 ROCHFORD, B.; for many years the renderer of signal service to commercial growers of glass-house crops.

1942 ROCHFORD, J. P. (d. 1965 in his eighty-third year); successful horticulturist in the Lea Valley and for twenty-eight years president of the Lea Valley Growers' Association.

1925 ROCHFORD, JOSEPH (d. 1932, aged 75); the last of five brothers who developed and brought to a state of great prosperity the well-known series of glass-house nursery businesses at Broxbourne, Herts.

1964 ROCHFORD, T.; head of the firm of Thomas Rochford & Sons Ltd., a remarkable cultivator of a very wide range of house plants and a superb exhibitor; member of Council of the Society.

1921 ROLFE, ROBERT ALLEN (d. 1921 in his sixty-sixth year); for forty years a botanist at the Royal Botanic Gardens, Kew, an expert orchidologist and founder of *The Orchid Review* in 1893.

1917 ROLLITT, SIR ALBERT KAYE (d. 1922 in his eightieth year); largely responsible for the institution of the National Diploma in Horticulture, for many years a member of Council of the R.H.S., president of the National Chrysanthemum Society, and closely identified with the horticultural activities of the Borough of Hull.

1943 ROSE, FRED J. (d. 1956 in his seventy-first year); gardener to Lord Swaythling, Townhill, Southampton, an outstanding exhibitor, and a raiser and grower of rhododendrons and lilies and for a time member of Council of the R.H.S.

1908 ROSS, CHARLES (d. 1917, aged 92); achieved wide fame chiefly as a raiser of new cultivars of apple, including 'Charles Ross', a cross between 'Cox's Orange Pippin' and 'Peasgood's Nonesuch'.

1929 ROTHSCHILD, LIONEL DE (d. 1942, aged sixty); creator of the famous garden at Exbury, near Southampton, a specialist in orchids, rhododendrons, and azaleas, and a staunch supporter of the R.H.S.

1897 ROTHSCHILD, LORD (d. 1937, aged 69); scientific-minded naturalist with a wide knowledge of plants, especially of orchids, and the creator of famous gardens at Tring.

1957 RUSSELL, J. L.; son of the following; succeeded his father as head of the firm of L. R. Russell Ltd., Windlesham, Surrey, an authority on trees, shrubs, stove and greenhouse plants, a member of Council of the R.H.S. and active on several of the Society's committees.

1929 RUSSELL, L. R. (d. 1942, aged 78); head of the firm of Messrs. L. R. Russell Ltd., Richmond Nurseries, Windlesham, Surrey, which for many years was the attraction for Continental and American nurserymen and noted especially for its tropical and economic plants.

1952 SALISBURY, SIR EDWARD J.; Director of the Royal Botanic Gardens, Kew, and a distinguished botanist and gardener.

1897 SANDER, H. F. C. (d. 1920, aged 73); senior partner and founder of the great orchid establishment of Sanders of St. Albans, employing at one time twenty-three collectors in various parts of the world.

1955 SAVILL, SIR ERIC; horticulturist and arboriculturist, the creator of the wonderful gardens at Windsor, a member of Council of the R.H.S. and active on several of the Society's committees.

1958 SCARLETT, ROBERT L.; market gardener who, in several ways, has made immense contributions to commercial horticulture in Scotland.

1897 SCHRÖDER, BARON SIR HENRY, BT. (d. 1910, aged 86); great collector and cultivator of orchids, benefactor of the R.H.S. ('The Father of the Hall') and of gardeners' charities.

1934 SCRASE-DICKENS, CHARLES R. (d. 1947); a keen amateur gardener and a successful grower of difficult plants, who was associated with the activities of the R.H.S. over a long period of years.

1936 SECRETT, FREDERICK AUGUSTUS (d. 1964, aged 78); the informed leader in the world of market gardening, devoted to the training of young horticulturists and active in the affairs of the R.H.S., on whose Council he served for many years.

1897 SEDEN, JOHN (d. 1921, aged 81); renowned cultivator and hybridizer and raiser of new plants, employed by the firm of Veitch.

1933 SHAWYER, GEORGE E. (d. 1943, aged 79); head of the finest and most extensive business in the world in the realm of cut-flower production—Lowe & Shawyer—and founder, with Mr. George Monro, of the British Flower Marketing Association.

495

1953 SHERRIFF, MAJOR GEORGE (d. 1967, aged 69); well-known plant collector, chiefly in south-east Tibet and Bhutan, the introducer of many fine garden plants and creator of a splendid garden near Kirriemuir, Angus.

1897 SHERWOOD, NATHANIEL NEWMAN (d. 1916, aged 70); head of the great firm of wholesale seedsmen, Messrs. Hursts, generous to gardening charities and to the Purchase Fund of the R.H.S.'s Hall.

1953 SHOESMITH, H. (d. 1967); chrysanthemum authority and the raiser of many fine new cultivars at his home at Woking.

1947 SIMMONDS, A. (d. 1968, aged 76); most devoted servant of the R.H.S., spending his entire working life in the service of the Society, finally in the post of Secretary, until retiring in 1962.

1943 SLADE, SIR JAMES (d. 1950, aged 88); head of the firm of Protheroe & Morris, who conducted sales of nurseries and of nursery stock in all parts of the country, and a keen horticulturist.

1964 SLOCOCK, O. C. A.; of the Goldsworth Nursery of Walter C. Slocock Ltd., Woking, and successful breeder of new rhododendron hybrids.

1916 SLOCOCK, WALTER C. (d. 1926, aged 73); nurseryman at Woking noted for the cultivation of conifers and of rhododendron hybrids, of which he raised many new cultivars.

1897 SMITH, JAMES (d. 1903, aged 68); for twenty-eight years head gardener to the Earl of Rosebery at Mentmore, Leighton Buzzard, and one of those who helped to form the Royal Gardeners' Orphan Fund in 1887.

1897 SMITH, MARTIN RIDLEY (d. 1908); the owner of one of the most famous collections of carnations in Europe, great raiser of new seedling carnations, and president of the National Carnation and Picotee Society.

1906 SMITH, THOMAS (d. 1919 in his seventy-ninth year); founder of the Daisy Hill Nurseries, Newry, Ireland, where he grew a unique collection of plants and where he did much to improve the state of gardening in Ireland.

1925 SMITH, PROFESSOR SIR WILLIAM WRIGHT (d. 1956, aged 81); Regius Keeper of the Royal Botanic Garden, Edinburgh, and Regius Professor of Botany at the University of Edinburgh, authority on rhododendrons and primulas, a Vice-President of the R.H.S. and its Honorary Professor of Botany.

1955 SNELLING, MISS L.; botanical artist famous for her contributions to the *Botanical Magazine*.

1897 SPEED, WALTER (d. 1921 in his eighty-sixth year); for nearly fifty-eight years head gardener at Penrhyn Castle Gardens, Bangor, to three successive Lords Penrhyn, specializing in the cultivation of indoor fruits, conifers, bamboos, rare shrubs and choice trees.

1953 STAIR, THE EARL OF (d. 1961, aged 82); the owner of the magnificent estate at Lochinch Castle, near Stranraer, Wigtownshire, and authority on rhododendrons.

1928 STAPF, O. (d. 1933, aged 76); Kew botanist, keeper of the Herbarium and Library at Kew 1908–22, editor of the *Botanical Magazine* and editor of *Index Londinensis* published by the R.H.S.

1965 STEARN, W. T.; botanist on the staff of the Natural History Division of the British Museum, and the Librarian of the R.H.S. for nearly twenty years.

1964 STENNING, L. (d. 1965, aged 63); employed at the Royal Botanic Gardens, Kew for forty years, holding the position of assistant curator of the tropical department for thirty-one years and Curator of the Gardens for nearly five years.

1940 STERN, SIR FREDERICK (d. 1967, aged 83); great amateur gardener who, in his famous garden, 'Highdown', Worthing, Sussex, taught the horticultural world what could be grown on chalk.

1939 STEVENSON, J. B. (d. 1950, aged 68); creator, at Tower Court, Ascot, of one of the finest rhododendron gardens in the country, a member of Council of the R.H.S. and chairman of the Society's Rhododendron and Publications Committees.

1937 STOKER, DR. FRED (d. 1943, aged 64); great amateur gardener, cultivator of a wide range of plants, and writer on his gardening experiences.

1954 STOUGHTON, R. H.; the first Professor of Horticulture at the University of Reading, an authority on hydroponics, and for some years a member of the Council of the R.H.S. and of the Society's Examinations Board.

1943 STREDWICK, HARRY (d. 1966, aged 89); outstanding cultivator of dahlias and raiser of several new cultivars.

1945 STREETER, F.; great gardener at Petworth House, Sussex, a highly successful cultivator and exhibitor of fruit, a member of several R.H.S. committees, and for many years a well-known radio personality.

1897 SUTTON, ARTHUR WARWICK (d. 1925, aged 71); senior partner in the firm of Messrs. Sutton & Sons, Reading, for some years a member of Council of the R.H.S.

1925 SUTTON, E. P. F.; one of the leading members of the seed trade and staunch supporter of the R.H.S., for many years being a member of Council and Vice-President of the Society.

1901 SWEET, JAMES (d. 1924, aged 85); founder of the firm of James Sweet & Sons Ltd., specializing in decorative plants for market, and an authority on ericas.

1955 TAYLOR, SIR GEORGE; botanist, Keeper of Botany at the British Museum, 1950–6, Director of the Royal Botanic Gardens, Kew, from 1956, authority on the genus *Meconopsis* and for several years on the Council of the R.H.S.

1937 TAYLOR, HAROLD VICTOR (d. 1965, aged 78); in the service of the Ministry of Agriculture from 1913, he was appointed first Senior Adviser to the National Agricultural Advisory Service; for many years a member of Council of the R.H.S. and chairman of its Examinations Board.

1926 THEOBALD, PROF. F. V. (d. 1930, aged 61); a great authority on injurious insects.

1948 THOMAS, HARRY H. (d. 1956, aged 79); horticultural journalist who was editor of *Popular Gardening* from 1907 until he retired in 1947.

1897 THOMAS, OWEN (d. 1923, aged 80); one with wide experience as a cultivator and for many years gardener to Queen Victoria.

1897 THOMPSON, DAVID (d. 1909 in his eighty-seventh year); great Scots gardener who for nearly thirty years maintained the Duke of Buccleuch's garden at Drumlanrig in the fore-front of British horticulture, specializing in almost every aspect of gardening.

1897 THOMPSON, WILLIAM (d. 1903 in his eighty-first year); founder of the famous establishment at Ipswich which later was to be known as Thompson & Morgan.

1952 TROTTER, R. D. (d. 1968, aged 80); skilful amateur gardener and three times Treasurer of the R.H.S.

1897 TURNER, HARRY (d. 1906); succeeded, with his brother, to the firm of Charles Turner of the Royal Nurseries, Slough, in 1885; particularly interested in carnations and auriculas.

1956 TURRILL, W. B. (d. 1961, aged 71); Kew botanist and keeper of the Kew Herbarium and Library from 1946 until he retired in 1957, authority on the flora of the Balkans and editor of the *Botanical Magazine*.

1906 VEITCH, SIR HARRY J. (d. 1924, aged 84); for fifty years the outstanding figure in horticulture, exercising more influence than any other on all things pertaining to gardening.

1916 VEITCH, PETER C. M. (d. 1929, aged 79); great-grandson of the founder of the house of Veitch, cousin of Sir Harry Veitch, and head of the firm of Robert Veitch & Sons.

1958 VINTEN, ALBERT GEORGE (d. 1962, aged 91); eminent chrysanthemum grower of Balcombe, Sussex, and a Vice-President of the National Chrysanthemum Society.

1936 WAKEHURST, LORD (d. 1936, aged 71); President of the R.H.S. and owner of Wakehurst Place, Sussex, one of the great gardens of the country.

1923 WALLACE, ROBERT W. (d. 1955, aged 88); an authority on lilies, narcissus and other bulbs, head of the nursery at The Old Gardens, Tunbridge Wells, exhibitor of formal and informal gardens at R.H.S. Shows and a one-time member of the R.H.S. Council.

1952 WALLACE, PROF. T. (d. 1965, aged 64); a member of the staff of Long Ashton Research Station for close on forty years and Director of the station from 1943 until he retired in 1958.

1926 WALLACE, W. E. (d. 1941); one of the pioneers of the cultivation of perpetual flowering carnations and raiser of many novelties.

1926 WATKINS, A. (d. 1937, aged 91); founder of the firm of Messrs. Watkins & Simpson, Wholesale Seedsmen, Drury Lane, London.

1916 WATSON, W. (d. 1925, aged 67); associated with the Royal Botanic Gardens, Kew, from 1879 until 1922, acting as Curator for twenty-one years.

1946 WEISS, PROF. F. E. (d. 1953, aged 88); for thirty-eight years Professor of Botany at the University of Manchester; after retiring he served the Linnean Society as president and the R.H.S. as a member of Council.

1920 WHITE, EDWARD (d. 1952); distinguished landscape gardener who planned the first Chelsea Flower Show and advised on the construction and alteration of many famous gardens.

1927 WHITE, H. (d. 1938, aged 81); noted cultivator and propagator, especially of Himalayan and Chinese rhododendrons, at the Sunningdale Nurseries, Windlesham, Surrey.

1927 WHITE, J. T. (d. 1930, aged 82); founder of the firm of Messrs. J. T. White & Sons, Daffodil Nurseries, Spalding, and one of the pioneers of the Lincolnshire bulb industry.

1952 WHITELEGG, G. G. (d. 1957, aged 80); noted landscape gardener, famous for his rock and water gardens at the Society's shows at Chelsea.

1912 WHITTON, JAMES (d. 1925 in his seventy-fifth year); Director of Parks under Glasgow Corporation, and strong supporter of horticultural and arboricultural causes in Scotland.

1914 WHYTOCK, JAMES (d. 1926, aged 81); gardener to the Duke of Buccleuch at Dalkeith, for a number of years president of the Scottish Agricultural Society as well as of the Botanical Society of Edinburgh.

1912 WILKS, THE REV. WILLIAM (d. 1923 in his eightieth year); for over half a century held a foremost position in horticultural activities, and for thirty-two years was Secretary of the R.H.S.

1927   WILLIAMS, P. D. (d. 1935, aged 70); in large measure the creator of the famous garden at Lanarth on The Lizard, and for forty years a successful hybridizer of daffodils and vice-chairman of the Society's Narcissus and Tulip Committee.

1897   WILLMOTT, MISS E. (d. 1934, aged 74); great gardener who made Warley Place, in Essex, formerly the home of John Evelyn, famous for its collection of trees, shrubs, alpines, lilies and daffodils; author of the magnificent work *The Genus Rosa.*

1943   WILSON, A. GURNEY (d. 1957, aged 79); outstanding orchidologist and benefactor to the R.H.S.

1912   WILSON, E. H. (d. 1930, aged 54); botanist, horticulturist, plant collector, introducer of many plants from China and Japan, author of important works on lilies, conifers and azaleas, and for over ten years associated with the Arnold Arboretum, U.S.A.

1897   WILSON, G. FERGUSON (d. 1902 in his eightieth year); a great amateur gardener, whose estate and woodland garden at Wisley was to become the Garden of the R.H.S., and for several years a member of the R.H.S. Council and various R.H.S. committees.

1950   WILSON, GUY LIVINGSTONE (d. 1962, aged 77); eminent breeder of daffodils, who, on seven occasions between 1922 and 1957, won the R.H.S. Engleheart Cup for the best exhibit of twelve daffodils raised by the exhibitor.

1897   WOLLEY-DOD, THE REV. C. (d. 1904, aged 78); renowned amateur gardener who cultivated a wide range of plants at his home at Edge Hall, Cheshire.

1897   WRIGHT, JOHN (d. 1916, aged 80); beginning his career in gardening and horticulture at the age of eight, he was for over twenty years sub-editor and editor of the *Journal of Horticulture,* became an expert on fruit culture, and pioneered school gardening.

1920   WRIGHT, SAMUEL T. (d. 1922 in his sixty-fourth year); first Superintendent of the R.H.S. Garden at Wisley, and renowned exhibitor of flowers, fruits, and vegetables.

1965   WYATT, O. E. P.; amateur gardener, particularly successful with the cultivation of lilies and other bulbous plants, and Treasurer of the R.H.S.

1897   WYTHES, GEORGE (d. 1916, aged 66); gardener to the Duke of Northumberland at Syon House, Brentford, and Alnwick Castle, Northumberland, and successful exhibitor of plants, fruits, and vegetables at the shows of the R.H.S.

1925   YELD, G. (d. 1938, aged 95); the great breeder of new cultivars of hemerocallis and bearded irises.

PAST AND PRESENT ASSOCIATES OF HONOUR

1954   ABBISS, H. W. (d. 1966); in the forefront in the commercialization of the daffodil and broccoli business in Cornwall.

1951   ALESWORTH, F. W. (d. 1966); horticultural journalist.

1933   ALEXANDER, J. (d. 1940); head gardener to Mrs. Wauchope, of Niddrie, Craigmillar, near Edinburgh.

1933   ALLEN, DONALD (d. 1955); manager of Messrs. Dobbie & Co.'s Seed Farms at Marks Tey, Essex.

1931   ANDERSON, T. W. (d. 1949); thirty-six years with Messrs. Laxton Bros. of Bedford, supervising the growing of the nursery stock including the firm's famous new fruits.

1931   ANDREWS, A. (d. 1937); Superintendent of Public Parks, Plymouth.

1930   ASHMORE, A. J. (d. 1959); Superintendent of Peckham Rye Park, London.

1957   AUSTIN, W.; Superintendent of Regent's Park.

1955   AYRES, W. G. (d. 1956); Superintendent of Parks, Nottingham.

1936   BAILEY, WILLIAM (d. 1955); head gardener at Crooksbury House, Farnham.

1942   BAKER, F. (d. 1945); Superintendent of Parks, Bournemouth.

1932   BAKER, W. G. (d. 1945); Curator of the Botanic Garden, Oxford.

1943   BALFOUR, A. P.; Superintendent of Messrs. Sutton & Sons' Seed Trial Grounds and Experimental Stations at Slough.

1942   BALL, H. (d. 1952); foreman of J. C. Allgrove Ltd.

1930   BANKS, G. H. (d. 1948); Curator of the Botanic Gardens, Glasgow.

1959   BARBOUR, T. C.; Superintendent, Central Royal Parks, London.

1953   BARNETT, M. J. (d. 1964); Director of Botanic Gardens, Parks and Reserves, Christchurch, New Zealand.

1934   BARRON, F. S. (d. 1959); manager of the seed department of Messrs. Bath Ltd., Wisbech.

1947   BARTLETT, A. C. (d. 1950); on the staff of the *Gardener's Chronicle*.

1964   BASSETT, G. B.; a director of Watkins & Simpson, where he served for many years.

1933   BEATTY, THOMAS (d. 1966); foreman of Messrs. Ben R. Cant & Sons.

1930   BEDFORD, A. (d. 1934); gardener to Lionel de Rothschild, Esq., Exbury, Hants.

1930   BENBOW, J. (d. 1939); former gardener to Sir Thomas Hanbury at the celebrated gardens at La Mortola.

1930   BENNETT, W. (d. 1941); Superintendent, Marine Parks, South Shields.

1931   BESANT, J. W. (d. 1944); Keeper of the Botanic Gardens at Glasnevin.

1941   BESANT, W. D. (d. 1946); Director of Parks and Botanic Gardens, Glasgow.

1945   BIRCH, F. E. (d. 1958); Superintendent of Greenwich Park.

1950   BISHOP, W. V.; Superintendent of Parks, Harrogate.

1954   BLACKBURN, A. (d. 1960); for over thirty years in charge of parks in Blackpool and one of the founder members of the Institute of Park Administration.

1931   BLAIR, C. (d. 1948); head gardener to Mr. Seaton Murray Thomson from 1901.

1931   BLAIR, P. C. (d. 1936); in charge of the gardens at Trentham, belonging to the Duke of Sutherland, from 1887 until they were closed in 1915.

1938   BLAKEY, W. J. (d. 1952); superintendent of the floral department, and later keeper of the Garden at Wisley.

1930   BLISS, D. (d. 1939); Superintendent of Public Parks, Swansea.

1961   BLOWERS, J. W.; head gardener to Hon. Mrs. Ionides at Buxted Park, and editor of *Orchid Review*.

1966   BODDY, F. A.; Director of Parks at Ealing.

1936   BOLAS, T. W. (d. 1958); head gardener at Mount Stewart, Newtownards, Co. Down.

1952   BOND, J. (d. 1957); gardener to Mr. Loudon of Olantigh, Wye, Kent, and successful exhibitor of fruit.

1953   BOYES, D.; noted for his outstanding breeding work on strawberries and other horticultural crops at the (now defunct) Horticultural Research Station at Cambridge.

1937   BRACE, JOSH (d. 1950); foreman at Messrs. Rivers' Nurseries.

1931   BREW, E. U. (d. 1946); foreman to Messrs. Charlesworth from 1899.

1964   BREWER, M. E.; manager for eighteen years of the Home Nurseries of Messrs. Carters Tested Seeds Ltd.

1949   BROOKS, A. J.; former Curator of the Botanic Gardens, St. Lucia.

1949   BROWN, F. C. (d. 1951); the Society's trials officer at Wisley.

1930   BROWN, J. (d. 1930); gardener to A. A. H. Speirs, Esq., Houston House, Houston, Renfrewshire.

1930   BROWN, W. T. (d. 1952); of the Horticultural Section of the Ministry of Agriculture in Egypt.

1951   BUCKHURST, C. T. (d. 1961); forty-seven years of service with Messrs. Carters Tested Seeds Ltd.

1938   BUCKMAN, J. (d. 1959); head gardener at Highdown, Goring-by-Sea.

1931   BULLOCK, A. (d. 1957); head gardener at Copped Hall Gardens for thirty years.

1945   BURGESS, A. E. (d. 1950); formerly Horticultural Superintendent to the Surrey County Council.

1934   BURTON, MISS MARY (d. 1944); late head gardener to the Private Mental Institution, New Saughtonhall, Polton, Midlothian, and one-time president of the Scottish Horticultural Society.

1946   BUSH, F. A.; formerly head gardener at Dell Park, Englefield Green.

1930   BUSS, F. (d. 1930); foreman to Messrs. George Bunyard & Co., The Royal Nurseries, Maidstone, Kent.

1957   CALLER, J. T.; assistant nursery manager, Messrs. John Waterer, Sons & Crisp Ltd., Bagshot.

1931   CAMERON, J. (d. 1935); served as head gardener for three proprietors at Auchterarder.

1937   CAMPBELL, D. (d. 1950); Superintendent of Regent's Park, London.

1930   CARPENTER, G. (d. 1935); gardener to F. Stoop, Esq., West Hall, Byfleet.

1951   CARTWRIGHT, W. D.; chief clerk at R.H.S. Garden, Wisley.

1932   CHISHOLM, J. S. (d. 1942); head of Department of Horticulture in the Edinburgh and East of Scotland College of Agriculture.

1933   CHRISTY, J. S. (d. 1961); Park Superintendent for the Metropolitan Borough of Camberwell.

1933   CLARK, W. B. (d. 1938); Park Superintendent for the City of Aberdeen.

1939   CLARK, WILLIAM (d. 1963); Superintendent of Parks and Cemeteries, Southport.

1931   COATES, A. W. (d. 1967); head gardener to Mr. G. W. E. Loder for twenty-seven years.

1950   COCKER, H.; gardener to Captain N. McEacharn, Villa Taranto, Pallanza, Italy.

1930   COMBER, J. (d. 1953); gardener to Lieut.-Col. L. C. R. Messel, Nymans, Handcross, Sussex.

1957   CONINGSBY, A. R. (d. 1966); for twenty-three years on the staff of Messrs. Sanders (St. Albans) Ltd., St. Albans.

1958   CONN, P. W. H.; Superintendent of Parks and Gardens, Liverpool.

1931   COOK, C. H. (d. 1963); head gardener at the Royal Gardens at Windsor.

1944   COOK, H. H. (d. 1957); Superintendent of the Reading University Horticultural Station at Shinfield.

1946   COOK, L. J. (d. 1959); of the Stuart Low Co.

1930   COOK, T. H. (d. 1947); gardener to H. M. The King, Sandringham, King's Lynn, Norfolk.

1966   COOLING, F. W.; head gardener at Wergs Hall, where he has served for over forty years.

1930   COOPER, E. W. (d. 1950); foreman to Messrs. Sanders, St. Albans, Herts.

1947   COUSINS, F. G. (d. 1963); late Superintendent of Parks, Torquay.

1930   COUTTS, J. (d. 1952); Senior Assistant Curator, and from 1932 to 1937, Curator, Royal Botanic Gardens, Kew, Surrey.

1965   COWARD, E. J. H.; in charge of parks and gardens of Douglas, Isle of Man.

1966   COX, S.; senior foreman at Messrs. Hillier, with whom he has worked for over thirty-six years.

1966   CRAMP, K. V.; for over thirty-five years has been occupied with horticultural teaching and advisory work, almost entirely in Cambridgeshire.

1961   CRANE, H. S. J.; director of R. C. Notcutt Ltd., Woodbridge.

1932   CRAVEN, W. (d. 1946); head gardener to the Weymouth Corporation.

1946   CREASEY, W. G. (d. 1966); of Thomas Rochford & Sons Ltd.

1966   CROSS, J. (d. 1967); in gardens for seventy years and for thirty-five years head gardener to Sir Frederick Wills.

1950   DAKERS, J. S.; late assistant editor of *Amateur Gardening*.

1931   DAVIDSON, J. J. (d. 1947); head gardener for twenty-six years to Sir John Reid of Ardencraig.

1962   DEE, R. E.; nursery manager to Messrs. Waterer, Sons & Crisp Ltd.

1946   DEW, C. J.; of Messrs. George Monro Ltd.

1961   DODSON, H. J.; head gardener to Colonel Ward and successful cultivator and exhibitor of vegetables.

1953   DOWNES, E. G. (d. 1957); Superintendent of Public Parks, Jamaica.

1949   DREW, R. J. (d. 1965); of Messrs. Alex. Dickson & Sons Ltd. (Hawlmark), Marks Tey, Essex.

1963 DYKES, P. J. (d. 1964); superintendent of the glass-house department at Wisley.

1938 ELPHICK, H. (d. 1966); nursery manager of Messrs. R. Wallace, Tunbridge Wells.

1960 EVISON, J. R. B.; Director of Parks, Brighton.

1945 FALCONER, A. (d. 1961); Superintendent of Stamford Park, Stalybridge.

1949 FARMER, R. E.; orchid grower to H. W. B. Schröder, Esq., Dell Park, Englefield Green, Surrey.

1957 FINDLAY, T. H.; head gardener, Windsor Great Park.

1940 FITT, J. E. (d. 1962); head gardener to the Hon. Mrs. E. S. Montagu.

1953 FLEMING, W. (d. 1965); gardener to Col. R. S. Clarke at Borde Hill, Haywards Heath, Sussex.

1946 GAULT, S. M.; head gardener at St. Andrews Hospital, Northampton; later Superintendent at Regent's Park, London.

1932 GIBSON, E. (d. 1945); of the headquarters staff of the London County Council Parks Department.

1930 GILES, W. F. (d. 1962); vegetable expert to Messrs. Sutton & Sons, Reading.

1934 GINGELL, W. B. (d. 1936); late Superintendent of Dulwich Park (L.C.C.).

1956 GOODCHILD, H. J. (d. 1961); gardener at Queen Anne's School, Caversham.

1950 GOULD, N. K. (d. 1960); the Society's botanist at Wisley.

1948 GOWER, A. H. (d. 1958); gardener to Col. C. B. Krabble, and expert sweet pea grower.

1946 GRANT, J. M. (d. 1961); head gardener at Grayswood Hill, Haslemere, Surrey.

1943 GREENFIELD, R. (d. 1956); representative and horticultural adviser of Messrs. John Peed & Son.

1959 GREENSMITH, H. P.; Superintendent of Parks, city of Nairobi.

1960 GROVES, G.; Director of Agriculture, Bermuda.

1930 GUTTRIDGE, J. J. (d. 1952); Chief Superintendent and Curator of Parks and Gardens, Liverpool.

1966 HABGOOD, H.; chrysanthemum expert in the service of Woolmans.

1932 HALES, W. (d. 1937); Curator of the Chelsea Physic Garden.

1949 HALL, H. J.; gardener to the Earl of Harewood, Harewood House, Leeds.

1941 HALLETT, G. F. (d. 1966); head gardener at Lilford Hall, Oundle, Peterborough.

1939 HANGER, F. E. W. (d. 1961); head gardener at Exbury House, Exbury, Southampton; later Curator at Wisley.

1964 HANVEY, J.; for more than thirty years head gardener at Rowallane, Northern Ireland.

1934 HARRISON, A. T. (d. 1949); head gardener at the Training Centre of the National Committee for the Training of Teachers, Jordanhill, Glasgow.

1964 HARRISON, A. T.; Superintendent of Parks, Edinburgh.

1930 HARROW, G. (d. 1940); late foreman to Messrs. Veitch, Coombe Wood, Kingston Hill.

1953 HELLYER, A. G. L.; editor of *Amateur Gardening* and *Gardening Illustrated*.

1962 HENLEY, G.; nursery manager to W. E. Th. Ingwersen Ltd.

1930 HILL, J. (d. 1954); gardener to Andrew Arthur, Esq., Rosemount, Monkton, Ayrshire.

1948 HILLS, B. (d. 1960); orchid grower to Edmund de Rothschild, Esq., at Exbury, near Southampton.

1931 HOARE, J. (d. 1932); foreman to Messrs. J. H. White of Worcester for fifty-four years.

1956 HOBBIS, E. W.; Plantation Officer, Long Ashton Research Station, Bristol.

1967 HOGG, R. D.; on the staff of the Commonwealth War Graves Commission and for many years the Commission's Regional Horticultural Officer in Rome.

1958 HOLDER, R. J. (d. 1968); superintendent of the Rock Garden at the Society's Garden at Wisley.

1957 HOLLOWAY, W. H. (d. 1963); sometime gardener to Lady Beit at Tewin Water.

1930 HOLTON, R. H. (d. 1946); fifty years' service in the firm of Messrs. J. Cheal & Sons Ltd., The Nurseries, Crawley, Sussex.

1930 HONESS, W. H. (d. 1937); head gardener at Walkempton, Lymington, Hants, and a specialist in rare trees and shrubs.

1944 HOPE, J.; head gardener at Ness, Neston, Wirral, Cheshire.

1932 HORWOOD, F. (d. 1962); foreman to Messrs. Kelways Ltd.

1931 HOSKING, A. (d. 1938); on the staff of the John Innes Horticultural Institute from 1919 to 1931.

1930 HOWE, W. (d. 1930); gardener at 65 Nimrod Road, Streatham Park, London S.W.16.

1966 HUGHES, J. J.; head gardener to the Bristol and West of England Zoological Society.

1963 HUNTLEY, R. J.; for nearly forty years with Messrs. Sutton & Sons Ltd., and for ten years head of their Slough nurseries.

1933 INGRAM, GEORGE J. E. (d. 1935); secretary of the Gardeners' Royal Benevolent Institution.

1930 IRVING, W. (d. 1934); late Assistant Curator, Royal Botanic Gardens, Kew, Surrey.

1930 ISBELL, W. (d. 1943); fifty-three years with the firm of Messrs. Hugh Low & Co., latterly Messrs. Stuart Low & Co.

1951 IZZARD, J. P. (d. 1966); gardener to the Rev. Canon Rollo Meyer, of Little Gaddesden, Herts.

1934 JANES, E. R. (d. 1958); of Messrs. Sutton & Sons Ltd.

1931 JEARY, T. J. P. (d. 1943); thirty-two years of service with Messrs. George Monro.

1939 JEFFREY, J. (d. 1955); head gardener at Lowther Castle, Penrith.

1940 JEFFREY, J. T. (d. 1961); Superintendent of City Parks, Edinburgh.

1930 JENKINS, W. A. (d. 1941); Curator of Stockton Park.

1964 JEOFFROY, R. A.; for nearly forty years employed by Messrs. Sutton & Sons Ltd.

1938 JOHNSON, G. F. (d. 1954); head gardener at Waddesdon Manor, Aylesbury.

1958 JOHNSON, J. (d. 1963); head gardener at Dartington Hall.

1930 JOHNSON, W. E. (d. 1937); for fifty-two years foreman with Messrs. W. Fuller & Son at Newton Abbot.

1931 JONES, J. (d. 1934); former Curator of the Botanic Gardens at Dominica.

1932 JONES, J. (d. 1933); head gardener to R. J. Corbett, Esq., of Ynys-y-Maengwyn, Towyn.

1930 JORDAN, F. (d. 1958); gardener to Lieut.-Col. H. Spender-Clay, Ford Manor, Lingfield, Surrey.

1956 KEIR, R.; gardener to Mrs. R. M. Stevenson at Tower Court, Ascot.

1930 KETTLETY, A. (d. 1951); forty years with Messrs. Blackmore & Langdon of Bath.

1957 KING, J. H.; for thirty-six years head gardener at the University of Leeds.

1950 KITCHING, W. H.; gardener to the Hon. George Vestey, Warter Priory Gardens, Pocklington.

1947 KNELLER, J. (d. 1951 or '52); late head gardener at Penrhyn Castle Gardens.

1964 KNIGHT, L. G.; Director of Parks Department, Leeds.

1931 LANE, G. T. (d. 1936); retired Curator of the Royal Botanic Gardens, Calcutta (1895–1924).

1952 LAVENDER, W. L.; of Messrs. Carters Tested Seeds Ltd.

1965 LEE, A.; show manager for Messrs. Carters Tested Seeds Ltd.

1956 LINDORES, T. (d. 1963); gardener to the Earl of Rosebery at Mentmore, Leighton Buzzard.

1930 LOGAN, W. (d. 1942); foreman at Messrs. Perry's Hardy Plant Farm, Enfield.

1931 LONG, E. (d. 1947); Superintendent of the Government Gardens, Simla, India.

1932 LONG, F. R. (d. 1962); Superintendent of Public Parks, Port Elizabeth, South Africa.

1956 LORD, S. L.; for many years Superintendent of Shenley Hospital Gardens, and successful cultivator and exhibitor of fruit.

1962 LUXTON, H.; for more than forty years with the British War Graves Commission overseas.

1931 McDONALD, F. W. (d. 1940); fifty years of service with Messrs. Sutton, from 1869.

1931 MacDONALD, J. V. (d. 1936); gardener to Sir George Kenrich.

1930 MacFIE, J. B. (d. 1938); manager of seed department of Messrs. Dobbie & Co. Ltd. (thirty-nine years in service).

1932 McINNES, D. (d. 1955); head gardener to the Earl of Strathmore, Glamis Castle.

1931 McINTOSH, D. F. (d. 1959); foreman with Messrs. Bath of Wisbech.

1966 MacKENZIE, M.; head gardener at Ilnacullin, Garinish Island, Eire, now belonging to the Commissioners of Public Works.

1954 MacKENZIE, W. G.; Curator of the Chelsea Physic Garden.

1930 McLAREN, J. (d. 1943); Superintendent, Park of the Golden Gate, San Francisco, U.S.A.

1934 McLEOD BRAGGINS, S. W. (d. 1960); superintendent of the gardens of Mr. Cecil Hanbury at La Mortola, Ventimiglia, Italy.

1942 MacMILLAN, H. F. (d. 1948); formerly Superintendent of the Royal Botanic Gardens, Ceylon.

1960 McMILLAN, R. C.; Director of Parks, Manchester.

1931 MACRAE, A. (d. 1946); Chief Superintendent of the Parks Department, Dundee, from 1908.

1931   MAITLAND, T. D.; Superintendent of the Botanic Gardens at Victoria in the British Cameroons.

1945   MALTHOUSE, G. T. (d. 1952); formerly horticultural adviser to the Salop County Council.

1932   MANN, P. (d. 1937); horticultural instructor and adviser to the Buckingham County Council.

1932   MARKHAM, E. (d. 1937); head gardener to Mr. Wm. Robinson of Gravetye Manor, East Grinstead.

1932   MARKHAM, H. (d. 1943); head gardener to the Earl of Strafford, Wrotham Park.

1930   MARLOW, W. J. (d. 1955); Superintendent of Hampton Court Gardens.

1964   MARTIN, D.; Australian horticulturist and authority on *Eucalyptus*.

1957   MASON, C. E. (d. 1959); for twenty-six years head gardener at Cheadle Royal Hospital.

1931   MATTHEWS, J. W. (d. 1949); Curator of the Botanic Gardens, Kirstenbosch, South Africa.

1943   MESSENGER, W. A. (d. 1945); formerly head gardener at Woolverstone Park.

1930   METCALFE, A. W. (d. 1961); head gardener, Luton Hoo, Luton, Bedfordshire.

1945   MICHAEL, F. C.; head gardener at Caerhays Castle, Cornwall.

1937   MIDDLETON, C. H. (d. 1945); horticultural instructor to the Surrey County Council.

1946   MILLER, G. J.; head gardener at Bayham Abbey.

1961   MILLS, H. G.; for over fifty years with the firm of Messrs. Baker.

1940   MILLS, W. E. (d. 1958); foreman to Messrs. Cheal & Sons Ltd., with whom he served for over fifty years.

1940   MITCHELL, W. J. (d. 1965); of the Arboretum, Westonbirt, Tetbury, Glos.

1935   MOORE, H. J. (d. 1946); horticultural consultant to the Ontario Government.

1959   MORGAN, L. E.; horticultural adviser, Ministry of Transport.

1930   MUDGE, E. C. (d. 1962); foreman to Messrs. Barr & Sons, Covent Garden, London W.C.2.

1945   MULLINS, C. (d. 1950); head gardener at Eastnor Castle.

1933   MUSTOE, W. R. (d. 1942); late Superintendent of the Agricultural and Horticultural Department, Delhi.

1930   NEAL, E. (d. 1951); gardener to C. G. A. Nix, Esq., Tilgate, Crawley, Sussex, for thirty-four years.

1946 NELMES, W.; Superintendent of Parks at Cardiff.

1959 NEWELL, J.; Curator, The John Innes Horticultural Institute, Herts.

1934 NOBBS, G. (d. 1945); head gardener at Osborne House, Isle of Wight.

1930 OLIVER, W. (d. 1945); foreman to Messrs. John Forbes of Hawick for forty years.

1940 OSBORN, A. (d. 1964); Deputy Curator at the Royal Botanic Gardens, Kew.

1960 PAGE, MISS MARY; horticulturist, Wye College.

1930 PAGE, W. H. (d. 1949); gardener to Miss Moore, Chardwar, Bourton-on-the-Water, Glos.

1963 PARR, J. H.; for some forty years with Messrs. Carters Tested Seeds Ltd.

1958 PARSONS, H.; head gardener to Her Majesty the Queen at Sandringham.

1931 PATEMAN, T. (d. 1933); head gardener, first at 'The Node' and then at Brocket Hall, with Sir Charles Nall-Cain, Bt., from 1906.

1962 PATRICK, E.; Parks Superintendent at Southport, and showground manager for the Southport Flower Show.

1958 PEARCE, S. A.; Assistant Curator, Royal Botanic Gardens, Kew.

1933 PERFECT, BERTRAM F. (d. 1954); orchid grower to Sir Jeremiah Colman, Bt., at Gatton Park, Surrey.

1950 PHILLIPS, A. (d. 1957); of Messrs. Stuart Low & Co., for whom he worked for fifty-six years.

1954 PHILLIPS, W. (d. 1960); gardener to F. W. J. Fox, Esq., of The Hall, Leighton, Shrewsbury.

1955 PINKER, R. D. (d. 1968); of Messrs. Sutton & Sons Ltd., Reading.

1961 POTTER, F. G.; for over forty years with Sutton & Sons Ltd.

1967 POULTON, A. L.; for more than twenty-five years a member of the Parks Department of the Brighton Corporation.

1936 PRESTON, F. G. (d. 1964); Curator of the University Botanic Garden, Cambridge.

1954 PRINCE, H.; of Messrs. Sutton & Sons Ltd., Reading.

1938 PRIOR, J. (d. 1947); foreman of Messrs. D. Stewart, Ferndown, Dorset.

1959 PRIOR, W. A.; head propagator, Messrs. Hillier & Sons.

1931 PRITCHARD, W. J. (d. 1941); foreman and right-hand man to Mr. Beckett, the veteran gardener to the Hon. Vicary Gibbs at Aldenham House.

1965 PROCTER, J. R.; editor of the *Home Gardener*.

1957 PUDDLE, C. E.; head gardener to Lord Aberconway and the National Trust at Bodnant, Tal-y-cafn, Denbighshire, North Wales.

1930 PUDDLE, F. C. (d. 1952); gardener to Lord Aberconway, Bodnant, Tal-y-cafn.

1933 RADLEY, SAMUEL (d. 1946); foreman of Messrs. Robert Veitch & Son Ltd.

1934 RAFFILL, C. P. (d. 1951); Assistant Curator at the Royal Botanic Gardens, Kew.

1960 RAMSEY, E. G. (d. 1962); general manager to Mr. Stuart Ogg.

1948 READER, C. H. (d. 1965); lately Superintendent of the Viceregal Gardens, New Delhi.

1958 REEVES, B. (d. 1961); for over forty years on the staff of Messrs. R. W. Wallace & Co.

1950 RICHARDS, WILLIAM (d. 1951); of Messrs. Bees Ltd.

1946 RICHARDSON, J. (d. 1961); Superintendent of Parks at Manchester.

1962 RIVERS, W. G. (d. 1967); spent the whole of his career with Messrs. Blackmore & Langdon; senior foreman in the begonia department.

1946 ROBINSON, G. W.; Curator of the University Botanic Garden, Oxford.

1943 ROGERS, F. M. (d. 1952); formerly Curator at the Amani Institute, Tanganyika.

1930 ROGERS, J. (d. 1946); late Superintendent of Battersea Park.

1937 ROSE, FRED J. (d. 1956); head gardener at Townhill Park, Southampton.

1964 ROSE, J.; has spent the whole of his working life with Waterer, Sons & Crisp Ltd.

1967 RUDD, C.; for twenty years Park Superintendent at Wood Green and for long played a prominent part in the affairs of the Institute of Park and Recreation Administration.

1951 RYE, R. S. (d. 1967); gardener to the Earl of Stair, Lochinch Castle, Stranraer, Wigtownshire.

1940 SAUNDERS, ARTHUR (d. 1964); late foreman to Messrs. Hillier & Sons.

1960 SAYERS, R.; gardener to Mr. Maurice Mason, King's Lynn.

1930 SCOTT, J. W. (d. 1938); grower with Messrs. Lowe & Shawyer of Uxbridge for thirty years.

1952 SETFORD, T. H. (d. 1965); gardener to Captain A. Granville Soames, Sheffield Park, Sussex.

1966 SHEFFORD, R. W.; foreman of the Savill Garden, Windsor, for over thirty-five years.

1967 SHEPPARD, A. L.; for twenty-five years with the firm of Messrs. Black-more and Langdon.

1930 SHILL, J. E. (d. 1940); orchid grower to Baron Schröder, Dell Park, Englefield Green, Surrey.

1938 SILLARS, R. K. (d. 1946); late foreman of Messrs. Samsons, Kilmar-nock.

1930 SILLITOE, F. S. (d. 1957); Superintendent, Palace Gardens, Khartoum.

1946 SMITH, ROLAND D.; head gardener at Weston Hall.

1933 SMITH, S. (d. 1946); head gardener to H. B. Fox, Esq., at Penjerrick, Falmouth, Cornwall.

1961 SPENCER, H.; for many years assistant to F. Rose, Esq., and later to F. Streeter, Esq.

1955 STENNING, L. (d. 1965); Assistant Curator, and later Curator, at the Royal Botanic Gardens, Kew.

1930 STEWART, L. B. (d. 1934); propagator, Royal Botanic Garden, Edinburgh.

1938 STEWART, W. (d. 1938); Superintendent of the Grounds, Royal Hospital, Chelsea.

1930 STREET, C. (d. 1946); head gardener at Floors Castle, Kelso, Roxburghshire.

1941 STREETER, FRED; head gardener at Petworth Park, Petworth, Sussex.

1949 STUDLEY, E. W.; Parks Superintendent, Alexandra Park, Portsmouth, Hants.

1930 TANNOCK, D. (d. 1953); Superintendent, Reserves Department, Botanic Gardens, Dunedin, New Zealand.

1932 TAYLOR, G. (d. 1941); head gardener to Sir John Ramsden, Bt., of Bulstrode Park.

1932 TAYLOR, G. M. (d. 1955); of Messrs. Dobbie & Co. Ltd.

1961 TAYLOR, H.; horticulturist to L.C.C.

1931 TAYLOR, T. W. (d. 1932); Curator of the Royal Botanic Gardens, Kew.

1966 TETHER, N. L.; joint managing director of Watkins & Simpson, with his entire working life spent in the seed trade.

1955 THODAY, R. E.; gardener to St. John's College, Cambridge.

1952 THOMAS, J. (d. 1954); of Messrs. McBean's Orchids Ltd., and breeder of cymbidiums.

1962 THROWER, P. J.; Parks Superintendent at Shrewsbury and television gardening personality.

1943 TOMALIN, T. E. (d. 1954); head gardener at Stansted Park.

1932 TROUGHTON, F. (d. 1951); nursery manager to Messrs. J. H. White & Co. Ltd.

1933 TUCKER, S. W. (d. 1948); head gardener to the Earl of Radnor at Longford Castle, Salisbury, Wilts.

1962 TUFFIN, H. R.; the Society's garden adviser.

1961 TURK, W. T.; nursery manager to the firm of L. R. Russell Ltd.

1935 TUSTIN, F.; head gardener at Abbotswood, Stow-on-the-Wold.

1934 USHER, A. E. (d. 1954); head gardener to Sir Randolf Baker, Bt., at Ranston House, Blandford, Dorset.

1932 VASEY, A. E. (d. 1934); of Messrs. Carter Page & Co. Ltd.

1942 VINE, J. E. (d. 1946); late garden adviser to the Society.

1936 WADDS, A. B. (d. 1946); head gardener at Englefield House, Reading.

1930 WAKELY, C. (d. 1932); of the horticultural department of the East Anglian Institute in Agriculture.

1965 WALKER, P.; vegetable trials superintendent and trials recorder at Wisley.

1956 WALLIS, R. J. (d. 1966); gardener to Sir Henry Price, Bt., at Wakehurst Place, Ardingly, Sussex.

1964 WARD, E. F.; has spent the whole of his working life with W. J. Unwin Ltd.

1961 WATSON, J. W.; Superintendent of the Parks Department, Leicester.

1930 WEBSTER, C. (d. 1939); gardener to the Duke of Richmond and Gordon, Gordon Castle, Fochabers, Morayshire.

1967 WELLS, D. V.; since the war with the Horticultural Advisory Service and the giver of much counsel to the Ministry of Transport, the Middlesex County Council, and the Roads Beautifying Association.

1953 WELLS, T. S. (d. 1960); Superintendent of Parks, Derby.

1930 WESTON, J. G. (d. 1943); head gardener to the Duke of Devonshire at Chatsworth, Bakewell.

1952 WHITNER, H.; gardener to Sir Giles Loder, Bt., of Leonardslee, Horsham, Sussex.

1945 WILKIE, DAVID (d. 1961); Deputy Curator, Royal Botanic Garden, Edinburgh.

1965 WILLARD, F.; for more than forty years with Messrs. Goatcher of Washington, Sussex, and foreman in charge of propagating department.

1931 WILLIAMS, R. O. (d. 1967); Superintendent of the Royal Botanic Gardens, Trinidad.

1947 WILSON, J. (d. 1957); the garden adviser of the R.H.S.

1941 WINDIBANK, H. (d. 1955); head gardener at Frensham Hall, Haslemere, Surrey.

1954 WISEMAN, P.; of Messrs. John Waterer, Sons & Crisp Ltd., Bagshot, Surrey.

1946 WITT, A. W. (d. 1956); formerly at the East Malling Research Station.

1932 WOOD, G. F. (d. 1943); gardener to E. M. Preston, Esq., of The Warren, Hayes.

1957 WOODHAMS, H. J. (d. 1957); of Messrs. Armstrong & Brown, Tunbridge Wells, where he served for over fifty years.

1930 WOODWARD, J. G. (d. 1941); gardener to Colonel Sir Charles E. Warde, Bt., Barham Court, Teston, Maidstone.

1935 WORT, J. (d. 1940); of Messrs. Dickson & Robinson Ltd., Manchester.

1961 WYNNIATT, F.; for many years gardener to Mr. Edmund de Rothschild, at Exbury, and successful cultivator of rhododendrons.

1962 YOUNGER, R. W.; Superintendent of the University Botanic Garden, Cambridge.

VEITCH MEMORIAL TRUST

1922 MR. W. J. BEAN. Silver Medal and £50 for his work on trees and shrubs.

DR. LLOYD PRAEGER. Silver Medal and £50 for his monograph, *The Genus Sedum.*

1923 MR. E. A. BOWLES. Gold Medal for his work on crocuses, colchicums, and other garden plants.

MR. R. IRWIN LYNCH. Gold Medal. Late Curator of the Cambridge Botanic Garden.

MR. JOHN HEAL. Gold Medal. Late foreman to Messrs. James Veitch and Sons.

MR. J. O'BRIEN. Silver Medal for his work on orchids.

MR. S. MORRIS. Silver Medal for raising new montbretias.

MR. T. G. HODGSON. Silver Medal. Chairman of the Council of the York Gala.

MR. A. B. JACKSON. } Silver Medal and £25 each for their work on
MR. W. DALLIMORE. } the Coniferae.

1924 ABERDEEN EXHIBITION. { Medal and £5 to the VISCOUNTESS COWDRAY (gardener: Mr. W. Smith), for the best exhibit of fruit.

MR. H. CORREVON. Gold Medal for his work on alpines.

MR. J. M. C. HOOG. Gold Medal for his work in introducing into cultivation many good garden plants.

MR. W. R. DYKES. Silver Medal and £50 for his monograph, *The Genus Iris.*

MISS L. SNELLING. Silver Medal and £25 for her botanical illustrations.

1925 EDINBURGH INTERNATIONAL SHOW { Silver Medal and £5 to the VISCOUNTESS COWDRAY (gardener: Mr. W. Smith), for stove and greenhouse plants.

Medal and £2. 10s. to EARL BALFOUR (gardener: Mr. G. F. Anderson), for dessert fruit.

MR. E. H. WILSON. Gold Medal for his introductions to gardens and his books.

MR. W. P. THOMSON. Gold Medal for his journalistic work in connection with horticulture.

1926 MR. MARK FENWICK (gardener: Mr. F. Tustin). Gold Medal for alpines.

DUNDEE CENTENARY SHOW
{
Silver Medal and £5 to the EARL OF STRATHMORE (gardener: Mr. D. McInnes), for grapes.

Medal and £2. 10s. to MR. P. DONALDSON, for vegetables.
}

MR. GEORGE FORREST. Gold Medal for his explorations and introductions.

MR. JAMES HUDSON. Gold Medal for his general services to horticulture.

THE REV. G. H. ENGLEHEART. Gold Medal for his work on daffodils.

MR. H. B. MAY. Gold Medal for his general services to horticulture.

MISS M. SMITH. Silver Medal and £25 for her botanical draughtsmanship.

MR. W. CAMP. Silver Medal and £25. Late foreman to Messrs. T. Rivers & Son.

1927 IRIS SOCIETY'S FIRST SHOW. Silver Medal to MR. B. R. LONG for irises.

PROFESSOR L. H. BAILEY. Gold Medal for his scientific work on behalf of horticulture.

MR. JOHN BASHAM. Gold Medal for his general services in fruit cultivation.

MR. FREDERICK J. HANBURY. Gold Medal for his work in the preservation and cultivation of the British flora and the raising of orchids.

MR. FRANK READER. Silver Medal and £50 on his retirement from the service of the Society.

1928 HARROGATE SHOW
{
Silver Medal and £5 to DR. W. L. SPINK and MR. C. F. SPINK for a group of plants.

Medal and £2. 10s. to MR. R. JONES for begonias.
}

MISS GERTRUDE JEKYLL. Gold Medal and £50 for her services to horticulture.

MR. C. G. A. NIX. Gold Medal for his services to the Society.

MR. JOHN FRASER. Silver Medal and £50 for his work on *Pelargonium, Salix* and *Mentha*.

MR. SAMUEL SMITH. Silver Medal for his work in hybridizing rhododendrons.

MR. W. REYNOLDS-STEPHENS. Silver Medal for his work in connection with the Sculpture Section of the International Exhibition of Garden Design, 17–24 October 1928.

1929   CORNWALL SPRING FLOWER SHOW, TRURO   { Silver Medal and £5 to REV. A. T. BOSCAWEN for group of twelve shrubs.

Medal and £2. 10s. to MISS WINGFIELD for Kurume azaleas. }

NORFOLK AND NORWICH HORTICULTURAL SOCIETY'S CENTENARY SHOW   { Silver Medal and £5 to MR. G. LANG for delphiniums (gardener: Mr. F. Sheldrake).

Medal and £2. 10s. to MR. GORDON WINTER for seedling pinks. }

DR. A. B. RENDLE. Gold Medal and £50 on his retirement from the keepership of Botany at the Natural History Museum and for his services to the Society.

PROFESSOR W. WRIGHT SMITH. Gold Medal for his work on the genus *Primula*.

MR. E. BECKETT. Silver Medal and £25 for his services to horticulture.

1930   MR. W. HALES. Silver Medal and £25 for his work at the Physic Garden, Chelsea.

CAPT. J. S. PARKER. Silver Medal and £25 for his work on the war cemeteries in France, Belgium, and Italy.

DR. M. J. SIRKS. Silver Medal for his work in connection with the International Horticultural Congress, 7–15 August 1930.

1931   THE MARQUIS OF HEADFORT. Gold Medal for his paper and exhibits at the Conifer Conference, together with £5 to his gardener, Mr. J. A. Boyle.

DR. O. STAPF. Gold Medal on the completion of the publication of the *Index Londinensis*.

DR. L. COCKAYNE. Silver Medal and £25 for his services to horticulture.

1932   SIR DAVID PRAIN. Gold Medal for his services to horticulture.

SIR FREDERICK MOORE. Gold Medal for his services to horticulture.

DR. R. LLOYD PRAEGER. Silver Medal and £50 for his work on sempervivums.

1933   SIR HERBERT MAXWELL. Gold Medal for his writings, paintings, and other work for horticulture.

MR. A. GROVE. Gold Medal for his work on lilies.

MR. W. J. BEAN. Silver Medal and £25 on the publication of Volume III of *Trees and Shrubs Hardy in the British Isles.*

MR. A. SIMMONDS. Silver Medal and £25 for his work in connection with the organization of the Lily Conference.

MR. H. R. HUTCHINSON. Silver Medal on his retirement from the Lindley Library.

1934 MR. E. A. BUNYARD. Gold Medal for his contributions to pomology.

MR. F. KINGDON WARD. Gold Medal for his explorations and the introduction of new plants.

DR. GEORGE TAYLOR. Silver Medal and £25 for his work on *Meconopsis.*

1935 LORD WAKEHURST. Gold Medal for his services to horticulture.

DR. E. J. SALISBURY. Gold Medal for his book, *The Living Garden.*

MR. A. D. COTTON. Gold Medal for his services to horticulture.

MR. E. H. WOODALL. Silver Medal for his services to horticulture.

1936 SIR ARTHUR HILL. Gold Medal for his services to horticulture.

MR. R. W. WALLACE. Gold Medal for his services to horticulture.

MR. R. L. HARROW. Silver Medal and £25 for his services to horticulture.

1937 MR. C. H. CURTIS. Gold Medal for his journalistic work in connection with horticulture.

MR. J. COUTTS. Silver Medal and £25 for his work in connection with the Empire Exhibition at Chelsea Show.

MR. DAVID WILKIE. Silver Medal and £25 for his book, *Gentians.*

MR. G. RUSSELL. Silver Medal for his work in selecting the Russell strain of lupins.

1938 MISS ISABELLA PRESTON. Gold Medal for her work in raising good garden plants.

MR. M. B. CRANE. Gold Medal for his work on the genetics of fruit trees.

1939 SIR DANIEL HALL. Gold Medal for his services to horticulture.

DR. KATE BARRATT. Silver Medal for her services to horticulture.

1940 MR. T. HAY. Gold Medal on his retirement from the position of Superintendent of the Royal Parks and for his introduction of new plants.

MR. W. C. WORSDELL. Silver-gilt Medal and £25 on the completion of his work for the Supplement to the *Index Londinensis.*

MR. L. R. RUSSELL. Silver Medal for his long services to horticulture.

1941 MR. DONALD MacKELVIE. Gold Medal for his work in connection with potato breeding.

MR. B. Y. MORRISON. Gold Medal for his work for horticulture both in America and England.

MR. R. F. WILSON. Gold Medal for his work in connection with the Horticultural Colour Chart.

MRS. MALBY. Silver Medal and £25 for her photographic work on garden subjects.

MR. W. H. DIVERS. Silver Medal in recognition of his fifty years of service on the Society's Fruit and Vegetable Committee.

1942 MR. COURTNEY PAGE. Gold Medal in recognition of his work as honorary secretary of the National Rose Society for twenty-eight years.

DR. C. T. HILTON. Gold Medal for his work in connection with daffodils and lilies.

MR. A. T. JOHNSON. Silver Medal and £25 in recognition of his writings in connection with horticulture.

MR. P. W. D. IZZARD. Silver Medal for his journalistic work for horticulture.

1943 PROF. B. T. P. BARKER. Gold Medal for his work done while Director of the University of Bristol Research Station, Long Ashton, Bristol.

DR. WILFRID S. FOX. Gold Medal for his work for the beautifying of the roads of England.

MR. C. T. MUSGRAVE. Gold Medal for his long and distinguished service to horticulture and in particular for his work on gentians.

1944 COL. STEPHENSON R. CLARKE. Gold Medal for his work for horticulture.

MR. WM. H. JUDD. Gold Medal for his work in the Arnold Arboretum.

DR. J. RAMSBOTTOM. Gold Medal for his work on edible and other fungi.

1945 MR. J. M. C. HOOG. Gold Medal for his introduction of choice and rare bulbs into this country.

DR. J. HUTCHINSON. Gold Medal for his horticultural writings.

DR. H. V. TAYLOR. Gold Medal for his work for horticulture.

1946 MR. R. L. HARROW. Gold Medal for his general services to horticulture and also for the work he accomplished while Director of the Society's Gardens.

MR. F. C. PUDDLE. Gold Medal for his services to horticulture in the hybridization and the development of new plants of garden merit.

MISS L. SNELLING. A silver Veitch Memorial Medal in 1924. A grant of fifty guineas in recognition of her further services to botany and horticulture as an illustrator in the *Botanical Magazine* and other publications.

1947   MR. F. J. CHITTENDEN. Gold Medal for his outstanding services to horticultural education and literature.

MAJ. LAWRENCE W. JOHNSTON. Gold Medal for his work in connection with the introduction and cultivation of new plants.

1948   CAPT. COLLINGWOOD INGRAM. Gold Medal for his services to horticulture and his book *Ornamental Cherries*.

LADY MURIEL JEX-BLAKE. Silver Medal for distinguished services to horticulture in the colony of Kenya.

MR. F. LUDLOW. Silver Medal for his work in collecting and introducing new plants.

MAJ. G. SHERRIFF. Silver Medal for his work in collecting and introducing new plants.

1949   HAMILTON (ONTARIO) HORTICULTURAL SOCIETY. Silver Medal on the occasion of their centenary.

MR. THOMAS SMITH. Gold Medal for his book, *The Profitable Culture of Vegetables*.

PROF. WEN-PEI FANG. Silver Medal and £25 for his work as editor of *Icones Plantarum Omeiensium*.

1950   HAYDON BRIDGE FLORAL HORTICULTURAL AND INDUSTRIAL SOCIETY'S CENTENARY SHOW. Silver Medal to Mr. J. W. Ferguson, the most successful competitor in the open horticultural classes.

MR. W. E. TH. INGWERSEN. Gold Medal for his services to horticulture and in particular for his contribution to the knowledge of alpine plants.

MR. AMOS PERRY. Gold Medal for his services to horticulture and in particular for his work in connection with the genus *Hemerocallis*, ferns, aquatics and other hardy plants.

1951   MR. WILFRID BLUNT. Gold Medal for his book, *The Art of Botanical Illustration*.

DR. J. MacQUEEN COWAN. Gold Medal for his services to horticulture, and in particular for his work in connection with the genus *Rhododendron*.

1952   MR. E. B. ANDERSON. Gold Medal for his work in connection with alpine-house and rock-garden plants.

PROF. R. H. COMPTON. Gold Medal for his work in connection with the study and cultivation of African plants.

MR. CHARLES C. ELEY. Gold Medal for his book, *Twentieth Century Gardening*.

MR. J. L. RICHARDSON. Gold Medal for his work in raising new daffodils.

MR. GURNEY WILSON. Gold Medal for his services to horticulture in connection with orchids.

1953   MR. E. F. HAWES. Gold Medal for his work on behalf of the chrysanthemum.

MISS NELLIE ROBERTS. Silver Medal and twenty-five guineas for her work in figuring certificated orchids.

DR. W. B. TURRILL. Gold Medal for his services to horticulture, especially as editor of Curtis's *Botanical Magazine*.

MR. FRANK BARKER. Silver Medal for his work in connection with alpine plants.

1954   MR. G. H. JOHNSTONE. Gold Medal for his book, *Asiatic Magnolias in Cultivation*.

DR. A. W. E. SOYSA. Gold Medal for his work in connection with orchids.

MR. CLARENCE ELLIOTT. Silver Medal and £25 for his work in introducing new plants and extending the knowledge of rock-garden plants.

MR. HOWARD H. CRANE. Silver Medal for his work in connection with *The Fruit Garden Displayed*.

MRS. W. G. KNOX FINLAY. Silver Medal for her work in connection with the introduction and cultivation of new plants.

MRS. J. RENTON. Silver Medal for her work in connection with the introduction and cultivation of new plants.

1955   THE HON. V. SACKVILLE-WEST. Gold Medal for her writings and general encouragement of horticulture.

DR. W. F. BEWLEY. Gold Medal for his work while Director of the Experimental and Research Station, Cheshunt.

MR. RALPH S. PEER. Gold Medal for his work in connection with camellias.

MR. R. REID. Gold Medal for his work in raising new strawberries.

MR. R. B. COOKE. Silver Medal for his work in connection with the introduction and cultivation of new plants.

MR. J. H. BRANDALL. Silver Medal and £25 for his work in connection with the floral trials at Wisley.

1956   MR. A. BURKWOOD. Gold Medal for his work in raising hybrid shrubs.

MR. JAMES C. HOUSE. Silver Medal and £25 for his work in raising varieties of scabious.

MR. J. L. MOWAT. Silver Medal and £25 for his work as Curator of the University Botanic Garden, St. Andrews.

MR. FRANK BISHOP. Silver Medal for his work in raising delphiniums.

1957 MR. ROY HAY. Gold Medal for his services to horticulture.

MR. H. ROBINSON. Gold Medal for his work in raising new roses and pyrethrums.

MR. P. M. SYNGE. Gold Medal for his work as editor of the Society's publications.

PROF. T. WALLACE. Gold Medal for his services to horticulture and particularly his work on trace elements.

MR. W. J. W. MITCHELL. Silver Medal and £25 for his work at the Westonbirt Arboretum.

1958 MR. A. A. CLUCAS. Gold Medal for his services to horticulture in raising improved varieties of vegetables.

PROF. J. R. MATTHEWS. Gold Medal for his services to horticulture.

MR. J. M. S. POTTER. Gold Medal for his services to horticulture in connection with the National Fruit Trials.

MR. J. R. SEALY. Silver Medal and £25 for his book, *A Revision of the Genus Camellia*.

1959 MR. A. GORDON FORSYTH. Gold Medal for his journalistic work.

MISS B. HAVERGAL. Gold Medal for her services to horticulture, especially in the field of horticultural education.

MR. G. W. LEAK. Gold Medal for his services to horticulture as a member of Council and as chairman of committees.

MR. LANNING ROPER. Silver Medal for his writings on gardens.

1960 SIR FREDERICK STERN. Gold Medal for his contributions to literature and other services to horticulture.

DR. H. HAROLD HUME. Gold Medal for his work for the advancement of horticulture and in particular for his work in connection with camellias.

DR. LESLIE W. A. AHRENDT. Silver Medal and £25 for his work on the genus *Berberis*.

MRS. C. B. SAUNDERS. Silver Medal for her work in connection with species of *Cyclamen*.

MR. THEO. A. STEPHENS. Silver Medal for his contributions to horti-cultural literature.

1961 DR. PETER DAVIS. Gold Medal for his work in introducing new plants from eastern Europe and the Middle East.

MR. D. E. GREEN. Gold Medal for his mycological work.

MR. T. JOHNSON. Gold Medal for his work in raising new chrysanthemums.

MR. T. ROCHFORD. Gold Medal for his exhibits of greenhouse plants.

MR. A. SIMMONDS. Gold Medal in recognition of distinguished services rendered to the Society over a period of forty years.

MR. H. H. DAVIDIAN. Silver Medal and £50 for his work in connection with the genus *Rhododendron*.

DR. R. A. H. LEGRO. Silver Medal and £25 for his work on the breeding of red and yellow delphiniums.

MR. J. E. DOWNWARD. Silver Medal for his work as a horticultural photographer.

1962 MR. H. FRASER. Gold Medal for his work in the field of horticultural education.

MR. H. G. HILLIER. Gold Medal for the wide variety and the many rare plants included in his exhibits.

MR. F. REINELT. Gold Medal for his work in connection with the breeding of delphiniums, begonias and polyanthuses.

DR. A. S. THOMAS. Gold Medal for his work in connection with roses.

MR. O. POLUNIN. Silver Medal and £50 for his work in introducing new plants.

MR. R. C. ELLIOTT. Silver Medal for his work in connection with alpine plants.

1963 MR. PERCY S. CANE. Gold Medal for his work as a designer of gardens and as a landscape architect.

PROF. H. B. RYCROFT. Gold Medal for his work as Director of the Botanic Gardens at Kirstenbosch.

SIR ERIC H. SAVILL. Gold Medal for his great work carried out at the Savill Gardens and for his services to the Society.

MR. F. A. SECRETT. Gold Medal for his work in connection with developments in market-gardening techniques and the training of young people in horticulture.

SIR GEORGE TAYLOR. Gold Medal for his contribution to horticulture as a member of many international committees, for his guidance in research and development, and for his outstanding success as Director of the Royal Botanic Gardens, Kew.

MR. J. WOOLMAN. Gold Medal for his work in connection with chrysanthemums.

MR. C. A. CAMERON BROWN. Silver Medal for his pioneer work and continuing direction of research into the application of electricity to horticulture.

MRS. MARGERY FISH. Silver Medal for her work as an author and lecturer on horticulture.

1964 DR. H. R. FLETCHER. Gold Medal for his work in connection with rhododendrons and the preparation of a classified list of rhododendrons.

MR. C. MEIRING. Gold Medal for his work in building up the Caledon Wild Flower Garden in South Africa.

MRS. FRANCES PERRY. Gold Medal for her contribution to the practice of horticulture and to literature on gardening subjects.

DR. W. T. STEARN. Gold Medal for his contribution to botanical literature and his services to the Society.

MR. W. D. CARTWRIGHT. Silver Medal and £50 for his services to the Society as secretary to Floral Committee A for fifty-four years.

MRS. M. WREFORD. Silver Medal and £50 for her work in connection with the preparation of the *Addendum* to *Sander's List of Orchid Hybrids*.

1965 MR. C. F. COLEMAN. Gold Medal for his work in connection with daffodils.

MR. W. DOUGLAS COOK. Gold Medal for his services to horticulture particularly in New Zealand.

MR. R. T. PEARL. Gold Medal in recognition of his services as a member of the Examinations Board and as a supervising examiner in the Society's examinations.

MR. G. L. PILKINGTON. Gold Medal in recognition of his unfailing readiness to devote so helpfully his time and knowledge to the interests of horticulture and of the Society.

MR. J. B. STEVENSON. Gold Medal for his contribution to the development of chrysanthemums.

MR. W. J. C. LAWRENCE. Silver Medal and £50 for his contribution to horticulture in connection with the development of the John Innes series of composts.

MR. A. H. NISBET. Silver Medal and £50 for his work in connection with dwarf and other garden conifers.

1966 DR. L. BROADBENT. Gold Medal for his services to horticulture in education and research.

MR. V. C. DAVIES. Gold Medal for his services to horticulture in New Zealand.

MR. J. S. L. GILMOUR. Gold Medal for his services to horticulture, in particular in the field of nomenclature.

MR. JAN DE GRAAFF. Gold Medal for his outstanding work in growing, hybridizing, and the development of lilies.

MR. A. F. MITCHELL. Gold Medal for his work in connection with the collection and recording of data on conifers.

MR. GRAHAM THOMAS. Gold Medal for his contribution to horticulture as adviser to the Gardens Committee of the National Trust, and as a writer.

PROF. E. G. WATERHOUSE. Gold Medal for his work in connection with camellias and for his services to horticulture in Australia.

1967   MR. ALAN BLOOM. Gold Medal for work in connection with the production and distribution of a very wide range of hardy herbaceous plants.

MAJ. T. H. BRUNN. Gold Medal for services to horticulture in Australia.

MISS ELIZABETH HESS. Gold Medal for services to horticultural education.

MR. E. R. LUCKHURST. Gold Medal for work with dahlias.

MR. E. LEYSHON. Silver Medal and £50 for work carried out in restoring the Westonbirt Arboretum.

INDEX

278, 302; introductions, 296, 301–2, 376, 388; popularity, 277; at Wisley, 277, 387–9, 399
Althorp Park, 308
Alton Towers, 274
Amaryllis: *see* Hippeastrums
America (*see also* North America; United States), and dahlia classification, 421; Douglas's visits, 100–5, 189; fruits from, 100–1, 173; plants from, 8, 10–11, 25, 42, 88–9, 100–5, 146, 148, 152, 304, 345; trees from, 89, 102, 104, 179
American Horticultural Society, 370
American nurseries, 303, 305
American Orchid Society, 381
Amherst of Hackney, Lord, 306
Amherstia nobilis, 128, 142–3, 174
Ammal, Dr. E. K. Janaki, 362; Plate 20
Amory, Sir John Heathcoat-: *see* Heathcoat-Amory
Amsterdam, physic garden, 415
Anderson, Dr. James, 40, 41
Anderson, Dr. William, 9
Anderson, Mr. William (of Chelsea), 72
Andes, plants from, 339, 346–7
Andrews, Henry C., 5–6
Androsace, 25
Anemones, 16, 50, 150–1, 272, 301, 377
Anniversary Dinners, 52–53, 84–85; dessert provided by members, 52–53, 367; ladies admitted to gallery, 52, 367
Anniversary Meetings of the Society, 39–40, 48–49, 51–52, 72, 117–18, 131, 164–5, 188, 190; 'Annual Meeting' (*q.v.*) substituted (1862), 190–1
Annual Meetings of the Society, instituted (1862), 190–1; mentioned, 194–5, 208, 259, 265, 328, 332, 384, 424, 432–6 and *passim*
Anthony, Cornwall, 15
Antiquaries, Society of, 75
Antirrhinums, 387
Apospory, 241
Apothecaries Company, 1, 77; Garden: *see* Chelsea Physic Garden
Apples, 21, 29, 45, 47, 49, 54, 64, 110, 184, 244, 306, 312, 314, 327; from abroad, 100, 173, 236; canker, 26; conferences on (1883), 224, 241, (1934), 339; Cox's, 223, 241; cross-breeding, 223–4, 241; Laxton's, 223; varieties, 12, 15, 24, 50, 68, 140, 147, 211; Wisley storm damage, 391–3
Apricots, 15, 87, 111, 147, 211, 216, 273
Aquatics, 149
Aralias, 69
Araucarias, 105

Arboretums: *see under* Chiswick Garden, Kew Royal Botanic Gardens, Westonbirt, Winkworth; *see also* Arnold Arboretum
Arbor-vitae, 180
Arbuthnot, Sir Alexander, 255
Arbutus, 8, 12
Arctic, 101
Ardingly, 427
Ardisia punctata, 94
Argentine, plants from, 347
Army and Navy Stores site, 65
Armytage-Moore, Hugh, 300, 351
Arnold Arboretum in United States, 296, 299, 344
Arnott stove, 148
Arran, Earl of, 100
Arthur, Prince: *see* Connaught, Duke of
Arthur Seat: *see under* Edinburgh
Artichokes, 394
Arts and horticulture, 191, 193–5, 199, 206, 211, 322–3
Arundel, 154, 219
Ascroft, R. W., 314, 325
Ashburton, Lord, 162
Asia, plants from, 138, 301, 351
Aske Park, 154
Aslet, W. K., 399
Asparagus, 394
Aspidistra lurida, 81, 99
Assam, 345
Assistant Secretary of the Society, 42–43, 65–68, 72, 116–19, 232, 402, 405–6
accounts disorder due to (1815), 66–67
Chiswick Garden, separate appointment for, 80, 95, 163, 168, 402; Assistant Secretary of Society acts in dual capacity, 118, 125, 402
duties, 65, 68, 74, 406
embezzlements leading to dismissal (1826), 116–19
holders of post, 43, 66, 68, 108–9, 118, 136, 170, 189–90, 199, 240, 261, 292, 313, 325, 357, 364, 405–7
residence for, 71
salary, 43, 68, 80, 108, 199; offer to give up (1856), 168; guaranteed by Fellows (1885), 233
Associates of Honour, honour instituted (1930), 329, 433; awards, 329, 346, 353, 357, 385–7, 397; past and present holders: *see* Appendix IV (pp. 501–514)
Asters, 12, 189, 269
Athenaeum, quoted, 131
Atholl, Duke of, 12, 14, 80
Atlas (ship), 98
Atmospheric pollution, 347